SIN AND CENSORSHIP

FRANK WALSH

Sin and Censorship

The Catholic Church and the Motion Picture Industry

YALE UNIVERSITY PRESS NEW HAVEN AND LONDON

Frontispiece: Jane Russell in a controversial dance scene in *The French Line* (1953). (Courtesy of the Museum of Modern Art)

Published with assistance from the Kingsley Trust Association Publication Fund established by the Scroll and Key Society of Yale College.

Printed in the United States of America.

Library of Congress Cataloging-in-Publication Data
Walsh, Frank, 1934–
Sin and censorship : the Catholic Church and the motion picture industry / Frank Walsh.
p. cm. Includes bibliographical references and index.
ISBN 0–300–06373–3 (alk. paper)
1. National Legion of Decency. 2. Motion pictures—Moral and ethical aspects. 3. Motion pictures—Censorship—United States. I. Title.
PN1995.5.W27 1996
363.3′1—dc20 95–266 CIP

A catalogue record for this book is available from the British Library.

The paper in this book meets the guidelines for permanence and durability of the Committee on Production Guidelines for Book Longevity of the Council on Library Resources.

10 9 8 7 6 5 4 3 2 1

CONTENTS

ACKNOWLEDGMENTS

■■■

In writing this book, I have, like Blanche DuBois, depended on the kindness of strangers; in the process, I have made a number of new friends. This is an opportunity to thank them. Among the many archivists and their staff who helped me, I wish to thank especially Leith Adams and Ned Comstock at the Doheny Library at the University of Southern California; Ted Baehr of the Christian Film and Television Commission; Charles Bell of the Harry Ransom Humanities Research Center at the University of Texas at Austin; Mary Belle Burch at the Indiana State Library in Indianapolis; James D'Arc of the Harold B. Lee Library at Brigham Young University; Sam Gill and Howard Prouty at the Margaret Herrick Library of the Academy of Motion Picture Arts and Sciences; Brigitte J. Kueppers of the Theater Arts Library at the University of California, Los Angeles; Carl Roesch at the Archives of the Diocese of Syracuse; Nicholas B. Scheetz and Michael North at the Special Collections Division of Georgetown University; Father Paul Thomas of the Archives of the Archdiocese of Baltimore; Msgr. Francis J. Weber of the Archives of the Archdiocese of Los Angeles; H. Warren Willis at the United States Catholic Conference of Bishops; Anthony Zito at the Catholic University Archives; and all the people at the Motion Picture Division of the New York State Archives in Albany. I am especially indebted to Henry Herx at the Department of Communications of the United States Catholic Conference for Film and Broadcasting, who not only opened the archival material of the Legion of Decency to me but also proved to be a delightful luncheon companion.

I also wish to thank the many individuals who were kind enough to take time away from their own work to talk to me: Msgr. Paul J. Hayes, the late Cardinal Timothy Manning, Msgr. John McClafferty, Paul J. McGeady, Father Hugh Nolan, James O'Toole at the University of Massachusetts at Boston, and Margaret Reher of Cabrini College. Two people were indispensable. Martin J. Quigley, Jr., gave me an appreciation of his father's role in the history of motion pictures that I could not have gained anywhere else. I owe a special thank-you to Father Paul J. Sullivan, S.J., who shared his experience at the Legion of Decency and the National Catholic Office for Motion Pictures with me. My meetings with him, his cards, and his notes did much to make the research for this book enjoyable.

Any scholarly study builds on the efforts of others. I want to acknowledge the work of four who are mentioned in the bibliography: Gregory Black, Garth Jowett, Leonard Leff, and Jerold Simmons. I should also like to thank the many people who answered my author's query in the *New York Times.*

I am indebted to Noreen O'Connor, who did a truly remarkable job of manuscript editing. The best thing I could wish for any author is to have an editor like Gladys Topkis. Where else could you find in one person someone who knows the book business inside out, is an enthusiastic supporter, and a great dinner companion?

Old friends are always indispensable, especially in a seven-year project like this. Dick Comeau always asked how my work was progressing and, more important, was willing to listen. Too bad he couldn't have stayed around for the finish. Don Jacobs, who has been a good friend since graduate school days, read parts of my manuscript at a crucial stage. Al Richard's careful scrutiny of every page did much to improve the final product. Equally important, his dedication to one-upmanship was a great motivator. With this book, I declare the competition over and myself the winner.

Finally, I want to thank my wife, Mary Roth Walsh. It's wonderful to have a great date for the movies. Her ideas, enthusiasm, and support not only made this book possible, but everything else in my life worthwhile.

SIN AND CENSORSHIP

INTRODUCTION

■■■

Early in *Cinema Paradiso,* a little boy peeks from behind a curtain as the local priest sits alone in the orchestra of the small Italian town's only movie house. The priest tenses as the couple on the screen move to embrace; his fingers toy with the bell at his side. Then, as they start to kiss, he sounds the alarm, and the projectionist dutifully attaches one more sticker to the reel of film. After the priest leaves, the boy watches as his friend the projectionist carefully eliminates the objectionable frames, splicing together what remains of the story. Later that evening, one audience member complains after an especially obvious cut: "Twenty years I've been going to the movies, and I've never seen a kiss."

By the end of the film, the little boy has grown up to be a successful director, who returns to his hometown for the first time in thirty years to attend the projectionist's funeral. With the old movie house torn down, all he has left of his boyhood is a reel of film bequeathed to him by his friend. As he views the clips in his studio, the screen fills with a montage of screen kisses: Rudolph Valentino, Agnes Ayres, Cary Grant, Rosalind Russell, and dozens of other stars enjoy a seemingly endless series of embraces, lovingly saved over the years from the accumulated cuts ordered by the village priest.

Working in the national office of the Legion of Decency in New York, a small group of priests and laywomen performed a task very similar to that of the lone cleric in *Cinema Paradiso*; however, they assumed the burden of safeguarding the morals, not of a small town, but of an entire nation. And anyone who tried to splice together all the cuts Hollywood made in the 16,251 feature films classified by the Legion and its successor, the National Catholic Office for Motion Pictures, would face a much more formidable task than the one undertaken by the *Cinema Paradiso* projectionist.

This book explains how the Catholic church became the most successful pressure group in the history of the movies and why it was eventually forced to relinquish its power. One movie insider claimed that "among all the pressure groups the Legion of Decency is the one with teeth." It played a major role in determining both what Americans saw and what they didn't see on the silver screen during the golden age of Hollywood.[1]

The story of the Catholic church's role in the motion picture industry, however, begins two decades before the formation of the Legion in 1934. Although film historians have long acknowledged the Legion's powerful influence, they have been at a loss to explain what they perceive to be the Catholic church's sudden interest in motion picture morality in the early 1930s. It seemed to them that, like Paul on the road to Damascus, church leaders underwent some mystical conversion to the ranks of movie reformers on the way to the annual bishops' meeting in 1934. This perception stems from the popular assumption that the church largely ignored the topic of movie reform before the formation of the Legion of Decency. In reality, the decision to launch the Legion was the culmination of a struggle to shape the content of American films dating back to World War I, when the Catholic church embarked on its first national film campaign, a battle to prevent the release of government-sponsored movies trying to check the spread of venereal disease among the military.

The events leading to the Legion's decline have similarly been neglected. Recognizing that the Legion was losing touch with a new generation of better-educated Catholics in the postwar years, church leaders first liberalized its classification system and in 1965 changed its name to the National Catholic Office for Motion Pictures (NCOMP). It didn't work. While a small group of conservative Catholics longed for the good old days of the Legion, the rest of the laity went its own way. Finally, dwindling interest in NCOMP's reviews forced the bishops to close it down in 1980. Ironically, NCOMP left the scene just before a new movie crusade began to take shape. Although individual Catholic leaders continue to speak out against what they consider objectionable content in today's films, much of the current criticism is coming from conservative fundamentalist Protestant groups who have adopted many of the Legion's old tactics, including letter-writing campaigns, decency oaths, film morality ratings, boycotts, and pickets.

In traveling to twenty-four cities in the course of writing this book, I have been surprised by the number of people who have asked me, "Where is the Legion of Decency now that we need it?" Some of today's movie reformers even attribute Hollywood's "moral collapse" to the Legion's disappearance. Ted Baehr, head of the Christian Film and Television Commission, has called for a return to the days when Joe Breen and his staff at the Production Code Administration scrutinized every film script. Baehr claims that the dramatic increase in objectionable films in the past twenty years stems not so much from Hollywood turning its back on religion as from religious pressure groups like the Legion turning their backs on Hollywood.[2]

I hope this exploration of the relation between the Catholic church and the motion picture industry sheds new light on the current debate over censorship. Although I am gratified by the growing interest in this topic, those who yearn for a revival of some version of the Legion of Decency should take a careful look at the Catholic crusade to clean up the screen. Sometimes the cure can be worse than the disease.

ONE

In Search of Censors

The people who peered at the flickering shadows in the peep shows and nickelodeons at the beginning of the twentieth century didn't realize that they were participants in an experiment that would revolutionize the way Americans spent their leisure time. All they wanted in exchange for their nickel was a few minutes of fun and escape from the drudgery of everyday life. As one advertising jingle put it: "If you're sick of troubles rife, go to the picture show; you'll forget your unpaid bills, rheumatism and other ills, if you'll stow away your pills, and go to the picture show." If you lived in a big city like New York or Chicago, five cents and a short walk could whisk you away into another world. And you didn't even have to speak the language! The absence of dialogue in those early films made it possible for any immigrant to understand the simple plots. One commentator explained: "Its very voicelessness makes it eloquent for Letts, Finns, Italians, Syrians, Greeks, and pigtailed Celestials."[1]

Some dismissed the new craze as "nickelmania," but it quickly became apparent that the nickelodeon was more than a fad. By 1910, weekly attendance in Manhattan alone had reached 900,000, and movies were here to stay.

But there were a lot of questions about the effect these images had on audiences. Some observers hailed movies as a potential source of good, especially among the poor, providing for the first time in history "a means of relief, happiness and mental inspiration to people at the bottom." In pursuit of that goal, Vitagraph made a number of "quality" films based on Shakespeare and Dante between 1907 and 1910.[2]

The Nation in 1918 rhapsodized over movies as the realization of Walt Whitman's hope for a genuine American art form. Vachel Lindsay took a more pragmatic approach, optimistically viewing the nickelodeon as a substitute for the saloon: "the first enemy of King Alcohol with real power where that King had the deepest hold." A few harbored the hope that movies might even offer a cure; the alcoholic in one temperance pamphlet, after seeing a drunk on the screen, exclaimed: "I never knowed just what a bum I'd gone and got to be—until those movin' pitchures went an' showed myself to me."[3]

But reformers interested in movies as a means of cultural enrichment for the masses were soon disappointed. Jane Addams, for example, discovered that the film adaptations of literary classics shown in her Hull House theater could not compete with such nickelodeon offerings as *The School Children's Strike*, *The Pirates*, and *The Defrauding Banker*. The problem with Hull House films, one young viewer pointed out, was that they were just plain dull. "People," he confided, "like to see fights and fellows getting hurt, and robbers and all that stuff."[4]

For every observer who saw something positive in movies, a hundred worried about their negative effects. Because there was no hope that movies would disappear, concerned citizens felt that the only way to render them harmless was to eliminate what was dangerous. That was easier said than done; it seemed that every topic the movies dealt with annoyed some group or other. Bankers saw nothing entertaining in a film like *The Defrauding Banker*, and the International Association of Chiefs of Police failed to see the humor in the *Keystone Kops* comedies. In 1910, an American Federation of Labor convention condemned films that made heroes of bosses and villains of union workers. Conversely, the Ohio Industrial Relations Committee denounced *The Strike at Coaldale* (1916), which portrayed a successful walkout by the miners, as a threat to American industry.[5]

Moviemakers quickly learned that race and religion were even more troublesome. The best known of the early controversies involved the NAACP's protest of D. W. Griffith's film *The Birth of a Nation* (1915). Some Protestants complained about *The Scarlet Letter*, whereas Catholics denounced *The Story of the Nun*, which portrayed a young girl forced into a convent against her will. Jews were unhappy about the negative stereotypes in *Bertha the Sewing Machine Girl*, and lines like "I'd rather take my chances with the Indians than the

Mormons" led the Mormon church to call for the suppression of *The Mormon Maid*.[6]

But sex and crime generated the greatest concern. The first "sex film" to cause a sensation was *The Kiss* (1896), starring May Irwin and John C. Rice, who re-created in forty-two feet of film—less than a minute of viewing time—a scene from their play *The Widow Jones*. It was one thing to view a kiss on the stage from a distance, but the intimacy of seeing it on a screen shocked many viewers. According to one magazine, "The spectacle of the prolonged pasturing on each other's lips" was "beastly" enough in life size on the stage, but "magnified to Gargantuan proportions and repeated three times over it is absolutely disgusting." A year later, the New York police banned *Orange Blossoms*, which featured an actress pantomiming a bride changing into her nightgown on her wedding night, and arrested the exhibitor. The Reverend Frederick Bruce Russell took matters into his own hands and raided any Coney Island peepshow that dared to show such "dangerous" films as *What the Girls Did with Willie's Hat* and *Fun in a Boarding House*. As filmmaking became more sophisticated and thirty-second film strips gave way to feature films, including those depicting prostitution in *Traffic in Souls*, venereal disease in *Damaged Goods*, and abortion and birth control in *Where Are My Children?* moralists stepped up their attacks. The proliferation of true-crime stories added fuel to the fire. Three treatments of one infamous case, the murder of Stanford White by Harry K. Thaw, led to a storm of opposition. The Chicago police closed *The Thaw-White Tragedy*, and a New York judge fined a nickelodeon manager $100 for showing *The Great Thaw Trial* to an audience made up largely of schoolchildren.[7]

These actions reflected a growing concern on the part of the industry's enemies: what were the movies doing to the youth of America? Jane Addams, who had used movies to try to win over the neighborhood children, soon became convinced that they were taking an enormous moral toll among the young. Not only were the films inflaming children's desires for a life they could never achieve, they prevented the children from preparing themselves to deal with the responsibilities of adult life. According to Addams, a good deal of juvenile delinquency stemmed from the children's desperate effort to obtain the price of admission. "Out of my twenty years' experience at Hull House," she later wrote, "I can recall all sorts of pilferings, petty larcenies, and even burglaries, due to that never ceasing effort on the part of boys to procure theater tickets." An Illinois judge agreed, noting that movies were responsible "for more juvenile crime coming into my court than all other causes combined." In 1910, *Good Housekeeping* concluded that the movie theater was fast becoming "a primary school for criminals . . . teaching obscenity, crime, murder and debauchery for a nickel." A few years later, an "anonymous source" told an investigator that her son and his friends, imprisoned for burglary, had "got the ideer . . . from de movies." And how could she be sure, she asked, that her daughter would be content to settle down in marriage after a steady diet of matinee idols?[8]

As early as 1906, the editor of the first movie magazine, *Views and Films Index*, raised what became a standard industry defense, pointing out that because the criminal was always caught in the end, such films were actually deterrents. And to those who claimed that movies were undermining the country's morals, he pointed out that, when compared to the fully clothed actresses on the screen, the undraped statues in public museums were far more likely to "arouse prurient thoughts." But the nickelodeon's enemies knew that no one had ever gone wrong in a museum. Reformers had always viewed the city as a difficult place in which to raise children; these fears were now exacerbated by the sight of boys and girls lining up to enter the dimly lit theaters. Many cities decreed that there should be enough light for patrons to read a newspaper while the movie was being shown, but what could be done to ward off the evil thoughts that darkened their souls?[9]

The police continued to seize "dangerous" movies, but some critics felt the need for a more systematic form of control. On November 4, 1907, Chicago became the first major city to establish a system of prior censorship by authorizing the police department to deny a permit to any film it judged "immoral" or "obscene." The police took action almost immediately, refusing permits for two westerns, *The James Boys in Missouri* and *The Night Riders.* Recognizing the threat to their livelihood, the moviemakers went to court in a futile attempt to overturn the law. According to the Illinois Supreme Court, the city's right to ensure decency and morals was especially clear in the area of movies because the low admission price attracted children and the lower classes. The Court anticipated no difficulty in enforcing the law because the "average person of healthy and wholesome mind" knew what "immoral" and "obscene" meant.[10]

A year later, the issue of the movies' effect on children was raised again, this time by a number of New York clergymen, including Father Michael Lavelle, vicar general of the New York diocese. Canon William Sheafe Chase of Christ Church, Brooklyn, coordinated the growing protest and pressured Mayor George B. McClellan to hold a public meeting. After listening to a group of clergymen, including a representative of the Catholic archbishop, the mayor ordered all the movie houses closed on the day before Christmas. This time the industry owners were more successful, obtaining an injunction on December 26 restraining the mayor and reopening the movie houses.[11]

Mayor McClellan's challenge to the industry had been easily thwarted, but his action did focus attention on the "movie problem." The result was a careful study of the issue by a civic organization, the People's Institute, which led to the establishment of the National Board of Censorship of Motion Pictures in March 1909. Although the board had no legal power, the producers voluntarily decided to submit their films to it for approval before they were released as a means of heading off government censorship. The cost of the operation would be underwritten by the cooperating companies, which paid a fee to the board for each evaluation. At its first meeting, which lasted six hours, the board viewed some 18,000 feet of film, rejected 400 feet, and temporarily refused to grant a permit to D. W. Griffith's *Heart of an Outlaw*. Nevertheless, the industry's view of the board as the lesser of two evils was rewarded over time as its reviewers approved 95 percent of the films submitted to them in the next five years. In fact, the board, which opposed censorship from the beginning, changed its name in 1916 to the National Board of Review of Motion Pictures to underscore its faith that it could help educate the public to patronize good films, thus driving bad movies out of the market.[12]

Local exhibitors breathed a collective sigh of relief when Mayor McClellan was succeeded by William Gaynor, a friend of the movie business. Convinced that the board had done a good job of cleaning up the screen, New York's new mayor had little sympathy with those who called for greater restrictions. Censorship, he told one minister, might do a little good, but it would do infinitely more harm. It could even, he added slyly, bar a movie showing Martin Luther nailing his theses to the cathedral door. Gaynor was no more receptive to a complaint from the president of St. John's College that new movie houses were too close to the city's Catholic schools. "When I came into office," the mayor told Father Moore, "many . . . clergymen asserted that these shows were indecent . . . but I have proved that to be baseless." Fearing that the reformers might invoke the city's fire laws as a means of closing down some of the more crowded movie houses, Gaynor told his fire commissioner to choose discreet inspectors, since "these shows are a great solace and benefit to poor people."[13]

Gaynor may have been satisfied, but the board's existence did not convince the skeptics that nothing more needed to be done. The fact that the film industry financed the board through a fee system caused some critics to brand it a tool of the moviemakers, but its liberal reviewing policy was at the heart of the moralists' continued call for government censorship. A comparison of the board's actions with those of the Chicago censors indicated that the two groups were applying dramatically different standards. During a five-month period in 1914, Chicago turned down 100 films and ordered 928 eliminations, as compared to the New York agency's 13 rejections and 198 recommended cuts.[14]

Even more irritating to the reformers, the New York censors concentrated on excessive violence and lawlessness while ignoring sex scenes. In fact, the board passed films dealing with such controversial subjects as birth control, prostitution, and even nudity, as long as they were not presented in "a crass, crude and commercial manner." Typical of the criticism that flowed into the New York office was a complaint from a Milwaukee citizens' group about New York's approval of *The Little Girl Next Store*, a film dealing with prostitution. Although the women were sentenced to a thirty-day jail term at the end of the film, the Milwaukee group argued that the fact that throughout most of the picture they "were so attractive, well-dressed and apparently happy" taught a "dangerous lesson to youth."[15]

The Board of Review's record did not persuade the industry's enemies like Canon Chase and the Reverend Wilbur C. Crafts (another film crusader) that government regulation was unnecessary. A censorship bill received a favorable report from the House Committee on Education in 1915 but failed to pass the entire House. Industry leaders were so grateful to Massachusetts Congressman Frederick W. Dallinger, who was credited with blocking the legislation, that they provided him with inside information to buy Triangle Film stock, which they told him would make him rich. They proved to be better filmmakers than investment counselors: the stock turned out to be a disaster. Facing financial ruin six years later, Dallinger persuaded the still-grateful industry to compensate him for his original $2,000 investment. Sensing that the film industry needed to make a better case for itself, the industry journal *Moving Picture World* offered theater owners a set of slides designed to turn the public against the idea of government regulation. Despite the industry's best effort, four states—Pennsylvania (1911), Ohio (1913), Kansas (1914), and Maryland (1916)—created censorship boards before World War I. Supporters of government intervention were especially heartened by the Supreme Court decision in *Mutual Film Corporation v. Industrial Commission of Ohio* (1915), which denied the industry's contention that films were protected by First Amendment guarantees of freedom of speech and freedom of the press. The industry now faced the possibility of a proliferation of censorship boards and death by a thousand cuts.[16]

The heart of the problem was that, although most of the city and state boards were not as effective as their supporters had hoped, filmmakers could never be sure just what scene or title would fall prey to the censor's scissors, in part because the censors themselves were not always sure what "illicit," "indecent," "obscene," "salacious," and "gruesome" really meant. The Maryland censors solved this dilemma by deciding not to adopt any rules or guidelines; it would be impossible, they said, "to apply the same yardstick or standards to every film." The result was that cuts ordered by the various boards often reflected the prejudices of the members. In its early years, the Chicago censorship board was headed by the colorful Major Metullus Lucullus Cicero Funkhauser, who claimed that he always censored pictures with a child's viewpoint in mind. He also eliminated scenes that "the male sex could stand" but that "might cause women to brood and lose their reason." He even ordered a scene involving a piece of nude statuary cut from one picture. But most Chicagoans were willing to put up with Funkhauser's capricious leadership until his efforts to cut scenes depicting German brutality against the French and Belgians during World War I invited questions about his Teutonic heritage and his loyalty to the Allied cause. When charges were also raised that he had used his position to employ "persons of ill-repute" to shadow many of the city's leading citizens, including the chief of police, the city decided that it had had enough and he was forced out of office.[17]

Chicago was not the only place where films were subject to the vagaries of the local censor. In his first two weeks on the job the police censor in Worcester, Massachusetts, in 1910, cut the dueling and Hell scenes from *Faust* and the murder of Julius Caesar in filmed adaptations of the two classics. The Pennsylvania board, in contrast, dictated that a kiss could last no longer than a yard of film strip, a more liberal standard than its attitude toward childbirth. Even a scene showing a woman knitting clothes for her unborn child could not be shown in the state because, as one board member explained, "Movies are patronized by thousands of children who believe that babies are brought by the stork, and it would be criminal to undeceive them."[18]

In spite of their differences, censors agreed that their main job was to protect American morals. The people who had led the fight to establish the various censorship boards were businessmen and clubwomen, urban reformers and politicians, educators and social workers; their motives ranged from a suspicion that anything that was entertaining must be evil to an honest, if misdirected, desire to safeguard the morals of their fellow citizens.[19]

Ministers like William Sheafe Chase and Wilbur C. Crafts, combined with the Catholic church's suspicion of secular censorship, gave the movie reform effort a distinctly Protestant cast in the early decades of the twentieth century. Nevertheless, the Catholic church did not completely ignore the issue during these years. A good deal of activity has gone undetected because it took place at the local parish level, the focal point of Catholic life before World War I. As early as 1907, the *Michigan Catholic* accused the film industry of being in league with the devil in an effort to destroy the souls of America's children. That same year, the *Catholic Messenger* in Worcester, Massachusetts, denounced movie houses as "the devil's lights" and "a chamber of horrors," the breeding places of moral plague far worse than any physical ills. It wondered why anyone would hesitate to close the nickelodeons and called upon the police to use their axes if necessary. The *Messenger* kept up a steady attack over the next few years, characterizing the theaters as stations of vice and informing its readers that in one month alone, procurers had picked up twenty-three young girls and shipped them to a brothel in Texas. The manager of one of the Worcester movie houses later recalled, "If you played a movie that wasn't fit to be seen, they [the Catholic clergy] would crucify you by saying 'don't go to see it.'"[20]

Yet Catholic concern about the movies was not limited to the parish level. In the years before World War I, influential Catholic newspapers like the *Boston Pilot*, national publications like the Jesuit magazine *America*, and the Federation of Catholic Societies (an association of lay organizations) called for federal film censorship at one time or other. "The dime novel of other days was a real danger," the *Pilot* proclaimed, "but some of the moving pictures of today are a positive menace." Director Cecil B. deMille was so concerned about Catholic criticism of his handling of the Inquisition in *Joan the Woman* (1916) that he suggested that distributors offer two versions of the Joan of Arc story to the public: a sanitized rendition, minus Bishop Cauchon and his coterie of sadistic priests, would be circulated in heavily Catholic areas, while the rest of the country would see the unexpurgated story.[21]

There was no single Catholic position on films in the early years. Before 1917, the church lacked any sort of unified national structure, with no agency that could speak for it on national issues. In David O'Brien's words, the prewar church was a "States Rights church, dominated by the local bishop." All this began to change with America's entry into World War I. Because there was no organization to act for the church in responding to the government's request for chaplains as well as looking after the needs of Catholics in the military, the bishops formed the National War Council, the first Catholic organization in the United States that was controlled by the hierarchy and capable of commenting on social issues. Headquartered in Washington with Father John J. Burke as its chairman, the War Council provided the armed forces with chaplains and tried to protect the faith and morals of both service personnel and young women living near military bases.[22]

One of the council's major tasks was to work with the government's Commission on Training Camp Activities (CTCA), headed by Raymond Fosdick. Fosdick was especially concerned with combating the spread of venereal disease, which he attributed to the streetwalkers and brothels that surrounded every military base. The national concern about prostitution, which had emerged at the turn of the century, reached hysterical proportions after the United States entered the war. Warnings that a "diseased woman can do more harm than any German fleet of airplanes" coupled with predictions that the "army and navy which is the least syphilized" would win the war provided the rationale for government involvement in the prevention of venereal disease.[23]

At first the War Council was gratified by the army's declaration that abstinence was the best safeguard against infection. Charles P. Neill, a council member, hailed the military's pronouncement as the first time in history that medical science had "laid down with exactness the principle which the Catholic Church has taught for two thousand years." But the CTCA also believed that the military had to develop a second line of defense, including prophylactic distribution and the creation of prophylaxis stations, for those who lacked the necessary self-control.[24]

The military's extensive reliance on prophylaxis touched off a storm of criticism. Church leaders denounced the practice as immoral; some social hygienists argued that it would increase infection by promoting sexual activity; and women attacked it as a reinforcement of the double standard. The sensitive nature of the topic was underscored by an incident at Fort Taylor, Kentucky, on May 2, 1918, when Captain Lee A. Stone gave a lecture on the army's campaign against venereal disease to a group of clergymen. Stone spiced up his presentation that evening by adding some material on phallic worship and the history of prostitution. According to Stone, in Genoa and Naples one could still see women carrying "waxen and dough images of the penis to the shrines of the saints." Several priests attacked Stone's credibility and demanded to know the names of the saints in question. Dissatisfied with his response, the Catholic chaplains complained to the War Council, which brought the matter to the attention of Secretary of War Newton D. Baker. Stone was eventually forced to write a letter of apology to the War Council in which he explained that he was glad to stand corrected and that he had not meant to cast any reflections on the Catholic church. After all, he pointed out, some of his best friends were Catholics.[25]

Stone's apology ended the affair, but the fact that such a minor incident could reach the office of a cabinet member indicates the growing tension between the War Council and the CTCA over how to protect military personnel against the dangers of venereal disease. In an effort to find some middle ground, the CTCA distributed to Catholic soldiers a War Council pamphlet entitled "The Honor Legion," which promoted sexual continence. But it issued another booklet, "Keeping Fit to Fight," which embodied "man-to-man-talk, straight from the shoulder." Treating venereal disease as a health problem rather than a moral issue, the booklet was aimed at those men who were "habitually promiscuous" and who either lacked self-control or would not be influenced by "moral or idealistic arguments." But church leaders charged that pamphlets like these created the very problem they sought to solve. Accusing the authors of using "the language of the pimp and prostitute," one Catholic critic claimed to have heard a soldier remark after reading the booklet, "It sure is great stuff. I'll bet the guy who wrote it was some whore-hound himself."[26]

The conflict came to a head over the production of two educational films developed by the American Social Hygiene Association, *Fit to Fight*, directed at the armed forces, and *End of the Road*, which was to be shown to young women living near military camps. *Fit to Fight* followed five young men from their entry into the army: the hero, Billy Hale, a college football player, shows he has the right stuff from the start by beating up a pacifist; Kid McCarthy is a boxer and a self-styled ladies' man; Hank Simon is fresh from the farm; Chick Charlton is rich in material things but weak in character; and Jack Garvin is a traveling salesman. Billy's sweetheart, who wants him to save himself for their marriage, writes him a letter about the dangers of venereal disease. Nevertheless, it is the army hygiene lecture that saves him and Kid McCarthy when the five soldiers go on leave. Only Billy refuses to go into a brothel; all the others, including Hank, who only kisses one of the women, contract either gonorrhea or syphilis. Happily, McCarthy remembers the hygiene lecture and is successfully treated at a chemical prophylaxis station. Kid clearly had learned the value of self-protection, but he also has to be taught some manners. When he sneers at Billy, "Ain't youse afraid that you will have a wet dream tonight?" the hero's answer is to knock him out with a single blow, winning not only the respect of the other soldiers but, in the best movie tradition, Kid's friendship, too. At the end of the film, only Billy and Kid are fit to fight; the other three are left behind in an army hospital.[27]

News of the film provoked a wave of protests, and not only from Catholics. One Protestant minister characterized it as "the vilest thing that I have ever seen," while a colleague declared: "I felt as though I had been obliged to listen to a smutty story and, though I heard it against my will, it will stick and dirty me." At first, Father Burke of the War Council tried unsuccessfully to block the release of the film, arguing for a more positive approach based on morality and idealism rather than fear. Rebuffed by Fosdick, Burke urged the army at least to eliminate any titillating scenes from the picture, such as the interior of the brothel, along with all shots of contact between the men and the prostitutes, for "such caresses," he argued, "are calculated . . . to arouse in every man who beholds them, sexual feelings, particularly . . . for men who have visited houses of prostitution." Even the letter from Billy's sweetheart on the need to remain pure was out of bounds. "We discuss such things in social hygiene circles," he exclaimed, "but we don't discuss them with the women we love." Fosdick made a few concessions—interior brothel scenes were shortened, and the letter from Billy's sweetheart was eliminated—but he refused to meet the priest's other demands because they would have cut the heart out of the picture.[28]

Father Burke could draw some comfort from the fact that *Fit to Fight* was to be shown only to male audiences; the second government film, *End of the Road*, didn't offer even that small consolation. Fosdick had become alarmed by the large number of complaints like the one from Decatur, Illinois, that half the young women in the senior class of the local high school had become pregnant after the construction of a military base in the area. It wasn't the plight of the women that bothered the CTCA; its only concern was the increased risk that military men might contract venereal disease.[29]

Again Fosdick decided that a movie would be the best way to deal with the issue. This time, the story would focus on what he considered to be "the source of the problem": the false modesty that left young women unprepared to deal with their sexuality. *End of the Road* told the story of two recent high school graduates: Mary Lee, whose mother tells her the "facts of life," and Vera Wagner, whose mother is interested only in having her daughter snare a wealthy husband. Both girls go to New York, where Vera, a shop girl, becomes a kept woman, thus taking the first step on the "road that leads to disease, desertion, and disgrace." Mary, in contrast, becomes a nurse and takes the high road, rejecting her boyfriend's request to have sex on the eve of his departure for France.[30]

Several other stories were woven into the film to demonstrate that what the CTCA referred to as "the girl problem" was a threat to everyone. An Irish maid who is impregnated by a chauffeur shoots him when he refuses to marry her and then, in remorse, holds a rosary to the dying man's lips. And social class was no protector against the ravages of the disease: a socialite whose young husband has contracted gonorrhea commits suicide after their child is born blind.

Vera, embittered by her experience, wants to wreak revenge on all men for the syphilis she has contracted. Fortunately, she runs into Mary, who convinces her to visit the physician she works for. Dr. Bell takes Vera on a tour of a hospital filled with female victims of venereal disease whose symptoms range from body sores to motor problems. Vera is somehow cured, and the picture ends with a shot of Mary and the doctor becoming engaged.

The CTCA tried to avoid another fight with the War Council by arranging a preview of the film for Father Burke on October 11, 1918. To no one's surprise, the priest could find nothing redeeming about the movie except its artistic quality. The film's technical superiority rendered it all the more dangerous in his eyes, for it made illicit sex that much more alluring. Charging that sex dominated the entire film, he pointed out that even Mary, the heroine, was depicted as "sexed from her school days" because her mother had given her a sex education book for teen-aged girls. A young woman seeing the film, he declared, could only conclude that sex was the greatest factor in life, an "abnormal" and "perverted" attitude. A case in point was the young man who asked Mary to go to bed with him on the eve of his departure for France. Despite Mary's refusal, Father Burke argued that young women would get the idea that such requests from soldiers were frequent. "If a pro-German hinted at this we would put him in jail," he said. But the maid's affair with the chauffeur especially enraged him. Although several other women in the film had also lost their virtue, the maid's fall from grace was apparently the only episode that did not ring true because, as he pointed out, "the moral virtue of the Irish girl is proverbial." Her use of the rosary in the death scene only added "one more vicious element in a film that had lost its moral compass."[31]

According to the priest, the most dangerous part of the film was its message that "knowledge is virtue and ignorance is sin." Young women in the audience, he pointed out, would conclude that "sexual intercourse is not bad if one knows how to avoid the consequences." Rather than trying to appeal to the female audience's better instincts, he claimed, the film sought to frighten them straight by showing them scenes of diseased women. "Has our civilization become so beggared of worthy motive," he wrote, "that we must ask the derelicts of humanity to parade themselves . . . exposing their rotting diseased limbs that we might be inspired to virtue?" Although Father Burke's comments left little room for negotiation, the CTCA reviewed the film to determine if it could make enough changes to get the priest to drop his opposition. The filmmakers eliminated a few scenes, including the chauffeur's murder, but the military lost interest in the project when the war ended a few weeks later.[32]

Convinced that these films offered a golden opportunity to combat a major social problem, the American Social Hygiene Association, the developer of the two movies, was able to win the backing of the U.S. Public Health Service to show them to the public. In order to give it a broader appeal, *Fit to Fight* was updated by adding a scene showing what happened to the five soldiers. In the revised version, retitled *Fit to Win*, the audience learns that Kid McCarthy died a hero's death in France. And in what must be one of the most unusual farewells of an officer to his troops, Billy, now a captain, advises his men to avoid prostitutes and to keep morally clean in civilian life. With his mission accomplished, the movie fades to a close with Billy at the altar with his sweetheart.[33]

To obtain maximal exposure, the association distributed the films to the public through an independent company, Public Health Films. In an effort to head off any problems, the Assistant Surgeon General sent a letter asking state and municipal governments to suspend any censorship that "might impede this very essential missionary work." To reduce the discomfort of the more sensitive souls, men and women were admitted to the films on alternate days or seated separately, with one group in the orchestra and the other in the balcony. To reinforce the serious nature of the presentation, the distributor also tried to arrange for a doctor to attend each showing and answer questions.[34]

Public Health Films was encouraged by the National Board of Review's approval of both movies, although the board's spokesman made it clear that it had passed the film on the basis of the filmmakers' "sincerity and artistic skills," and that the board was in no position to judge the "pathological detail . . . or the efficacy of treatment." Some of the board's reviewers had, in fact, been bothered by the graphic nature of a few scenes in *End of the Road.* One woman found the shots focusing on syphilitic lesions "unendurable," but the majority agreed with another reviewer, a physician, that although the effect of these scenes was "sickening . . . that was precisely what was wished."[35]

The two major trade journals were divided over the merits of the films. *Moving Picture World* felt that as long as the movies were shown to separate male and female audiences, they would do more good than harm; however, *Exhibitor's Herald* warned theater owners that unsuspecting patrons in search of "sweet romance" would be disgusted by the "sickening exposure of the ravages of the social evil." The *Herald*'s position on the films probably came as no surprise to its readers as its Catholic owner, Martin Quigley—later a coauthor of the 1930 Production Code—had refused to publish any social hygiene film advertisements since 1915. He rejected the notion that such pictures had any educational appeal. "For every person who comes to be instructed," he wrote, "a thousand come to wallow in the filthy thoughts suggested."[36]

Quigley may have overstated the case, but most of the people who thronged to the films did come in search of sexual excitement rather than medical information. Ads like those posted in front of a Chicago theater for *End of the Road*, promising to show "immorality exposed . . . how syphilis can be contracted by a kiss" while giving the answer to "where babies come from," reinforced such hopes. The films drew huge crowds in small and large towns alike. Two thousand people turned out to see *Fit to Win* in Pittsfield, Massachusetts, on a single Sunday afternoon in August. In Saint Paul, Minnesota, four thousand disappointed customers, denied seats because of a full house, rioted for almost two hours outside the theater.[37]

Commercial release of the films galvanized the War Council. Evil was evil, Father Burke maintained, whether men and women experienced it separately or together. Nor did the presence of a physician make it any more acceptable.

The council immediately appealed to the various Catholic societies across the country, declaring that these films had to be "squelched." Members were asked to send their protests to the Surgeon General. "Do not delay a single day," urged one council member; "although we are a patient people, we shall not tolerate any violation of the standards for which Catholic manhood and womanhood stand."[38]

The first major challenge to the public exhibition of both films came in New York, where Father Burke had a good deal of influence, having once been head of the Catholic Theater Movement and a member of the Commissioner of Licenses' advisory committee. On the priest's advice, Commissioner John F. Gilbert threatened to revoke the license of the Grand Opera House of Brooklyn if it continued to show *Fit to Win*. After a series of appeals and counterappeals, U.S. District Court Judge Learned Hand allowed *Fit to Win* to be shown on the condition that the interior scenes of the brothel and any suggestion that the madam had paid off the police were eliminated.[39]

Unwilling to give in, Gilbert sought the counsel of a number of civic organizations. Most recommended that the films be shown, although there was considerable disagreement over who should control the distribution of the films and who should be allowed to see them. John B. Peters, chairman of the Committee of Fourteen, one of the city's many reform groups, recommended that the movies be distributed by the federal government instead of Public Health Films in order to avoid exploitation. He also commented that the films were appropriate for men and boys but not for women, who would go to see it "either through misunderstanding or for an improper reason."[40]

Father Burke sought to stiffen Gilbert's resolve by providing him with a lengthy analysis of the "gratuitous evil" in *Fit to Win*. He argued, the film failed to accomplish its main objective: to persuade its viewers to avoid temptation. Instead, he noted, the most dramatic parts of the film were those centered on the brothel, which only served to excite the viewer's sexual imagination. Even if all of his objections were honored, he told Gilbert, he would still oppose the film because moral education could be given effectively only in the home or the church, not in a place of entertainment.[41]

Swayed by the priest, Gilbert launched an appeal arguing that the picture was so "extremely revolting" that it would endanger public morality. In a reversal of Judge Learned Hand's decision, the U.S. Court of Appeals found that Gilbert had acted on reasonable grounds in blocking the film. Judge Kapper noted that the film's titles, which he refused to read aloud in court in order not to offend public decency, were enough to support the commissioner's contention. Although the film had played an important role during the war, he concluded, a public exhibition would constitute "a gross impropriety."[42]

The Catholic War Council followed up the New York victory with a mass mailing. A pamphlet entitled "Fit to Win," based on Father Burke's critique, was sent to some 15,000 Catholic organizations across the country. In Philadelphia, Cardinal Dougherty's denunciation resulted in an order by the city's health commissioner to pull the film from distribution; the Pennsylvania Board of Censors soon barred all showings of *End of the Road* within the state. The final blow came when the National Board of Review withdrew its approval and said that henceforth it would pass only social hygiene films endorsed by a public health agency. Recognizing the rising tide of protest, the Public Health Service retracted its endorsement of the two films.[43]

The War Council's campaign against these films marked the church's first significant success in combating films it found objectionable. Father Burke cited it in his effort to convince the hierarchy of the need to continue the organization after the war. As a result, the War Council, which had been devised as a temporary operation to deal with war-related problems, became the National Catholic Welfare Council in September 1919.

The decision to continue the council reflected a growing consensus within the church that it should play a more active role in national affairs. The council would lobby for Catholic interests and advise the bishops who met each year in the nation's capital. Father Burke also viewed it as the logical agency to coordinate the church's efforts to combat anti-Catholicism. "Now whatever our strength may be, if it is scattered, dissipated, unable to summon its entire self it will be weak and helpless before the trained, organized, watchful enemy," he wrote. Consequently, when the Vatican terminated the council on February 25, 1922, in response to the complaints of Cardinals Dougherty and O'Connell that it was a threat to their local autonomy, its supporters, citing the resurgence of the Ku Klux Klan, were able to get the pope to reverse his decision by arguing that America's Catholics were "on the eve of a prolonged and virulent persecution." The National Catholic Welfare Conference (renamed again in the fall of 1922) (NCWC) improved communication within the church and provided it with a national voice when the hierarchy agreed on an issue. Although the Catholic church was never as unified as people thought, the NCWC reflected the beginning of a trend toward greater centralization within the church. Although the bishops were free to go their own way, the conference's various pronouncements on social issues reinforced the popular image of a church with the power to direct and control its members unrivaled by any other religious group in America.[44]

Although church leaders had worked together to curtail the distribution of the two public health films, there was little agreement among the bishops on how to deal with Hollywood's growing influence during the 1920s. A few bishops, like John Murray of Portland, Maine, believed that the only way to deal with the movies was to quarantine them. Characterizing the industry as the "most destructive element that ever entered into the life of this country," he refused to have anything to do with it. "You might as well ask me to approve a committee of the hierarchy to supervise properly conducted saloons and road houses," he declared, "as to ask me to approve of any kind of committee to supervise films." Murray's distrust of films was so deep-seated that he even opposed exhibiting Catholic films in church recreation halls for fear that they would stimulate a taste for the new medium among the faithful.[45]

Most bishops took a more realistic position, recognizing that Catholics had already acquired the "movie habit." The *NCWC Bulletin* declared, "The influence of motion pictures upon the lives of our people is greater than the combined influence of all our churches, schools, and ethical organizations." Especially disturbing was the threat that the movies posed for Catholic children. The church had made a major commitment to building its own school system, only to find that a few hours at the local movie house could undermine everything it had tried to accomplish. One Ursuline nun exclaimed: "Even the youngest student will tell you that she 'just adores Theda Bara' . . . and that she's going to be a movie actress when she grows up 'because they make lots of money.'" Even more alarming were the older girls she encountered who were "half-convinced that 'love' justifies anything. That a 'woman has the right to live her own life as she pleases.'"[46]

Catholic fears were also sparked by the anti-Semitism that characterized much of the general opposition to the film business. Karl K. Kitchens, writing in *Columbia*, the official publication of the Catholic Knights of Columbus, claimed that the industry was controlled by "foreign-born Jews of the lowest sort" who were willing to "glorify crime and make heroes of seducers and heroines of prostitutes for a dollar." Similarly, Pat Scanlan, editor of the *Brooklyn Tablet*, declared that the moviemakers had no interest in cleaning up the industry because they were nothing "more or less than alien ex-buttonhole makers and pressers" who had brought the principles and ideals of "the cloak and suit trade" with them to Hollywood.[47]

Catholic leaders' positions on "the movie question" during the 1920s covered a broad range. Priests like Father Edward Garesche, a regular writer for the *Ecclesiastical Review*, the *Brooklyn Tablet's* Pat Scanlan, and Father Frederick Siedenberg, dean of Chicago's Loyola University, were just a few who felt that the "filth" emanating from the screen justified state censorship. In an article warning pastors about the "wholesale corruption" infecting their parishes, Garesche found it difficult even to discuss the type of material cut by the Pennsylvania Censorship Board, including: "scenes of a woman pulling the trousers off a preacher while he is caught in a tree; a view of a woman holding up the preacher's trousers; and a view of girls dancing around the preacher in his undergarments." Sadly, the priest reminded his readers, only a few states were protected against such sordid stuff. Scanlan and Siedenberg were especially concerned about what was regularly referred to as "the slaughter of the innocents." Pointing out that films promoted promiscuity and "moronism" among the young, they argued that the state's power to confiscate obscene literature should be extended to the screen. Others, like Cardinal James Gibbons of Baltimore and his successor, Archbishop Michael J. Curley, favored Sunday closing laws, not because the clerics opposed movies per se, but because the stories that were shown on the Lord's day focused on "illegitimate love affairs, triangles, marital infidelity, and sex problems, ad nauseam."[48]

Yet some Catholic clerics took a surprisingly liberal position on censorship. Father Thomas M. Schwertner, editor of *The Rosary* magazine, argued that censorship was a violation of American liberties and that legislation would accomplish little beyond breeding a race of hypocrites. For Father Francis Finn, censorship had a dangerous tendency to kill the creativity and originality in the art of the motion picture. But most of the Catholic opposition to censorship stemmed from distrust of government interference in moral issues and the belief that censorship was counterproductive because it publicized evil films that might disappear if left alone.[49]

In the absence of a consensus on how to deal with the film problem, the NCWC tried to forge a policy that would not alienate the bishops. The initial organized Catholic approach to the film industry emerged in the fall of 1919 with the creation of the Motion Picture Committee, under the leadership of Charles McMahon, who reported directly to Father Burke. McMahon was directed to work quietly with the producers to eliminate indecent pictures. If they refused to cooperate, he was free to carry the battle to the pages of the *NCWC Bulletin*. McMahon's opening barrage was directed against the sex-hygiene films that were based, he said, on the premise that "if you cram young people with sex knowledge, you will keep them honest and pure." The first films to incur his wrath were *Know Thy Husband* (1919) and *Open Your Eyes* (1919), the latter relating the tale of a young woman saved at the last moment from marriage to a syphilitic playboy who ends up in an insane asylum. McMahon dismissed it as a "rotten . . . vile hodge-podge of obscene gestures, motions, embraces . . . interspersed with a few foolish, futile slices of moral fudge."[50]

He directed most of his committee's opposition, however, to *Know Thy Husband*, in which a young man goes to the city for excitement and contracts a "loathsome disease" that prevents him from marrying his sweetheart. When he learns that an old friend plans a night filled with wine, women, and song before joining the navy, the sadder but wiser hero tries unsuccessfully to dissuade him by relating his own experience. Desperate to save his friend, the hero convinces a group of models to pretend to be prostitutes and then drugs the aspiring rake before anything happens. When the reveler's head finally clears, he is told by a cooperating doctor that he has contracted the worst form of syphilis. Once he has learned his lesson, he is informed of the ruse and joins the navy with a light heart. Obviously more successful than the public health system in treating the dread disease, Hollywood cures the hero, enabling him to marry his sweetheart. Characterizing the film as just another effort to exploit the topic in order to make money, the *Bulletin*'s reviewer went on to argue that the movie's purported message was, in fact, contradicted by its own plot. When the hero first related his experience "in all its awful details," his story only made his visitor more eager to plunge into the same stream of sin. The only logical inference one could make from all this, the reviewer concluded, was that knowledge of the possible consequences of evil did not dissuade anybody but apparently made people more determined to try it themselves.[51]

The NCWC's Motion Picture Committee did not limit itself to blacklisting dangerous films; McMahon also encouraged the hierarchy to harness the power of movies for the good of the church. Bishop William T. Russell of Charleston, South Carolina, one of several members of the hierarchy to respond to the challenge, hoped to fund a series of films to spread "concealed propaganda" on issues like divorce. McMahon himself talked grandly of enlisting the best Catholic writers in the country to tell the real history of the church in America: stories of the Catholic founding of California, the Jesuit missionaries in the Mississippi Valley, and the Catholic soldiers of the American Revolution. Yet the few movies the church did turn out, including a four-reeler documenting the work of the New York Archdiocese's charities, had little appeal beyond parish recreation halls. The NCWC's own effort was a five-reel film in 1919 entitled *American Catholics in War and Reconstruction*, which it hoped would silence anti-Catholic bigotry forever by documenting the church's role on the battlefield, the home front, and the revitalization of Europe. Unfortunately, a preview at the annual bishops' meeting in Washington indicated that the film itself was in desperate need of revitalization. A number of viewers complained that it omitted some of the most important contributions like the work of church chaplains; others objected to the heavy dose of text and statistical information that made the movie seem more like a book than a film. Ed Murtaugh, a reporter who attended the screening, told his sister, who worked at the NCWC, that the film was "frightfully dull." It might appeal to the "highbrows of the church," but the "hoi polloi won't understand it," and "you know the Catholic Church is nine-tenths poor people." He added that what the film really needed was a "few good looking women . . . to relieve the monotony of the plain girls that are screened."[52]

In response to the overwhelmingly negative audience reaction, the film was revised by shortening some of the text and adding eighty-nine new scenes. The second version was shown in 1920 to some 900,000 viewers, but it never lived up to McMahon's expectation that it would become a major weapon in the church's battle against anti-Catholicism. Clearly, if the church had any hope of affecting the type of films Hollywood was turning out, it would have to influence the choices Catholics were making at the box office.[53]

TWO

When Irish Eyes Weren't Smiling

In the spring of 1919, leaders of the fight against the public exhibition of *Fit to Win* and *The End of the Road* received some help from an unexpected source: the National Association of the Motion Picture Industry (NAMPI), which had been formed in 1916 to enable filmmakers to present a united front against attempts to establish federal censorship of the movies.

In an effort to convince the public that the industry was capable of regulating itself, NAMPI announced that it would promptly begin to police all films produced by its members. Part of its plan called for members not to release any movies to theaters exhibiting films that had not been passed by the association. Although it heralded this step as part of its cleanup campaign, NAMPI was actually attempting to reduce competition by driving social agencies like the American Social Hygiene Association, which had produced the military's anti–venereal disease movies, out of the commercial market. Choosing to ignore NAMPI's hidden agenda, Martin Quigley's *Exhibitor's Herald* hailed the plan as marking the death of both indecent films and the need for political censorship.[1]

It would take more than promises to win over the reformers. Although films like *Don't Change Your Husband*, *The Married Virgin*, and *Forbidden Fruit* promised much more than they delivered, their titles alone alarmed the industry's enemies. Moreover, critics found fault with any film if they looked hard enough. After the Pennsylvania board of censors had ordered twenty-two cuts in Cecil B. deMille's *Why Change Your Wife?* the Rev. Clifford G. Twombly was still dissatisfied, noting that the state reviewers had missed a shot of a naked kewpie doll on the mantelpiece performing "a suggestive dance."[2]

The filmmakers' earlier hope that their agreement with the National Board of Review would protect them had faded in the face of their enemies' complaints about the board's lax standards. A 1920 study comparing 228 films passed by both the National Board of Review and the Pennsylvania censors revealed that the board had made only forty-seven cuts as compared to 1,464 ordered by the state agency. While a disinterested observer might question the Pennsylvania censors' performance, reformers cited the numbers to show that the board had outlived whatever usefulness it may have had. The filing of censorship bills in thirty-seven states in 1921 convinced the industry that it had to do more than talk about reform. In March 1921, the major film companies adopted an industry code known as the "Thirteen Points," the first of several efforts over the next decade to convince the public that they could be trusted to clean their own house. The signers of the pact pledged not to produce or exhibit films on such topics as white slavery, illicit love, bloodshed, and violence. They also promised not to ridicule religious leaders or public officials or to undermine respect for the law, all subjects that had caused trouble with state censorship boards. The Thirteen Points were aimed at blocking any pending legislation in the states, but industry leaders were especially concerned about the situation in New York, where passage of a censorship bill could create a domino effect in other states. A New York regulation board also posed another threat: because most films opened in New York, films would have to meet that state's standards, making it a kind of national censor.[3]

The filmmakers treated the proposed New York bill as a life-or-death struggle. A short subject entitled *The Non-Sense of Censorship* was shown in all the state's theaters. In one scene, an actor playing poet Rupert Brooke is reading a booklet entitled *The Rules of Censorship*. A pained expression crosses his face as he declares: "The Motion Picture is about fifteen years old. Sin is somewhat older than that, yet the censors would have us believe that it was not Satan but Thomas Alva Edison who invented 'The Fall of Man.'" In another segment, Douglas Fairbanks, Sr., who is being pushed around by a tough, finally musters a sickly grin and declares: "Say, I'd like to mop up the floor with this bird, but the censors won't let me fight."[4]

But even Fairbanks was no match for the reformers; the legislature passed the bill. An effort to persuade Governor Nathan Miller to veto it was undermined by heavy-handed lobbying by industry representatives, combined with their admission that objectionable films had been produced since the adoption of the Thirteen Points. The lobbyists' task was made all the more difficult because Miller had been offended by a scene in D. W. Griffith's *Way Down East* in which the birth of the heroine's baby was introduced by the words "Maternity; Woman's Gethsemane." In signing the bill, the governor rejected the industry's last-ditch promise to reform, noting that the public "had heard that old story before."[5]

The establishment of the New York State Motion Picture Commission was a bitter defeat for the industry. No longer able to rely on the cooperative National Board of Review, which continued to work in the shadow of the state agency, moviemakers now had to submit their work to more rigorous reviewers. The new board ruled on the first day that westerns could be "wooly" but not "wild" and cut out all scenes of the interior of a frontier barroom. A shot in *Bad Boy*, another cowboy film, of the villain impaling a beetle on a pin, and a view of the heroine's leg from ankle to knee were also apparently more wild than wooly, and both were removed. But when the censors ordered the elimination of a group of Atlantic City bathing beauties from a Pathé News clip, *Variety* felt that this time they had gone too far, pointing out that the city's mayor, who also appeared in the shot, didn't seem to mind the company.[6]

Just one month after the New York censors began to apply their scissors, the public learned that the popular comedian Fatty Arbuckle had been charged with manslaughter in the death of a young actress, Virginia Rappe, at a drunken Labor Day weekend party in San Francisco. Arbuckle's popularity with children added to the notoriety of the case, and although he was acquitted at his third trial (the two previous ones ended in hung juries), many people continued to believe that Rappe's ruptured bladder was caused not by periadenitis, as the defense claimed, but by the comedian's great weight as he forced himself on her. Even if Rappe had died of natural causes, William Jennings Bryan charged, Arbuckle was still guilty of the worst type of depravity and should be banished from the screen. Despite the actor's final acquittal, public outrage forced the industry to withdraw his films from exhibition. Apparently fearful that even hardened criminals might be harmed by exposure to such a nefarious role model, the warden at Sing Sing prison refused to show Arbuckle's movies to the prisoners.[7]

The industry received another blow on February 1, 1922, when Hollywood director William Desmond Taylor was found slain in his home. Although his murder was never solved, the case ruined the careers of two actresses who were romantically linked to the director: Mabel Normand, the popular comedienne, and starlet Mary Miles Minter. Rumors that Taylor had used drugs added to the industry's woes. And when actor Wallace Reid died of a drug overdose a year later in a sanatorium where he had sought a cure for his addiction, Hollywood was castigated as the Sodom of the Western world. According to one magazine story, the reason movies cost so much to make was that scores of blackmailers were kept on industry payrolls to keep them quiet about the private lives of the stars.[8]

At first the industry tried to distance itself from the scandals. The *Exhibitor's Herald* argued that moviemakers were the victims of a double standard, pointing out that when the head of a large financial institution had been involved in a sensational case at the time of the Arbuckle trial, no one had called for an investigation of the banking business. *Moving Picture World* declared that the film industry was similarly no more responsible for the Arbuckle affair than the "reverend clergymen were responsible for the minister of the gospel who, in cold blood, murdered a young woman of his parish in Boston not so long ago." But nothing seemed to work; the filmmakers who had exploited the public's fascination with movie stars found it impossible to argue that their foibles had nothing to do with the system that had created them. As the anonymous author of *The Sins of Hollywood* put it: "There is something about the pictures which seem to make men and women less human, more animal like."[9]

Hoping to restore public confidence, the moviemakers decided to emulate the baseball owners, who had salvaged the sport in the wake of the 1919 Black Sox scandal by hiring an outsider, Judge Kenesaw Mountain Landis, as commissioner. Hollywood, concerned about the danger of federal censorship, found its outsider among one of Washington's most powerful insiders. In March 1922, Will Hays, postmaster general in the Harding administration and an elder in the Presbyterian church, became president of the newly formed Motion Picture Producers and Distributors of America (MPPDA), the successor to NAMPI.

Hays was a master politician whose first major task was to deal with the calls for censorship that continued to sweep the nation. His initial challenge came in Massachusetts, where the state legislature's bill establishing a film censorship board had been slated to take effect on January 1, 1922. Fortunately, the industry had been granted a stay of execution when the commonwealth's Allied Theaters Association gathered 25,000 signatures postponing implementation until the voters decided the question in a state referendum. Hays coordinated a massive campaign to reverse a national trend toward state censorship. Once again, the industry drew on its own resources, bombarding movie audiences in Massachusetts with filmed arguments against censorship, including one featuring young Jackie Coogan appealing to voters to defeat the bill in the name of patriotism.

But the politically astute Hays did not repeat the mistakes of the industry lobbyists who had failed to block the New York bill. Leaving nothing to chance, public officials were put on the MPPDA's payroll, including one justice who received a $2,500 retainer and $250 a week during the course of the campaign. Other industry friends, including Joseph P. Kennedy, the father of the future president, offered their help to Hays. John M. Casey, Boston's commissioner of licenses, induced the city council that made "Banned in Boston" famous to pass a unanimous resolution denouncing censorship.[10]

Hays also sent Courtland Smith, the association's secretary, to visit all the Massachusetts newspapers to enlist them in the anti-censorship campaign. Smith made several trips across the state to identify those editors who opposed censorship and those who needed persuading. Some papers, like Hearst's *Boston American*, which offered a $1,000 prize for the best essay on "Why Massachusetts should not have political censorship," clearly needed no prodding. Smith suggested to Hays that he use his connection to Senator David I. Walsh to get to papers like the *Boston Globe*, which had yet to take a stand. And if all else failed, Smith reminded his boss, the promise of some additional movie advertising might move a paper into the anti-censorship camp.[11]

Although several Catholic men's and women's groups were among the 406 organizations supporting the censorship bill, the church itself did not take an official position on the question. Its silence, however, coupled with an editorial in the archdiocesan newspaper, the *Pilot*, noting that the MPPDA seemed sincerely interested in reform, was generally interpreted as a sign that the church opposed government regulation. Nevertheless, despite all Hays's efforts, *Variety* predicted that the state would overwhelmingly vote in favor of censorship.[12]

Aware that the heavy Catholic vote could be crucial, Hays needed something more than benign neutrality from the church. One possible solution was an endorsement of the MPPDA's cleanup efforts from the NCWC. Prior to the industry's appointment of Hays, Charles McMahon, head of the NCWC Motion Picture Committee, had regularly criticized Hollywood's habit of "dragging into otherwise harmless pictures, two or three hundred feet of cabaret scenes, nakedness, oriental dances, suggestive bed room and bath room situations and other forms of filth." At one point, a frustrated McMahon had even tried to persuade Father John J. Burke that the NCWC should lead an interfaith effort to sponsor a national censorship bill, but the priest turned him down, declaring that he opposed any type of government censorship.[13]

McMahon quickly changed his views after the appointment of Hays. As part of his plan to win the support of a number of organizations including the National Organization of Parents and Teachers and the Federal Council of Churches, Hays had contacted McMahon during the summer of 1922 to solicit the NCWC's help. In July, Hays was rewarded by an editorial in the *NCWC Bulletin* praising him for making good on his promise to clean up the movies. The MPPDA distributed some 200,000 copies of the editorial to Massachusetts priests, Catholic leaders, and voters.[14]

When the vote on the referendum was announced, it was clear that the film industry had made the right decision in choosing Hays. In the only state referendum on film censorship ever held in the United States, the voters soundly rejected the idea 563,173 to 208,252. Boston, a city with a large Catholic population, voted against the bill by a similar margin, 104,824 to 38,240. The referendum's impact was felt far beyond Massachusetts as the vote broke the momentum in favor of state censorship. Although the threat could never be ignored, no state censorship boards were established after the industry's 1922 victory. As far as the film industry was concerned, the Massachusetts vote proved once and for all that the public opposed government regulation. As late as 1953, industry representatives were still citing the 1922 vote as the only true test of America's view of state censorship.[15]

Hays and the MPPDA, however, had little time to savor their success. Seven states and a number of cities had censorship boards, each with its own peculiar concerns. Pennsylvania cut childbirth and shooting scenes, Kansas prohibited on-screen smoking by women, Ohio tried to stamp out sex, while Chicago seemed to be trying to compensate for its reputation as America's crime capital by coming down hard on sex and violence. The censorship boards in Virginia and Atlanta, Georgia, were especially concerned with racial matters. Virginia prohibited the showing of black filmmaker Oscar Michaux's *The House behind the Cedars* because it dealt with miscegenation. A year later, Atlanta barred *Uncle Tom's Cabin* on the ground that "it painted a false and exaggerated picture of the south and slavery, making an isolated case of brutality appear as typical." The New York board, in contrast, seemed to be on the lookout for anything and everything, eliminating 3,244 scenes and 566 titles from 627 pictures in 1924 because they either "incited to crime" or were "inhuman," "immoral," "indecent," "sacrilegious," or "obscene." Moreover, the small number of states with censorship boards did not mean that the industry had a free ride elsewhere. Several states ordered the local distributor to adhere to the alterations made by a neighboring state board. The cuts occasionally rendered the film incomprehensible; they always added to its cost. *Variety* estimated that the time and effort involved in making the ordered eliminations added more than $3 million each year to the industry's expenses.[16]

The industry celebrated the Massachusetts victory, but it could not let down its guard. All it took was some scandal or a star's divorce to spur some local solon to file a censorship bill in the state legislature. Nor were politicians above raising the issue in order to extort funds from the film industry. As early as 1919, the chair of NAMPI's campaign committee complained to producer Hal Roach about the "enormous cost" involved in electing friends of the industry in the past three years. Charles Pettijohn and Fred Beetson, two of Hays's key assistants, regularly complained about censorship bills that were filed to "shake down" the industry. In Oregon, a proposal to regulate films prompted the usual outpouring of offers to "help" the industry. A state legislator demanded $2,000 to kill the bill before it reached the floor, while the chairman of the Senate Judiciary Committee traded his support in the hope of obtaining a monopoly of the MPPDA's legal work in the state. In some instances the price of a vote was as small as promising a screen test for a senator's niece who was an aspiring actress. Politicians, of course, were not the only ones to recognize the opportunities connected with censorship. A Portland newspaper editor, who warned Beetson that all the talk about money and censorship was hurting the industry, promised to line up public sentiment against any future bills if he were given a suitable retainer.[17]

Although Hays was not above rewarding the industry's "friends," his major job was to convince the public that outside regulation was unnecessary. In pursuit of this goal, he established the Public Relations Committee in 1922. The committee, headed by Jason Joy, the former national secretary of the American Red Cross, had two major tasks: a behind-the-scenes effort to head off any future scandals and a much-publicized campaign to encourage the channeling of complaints directly to the studios rather than the legislatures. Each producer was to appoint a studio contact who would be available at any hour to deal with local police, prosecutors, coroners, and reporters in order to squelch potentially damaging stories. The committee derived much of its success from the cooperation of the local police departments, whose efforts ranged from warning a studio to keep its people out of a neighborhood speakeasy that was about to be raided to hushing up drunken driving charges against some star. Had the system been in effect at the time of the Arbuckle scandal, the Hays Office declared, its skill at damage control would have justified the committee's entire yearly budget.[18]

The committee's main objective, however, was to co-opt, or at least neutralize, those organizations that could sway public opinion for or against the industry. It was made up of representatives from a number of organizations including the Girl Scouts, the General Federation of Women's Clubs, the Federal Council of Churches, the Daughters of the American Revolution, the National Catholic Welfare Conference, and the International Federation of Catholic Alumnae. In what became known as "the open door policy," committee members were encouraged to forward their complaints to the Hays Office, which would distribute them to the offending studios. The industry, in turn, financed the printing and distribution of lists of recommended films prepared by some of the member organizations. It was in theory the best of both worlds for the filmmakers, as complaints were handled privately while each new list of endorsed films would prove that Hollywood was keeping its promise to reform itself.

Unfortunately for Hays, the committee didn't always work according to plan. The first breach occurred shortly after its formation, when Hays decided to allow Fatty Arbuckle to resume his career. The wave of public protest, coupled with the committee's resolution urging the industry not to release any of Arbuckle's old films, made the comedian realize that his acting days were over, and he took a job behind the cameras. Nevertheless, the fact that Hays had even considered bringing Arbuckle back was enough to cause several members to charge him with betrayal of the public trust.[19]

The rift between some members and Hays widened when Famous Players–Lasky Studios decided to ignore the committee's advice against filming *West of the Water Tower*, a best-selling novel about small-town life which included illegitimacy, robbery, a dissolute clergyman, and a host of mean-spirited townspeople. Convinced now that the committee was a sham, several groups, led by the National Congress of Parents and Teachers and the General Federation of Women's Clubs, resigned.[20]

Hoping to avoid a repeat of the *West of the Water Tower* incident, Hays persuaded the members of the MPPDA to give him a summary of each play, story, or book they planned to put into production. Applying what became known as "the Formula," the Hays Office developed a list of unsuitable books and plays that were likely to run into trouble with the censors. By 1926, the list comprised ninety-two works, including *Desire under the Elms*, *Kongo*, *Shanghai Gesture*, *White Cargo*, and *The Green Hat*.

Hays's claim that the Formula had kept 160 books and plays from the screen in 1925 alone did little to appease the industry's critics. Part of the problem was structural. In order not to violate the antitrust laws, Hays's decision to block a particular story had to be made behind the scenes, which robbed the process of much of its public relations value. Meanwhile, authors and playwrights accused Hays of denying them a chance to cash in on their work. The author of *Kongo*, a tale of revenge set in Africa, claimed that the Formula had cost him between $50,000 and $75,000. Faced with an antitrust suit from the Authors' League of America, Hays worked out an agreement that allowed any author to rework a rejected story and present it to a studio again under a new title. But because the film reviewers usually identified the source of the newly titled film, industry opponents dismissed this plan as just one more effort by Hays to hoodwink the public.[21]

The Maryland Citizens' League for Better Pictures agreed, declaring in 1925 that, far from improving, movies had become more objectionable under Hays's leadership. Although he continued to boast of the reforms he had instituted, an internal report analyzing the cuts made by the New York censors that year seemed to confirm that the studios had not cleaned up their act. A man biting another man's hand or trying to gouge out his eyes, women in various stages of undress silhouetted behind a screen, and women in the "agonies" of childbirth were just some of the eliminations ordered by New York. Although it suggested that a few of the cuts were unjustified, including a close-up of three girls swinging their skirts to show their rolled-up stockings, the report concluded that had none of the cuts been made, the films would have played into the hands of those who favored federal censorship.[22]

Even though a number of organizations eventually withdrew from the Public Relations Committee after the *West of the Water Tower* flap, the NCWC and the International Federation of Catholic Alumnae stayed until the committee was reorganized. In fact, the NCWC's Charles McMahon, who was appointed to the Public Relations Committee's executive board in 1922, was for a time one of Hays's most outspoken supporters.

In a sense, Hays's wooing of the Catholic church was part of his general plan to drum up industry support wherever he could find it. But his failure to draw any significant backing from the Protestant churches, which should have been the natural constituency of someone who was a Presbyterian elder, made Catholic cooperation all the more necessary. Although few ministers went to such extremes as the Reverend Leo Hooper of Franklin, Michigan, who smashed a projector in the local town hall because movies were the "work of the devil," Protestant ministers constituted the core of Hays's opposition in the 1920s.[23]

Seeking to draw the Catholic church into a closer tie with the film industry, Hays suggested to McMahon that the MPPDA would be willing to contribute $10,000 a year to a committee made up of film industry representatives and the NCWC, which would provide the studios with a Catholic point of view. Although McMahon was vague about the particulars, he urged Father Burke to accept the offer. The priest, however, refused, pointing out that taking Hollywood money would undermine the NCWC's independence. But McMahon, who saw himself becoming a key player in the movie business, persisted. He told Burke that if industry money was the problem, Hays had said that he could find a wealthy Catholic to finance the operation and that additional funds could be raised by asking Catholic actors and directors for donations. But Burke refused to budge, forcing McMahon to settle for a stipend from the Hays Office for his work on the committee.[24]

What made McMahon so attractive to Hays was his role as chair of the NCWC's Motion Picture Committee, which by 1923 was issuing monthly lists of approved films. McMahon would claim in his later years that the Legion of Decency's classification system could be traced back to his committee's film evaluations. However, unlike the Legion, the *NCWC Bulletin* followed the approach of the Catholic Theater Movement, which evaluated plays and issued a "white list" of recommended films while ignoring the bad ones. In this sense, McMahon's position mirrored the consensus among that era's film reformers that the best way to clean up the movies was to educate the public to appreciate quality films. It also reflected the church's concern that negative evaluations might boost ticket sales. "Many of our people," declared Father Charles Gainor, "are just as much inclined to 'see for themselves' as the general public." The *Bulletin* usually summarized the plots of the recommended movies; the few long reviews were reserved for films with a religious theme. While generally endorsing Vitagraph's *From the Manger to the Cross* because of its faithfulness to the Bible and suitability for Catholic and Protestant audiences, the reviewer had a few reservations about the film's numerous title cards and the difficulty of reading the scriptural text in Old English type. The actor who played Christ was criticized for his air of "self-satisfaction and smugness" in the scenes depicting his miracles.[25]

The *Bulletin*'s monthly list was aimed at overcoming its readers' passive habit of going to their neighborhood theater without any thought to the film's content. As Father Gainor noted: "The same parents who so carefully watch the diet of their children permit them to absorb a menu of visual hodge podge that sickens the minds and dwarfs the souls of those same children." Even McMahon had to admit that one of his major problems was finding enough movies to recommend to his readers. Noting that the *Bulletin* had recommended only half of the four hundred pictures it had carefully chosen to review, McMahon lamented that only a few of even the endorsed films would be entitled to a place on a true white list. The only solution, he argued, was for Catholics to restrict their box-office dollars to truly worthwhile material in the hope that this would stimulate the studios to reform.[26]

Even McMahon's careful screening didn't please everyone. Father Placid Schmid, writing from Conception, Missouri, complained that he and several other priests had walked out of *Potash and Perlmudder*, which the *Bulletin* had recommended, when shots of "half-naked young women" being dressed by young men were flashed on the screen. All Father Burke could offer in the *Bulletin*'s defense was the suggestion that the priest may have seen a different print than the one it had recommended and the reminder that the *Bulletin*'s evaluations were never meant to take the place of an individual's conscience.[27]

Conscientious Catholic moviegoers could consult another list of recommended films, put out by the Motion Picture Bureau of the International Federation of Catholic Alumnae (IFCA). Concerned about reports that 30 to 40 percent of movies displayed scenes of "illicit love and adultery," the IFCA had begun advising Catholic schools in 1922 about what was suitable entertainment for their children. Under the leadership of Rita McGoldrick, a graduate of Rosary College in Illinois, the IFCA quickly eclipsed the NCWC as the major source of Catholic film information. By the mid-1920s, the NCWC could only evaluate some four hundred films each year, while the IFCA, with a large staff of volunteer graduates from Catholic high schools and colleges, annually reviewed 11,000 releases, including foreign films, documentaries, and short subjects. Strong differences of opinion among the staff were referred to McGoldrick, who screened the questionable material before making a decision. Controversial pieces, especially those with theological implications, were handed over to a committee headed by Father Francis X. Talbot, the Motion Picture Bureau's adviser and the literary editor of *America;* Father Wilfrid Parsons, the magazine's editor; novelist Kathleen Norris; and playwright Myles Connolly. Like McMahon's committee, the IFCA issued only a white list of recommended films, subdivided into those considered suitable for church entertainment or Catholic schools and those appropriate for mature audiences. Each film was also given an aesthetic rating of "good," "very good," or "excellent."[28]

The IFCA's growing influence led to McGoldrick's appointment to the National Board of Review's central committee in 1926, enabling two to four of the thirty regular IFCA reviewers to attend each preview at studio offices in New York. Members filled out two evaluation sheets, one for the board and one that responded to the IFCA's special guidelines, which prohibited, among other things, recommending any films that dealt with divorce. This dual responsibility occasionally colored their responses on the board's form. At times, Wilton Barrett, the board's executive secretary, had to remind McGoldrick that her reviewers had a tendency to become overzealous in rooting out evil. Noting that one woman had objected to a movie because of an immoral bedroom scene, he pointed out that the film was a farce and that a person concealed under a bed did not violate the sanctity of marriage.[29]

Because they chaired the only two national Catholic film committees, McGoldrick and McMahon often served as consultants to the major studios for films that touched on church matters. One of their earliest contacts arose from Universal Pictures' decision in 1923 to produce *The Hunchback of Notre Dame*. Victor Hugo's novel *Notre Dame de Paris*, on which the film was based, was on the index of books forbidden to be read by Catholics. Careful not to reveal that Universal had made a number of cuts at the suggestion of Catholic advisers, the studio's president, Carl Laemmle, presented the numerous revisions of the novel as a "surgico-screeno-literary operation [performed] without killing the patient" in order to make the story more palatable to the general public. Happy that the villain of the story was no longer a priest, the *NCWC Bulletin* recommended the film to its readers without reservation. Universal also used McGoldrick as a consultant on its adaptation of Edna Ferber's novel *Show Boat* after Cardinal George Mundelein of Chicago threatened to lead a boycott of Ferber's publisher because the story contained a negative description of a convent school. McGoldrick's assignment was to supervise the filming of the convent school scene to ensure that Catholic filmgoers would not be angered.[30]

Studios began to realize that they could avoid a lot of trouble and perhaps earn a place on a Catholic white list merely by making a few simple alterations. Sometimes all it took was the removal of a crucifix from a café wall, as in *Merry Widow*, or the addition of a scene to *Bobbed Hair* to make it clear from the start that the criminal is not a nun but someone using a religious habit as a disguise. The changes weren't limited to religious issues. In the 1927 comedy *Foiled*, removal of the line "His father was so lazy he married a widow with six children" was enough to win IFCA approval. Other films, however, required more extensive revision before they earned a place on the organization's white list. Two titles and two scenes, one showing the star in her underwear and the other a woman whose dress gets caught, revealing her "legs above the knee," had to be eliminated from *Ankles Preferred*. The studio had to agree to several requested cuts in *Tender Hour*, including a scene in which a girl in a hula skirt climbs on a table while a man walks across a room with a woman on his back. The provocative nature of hula skirts apparently transcended gender roles as a shot of two men in hula skirts was also removed.[31]

As a sign of the IFCA's growing power, McGoldrick reported to its members that Universal had made several requested changes necessitating the reburning of a building at a cost of several thousand dollars before it released *The Flaming Arrow* in 1926. Hollywood's courting of Catholic interests made some Protestants wonder if their concerns were being overlooked. The *Texas 100% American* charged Hays with playing into the hands of the Catholic hierarchy, while the editor of the *National Republic* asked him to explain "why it is that when a Protestant minister . . . is shown on screen, nine times out of ten, he is portrayed as a sap or a sissy."[32]

By 1926, McMahon and McGoldrick were among Hays's most dependable supporters. Outlining the benefits of the free advertising that could be gained from cooperating with independent organizations such as the NCWC, Hays singled out McMahon's work in a report to the MPPDA directors. McMahon, in turn, clearly hoped that he would eventually secure a position within the Hays Office. Aware of McMahon's goal, Jason Joy of the Public Relations Committee told Hays that he had spent all of his time on a trip to New York for the NCWC "on our business."[33]

McMahon and McGoldrick opposed any call for government censorship, especially in the Catholic press. When the Buffalo diocesan newspaper the *Echo* called for a "black list" of censored films, McMahon rushed to the industry's defense, declaring that the only answer to movie immorality was educating the public to support Hays's efforts to secure better films through self-regulation. He also rejected the *Brooklyn Tablet*'s push for government regulation, arguing that such a move would be an admission that Catholic education had failed to prepare children adequately to avoid the occasion of sin. McMahon and McGoldrick were two of the eleven witnesses who spoke on behalf of the industry before a 1926 Congressional committee investigating federal censorship. McMahon denounced the idea as the "most reckless intrusion upon the rights of [the American people] since the passage of the Volstead Act." And when the MPPDA sponsored a series of radio broadcasts highlighting the artistic contributions of the movies, McMahon was one of the first speakers. A good deal of McGoldrick's support took place behind the scenes. When a New Jersey convention of Holy Name societies passed a resolution in favor of state censorship, she got the names of all the delegates for Hays. Within a few weeks, each member was mailed a copy of McMahon's "American Public and Motion Pictures" and McGoldrick's "Getting Results in Motion Picture Work," both of which extolled the industry's cooperation with the Catholic church.[34]

Hays, who had been appointed head of the MPPDA in part because of his ties to the Protestant churches, began to count the IFCA and the NCWC among his most dependable allies. Noting in 1926 that they were "working just as hard for us as we are working for ourselves," he contrasted their open praise for his attempts at reform to the hesitancy of even friendly Protestant churches to say something positive about his efforts.[35]

Not all Catholics were as convinced as McGoldrick and McMahon about Hays's ability to reform the film industry. In a prescient article in the May 1927 issue of the *Ecclesiastical Review*, Father Edward Garesche argued that local pastors and priests had to be the ultimate monitors of what was shown on the screen. "Since our standards of morality are higher and purer," the priest declared, "it is up to us to protest, and if necessary, boycott 'bad films' at the neighborhood theaters."[36]

Unfortunately for Hays, MGM's release of a seemingly innocuous comedy, *The Callahans and the Murphys* (1927), threatened to undermine his campaign to cultivate Catholic support. At first glance, *The Callahans and the Murphys* seemed an unlikely candidate for protests and boycotts. Both Marie Dressler and Polly Moran, the two female stars, were using the film to make a comeback after a lengthy absence from the screen. The Irish-American press had complained now and then about Hollywood's willingness to resurrect the "stage Irishman" to get a few laughs. As Thomas J. Ford, an Irish-American journalist, noted, some producers believed that an Irish picture without a pig would be like *Hamlet* without the prince, but there didn't seem to be any harm in making one more Irish-American comedy. Nevertheless, in the summer and fall of 1927, protests over the MGM film reached a fever pitch in such heavily Irish-Catholic sections of the nation as Boston and New York. According to Boston city censor John Casey, the film caused more complaints than any picture since *Birth of a Nation*. It also led to a split between the Hays Office and one of its staunchest supporters, Charles McMahon.[37]

The film's plot was loosely based on a series of short stories by Kathleen Norris, a member of McGoldrick's advisory committee, and adapted to the screen by Frances Marion, MGM's highest paid writer. Budgeted at $350,000, it was billed as "the mirthquake of 1927." The studio had high hopes for the film, which was advertised as introducing Hollywood's first female comedy team; box-office success could lead to a series starring the two women.[38] The story involved two families, the Callahans and the Murphys, who live on opposite sides of Goat Alley. Mrs. Callahan and Mrs. Murphy are alternately the best of friends and the worst of enemies, who are not above thumbing their noses at each other across the alley. The subplot centered on a love affair between Mrs. Callahan's daughter Ellen and Mrs. Murphy's son Dan, a bootlegger. The audience is also introduced to the other members of the two families including Jim Callahan, who works as a sewer digger. A number of scenes highlighted Hollywood's version of Irish tenement life, including one in which Mrs. Callahan searches herself for fleas acquired from the dog that sleeps in her bed. The absence of indoor plumbing is underscored by several shots of a chamber pot, including one of young Terrance Callahan, Hollywood's stereotype of the irrepressible Irish urchin, parading around with it on his head.

It is clear to the audience that both families are Catholic. Mrs. Callahan regularly punctuates her conversations with the sign of the cross, correctly when sober and incorrectly when intoxicated. The humorous high point of the film is the St. Patrick's Day picnic, when the two mothers get uproariously drunk, pouring schooners of beer down the front of each other's dress. The picnic ends in the obligatory Irish donnybrook with police wagons and ambulances called to the scene. Meanwhile, Ellen Callahan is forced to go to the country to have a baby that the audience is led to believe is illegitimate. Unwilling to tell her mother about the impending birth, she arranges to have it left at Mrs. Callahan's door, which leads to a discussion of the infant's identity. Mrs. Callahan wonders: "Maybe it's a black Protestant." Her son suggests: "It might be a Jew baby." With that, Mrs. Callahan lifts the baby's diaper, winks broadly, and announces, "It ain't a Jew baby." Later the audience learns that the child is, in fact, legitimate since Ellen had married Dan Murphy earlier but had refused to live with him until he quit bootlegging. When he gives up his criminal ways and is united with his wife at the end of the film, the remaining question is whether they should reclaim their child in light of Mrs. Callahan's attachment to the infant. With a glance toward a picture of a large Irish family on the wall, Dan tells Ellen not to say anything, noting that one baby more or less makes no difference. She responds: "Thank heaven we're Irish."[39]

The initial reaction to the film seemed to augur well. Frances Marion later recalled that the favorable audience reception at a sneak preview indicated that MGM had hit the jackpot. Apparently no one at the time realized that the preview had been held in a section of California with few Irish-Americans. Further encouragement came from Charlie Chaplin and Harold Lloyd, who called it one of the funniest films ever made. Nor did the cuts requested by the several state boards of censors—minor deletions that centered on shortening the drinking scenes—pose any serious problems. After requesting the elimination of two titles, the National Board of Review recommended it for general audiences. While conceding that it did contain some roughhouse humor, the board's reviewer concluded that "in the end the better nature of the Irish is exerted."[40]

Confident that it had a hit on its hands, MGM held a gala opening night celebration on June 16 in Los Angeles with free tickets for all the Callahans and Murphys in the city's fire and police departments. The initial round of reviews appeared to confirm the studio's high hopes. *Variety* labeled the picture a "wallop" and "a fine-faithful transcript from life." *Film Daily* reported that the audience was in "what sounded like near convulsions," and the *Los Angeles Record* predicted that the film would be one of the big box-office successes of the year. The only sour note in this first round of reviews came from film critic Robert Sherwood, who characterized the story as "loathsome" and the film as "the most terrible picture I have ever seen."[41]

The first sign of trouble emerged in Los Angeles, where several local Irish-American organizations, including the Ancient Order of Hibernians, met with representatives of MGM and asked them to recall the film. Their protest was picked up by the Los Angeles archdiocesan newspaper. Noting that "the farfetched vulgarity and scenes of debauchery would insult any group," the church's reporter declared that when "saddled upon one of the cleanest races in America, it is the absolute limit of mendacity."[42]

Convinced at first that the criticism was nothing more than the usual handful of complaints engendered by any ethnic comedy, MGM treated the objections lightly. Frances Marion suggested, tongue in cheek, that the critics might be satisfied if the title were changed to *The Browns and the Joneses.* The studio's position was that only the most sensitive viewer could find anything offensive in the film, and, in any event, that recalling it would be financially disastrous.[43]

But the problem was not to be dismissed so easily. Objections began to pour in from Irish-American organizations around the country. Recognizing that events could easily get out of hand, MGM embarked on a major public relations effort. The studio contacted representatives of Los Angeles Irish societies to show good faith, suggesting the formation of a committee that could point out "in a friendly way" scenes in future films that might be offensive to the Irish. An MGM official reminded the Irish leaders, however, that the members of such a committee must be broad-minded enough to accept a "certain amount of good natured humor." After all, he pointed out, "the man who makes the world laugh is the man whom the world loves."[44]

Unfortunately for MGM, Irish eyes weren't smiling, much less laughing, by that point, when the studio learned that the Ancient Order of Hibernians at its annual convention was discussing how to stop the film. Moreover, MGM's problem began to affect other studios. Films released earlier in 1927 like *McFadden's Flats*, which had not attracted any attention, and *Irish Hearts*, which had been criticized by a few obscure groups, now came in for serious reappraisal. As one spokesperson for the United Irish Organizations of Los Angeles put it, *Irish Hearts* would have been acceptable had the country not been flooded with pictures like *The Callahans and the Murphys.* An alarmed MPPDA official warned all the studios to take special care with any films planned or in production dealing with the Irish or the Catholic church.[45]

In an effort to head off further embarrassment, MGM discussed possible cuts in the film with twenty-two representatives of Los Angeles Irish-American organizations. One executive who had attended the meeting came away convinced that the Irish only wanted a little attention and that they would make no further trouble. Two leaders retracted some of their original complaints in an open letter to the Catholic press in recognition of the studio's willingness to meet some of their demands. MGM also asked Rita McGoldrick and Father John Kelly of the Catholic Theater Guild to view the film and suggest revisions. The two reviewers recommended deleting all references to the Catholic church, such as the sign of the cross, crucifixes on the wall, and the identification of the picnic as a celebration of St. Patrick's Day.[46]

Any hope that the studio's conciliatory stance would end the crisis was dashed by the response of Charles McMahon and Father Burke of the NCWC. McMahon complained to the Hays Office that he had never before "been so disgusted with a picture and so incensed at a company that could . . . produce such a picture." Neither he nor Father Burke believed that the film could be saved by "any process of editing or deletion of scenes or subtitles." Without waiting for a response, McMahon denounced the film, in a statement to the Catholic press around the country, as a "hideous defamation of the Catholic faith" aimed at discrediting the church. Although parts of the film were insensitive, it was not the first to exploit Irish stereotypes, and it is hard to believe that McMahon really felt that MGM intended to defame the Catholic church. One of Hays's close associates believed that McMahon felt he had not been properly rewarded for his past support of the film industry, and he may have been passed over for an important job in the Hays Office.[47]

The mounting tide of criticism also caused state and local censor boards to have second thoughts about the film. In Boston, the city censor ordered its withdrawal following complaints from the Knights of Columbus and local Irish societies. The most significant reversal took place in New York, where the state board, in a highly unusual move, yielded to public pressure by rescreening the film after having approved it. After taking a second look, the board ordered MGM to either make a series of cuts or withdraw the film from the state's movie houses. The cuts began with the opening title, which introduced the audience to Goat Alley, where "a gentleman takes off his hat before striking a lady." MGM replaced it with: "This is the story of the Callahans and the Murphys—both of that fast fading old school families to whom the world is indebted for the richest and rarest of wholesome fun and humor." The remaining twenty-three changes ordered by the New York board eliminated, among other things, Jim Callahan's job description as "sewer-digger," all scenes involving the thumbing of noses, and all references to "black Protestant" or "Jew babies." The removal of all shots of Mrs. Callahan making the sign of the cross, correctly or incorrectly, along with any connection between the picnic and St. Patrick's Day eliminated all explicit references to the Catholic church. In addition, the beer-drinking scene involving the two mothers was shortened, although the studio refused to eliminate the entire episode.[48]

Hays convinced Los Angeles Bishop John Cantwell to make a statement that in view of MGM's cuts it was ridiculous to continue to object to the film on the grounds of anti-Catholicism, but his announcement received little play in the Irish-American or Catholic press. Instead, each new round of complaints seemed to uncover additional defects in the film. In August, the *Milwaukee Journal* summed up the charges against the picture when it identified the various scenes that had troubled one group or another, including those depicting: "drunkenness, indecency, immodesty, rough-house dancing, depravity, stealing, sewer-digging, street-sweeping, jilting, thuggery, lies, cheating, quarreling, and irreligion."[49]

The studio's last chance to avoid further damage was to try to win over the powerful Irish-American societies of New York, where a screening was hurriedly arranged at the MPPDA office. According to an MGM executive who attended the meeting, most of the Irish viewers sat chuckling at the edited version, but in the subsequent discussion they maintained that it was still unacceptable. According to one of New York's Irish papers, the *Gaelic American*, nothing was resolved at the meeting: the new version remained "the most insulting characterization of the Irish ever put on the screen." A new, more ominous note was introduced as the paper went on to warn the studio that if the film was not withdrawn, people would take matters into their own hands.[50]

Meanwhile, McMahon encouraged the executive secretaries of the National Councils of Catholic Men and Catholic Women to urge their members to protest the showing of the film at their local theaters. Although MGM had, in effect, de-catholicized *The Callahans and the Murphys* through its cuts, the Catholic press kept up its criticism into the fall of 1927. The continuing church hostility was due in part to the disproportionate number of Irish-Americans among the hierarchy who tended to equate an attack on the Irish with an attack on the church. After several weeks of controversy, the two families were firmly identified in the public mind as Irish and Catholic, whether or not Mrs. Callahan made the sign of the cross.[51]

At this point, MGM announced that it would not make any more changes. Instead, it launched a public relations campaign intended to present the studio as the innocent victim of an unfounded attack. MGM instructed Will Hays to respond to each criticism that reached his office by explaining that the film simply highlighted one of the admirable characteristics of the Irish: "the ability to fight at the drop of a hat in any just cause." In its public pronouncements, the studio constantly pointed out that Eddie Mannix, the film's production supervisor, Polly Moran, who played Mrs. Murphy, and the actors who portrayed Ellen Callahan and Dan Murphy were all Irish. Marie Dressler, who played Mrs. Callahan, was conveniently discovered to have Irish blood on her mother's side and was identified in a number of press releases as a major contributor to Irish and Catholic charities. This attempt to give the film an Irish pedigree failed to convince its critics. "The worst enemies of the Irish in America," sneered one writer, "have been the grotesque buffoons on the stage."[52]

By early August, there was little MGM could do—short of withdrawing *The Callahans and the Murphys*—to placate critics who saw the film as a vicious assault on Irish-Catholic family life. The *Irish World and Independent Liberator* charged that Marie Dressler had "successfully impersonated a gorilla" rather than an Irish mother. The *Gaelic American* not only joined in denouncing the ape-like countenances of the players but also charged that they had been given the manners of "Fiji Islanders." Equally objectionable was the film's casual treatment of Ellen Callahan's relationship to Dan Murphy, which suggested that the Irish were "so immoral that the arrival of an illegitimate offspring was an everyday occurrence." By late August, the mounting furor over the picture caused Kathleen Norris to repudiate Hollywood's treatment of her story.[53]

A siege mentality gripped the film's opponents. Especially alarming were the rumors that *The Callahans and the Murphys* was the first of a planned series of pictures holding up the Irish and the Catholic church to ridicule and contempt. All this naturally forced the Irish to question why Hollywood had unleashed this dastardly attack on such an innocent people. One popular answer was rooted in American politics. Noting that Will Hays was a leading Republican, some critics saw the campaign to discredit Irish-Catholics as part of an attempt to deny Al Smith the presidency in the next election. Others found a larger meaning in the rumored wave of anti-Irish films and traced the plot to an institution even more nefarious than the Republican party: the British government. Claiming that MGM's representative in England had served as the chief of British propaganda during the war, the *Irish World and Independent Liberator* predicted that *The Callahans and the Murphys* would soon be distributed to every overseas hamlet as part of a scheme to prevent the unification of Ireland. Moreover, the deaths of Marcus Loew, president of MGM, and Samuel L. Warner, vice-president of the company that produced *Irish Hearts*, followed the release of *The Callahans and the Murphys* and convinced the film's critics that God was on their side. Reminding its readers that the revised version of the film was playing in New York and Brooklyn, the Irish press began to call for direct action. A series of blistering articles in the *Irish World and Independent Liberator* ended with the same question: "What are you doing about it?" One reporter for the *Gaelic American* reminded his readers that rotten eggs had done wonders in helping to remove the stage Irishman from New York playhouses.[54]

The first disturbance occurred in New York City on August 24, 1927, when a man stood up in the middle of a showing of *The Callahans and the*

Murphys at the Loews American theater and denounced the film. The *New York Times* reported that the police were summoned but no arrests were made. The following night at the Loews Orpheum, another man stood up in the middle of the mothers' drinking scene and shouted, "My mother never acted like that." On August 26, light bulbs, fireworks, and a "malodorous chemical bomb" exploded at another location. The first arrests were made on the twenty-seventh, when four women were detained at one theater; it took twenty police officers to bring in an additional protester, John O'Houllihan, from another movie house. Much more alarming was the report in a Bronx newspaper that acid had been thrown at the screen of a local theater, burning the arm of an audience member. A combination of ink and rocks destroyed a $400 screen at the Strand Theater in Yonkers, New York. And the protests weren't limited to *The Callahans and the Murphys.* The *New York Daily News* reported that at a showing of *Irish Hearts*, "While petite May McAvoy was chasing a flock of sheep in the picture, someone hurled a paint container. The sheep became very black sheep immediately." When the paint was followed by tear gas, the theater manager narrowly averted a stampede by ordering all the doors to be thrown open. By September 3, the *Gaelic American* chortled that New York's Loews theaters were under police guard. Noting that the Irish had been angered by a film depicting them as brawlers, one film trade paper pointed out that in order to repudiate the charge, they had started fights all over the city. *Life* carried the following exchange: "Mr. Callahan: 'Did you protest against showing the movie that represents the Irish as disorderly?' Mr. Murphy: 'Did we? We wrecked the place!' "[55]

The battleground then shifted to the courts, where the Irish-American press waited to see what would be done to those demonstrators who had been arrested. To their outrage, a series of "traitorous" Irish-American judges fined all the nonviolent protesters and released the others on bail, pending charges of inciting a riot. But the actions of the one Jewish magistrate especially enraged the *Gaelic American.* The paper charged that Judge Elperin could not have treated the prisoner any more harshly if he had been a firebug. When Tim McGloin, the prisoner in question, refused to pay his fine, the judge took the "outrageous step" of ordering the defendant to jail handcuffed to a black prisoner, thus "express[ing] his opinion of the entire Irish race."[56]

The identification of Judge Elperin as Jewish touched on the darker side of *The Callahans and the Murphys* controversy. The pages of the Irish-American press were filled with charges that the "Jewish Trust" was waging war on the Irish. The *Gaelic American* claimed that the recent glut of Irish-American films constituted an all-out attack on "the family—the very citadel of Christian Civilization." The *Irish World and Independent Liberator* warned that if Hollywood's moviemakers wanted to make money by ridiculing women, "let them confine their talents to the Rebeccas and Marthas of their own families. If they want grotesque figures, Hester Street is full of them. . . . But they are not going to put their filthy hands on Irish women any more."[57]

Although the battle to recall *The Callahans and the Murphys* was centered in New York City, within a week of the film's initial release, the MPPDA had received 125 letters of complaint from around the country. According to reports in two trade papers, the *Exhibitor's Herald* and the *Exhibitor's Daily*, the film encountered opposition in small towns as well as large cities. The owner of the Palace Theater in McGehan, Arkansas, for example, warned other exhibitors: "If you are Irish and have any spark of Irish pride do not run this picture. It's the lowest order of filth." Similarly, the manager of a theater in Valparaiso, Nebraska, reported that his audience had found the film "too raw." As opposition to the picture spread, a California newspaper suggested that Will Hays should consider getting a bodyguard.[58]

In a bow to public pressure, *The Callahans and the Murphys* was eventually withdrawn in a number of cities, either voluntarily by theater owners or under orders from the local government. Individual Catholic priests condemned the film in Sunday sermons, and the Norfolk, Virginia, diocese urged parishioners to boycott it. The pastor of St. Anne's church in San Francisco persuaded the manager of the Irving Theater to withdraw it. *The Callahans and the Murphys* was also pulled in San Antonio, Cincinnati, Syracuse, Jersey City, Washington, D.C., and Bridgeport, Connecticut. Concerned over the effect of the protests on their public image, the Independent Theater Owners of Western Pennsylvania and West Virginia passed a resolution urging members to cancel the film. Other cities, like Chicago, ordered major cuts in the picture. In late August, a desperate New York State board, reeling under the attacks of the Irish and Catholic press, ordered a third round of deletions in the film.[59]

The stakes were raised in October by two separate events. The New York board of censors rebuffed continued requests that the state order the film withdrawn from exhibition, claiming that it had no power to revoke a license after it had been issued. The film's frustrated opponents persuaded the New York Board of Aldermen to hold hearings on the McKee bill, which would prohibit the showing of films that "disparaged any race, creed or nationality." *Variety* reported that the bill sent shock waves through the film industry. One danger was that cities with large Irish-Catholic populations, like Boston, Chicago, and Philadelphia, would soon follow with their own legislation. A more immediate threat came from Wall Street, where a loan to one of the largest studios was delayed pending a vote on the McKee bill.[60]

The second blow came in the form of a demand from Philadelphia's Cardinal Dougherty that MGM withdraw the film from distribution entirely.

In August, the Stanley theater chain, the largest purchaser of MGM films in the Philadelphia area, promised not to exhibit *The Callahans and the Murphys* after a protest from the archdiocese. But on October 24, the chain reversed its earlier decision, which in turn prompted the cardinal's action. MGM, facing possible political action in New York and pressure from one of the most influential prelates in the country, surrendered. In a letter to Cardinal Dougherty which was published in Catholic newspapers around the country, MGM head Nicholas Schenck announced that, in spite of the financial cost, he felt that he had to recall the film. Although the New York Irish press continued to warn its readers that Hollywood was simply holding back other films "far more insulting" until the coast was clear, the public quickly lost interest. After MGM surrendered, the NCWC and the Catholic press dropped the matter. The McKee bill never came to a vote, and efforts to revive it in the spring session failed.[61]

It is not clear why *The Callahans and the Murphys* triggered such an uproar. Some members of the Hays Office suspected that the entire affair was generated by a disgruntled applicant for the job of counsel to the MPPDA, William Marston Seabury, the brother of Judge Samuel Seabury. Hollywood had produced more Irish-Catholic films in 1927 than in any other year since 1921, so that the release of even a few insensitive films may have been interpreted by some Irish-Americans as a concerted attack on their ethnicity and religion. After the controversy had erupted, others simply joined in pursuit of their own political interests.[62]

It is difficult to determine if MGM was hurt by the protests or benefited from the ensuing publicity. Box-office receipts in Pittsburgh, for example, fell off $750 in two days after protests by the local Council of Catholic Women and the Ladies Auxiliary of the Ancient Order of Hibernians. Yet the trade papers reveal as many managers reporting good box-office receipts as complaining that they had been hurt by the film's notoriety. Furthermore, a survey in *Motion Picture News* showed that the picture was doing better when it was withdrawn on October 24 than it had done in early September.[63]

Nevertheless, the film's critics could derive some satisfaction from having forced MGM to withdraw a major motion picture against its will. Subsequently Warner Brothers made several cuts in *Irish Hearts* after first refusing to do so on the ground that it would be impossible to recall all the prints in circulation. Threats of a blacklist forced MGM to bring in a Catholic priest as a technical adviser on another Irish-American film, *Bringing Up Father.* The New York state censors also appeared to demonstrate a new sensitivity in reviewing other Irish films in the fall of 1927. Several lines from *Finnigan's Ball* (including "when friendly enemies get together without fighting it's a reunion. When the Irish do—it's a miracle") were removed from the film. A number of scenes were also cut, including one showing Finnigan and a friend eating with knives, Finnigan spitting on the floor, and another in which a child accidentally wets his pants, which, the censor noted, "might be interpreted as a reflection on Irish family life." And when *Mother Machree* was released by Fox in the following year, advertisements prominently featured letters of endorsement from leaders of the fight against *The Callahans and the Murphys*, including Charles McMahon, who found the film "free from offense, religious or racial" and "powerfully appealing in its stressing of traditional qualities of the true Irish nature."[64]

The campaign against *The Callahans and the Murphys* taught Irish and Catholic organizations that united action could force Hollywood to bend. As a member of Hays's staff prophetically remarked at the end of 1927: "I am inclined to think the withdrawal of *The Callahans and the Murphys*, while at the time it seemed the only feasible thing to do, has established a precedent which will rise up to plague us in the future." A few months later, Jason Joy, still disturbed about what MGM's surrender might lead to, sent a confidential memo to Will Hays warning him that in the future a powerful pressure group could be more of a problem to the industry than state censorship. Seven years later, his worst fears would become a reality with the formation of the Legion of Decency.[65]

THREE

A New Moral Code

Although *The Callahans and the Murphys* had caused a momentary stir, the big film news in 1927 was the premiere of *The Jazz Singer*, starring Al Jolson, in New York on October 6. The immediate success of movies with sound surprised many experts. A year earlier, Thomas Alva Edison had predicted that Americans wouldn't be interested because they preferred "a restful quiet in the theater." Mary Pickford likened sound in films to putting "lip rouge on the Venus de Milo." Even Sam Warner, whose studio had produced the Jolson film, had once responded to the idea of "talking movies" with: "Who the hell wants to hear actors talk?"[1]

As it turned out, a lot of people did, but they had to wait until their local theaters were equipped to offer sound. It was December 31, 1927, before Milwaukeeans could hear Jolson sing at the downtown Garden Theater, and his songs didn't reach the city's neighborhood houses until May 13. Although audiences flocked to see the "talkie," a survey in January 1929 found that only half of Syracuse movie audiences would rather see a talking picture, and just 7 percent hoped that talkies would replace silent films entirely. But there was no turning back: by the middle of 1928, more than three hundred theaters had converted to sound, and it was predicted that one thousand would do so by the end of the year.[2]

The Jazz Singer opened with "Wait a minute, you ain't heard nothing yet!" This line had more than one meaning for the censors, who, in addition to guarding against improper scenes and titles, now had to listen for racy songs and objectionable dialogue, as well as to the actors' intonations. As Effie Sigler, head of the Chicago censor board, explained: "Very often a written remark will not be offensive. The voice can change the entire meaning of a statement and we have to be on the watch constantly for . . . double meanings." The studios, in turn, found it much more difficult to handle the censors' cuts. Instead of simply eliminating the offending scene or title, they now often had to reshoot a scene to compensate for the missing dialogue.[3]

Hays had formed the Studio Relations Committee in 1926 under the direction of Jason Joy, the former head of the Public Relations Committee, to help producers identify potentially troublesome script material. In the same month in which *The Jazz Singer* opened, Joy, in cooperation with a committee headed by MGM's Irving Thalberg, drew up what became known as the "Don'ts and Be Carefuls," a codification of the most common city, state, and foreign rules for elimination. The "Don'ts" consisted of eleven topics, including profanity, white slavery, sex hygiene, sex perversion, and "scenes of actual childbirth," which were prohibited from the screen. The twenty-five "Be Carefuls" contained such items as crime methods, rape, and wedding-night scenes which were to be handled with special care to avoid "vulgarity and suggestiveness." In order to keep the regulations current, Joy visited the major censor boards twice a year.[4]

Despite the fanfare surrounding the introduction of the Don'ts and Be Carefuls, they suffered the same fate as NAMPI's Thirteen Points, which they strongly resembled. Originally hailed as a panacea that would cleanse the screen of immorality, they quickly became in the eyes of the reformers one more example of industry double-talk. A few years after the new regulations were adopted, *Colliers* dismissed them as "don't forget to before you have gone too far" and "if you can't be good, be careful." The Don'ts and Be Carefuls, as with all Hays's previous reform efforts, relied on the studios' willingness to cooperate. Hays had hoped that the moviemakers' self-interest in avoiding the costs of complying with the censors' cuts would ensure success for the new guidelines. Indeed, when the studios followed Joy's advice, it proved helpful. In 1927 his staff reviewed 349 stories and treatments. Of the 163 films that incorporated his recommendations, 161 passed state and city censors with no major eliminations. Nevertheless, most producers resented any outside interference and ignored the Studio Relations Committee, submitting fewer than 20 percent of their films to Joy's staff in 1929.[5]

The result was a steady stream of cuts ordered by the increasingly active censorship boards. In 1928, the New York State censors ordered the elimination of more than four thousand scenes, while Chicago's found some six thousand that posed a danger to the morals of its citizens. Most of the cuts, according to Joy, related to the same old problems: crime and sex. Censors, especially sensitive to anything that might teach would-be criminals how to hone their craft, regularly eliminated scenes involving planning a robbery or disabling an alarm system. Similarly, any "suggestive" shots of a couple lying on the floor or kissing on the neck invariably fell victim to the censor's scissors. As United Artists found out, ignoring Joy's office could be costly: by the time all the censors' demands were satisfied, the length of *Two Arab Knights* had been reduced from 8,250 feet to 4,000 feet.[6]

Producers recognized that Joy's staff could help them reduce the expensive overhead associated with censorship, but they feared that too much sanitizing meant death at the box office. Carl Laemmle, president of Universal, confided to a colleague that "our pictures are too namby-pamby and . . . the public knows that [they] . . . are too damn clean and they stay away on account of it." Nevertheless, the producer promised to cooperate fully with the Don'ts and Be Carefuls, posting copies of the regulations around the studio lot.[7]

But did the public really want movie reform? According to *Variety*, by 1929 even the farmers in rural areas wanted pictures with excitement and chorus girls. Furthermore, studio heads could always justify their disregard of the Don'ts and Be Carefuls by claiming that they had to keep up with the competition. A Universal spokesman charged that the increase in "dirty" pictures could be traced to the "natural lasciviousness" of Paramount's Ben Schulberg and MGM's inability to "tone down" Irving Thalberg. Similarly, Harry Warner, whose studio was often criticized for ignoring the Hays Office guidelines, charged that the vulgarity of the Fox studio threatened to undermine the film industry.[8]

While the studio heads were busily pointing their fingers at each other, industry critics blamed everyone from the actors and screenwriters to the company heads and the Hays Office. Protestant journals like the *Churchman* became increasingly vituperative, charging Hays with being a "seller of swill and an office boy" for the producers who were transforming American society into a "brothel house." The industry's response—that it was giving the public what it wanted and that practically every picture recommended by the *Churchman* had lost money—played into the hands of those who accused Hollywood of being willing to sell any kind of filth for the right price. To refute the accusation that most of the country's social problems could be traced to the movies, Hays argued that films were far cleaner than stage plays or popular novels and were held to a far higher standard than the daily press. The newspapers, he pointed out, were free to print intimate details of notorious trials, which would never be allowed to reach the screen. He argued that the movies, unlike the press, deterred crime because the villain was always punished before the lights came on. The real causes of crime, said Hays, were a sensational press, immigration, prohibition, lax law enforcement, and the automobile.[9]

Convinced that Hays and the filmmakers would never clean up the industry and frustrated by the piecemeal approach of state and local censorship, industry critics increasingly turned to the idea of federal control. In 1927 the Brookhart bill was filed in the Senate in an attempt to eliminate the industry practice of block-booking and blind-selling. Under this system, which dated to 1917, independent theater chains and local exhibitors had to buy a group of films sight unseen from a studio rather than being able to select individual pictures. If the local theater owners had the right to pick and choose, the reformers reasoned, they would not buy any objectionable films, either because the movies violated their own moral standards or because of community pressure. Although the Brookhart bill was easily defeated, the elimination of block-booking and blind-selling became a rallying cry for the industry's enemies.

Despite Hays's public attempts to portray the filmmakers as committed to reform, his office's internal reports told another story. Angered by the unremitting criticism of journals like the *Churchman*, Hays retorted: "For six years I have been personally blamed for every mistake, every bad line and every bad shot in every picture. . . . There is a limit to which I propose to stand for this." In the final analysis, the producers would be the ones to pay the price for failing to abide by the Don'ts and Be Carefuls. "Remember," he warned them, "every time a picture is banned or cuts are made, censorship is justified that much more in the minds of the people."[10]

Under the steady barrage of criticism from many Protestant leaders, the beleaguered Hays increasingly valued the support of the International Federation of Catholic Alumnae. Unlike the NCWC's Charles McMahon, the IFCA's Rita McGoldrick had remained loyal during *The Callahans and the Murphys* controversy. Moreover, during the Depression, the NCWC could not afford to fund McMahon's Motion Picture Committee, leaving the IFCA the sole Catholic reviewing agency. The IFCA's policy of "praising the best and ignoring the rest" was all Hays could have asked for. Although the Daughters of the American Revolution and the General Federation of Women's Clubs adhered to a similar policy, the Hays Office regularly held up McGoldrick's group to the studio heads as a model of how the industry could benefit from cooperating with public organizations. A case in point was McGoldrick's role in helping to ensure that *The Garden of Allah* did not run into trouble with Catholic moviegoers. The film told the story of a monk in an Algerian monastery who forsakes his vows and marries a woman who is unaware of his background. When his wife eventually learns the truth, she persuades him to return to the church. McGoldrick was asked to critique the novel before the producer bought the rights to the story. She also monitored the production process, reminding the studio, among other points, to keep scenes of desert dancing girls to a minimum. When it was finished, McGoldrick arranged a private showing for a number of distinguished Catholic clergymen, who praised the movie. With the studio still fearful of a repeat of *The Callahans and the Murphys* affair, McGoldrick published a recommendation in the Catholic press to head off any opposition.[11]

By the end of the 1920s, the IFCA's Motion Picture Bureau had gained considerable visibility. In 1928 alone, McGoldrick's staff mailed out more than 200,000 pieces of film literature to 5,260 groups in the United States and fifteen in foreign countries. In addition, the IFCA list appeared in twenty-one Catholic and two large-city newspapers, and McGoldrick's weekly broadcast of film recommendations was carried on radio stations in New York, Cleveland, Milwaukee, St. Louis, Cincinnati, New Orleans, and other cities.[12]

Despite its support of the Hays Office, the IFCA refused to recommend 49 percent of the 1,472 feature films and short subjects it reviewed in 1929. Suggestive dialogue and scenarios justifying divorce were obvious targets for rejection, but so were scenes of excessive drinking, which made the United States "look ridiculous in the eyes of other countries." Titles like *Dance Hall Marge* were also guaranteed to remove a film from the recommended list. Little escaped the reviewer's eye, even a shot of a goat's udders in a Terry-Toons cartoon. Although the IFCA was hardly in a position to dictate to the studios, producers were usually willing to cut a few scenes if this meant that the film was recommended. A series of negotiations with Columbia Pictures led to the approval of *Flight*, although the studio's refusal to eliminate a reference to "lousy dames," the mouthing of "son of a b," a woman bargaining with a man for money (with its implication of prostitution), and a hula dance prevented it from being recommended for college and high school students. By 1928, the IFCA was becoming a force in motion pictures. As a writer for the *London Daily Express* put it, every American parent owed a debt of gratitude to McGoldrick and her "fighting forty" for molding the movies through their reviews.[13]

The IFCA was always on the lookout for material that might reflect negatively on the Catholic church. In one film, Helen Morgan, playing a nightclub singer, responds to her daughter's concern about the skimpily attired dancers in her show. "It ain't what you do so much as what you are," she tells the little girl. "Why, there's a couple of dames in this troupe just as good Catholics as you ever expect to see." After McGoldrick asked why the two dancers couldn't have been Baptists or Methodists, the studio added some additional background noise to blot out their religious affiliation before the film was released.[14]

IFCA policy also reflected the church's opposition to anything in the movies that could undermine the parents' role in sex education. Claiming that "our celluloid teachers" were forcing children to become unnaturally precocious, Philip Burke, writing in the Knights of Columbus journal *Columbia*, declared: "Until children are no longer children, the best sex education is the forgetting of sex." When Margaret Sanger, who, according to one priest, was nothing more than a "rubber goods saleswoman" working for the condom manufacturers, appeared in a Fox Movietone newsreel, McGoldrick went into action. In a brief clip, Sanger predicted that birth control would be the "keynote of a new moral program [advocating] fewer and healthier children, children by choice and not by chance." As one of McGoldrick's staff complained in her review, it was frustrating to "sit and listen to a woman voice a theory extremely objectionable to me and to be unable to answer her because she is not there in person." But Fox had to answer to McGoldrick. Noting that the IFCA had endorsed many of its pictures, which resulted in a good deal of free advertising, McGoldrick pointed out that it would be just as easy to lead a nationwide campaign against the studio. Fox hurriedly arranged a meeting with Courtland Smith, its chief executive officer, who told McGoldrick that Fox Movietone was in the news business and that Sanger's "theories" were news. Nevertheless, fearful of a fight with the IFCA, he promised to withdraw the clip from circulation. In a further effort to make amends, he invited the IFCA to select a representative who would go before the cameras to rebut Sanger, but the offer was politely rejected, for, as McGoldrick told one of her colleagues, it was a subject "Catholic women cannot talk upon without offending the delicacy which is our pride."[15]

Even though the IFCA had a large staff of volunteers, the MPPDA paid for the mailing of the IFCA lists, which it regarded as a relatively inexpensive form of advertising. As the organization did not issue a list of objectionable films, the film industry did not have to worry about negative publicity. The list was ambiguous, as a film's absence could mean that reviewers had simply not yet evaluated it. McGoldrick was also one of eleven speakers who were granted travel expenses by the MPPDA to defend Hays's reform efforts. In one four-month period, she gave some thirty public addresses to groups ranging from a Catholic women's study club to a dinner for banking executives. Wherever she went, she delivered the same message: self-regulation was working "thanks to the dedication of the industry in general and Hays in particular."[16]

Although producers occasionally contacted Rita McGoldrick or a Protestant minister for advice on some religious question in their films, no one had ever gone to the lengths taken by Cecil B. deMille in filming his 1927 epic *King of Kings*. Recognizing the sensitive nature of a story about the life of Christ, deMille asked Will Hays to help him find religious consultants. When Hays's recommendations, which were supplied by the Rev. William C. Covert (a fellow Presbyterian), proved to be too narrow, deMille secured an adviser from each of the three major faiths. The Reverend George Reid Andrews, a leader of the Federal Council of Churches and chairman of its Church and Drama Association, representd the Protestant church, and Rabbi J. M. Alkow of California advised deMille on matters relating to the Jewish faith. When deMille contacted the NCWC, Father Burke recommended Father Daniel Lord, a Jesuit who was a drama teacher at St. Louis University. Lord seemed an ideal choice. An accomplished pianist and a movie fan since his boyhood in Chicago, Lord loved to produce musicals at his university. A popular speaker and the author of a number of articles and religious pamphlets, he was serving as assistant editor of the *Queen's Work*, the magazine of the Sodality of the Blessed Virgin, when Burke contacted him.[17]

Lord joined deMille and the others on Catalina Island, off the California coast, where the story was to be filmed. DeMille did seek some advice from his consultants, but his decision to bring them in was more of a publicity stunt aimed at defusing future criticism. His tactics worked from the start, with the press treating the production as a religious experience. Even *Variety* struck an unusually solemn tone when it reported that the producer had dictated that there was to be no profanity on the set. When the musicians had nothing else to do, they were to play "Onward, Christian Soldiers," which was performed every morning as deMille made his appearance, "with all the players standing with bowed heads in reverence" until the director took his position.[18]

Lord and deMille developed a close friendship during the shooting, and the priest spent several nights on the director's yacht. Although critics viewed deMille's fondness for biblical stories as a cover that allowed him to get away with scenes that would have been eliminated in a secular context, Lord believed the director when deMille told the cast and crew on the first day that he was making the film because he wanted to "do good and make people know and love Christ." The notoriously egotistical deMille, who viewed the priest's daily mass on the set as a "continued benediction of our work," asked Lord if it was possible to get Catholics to pray for the success of the picture.[19]

Because of his theater experience, Lord was not particularly bothered by the liberties deMille took with the chronology of Christ's life, noting that the authors of the passion play at Oberammergau had also reordered history for dramatic effect. What did bother Lord was deMille's characterization of

Mary Magdalen. Initially concerned over the actress's scanty dress (she was "nude from the waist up except for large jewelled plates at her breast and a loose robe over her shoulders"), he eventually conceded that her costume was an integral part of the story. However, he persuaded the director to cut the Magdalen sequences from two thousand feet to five hundred feet, eliminating a number of shots including a "sensual kiss," an old man leering at her leg, and a procession of dancing girls while toning down a scene suggesting that she was Judas's mistress.[20]

DeMille, remembering the trouble he had had with *Joan the Woman*, told Lord that he would do anything to satisfy the church, including eliminating the Protestant ending to the Lord's Prayer when the picture was shown in the United States and in Catholic countries. Noting that deMille was "the only real Christian company producing films" and concerned that the Federal Council of Churches would gain influence with the film industry through Rev. George Andrews's advisory work on *King of Kings*, Lord persuaded Father John Burke to set up an NCWC committee to evaluate the film. The priest wanted to avoid second-guessing by his fellow priests, but he also believed that an endorsement would give the Catholic church some leverage in Hollywood.[21]

Only one committee member, Father Joseph Husslein, also a Jesuit, had serious reservations about deMille's film. Although he felt that the picture was an artistic success and praised the treatment of Christ and his mother, as well as the "very Catholic" communion scene, Husslein objected to the overly sensuous nature of the film and was appalled by the director's historical license. The result, he said, was a story filled with such errors as Christ rising through a sealed tomb instead of walking out after the door opens. Conceding that the changes may have been made for economic or technical reasons, he nevertheless maintained, "It is the movies that must yield to the scriptures and not the scriptures to the movie," a concept that Hollywood would have branded as heresy. Husslein's negative critique persuaded the NCWC not to endorse the film, although the IFCA recommended it.[22]

DeMille, however, failed to anticipate Jewish objections to *The King of Kings*. He appears to have at first believed that they would be both astonished and enthusiastic to learn that Jesus was a Jew. In all fairness, Rabbi Edgar Magnin, a favorite of Hollywood's Jewish community, had told the director that he had no problem with the picture. Lord also claimed that Rabbi Alkow, a consultant on the film, had dismissed the question of his people's involvement with the crucifixion with the comment, "It is history and it cannot be helped." However, the B'nai B'rith and a number of Jewish papers were more difficult to deal with. Citing MGM's capitulation a few weeks earlier in the case of *The Callahans and the Murphys*, they demanded that *King of Kings* be withdrawn because it would create Christian prejudice against the Jews. When the protest leaders became convinced that suppression of the film would probably generate even greater hostility, they settled for a series of compromises. DeMille cut several of the more objectionable scenes and agreed to prepare a foreword that exculpated the Jews for the death of Christ.[23]

The IFCA, which was always sensitive to the slightest anti-Catholic nuance, had no sympathy for Jewish concerns. Rita McGoldrick deplored the concessions that had been made to the B'nai B'rith because "some of the most exquisite Catholic references" were lost. She also actively joined in the MPPDA's effort to counter any further objections to the film. Whenever news of a local Jewish protest reached the Hays Office, a staff member contacted McGoldrick, who would write to Catholic clergymen around the country to get them to boost the film in their area.[24]

But deMille's choice of the Reverend George Reid Andrews as a consultant gave the industry its biggest headache. Lord had feared that the Federal Council of Churches, through Andrews, would use the film to its own advantage. Andrews had hoped to use his involvement with the film to obtain financial support for his Church and Drama Association, but Hays refused. Embittered by his experience, Andrews became a leading critic of Hays and the film industry.[25]

As Hays's relationship with the Protestant church continued to deteriorate during the late 1920s, he increasingly courted the Catholic church. Los Angeles's Bishop Cantwell, who had supported MGM in *The Callahans and the Murphys* controversy, complained to Jason Joy that his effort had gone unappreciated. The bishop reported that movie advertising in the diocesan paper, the *Tidings*, which had amounted to three to four thousand dollars a year through 1927, had fallen off sharply in 1928. Joy, citing the advantage of having a friendly bishop whose diocese included Hollywood, recommended that the MPPDA encourage the studios to increase their advertising in his paper or make a yearly donation. Hays also developed a strong friendship with Cardinal Patrick Hayes of New York, who supported him whenever he was under fire. In the midst of the mounting attack on Hays by the Protestant press in 1929, the cardinal was one of the few church leaders to praise the MPPDA president for enabling the movies "to stand out like a shining light of great potential goodness in America."[26]

But Chicago would have the greatest part in forging the film industry's ties to the Catholic church. Five of the six key players in the development of the 1930 Production Code and the Legion of Decency were connected in one way or another to the Chicago archdiocese: Cardinal George Mundelein; Martin Quigley, publisher of the *Exhibitor's Herald;* Joseph I. Breen, a Catholic layman; and two Jesuits, Daniel Lord and FitzGeorge Dinneen.

The Chicago connection began in 1926, with the filming of the first Eucharistic Congress held in the United States. A year earlier, 50,000 Ku Klux Klan members had paraded down Pennsylvania Avenue in Washington. Cardinal Mundelein saw the Eucharistic Congress as a means of countering anti-Catholic groups like the KKK while forging a sense of self-confidence among the faithful. It was a formidable display of Catholic power: Cardinals and bishops from Europe and the United States arrived in Chicago, where, on the last night of the congress, they were joined by almost a million worshipers. Martin Quigley, at Mundelein's request, had arranged to have Fox make a movie of the congress. Quigley, who was born in Cleveland in 1890, had attended Niagara University and Catholic University of America before becoming a newspaperman in 1910. His marriage to the wealthy Gertrude Schofield of Chicago in 1913 enabled him to become the editor and then the publisher of the *Exhibitor's Herald*, which he merged with *Moving Picture World* in 1931 to form *Motion Picture Herald*, the largest trade paper in the business. Fox covered the congress from beginning to end and then donated the film, which was estimated to have cost between $50,000 and $100,000, to Cardinal Mundelein. Joe Breen, who had served as public relations director for the congress, was given the job of distributing the film to Catholic schools and organizations around the country.[27]

The congress marked the first experience with the film business for Breen, who later headed the Production Code Administration in Hollywood. Breen, who was born in Philadelphia in the same year as Quigley, had dropped out of St. Joseph's College to become a reporter before serving four years at the U.S. consulates in Kingston, Jamaica, and Toronto. A devout Catholic, father of six children, and brother of a priest, Breen maintained close ties with the church, having spent several years overseas as chairman of the NCWC's department of immigration and writing for *America* under the name Eugene Ware.[28]

Meanwhile, as complaints about movie immorality grew, calls for federal censorship continued to mount. Word reached Hays in February 1929 that William Randolph Hearst was going to join the Protestant press in asking for government intervention. A month later, Senator Smith Brookhart of Iowa filed a bill to place the film industry under the control of the Federal Trade Commission. To the film industry, facing another Washington battle, news that state and local censorship boards were ordering more deletions than ever was hardly encouraging. Even Charles Pettijohn, counsel to the MPPDA, wondered if federal censorship might be preferable to the task of maneuvering through the maze of local boards.[29]

In September 1929, Hays talked to Jason Joy about modifying the Don'ts and Be Carefuls to reduce the growing criticism of the film industry. Meanwhile, Martin Quigley had become increasingly alarmed, not only about the need to clean up the films, but also by the remedies that were being discussed. Quigley had, in his early years, expressed a variety of views on censorship, ranging from denouncing it as "un-American and unnecessary" to defending its necessity in Chicago "as long as . . . indecent pictures remain." The only way for the industry to avoid outside interference, he maintained, was to eliminate immorality from the screen itself. Real reform, Quigley insisted, would not be realized through gimmicks like the Formula and the "open door policy." He felt that the organizations associated with the Hays Office, which included such diverse groups as the Boy Scouts and women's clubs like the IFCA, had little to contribute. He conceded that the Don'ts and Be Carefuls were a step forward but were too vague to be useful. For example, when, he asked, did a description of criminal methods become too detailed, and at what precise moment did "excessive or lustful kissing" begin?[30]

In contrast, Father FitzGeorge Dinneen, a Jesuit who was the pastor of Quigley's parish on the north side of Chicago, shared none of the publisher's opposition to government regulation. Appointed a member of the Chicago Board of Censorship in 1918, Dinneen believed that its work was more important than the health commissioner's because the censors had a far more important task: to save the souls of the city's children, which were being jeopardized not only by too much attention to sex but also by Wild West films with their barroom scenes and gun fights, which tended to make criminals of young people. One night in 1929, Dinneen stormed into a meeting of the Loyola University board of trustees, on which he and Quigley served, exclaiming: "I'm going to teach some people in town a lesson. I'll stop these filthy pictures from coming into my parish." What had enraged Dinneen was the Board of Aldermen's decision to allow the showing of *The Trial of Mary Dugan*, MGM's first all-talking picture, starring Norma Shearer as a woman unjustly accused of murder. Jason Joy had been warned that Dugan's courtroom admission that she had been a mistress to four men was bound to cause trouble with the censors, but he lacked the power to block it.[31]

Few people were satisfied with the censorship situation in Chicago. Although Dinneen might be unhappy with a system that let a *Trial of Mary Dugan* slip by, the film industry had long regarded the city's censorship board as a thorn in its side. Industry lawyers usually were able to block the censors' cuts in local jury trials, only to see the favorable decision overturned on appeal. Filmmakers wondered if there was some way to avoid the cost associated with 6,470 eliminations in 1928 alone. Three years earlier, the MPPDA had seriously considered launching a referendum similar to the one that had led to the defeat of censorship in Massachusetts. The cost of the Chicago campaign was estimated at $150,000, but the idea never went beyond the discussion stage.[32]

Hays decided that the best way to deal with the problem was to make an end run around the city officials. Charles Pettijohn, the MPPDA counsel, knew he would have to overcome the Catholic church's support of film regulation in the city. Pettijohn, a Protestant who had married a Catholic and had agreed to raise their two children in her faith, had developed a friendly relationship with Cardinal Mundelein. He also hoped to capitalize on the Fox studio's cooperation in filming, at no expense to the church, Mundelein's elevation to the cardinalate in 1924 as well as the Eucharistic congress in 1926. In June 1929, Pettijohn presented the cardinal with a solution to the problem. Claiming that only Chicago and two minor cities had censorship boards, he argued, it was clear that government regulation was unnecessary. If the cardinal would help to eliminate the city board of censors, he said, the industry promised to abide by any objections he or his representative raised over any movie. Although he was vague about the details of the plan, Pettijohn had orchestrated a careful campaign to convince Mundelein. Shortly after he made his proposal, the cardinal received a petition from the Chicago Exhibitors Association declaring that the advent of sound had made the present censorship system "mechanically and economically impossible." Claiming that there was no other solution, they urged the cardinal to accept Pettijohn's proposal.[33]

The cardinal consulted Father Dinneen, who warned against going along with the industry's offer. The priest pointed out that Chicago was hardly an anomaly since, contrary to Pettijohn's assertion, there were three hundred cities and seven states with some form of censorship. Reminding the cardinal that censorship in the city had been saved more than once by Catholic pressure, Dinneen listed the dangers inherent in having the church replace the city's board of censors, including inspecting and supervising films, incurring the animosity of those who preferred the present form of censorship, and being uncertain of how long the new arrangement would last. Dinneen, in fact, had long since given up on the good intentions of the producers. An anonymous editorial in the archdiocesan newspaper, the *New World*, which he probably wrote, stressed the need to maintain the board of censors as the only way to prevent a "riot of indecency." The author explained that the industry was incapable of self-regulation because the men who made the movies "were not artists [but] ex-pants pressers and ex-push cart merchants of the lower east side of New York," few of whom were "real Americans."[34]

In spite of Dinneen's advice, the cardinal was apparently still toying with the idea in September 1929. Mundelein told Pettijohn that his major reservation was that films inimical to the church would be made, and that once they were completed, it would take more than a gentleman's agreement to prevent them from being shown in some theater. Pettijohn responded that the MPPDA would either invite Bishop Cantwell of Los Angeles to preview films before they were released or give him veto power over films dealing in any way with the Catholic church. Jason Joy, who studied the plan, advised Hays that, without Cantwell's good will, such a plan would be not only useless but probably dangerous. Nevertheless, Joy pointed out, the crux of the problem was not the mechanics of the proposal, but what non-Catholics would say about the pact. Recognizing that even the hint that Hollywood was entertaining such an idea was potentially explosive, he urged Hays to burn his memo after reading it.[35]

Martin Quigley felt that Pettijohn's offer was nothing more than a Machiavellian plot to get rid of censorship in Chicago: big on promises but fuzzy on implementation. At the same time, Quigley was convinced that the power of film threatened to shatter "those principles upon which home and civilization are based," thus becoming "the curse of the modern world." No government, he declared, could stand by and let that happen. Quigley was in a difficult position, one that would crop up time after time in his career. A devout Catholic who sincerely wanted to eliminate movie immorality, he made his living by advertising some of the very films he thought were evil. Father Wilfrid Parsons, the editor of *America* and a close friend of Quigley's, wondered at times how the publisher coped with his conscience when he printed magazines that he had to hide from his children. At one point, Quigley told the movie executives that he was committed to protecting their interests. Without their business, his publishing firm would never survive, and he knew full well what it meant to run afoul of a studio. In the early 1920s, a cartoon critical of Adolph Zukor's growing power had so angered the head of Famous Players–Lasky Corporation that he temporarily withdrew all his advertising from the *Exhibitor's Herald.*"[36]

Toward the end of 1929, Quigley intensified his search for a plan to clean up the movies that would benefit both sides. Sensing an opportunity in Pettijohn's negotiations with Cardinal Mundelein, he began talking to Father Dinneen about how they could turn the discussions to their advantage. The answer, Quigley believed, lay in an effective system of self-regulation that would "stop the sewage at the source." If all the objectionable material could be weeded out in the production stage, he contended, censorship boards would soon become superfluous. The two men began to meet in early October to design a new system of self-regulation intended to replace the Don'ts and Be Carefuls. More than a new set of rules, what was needed was a philosophy of morality that would help the producers understand why the rules were necessary. To obtain other points of view, they sent an outline of their notes to Joe Breen and Father Wilfrid Parsons for comment.

In the course of the discussions, Quigley wanted to consult a trained moralist who hopefully would have some understanding of the movie industry. Dinneen recommended his former pupil and friend Father Daniel Lord, who had already gained something of a reputation as the leading Catholic expert on films because of his work on *King of Kings*. Lord liked movies, but he took a narrow view of what should be shown on the screen. Films, he argued, should be a force for good, and he fondly remembered the movies of his youth, when "virtue was virtue and vice was vice, and nobody in the audience had the slightest doubt when to applaud and when to hiss." Lord, like Quigley and Dinneen, had become increasingly frustrated with the proliferation of what he regarded as indecent films. A visit to a neighborhood theater, he told Quigley, meant having to listen, for example, to a discussion of eugenics in *The Very Idea* (1929). Broadway audiences might enjoy such "sophisticated stuff," he grumbled, but it was a source of both shock and discomfort for the audience at a small uptown theater in Saint Louis. Especially disturbing was the presence in the audience of a large number of teenagers, who giggled nervously or made comments like "gee, this is getting hot" and "this is certainly dirty stuff."[37]

Lord turned the notes Quigley had prepared in cooperation with Dinneen, Parsons, and Breen into the Motion Picture Production Code. The code was divided into two sections, a set of general principles and their application and—the part Lord and Quigley regarded as the heart of the document—"a detailed exposition of the relation of basic moral principles to motion picture production." "Correct entertainment raises the whole standard of a nation," Lord wrote; "wrong entertainment lowers the whole living conditions and moral ideals of a nation." Because movies were meant for the masses, Lord noted, they could never be given as wide a latitude as books, plays, and even newspapers.[38]

The revised draft was back in Quigley's hands within three days. He and Dinneen felt that the best hope of getting the industry to accept the new system was to enlist Mundelein on their side. They first had to overcome the cardinal's dislike of Lord even though he had played a key role in putting the Code together. In the course of expanding the property holdings of the Chicago diocese, Mundelein had developed a close relationship with the investment firm of Halsey, Stuart and Company, which had played a major role in financing the film industry's expansion in the 1920s. The transition to sound required heavy borrowing from banks in order to equip the studios with soundproof stages and new cameras as well as wiring the theaters at an average cost of $8,000 to $15,000 in 1927. The banks' involvement in the movies set the stage for a shift in the control of the film industry a few years later.[39]

The stock market crash in late October 1929 did not affect the movie business immediately, but it eventually put many studios in a vulnerable position. The experience of William Fox, head of the Fox Film Corporation, was a portent of the increased involvement of investment and banking interests in the movies that was to come. Fox had financed much of the expansion of his company in the 1920s through loans from Halsey, Stuart and was badly overextended when the Depression hit. Unable to bail out, he was forced to accept a three-man trusteeship made up of himself, Harold Stuart and another major creditor.[40]

Working through Dinneen, Quigley and Lord were able to persuade Mundelein to pressure the bankers to induce Hollywood to accept the new Code. The cardinal met with Harold Stuart on January 2, 1930, and convinced him that the new regulations would stave off government interference and bring stability to the industry. A week later, Pettijohn told Quigley and Lord that the backing of Stuart and Paramount head Adolph Zukor, whose support had also been lined up by Mundelein, meant that the producers would accept the new Code.[41]

Quigley went to Hollywood in late January, but despite Pettijohn's assurances he found that the producers were not yet ready to surrender. Irving Thalberg countered with a draft of a new code that he had been working on with several other producers. The crux of Thalberg's version was that the box office should be the ultimate arbiter of which movies were produced, not their potential contribution to raising moral standards. Thalberg's proposal probably expressed the sentiments of the other producers, as well; nevertheless, according to Quigley, "it was passed around, glanced at by those present and was never even discussed." Sensing the need for reinforcement, Quigley wired Lord on February 2 asking him to come to Los Angeles as soon as possible. Quigley felt that Lord's presentation to the major studio executives there made "an extremely favorable impression," and a subcommittee of executives was formed to work with the priest and Hays to streamline the new document. After several minor revisions and an agreement to incorporate the Don'ts and Be Carefuls, the executive group recommended the new Code to the full board of company executives. Heading home on the train, Lord wrote to Mundelein crediting him with facilitating the adoption of what he referred to as "the Cardinal's Code." On March 31, 1930, the MPPDA's board of directors formally ratified the Production Code.[42]

Only the first half of the Code, a longer and somewhat more specific version of the old Don'ts and Be Carefuls, was published. "The technique of murder" was to be handled in such a way as not to inspire imitation. "Impure love" was never to "be presented as attractive and beautiful," and passion was to be treated so that it did not "stimulate the lower and baser element." It is not entirely clear why the second half, "The Reasons" supporting the Code, which Lord and Quigley believed supplied its moral underpinning, was not made public. Hays's reluctance may have reflected his desire to placate the producers who had objected to Lord's argument that the subject matter of films had to be limited because they were made for a mass audience. It is also likely that Hays did not want to call attention to the fact that a set of rules aimed at regulating an entire industry had been written by a Jesuit priest and a Catholic layman.[43]

Quigley, who was also aware of the danger of associating the Code with the Catholic church, warned his colleagues that it would be unwise for *America* or any other Catholic publication to take the lead in supporting the new regulations. Rita McGoldrick, a supporter of Hays, was cautioned by Father Wilfrid Parsons to curb her enthusiasm. "She didn't like it," he told Quigley, "but she always does what we ask of her, even though she doesn't know why." Even Quigley omitted any reference in his journal to his own role in helping to devise the Code. Instead, he announced that it "was formulated after intensive study by members of the industry and, according to Will H. Hays, by church leaders, leaders in the field of education, representatives of women's clubs, educators, psychologists, dramatists and other students of our moral, social and family problems."[44]

Public reaction to the Code was mixed. A few papers felt that the attempt to purify the screen had already gone too far. Even before the formulation of the Code, some editors had wondered how Hollywood could satisfy a twelve-year-old and an adult with the same picture. "Thus far," one paper declared, "censors have spent all of their time protecting children against adult movies—they might better protect adults against childlike movies." Warning that "we are rapidly developing into the most censored and reformed nation on earth," the *New Britain Herald* suggested that it might be better if the Hays Office could concentrate its efforts on trying to reform the reformers.[45]

The press was evenly divided over whether or not the Code constituted a real change in the way Hollywood did business. The *Atlanta Constitution* interpreted it as ensuring "high-class" entertainment, and the *Boston Traveler* said it was "the best news we have heard in a long time." Jesse Henderson of the *Baltimore Sun* gave his readers fair warning that they had seen the last of the "excessive screen kiss, . . . the bed, the bathtub, and the hula skirt." Others were more skeptical, seeing little difference between the Code and the Don'ts and Be Carefuls. John Rosenfield, movie critic for the *Dallas Morning News*, predicted that nothing would change since he couldn't think of a single motion picture within the previous few seasons that seriously violated the new regulations. Yet many commentators who hailed the Code as a step forward wondered whether the producers would abide by it and if Hays had the power to make them. Skeptics predicted that the producers would quickly go back to their old ways. Some held that the producers simply had no choice inasmuch as they were giving the public what it wanted. As a reader of a western Massachusetts newspaper put it, it was no sin to supply the public with grown-up films in an "age of jazz and pep." What else could they do, asked Neil O'Hara in the *New York Evening World;* if the producers stopped making "sex talkies . . . Clara Bow will have to play Little Eva in *Uncle Tom's Cabin.*"[46]

Boston's city censor Wilton Barrett, a strong supporter of the National Board of Review, summed up the thoughts of some of the Code's critics when he branded the new guidelines "absurd and ridiculous," predicting that if they were implemented they would reduce future pictures to "pap." But for Barrett, if it came to a choice between honoring the Code and catering to an audience that with the advent of sound demanded more mature films, the new system would lose every time. One of many signs that the reformers were out of touch with the public was the response to a question in *Photoplay* as to whether Fatty Arbuckle, who had been working as "William Goodrich" for a film exchange, should be allowed to return to the screen under his own name. Although a few stalwarts like Canon William Sheafe Chase thought this would be unwise, an overwhelming number of the respondents favored his return, including the foreman of the first Arbuckle jury and the district attorney who prosecuted him.[47]

It is not clear what the studio heads thought they had committed themselves to when they signed the Code agreement. Most probably hoped that it would go the way of the previous reforms they had signed, while satisfying their critics. Nearly all of some thirty studio executives Quigley surveyed two months after the Code was adopted treated his inquiry as a public relations opportunity, declaring that the Code could curb the occasional excesses. Nevertheless, one producer touched on the fears that probably troubled most of his colleagues. Noting that the movies had to compete with other media, he argued that the industry wouldn't have a chance if "we are obliged to . . . drive with our brakes on" while the newspapers catered to men with stories of crime and gangsters and magazines furnished women with "lecherous . . . trashy, and salacious fiction."[48]

Quigley's initial fear that too much Catholic enthusiasm for the Code would taint it quickly gave way to the realization that it had little support outside the tight circle of Dinneen, Lord, Parsons, Breen, McGoldrick, and himself. As Parsons put it, the reaction was "a perfect dud." Some Catholic magazines were openly hostile. *Commonweal* argued that any reform that had to rely on Will Hays for enforcement was bound to fail, while the editor of *Columbia* dismissed the Code as "just a bright idea that someone had to make a bad business look good." One sign of the industry's duplicity, he continued, was the announcement that the public should not expect instant improvements because a number of films that were about to be released had been made before the Code was adopted. It sounded to this editor like "the butcher who pleads that he must be allowed to peddle all the rotten meat in his shop before offering the good meat."[49]

Quigley and his allies realized that the skepticism and indifference of the press's response to the Code would eventually destroy it. Without any public support, they reasoned, there would be no incentive for the studios to abide by the agreement. And it was, after all, not just any code, it was *their* Code. Although Quigley and Breen always publicly declared that the Code was an ecumenical document based on the Ten Commandments, they believed that its Catholic origins made it different from the industry's previous attempts at reform. "Our ideas of morality in entertainment," Quigley told one bishop, "differ radically from those held by the vast majority of the public." Similarly, Breen privately maintained that the Code was based on Catholic philosophy and ethics that were in conflict with some of the teachings of Protestant philosophers and theologians. In light of this, there was no question in the minds of its Catholic backers that the Code held the key to meaningful movie reform. As Father Parsons put it, "What we must do . . . is to create in the industry's minds an impression that influential people expect the Code to be obeyed; if that happens it will be obeyed." The IFCA needed no prompting. Carefully avoiding any mention of its Catholic origins, Rita McGoldrick hailed the Code on her radio show. She admitted that it bore some similarity to the Don'ts and Be Carefuls but noted that the old guidelines were subject to a variety of interpretations whereas the new Code was "steel ribbed in its definiteness."[50]

The major effort to rally Catholic support behind the Code was coordinated by Joe Breen and Father Parsons. Using an office in Quigley's publishing house, Breen went to work for the industry as public relations man for the Code. Early on, Breen suggested to Hays that if he wanted Catholic support, he should consider paying for it. He hastened to add that the $50,000 he asked for would be used not as a bribe but for advertising in Catholic newspapers around the country. Fearful that such an obvious move might backfire, Quigley and Parsons vetoed the idea. Breen's job was to drum up support among the editors of Catholic newspapers, and he personally contacted 75 percent of them between June and October 1930. Although he found that many were initially skeptical about the Code's value, more than half of them endorsed the new guidelines. He even secured the approval of

L'Osservatore Romano by telling the Vatican that the Protestant clergy in America favored government censorship whereas the Code was rooted in Catholic philosophy.[51]

While Breen was wooing the Catholic press, Parsons used *America* to drum up support for the Code among his readers. Editorials argued that state control, which left moral decisions in the hands of political appointees, would never work and that self-regulation was the only answer. But his major task was to win public endorsements from Cardinal Mundelein of Chicago and Cardinal Hayes of New York. Hayes did not want to endorse the Code until Mundelein had spoken, and tensions among the members of the original coalition made Parsons's task more difficult. After *Variety* scooped the other trade journals, including his own, on Hollywood's adoption of the Code, Quigley was convinced that the "worm" Hays had slipped the news to *Variety* in a "conniving and double dealing" attempt to deny him what he believed to be rightfully his story. Quigley in his anger had told the cardinal to avoid the Hays Office "as he would poison," a warning that understandably made Mundelein think twice about being publicly associated with the Code.[52]

The situation was further complicated by Quigley's discovery that Father Lord had accepted a $500 honorarium from Hays for his work on the Code. A contrite Lord offered to send the money back, but Quigley told him that would only make matters worse. When Parsons learned about the episode, he immediately pulled an article on the Code that Lord had written for *America*. "Wouldn't we have looked nice," he told a colleague, "publishing an article by one of Mr. Hays' hired men." He was so disturbed about the incident that he felt it disqualified Lord from ever again writing about the movies in his magazine. Lord had also told Hays that Mundelein had wanted credit for the Code; this undermined Quigley and Parsons's original strategy, which was to convince Hays that the cardinal was reluctant to become involved. Now, instead of pursuing the cardinal, Hays had reason to believe that Mundelein wanted publicity from him.[53]

Convinced that he was now in a better bargaining position, Hays revived the Pettijohn plan. Noting that the cardinal's original worries had been taken care of by the Code, Hays asked him to use his influence to eliminate the Chicago board of censors. But Father Dinneen cautioned Mundelein to proceed slowly, as a sudden change of course would open him up to the charge that he had sold out to Hays and the movie magnates. Quigley favored the Chicago board's eventual elimination, but he agreed with Parsons, Lord, and Dinneen that the time was not right. Nevertheless, his criticism of the board was Dinneen's first inkling that the publisher would side with the film industry. The group's advice to stand fast, coupled with the news that some local movie houses were still displaying indecent movie ads, not only led

Mundelein to turn down Hays's request but made him all the more reluctant to endorse the Code.[54]

Convinced that Mundelein's silence would be interpreted as a rejection of the new regulations, Parsons redoubled his efforts. Months of subsequent negotiations finally yielded a letter of support. With Mundelein in line, Parsons persuaded Cardinal Hayes to offer his backing. Finally, on November 15, seven and a half months after the Code's adoption, Parsons was able to publish the cardinals' endorsements in *America*.[55]

The coalition that had brought about the Code, however, would never be the same. Mundelein, Lord, and Dinneen began to doubt Quigley's true loyalties. Quigley, in turn, came to believe that Mundelein's delay in endorsing the Code had convinced the producers that the church was not really interested in cleaning up the movies. Parsons had found Lord wanting—"clever all right, but not in any practical way." He concluded that Lord should not be allowed to deal with the moviemakers on his own. The only thing they all agreed on was not to trust "that slippery gentleman" Will Hays. In spite of their differences, Quigley and the others had to work together over the next three years to ensure the Code's success.[56]

Historians have wondered why the Catholic church "suddenly decided" in 1934 that it would have to exert outside pressure in the form of the Legion of Decency in order to clean up the screen. The shift to a more adversarial approach three years after the adoption of the Code derived in good measure from the growing conviction on the part of its original Catholic champions that they had been used by the film industry. By publicly supporting new guidelines, they had put their reputations on the line. Eight months into the new system, Father Parsons told Will Hays that he was worried that his position would be damaged severely if the Code did not work. There were already signs: his letter to Hays had been prompted by an editorial in the *Baltimore Catholic Review* charging him with being naive to believe in Hollywood's promises. Noting that "movie filth" was still playing to big crowds, the paper declared that "no one with an ounce of sense has faith in the sincerity of the producers of the Code of morals. . . . Father Parsons has a lot of explaining to do when he gets back to normal," the writer concluded. Parsons and the others had persuaded the church to join the Code bandwagon. If the wagon took a wrong turn, they would have to take the lead in pointing the right way.[57]

FOUR

■■■

Disillusion

The ultimate success or failure of the Code rested on the performance of Jason Joy and the Studio Relations staff who were charged with its enforcement. Joy and two assistants concentrated on feature films while a third assistant monitored all comedies. Before the Code was adopted, Joy could plead with the producers to abide by the Don'ts and Be Carefuls or persuade them that it was in their best interest to seek his advice, but there had been nothing in the regulations to force them to cooperate. Now, every movie was supposed to obtain Joy's approval before it could be released. Joy could refuse to approve the film, but the studio had the right to appeal his decision to a jury of three West Coast producers. Because the jury members served on a rotating basis, the producer whose appeal they were listening to today could be judging them when it was their turn to challenge Joy. Nevertheless, a comparison of the nine months of 1930 in which the Code was in operation with the previous year indicates that the producers were making an effort to cooperate. In 1929 there had been only 48 consultations with Joy's office before and during the preparation of stories, compared to 1,271 in 1930, while the number of films viewed prior to release went from 323 to 564.[1]

For a time, Joy's power to hold up a film until the producer had made whatever changes were needed to satisfy the Code created the impression that movie immorality was a thing of the past. *Bad Girl* (1931), one of the first pictures produced under the new code, was shown at the Fox studio's office in New York to several priests, members of the Catholic press, and a few movie critics, who gave it unanimous approval. There was one momentary snag: in the press book that accompanied the film, Fox's advertising department had exploited the title of an otherwise innocent film about a young married couple expecting a baby, giving the impression that the blessed event had originated with a petting party on the sofa. The objectionable ads, which were pulled at the last moment, led to an internal Fox memo declaring: "Let us understand once and for all time that it is not for us to try to beat the Code nor even see how close we can come to the border line of its restrictions." Sex and crime weren't the only topics purged from the screen. At Joy's insistence, RKO made its contribution to national confidence in the banking system by dropping a scene in *Drifting Souls* in which a reporter asks the heroine: "Do you know that the bank in which your husband had all his money closed?"[2]

Not everyone was satisfied. Concerned that the Code would reduce them to making films about Jack the Giant Killer and Cinderella, the filmmakers scrutinized each release to see what other studios were able to get away with. Any sign of laxity became a precedent for greater leniency. As a Paramount executive told the studio's chief, Ben Schulberg, because Joy had ignored the Code when he allowed MGM to show explicit crime methods in *Paid* (1930), he was in for trouble if he asked Paramount to toe the line. Yet there was always someone who felt that the Hays Office wasn't doing enough to protect the public. A woman from White Plains, New York, complained to the Hays Office that she had stopped a young boy running hysterically through the streets crying, "I knew he was going to kill her." Asked what was disturbing him, he answered, "Frank somebody was going to kill the girl." It dawned on her that he had just seen *Frankenstein*.[3]

In spite of the occasional complaints from a handful of zealots, Quigley wrote on the first anniversary of the Code's adoption that "an examination of the record very definitely proves that . . . it has been enormously successful." Joy was trying, having recommended 975 major changes in 286 scripts during his first year as guardian of the Code. As proof of Hollywood's new spirit of cooperation, Rita McGoldrick reported that the IFCA had endorsed 61 percent of the films released in 1930, a jump of 10 percentage points over the previous year. "These are the days," she declared, "when the most fastidious person may have a wide variety of splendid films to select from." Best of all, "Everything Catholic on the screen has been, and is being, protected one hundred percent."[4]

However, the studios' insistence on basing many films on "pre-tested" material like novels and Broadway plays continued to pose problems for Joy. Paramount had purchased the rights to Theodore Dreiser's novel *An American Tragedy* a few months after the Code's adoption, in spite of the opposition of the National Board of Review and the Daughters of the American Revolution. The book (banned on three separate occasions in Boston in the 1920s) told the story of Clyde Griffith, a son of street evangelists who hungers for wealth and position. While carrying on an affair with Roberta Alden, a co-worker, he falls in love with a wealthy young woman who can open the door to a new life. When all this is threatened by Roberta's pregnancy, he plots to drown her in a lake. Although he decides not to carry out his plan, the boat accidentally capsizes and he swims away, leaving her to die. The novel ends in a lengthy court trial where Clyde is sentenced to death.

Joy predicted that Paramount's purchase could become "as Arbuckle did, a symbol of everything objectionable in the industry." *An American Tragedy* was just the kind of "polluted novel" that Father Daniel Lord had argued had no place in a mass entertainment medium like the movies. But with Paramount's heavy investment, there was no question that the story would be filmed. Joy worked for the studios, not the reformers, and he did his best to make the film conform to the Code. The studio agreed early on to shorten Clyde's seduction of Roberta. It also transformed Clyde: initially ashamed of his mother, a street preacher, he comes to love her for standing beside him during the trial. After being found guilty, Clyde tells his mother that he wishes he had his life to live over, and she responds, "They may not understand on earth, but there is One above who will understand and redeem you." As Ben Schulberg put it, her words gave the picture "a spiritual lift at the finish and even the semblance of a happy ending."[5]

But Lamar Trotti, one of Joy's assistants, warned his boss that "we'll catch hell" over the two scenes in which Roberta tries to obtain an abortion. Although the producer claimed that the film would show the "tragic consequences" of abortion, Joy's staff feared that even this would cause a major problem with the Catholic church. Joy contacted Will Hays, who admitted that there was nothing in the Code that prohibited abortion, but that he was firmly opposed to any on-screen reference. Hays personally lobbied Ben Schulberg, telling him that five abortion stories being considered by other studios would be dropped if Paramount excluded it from *An American Tragedy*. A small group including Hays, Joy, and Lord screened the completed film. Schulberg thought he had resolved the abortion problem by eliminating one scene and cutting a few key lines in Clyde's cross-examination at his trial. In the revised script, Clyde admits that he and Roberta had gone to a druggist, leaving what they were seeking to the audience's imagination. But Hays was still not satisfied, and Paramount had to eliminate even indirect references to abortion before the film was approved.[6]

Authors were usually dissatisfied with what Hollywood did to their books, and Dreiser was no exception. Convinced that Paramount had turned his indictment of society into an ordinary murder mystery, he sued the studio. But the court, which had little use for social realism, rejected his claim and praised the producer for recognizing that the great majority of moviegoers would be more interested in seeing justice prevail than in figuring out what forces had destroyed Clyde.[7]

Despite his struggle with Paramount, Joy was generally satisfied with the studios' cooperation during the first year of the Code, but he was worried that their efforts had gone unnoticed by censorship boards. He told Hays that despite the improved quality of pictures, local boards requested more cuts in 1931 than any previous year. Good pictures, he reported, had been "mutilated beyond belief in the most fault-finding and childish way by some censors," particularly New York, Pennsylvania, and Ohio. His department had worked closely with RKO to turn *Are These Our Children?* into "a powerful preachment against liquor, loose living and the evil consequences of bad companions" and was shocked when the New York censors rejected it. If the censors continued their nit-picking, he warned Hays, the producers might decide to give them something they would really object to.[8]

Lord carefully evaluated the Studio Relations Committee's progress when he traveled to Hollywood at Hays's invitation in the spring of 1931. Still smarting over Quigley's criticism, however, the priest refused to accept any money from Hays and insisted on paying his own expenses. Lord found much to praise, pointing out in a report to Cardinal George Mundelein that, without the Code, "conditions in the motion pictures this year would have been beyond description." Nevertheless, Lord identified three problems that he predicted would undermine the Code's effectiveness if they were not resolved. One was that the industry's increasing tendency to draw its material from Broadway plays and novels designed for more sophisticated audiences too often lowered the moral standards of the public, in direct violation of the Code. He pointed out that twenty-eight of sixty films in production in the spring of 1931 dealt with infidelity, adultery, illegitimacy, or seduction. The effect, he concluded, was that mistresses were presented as heroic, the virtuous were drudges, and premarital and extramarital relations were the norm. In one of several examples cited by Lord, a "college sheik" seduces a fellow student but is expelled from school before she discovers she is pregnant. She marries a studious classmate in order to give the child a name, but she and her lover are reunited at the story's end. This sort of image of college life, Lord declared, was bound to offend college students. According to the priest, the students were hungering for "wholesome and clean . . . national heroes like Lindbergh, Bobby Jones, Knute Rockne, Babe Ruth and even Al Smith" who would replace the "degenerates, libertines, prostitutes and unfaithful husbands and wives."[9]

Nevertheless, Lord suspected that there were likely to be far more libertines than Lindberghs during the next year. Noting that the Depression had put many studios on shaky financial ground, he found that a number of producers were turning to sex and gangster pictures to save them from bankruptcy. Lord was right; initially, movie attendance had withstood the effects of the downturn, and there had been a great deal of talk that the industry was Depression-proof. Hollywood had experienced record admissions and profits in 1930, the first full year after the stock market collapse. But as the lines at the soup kitchens lengthened, the lines at the box office began to shrink. And although some studios continued to make money in 1931, Fox lost $3 million, RKO, $5.6 million, and Warner, $7.9 million. The downward spiral continued over the next two years. By the end of 1933, according to one estimate, attendance had fallen 40 percent since 1929, and *Film Daily* reported that 5,000 out of 16,000 theaters had closed.[10]

The studios' commitment to the Code would have waned in any event, but the economic plight of the industry accelerated the slide. One of the studios' first steps was to revive the practice of using movie ads that promised more sex than the film delivered. *Abraham Lincoln*, a rather dull story of the President's alleged romance with Ann Rutledge and his path to the White House, sounded much more exciting in an ad in the *Albany Evening News:* "She taught Lincoln how to love—and like it." Hoping to stimulate more truth in advertising, Father Wilfrid Parsons of *America* told the Hays Office that when one of his friends looked for a film to which he could bring his wife and children, he always chose the one with "the most salacious title, since he was pretty sure it would be clean." Parsons wondered whether the very existence of the Code had spawned a trend toward deceptive advertising in the industry.[11]

Instead of toning down their ads, however, the studios began turning out films that delivered some of what the titles and posters promised. First to assault the Code was a wave of gangster films that began with *Little Caesar* (1930), a tale of the rise and fall of a hoodlum, played by Edward G. Robinson, who dies unrepentant in a shootout with the police. The story, which had gone into production before the adoption of the Code, had not been presented to the Studio Relations Committee, but a chorus of protests forced Joy to see the film in a local theater. Satisfied that the movie's ending demonstrated that crime didn't pay, Joy locked horns with the New York state censors, who refused to pass the film until Warner eliminated much of the violence. Joy warned the censors that their demands were counterproductive because "the more ghastly, the more ruthless, the criminal acts, the stronger will be the audience reaction against men of this kind." The New York censors settled for a series of minor changes, including the elimination of a shot of stolen money, a scene of a gangster's funeral, and a few lines like "my gun's gonna speak its piece."[12]

Crime may not have paid on the screen, but it paid off at the box office. *Little Caesar* was soon followed by *Public Enemy* (1931), starring Jimmy Cagney. Shot in twenty-one days at a cost of $151,000, it earned in excess of a million dollars in its initial release. By the end of the year, Hollywood had turned out more than fifty gangster films. According to Father Lord, although a single such film might be harmless, the constant repetition of these stories was bound to make a mark on the audience. When a police court judge declared that the case of seventeen-year-old Joseph Wilkinson, who had been arrested for robbery, was typical of the juvenile crimes caused by the movies, the boy scoffed at the judge's comment, claiming that a picture like *Little Caesar* would make him want to stop before he was gunned down like Edward G. Robinson's character. If anything, he blamed his delinquency on the fact that his mother had not let him go to the movies until he was twelve, forcing him to hang around with a street gang.[13]

But no less an expert than Al Capone, in one of his last press conferences before entering federal prison, recommended throwing all gangster films away. "They're doing nothing but harm to the younger element," he declared. "[They] are making a lot of kids want to be tough guys, and they don't serve any useful purpose." The censors agreed. Having passed *Scarface* after producer Howard Hughes had consented to a number of cuts, Jason Joy was forced to convince one censorship board after another to allow it to be shown. It took four months of negotiating before New York agreed to its release under a compromise title, *Scarface, Shame of the Nation.* With the chair of the Studio Relations Committee going around the country lobbying for crime films, Code supporters began to wonder if the fox had been appointed to protect the henhouse.[14]

The Hays Office tried to defend itself by arguing that because all of these films ended with the gangster's death, the industry was doing its part to fight wrongdoing. Crime experts like August Vollmer were enlisted to argue that movies like *Public Enemy* did not cause crime, but critics retorted that Cagney's death at the film's end seemed to many to be a small price to pay for the excitement of criminal life and a chance to date Jean Harlow. As Walter Lippmann noted, "the damage is done long before . . . the gangster has been handcuffed. The damage is done when . . . the gangster [is] shown living in splendor, wearing magnificent clothes and riding around in great limousines." Recognizing that the concern about crime films was reaching dangerous proportions, Hays convinced the MPPDA to halt their production in September 1931.[15]

The Hays Office quickly learned that it had traded one problem for another. As Jason Joy admitted, "with crime practically denied them, with box-office figures down . . . it was almost inevitable that sex, the nearest thing at hand and pretty generally sure-fire, would be seized upon." A sanctimonious Cecil B. deMille complained that the producers were "in a state of panic and chaos. . . . And like little children, they rush for the bedspring and the lingerie the moment the phantom of empty seats rises to clutch them." According to the *Cleveland Plain Dealer*, it was a matter of arithmetic: "two plus two makes four, four and four, eight, and sex and sex make millions." Lord complained to Hays that producers seemed to be competing to give each picture a little more "kick" in order to attract a jaded audience so that romance gave way to "lust" and then "to open infidelity."[16]

The result was what came to be known as the "fallen woman" film, in which the star took to the streets or became the mistress of some successful man in order to survive. More alarming to Hollywood's critics than the stories was that the woman didn't always fall, or fall far enough, to convince the audience that she had paid for her sins. The release of *Possessed*, starring Joan Crawford and Clark Gable, toward the end of 1931 touched off a cycle of similar stories. It also marked the beginning of Joy's real problems in trying to enforce the Code.[17]

In *Possessed*, a poor factory worker (Crawford) leaves the drudgery of small-town life and eventually becomes the mistress of an ambitious lawyer (Gable), who is separated from his wife. When he decides to run for governor, they part in order to protect him from scandal. After the relationship is revealed at a political campaign rally, Crawford's character, who happens to be in the audience, stands up and announces that she left him so that he could be free to serve the public. Her bravery wins over the crowd, and the candidate follows her out of the hall. Win or lose, the audience knows that he will never let her leave him again. MGM had failed to furnish the Studio Relations Committee with the script, and Joy's people did not see the film until it was finished. Lamar Trotti reported back that it worried him more than any picture he had seen since joining the staff. The studio, however, rejected most of Joy's requests for dialogue and scene changes, although it agreed to add a clumsy moralizing speech by Crawford's character stressing the importance of marriage. Unwilling to get into a fight that he was likely to lose, Joy passed the film.[18]

Producers treated each concession as an invitation to bend the regulations a little more. If Joan Crawford could be sexy, self-sacrificing, and brave at the same time, then Tallulah Bankhead could take to the street to support her ailing husband in *Faithless*, Marlene Dietrich could sleep her way to the top of the cabaret circuit to save her dying husband in *Blond Venus*, and Irene Dunne could fruitlessly beg John Boles for a child while waiting twenty years in vain for him to leave his wife in *Back Street*. But there was nothing ennobling or self-sacrificing about Jean Harlow's portrayal of a small-town secretary who sleeps her way to the top, man by man and floor by floor, in *Red-Headed Woman* (1932). Trying on a dress in a shop, she asks the saleswoman, "Can you see through this?" When the clerk responds, "I'm afraid you can, ma'am," Harlow cracks, "I'll wear it." The wages of sin turn out to be a French aristocrat's luxury apartment in Paris with Charles Boyer as her chauffeur. A worried Joy knew that someone would pay the price for Harlow's sins and he suspected it would be him—he told Hays, "half the other companies are trying to figure out ways of topping this particular picture."[19]

If, as the reformers presumed, gangster films turned viewers into criminals, what were the fallen woman films doing to America's women? "Is there nothing interesting about a good woman?" asked Mrs. Alonzo Richardson, secretary to the Atlanta Board of Review. Sitting in a theater showing *Possessed*, she heard one young girl whisper to another that she would be willing to live with Clark Gable under any conditions. In 1932, *Christian Century* began to count the number of "strumpets" in "another year of the 'Hays-cleaned' movies." Even Irving Thalberg, whose studio had started the cycle with *Possessed*, feared that the industry was suffering from a surfeit of sex and crime pictures. He suggested as an antidote that each major studio should make ten important movies each year without any sex or crime angles, but no one, including Thalberg himself, volunteered to take the lead.[20]

One measure of the Code's ineffectiveness was the increasing number of cuts ordered by state and city censors. Joy could call it nit-picking, but at the end of 1931, James Wingate, head of the New York state board, warned Hollywood that unless something was done, he would have to clamp down. Although Wingate claimed that his reviewers had been lenient in light of the shaky economic situation in Hollywood, they had ordered almost one thousand more cuts in 1931 than in the previous year. By the summer of 1932, fallen women were dropping into more and more stories, and Joy's office was to blame. According to Pete Harrison, editor of the trade paper *Harrison's Reports*, "In pre-Code days a producer felt personally responsible for the filth he put in his picture—now he cloaks himself in the Code."[21]

News that Paramount had decided to put aside the conservative policy it had followed for years and purchase the rights to Mae West's play *Diamond Lil*, one of the properties that Hays had personally banned, was the last straw. When Joy was offered a job as story consultant at Fox studios, he jumped at the chance and left the Hays Office in September 1932. As Geoff Shurlock, one of his assistants, explained, the Code was not working, and Joy "was not going to spend his life fighting a losing battle." Hays asked Carl Milliken, former governor of Maine and head of the MPPDA's public relations department, to take over Joy's job. Milliken claimed that he lacked the ability to analyze scripts in order to bring them in line with the Code and rejected the offer. Asked by Hays to recommend a replacement, Martin Quigley told him that no one could perform the job in the present atmosphere. A year earlier, publisher William Randolph Hearst had warned Hays that once the studios lost their respect for his office, he wouldn't last "as long as a drink of whiskey in Kentucky." Now Quigley warned him that unscrupulous moviemakers might continue to make money, but he would be the one held responsible.[22]

With his reputation on the line, Hays sought to prove his commitment to reform by appointing Wingate as Joy's successor. Wingate proved to be the wrong man for the job. He could identify the Code violations in a picture, but because he didn't know how to fix them, he felt more comfortable ordering cuts than trying to negotiate an acceptable alternative. Moreover, producers often complained that he was so tardy in sending in his responses that the picture was half-finished by the time they were received.[23]

In fairness to Wingate, he took over Joy's job at a time when Paramount and RKO were only a few months away from being placed in receivership, and all the other studios were experiencing some financial difficulty. To make matters worse, one of Wingate's first jobs was to deal with Paramount's version of *Diamond Lil*, which began shooting two months after his arrival in Hollywood. Paramount executives had originally backed off from filming the West play at Hays's request, but they were now willing to risk his ire if it would help them dig out of their financial hole. Wingate's staff worked on the film, retitled *She Done Him Wrong*, in an unsuccessful effort to distance it from the play. Although the studio made several concessions, West's famous double entendres survived. She was also able to get away with her musical tribute to foreplay in "A Guy What Takes His Time." Nor could anyone restrain the full-figured West, who had only to roll her eyes to transform an innocent exchange into a sexual encounter. What probably bothered her critics the most was that she displayed as much interest in sex as any man. With Paramount teetering on bankruptcy, Wingate characterized the film as "rowdy amusement," crossed his fingers, and passed it.[24]

The reaction to *She Done Him Wrong* was one more measure of the gap that existed between the reformers and the public. Censors around the country protested so much that Paramount voluntarily cut a hundred feet of film from "A Guy What Takes His Time," leaving a scar across the picture. But the public loved it. The *New Haven Register* asked its readers, "What star stands out above all the others? Is it demure Janet Gaynor or perhaps sweet little Marion Nixon? . . . No! . . . It is none other than buxom Mae West, the lady whose pictures . . . had to be run on asbestos film." An embarrassed Martin Quigley was forced to include West in the *Motion Picture Herald*'s ten biggest box office stars for the 1932–33 season.[25]

While West's popularity soared, Wingate's reputation plummeted. By the end of 1932, religious and educational groups across the country were adopting resolutions calling for federal regulation of the movie industry. To add to Wingate's woes, a series of twelve studies financed by the Payne Fund on the effects of moviegoing on children was released in 1933. The investigators sought to measure how the movies influenced the attitudes, beliefs, and character of elementary and high school students. Although their research was based on interviews and questionnaires, occasional references to investigative tools like the psycho-galvanometer, which measures the effect of movies on children's sleep patterns, convinced reformers that at last they had scientific proof of the necessity for federal censorship.[26]

The studies were condensed into a single book for the general public, Henry James Forman's *Our Movie-Made Children*, a sensational exposé that purported to document the terrible consequences for children of unregulated filmgoing, ranging from lowered grades to deteriorating moral standards. The book suggested that all the nation's ills could be traced to the evil influence of the neighborhood theater, which had become "not merely a school but a university of crime." And how could any responsible parents let their daughters go to the theater after reading the story of one young woman who was "addicted" to the movies because they taught her "how to love and kiss": after seeing a passionate movie, this young woman told the interviewer, she usually went out "to some kind of road house or an apartment with [her] man to get [her] wants satisfied." Most people learned about the studies from popular magazines like *McCall's*, *Saturday Review of Literature*, and *Parents' Magazine*. The "Payneful studies," as they were known in the Hays Office, threw the industry on the defensive. Hays might have found some small solace in the occasional newspaper story that characterized the studies as quackery, but overall the reports seemed to hold the movies responsible for the decline of Western civilization.[27]

In early March, Joe Breen warned Hays that Quigley, who had visited Hollywood, believed that the producers who were ignoring the Code had to be reined in. On March 5, a beleaguered Hays called a meeting of the MPPDA board of directors which lasted through the night. He warned the members that if they continued to do business as usual, federal legislation would soon compel them to do what they had voluntarily agreed to do when they signed the Code three years earlier. Faced with a series of hostile bills in Congress, including one calling for an investigation of the entire industry, and with the new Roosevelt administration in the White House, the directors signed an agreement reaffirming the Code. Armed with the new accord, Hays traveled to the West Coast in April and bluntly told the producers that if they wouldn't cooperate, the company presidents back east would have no trouble finding replacements for them.[28]

Although the agreement was not made public because it would be an open admission that the industry had been ignoring the Code, Hays tightened control over production. He first persuaded Fox Studios to let him borrow back Jason Joy for the rest of the year. Joy was to coordinate the work of the Studio Relations Committee, while Wingate, assisted by Breen, who had moved to Hollywood to handle press relations for the Hays Office, would review the scripts and films that were sent to them. The Studio Relations Committee had always tried, with mixed success, to portray criminal or immoral behavior as wrong. Now, as Wingate and his staff redoubled their efforts, they demanded tangible proof: criminals were to be killed or jailed, gold diggers stripped of their ill-gotten gains, and adulterers punished.

Hays's attempt to reinvigorate the Studio Relations Committee came too late to satisfy his critics. Even Alice Ames Winter, a loyal member of Hays's staff, complained that the producers continued to regard the Code as something to be "got around." When Hays invited Father Daniel Lord to come out to Hollywood to help Wingate during the summer of 1933, the priest turned him down. Lord, who had begun to lose faith in the producers' promises, had gone to a neighborhood theater to see a film recommended by a friend and arrived in the middle of the second feature, *No Man of Her Own*, starring Clark Gable and Carole Lombard. Gable plays a crooked gambler who marries a woman (Lombard) because of a bet with a friend. Realizing that he has fallen in love with his wife, he decides to start a new life by turning himself in. After his brief stint in jail, the couple reunite for the usual happy ending.

Lord wrote a blistering letter to Hays in which he identified five distinct Code violations in the picture. One involved Lombard's character removing her dress in front of her husband, prompting Lord to ask if the movie producers had stock in lingerie companies. How William Powell, Lombard's husband at the time, could allow her to appear in such "filthy stories" was beyond him. And as for her costar, Lord declared that he was glad that he was not "responsible for turning loose upon the public a menace to morals like Clark Gable." He told Hays that pictures were now worse than before the enactment of the Code. A case in point was *She Done Him Wrong*, which he declared was just the type of picture that the Code had been designed to prevent. "Sick and more than a bit tired," Lord warned Hays that the producers were about to "face a day of reckoning." Lord primarily blamed

Wingate. While he agreed with Alice Winter that the producers could not be trusted, Wingate was being paid to keep them in line. According to Lord, Wingate's failure stemmed from his practice of trying to elevate a film's moral stance by cutting a line here and adding a line there while ignoring the movie's message. Wingate would excise an occasional "damn" or "hell" while ignoring a scene where "a young man seduces a young woman and is shown at the breakfast table the next morning." "One feels," Lord complained to Breen, "that there is a straining at gnats and a swallowing of camels." Trying to put everything right with a bit of moralizing in the last hundred feet of film, the priest warned, did nothing to wipe out the previous seventy-five minutes of indecency. With a sense that he had been personally betrayed by Hollywood, Lord told friends in the summer of 1933 that he was "off" the Hays Office for life.[29]

Lord's break with Hays marked a major shift in Catholic attitudes toward the film industry. The spirit of cooperation that had pervaded the previous decade had stemmed, in part, from a belief that, despite all his scheming, Hays was committed to reform. Now Catholic leaders were no longer so sure. At their annual fall meeting in 1932, the Catholic bishops declared that the greater leisure time stemming from unemployment is "one of the gravest problems presently facing our nation." The church could no longer stay on the sidelines. As Father FitzGeorge Dinneen noted in a letter to Father Wilfrid Parsons, "Everything in the moral order that we stand for and are working and fighting for in the church is at stake." The church's decision to launch a national attack on Hollywood was part of a larger trend toward a greater Catholic involvement in economic and social affairs that had emerged in the early 1930s. The Great Depression seems to have spurred the church to come up with its own solutions to the nation's problems. Monsignor Francis Lally noted that it was not until the 1930s that "we can really speak in realistic terms of a widespread Catholic social consciousness and with it a willingness not simply to adapt to community life but also to work to transform it." Many Catholic leaders traced the economic collapse to the failure of the laissez-faire policies of the Protestant establishment. In contrast, Pope Pius XI's 1931 encyclical, *Quadragesimo Anno*, on social justice and the obligation of the government to work for the common good, put the church in tune with the more activist policies of the New Deal. Even Cardinal Mundelein's close friendship with President Franklin D. Roosevelt seemed to symbolize a larger role for Catholic social policy.[30]

By 1933, the church had the will to "clean up the movies"; all it needed was someone to show it the way. That task fell to the original Catholic supporters of the Code, who found little to celebrate on the third anniversary of its adoption. Father Parsons, who had gone out on a limb to support the Code openly, observed the date by warning his readers to abandon whatever hope that they might have that the moviemakers were interested in reform. Although still suspicious of federal censorship, he was willing to entertain the idea, noting that the time may have come for society to take control of the movie industry, as it was doing in banking and investment. Parsons and Quigley thought that moment had come with the establishment of the National Industrial Recovery Act in June 1933. The act was designed to revive economic activity by encouraging major industries to develop agreements eliminating cutthroat competition and establishing minimum wages. If the Production Code could be incorporated into the motion picture industry's agreement, the Code would have the force of law. Hays gave Parsons and Quigley the impression that he favored the idea, but the final document not only ignored the Code but had little to say about movie morals in general. In the end, it seemed like just one more of Hays's double crosses.[31]

Meanwhile the Catholic press kept up a steady attack on Hollywood in the spring and summer of 1933. *America*'s Father Gerard Donnelly, who six months earlier had defended Hays, took him to task on May 20 for failing to halt the trend toward movie immorality. Donnelly listed fifty recent pictures that had subverted decency through "offensive situations, smutty dialogue and obscene wit." What was especially disheartening, he said, was that even Will Rogers had begun dealing in double entendres in his latest picture, *State Fair*.[32]

A case in point was what some Catholic critics believed to be Cecil B. deMille's gratuitous introduction of sex into his 1932 religious epic *The Sign of the Cross*. It wasn't the first time he had used the Bible as a source of safe sex, but the film's release in the midst of the growing distrust of Hollywood touched a raw nerve in Catholic circles. Although it would be simplistic to trace the subsequent formation of the Legion of Decency to one single Hollywood production, *The Sign of the Cross* played a significant role. The furor that surrounded the film was especially embarrassing to Lord, who had maintained a close friendship with the producer since their collaboration on *King of Kings*. They exchanged letters frequently, and Lord regularly acted as a consultant for deMille on his religious projects. Consequently, when deMille asked Lord to help him with his latest enterprise in early 1932, Lord jumped at the chance.[33]

After reading the original script, Lord told the director that the story had "grand dramatic possibilities" but the major problem, as Lord saw it, was that the pagans with their orgies and banquets seemed "alive, modern, 'night-clubish,' making sin fascinating as it often seems to be." The Christians, in contrast, came off as "dull, plodding, and uninspiring," which robbed their subsequent martyrdom of any dramatic interest. DeMille encountered a similar reaction from the Studio Relations Committee when Wingate questioned some of the Roman revelries, especially an "indecent" dance that later caused much of deMille's difficulties with Catholics. The director rejected Wingate's objections, sanctimoniously pointing out that the pagan excesses had been introduced only in order to highlight the purity of the Christians. In the end, deMille's few token cuts satisfied Wingate. DeMille "refrained from running wild with Roman orgies," he told Hays, predicting that the film would cause little difficulty.[34]

Wingate couldn't have been more mistaken. The first sign of trouble came after Paramount's advertising department asked the Reverend Christian Reisner, an important New York minister, to preview the film in the hope that he might recommend it. Instead, Reisner fired a letter back denouncing the film as "repellent, nauseating, lewd, cheap and disgusting" and declaring that only an "ignoramus" could have come up with such a script. Meanwhile Lord, who had not previewed the film, wrote to deMille that he was eagerly awaiting its release but was puzzled by the ad he had seen announcing its opening at the Roosevelt Theater in Chicago. The ad, which covered an entire building, included a "picture of a Roman orgy with a nude woman and a drunken man in each other's arms and [a dancer] inflaming their passions." Lord's worst fears were realized when he saw the film. With scenes of seduction, sensuous dancing, a revealing milk bath, and hints of homosexuality and lesbianism, *The Sign of the Cross* was deMille at his best—or worst. Lord tried to explain to his friend what was wrong with his film. Declaring that Catholics began and ended each day with the sign of the cross, he suggested that anything related to that subject had to be handled with great sensitivity. He felt that with the exception of one scene in which a female dancer tries to excite the Christian heroine, which he felt bordered on "sex perversion," most of the problems could be handled by cutting three hundred to five hundred feet of film.[35]

Other Catholic critics were not so gentle. *America*, *Commonweal*, and the *NCWC Bulletin* were among the journals that excoriated the film. The scene that captured the most criticism became known in Catholic circles as "that lesbian dance." *America* called it one of "the most unpleasant bits of footage ever passed by the Hollywood censors," and Cleveland Bishop Joseph Schrembs took the unusual step of denouncing the film in his New Year's Eve sermon, which was picked up by the National Catholic News Service and reprinted around the country. As a result, Mary McGill, writing in *Our Sunday Visitor*, warned her readers away from the film (even though she had not seen it) because "authorized Catholic critics" had condemned it.[36]

DeMille, who claimed that he had never before responded to criticism in his twenty years in the industry, was so stung by the attack that he sent a defense of the film to several Catholic critics. Noting that the dance scene accounted for only 148 feet in 11,000 feet of film, he reminded them that sexual irregularities did not originate in Hollywood. "I seem to remember in the Bible," he said, "a story of Sodom and Gomorrah." Yes, wrote Martin Quigley in response, "and as for Sodom and Gomorrah we seem to remember from that same Bible that they got hell and lots of it."[37]

In fairness, the Catholic reaction to *The Sign of the Cross* was not unanimous. A group of fifty priests at a special showing in the New Orleans diocese liked it and seemed to have no problem with deMille's use of vice to accentuate virtue. One elderly bishop even publicly recommended the film until he was embarrassed to learn about the "lesbian implications" of the dance sequence from a colleague. Nevertheless, almost every influential Catholic newspaper condemned it and urged its readers to boycott the film. It is not clear whether their readers responded to the call. Parsons and Quigley claimed that ticket sales were damaged seriously, whereas Paramount insisted that the film grossed more money than any picture in the previous five years. It made no difference who was right. Catholic leaders believed that their efforts had seriously damaged the film's success and that they could do the same to other films.[38]

To many Catholics, *The Sign of the Cross* symbolized an industry out of control. If a studio could transform a beautiful story of the triumph of the Christian martyrs over the Roman Empire into something sordid and evil, the critics reasoned, what hope could they have that the industry could be trusted to regulate itself? Unfortunately for deMille, his film coincided with a revival of the type of newspaper stories that had bedeviled Hollywood during the Arbuckle scandal. Accounts of high salaries and low morals, made all the more reprehensible in the midst of an economic collapse, filled the papers. According to the *Buffalo Catholic Union and Times:* "Herod's court had nothing on the alley urchins and ladies of loose morals who have risen high in movie fame."[39]

The publication of the Payne studies, which declared that 72 percent of movies were unfit for children, was the last straw. The Catholic church, which had opposed child labor legislation for fear that it would undermine parental control, spent millions of dollars developing a separate school system to inoculate its children against the evils of a secular world. And yet a series of sexual images on a silver screen seemed to threaten everything the church had tried to accomplish. Likening the movies to a Pied Piper that was leading children to perdition, *Columbia* declared that the current trend had to be stopped. Suddenly the Catholic press was filled with calls for action. On July 8, the *New York Catholic News,* noting the death of Fatty Arbuckle, asked why Hays, who had kept the comic off the screen, couldn't do the same thing with the people who were befouling the industry. "What answer does Catholic action have for this problem?" asked another paper. Uncoordinated responses in various dioceses indicated that the challenge would not go unanswered. In Buffalo, the diocesan paper called for a boycott of pictures featuring divorce, while the students of St. Catherine's High School in Racine, Wisconsin, presented a petition demanding cleaner pictures to the local theater owners.[40]

The Catholic hierarchy had largely ignored the movie problem until the summer of 1933. The industry would respond, Dinneen argued, only if the hierarchy asserted itself. A good example of how the producers bent to pressure, he told Parsons, was their response to Mussolini's threat to ban *A Farewell to Arms* if it showed the Italian army in retreat. We could exert the same type of pressure, he argued, if we worked together. Dinneen, who had never trusted the moviemakers, found a new ally in Lord. By early summer, according to Breen, the two priests were "very much up in arms with fire in their eyes."[41]

As criticism of Hollywood mounted, Dinneen, Lord, Parsons, Quigley, and Breen sensed that this was their last chance to save the Code they had devised, but they needed someone in the hierarchy to lead the way. Cardinal Mundelein was the logical choice, but he had been burned by the Code's failure and was unwilling to lead on the movie issue again. The other three cardinals offered little hope: Hayes of New York was too cautious; Dougherty of Philadelphia was too independent; and O'Connell of Boston was too unpopular with the other members of the hierarchy. Their best hope seemed to be Bishop John J. Cantwell of Los Angeles. Cantwell had been appointed bishop in 1917 after a two-year interregnum during which the church had difficulty finding someone willing to take over what was at the time an insignificant diocese. The growth of the movie industry in the 1920s had changed all that. At first glance, Cantwell seemed to be an unlikely candidate to lead the reform effort. The Irish-born prelate was a conservative who, while championing the reunification of his native land, applauded the efforts of Mussolini and Franco during the 1930s. Although he supported the church-instigated Christero revolution in Mexico in the 1920s, he had ignored the movie question, limiting his activity to the establishment of the Catholic Motion Pictures Actors' Guild, which had never become a force in the industry. The diocesan newspaper, the *Tidings*, barely acknowledged a problem during the period between the adoption of the Code and the end of 1933. Nevertheless, with the movie business located in his diocese, he had more contacts with industry representatives than any other bishop. If Cantwell, who Quigley thought had been "grossly negligent," could be made to feel partly responsible for the type of films that emanated from his city, he might agree to spearhead the new campaign.[42]

The task of enlisting the bishop was given to Joe Breen, who had already proved his ability to excel at Hollywood politics. As early as the fall of 1929, when the Code was still in an embryonic stage, he had urged Quigley to include a new board of examiners in the proposal to evaluate the scripts before they were turned over to the producers. Eager to improve his situation after completing the job of enlisting Catholic support for the Code, he wrote Hays, "I am so enthusiastic about the whole business and so willing to work that I'd be tempted to bite the legs off anybody who might dare to cross us at this stage of the game." Rewarded with a job in the Hays Office, he began to look around for a chance to advance himself. Less than a year later, he wrote an eight-page letter to Hays pointing out the industry's need to get "the best man in America" to control publicity. A shameless paean to the industry, his letter identified the type of man who could do the job: "a crusader . . . with the vision before him of saving a great industry in which the lives and destinies, the hopes and the dreams of thousands of our people are inextricably involved." He concluded, "Don't you see what an opportunity such a job offers?" He modestly added that he didn't know who that man was, but he suggested that he might be buried in some department in Hays's office. A few months later Hays appointed him head of West Coast public relations.[43]

Wingate's failure provided him with his next opportunity. Breen had begun helping out with script reviews shortly after his joining the Hays Office. Word that Universal was considering making a film of Charles G. Norris's novel *The Seed* had prompted an immediate protest from the editor of the *Western Catholic* charging the studio with spreading birth control propaganda. Breen quickly intervened and pressured the studio to rewrite the script, which was then sent to Lord for final approval before it went into production. Breen informed Cardinal Mundelein that Universal accepted "our Catholic viewpoint against the sneers of the opposition. When these contemptible apologists for birth control appealed to the senior Laemmle 'not to spoil a masterpiece . . . of literature by permitting ignorant papists to tell him how to run his business,' he turned them down."[44]

Appointed Wingate's assistant in March 1933, Breen quickly displayed a gift for helping producers rewrite their scripts to meet Code requirements—just the talent Wingate was lacking. Self-confident, aggressive, blustering at times, he had no fear of dealing with directors, producers, or studio heads. One of his first assignments in his new job was to work on *Ann Vickers*, based on the Sinclair Lewis novel about a social worker who has had an unsuccessful marriage and an out-of-wedlock child. She then meets a married judge with whom she has a second child. When the judge is sent to prison, she abandons her career and waits until she and the judge are reunited upon his release. *America* had warned Hollywood not to touch the story. Although Lewis had in 1930 become the first American to win the Nobel Prize in Literature, Breen wasn't impressed. He told Wingate that he had never read anything quite so "vulgarly offensive" and that it would have to be radically changed. Breen was able to persuade RKO to eliminate Ann's marriage and her first child, although he had to allow the hint of an earlier abortion. The studio balked, however, at his request for additional lines that would have Ann express her remorse for having "broken the laws of God and man." B. B. Kahane, RKO's president, argued that there was nothing in the Code requiring a character to say that adultery was wrong. Convinced that he had satisfied the letter of the law by not justifying the couple's relationship, he threatened to appeal. Although no one had ever appealed an unfilmed script, Kahane claimed that with a $700,000 investment, he didn't want to shoot the movie and then run the risk of having to make extensive cuts. Will Hays, who was able to persuade Kahane to back down, arranged a compromise that Breen felt was the best they could get, considering the jury's partiality to the producers' interests. Ann would pay for her indiscretions by losing her job and being forced to support herself in humble circumstances until the judge was released.[45]

As protests continued in the summer of 1933, it was clear to Hays that Breen had much more to offer than Wingate: he was tougher, he was much better at solving script problems, and, best of all, he was Catholic. As the church's clash with Hollywood began to reach a crisis point, Breen and Quigley were the two indispensable men who could explain the industry to the church and the church to the industry. But Breen was something of a Trojan horse within the industry. Whether out of conviction or because he saw a chance to use the Catholic crusade to improve his situation, he never missed an opportunity to tear down Hays and the producers to his Catholic colleagues. A few months before his break with Hays, Lord came away from a meeting with Breen feeling that he had never met anyone more pessimistic about the operation of the Code. And according to Parsons, Breen more than anyone else engineered Quigley's distrust of Hays. "He raves and rants," Breen told Quigley, "but seems to be in abject fear" of some studio heads. In a letter to Parsons, he observed that Hays was a compromiser who "sold us a first class bill of goods when he put the Code over on us" and who now lacked the "guts" to clean things up. Dinneen's prejudices about Hollywood were confirmed by letters from Breen that the industry simply didn't understand what they were complaining about. "Most . . . are a foul bunch, crazed with sex, dirty-minded and ignorant in all matters having to do with sound morals. I don't suppose five percent have a shred of religion."[46]

Much of Breen's criticism of Hollywood stemmed from a streak of puritanism saturated with a strong strain of anti-Semitism. Hollywood, in his eyes, was a den of iniquity filled with "perverts," including a "lady star who admitted to being lesbian," studio heads who jumped into bed with their neighbor's wife, and birthday parties where the place cards for men were "condrums" (*sic*) and Kotex with a dash of ketchup for the women. Little wonder that they cared nothing about the Code "except to sneer and laugh at it as a first rate gag to fool the 'blue noses' and the 'church people.'" The abandonment of the Code, the filthy pictures, and the immoral lifestyles, he claimed, could all be laid at the door of those "lousy Jews . . . 95 percent of whom are Eastern Jews, the scum of the earth . . . whose only standard is the box office." Breen didn't have a corner on anti-Semitism. Despite their success in the motion picture industry, Jewish executives couldn't join the local country clubs, and their children were refused admission to the better schools. Nevertheless, none of the bishops or priests with whom Breen communicated regularly ever rebuked him for his attacks.[47]

Complaining that he was feeling isolated, he told Parsons that he was going to mass four times a week and praying to the Holy Ghost to "sort of tip [him] off" as to the proper thing to do, "but so far little light." Whether it came from divine inspiration or from the memory of Cardinal Mundelein's successful employment of Halsey, Stuart in pushing the Code, Breen conceived the idea of using Bishop Cantwell to "work on the American (not Jewish) bankers to bring pressure on the industry." His plan was to persuade them to stop making loans to Hollywood, which was using the money to "paganize the nation." Breen had been meeting with Cantwell on a regular basis during the summer and his efforts had begun to pay off. As the bishop later told Cardinal Dougherty, he could no longer ignore the problem that existed in his own backyard: something had to be done to "dam this noisome sewer." The bishop took Breen's advice and contacted two prominent Catholic laymen in Los Angeles: Joseph Scott, a successful lawyer with industry ties, and Attilo Henry Giannini, chairman of the Bank of America, a pioneer in financing the film industry. Echoing Breen, Cantwell told Scott and Giannini that the bankers had to stop loaning money to perpetuate evil movies. He warned them that unless something was done to improve the situation, the Catholic bishops might issue a joint pastoral letter at their annual meeting in November, censuring the film business. Fired up by Scott and Giannini's positive response, Cantwell sent off a letter to Cardinal Patrick Hayes of New York urging him to use his influence to persuade John D. Rockefeller, Jr., to work on MGM, Fox, and RKO. Having once complained about the bishop's lack of fire, Quigley soon found himself urging Breen to keep Cantwell "from going off half-cocked."[48]

The Catholic mobilization against the movies that took shape during the summer of 1933 couldn't have been better timed. The studios' shaky financial condition made them vulnerable. The leaders of the campaign also felt that the rise of Adolf Hitler had made the industry more susceptible to outside pressure. As Cantwell argued in a letter to the archbishop of Cincinnati, "Jewish control of the industry is alienating many of our people" just at the time when "Jews are afraid of things that may possibly happen in this country to them."[49]

Cantwell's warning that the bishops would release a statement condemning Hollywood for corrupting America's children spurred Hays into action. Halfway through a dinner meeting of the studio heads and his staff he arranged on August 1, Hays reminded the executives that he had warned them, when they reaffirmed the Code in March, that he was willing to take any future violations to the public if that was the only way to reform the industry. After recalling some films that had recently caused problems, he identified those pictures in or about to go into production that were "dangerous to the Code," including a new Mae West film, the Marx Brothers' *Duck Soup*, and *Of Human Bondage*. At 8:15 P.M. Attilo Giannini and Joseph Scott were invited into the meeting. Giannini told the audience that they could not afford to alienate the church by continuing to make the wrong kind of pictures. He then introduced Scott, "unquestionably one of the outstanding public speakers in America," according to Breen. Scott started off slowly, explaining the hierarchy's responsibility on moral issues, and then read a letter from Cantwell condemning the industry's irresponsibility. He reminded the Jewish members of their glorious religion and drew a parallel between the persecution of the Irish Catholics and their people in America. At that point, according to Breen, he changed his tactics and "lashed into the Jews furiously." Lumping the studio heads in with Jewish Communists and anarchists, he charged them with ingratitude and disloyalty to the country that had taken them in. Reminding his listeners of the Nazi success in Germany, he warned them that they were on the spot, that similar organizations were readying themselves to carry on the fight in America. If the Catholic church were to condemn the movies openly, he concluded, it would mean that all the organized Christian forces in the country would be lined up against the industry. At that point, he implied, box-office receipts might be the least of their worries. Breen reported that almost everyone at the table rose and cheered Scott's lecture. Adolph Zukor told the others that although "dirt and filth" had been allowed to creep into his pictures because he had become too involved in the financial end of the business, he would do everything possible to clean up his studio once and for all. The heads of MGM, Warner, Universal, Columbia, RKO, and Fox agreed that Wingate would be given additional help to enforce the Code. Only independent producer Sam Goldwyn and Joe Schenck, head of United Artists, disagreed. Schenck attacked the bishops as narrow-minded bigots and stated that he for one intended to continue to make the kind of pictures the public wanted to see.[50]

A few studios tried to appease Cantwell: Paramount hired a Catholic to serve as a studio censor, and MGM asked him to recommend someone for a similar position on its lot. But despite the pledges of reform made at the August 1 meeting, Quigley, Breen, and the others felt that there would be little change without additional pressure. During August, Quigley, Breen, Parsons, Lord, and Dinneen considered applying direct pressure on the company presidents in New York, asking Jewish leaders in the East to join the campaign, and including the Code in the trade regulations that were being established as part of the National Industrial Recovery Act. But none of this, they feared, would force the studios to change. The only answer, they concluded, was to get the bishops to follow through on Cantwell's idea of a pastoral letter condemning the industry. The question was what should the bishops do afterward. Breen and Parsons favored Quigley's idea of a national protest week during which Catholics would refrain from going to the movies. Lord and Dinneen felt that a more permanent approach was necessary. Mindful of Hollywood's tendency to backslide after the shouting stopped, they proposed a permanent reviewing committee that, in contrast to the IFCA, would identify objectionable films. Lists would be prepared and sent to parish priests, who would warn their parishioners on the Sunday before the film was scheduled to be shown in their area.[51]

While Quigley and the others were trying to come up with a common strategy, Cantwell developed cold feet. By mid-August, the bishop, who only a few weeks earlier seemed eager to take their case to the November meeting, became convinced that his colleagues would do nothing and began to look for a way out. With time running out to get the issue on the agenda of the November bishops' annual meeting, the plotters met in early September. To broaden their base they invited Monsignor Joseph Corrigan, the rector of St. Charles Seminary in Philadelphia, to join them. Corrigan suggested that the Reverend Amleto Giovanni Cicognani, the newly appointed apostolic delegate to the United States, might be able to get Cantwell involved "in spite of himself" while at the same time lighting a fire under the other bishops. Cincinnati's Archbishop John T. McNicholas arranged for the delegate to meet with Quigley and Breen, who persuaded him to tack on an indictment of the movies to a speech he was scheduled to give on October 1 in New York.[52]

Charging that the film industry was involved in a massacre of youth, hour by hour, the papal delegate declared, "Catholics are called by God, the Pope, the bishops and the priests, to a united and vigorous campaign for the purification of the cinema, which has become a deadly menace to morals." Cicognani's speech, reproduced in a number of Catholic papers, was a major turning point in the struggle because it meant that the bishops could not ignore the question at their annual meeting. Meanwhile, Breen, urging action, seemed to be everywhere, meeting with Mundelein in Chicago, McNicholas in Cincinnati, Thomas Purcell (president of the National Council of Catholic Men) in St. Louis, and in San Francisco with Archbishop Edward J. Hanna, who was slated to preside over the November meeting. As the date for the meeting drew close, however, Breen and his allies still lacked a specific plan to put before the bishops. He and Quigley adamantly opposed any blacklist while Lord and Dinneen were convinced of the need to establish a reviewing system that would identify the objectionable films for Catholic moviegoers. Neither side, however, was willing to risk a divided meeting. An additional difficulty was that each bishop was free to administer his own diocese as he saw fit, an autonomy reflected by the bishops' frequent use of "Boston," "Chicago," or "Albany" as a means of referring to each other. As Lord reminded Breen, the bishops' conference was like "a symphony orchestra without a director, and that doesn't always make for music."[53]

With the two sides of the reform issue at loggerheads and with Cantwell growing more nervous by the minute, Breen suggested a compromise. Cantwell had earlier agreed to Archbishop McNicholas's suggestion that he write an article on the movies for *Ecclesiastical Review* which would also serve as the basis of his report on the problem to the rest of the hierarchy. Breen, who ghosted Cantwell's report, knew that it would take time to induce the bishops to act. Consequently, he convinced Cantwell to conclude his remarks with a recommendation that the hierarchy form a committee to study the movie problem "to keep the Jews worried." There was no sense letting the producers know they didn't have a plan, and a standing committee would "keep suspended over the heads of the producers the sword which is now threatening to decapitate them."[54]

Cantwell's report was an eye-opener, as few of the bishops knew anything about the movie industry. With the studios in a race to produce the most sordid films in an effort to offset declining receipts, he explained, theaters were inundated with stories of sexual irregularity, free love, prostitution, illegitimate children, race suicide, native nudity, and the freedom of women. According to Cantwell, the Jewish studio owners were partially to blame because the filth was created by the directors and writers, 75 percent of whom were pagans. Yet the public, including Catholics, had to share the guilt. After

150 years of the church's highly touted educational system, he noted, some Catholics cared "for nothing higher than the vaporings of the pig-sty." The only bright note, he concluded, was that clean pictures were more popular than the vile films, a common view among movie reformers. No one ever explained why the "money-hungry" studios continued to make so many objectionable films if they did so badly at the box office.[55]

Shocked by Cantwell's report, the bishops voted to establish a special Episcopal Committee on Motion Pictures to study the problem. Although Cantwell agreed to serve, he declined the chairmanship because he felt it might make it too easy for the local movie people to lobby the committee through him. Instead, Cincinnati's Archbishop John T. McNicholas agreed to head the committee with Bishop Hugh Boyle of Pittsburgh and Bishop John Noll of Fort Wayne, Indiana, as the other two members. The conservative McNicholas, an archbishop since 1925, believed that society needed a "fixed moral code" that only the Catholic church could provide. Critical of what he saw as an increasingly permissive society, he once condemned a local newspaper's defense of divorce, declaring that "liberty of the press can in no sense justify the degradation of the reading public." When asked after criticizing the movies if he ever went himself, he answered that he didn't have to go; the lurid billboards advertising the latest films that he passed going from home to office convinced him that something had to be done.[56]

After the bishops' meeting there was another reorganization of the Hays Office. In December, with Joy slated to return to Twentieth Century-Fox, Breen was placed in charge of enforcing the Code while Wingate was relegated to reading scripts along with the other members of the Studio Relations Committee. Breen immediately took a more forceful approach to the job, refusing on several occasions to approve a film's release until cuts had been made. Most of his problems, he told Dinneen, came from MGM and Warner, who "makes a cheap, low-tone picture with lots of double meaning wisecracks and no little filth." In his new capacity, Breen was able to remove all references to abortion from MGM's *Men in White* and Warner's *Doctor Monica*, a tearjerker about an obstetrician who is forced to deliver the baby of her husband's mistress. He also persuaded Warner to drop a discussion of the difficulties of childbirth as well as a reference to breast-feeding, which he considered to be a gratuitous introduction of an unpleasant subject. Speaking ex cathedra, he declared: "While I have never been a mother, I do not think it is absolutely necessary for a mother to nurse."[57]

One measure of Breen's aggressive stance was the sharp increase in appeals in the months following his takeover. Only six pictures had been referred to the jury between the establishment of the Code in March 1930 and his takeover at the end of 1933, but in the next four months the studios appealed eight of his decisions. Although Breen was overruled in the case of MGM's *Queen Christina*, when he tried to cut the queen's recollection of her affair, he won more than he lost. Yet MGM's appeal of Breen's rejection of *Tarzan and His Mate* demonstrates that the studios didn't give up without a fight. The Studio Relations Committee had requested that MGM tone down the sex scenes, especially one in which Tarzan dragged Jane into their shelter, which was followed by her contented laughter. It also strongly objected to several shots of a naked Jane. When the jury, which met at MGM, supported Breen, Irving Thalberg protested that he remembered seeing at least fifty nude women in *White Shadows of the Silver Sea*. When the jury screened it, however, the fifty women failed to materialize. Unwilling to give up, Louis B. Mayer asserted that he had been on a jury that had approved a nude scene in *The Common Law*, but additional research also disproved that claim. In the end, the jury refused to overturn Breen's ruling, but jury member Winfield Sheehan recommended that they meet at a neutral studio in the future to avoid any "ganging up" by studio officials.[58]

Still feeling his way on the job, Breen approved a number of films that he thought were questionable but not worth fighting over. He reluctantly agreed to release *Affairs of a Gentleman*, but he told the studio that state censors were sure to delete several scenes. "I think it's a bad thing to do," he concluded, "but . . . it's your responsibility." While Breen was consolidating his position in Hollywood, the Episcopal Committee was trying to formulate a policy that the other bishops would support. Cantwell's report on the motion picture industry, which had appeared in the February issue of the *Ecclesiastical Review*, became a catalyst. McNicholas had one thousand reprints of the article distributed to church leaders across the country. In a cover letter, McNicholas reminded his colleagues that Cantwell had shown that protest letters alone had proven ineffective and that the studios must be approached at the local level, in a way that hurts their pocketbooks.[59]

Neither the bishops' November meeting nor Cantwell's article received much attention from the secular press. *Variety* reported the meeting under the headline "Bishops Protest Filth" but failed to follow up on the story. W. R. Wilkerson, the publisher of the *Hollywood Reporter*, was one of the few who responded to the Cantwell piece. Wilkerson, who identified himself as a Catholic, declared that the "pagan writers" Cantwell had denounced were giving the public what it wanted. The problem was, Wilkerson argued, that the church had failed to raise the moral standards of its people.[60]

Cantwell's article, however, did not go unnoticed in the Jewish community. Several Jewish leaders were alarmed by its references to a Jewish film industry, but they were advised by friends not to go public with their criticism. Carleton Hayes, a professor at Columbia University and the Catholic cochairman of the National Conference of Christians and Jews, who agreed to work on their behalf, suggested to Cantwell that he was inadvertently endorsing the anti-Semitic prejudice that was sweeping Germany. The bishop responded that he had not attacked the Jewish people but had simply stated a fact: the industry as a whole was largely in the hands of "our Jewish neighbors." One solution, he said, might be the establishment of some sort of film previewing board in New York made up of Jewish, Protestant, and Catholic representatives.[61]

Cantwell's article also stimulated a major attack on the movies in Catholic journals, including his own paper, *Tidings*. "What with nudist colonies, moron birth control propaganda, the 'romances' of libertines exploited for the edification of millions . . . the continuous caricaturing of old-fashioned homelife, the persistent mocking of the marriage ceremony, the joking about everything sacred, the tinseling of things immoral," one editorial read, it was little wonder that the nation was on the verge of a moral collapse. At the same time, the San Francisco diocesan paper, the *Monitor*, which had previously ignored the topic, launched a broadside against local theaters showing "dirty movies." The pictures they presented were "so vicious," one editorial declared, "that it is more than a sin of indecency to attend them . . . it is a public renunciation of the Catholic faith in moral teaching." Boston's Cardinal William O'Connell denounced movies as "the scandal of the world" and recommended publication of the names of the "movie magnates who countenance such filth." By early March, a worried Hays staffer reported that clerical criticism, much of it Catholic, had reached an all-time high.[62]

Almost all of the criticism focused on the sexual content of the movies. *Ave Maria* complained about films that presented divorce ad nauseam and everything from near nudity to "sex communism." Fort Wayne's Bishop Noll charged that the producers believed that the American public was made up of cannibals who wanted female flesh. Father James Gillis, whose columns were syndicated in the Catholic press, rejected Hollywood's defense that it was depicting life as it is. Commenting on *Nana*, Samuel Goldwyn's portrayal of Emile Zola's novel about a Parisian courtesan, Gillis wrote that if the producers would only speak the truth about sin like the Bible and Shakespeare, it might be tolerated. But, he said, if they made the prostitute "loathsome" instead of alluring, the theaters would be empty. According to one priest, the way to spell movies was *M* for "moral menace," *O* for "obscenity," *V* for "vulgarity," *I* for "immorality," *E* for "exposure," and *S* for "sex." According to the Catholic press, the movies were not only undermining America's morals, they were subverting Catholic missionary work throughout the world. Mary Hawks, president of the National Council of Catholic Women, back from a Catholic Cinema Congress in Rome, claimed that movie houses were multiplying so rapidly in the Far East that they threatened to nullify the "Oriental concept of Christian civilization," thereby undoing the efforts to save the "pagans" in India.[63]

The Episcopal Committee on Motion Pictures was to channel the increasingly vituperative criticism of the movies into an effective force for change, and its first major issue was whether the church should follow an independent course or advocate some form of federal intervention. There had been some support at the November meeting for the Patman bill, which would empower the President to set up a review commission that would prohibit the interstate distribution of any film that was not approved for "family use." A few bishops had wondered if block-booking was the root of the problem. The bishops had been so divided that they had turned both questions over to McNicholas's committee for further study. Dinneen, who favored some form of government intervention, and Quigley, who was convinced that a rejuvenated Code was the answer, competed to influence McNicholas. But the priest was at a disadvantage because Quigley was able to furnish the bishop with inside information about the movie business. When Quigley went to Cincinnati in April, he warned the bishop that a government censorship board that was subject to political pressures could conceivably approve pictures advocating divorce and birth control. He also dismissed anti-block-booking legislation as a fraud. He predicted that the local exhibitor would simply turn down unpopular movies while rushing to book the latest Mae West release.[64]

Quigley's advice tapped into the growing feeling among Catholics that their church was the logical choice to clean up the movies. Father Daniel Lord had long been arguing that it was high time that Catholics stop feeling like second-class citizens. Father Owen McGrath, a New York priest, declared that the church's minority status had forced it to remain silent while the forces of paganism and Protestantism had led the nation to its present plight, where day after day children were being corrupted by obscene movies. But now that the church had become a power, he thundered, "In the name of God let us see the battle to its glorious triumph." Church leaders like Bishop Noll regularly pointed out that demographics as well as God were now on their side. Although the ratio of Catholics to the total population was only one to five, the proportion rose to between one in two and one in three in most large cities east of the Mississippi, where box-office receipts were heaviest. "We must lay aside our inferiority complex," he declared, "and decide that we can do this job."[65]

As Father Gerard Donnelly pointed out in *America*, the Catholic church was the sole institution in a position to apply a moral yardstick to the evil spewed out by Hollywood. The *Boston Pilot* joined Donnelly, declaring that only the Catholic church had the necessary expertise in moral law to lead the movie crusade. In addition to its "infallible standards of conduct," the church possessed the solidarity to organize a movement. The producers could never be frightened by a crusade out of Wittenburg, for even if Protestant leaders warned their flock to avoid an objectionable film, individual Protestants, "with every man his own priest," were free in conscience to disobey them.[66]

In the end, McNicholas's opposition to a federal block-booking bill was based on strategic considerations; it would be easier to apply church pressure on eight studios to solve the problem at the source than to try to persuade some 14,000 theater managers not to show objectionable films. Reinforced by Cantwell's strong opposition to government censorship, McNicholas's committee also decided not to endorse the Patman bill. The bishops agreed not to make their decision public, reasoning that it would be better to keep the industry guessing; fear of government legislation might make it more willing to make concessions to the church in exchange for a promise not to support censorship. Consequently, the Episcopal Committee quieted Catholic Congressman Lawrence J. Connery of Lynn, Massachusetts, who opposed censorship at the hearings on the Patman bill. At Cantwell's request, Cardinal O'Connell, in a rare act of cooperation, not only persuaded Connery to withdraw from any further discussion of the bill but also induced him to send a letter, drafted by Father Michael Ready of the NCWC, urging the studios to clean up their films.[67]

Meanwhile, church leaders were still feeling their way toward a united policy. "We can settle on a common plan later," wrote Bishop Hugh Boyle, but "in the meantime it's best to swarm upon the enemy from all sides with all kinds of weapons." In spite of all the talk of Catholic solidarity, each bishop was free to run his own campaign against the movies, or, for that matter, to ignore the issue entirely. Some bishops singled out individual films or theater owners for attack, while others began to establish parish vigilance committees. In Fall River, Massachusetts, Bishop James E. Cassidy had a pastoral letter read at all masses calling on his people to subscribe to a "N.I.M. Code": no immoral movies. He also called for a boycott of the movies during the Lenten season. When a string of objectionable films, one of which depicted a nudist colony, was shown in his diocese, the local parish priests announced that they would refuse parishioners absolution if they patronized the offending theater.[68]

During February and March, the members of McNicholas's committee exchanged ideas on how to enlist their fellow bishops and the laity in a national organization that would pressure Hollywood to reform. Meanwhile, McNicholas and Boyle collaborated on a pledge, first tried out in Cincinnati, which obligated the taker to unite with others in protesting indecent and immoral films and to stay away from theaters that showed them on a regular basis. Hoping to build on this momentum, the Episcopal Committee on April 11 informed all the other bishops of their plan to form a Legion of Decency. The bishops were asked to explain the purpose of the campaign to their people and distribute the pledge cards. Some bishops embraced the campaign from the start, while others took a wait-and-see attitude. Nor did every priest fall into step. A pastor in Alhambra, California, informed his bishop that he was postponing pledge day because he had already prepared a sermon on the rosary for that date.[69]

Nevertheless, the response was far more positive than McNicholas's committee had expected. Bishop Joseph Schrembs of Cleveland made every effort to "get out the vote," ordering all pastors to make sure that there were enough pencils in each pew so that the pledges could be signed promptly at each mass. Each pledge came in duplicate so that signers could retain a copy as a reminder of their obligations. Soon the pledges began to pile up. Although the bishops never came out with a definitive statement about the penalty associated with breaking one's pledge, the solemn manner in which it was taken led many signers to believe that viewing an immoral film constituted a mortal sin. Meanwhile, the bishops quietly moved to make sure that their own house was in order. Cardinal Hayes's discussion of how best to clean up the movies had prompted a letter from one of his pastors warning him that "a visit to any large motion picture theater on any day would reveal the presence of a number of priests, no matter what the picture is." Soon, letters began to go out from the hierarchy warning clergy to set a good example by staying away from the movies.[70]

In order to keep the pressure up, the Episcopal Committee decided to hit the industry at the box office. The committee's action originated with a letter from the Reverend Philip Scher, bishop of Monterey-Fresno, to the managers of the Fox and Warner theaters in his diocese informing them of the church's campaign against indecent movies, particularly those corrupting the youth of the country. Recognizing that the managers' hands were tied by block-booking and other trade practices, the bishop asked them to bring the matter to the attention of the film producers. "You may assure them that it is not our wish to hurt their business," he wrote, "but we do insist on decent shows." To prove his good intentions, the bishop offered to advertise in the diocesan paper free of charge any films the managers guaranteed as wholesome. At first Scher's only response was a form letter from Fox Theaters with a list of the studio's movies that had been approved by several national organizations, including the IFCA. But Joe Breen learned that the bishop's letter had caused something of a panic within the industry. Charles Skouras, head of the Fox theater chain, had immediately sent a letter to all his managers reminding them of the national agitation against the industry and warning them not to place children's movies on the same bill as adult fare. News of the bishop's letter also prompted Warner to tell its producers that they would have to change the type of pictures they were making.[71]

Breen and Quigley met with Cantwell to prepare a letter modeled on Scher's that could be sent by every bishop to the theater managers in his diocese. Quigley supplied the names and addresses of all the exhibitors. "We hope to get 8,000 to 10,000 letters in reply," Breen told Dinneen. "The exhibitors will pass the buck back to the producer," he predicted, "and all these replies when assembled will make a terrific indictment of the producers and may be used with telling effect later." The lists were broken down by diocese and mailed in May to each bishop with a cover letter from Cantwell warning them that if they let up on this campaign, in a few years the producers would be making films featuring birth control and sterilization.[72]

While the letters were being prepared, *Variety* reported that McNicholas's committee had sent out a questionnaire to every parish in the country asking for the names of the banks with which their local theaters did business, whether any mortgages were held against theater property, and by whom. "What they will do with this information," the writer added, "we do not know." Neither did the studio heads, but the messages from local exhibitors reporting that they had received a complaint from the local bishop indicated that a major grassroots campaign was under way.[73]

FIVE

A Catholic Crusade

The pledge to avoid immoral films forced the bishops to confront the issue of which ones were immoral and who would make the determination. Initially, the members of the Episcopal Committee seem to have assumed that if right-minded people put their heads together, they could quickly come up with a list of objectionable films. They probably would have agreed with the exhibitor who, when confronted by a similar question, said, "I'll tell you what dirt is. Dirt is dirt. There are no two ways about it." What troubled Archbishop John T. McNicholas's committee, however, was what should be done about the objectionable films after they had been identified. The IFCA published a white list of recommended films, but the current crisis raised questions about the effectiveness of this approach.[1]

Bishop John J. Cantwell's shifting position on the question reflected the ambivalence of many other church leaders over the advisability of blacklisting. A month after the bishops' annual meeting in November 1933, Cantwell had told McNicholas that the Catholic people would have to be informed about which pictures to avoid. He had in mind a preview board located in Hollywood which would publish its list in the Catholic press. In order to build up support, at least in the beginning, he felt that the board should not condemn too many films but limit itself to the few that were "bad not only from the moral standpoint but from the standpoint of entertainment." After a few months, however, he switched his position. Blacklisting, he told another committee member, would instill in many young people a desire to see evil pictures; consequently, he was thinking about setting up a local committee that would issue only a white list.[2]

Baltimore's Bishop Michael J. Curley, on the other hand, had no qualms about blacklisting. In an effort to prove that films had become "filthier and filthier" after the first year of the Code, his diocesan paper had published a list of objectionable films, prompting Will Hays to dispatch his executive assistant Carl Milliken to Baltimore to ask him to stop. No movie magnate would ever come to see him if he singled out only good movies, Curley told McNicholas; if the bishops wanted to attract Hollywood's attention, a blacklist was the only way to do it.[3]

Unwilling to wait for the Episcopal Committee to make up its mind, some Catholic critics began to distribute their own blacklists. Detroit was the first diocese to condemn films openly in a systematic way. Complaining that 90 percent of Hollywood releases were unfit to be shown to the public, Monsignor John Hunt compiled a list of proscribed films including *George White's Scandals;* a Wheeler and Woolsey comedy, *Hips, Hips, Hooray;* and *The Story of Temple Drake*, a bowdlerized version of William Faulkner's *Sanctuary.* The prime mover behind the Detroit campaign was Arthur Maguire, a Canadian-born lawyer and cochairman of the Detroit Council of Catholic Organizations, which had been set up in late 1933 to combat film immorality. Maguire's inclination to blacklist objectionable films had been reinforced through his correspondence with Bishop Curley, who told him that after a decade of the IFCA's white list, "rotten movies were making money hand over fist. . . . If we 'boost the best'" as the IFCA recommended, "we should damn the rest." He pointed out that the Holy See had no compunction about condemning evil books, and it didn't waste its time coming up with a list of good ones. Encouraged by Curley's support, Maguire's council began to publish a combined whitelist and blacklist in the *Michigan Catholic* early in 1934, based on its analysis of film evaluations in eight journals and reviewing services, including the IFCA list, *Parents'* magazine, *Variety*, *Time*, *Harrison's Reports*, and the *Motion Picture Herald.* Maguire's group recognized that if separate dioceses developed their own lists, conflicting evaluations could result, but they hoped that their example would stimulate the Episcopal Committee to support a national effort.[4]

One of the first films the Detroit group condemned was *Queen Christina*, which the Hollywood jury had passed after MGM appealed Joe Breen's refusal to approve it. The queen's habit of wearing trousers while on horseback, according to the Detroit council, turned her into a "perverted creature." However, to the dismay of many theater owners, most of the condemned films, including *Viva Villa*, *Flying Down to Rio*, and *Tarzan and His Mate*, were listed without explanation.[5]

The Detroit lists showed the difficulty of distinguishing between moral and immoral films. George Trendle, owner of a chain of Detroit theaters, had announced his willingness to cooperate with the council but was bewildered by the condemnation of pictures like *Tarzan and His Mate:* "Is it possible to find out on what theory some of them are banned?" Maguire found that although no one on the council had seen the film, *Tarzan and His Mate* had been rejected on the basis of a review in *Harrison's Reports* because its brutal scenes were considered unsuitable for children and adolescents and because "sex had been brought into the story in a suggestive way."[6]

The movement to develop a national blacklist was soon bolstered by Father Daniel Lord's decision in May to begin condemning five objectionable films each month in the *Queen's Work*. In a series of articles in his journal that culminated in a pamphlet, "Motion Pictures Betray America," he explained that he no longer opposed blacklisting after finding out from *Our Movie-Made Children* (Henry Forman's book on the Payne studies) "how Norma Shearer and Joan Crawford introduce our little girls to the 'romance' of kept women . . . how George Bancroft and George Raft introduce our boys into the company of gangsters . . . and how undressed women whip with sharp lashes the passions of boys and girls." By reducing the Code to a "scrap of paper," Lord said, the film industry had engaged in the "most terrible betrayal of the public trust in the history of our country." Encouraging the industry to reform by issuing white lists was a waste of time, he maintained, since one could record all the recommended films "on the back of a postage stamp and have room left over for the Declaration of Independence." Catholics who saw objectionable films were as much to blame as anyone for the sorry state of the movies. But, he pointed out, "if in each of our 5,000 active Sodalities, 20 people stayed away from each offending film, that would cost the box-office over $35,000 a picture . . . enough to turn an ordinary film into a failure. . . . Suppose a half-million Sodalists stayed away," he continued, "that would bring any company to its knees."[7]

Lord went the *Michigan Catholic* one step better: in addition to identifying the objectionable films he told his readers where to send their letters of complaint. *The Trumpet Blows* starred the "absolutely unwholesome . . . George Raft . . . loose in his relationship with women and a thorough no-account. . . . The film is based on banditry without punishment, on seduction and general immorality. Protest to Paramount Studios, Hollywood, Cal.

[and] to George Raft, same address." An even more personal attack was launched against Irving Thalberg's wife, Norma Shearer, who had recently starred in *Riptide.* "It seems typical of Hollywood morality," Lord declared, "that a husband as productions manager should constantly cast his charming wife in the role of a loose and immoral woman. . . . We advise strong guard over all pictures which feature Norma Shearer." With the *Queen's Work* distributed across the country and with more and more Catholic papers reproducing his reviews, Lord's condemnations were the closest thing to a national blacklist that existed in spring 1934. By early June, *Variety* reported that letters signed by individual protesters, Knights of Columbus chapters, church organizations, and high school groups were pouring into Hollywood. Most of the messages were form letters excoriating a star for appearing in an objectionable film. "Being an admirer of your work," went a typical letter, "I want to inform you that I as a student at Canisius College in Buffalo have taken an oath not to patronize pictures of this nature." Students at the Academy of the Holy Name in Albany targeted a different group of stars each week.[8]

Quigley and Breen were appalled by Lord's campaign. Quigley had warned McNicholas when they met in April 1934 that the Legion of Decency's campaign could not be carried on at a high pitch indefinitely. Quigley and Breen argued that the only long-term solution was to strengthen the Studio Relations Committee and eliminate the Hollywood appeals jury, proposals that would have to be negotiated with the industry's representatives. Quigley thought that the presidents of the movie companies were ready to cut a deal, but he feared that Lord's guerrilla tactics would alienate them. His attack on Norma Shearer, for example, had so angered her husband that Thalberg personally complained to Bishop Cantwell, who had never liked Lord. The bishop warned McNicholas that the priest not only was doing a great deal of harm in Hollywood but also was sowing confusion among the faithful. He urged McNicholas to use his position as chair of the Episcopal Committee to persuade Lord's superior to curb the priest's activities.[9]

With two lists in use, Detroit's and Lord's, Quigley and Breen felt that there were bound to be conflicts that would in the long run undermine the church's credibility. Quigley pointed out that the Detroit list, which was compiled by amateurs, condemned many pictures that were acceptable entertainment. Even when the evaluations were correct, all they accomplished was to provide free advertising for filthy pictures. Equally damaging to the cause was Lord's pamphlet *Motion Pictures Betray America*, which, Quigley argued, was sloppily prepared and full of errors. Quigley also objected to Lord's mail campaign, arguing that the letters of protest presented a "confused state of mind" so that reasonably good pictures were condemned and others that were "definitely wrong" were ignored. Moreover, he predicted, the protest letters would soon lose their impact when Hollywood realized that many had been prepared by Catholic school teachers and copied by their students. An angry Lord responded that Quigley was nitpicking by pointing to a few inconsequential errors while ignoring the basic message in his pamphlet. And as for the argument that the letters wouldn't work, he retorted, "If I discovered that a sister in fourth grade had her class copy out and send to me a letter telling me that my business was rotten and that my product ought to be banned, I'd be scared stiff."[10]

Hoping to put a halt to the proliferation of blacklists, Quigley persuaded McNicholas's committee to discuss the idea of establishing a new Catholic review board that would issue a white list. The committee's willingness to take up his recommendation reflected its lack of confidence in the IFCA's reviewing process. Many were bothered by the women's group's continuing support of the Hays Office, which seemed at odds with the Legion campaign. The rise in the percentage of their endorsed films (71.5 percent in 1932 as compared to 61 percent in 1931) conflicted with the editorials in the Catholic press condemning the increase in screen immorality. Even Father Wilfrid Parsons, who had publicly defended the IFCA against Bishop Curley's attacks, recognized that its white list did not fit in with the campaign's focus on boycotting objectionable films. *Variety*'s assertion that if the church decided to set up a national reviewing board the IFCA would be the best choice from the industry's point of view only added to the bishops' suspicions.[11]

Some of the opposition reflected the church's distrust of women. Lord had long been critical of the IFCA's work, and the Philadelphia archdiocese had refused to carry its lists for several years because its evaluations were "morally unreliable." Quigley, who had little use for the IFCA leaders, complained that McGoldrick got on his nerves, a condition that he blamed on her difficulties with menopause. The IFCA may have been adequate in the days when the church ignored the movie question, but the national campaign to reform the industry was serious business, and serious business in the church belonged to men. The idea of adding a few priests to the IFCA reviewers' ranks was dropped in the face of a growing feeling among McNicholas's committee that McGoldrick and her staff had been so co-opted by Hays that a heavier hand was needed. The only viable option seemed to be Quigley's concept of a New York-based reviewing board that would issue only a white list. "I am told," McNicholas wrote the papal delegate, "that the immoral implications of many moving pictures are most subtle."[12]

Arthur Maguire of the Detroit council and Father Lord charged that the bishops' decision not to support a blacklist had been based on the advice of Hollywood insiders—clearly Quigley and Breen. Maguire conceded that a blacklist might lure some Catholics to objectionable films, but, he said, they would probably go anyway. To suppose that large numbers of Catholics would flock to objectionable films, he argued, was to assume that the entire system of Catholic education had been a failure. What had not worked, Lord declared, was the IFCA's white list. The major contradiction in the bishops' recommendation, Lord told McNicholas, was "We say, 'don't go,' but we don't say where they are not to go."[13]

The committee's work on a new reviewing system was slowed not only by the growing division over the advantages and disadvantages of blacklisting but also by the expense of such an undertaking. Committee members feared that many of their fellow bishops would balk at the cost, estimated at between $7,000 and $7,500 a year. Deferring its recommendation to the bishops, the committee concentrated on keeping the Legion campaign alive for the next few months until a consensus was reached. McNicholas's strategy was a simple one: he would send a recent copy of one bishop's speech to another in order to build national support for the Legion of Decency. Consequently, a public indictment of the movies from Bishop Michael J. Gallagher of Detroit, who charged the "Herods of our day" with carrying out a "massacre of the innocents," was immediately forwarded to Bishop Joseph Schrembs of Cleveland with a request for a similar statement. "If you could suggest some simple organization that would keep your people . . . away from movies for a month, or even a week," McNicholas wrote, "it would do incalculable good." Schrembs's blistering response incorporated parts of Gallagher's speech. This time the producers were "out-Herod[ing] Herod" in their "massacre of innocent souls," but Schrembs went on: "If the sale of black children produced the abolitionists, then the sight of children's souls sold to the devil by Hollywood must produce a new wave of abolitionists to destroy their spiritual bondage." Warning that lurid movie ads were turning the lobbies of theaters into modern Sodom and Gomorrahs, he predicted that the time was near when Catholics would have to give up movies or risk their immortal souls.[14]

Schrembs also staged a major demonstration of Legion power in June in a Cleveland stadium. The papal delegate spoke to a crowd of fifty thousand that included the city's mayor and the governor of Ohio. As the bishop and the papal delegate entered the stadium, the *Cleveland Plain Dealer* noted that they were followed by "two abbots, a group of monsignori in robes of purple, the Knights of St. Gregory in uniforms of green, secular priests in black cassocks, Franciscans in brown, Benedictines in black, Dominicans in gleaming white, hundreds of nurses in blue, gray and white uniforms and 800 acolytes in their surplices." After the clergy were seated, the Legion oath was administered and answered by a "thundering 'I do.'"[15]

With more and more bishops issuing their own condemnations, Mc-

Nicholas urged the four American cardinals to join the campaign. McNicholas had Breen draft a statement that Cardinal Mundelein, released in early June, recounting how he had helped to draw up the Code that the moviemakers had signed and then discarded. As a result of their perfidy, the cardinal declared, "in the last few years there has been no other medium or agency that has exercised so debasing an effect on public morals as the pictures." Mundelein hinted that events had reached such a pass that government censorship might be the only answer.[16]

No one was surprised when Cardinals O'Connell and Dougherty, the two most independent prelates, did not cooperate with the Legion campaign but decided to follow their own agendas. O'Connell asked Father Russell Sullivan, a Jesuit professor of philosophy at Boston College, to develop a strategy for the archdiocese. The priest's response, entitled the "Massachusetts Plan," called for the creation of a Catholic preview committee in Boston to decide which pictures could be distributed throughout the region. Theaters, distributors, and producers associated with the release of any objectionable films would be punished by a boycott not only of the picture in question but of all the offending studio's releases for at least one month. Sullivan envisioned his plan as a model for similar committees in Catholic centers across the country. Ignoring the bishops' committee, O'Connell sent a copy of Sullivan's plan to the Hays Office. For the cardinal, it was his chance to dominate the Legion campaign, but for Quigley, it was one more example of the fragility of the Legion crusade. He knew that a united front was the church's greatest weapon in dealing with the film industry; if the coalition splintered, the producers would pick them off one by one.[17]

O'Connell's effort to forge his own campaign was quickly eclipsed by events in Philadelphia. The formation of the Legion of Decency on April 11 had not been accompanied by any public announcement. Consequently, although the mounting Catholic criticism of Hollywood had been reported in the press, the Legion itself had been ignored. All this changed when Cardinal Dougherty released his own plan to end objectionable films on May 23, 1934. A few months earlier, Joe Breen had written to Monsignor Lamb, Dougherty's advisor on movie matters, recommending the establishment of a committee that could pressure Warner's theaters in the Philadelphia area. Breen suggested that the committee should include a couple of public prosecutors because, he pointed out, most of the exhibitors are "Jewish boys who are unfailingly . . . impressed and terrified by officials connected in any way with the police or the courts." Breen promised to supply a list of objectionable films that had been shown in the city in the previous six months. Armed with that information, the committee leaders would demand a meeting with Harry Warner in the "swellest and ritziest club in town," which would be arranged by Warner's district manager, "a kike Jew of the very lowest type." If Warner refused, he continued, the committee would tell him he would be brought in by court order or criminal action. When he arrived, he would be told that the committee was not interested in any "highfalutin gab about art and the movies" or "freedom of expression." He was to be given two choices: clean up his act or face a boycott.[18]

What Breen had not counted on was Dougherty's preference for action over negotiations. The corpulent cardinal, who was often referred to as "His Immense," held only two press conferences during his episcopacy. He had forced MGM to withdraw *The Callahans and the Murphys* in 1927 with a single pronouncement; he would now compel the entire industry to remove "the filth" that was polluting the nation's screens. On May 23, the cardinal called on Philadelphia's 823,000 Catholics to boycott all the movie houses in the diocese. In his message, read at all masses, Dougherty denounced the movies as the "greatest menace to faith and morals in America today." The cardinal declared, "experience has shown that one hour spent in the darkened recesses of a movie picture theater will often undo years of careful training on the part of the school, the church and the home." With so much in the balance, there was no room for compromise: a selective boycott of only the objectionable films would not work because the ticket sales from good movies financed the studios that produced the bad ones. The seriousness of the matter was underscored by the cardinal's pronouncement that the boycott was "a positive command, binding all in conscience under pain of sin." The boycott catapulted the Catholic campaign into the national news. On June 9, the *New York Times* mentioned the Legion of Decency for the first time, and for the rest of 1934 the press printed something about the campaign almost every day. The Hays Office noted an alarming increase in Catholic criticism beginning in May; by mid-June, it accounted for 80 percent of all articles dealing with film reform. On June 18, the front page of *Variety* reported that some 1,750,000 persons had already signed the Legion pledge. Worse, each week brought news that the Legion was picking up additional support from non-Catholics. One day it was a Methodist bishop, the next the president of Harvard, and then Sara Delano Roosevelt deploring unclean movies in a Mother's Day address.[19]

Edwin Schallert, in a three-part report for the *Los Angeles Times*, claimed that the Legion campaign, which he felt was different from all previous reform efforts, had thrown Hollywood into the most serious crisis in its history. The organizational strength of the Catholic church especially worried the filmmakers. "Protestant ministers may rave and rant" with little effect, *Box Office* added, but "when the Catholic church . . . decrees a certain action a sin, its members usually listen." Not only were the industry leaders panicked by the news that an estimated five million people were staying away from the movies, *Variety* declared, but they were bewildered over how to deal with the crisis. A few producers tried to brazen it out, suggesting that the industry challenge the church to a contest. A priest would be invited to the lobby of a theater ready to show two pictures: he would recommend one, the other would be a film that had been condemned by Lord or the Detroit council. He would find out, they declared, that "wishy-washy innocuous pictures die" and the others sell. But few people wanted to take on the church. As the *Cleveland Plain Dealer* pointed out, any attempt at a counterattack would make it look as though the industry were defending dirty films. And, *Variety* added, what producer or star would wish to debate the issue with a skilled speaker like Father Charles E. Coughlin, the radio priest, who had gained popularity by attacking international bankers as the cause of the Depression.[20]

As Catholic pressure mounted, industry leaders tried to find some gesture that might satisfy the church. At the time of the Code's adoption in the spring of 1930, Hays had discussed with Lord the idea of grading theaters as either adult or family entertainment centers. *Variety* now revived the scheme, adding that in towns with one movie house, adult and family films could be shown on alternate nights. Warner even considered categorizing films as either A for adult or F for family, but it would be another thirty years before Hollywood would be ready to implement such a plan.[21]

As summer approached, alarmed by reports that, in addition to box-office damage, the campaign was building up an enormous amount of ill will against the film industry, Hays, sensing an opportunity to strengthen his office, decided to negotiate with the church. On May 28, he met with Quigley and told him that the Catholic authorities could have anything they wanted. The studio heads were willing to put Breen in charge of a strengthened Studio Relations Committee and to replace the jury system with an appeals board that would support Breen's decisions. McNicholas dropped the idea of inviting Hays to a meeting of the Episcopal Committee scheduled for June 21 in Cincinnati when Cardinal Mundelein, still smarting over the collapse of the Code, objected strongly to Hays's presence. Dinneen warned McNicholas not to trust Hays. "He is a foxy boy," he said, "and will promise anything to stop the campaign. . . . My advice is to stall him off until after the meeting. . . . You will have them on their knees in another sixty days." Wary about Hays but persuaded that the time had come to negotiate a settlement, McNicholas invited Quigley and Breen to represent the industry at the meeting.[22]

Mundelein and Dinneen continued to caution McNicholas against entering into any deals with the filmmakers. Although they conceded that Quigley and Breen were "100 percent Catholic," they pointed out that both men owed their livelihood to the movie industry. When McNicholas's committee finally sat down with Quigley and Breen, they were joined by representatives of Cardinals Dougherty and Hayes. Noticeable by his absence was Lord, who was disliked by McNicholas and Cantwell. Dinneen argued that the only way to wring any real concessions from Hollywood was to launch a national boycott modeled after Dougherty's in Philadelphia. Although Bishop Hugh Boyle of Pittsburgh initially sided with Dinneen, he and the other participants eventually agreed with Quigley that such a boycott could never be sustained and would bring down the entire campaign. Dinneen suffered a second defeat when the bishops again listened to Quigley and decided against supporting a national blacklist.[23]

Quigley then presented Hays's plan to strengthen the administration of the Code. One could continue to pressure the industry, he argued, but some mechanism was necessary to guarantee the resulting agreements. The answer was a new Production Code Administration (PCA) under Breen which would replace the old Studio Relations Committee. In the new system, no film could begin production until the PCA had approved the script. Moreover, any picture that lacked the PCA seal of approval could not be shown in any MPPDA theater; any violation would result in a $25,000 fine. "At last," Hays later recalled, "we had a police department, or at least a civilian defense force." In order to strengthen Breen's office, the Hollywood jury system was scrapped; all future appeals were to be decided by the board of directors of the MPPDA in New York. As a further gesture of good will, theater owners would have the right to cancel any picture released before July 15, 1934, the date when the PCA seal became effective, if the local community protested it on moral grounds. Finally, to appease the anti-block-booking forces, exhibitors could cancel up to ten percent of each block of films from a studio without penalty.[24]

Although they recommended accepting Hays's offer, Quigley and Breen urged the bishops to preserve the Legion campaign in order to keep the producers honest. After all, the publisher pointed out, the reluctance of members of the hierarchy, including Cardinal Mundelein, to support the Code publicly after it was originally adopted was a principal reason for its failure. The Episcopal Committee gave the moviemakers a chance to make good on Hays's proposal. As Hays later recalled, everyone gathered at his office at 8:30 A.M. to await nervously the return of Quigley and Breen, "our two ambassadors." When the two men arrived at noon, "I knew everything was alright when I saw the 'cat-ate-the-canary' expressions on their faces: it told us the war had been called off."[25]

Dinneen came away from the meeting convinced that Quigley and Breen had sold out the church to the film industry. He suspected that Quigley was the source for an erroneous story that the bishops had suspended the Legion's campaign. He told Lord that he had never seen Mundelein so wrought up as after his report on the meeting, which included Quigley's charge that the cardinal bore some of the blame for the Code's ineffectiveness. Mundelein had just called on his priests to drum up support for the Legion in their parishes and felt that a suspension of the campaign would leave him out front and alone. "He was really wild about the prospect," Dinneen told Lord, "and said what he thought about the four bishops, but most of all Cantwell," whom he viewed as Quigley and Breen's puppet.[26]

Hays's hope that the June meeting had signaled the end of the Catholic campaign was quickly shattered by events in Chicago, where the church seemed to be gearing up for another attack. The first sign of renewed hostilities came on July 2, when Dinneen informed the nuns in his parish that there would be no more Saturday afternoon movies during the summer vacation. For some time the local distributor had been providing the films to the church at no cost, but Dinneen felt that this was no time to accept any favors. "Remember the words of Washington," he told the women, "'no entangling alliances.'" But the biggest blow came with the announcement that Mundelein, angered by Dinneen's report, began issuing his own blacklists and white lists on July 6. As the official opening of the new PCA drew near, not only was the Legion still in place, it seemed as though the industry faced a kind of guerrilla warfare. Confronted by lists from Chicago, Detroit, and St. Louis, with no halt to the Philadelphia boycott, and with Cardinal O'Connell apparently intent on setting up his own preview committee in Boston, the moviemakers wondered who really spoke for the church. An editorial in *Variety* entitled "Fair Is Fair" complained that "each bishop is running his own show, and . . . it's become too much of a show." At this point, the industry's only hope was that Breen could convince the church that this time the filmmakers meant what they said.[27]

Joe Breen had a lot to be thankful for as he prepared to take over his new office. In four short years, he had maneuvered himself into a powerful, well-paying position that enabled him to hire two servants and provided him with a chauffeur-driven car. *Variety* referred to him as Will Hays II; *Film Weekly* went even further, dismissing Hays as a "mere Hindenberg" who was about to be eclipsed by "the Hitler of Hollywood," Joe Breen. If he tuned in Eleanor Roosevelt's first radio broadcast, he would have heard the First Lady congratulating the film industry on his appointment. It was all heady stuff for the ex-newspaperman, but even the self-confident Breen must have worried about the problems with enforcing the Code. His predecessors' record was hardly encouraging: Joy had quit in despair and fled to Fox, and Wingate's lack of success had led to his demotion. Moreover, Dinneen to the contrary, Breen had to serve two masters if he was going to succeed. To some Catholics, he was a modern Saint George on a mission to slay the Hollywood dragon. Others saw him as the "fighting Irishman" who had gone west to stop the "smut, glossed vice, faked romance [and] unhealthy sex appeal." A few thought that he was employed by the bishops to censor movies at the source. Breen told Lord that his mail was filled with accusations that he was an "agent of the Pope" or a "spy for the Papists," while critics like Dinneen and Arthur Maguire dismissed him as one of Hays's "special pleaders." Both sides were right, as it would be Breen's job to ensure that the industry was able to sell its pictures and that the pictures sold were morally acceptable to its Catholic critics.[28]

Breen was aware that the Catholic support that had catapulted him into the PCA could just as easily evaporate. When he was quoted as saying that the movie reform movement had reached "the lunatic fringe," a charge he denied making, several Catholic papers quickly attacked him for turning his back on his constituents. This angry response to what was at worst a chance remark indicated that Breen's Catholicism would not protect him if he stumbled in his new job. As Dinneen warned him a few weeks after he took over the PCA, "Watch your step. If the pictures are not cleaned up, you will be the most discredited man in the country."[29]

Nevertheless, Breen exuded confidence as he went off to slay the dragon. "Dragon" was as good a name as any for Harry Cohn, head of Columbia Studios. When Breen presented him with his resumé during his round of introductions, Cohn held it up and asked, "What's all this shit?" When Breen responded, "I take that as a compliment," the startled Cohn asked, "What does that mean?" Breen replied, "My friends inform me that if there's any expert in this town on shit—it's you. So if I have to be judged, I'm glad it's by professionals." Geoff Shurlock, who worked closely with Breen at the PCA, always thought that his style was just an act to enable him to deal with the rough-and-tumble world of Hollywood, but if it was, it put a lot of high-paid actors to shame.[30]

Breen had been in charge of administering the Code for several months before the PCA was established; nevertheless, the industry's concessions in the face of the Legion campaign strengthened his hand. With the elimination of the Hollywood jury system, the producers lost a major bargaining chip in the negotiations that surrounded the approval of any questionable film. The industry's willingness to increase Breen's staff to nine (it had previously not exceeded six) also meant that the PCA could broaden its review process to include a careful monitoring of costumes and set construction. Breen picked up additional leverage in dealing with producers when bankers began to require a letter from the PCA stating that a script was basically acceptable before they would finance its production. And although Breen occasionally grumbled over Legion criticism, it furnished him with his ultimate threat: if the producers tried to renege on their agreements, he could always count on the Catholic church to come to his aid.[31]

The real test of Breen's office, however, would be its ability to force the studios to comply with his stringent view of the Code. He made it clear from the start that he would not allow producers to justify immoral themes and indecent scenes "by the sophistry of the excuse of beauty" or claims of art. The first film to receive a seal of approval was *The World Moves On*, which fortuitously included a priest in the story. Breen's first real challenge came over a Mae West screenplay that had gone into production before the PCA was formed. Paramount had begun filming *It Ain't No Sin* even though Breen had rejected two revised scripts in February and March 1934, but the studio hadn't moved fast enough and he now had the trump card, the Production Code seal. Instructed by Paramount executives in New York to cooperate, the producer made several major changes in the film. All references to West's character's past as a prostitute, an affair with her boss, her theft of her employer's jewels, and her boyfriend's criminal record fell to the cutting room floor. And in what was perhaps the unkindest cut of all, Breen persuaded Paramount to marry off West at the end of the film. After close to one hundred alterations and cuts by Paramount, Breen was willing to overlook a few vintage West one-liners and awarded the movie PCA seal number 136. To his chagrin, the New York censors refused to go along, and he and Hays had to lobby them in order to get the film accepted. It may have been the Catholic priests responding to the early ads for *It Ain't No Sin* with signs declaring "IT IS" that caused New York to demand a title change. Mae West's name finally appeared on the Manhattan marquees in September under the title *The Belle of the Nineties.*[32]

Paramount's experience demonstrated that even big-budget films could no longer count on a free ride. After a row with Warner over the script for *Anthony Adverse*, Breen wrote to Quigley, "They seem to think the Code ought not to apply in a case where the picture cost one million dollars or when based on a widely read popular novel." Sam Goldwyn learned his lesson when a half-dozen rejected treatments of Herbert Asbury's *Barbary Coast*, a tale of crime and prostitution in old San Francisco, forced him to hire Ben Hecht for a rewrite that essentially eliminated everything from the original story but the book's title. Although he did not have to go that far, David O. Selznick was surprised by the number of requested script changes, "much more extensive than any formerly," in *Anna Karenina*. Breen eventually allowed the implication of Anna's adultery, but she would have to pay a price. After being lectured to by her husband about the sanctity of marriage, publicly insulted for her scandalous life-style, losing her son and her lover, who is driven out of the army for his sins, she eventually commits suicide. Selznick's experience with *Anna Karenina* made him much more cautious about other projects. "Fine," he noted on the script for *Man with a Load of Mischief*, but "how much will be left after Breen gets through with it?"[33]

While it often seemed that Breen's office was obsessed with sexual issues, no Code violation, real or imagined, could be ignored. Consequently, Jimmy Cagney's message to the airport in *Ceiling Zero*, "I'll be home soon, boys. I can smell Jersey City," ended up on the cutting room floor. The Code's prohibition of miscegenation also meant that Breen could not approve the script for *Pudd'nhead Wilson* unless Selznick agreed to make the "colored boy the son of a very white octoroon, without saying the father is black or white." Although nothing in the Code required Breen to protect the image of American business, he was always on the alert for stories that might be interpreted as an attack on capitalism. The original script of *Black Fury* was a hard-hitting indictment of the coal industry which began with a capsule history of mining disasters and bloody strikes and centered on a plot by the owners to break their contract with the workers in order to drive wages down.[34]

The executive secretary of the National Coal Association complained to Breen that an unfavorable story like *Black Fury* could damage the industry's attempt to shake off the effects of the Depression. Breen needed no prompting: as public relations director for Illinois Peabody Coal Company in the late 1920s, he had denounced a series of strikes at their mines as Communist inspired. Breen contacted Jack Warner immediately and recommended that the film be changed to show that working conditions were getting better and that the miners had little to complain about. He also asked Warner to make it clear that the owners opposed any police violence. In the released version, the company's labor relations are generally favorable, and the walkout is caused not by the owners but by a detective agency that foments strikes in order to expand the market for its guards and strikebreakers. The decision to strike is trivialized, there is little violence in the new version, the agency's plot is uncovered, and the strike is called off. At the end of the film, a government investigator looking into the cause of the strike delivers Breen's message: "There was never a real issue in this controversy."[35]

Nor did Breen think there was any real issue in Walter Wanger's antiwar film *The President Vanishes*, a story of a gang of avaricious capitalists who plan to make a fortune by involving America in a foreign conflict. Breen approved the film after a few changes had been made, but Will Hays exploded when he saw it. He was especially angered by a speech by a street agitator urging his listeners to join the Communist party, claiming that the "capitalist bloodsuckers" were after the workers' blood. Convinced that the film was "Communist propaganda . . . and perhaps treasonable," he ordered Breen to negotiate additional changes, including the elimination of the "bloodsuckers" line.[36]

Breen was not naive. He recognized from the beginning that he had acquired a job that invited second-guessing. A few weeks after taking over the PCA, he predicted to Vincent Hart, an MPPDA counsel, that with everybody in America so censor-conscious, he was in for a good "clouting" sometime in mid-September or early October. As it turned out, he was correct about the timing; what he didn't anticipate was that his ally Martin Quigley would administer the blows.[37]

Breen had approved *The Merry Widow*, an operetta produced by Irving Thalberg and directed by Ernst Lubitsch, in September after several deletions were made. The plot revolved around the efforts of Captain Danilo, played by Maurice Chevalier, who is assigned by his king to woo a wealthy widow (Jeanette MacDonald) who has left the kingdom of Marshovia for Paris, in order to bring her back and save Marshovia from economic collapse. Danilo, who gets his assignment after being caught in a compromising situation with the queen, goes to Paris, where he mistakes the widow for a prostitute in Maxim's. After several musical numbers, the couple are married and the kingdom is saved.[38]

After seeing the picture with Hays, Quigley wrote to Breen on October 12 that he couldn't believe Breen had passed a film that sharply violated the Code at several points. Double entendres in Maxim's, which was made to look like "a huge bordello," plus the intimation of the queen's infidelity had introduced a "lot of filth" into what should have been a delightful and charming Viennese operetta. "If this picture goes out," he warned Breen, "the jig is up; if MGM gets away with this, others will follow." Quigley, who had assured McNicholas that the church could count on Breen, felt that his own reputation was at stake. He informed the archbishop that although Breen had tried to dismiss his criticism, he and Hays were working to resolve the crisis. Hays summoned Breen to New York a week later, where the film was screened in the presence of Quigley, Father Wilfrid Parsons, Pat Scanlan (editor of the *Brooklyn Tablet*), and an MGM representative. After seeing the film again, a contrite Breen admitted that it was no longer the "light, gay, frivolous operetta" he remembered but a "French farce that is definitely bawdy in parts."[39]

Breen ordered thirteen additional cuts in the film totaling three minutes of screen time, but Thalberg was understandably miffed over being forced to cut a film that had received a seal of approval from Breen just a month earlier. All the state censorship boards had approved the film, and the only criticism seemed to be coming from Quigley and his friends. The publisher privately admitted to McNicholas that they were somewhat handicapped in the negotiations by the absence of any public clamor over the film, which he traced to a general lack of sympathy and understanding for their ideals in the big cities. The possibility that he may have exaggerated the film's deficiencies seems never to have crossed Quigley's mind. He warned MGM of possible reprisals from the Legion if it refused to accept Breen's second round of cuts and urged MGM to back down for the good of the industry. Thalberg gave in.[40]

After the *Merry Widow* affair, although Breen and Quigley worked closely together for the next twenty years, their relationship would never be the same. When the publisher visited Hollywood a few months later, he found Breen still smarting over his criticism and "too busy" to invite him to his home. Angered by Breen's rebuff, he told Father Parsons that Breen had gone Hollywood, living beyond his means with a butler and three cars.[41]

While Quigley was worrying about the PCA's laxity, some wondered if reform had gone too far. The movie critic for the *Dallas Morning News* noted that the average length of a screen kiss had dropped from 72 inches of film, or 4 seconds, to 18 inches, or 1.5 seconds, since the Breen takeover. A columnist for the rival *Dallas Times Herald* wondered what Hollywood was going to do with its sexy stars during the crackdown. Shall they be fired, he asked, "or shall they put, say, Mae West in pinafores?" The *New York Times* reported that large numbers of people hissed and booed the appearance of the Production Code seal at the beginning of each movie. After seeing the latest Mae West film, one movie fan wrote to Breen. "You certainly ruined that picture—didn't you," complained Ferrell Emmett Long, "You C-E-R-T-A-I-N-L-Y did. Who do you serve," he asked, "the American people or those social thieves and moralistic skunks, the agents of gang religion?" The sad thing, Long concluded, was "that we the people don't know the names and addresses of these prudes who are suddenly trying to rob us of our human rights by telling us . . . what we shall look at and what we shall listen to."[42]

Long's suggestion that the Catholic church was running the movies was supported by a few newspaper editorials criticizing the Legion for its un-American reliance on censorship and boycotts. It could ruin not only the movies, the *Poughkeepsie Star* declared, "but our own liberties as well." Heywood Broun, one of the few columnists who was willing to ridicule the Legion publicly, argued that as far as he was concerned, what the nation needed was "bigger, better and bawdier pictures." But as Roy Howard, chairman of the Scripps-Howard newspaper chain, acknowledged, "most newspapers are frightened to death of church sentiment and especially of Catholic church sentiment." In a survey of a hundred and seventy-two editorials regarding the Legion activities in early July 1934, the Hays Office found only twenty that disapproved of the church's efforts.[43]

Will Hays and the film industry heads had swallowed their own resentment in the hope that their cooperation with Breen's office would persuade the church leaders to call off their campaign. They were shocked when they realized that not only was the Legion not disbanding, it was busily adding new members. Catholic papers drove home the point by running pictures of piles of pledge cards on their front pages throughout the summer of 1934. By the end of the year, between seven and nine million Catholics had taken the pledge, and this didn't include the *Baltimore Catholic Review*'s report that seven Chinese converts had joined the campaign in Peking.[44]

What the industry did not know was that the church leaders had decided to transform the Legion into a permanent pressure group. Archbishop McNicholas, who was already tired of the movie business, told Quigley he wanted to leave the committee, but he recognized that the Legion was the only way to ensure that the industry leaders kept their word. Even Bishop Boyle, who thought the campaign had achieved its goal in August, felt that the Legion was necessary. As Father James Gillis put it, the millions of pledge takers hadn't signed up to go into "a Rip Van Winkle sleep for the next twenty years."[45]

Moreover, by the summer of 1934, the Legion campaign had developed a momentum, independent of the bishops' actions. It was, in the words of one priest, "Catholic Action's big opportunity." *Our Sunday Visitor* gloried in the magnitude of the campaign: "Twenty million strong—[led by] 18 Archbishops, 107 Bishops, 29,619 priests! And all of these captains are long trained in 'the science of the right.'" The days of sitting on the sidelines were over. "The Catholic church," the writer crowed, "could put anything through it wished, and could crush anything." Industry leaders never realized how little control McNicholas's committee had over the other bishops. "We must thank God that things are going as well as they are," McNicholas told Cardinal Hayes, "considering that there is activity in 80 or more dioceses, and that our Episcopal Committee has no authority whatever." He tried to get Hayes to issue a strong statement in support of the Legion, but the cautious New York leader released only a vague pastoral letter in July supporting wholesome entertainment while warning against extremism. No one had the temerity to try to advise any of the other three cardinals, each of whom seemed to be running his own campaign. O'Connell continued to try to negotiate a separate agreement with the industry while Dougherty showed no sign of calling off the total boycott he had initiated before the Cincinnati meeting. In the meantime, Mundelein was distributing his own black- and white lists in Chicago.[46]

Hays must have wondered what the industry concessions had bought as he read his staff's reports on the Catholic press coverage of Hollywood. Catholic attacks on the movies seemed to have grown more bitter after the June meeting. In a special movie edition, *Our Sunday Visitor* ran a series of vicious cartoons reviling the industry, including one that presented a movie house in the shape of a skeleton head named "Filthy Films, Inc." Another depicted Mae West holding a bag of profits and standing before a table of rotten eggs representing several divorced movie stars, including Douglas Fairbanks, Sr., and Mary Pickford. Four months after Breen took over, the *New World* charged that "whether indecencies be staged under the direction of unscrupulous directors of Hollywood or by command of the pagan kings of Babylon; whether scenarios be the composition of Boccaccio . . . or contemporaneous Hecht; whether theme music echo the debauchery of Jezebel . . . or reek with the jungle vulgarity of Duke Ellington, they all belong to the same category of filth."[47]

A few Catholics complained about the church's preoccupation with the movies. In a letter to the editor of the *Michigan Catholic*, "J. H. M.," an out-of-work father of seven, found the campaign against the movies humorous because he couldn't afford the price of a ticket. Rather than focusing on Hollywood, he argued, the church should do more to help the economy. But for every J. H. M. there were scores of Catholics, priests and lay people, who were willing to do their part. Father James Smith stood in front of the only theater in Sayville, Long Island, night after night scrutinizing every person who bought a ticket to see Mae West's *Belle of the Nineties*. After a few days, the nightly audience had dwindled to fifty, and the manager tore up the Mae West posters and tacked up ads for the latest Helen Hayes movie. In Herkimer and Ticonderoga, New York, priests stood outside their neighborhood theaters to prevent their flocks from seeing films like *Doctor Monica* and *Tarzan and His Mate*. Convinced that *Little Man, What Now?* (a movie about unemployment in Germany) was "not a fit subject," the pastor of a church in a neighboring town brought a local policeman to force the manager to stop showing the film.[48]

In some communities, the diocesan press took the lead. As Vincent dePaul Fitzpatrick, the *Baltimore Catholic Review*'s managing editor, reassured his readers: "Managers . . . have been told that the *Review* will cooperate with them if they do the right thing [and] will tear them apart if they try to oppose the Legion of Decency." When the *Review* denounced the Little Theater for showing *Lot in Sodom*, the manager apologized to Fitzpatrick, even though, as he explained, he had not anticipated any problem because the film had been awarded first honors at the Venice International Exposition and none of the published reviews had raised any questions about it.[49]

Catholic schoolchildren also enlisted in the campaign. Students at St. Stephen's School in Port Huron, Michigan, forced the local police commissioner to close a film that had been condemned in the local Catholic press. In September 1934, some 70,000 students marched through the streets of Chicago with banners proclaiming, "An admission to an indecent film is an admission to hell" and "Films we must see, but clean they must be."[50]

With the Legion unwilling to go away, a concerned Hays sent Lupton A. Wilkinson, a former journalist who worked for the MPPDA, to sound out newspaper editors in eighty-two cities. Wilkinson was to determine the effect of the Legion campaign in different parts of the country and convince the editors that it was in the interest of the media to downplay any notion that Catholic pressure had forced the film industry to reform. He found a few editors who were concerned about the Legion campaign. The editor of the *Boston Traveler* thought the industry should have told the church to "scram," while his counterpart at the *Christian Science Monitor* worried about a Catholic takeover of Hollywood. But most editors Wilkinson talked to felt that "sex-happy" Hollywood deserved the criticism. According to the drama editor of the *Philadelphia Public Ledger*, RKO was looking for trouble when it advertised *The Lost Patrol*, which had no female roles in it, as "lonely men longing for women." Most papers were especially concerned about what the movies were doing to children. The editor of the *Philadelphia Inquirer* charged that the root of the problem was not Mae West but pictures that undermined parental control by showing young people engaged in "anti-conventional behavior." The *Chicago Herald Examiner*'s Vic Watson, who claimed that a cycle of horror films such as *Dracula*, *Dr. Jekyll and Mr. Hyde*, and *The Black Cat* had driven parents away, told Wilkinson that he had almost sued the makers of *Frankenstein* for its effect on his eight-year-old son. According to Watson, the boy had suffered a nervous collapse in the midst of the picture and had been under a doctor's care for the two and a half years since he had seen it. If Hollywood keeps on making pictures like this, Watson warned, "a woman will have a miscarriage in a theater or Mrs. Jones will go crazy."[51]

The campaign appeared to have its greatest success in cities with a large Catholic population, especially in the neighborhood theaters. Although Hays may have derived some initial satisfaction from the news that the Detroit Legion had not boycotted any theaters, he must have blanched at Wilkinson's explanation that their inactivity was due to the theater owners' success in shifting the blame to Hollywood. In the South, where Catholics were in the minority, attempts to drum up support for the Legion usually foundered on anti-Catholic prejudice. In Jacksonville, Florida, for example, two ministers ripped up sermons favorable to the Legion after a colleague who belonged to the Ku Klux Klan denounced the campaign as a Popish propaganda plot. Wilkinson had a close call when a Richmond reporter called up a Catholic priest to get his reaction to a piece he was preparing that suggested that a local

20 percent box-office increase during the Legion campaign indicated that the crusade had failed. Wilkinson was able to stop the story, but he asked Hays to warn the trade papers not to rouse sleeping dogs by bragging about any improvement in attendance.[52]

Wilkinson's confidential reports soon found their way to the enemy camp. Breen secretly made copies of all his information and passed it on to Quigley, McNicholas's chief adviser. They must have smiled ruefully over a prediction by the editor of the *Chicago Daily News* that the Legion campaign was likely to outlast most movie reform movements because of the church's "genius for organization." From their vantage point, the church's only genius when it came to the movies seemed to lie in disarray. Knowing that Hollywood shared the common perception of the church as a monolithic institution, Quigley feared that once Hollywood detected the real internal divisions it would withdraw its support of the PCA. Equally worrisome was the continued Catholic criticism of Hollywood. Sooner or later, he argued, the moviemakers were going to conclude that because their concessions had gained nothing, they might as well produce any type of picture they wanted to.[53]

One of Quigley's chief concerns centered on Boston. Cardinal O'Connell had ignored the creation of the PCA under Breen and his blasts at "Hollywood, the scandal of the world" suggested that nothing had changed since the establishment of the Legion in April. Convinced, the Massachusetts Catholic Order of Foresters immediately called for criminal proceedings against anyone showing objectionable films. Meanwhile, O'Connell continued to encourage Father Russell Sullivan to strike a separate deal with the producers. Sullivan was the perfect choice to represent the irascible and autocratic O'Connell. Just as the other bishops disliked O'Connell, his fellow Jesuits had no confidence in Sullivan, who had gotten into a number of jams throughout his career. In what the *New York Herald Tribune* labeled the "most sensational castigation of the motion picture industry" ever, the priest characterized Jean Harlow, Norma Shearer, Barbara Stanwyck, and Joan Crawford as "teachers of the ways of prostitutes and kept women." Little wonder that young people were led astray, he continued, when Mae West showed them how to climb the ladder of success "wrong by wrong," while Clark Gable and William Haynes introduced them to the skills of the "insidious seducers." Sullivan, who had little use for lists, white or black, believed that the only solution was to boycott all the pictures of any producer or theater that showed even one film that a Massachusetts Knights of Columbus committee found objectionable. The Hays Office was stunned to find that O'Connell was still championing the Sullivan plan after the industry's concessions. Charles Pettijohn, the MPPDA general counsel, telephoned Massachusetts Senator David I. Walsh to complain that the plan was contrary to the

Episcopal Committee's understanding with the producers. But the cardinal was as likely to abide by the decision of the McNicholas committee as by a directive from the archbishop of Canterbury.[54]

In an effort to placate O'Connell, the Hays Office asked Quigley to inform Sullivan that the industry was interested in cooperation but that his plan was impractical. On July 25 Quigley tried to explain to the priest that any theater owner who refused to show films because some censor appointed by the cardinal had rejected them would be subject to a breach-of-contract suit by the distributor. And if the industry made an exception for Boston, he continued, it would be vulnerable to similar demands from the remaining one hundred four dioceses, not to mention other religious groups. The meeting ended after ten hours with Sullivan still insisting that the industry accede to his demands.[55]

Sullivan, who had questioned Quigley's motives in their discussion, carried the attack to the press in the following days. The damage to the Legion campaign was bad enough, Quigley told Father Parsons, but he was also afraid that Sullivan might even cause trouble for Quigley's son, who was studying to be a Jesuit. Appalled, Parsons wrote to a colleague in Massachusetts urging that the superior of the order be persuaded to go to O'Connell and tell him that Sullivan was not well and had to be replaced.[56]

More convinced than ever that O'Connell could derail the Legion campaign, Quigley asked Father Francis Spellman for advice. Spellman, who later became cardinal of New York, was the auxiliary bishop of Boston at the time and as such had spent several uncomfortable years under O'Connell. Spellman told Quigley that the only way to win the cardinal over was to butter him up by telling him that "some men, less experienced and less broad-minded than His Excellency is known by all the world to be," might, by making impossible demands, nullify all the progress they had made. Suggest to him, he added, that one of his "masterly, timely pronouncements on the subject" could make a significant contribution to the fight against movie immorality. Quigley immediately dashed off a letter to the cardinal stating that Sullivan must have misrepresented O'Connell, "knowing your tolerance, keenness of judgment and understanding of men and affairs." The day after O'Connell received Quigley's letter, the cardinal dropped his plan and Sullivan left on vacation. But within a few months Sullivan was back, unchanged, and this time Quigley was forced to ask Joseph P. Kennedy to travel to Boston and pressure the cardinal to put an end to Sullivan's scheme.[57]

Will Hays and Quigley were even more concerned over Cardinal Dougherty's continuing boycott of all the movie houses in Philadelphia: Hays for fear that it would succeed, Quigley out of a belief that it would collapse and undermine the Legion campaign. Like O'Connell, Dougherty had no use for black and white lists, which carried the implication that "movieland can have two kinds of groceries in stock, wholesome and tainted, and still get patronage." Unlike O'Connell, who had hoped to dictate the terms of Hollywood's surrender, Dougherty had no interest in negotiating with anyone from the industry.[58]

Most of the first-run theaters in Philadelphia were owned by Warner Brothers, whose appeal to Dougherty to ban individual pictures and not entire theaters fell on deaf ears. In an attempt to rally public opinion, Warner and the 409 independent theater owners charged that the boycott would force them to close 475 theaters and lay off more than 10,000 workers. Their strategy led to some public criticism of the cardinal, including an open letter signed by several Philadelphians likening him to the "stage Irishman, . . . ready for a fight at all costs, not too careful about rights, but determined to get in a wallop for the sake of a wallop." In a more respectful tone, the independent theater operators of the city asked the cardinal to recognize the progress that had been made under the PCA and to consider the effect his boycott would have on all those thrown out of work in the midst of a severe depression.[59]

But the Philadelphia hierarchy was unmoved. Dougherty left for six weeks in Europe after invoking the ban, and Bishop John O'Hara, his auxiliary, dismissed the theater owners' sudden sympathy for their workers. He reminded them that he hadn't seen any tears a few years earlier when the advent of sound had led them to dismiss the piano players who performed at each silent film presentation. Once it was clear that the church would not bend, Warner called off the threatened theater closings and waited to see how many Philadelphia Catholics would obey the ban.[60]

Lupton A. Wilkinson, who visited Philadelphia for the Hays Office that summer, reported that there had been an overall reduction of between 15 and 20 percent in ticket sales in the early stages of the boycott and that the independent owners in predominantly Catholic areas had been especially hard hit. In late July, *Variety* disclosed that Warner's Stanley Theater had taken in $7,000 in the previous week, down from its usual ticket sales of $41,000, and stories circulated that one could fire a cannon down the theater's center aisle without danger of hitting anyone. According to one account, Warner was losing $175,000 a week because of Dougherty's edict. When one local theater went out of business, the manager dedicated the closing to the cardinal.[61]

Years after the Philadelphia crisis, Joe Breen recalled meeting with the panicked president of Warner Brothers: "There was Harry Warner standing up at the head of the table, shedding tears the size of horse turds and pleading for someone to get him off the hook." Warner tried to arrange a meeting with

Dougherty, who said he was willing to talk to him about anything except the boycott. "I can't discuss pictures and the theater," he said, "as I have had more than enough of that subject." Will Hays thought he detected an opening when the diocesan paper declared that the boycott would not be called off until the industry capitulated. He immediately wrote to Dougherty, pointing out that the industry had, in fact, already capitulated, and that he and Quigley would explain what the Legion campaign had accomplished. Once again, the cardinal expressed a willingness to receive visitors as long as they did not come to talk about the movies. Moreover, he added, even if there had been some progress, in view of the moviemakers' past promises he would not call off the boycott until sufficient time had elapsed to convince him of their sincerity.[62]

Despite Dougherty's confidence, Quigley and McNicholas began to worry that Catholic support for the boycott might wane when the weather turned colder and there were fewer alternative amusements. If the Philadelphia boycott collapsed, they feared it would drag down the Legion campaign. Rumors that the executive committee of the Philadelphia Knights of Columbus had quietly voted not to endorse the cardinal's edict reinforced their concern. Quigley tried to get the apostolic delegate to suggest to Dougherty that he had won a moral victory and should call off the boycott, but he refused to get involved in diocesan affairs.[63]

Attendance began to pick up in the fall, and by October, the fifth month of the boycott, even the diocesan paper admitted that some Catholics were beginning to violate it. Lamenting the loss of Christian self-denial and Catholic solidarity, it urged its readers to use a little ingenuity to find other sources of entertainment. Noting that the increased box-office receipts in Philadelphia indicated that Catholics were returning to the movies, Quigley warned Dougherty that the failure of the boycott would shatter the church's reputation for discipline and reduce the industry's fear of the Legion. He offered to get the studios to promise to withdraw any picture that the cardinal identified as an "occasion of sin," but Dougherty refused.[64]

The cardinal issued one last blast at the movies in his New Year's address for 1935 and then dropped the issue entirely. It was a strange ending to the affair; without any further pronouncements from Dougherty, the boycott was technically still in effect when he died in 1951. The quiet that descended on Boston and Philadelphia was welcome news to filmmakers, but their problems were far from over.

SIX

Battle of the Bishops

Although the independent actions of Cardinals O'Connell and Dougherty posed a serious threat to church unity, the real danger in the summer of 1934 stemmed from the growing division over the advisability of blacklisting objectionable films. The failure of what one priest referred to as "the disappointed, subsidized, inefficient women of the IFCA" to clean up the screen had done much to discredit their policy of white listing. Nevertheless, Martin Quigley and Joe Breen continued to oppose any public condemnation of films, a stand that only confirmed their enemies' suspicion that their true loyalty lay with Hollywood.[1]

Their strongest support within the church came from Father Edward Schwegler, director of the Buffalo Legion of Decency. Schwegler, a nationally known contributor to the Catholic press, agreed with Quigley and Breen that blacklists only publicized objectionable films. Moreover, he pointed out, the subjective nature of film reviews made deciding which pictures to condemn a ticklish business. He dismissed Baltimore's Bishop Michael J. Curley's argument that a movie blacklist was just an extension of the church's Index of forbidden books, pointing out that Rome's list was prepared with considerable thought, contained a relatively small number of books dealing with some important doctrinal or moral issue, and had a limited circulation. In contrast, a movie blacklist had to be prepared quickly and could contain numerous films that would be viewed by millions. With so many chances for mistakes to be made, a white list at least erred on the side of Christian charity.[2]

In contrast, Pittsburgh's Bishop Hugh Boyle, a member of the Episcopal Committee, had no use for white lists, which, he argued, encouraged Catholics to go to the movies. As the *Pittsburgh Catholic* noted, 90 percent of the films on the IFCA's white list were "dull, trashy and boring," and some of them even conflicted with Catholic standards. The hero of *The Count of Monte Cristo* (1934), for example, was motivated by revenge. A simple blacklist, the paper concluded, was not only less troublesome but focused on what the church was most concerned about—immoral pictures.[3]

Adding to the confusion were people like R. Dana Skinner, drama critic for *Commonweal* magazine, who was opposed to both black and white lists. Arguing that screen immorality was too complex an issue to be reduced to lists of good and bad films, he called for comprehensive reviews that would alert Catholic moviegoers to a film's moral and artistic worth. But Skinner's stance had few backers since the cost and time involved made such an enterprise impractical. Father James Gillis, editor of *Catholic World*, argued that "subtle immoral pictures" were far more dangerous than flagrantly objectionable ones because Catholics would have no difficulty in recognizing the latter. Yet Gillis neglected to tell his readers how one identified these insidious films and whether he favored placing them on a separate gray list.[4]

After signing a pledge not to view objectionable films, laypeople wanted to know what they could and could not see. Schwegler, Quigley, Breen, and the IFCA claimed that any film that did not appear on its white list was not worth seeing. Conversely, Bishop Boyle said any film not on a blacklist was acceptable. But as critics of both approaches pointed out, the absence of a picture from a list could mean that it had yet to be evaluated. The surest method of educating the laity would combine recommended and not recommended films on a single slate, as the papal delegate indicated to Archbishop John T. McNicholas, who began to lean toward a combined white and blacklist. Yet he felt that his committee could do nothing until after the bishops' annual meeting in November.[5]

The move toward a comprehensive system picked up momentum with the publication on July 6 of the Chicago Legion's first list, which contained 123 films produced before the PCA's creation. Even a quick glance at the classifications must have given readers the feeling that the Legion had been formed in the nick of time: fifty-two, less than half, were on the A list of approved films; forty-one were found to be "offensive in spots" and relegated to the B category, suitable only for adults; and thirty were declared immoral and placed in the condemned, or C, category. Included among these thirty films were some, like *Doctor Monica*, that Breen thought he had cleaned up and others, like *Affairs of a Gentleman*, that he had passed against his best judgment. On July 13 four more pictures were added to the C list, including *Affairs of Cellini*, which Breen had approved, characterizing it as a "fine, high comedy . . . that handled some questionable material extremely well."[6]

The quick success of the Chicago list surprised even its most ardent supporters. Within a few weeks of having been condemned, Universal's *Little Man, What Now?* ran into trouble in neighborhood movie houses. As a result of visits from parish vigilance committees, several owners had canceled $3,000 worth of rentals under the terms of the industry's agreement that any movie released before July 15 could be withdrawn if the community protested it on moral grounds. In an effort to get the film back into circulation, Universal made a number of cuts on the spot and asked the Chicago Legion to reevaluate it. Father FitzGeorge Dinneen conceded that the new version was an improvement, but because the Chicago list had been adopted by other Catholic papers, he refused to notify the public about the reclassification until the studio agreed to show only the revised film throughout the country. Aware that Universal's acceptance of his offer had extended the influence of the Chicago Legion beyond the archdiocese, Dinneen asked McNicholas to sanction the negotiations. Without giving the matter much thought, the archbishop wrote back that the studio's concession could only help the campaign.[7]

Encouraged by Universal's operation, Dinneen began to promote the idea that the film industry should establish previewing facilities in Chicago. Breen had no wish to be second-guessed by Dinneen's committee, and Martin Quigley believed that any attempt to allow the Chicago group to screen films threatened the national movement's future. "I can conceive of no surer way in which the whole campaign might be wrecked," he told the president of Loyola University, "than to have the American public learn that a Catholic priest is setting himself up [as] a censor of motion pictures." The industry leaders, who were no more willing than Quigley to delegate power to Dinneen, politely fended off the priest's requests for previewing facilities. Nevertheless, with additions every week, the Chicago list captured national attention. Although most of the secular press applauded the Legion campaign, some papers began to wonder if the Chicago list was a taste of what was to come if the church got its way.[8]

One problem was Chicago's tendency to condemn what many people believed were some of Hollywood's best films. New York's *Daily Mirror* noted that six of the twenty-five pictures selected for President Franklin D. Roosevelt's cruise to Hawaii had been labeled immoral by the Chicago Legion. The *New York Times* even suggested that moviegoers might be better off if they reversed Chicago's rating system because twenty to twenty-five of the thirty-seven films on its A list were not worth the filmgoer's time and money, whereas seven to ten of the movies in the C category were artistically crafted films. The *Waterbury American* agreed, noting that if both the B and C categories were eliminated, only the "insipid, trite, shallow, trivial and dull" would remain.[9]

All this renewed the fear of some that the church would be satisfied only with a steady diet of children's pictures. If the Chicago Legion succeeded, one critic warned, movie houses would feature only an "all-decent life of Elsie Dinsmore, played by actors who say their prayers every night and never chew their fingernails." G. Stevenson of New Haven complained to *Time* magazine about the Legion "and all other forms of pernicious busy-bodying." He insisted on his inalienable right to see a "filthy show" if he so desired, and he was not alone. The same issue of *Time* featured a letter from R. B. Seitz of Cleveland Heights, Ohio, who wanted to know if an anti–Legion of Decency movement had been formed.[10]

With the press beginning to focus on the Chicago list, Quigley knew that it would not be long before someone began comparing it with the other Catholic classification systems. By midsummer there were several lists, ranging from those that were circulated nationally, like Father Daniel Lord's, the IFCA's, and the Chicago Legion of Decency's, to local ones in Pittsburgh, Detroit, Buffalo, and Omaha. Even Boyle, who sponsored his own blacklist, admitted to McNicholas that he recently had attended a breakfast where eight of the ten priests were divided over the danger to the laity in seeing *The Private Life of Henry VIII.*[11]

The creators of the Chicago list claimed that their greatest difficulty was trying to distinguish between an approved film and one that was "offensive in spots." When in doubt, they placed the movie in question on the B list, "to be on the safe side," a practice that sometimes got them into trouble. An outpouring of complaints that *Twenty Million Sweethearts*, an innocent musical starring Dick Powell and Ginger Rogers, should never have appeared on the first B list prompted the committee to review the film and place it on the A list the following week. The same picture caused even greater embarrassment for the Detroit Legion, which compiled its list from a number of sources. Unaware that *Twenty Million Sweethearts* had originally been entitled *Rhythm in the Air*, Detroit placed *Sweethearts* on its A list and *Rhythm* on its B list. It was all right for Boyle to declare that discrepancies were to be expected, but a film's classification could determine its success or failure in a heavily Catholic area. The bewildered manager of one local theater complained to Cleveland's

Bishop Joseph Schrembs that two of his films that had flopped because of Chicago's objections had been praised by both a noted Catholic film critic and the IFCA.[12]

A spot on the Chicago blacklist posed a special problem for films that had been released prior to the establishment of the PCA on July 15, 1934, since the local manager had the right to cancel any picture in this category that encountered a genuine protest on moral grounds. Industry leaders had been desperate when they made the promise to McNicholas's committee, but they soon realized that it could cost them a lot of money. United Artists' Paul O'Brien was busy throughout the summer and fall of 1934 handling requests to cancel films like *Born To Be Bad*, a story about a woman's attempt to seduce the man who adopted her illegitimate son. Early on, O'Brien had asked a theater manager for proof that there was a genuine protest, only to receive a copy of *Our Sunday Visitor*, which indicated that the film had been condemned by the Chicago Legion.[13]

O'Brien suspected that some managers were using the Chicago condemnations selectively as a means of ridding themselves of unpopular pictures without paying the usual cancellation penalty. Consequently, he argued that cancellation privileges should apply only when an exhibitor was experiencing a serious dip in attendance due to a militant local campaign and not just because a film appeared on a blacklist. When cancellation requests began to pour in accompanied by references to protests in the local Catholic press, O'Brien suspected that the owners were stirring up complaints to justify breaking their contracts. He warned them that this practice would only encourage local churches to believe that they could determine what pictures played in their area. Nevertheless, at the urging of Quigley, who was becoming the unofficial liaison between the church and the film industry, the studios usually agreed to pull any film without penalty where there was anything approaching a serious protest on the part of a local parish.[14]

But the studios drew the line when it came to films that had been approved by Breen's office after July 15. Much of the problem stemmed from dioceses that relied on the Chicago list, like Fall River, Massachusetts, where Bishop James Cassidy and his Legion adviser, Father Edward Gorman, pressured local theater owners not to show any film that had been condemned by the Chicago Legion even if it had the PCA seal. The owners complied and were slapped with a cancellation fee. In an effort to head off similar complaints from other dioceses, Quigley and Breen told Cassidy and Gorman that the Chicago list was unreliable and that some of the condemned pictures, like *Limehouse Blues*, had been approved by a group of priests appointed by Bishop Cantwell to review the work of the Chicago Legion, while other films, including *The Scoundrel*, had been recommended for family viewing by the IFCA.

Gorman complained to McNicholas that Fall River had based its entire campaign on the Chicago list. Moreover, he had seen *The Scoundrel*, which he summed up as sixty minutes of indecency followed by a feeble attempt to draw a moral from a sordid story.[15]

Gorman drew the wrong conclusion: if Chicago was so unreliable, he would take matters into his own hands. After viewing *Four Hours to Kill*, to which even Chicago had given a B, he wrote to Paramount demanding that the film be withdrawn from all theaters in the Fall River diocese. When a studio representative told Gorman he couldn't understand the basis of his request in view of the Chicago rating, the priest airily responded that Fall River made its own decisions. It was becoming apparent to Quigley that in Fall River, every priest was becoming his own movie critic. He advised Paramount to tell Gorman that although it was willing to listen to his concerns, it could not hand over the power to decide what movies could be shown to every bishop in the country. Quigley, the mediator, had to assure the church that Hollywood was willing to listen, but he recognized that if he pushed the producers too far, he could undermine all the progress that had been made. After all, they might eventually conclude that it was useless to conform to the Code if they then had to negotiate with any bishop who second-guessed Breen.[16]

In spite of this, Quigley treated a cancellation request from Father Edward Schwegler, director of the Buffalo Legion of Decency and one of the few priests who had publicly opposed blacklisting, with special care. Schwegler had come close to requesting a cancellation on several occasions but had pulled back in order not to add to Breen's problems. But to his mind, Paramount's *The Devil Is a Woman*, starring Marlene Dietrich as a Spanish femme fatale, had crossed the line. Breen ordered a number of cuts in the film and approved it when the writers made it clear that Dietrich's character abandoned her immoral lifestyle at the picture's end. What spurred Schwegler to act was a scathing review of the movie in one of Quigley's publications. In a letter denouncing Dietrich's character as "meretricious, faithless, unnatural and inhuman," Schwegler directed all Buffalo's pastors to ask their neighborhood theaters not to show the film. But when several theater owners complied, they encountered the same problem of cancellation fees that the Fall River exhibitors had run into when they had followed Gorman's advice. Quigley's argument that the local theater owners' contract with Paramount superseded their obligations to the public was the wrong tack to take with Schwegler. Contracts were all right, he wrote Quigley, but when they obligated someone to do something morally objectionable, they no longer had any binding power. Concerned about losing Schwegler's support, which he needed in his battle with the Chicago Legion, Quigley urged Will Hays to get

Paramount to forget the Buffalo cancellation fees. Since Schwegler and Gorman who had also objected to the Dietrich film were the only priests who had taken action, Quigley was able to convince Paramount to waive the fee quietly in order to help the two priests save face.[17]

Still, Quigley's major problem continued to be how to end the Chicago list without bringing down the entire Legion campaign. Each new discrepancy among the various lists suggested that the church was as fallible as anyone else when it came to evaluating films. The *New York Herald Tribune* evoked Quigley's worst fears when it declared, "These distinguished judges of what is fit to see are having an awfully tough time deciding just what is indecent." Father Wilfrid Parsons noted, "If the producers had any brains, they would have blown us out of the water long ago." The producers were aware of discord within the Legion ranks, but they were afraid of direct confrontation with the church. Their best hope was that the Legion would eventually lose its momentum or, better still, self-destruct over the list controversy. Consequently, the Hays Office was delighted to read the Legion's first "obituary" in the *Birmingham News*, which reported in September that people were starting to speak of the Legion in the past tense.[18]

The Chicago Legion received an important vote of confidence when Father Lord announced that he would substitute it for his own list. Nevertheless, Chicago's condemnations of quality films like *Of Human Bondage* continued to damage the campaign's credibility. Breen had worked hard on the film, persuading RKO to agree to give Bette Davis's character tuberculosis instead of venereal disease, before he passed it. But while *Commonweal*'s reviewer praised it as a "veritable sermon . . . that the wages of sin are death," Chicago added it to its growing list of indecent films. Chicago also condemned *The Life of Vergie Winters*, a movie that Breen had fought over with RKO in the months before the establishment of the PCA. The studio had finally made all the requested cuts in what turned out to be one more story of a mistress who is punished in the end. In this case, Vergie lets her lover, a rising politician, and his wife adopt her daughter. Father Wilfrid Parsons, who felt the film was "neither dirty, nor filthy, nor salacious, nor obscene," told Breen it was one of "the most beautifully acted and directed pictures I ever saw." He was not disturbed by the adulterous relationship between Vergie and her lover, he said, because she paid for her sins. The real danger lay in Chicago's tendency to condemn any film with an adult theme, thus playing into the hands of those who claimed that the church was out to destroy the film industry.[19]

Quigley and Parsons were not the only critics of the Chicago system. Pat Scanlan, editor of the *Brooklyn Tablet*, had no problem with the condemnations per se and had used the Chicago list until he also began to lose confidence in its evaluations. With so many pictures premiering in New York,

Chicago's lack of previewing facilities meant that a number of films playing in Brooklyn had yet to be evaluated while half of the classified films had already left town. Scanlan finally dropped the Chicago list in favor of the IFCA's recommendations, which were more up to date. By the end of the summer, two camps were beginning to take shape: a loose alliance of Quigley, Breen, Parsons, Schwegler, and Scanlan pitted against the Chicago coalition, which included the Detroit Legion of Decency and Lord.[20]

The quarrel between Quigley and Dinneen, which had its origins in the split at the June 1934 bishops' meeting, had intensified when Chicago's first list of condemned films included *It Ain't No Sin* (before its name change to *Belle of the Nineties*) and *Madame DuBarry*, both of which had not been shown in Chicago and were in the process of being revised. When the publisher asked Dinneen how his committee had placed the films on the C list sight unseen, the priest explained that the determination was based on their lurid ads and on the studios' request for adult permits from the city censors. After Quigley remonstrated with Dinneen over the fairness of evaluating films without having viewed them, Dinneen responded that the publisher must be losing his sense of humor. "I opened your letter this morning," he wrote Quigley, "and to my relief, the only criticism of our list is unfairness to Mae West and Madame DuBarry." Enraged by what he felt was the priest's patronizing attitude and tyrannical manner, Quigley informed Archbishop McNicholas that he was discontinuing all correspondence with Dinneen. Charles Pettijohn, the industry counsel (who hated Quigley and Breen), didn't help matters when he told Dinneen and Chicago's Cardinal George Mundelein that the PCA should never have approved *Girl from Missouri*, starring Jean Harlow. Breen had forced MGM to do a major rewrite of the film so that Harlow's character retained her virtue—a break with her previous films. Nevertheless, this didn't satisfy the Chicago Legion, which condemned the movie.[21]

Parsons suspected that Dinneen had his own agenda, for if Breen could be discredited, the Chicago Legion might become the moral arbiter of the American film industry. Nevertheless, Parsons made one last effort to heal the growing breach by reminding Lord and Dinneen of the need to maintain a united front in support of Breen, who was their only hope of success. Lord acknowledged that "the tragedy of the whole thing is that so many sincere and well-intentioned people [were] getting on each other's nerves." Encouraged by Lord's response, Parsons reminded Dinneen that Cantwell "would never have moved an inch" without Breen; that it was Quigley who had convinced the papal delegate to speak out against the movies; and that McNicholas would never have dreamed of launching the Legion except for the publisher's efforts. In a last attempt to reverse Dinneen's conviction that Quigley had tried to torpedo the Legion at the June meeting, Parsons persuaded McNicholas to inform Dinneen that the publisher had wholeheartedly supported the campaign from the start.[22]

But Dinneen and Lord remained convinced that Quigley and Breen had manipulated the Episcopal Committee for their own purposes. Had Dinneen known that Quigley's expenses for his work in connection with the Legion campaign were paid by the Hays Office, he would have launched a public attack. Quigley was nervous enough about the matter to report it to McNicholas in case it ever became known and some "busybody" placed it in an unfavorable light. The archbishop reassured him that he had no problem with the arrangement. "If Martin Quigley cannot be trusted absolutely," he said, "then no man can be trusted." Without any solid evidence, all Dinneen could do was to voice his suspicions to the others. "No man can serve two masters," he told Parsons, "and it would discredit our campaign to have it dominated by two movie men." When Parsons responded that Quigley could serve two masters by working within the industry for better films, Dinneen, resentful at being lectured to, sent him a notarized affidavit that all his charges were true. "This is simply fantastic beyond words," an exasperated Parsons told Lord. "One father here said it was paranoia."[23]

As the annual November meeting of the bishops approached, Quigley continued to lobby against blacklisting, while Dinneen urged McNicholas to adopt Chicago's classifications as the official church list. The archbishop, who knew that the topic would dominate the discussions, admitted to Cardinal Patrick Hayes that he was perplexed. He recognized the need to guide the vast majority of the faithful who had no source of recreation other than the movies, but he was concerned about having the bishops authorize a list that would rely on the moral evaluations of a committee. So far, McNicholas pointed out, all the problems had involved questions about the judgment of Chicago, Detroit, Lord, or the IFCA; if the bishops sponsored a national list, the final responsibility would be theirs. He was inclined, he told Hayes, to defer a decision in the hope that the need for a list would disappear within a year if the church kept pressing the industry to honor its commitments. Then, only a watchdog committee would be necessary to make sure that there was no backsliding. Such a stance, he told Hayes, would impress outsiders, who would say, "here is a church that cannot be intimidated by the producers, but how sane the Catholic church is! She is reasonable, she is kind, she is understanding. She does not wish to destroy or to injure the business of producing pictures."[24]

As a sign of the importance he attached to the movie question, Cardinal Mundelein, who had largely ignored the NCWC in the past, traveled to the

Washington meeting. Claiming that the prestige of the church was at stake, he called for a free and open discussion of the issues, yet the talks were not as broad based as they might have been. McNicholas declined to extend an invitation to Lord, who he believed was "an appalling instance of Catholic action gone wrong when uncontrolled by the bishops." Cardinal O'Connell, as usual, ignored the meeting, and although Cardinal Dougherty sent Bishop John O'Hara as his representative, he made it clear that he would not abide by any decision other than a call for a national boycott.[25]

O'Hara made a valiant effort at the beginning of the meeting to rally the other bishops behind Dougherty by arguing that anything short of a total ban would undermine the sacrifice of Philadelphia Catholics who had been boycotting the city's movie houses for six months. Bishop Cantwell of Los Angeles, mindful of the economic interests of his own diocese, pointed out that if the bishops adopted the Philadelphia plan it would destroy the film industry and put thousands of Catholics out of work. But Mundelein, who had originally warned against throttling any discussion, blocked serious consideration of the Dougherty plan. Aware that the support of the Catholic laity was already waning, he dryly noted that because none of the other bishops could count on the "splendid cooperation" Dougherty had received, it might be best to consider a more realistic method of dealing with the question. Bishop Walsh of Charleston, South Carolina, proposed the appointment of one well-trained Catholic censor who would work in close collaboration with the PCA, but his recommendation found little support. Mundelein, who argued that, unless the church adopted a unified approach, the "picture people will laugh at us," came up with the most comprehensive plan, a national reviewing committee that would replace all the local lists, including the IFCA's. Estimating that the annual cost of such an undertaking would be in the neighborhood of $12,000, for the reviewers' salaries, Mundelein volunteered to contribute $1,000 a year. Although most of the bishops shared Mundelein's concerns about disunity, they shied away from such an expense. Bishop Hugh Boyle spoke for most of his colleagues when he said that, in view of the progress that had already been made, he could live with the present situation.[26]

In an effort to reach some consensus, McNicholas, who had favored a New York-based reviewing system if one were necessary, persuaded the bishops to compromise. Chicago would continue to publish a weekly list of evaluations, which would be distributed to all the bishops. Bishop Gallagher, in a gesture of unity, declared that he was terminating the Detroit list in favor of Chicago's evaluations. To placate Cardinal Dougherty, the Episcopal Committee agreed to warn Hollywood that if it reneged on its pledge to maintain decent standards, the bishops would call for a national boycott of all movies for a period of time to be determined at a later date. Finally, the bishops agreed to have the pledge of the Legion of Decency publicly renewed each year at all Sunday masses within the octave of the feast of the Immaculate Conception.[27]

Industry leaders were disheartened by the bishops' decision to renew the pledge because it destroyed any hope that the Legion would fade away. They were especially dismayed by the announcement of Cardinal Hayes—who had previously held back in order to give Hollywood a chance to prove itself—that he would join the others in administering the pledge. Although unwilling to speak on the record, several producers told reporters that they saw the pledge renewal as a new assault that left them wondering just what the church wanted. But what the industry interpreted as betrayal the church leaders saw as good tactics. "Just when the producers thought we had gone to sleep," Boyle told McNicholas, "came the pledge, which they think is a new campaign." The leaders of the Chicago Legion were delighted by the bishops' vote, construing the decision to distribute the Chicago list nationally as an endorsement of their work. The *New World* informed its readers that in choosing Chicago before all others, the bishops had "voted the Chicago clergy and laity a citation *summa cum laude.*" As one local priest pointed out, it was Cardinal Mundelein's "brilliant and ever-to-be-cherished decision to launch the Chicago Legion that had led the way to reform."[28]

Yet the bishops' decision was more an economic matter than a ringing testimonial. Moreover, some bishops saw a tactical advantage in letting Chicago have the responsibility of preparing the list as any criticism would be laid at Mundelein's door. Bishop Cantwell's announcement at the November meeting that he was contemplating establishing his own reviewing committee in Los Angeles, staffed by members of the West Coast branch of the IFCA, should have told the Chicago Legion that the deep divisions over the movie question had merely been papered over at the November meeting. In December 1934, at Breen's suggestion, Cantwell had arranged to have Father John Devlin, his former secretary and head of the Los Angeles Legion, and an associate review four gangster films that had been approved by the PCA and condemned by Chicago. When the two priests reported that there was nothing indecent or immoral about the films, Cantwell could only conclude that they had touched a raw nerve among the Chicago reviewers, who were overly sensitive about the image of their city as the home of Al Capone. When Dinneen and four other Chicago priests visited Hollywood in early January, they did nothing to reassure Devlin. On tour of the studios they criticized everyone and everything. They refused to listen to Devlin's suggestions that greater care should be taken in preparing their list. He was astounded to learn that four of the priests had not seen any of the condemned films and the fifth had seen only one. They made it clear that the Chicago Legion had little use for either Breen or the Production Code, choosing instead to use their own undefined standards. In turn, the Chicagoans made it clear that they interpreted Devlin's defense of Breen as a sign that he had been co-opted by the producers. To cap the trip off, Dinneen got involved in a bitter argument with the chancellor of the archdiocese. By the time Bernard J. Sheil, Mundelein's auxiliary bishop, arrived to join the delegation, Cantwell had had enough of the Chicago Legion. He summoned Sheil to his office and criticized the boorish behavior of his colleagues. Sheil left Los Angeles on the next train while an angry Cantwell told the producers not to deal with any priests in the future before checking with him.[29]

The priests' admission that they had not seen most of the films they had condemned raised a question that had bothered Quigley and his allies from the beginning: just who was preparing the Chicago list? Earlier, Father Wilfrid Parsons worried that it had been put together on the advice of Pete Harrison, the editor of *Harrison's Reports*. "It would be dangerous," Parsons told Lord, "to make a non-Catholic the *de facto* maker of standards on films for the church." But the real source of Chicago's decisions was even more unsettling. Much of the list was prepared by a woman named Sally Reilly, who held a minor position on the Chicago censorship board. Reilly, who was a close friend of Dinneen and had once served as his secretary, took notes on the films previewed by the city board of censors and passed them on to the Legion committee. If there were any doubts about Reilly's evaluations, several committee members viewed the film before making a final judgment. When Father Gerard Donnelly leaked this information in an editorial in *America*, Dinneen was outraged. Claiming that his parishioners strongly resented the "slur" against Reilly, he prohibited the sale of the journal in his parish.[30]

According to Dinneen, the Chicago Legion had to rely on Reilly because Breen and Quigley had sabotaged Chicago's chance to get its own previewing facility. Angry over *America*'s revelation of Reilly's role, Mundelein complained to the apostolic delegate that the attacks were accomplishing for the movie producers what they could not do on their own, the destruction of the Legion. But it was Detroit's Father Joseph Luther, an ally of Dinneen, who launched the most bitter attack against Parsons. Characterizing the actions of *America*'s editor as "little less than lying treachery and traitorous," he charged Parsons with destroying the confidence of the Catholic people in the Chicago list. In Luther's mind, a priest would willfully engage in such sabotage only if he had been bought off by the producers. Quigley and his allies countered that the bishops had only recommended the Chicago list; it had never been made mandatory. The revelation about Sally Reilly's role convinced Quigley, who had steadfastly opposed a blacklist, that a consensus had developed on the need to identify objectionable films for the faithful.[31]

In an effort to put the task in more responsible hands than the Chicago Legion's, Quigley convinced Cardinal Hayes that the New York archdiocese should publish its own evaluations because films were often released there before they had been seen by the Chicago Legion. Another reason he didn't mention to the cardinal was that Quigley had moved the headquarters of his publishing business to New York. If the Legion list originated there, his influence within the Catholic film campaign would be enhanced. To keep the cost of the operation down, Quigley turned to the only available trained Catholic evaluators, the women of the IFCA, who agreed to do the New York diocese's evaluations secretly while they continued to publish their own white list. Parsons, working through the IFCA's adviser, Father Francis Talbot, overcame the organization's long-standing opposition to blacklists, a task made much easier by Rita McGoldrick's successor as head of the IFCA's Motion Picture Bureau. Mary Looram proved to be much more flexible than McGoldrick on the question of blacklisting. She had no reservations about putting her volunteers to work on the New York list, which was comprised of four categories: A–I, general approval; A–II, approved for adults; B, unsatisfactory in part, neither recommended nor condemned; and C, condemned.[32]

The establishment of a New York list involved a series of delicate negotiations. Quigley and Parsons had discussed the classification headings with Will Hays—something that, if leaked, would have been seized upon by Dinneen as further proof that the two men were in league with the filmmakers. In an attempt not to antagonize the Chicago Legion, Quigley and Parsons decided that the New York list should appear in the diocesan paper, the *Catholic News*, without any fanfare. The creators of the New York list also made every effort not to conflict with the Chicago list. Consequently, although they didn't agree with many of its evaluations, their first C list carried eleven films that had been condemned by Chicago, including six approved by the PCA. So as not to embarrass Breen, Parsons had tried in vain to get the six dropped from the condemned list, but Looram promised that they would be removed as soon as possible.[33]

Meanwhile, Quigley stepped up his efforts to undermine the Chicago list. In a series of letters to the hierarchy, he maintained it was not just the pictures the Chicago Legion condemned that raised questions about its judgment, but also the pictures it recommended. He claimed that such films on Chicago's A list as *The Count of Monte Cristo*, *Age of Innocence*, *Flirtation Walk*, and *What Every Woman Knows* were unsuitable for children. Especially troublesome was

Three Songs About Lenin; either none of the Chicago people had seen this "vicious, Godless, Soviet propaganda picture," Quigley told McNicholas, or it has been reviewed by a "particularly stupid person."[34]

Nevertheless, the major problem continued to revolve around Chicago's condemnation of films that had been approved by the Breen office. Likening such films as *Anna Karenina, The Scoundrel, Barbary Coast, Catherine the Great, The Mysterious Mr. Wong*, and *The Private Life of Henry VIII* to the deadly snakes in the city's zoo, the *New World* urged its readers to boycott any theater showing such "reptilian pictures." Because most of the condemned films were added to the list without explanation, it was often difficult to understand what standards Chicago was using. Now and then, the *New World* discussed a particularly reprehensible film, like *Anna Karenina*, which it claimed was "one of the most immoral and indecent films ever to be shown on the screen." Ironically, Breen had featured his work on that film in his annual report to Hays. According to Chicago, however, he had overlooked three fundamental problems: the harsh characterization of Anna's husband, which encouraged the audience to sympathize with her; her abandonment of her husband and child for her lover; and her suicide. Father Devlin, Bishop Cantwell's film adviser, disagreed, pointing out that the producer had not tried to justify Anna's adultery, nor was there any attempt to lessen the audience's respect for the sanctity of marriage. The IFCA reviewers did not recommend the film, but a spokesperson said they would have endorsed it under the heading of "adult discretion" if such a category existed. In fact, the IFCA reviewers who prepared the New York list gave it a B despite the Chicago condemnation.[35]

By the summer of 1935, each new Chicago list of condemned films seemed to contain at least one that left its critics baffled. Sam Goldwyn was so angry about the Chicago Legion's condemnation of his bowdlerized *Barbary Coast* that he threatened to sue its leaders. And Cantwell enjoyed the film so much that he wrote to McNicholas complaining about Chicago's judgment. Breen was especially incensed over Chicago's condemnation of *The Scoundrel*, a film about the return to earth of the ghost of a cynical writer who comes to realize the error of his ways. He had forced Paramount to make a number of changes in the film and had approved it only after a panel of three priests unanimously sanctioned its release. Father Schwegler of Buffalo told Breen he was astonished to see the film on Chicago's C list. Conceding the theological absurdity of the premise that a soul, having departed this life, could free itself from eternal damnation, he nevertheless maintained that it was an acceptable literary device. As such, Schwegler continued, the film drove home the message of the power of repentance, and therefore it was "idiocy" to condemn it. The IFCA reviewers for the New York archdiocese agreed, awarding the film an A–II rating.[36]

Chicago lost whatever credibility it had left when it condemned *The Informer*, a film about the betrayal of an Irish Republican Army leader by a compatriot, which eventually was nominated for the Academy Award for best picture and won Oscars for director John Ford and actor Victor McLaglen. Its critical success meant nothing to the Chicago reviewers, who branded it, among other things, "nauseating, beastly, un-principled, immoral, indecent and rotten." Father George McCarthy, secretary of the Chicago Legion, charged that the director's location of a brothel in Dublin constituted the most offensive and insulting attack on Celtic womanhood ever made in Chicago. Critics cited the condemnation as an example of why Chicago could not be trusted with evaluating films for the Legion. Schwegler dismissed McCarthy's attack as "unadulterated poppycock" and "twaddle." The IFCA's Mary Looram thought the film was great, and her committee gave it an A–II classification in the *Catholic News*. Even Lord, a supporter of the Chicago Legion, told Dinneen that *The Informer* was one of the greatest films he had ever seen and that he was flabbergasted by the condemnation. An embarrassed Dinneen privately conceded that the gloomy picture of Dublin had bruised the Irish sentiment of the reviewers, making them forget that their job was to protect American morals and not Ireland's reputation.[37]

Exasperated by the growing ridicule of the Chicago list and concerned that the differences between it and New York's list made the question of movie morality appear to be a matter of geography, Bishop Cantwell had Father Devlin set up a "jury" to evaluate several condemned films. The reviewers, who included the president of Loyola University of Los Angeles, the former president of Santa Clara University, and the assistant to the provincial of the Augustinian Fathers, screened *The Informer*, *The Scoundrel*, and *Anna Karenina* and reported back that, although these films dealt with adult themes, there was nothing indecent about them and they did not violate the Code. The growing criticism of the Chicago list began to take its toll. Three months after the November meeting, only eight of the more than one hundred bishops were still using it.[38]

The Chicago list's friends did their best to defend it against the attacks of Quigley and the others. Although Lord admitted to one of the members of the Episcopal Committee that some condemned films deserved a better fate, he insisted Sally Reilly was as good a judge of pictures as any woman he had met. Some of its other defenders, like Detroit's Father Joseph Luther and Arthur Maguire, did more harm than good. Luther leveled a series of unsubstantiated attacks on anyone who failed to support the Chicago list, claiming, among other things, that both Father Coughlin, the popular radio priest who had largely ignored the Legion campaign, and Pat Scanlan, editor of the

Brooklyn Tablet, had been bribed by Hollywood. Maguire broadened the attack against Chicago's "enemies" in a pamphlet entitled "An Epistle from a Layman to the American Hierarchy," which he modestly characterized as the first such document ever written by a layman to the bishops. The pamphlet was a diatribe against Quigley and Parsons, whom he called propagandists for the film industry and the major source of disunity in the Legion campaign. Dinneen, who had seen an advance copy, told Lord it was "dynamite" and that Cardinal Mundelein and Bishop Sheil were secretly pleased to see Chicago's critics publicly skewered. "We naturally thought that our fight was only against the producers and Will Hays," he declared, "but the enemy had cleverly sown seeds of division in the Catholic camp through the treasonous acts of Quigley and Parsons." Quigley was in no position to criticize Chicago, Lord continued, when he advertised "some of the most rotten pictures produced in Hollywood" in his magazine. And as for Parsons's criticism of Reilly, she was a far better judge of movies than his friend Joe Breen. An angry Quigley urged McNicholas to respond publicly to Maguire's attacks, but the bishop suggested that he should turn the other cheek. Although Maguire's assault hurt in the short run, McNicholas felt that it would eventually spiritualize them.[39]

As 1935 drew to a close, Lord's prediction that anyone who associated with the motion picture problem was "sure to get messed up" seemed to be coming true. One indication that everyone's nerves were fraying was Dinneen's reaction to Lord's proposed piece on Quigley for the *Queen's Work*. This innocent article almost destroyed the long-standing friendship of the two Jesuits. "I woke up at three o'clock this morning," Dinneen wrote Lord, "and my first thought was your remark last evening about an interview with Martin Quigley." He warned Lord that Mundelein and Sheil would be displeased to see Quigley featured in his magazine, but what bothered him even more was the effect it would have on Sally Reilly: "To say that she was shocked is putting it mildly." He made it clear that if the Quigley article did appear, he would be forced to do to the *Queen's Work* what he had done to Parsons's *America* and forbid its distribution in his parish.[40]

Lord considered writing a companion piece on Reilly to balance the Quigley article, but he dropped it, claiming that it was never intended to focus on the publisher but only to get Quigley's views on various screen personalities. "I couldn't think of hurting either you or Sally," he told Dinneen, and if Quigley was irritated, that was all right with him since "he certainly kicked my booklet [*Motion Pictures Betray America*] around the block." Quigley's discovery that the article based on his interview had been withdrawn because of Dinneen's intervention only added to the growing enmity between the co-authors of the Code. As the publisher told a friend after a bitter exchange of letters with Lord, "I hope . . . to keep as far away from the clergy as possible, except on Sunday mornings."[41]

It was clear to the bishops at the annual meeting in November 1935 that unless the church could agree on a single list, the Legion campaign would not survive. As one priest put it, "Those who see, as so frequently happens, a picture given one classification in Chicago and another in New York, are too likely to draw the conclusion that morality after all is only a matter of opinion and that since authorities differ . . . they are free to make up their own minds." He noted that he had just learned that the women students at one of the best Catholic colleges had concluded they were fully capable of deciding which movies to see.[42]

The battle that some expected never materialized. Tired of the conflict and concerned about the financial cost of distributing a list that he said "was not generally appreciated," Cardinal Mundelein wanted out. While the bishops breathed a collective sigh of relief over avoiding a divisive issue, many were worried about financing a new operation. Bishop John G. Murray claimed that it would increase their budget by 30 percent, but he persuaded the others they had no choice because their purpose was to save souls at any cost. In the end, Mundelein, who presided at the meeting, agreed to transfer responsibility for issuing a national list to a new national Legion of Decency, headquartered in New York, with one proviso: the new committee must agree to a graded listing of films similar to the one devised by the Chicago Legion.[43]

The crucial question was who would put the new list together. The decision was left in the hands of McNicholas's committee and Cardinal Hayes, who reluctantly agreed to house the new system in his diocese. Quigley politely suggested that the only Catholic film reviewers left on the field of battle were the IFCA's unpaid volunteers. If they were unacceptable, the church would have to hire a staff of paid reviewers, who, Quigley argued, would need at least three years to reach the IFCA's level of experience. Aside from the considerable cost of setting up a new system, the church would still have two rival lists unless the hierarchy wanted to abolish the IFCA through some sort of episcopal injunction, which would raise a new set of problems.[44]

The IFCA had, in fact, for several months successfully incorporated a blacklist into its work on the New York list. Monsignor Joseph Corrigan of Philadelphia interviewed Mary Looram, chair of the IFCA reviewers, who assured him that her organization would meet Mundelein's demands. Although Rita McGoldrick had personally opposed blacklisting, Looram told Corrigan that the IFCA women had issued a white list when the hierarchy seemed opposed to blacklists; now that the hierarchy had changed its policy, the IFCA was happy to cooperate. In order to ensure a smooth transfer, potentially troublesome members of the hierarchy including O'Connell in Boston, Dougherty in Philadelphia, Gallagher in Detroit, and Curley in Baltimore were reassured that under Looram's leadership all ties to the Hays Office, which had once included printing and mailing the IFCA white list, had been severed. A few months earlier the IFCA had terminated the last link—using the MPPDA office boys to fold, insert, and seal its lists in envelopes supplied by the Hays Office. Even Curley, the IFCA's most outspoken critic, was satisfied. Dinneen also gave the new system his blessing, although he warned that the Chicago Legion would be monitoring the women's work closely. The only outward sign of sour grapes was the sudden termination of a weekly column in the *New World* which had highlighted the success of the Legion campaign since the beginning of the Chicago list.[45]

The new system was put in place quickly. The national list was to be prepared under the direction of the New York archdiocese's Legion of Decency, chaired by former Governor Al Smith. While the system was to be under the nominal control of Cardinal Hayes, any expenses connected with it would be paid for by the NCWC through donations from all the bishops. McNicholas, who had little faith in his fellow bishops' largess, privately told one of his committee members that he hoped that expenses would be kept to a minimum. Everyone agreed with McNicholas that the key to the Legion's success was finding an executive secretary "of splendid judgment" who would supervise the work of the reviewers and stand up to the producers. After careful consideration, Cardinal Hayes appointed Father Joseph Daly, Ph.D., who had taught psychology at New York's Mount Saint Vincent College. Daly, who was well known in Catholic circles because of his broadcasts on the national weekly radio program "The Church of the Air," seemed ideal for the job.[46]

The national list also needed a classification system. Bishop Mooney, chairman of the NCWC, distrusted anything that originated in Hollywood and, under his plan, even the A–I category would be labeled "not disapproved." Cardinal Hayes favored being a little less negative, so the new Legion rating system reflected a compromise. A–I covered those films "morally unobjectionable for the general public," whereas A–II included those unobjectionable for adults. B was reserved for movies that were "morally objectionable in part." Finally, C was applied to stories that because of theme or treatment, were immoral.[47]

Although the Legion's ratings never had the force of ecclesiastical law, there was a general consensus among church leaders that willful disregard of the ratings was a grave matter. The solemn manner in which the annual pledge to avoid immoral films was given led most Catholics to believe that going to see a condemned film constituted a mortal sin. There was much less agreement over whether Catholics were obligated to avoid B films. The category was clarified only with considerable difficulty: there had already been five definitions before the establishment of the final classification system by 1936. A few priests, like Father Edward Schwegler, tended to view B films as acceptable fare for mature adults, but most priests seemed to agree with a 1936 editorial in *America* that Bs differed from Cs only "in quantity, not in quality of the filth purveyed." As Father Aloysius McDonough explained in the *Sign Post:* "It is not far fetched to say that moral harm can be occasioned by a few inches of cinematic film projected on the screen in minutes." One overly scrupulous Legion member from Glendale, California, even asked Bishop Cantwell if he would commit a serious sin by using the classification system. "As I understand my obligations to Almighty God," he wrote, "If I hire a person to perform an immoral act, I am equally responsible for his sin." By relying on the Legion list, which required the reviewers to look occasionally at indecent films, was he not an accomplice in an immoral act? The bishop explained that the "virtue and judgment" of the women who did the reviewing guaranteed that they were not placed in an occasion of sin.[48]

All that was left was a smooth transfer from Chicago to New York. The news release, drafted by Quigley, announced that beginning in February 1936, New York would publish a national list at "the urgent request" of Cardinal Mundelein, who could no longer bear the heavy financial burden alone. Schwegler probably expressed the real feelings of the anti-Chicago coalition when he wrote: "If it did not smack of boasting and a lack of charity, we should be tempted to head this column 'We Told You So.'" The only public objection to the move came from the indefatigable Arthur Maguire, who had the Detroit Council of Catholic Organizations declare that the IFCA was under Will Hays's thumb and that the job of detecting immoral films was too important to be left to women. Maguire's move angered the usually reserved Cardinal Hayes. "Is there no possible way of keeping that fellow quiet for a while?" his spokesman asked McNicholas. "He may wreck everything just as we are getting organized." But Hayes had little to fear; the turmoil of the previous eighteen months had so exhausted everyone that there was no interest in launching another battle.[49]

There was one casualty, however. Father Wilfrid Parsons, whose open criticism had alienated the Chicago Legion, was forced to resign his twelve-year editorship of *America*. As Parsons later told Quigley, "Mundelein never forgave me for helping to 'steal' the Legion away from Chicago . . . and he never let up, here or in Rome. . . . So I got ulcers . . . and a mercifully short nervous breakdown." The banishing of Parsons proved to be Chicago's parting shot.[50]

Much of the credit for ending the turmoil within the Legion ranks, however, must go to Breen. His success in administering the Code convinced the church leaders that real reform had finally come to Hollywood. Father Francis Talbot, who visited Hollywood, reported to Rome that Breen had imposed his morality on his staff so that even the one Jewish member, "in reporting on a picture, spoke as a Catholic would." In the fifteen months after the establishment of the PCA, Breen and his staff reviewed 1,275 movie scripts, sat through 1,440 screenings, held 1,812 consultations, and turned out more than six thousand corrective notes and comments. However, as Father Devlin told Bishop Cantwell, the easiest part of Breen's job was the long hours. "Much more difficult [was] the matter of thought and judgment, since it involve[d] the continuous and consistent application of eternal principles of ethics to the ever varying practical problem of life and conduct." But, he said, divesting sex of its "glamour" and the gangster of his glory was worth the effort. Others, like *America*'s Father Gerard Donnelly, agreed that the improvement was truly remarkable. In March 1935, Mary Looram announced in her weekly radio report that the Legion had endorsed 95 percent of the films approved by the PCA.[51]

Breen's decision to clamp down on pre-Code films also reassured any doubters. Although he rejected the *New World*'s suggestion that the industry should follow the precedent of those governments that had destroyed their deadly weapons after World War I and burn all films made before July 1934, Breen ordered a number removed from circulation. Several, including *I'm No Angel* and *Hips Hips Hooray*, a traveling-salesman comedy, were allowed to play out their contracts before being sealed away in a Hollywood vault, never again to see the light of a theater projector in Breen's lifetime. Others, like *Baby Face* and *Affairs of a Gentleman*, which were still being shown in theaters, were apparently so dangerous that even one more day on the screen posed a serious threat to public morals, and they were immediately withdrawn from circulation.[52]

Breen allowed the studios some leeway by establishing a separate category of films that could be re-edited to meet the PCA's new standards and then submitted for a seal. Nevertheless, many sanitized films still didn't satisfy the new requirements. A revised version of *Are These Our Children?*—a 1931 story that traced a teenager's road to the electric chair—failed to please Breen. Noting that scenes of high school students engaged in drinking and "suggestive love making" tended to lower the moral values of those who saw it, he refused RKO's request to approve its re-release. Another RKO film, *Ann Vickers*, over which Breen had quarreled with Wingate, suffered a similar fate because the expurgated version still justified adultery. Nor did Jason Joy's admiration for Marlene Dietrich's *Blue Angel* help to save the Paramount film. It remained in Breen's eyes a "sordid story based on [an] illicit sex relationship." Producer Howard Hughes tried to argue that he shouldn't be forced to resubmit *Scarface* for approval because it had never been out of circulation since its initial release. Nevertheless, Carl Milliken's report to Hays that all the studios had withdrawn a large number of pictures "without a whimper and at a substantial loss" was a sign of how much the Legion had frightened the moviemakers.[53]

Although Breen seemed to be the right man for the Hollywood job, Quigley and McNicholas began to have second thoughts almost immediately about the selection of Father Joseph Daly as the Legion's executive secretary. Characterized by one commentator as a level-headed scholar with considerable communications skills, Daly's first appearance on the national scene provided Quigley with his first inkling that the Legion's troubles were not yet over. Daly had been in office only a few weeks when he represented the Legion at Congressional hearings in mid-March on the Pettengill bill, which outlawed block-booking. Although most church leaders were suspicious of government involvement, several prelates, including Bishop Gallagher of Detroit, endorsed some aspect of the bill. Bishop Noll, a member of the Episcopal Committee, had been recorded on both sides of the issue. Quigley, who had always championed industry self-regulation, tried to persuade McNicholas to oppose the bill, but he refused, pointing out that he had no mandate from the bishops on the issue.[54]

Nevertheless, everyone agreed that it would be unwise to refuse to participate in the hearings. Quigley drafted an ambiguous statement that seemed to indicate that the church had decided not to focus on the question of block-booking for tactical reasons. "The National Legion of Decency has not dealt with the exhibitor, but with the producer. To deal with the former would mean conducting the campaign on 12,000 fronts rather than confining it to one front—the producers." The rest of the declaration trailed off into a tortured discussion of the business and moral aspects of block-booking. Because even Bishop Edward Mooney, the NCWC's chairman, didn't know how to interpret the Episcopal Committee's pronouncement, Daly's testimony at the hearing would be crucial. Quigley persuaded McNicholas to direct Daly to make clear to the congressional committee that the Legion did not want to get involved in the battle over the Pettengill bill. Recognizing that the priest had never testified before, Quigley prepped Daly for the hearings by supplying him with written answers to any questions that might be raised about block-booking.[55]

At first, everything went as planned: Daly read the bishop's statement to the committee. But the priest, when questioned by the congressmen, displayed an unsuspected fondness for hyperbole and gave the committee members the impression that McNicholas intended to function as the "czar of all the motion pictures." But what really incensed Quigley was Daly's bungling of the key question regarding the Legion's position on block-booking. All he had to do was to read the answer prepared by Quigley—"We are not concerned with block-booking as a trade practice. We are against any effort to cure moral problems in pictures by legislation." But Daly blurted out instead that the Legion favored the bill. Quigley was eventually permitted to correct the record, but it was too late to head off an article in the *Hollywood Reporter* recounting Daly's testimony.[56]

While Quigley was still fuming over Daly's congressional performance, the new Legion system experienced its first crisis over one of its ratings. The picture in question was Paramount's *Klondike Annie*, starring Mae West as a woman who flees to Alaska after killing in self-defense the nightclub owner who has held her captive. Aware that his reputation was on the line, Breen had ordered a number of cuts in the script, including several vintage West lines like "men are at their best when women are at their worst." The result, according to Breen, was "a new type of characterization [for West], depending for entertainment less on her wisecracks and more on a legitimate story." Breen's precautions seemed to have paid off. On February 17, 1936, six of the most experienced Legion reviewers saw the film and gave it a B. Aware of the notoriety that a Mae West film always generated and hoping to dissolve any lingering suspicions of the New York Legion the supporters of the old Chicago list might still harbor, Daly arranged a second review two days later. This time five reviewers, including three priests, unanimously confirmed the original B rating, which was then made public.[57]

But Breen had not counted on William Randolph Hearst, whose newspaper chain not only attacked *Klondike Annie* in a series of blistering articles but also refused to advertise it. It was never quite clear why the publisher, who was hardly a paragon of virtue, unleashed the attack. Rumors ranged from a battle over advertising rates to a row between Mae West and Marion Davies, Hearst's mistress. Whatever the cause, the resulting furor threatened to make Hearst appear, if not holier than the pope, at least holier than the Legion. Father Edward Moore, Cardinal Hayes's liaison with the Legion, hurriedly arranged a third review of the film two days after the Hearst attack. This time the reviewers, who included two priests, two physicians, a judge, the dean of Fordham Law School, and a businessman, split, with four voting for a B rating and three recommending condemnation. All seven agreed with Father Moore that any attempt to change the original rating would be impolitic. Apparently prodded by Breen, Father Devlin urged Daly to stand fast. "If you change to C," he told him, "you will never escape the charge that you were influenced by Hearst. If the producers realize the Legion can be stampeded," he warned, "we can never regain their confidence." Daly decided to soft-pedal the matter in the hope that it would blow over. To add to the confusion, two priests chose this moment to write Paramount about how much they liked the film. One thought it was Mae West's "best film yet . . . with a fine plot; excellent dialogue; and delightfully humorous." The other applauded the studio for keeping the picture clean. "As far as I could judge," he wrote, "there was only one remark which the censors might delete."[58]

Recognizing that the Legion could not survive another failure on the heels of the Chicago Legion's disaster, McNicholas decided that the other dioceses had to be made more confident about the New York evaluations. Quigley, who thought the film was "a foul mess from start to finish," persuaded the Legion, against Daly's better judgment, to issue a press release clarifying its views on the picture. The Legion declared that "the appearance of a performer [West was never identified] who . . . has in several instances been associated with plays which have elicited widespread disapproval, creates an apprehension that unless there is renewed vigilance . . . the excellent progress in the improvement of the moral character of films in the past several months may be lost." Noting that since the film had been classified as "objectionable in part," the Legion advised all Catholics to avoid it.[59]

Had the matter stopped there, the publisher might have been willing to give Daly the benefit of the doubt. But when Quigley, whose business relied on the film industry's good will, learned that Daly had told Will Hays that Quigley had pushed for condemnation of the West film, he gave up on the priest. "He is lacking in the kind of intelligence required in this work," Quigley complained to McNicholas, as well as "the necessary prudence." Daly was not only temperamentally unfit for the job, he continued, but he might be about to suffer a nervous breakdown. And when *Harrison's Reports* criticized the Legion for recommending *Robin Hood of El Dorado* as family fare, Quigley insisted that Daly take a second look. The film, which told the story of the bandit Joaquin Murieta's efforts to avenge his wife's murder, was a standard western that included several scenes of men and women drinking and flirting in a saloon. Under pressure from Quigley, the Legion announced that it had reclassified the film as B, a move hardly designed to enhance Daly's self-confidence.[60]

Quigley's behind-the-scenes maneuvering, which was meant to strengthen the Legion's evaluation system, led to another attack on him by Detroit's Arthur Maguire and Father Luther, who suspected a sellout. Never one to let facts get in the way of a diatribe, Luther told a meeting of the Detroit Legion that the industry had set up a $100,000 "slush fund" to bribe Quigley, Daly, and Mary Looram to give *Klondike Annie* and *Robin Hood of El Dorado* B ratings instead of the C they so richly deserved. Once again, to Quigley's dismay, Daly apprised Will Hays of this latest division within the Legion ranks. Although the publisher complained privately to McNicholas that Daly was "hopeless," he tried to explain to the priest that the Legion's greatest asset was Hollywood's belief in the Catholic church's unity and discipline. Daly, who obviously wanted to open up his own lines to the industry, told Quigley that he was within his rights in dealing directly with the Hays Office. Rebuffed, Quigley asked McNicholas to put Daly on a tighter rein or risk ruining the Legion, claiming that the priest would be "putty" in the hands of the "slick operators" in the Hays Office.[61]

What finally did Daly in was his decision to expand the Legion's classification system by awarding a monthly "Golden Seal" to the picture that came closest to its ideals. Quigley thought he had convinced Daly that the Legion should restrict its activities to moral evaluations, but Daly soon began publishing a monthly list of entertainment and artistic evaluations in addition to the Legion's regular classification lists. By the summer of 1936, Quigley was complaining to McNicholas that, although Catholic views on morality were certain "as to their correctness at all times and under all circumstances," artistic judgments lacked "fixed [and] unvarying standards." If Daly continued on his present course, he warned the bishop, the Legion would appear ridiculous. The heart of the problem, according to Quigley, was that Daly's comments did not always correspond to the film's moral classification, so that an A movie might be described as artistically deficient while a B might be judged a dramatic success. *Song of the Saddle*, which had been classified objectionable in part because the film's theme of revenge was "ethically unsound," was pronounced "a good western with fine singing and photography." Similarly, the Legion reviewers classified the French film *Itto* as a B because of its treatment of illegitimacy, but Daly thought it was "very good" artistically. Some wondered if they could ignore the church's recommendation to avoid Bs if a quality film was involved, or was Daly just filling them in on what they were missing?[62]

In some instances, no moral justification explained the Legion's classification. *The Man Who Lived Again* was classified as objectionable in part with the comment: "A horror picture that provides unwholesome entertainment." Similarly, *The Girl from Maxim's* was restricted to adult viewing along with the notation, "A cheap production that has little or no entertainment value." This system is "utterly stupid," Quigley told McNicholas. "It makes no effort to make any sensible estimate of the pictures from the moral viewpoint."

Equally troublesome was what Quigley termed Daly's garbled comments. He pointed out that the only justification for classifying the Scandinavian film *Walpurgis Night* as objectionable in part was the comment, "An unhappy marriage, an operation, a murder and a suicide solving the inevitable triangle provides a rather unsavory plot." What did that mean, asked Quigley, "that the Legion is opposed to any operation or suicide?"[63]

Criticism of some of the Legion's evaluations began to spill over into the trade papers. *Harrison's Reports* pointed out that *Killer at Large* had been recommended for the entire family with the comment: "A jewel robbery, a murder, a sinister looking culprit and a wide-eyed girl detective—a combination of exciting elements that results in a rather dull mystery." Yet *The Country Doctor*, the story of the Dionne quintuplets, was classified as A–II and therefore not recommended for children. The result, Harrison pointed out, was that children could be exposed to murderers and thieves but not to the Dionne quintuplets.[64]

By the summer of 1936, McNicholas was so concerned about the Legion's credibility that he suggested to Quigley that the Episcopal Committee issue its own evaluation of three films to establish the proper criteria for future recommendations. The evaluation would be prepared by Quigley, Monsignor Corrigan, and himself. He asked Quigley to identify two that they could recommend and one that they could strongly condemn. In order to avoid further division within the ranks, the three films would not have been classified by Daly's reviewers. Quigley wrote back that there was no difficulty in locating good films, but the problem was to find an indecent one that had not already been condemned by the Legion. The only one he could think of was *Ecstasy*, a Czechoslovakian movie starring Hedy Lamarr which had been rejected by Breen's office because of a nude swimming scene and a close-up of Lamarr's face as she experienced orgasm. Quigley pointed out that condemning the film would publicize a picture that would ordinarily be limited to the handful of theaters that showed unapproved films. Instead, Quigley modestly proposed that a clear articulation of standards could best be accomplished by a pamphlet he was preparing entitled *How to Judge the Morality of Motion Pictures*. Convinced that the publisher knew best, McNicholas dropped the idea of an evaluation by the Episcopal Committee.[65]

By the fall of 1936, Daly's days were numbered. Quigley, who regularly characterized him as "inexperienced and impulsive," told McNicholas that he was more and more pessimistic about Daly's chances of working out. Daly, in turn, was feeling increasingly depressed and isolated. When he reluctantly bowed to the pressure from McNicholas and agreed to discontinue the comments on the artistic and entertainment values of the films classified by the Legion, he sent along a spirited defense of his actions. McNicholas wrote to

Father Edward Moore in New York that he couldn't work with Daly if he were in his diocese, adding that he had no alternative but to bring the matter up at the next bishops' meeting. Daly was finished. After Cardinal Hayes asked him to vacate his office, Daly resigned on November 2, 1936. With the Legion still dangerously adrift, the need to find a replacement for Daly became a paramount issue for McNicholas and Hayes.[66]

SEVEN

■ ■ ■

Success

Cardinal Patrick Hayes was fortunate when he selected Father John McClafferty to succeed Father Joseph Daly as the Legion's executive secretary in December 1936. After seminary, McClafferty had earned a master's degree in anthropology at Catholic University and a diploma from the New York School of Social Work. At the time of his appointment, he was thirty years old and an assistant director of the Division of Catholic Action at the Catholic Charities of New York. Unlike his predecessor, McClafferty had no media experience, but his work in Catholic Charities had caught the eye of Father Edward Moore, the cardinal's liaison to the Legion. "He has shown stability, good judgement and the willingness to be advised," he told Archbishop McNicholas, "and I feel that he is admirably suited for the post." After his experience with Daly, McNicholas may have viewed McClafferty's willingness to take advice as his most attractive feature. McClafferty's own view was that his experience in social work, with its special emphasis on casework and problem solving, was probably his greatest asset for the job. Bright, articulate, and able to work well with McNicholas's committee, as well as with Quigley,

Breen, and the Hollywood producers, McClafferty helped turn the Legion into a major force in the motion picture business over the next decade.[1]

Support for the Legion varied. In Philadelphia the local organization was active, while Boston's Cardinal O'Connell showed little interest. The steady stream of complaints from local parishioners about the failure of diocesan newspapers to publish the Legion's classifications and about local pastors who neglected to publicize the latest lists suggests that the organization was far from monolithic, as most people thought it was. Within a few years of McClafferty's takeover, communication between his office and the secretaries of the local Legions had largely become routine. In the absence of some specific crisis, the New York office would mail its list and remind its constituents of the need to administer the annual pledge along with suggestions on how to invigorate diocesan organizations.[2]

Because each diocese was autonomous, McClafferty's office had no direct control over the local Legions. He could try to correct diocesan practices that were at odds with national policy, but questions related to accepting advertisements for B films in diocesan newspapers or publishing the Legion's classifications during Lent could be resolved only at the local chancery office. Father Edward Schwegler, for example, waged a battle for several years with the editor of the Buffalo diocese's *Union and Echo* over the latter's willingness to advertise objectionable films. Schwegler reported to his bishop that mothers told him their arguments against attending B pictures fell apart when their children pointed out that the films were listed in the diocesan newspaper. On the other hand, Schwegler felt that the paper's policy of not reprinting the Legion's evaluations during Lent was a waste of time since he couldn't even persuade the "best of our Catholic people" to abstain from films during that period. Noting that *Pinocchio* had been released during the 1940 Lenten season, he argued that the faithful would be better served if they were steered toward superior pictures like the Disney film, rather than being left on their own.[3]

The Legion received a strong endorsement in 1936 when Pope Pius XI issued an encyclical on motion pictures entitled *Vigilanti Cura*, urging Catholics in other countries to form similar organizations. The special praise for the "holy crusade" begun by American Catholics may have been due to Quigley's influence. His son later claimed that the encyclical came from his father's mouth, and McClafferty indicated that at the very least Quigley had supplied the pope with the technical data. Although the Legion campaign had boasted that the Catholic church's fixed ethical standards made it the logical arbiter of film morality, church leaders were wary about establishing a worldwide evaluation system. As the pope noted in *Vigilanti Cura*, "circumstances, usages and forms vary from country to country, so it does not seem practical to have a single list for all the world." The pope also granted the bishops the power to apply stricter ratings than their national reviewing system. Consequently, if a prelate decided that the Legion had erred by awarding a movie a B, he was free to classify it as a C in his diocese.[4]

Nevertheless, a year later the Vatican Secretariat of State asked Archbishop McNicholas if the Legion's list of recommended films could be brought in line with "Italian sensibilities." McNicholas asked Father Moore to look into a list of forty films that had been supplied by Rome. Moore tried to re-rate them from an Italian point of view, but the project was quickly terminated by Cardinal Hayes. Noting that even though the Legion based its evaluations on moral law, which is "the same at all times and places," he also noted that American and Italian mores differed so much that it would be impossible, even with the aid of knowledgeable Italian-Americans, to correctly classify films intended for Italy. Moreover, with so many American pictures being banned by the Mussolini government, any effort to provide Rome with a separate list might also lead Hollywood to scapegoat the Legion for its difficulties.[5]

Although the church continued to present the Legion as a Catholic grassroots movement, its day-to-day operations were all handled by McClafferty and Mary Looram. Looram's years with the IFCA made up for McClafferty's initial lack of film experience, and she assigned reviews to between sixty and one hundred female volunteers. For a two-year period ending in 1936, her committee reviewed and classified 3,740 films, which required 179,520 hours of work. New reviewers had to take a six-month training program that included sitting in on the weekly previews. The course material consisted of two short guidebooks: *How to Judge the Morality of Motion Pictures* by Martin Quigley and *The Morals of the Screen* by *Commonweal*'s dramatic critic, Richard D. Skinner. After a brief introduction to the Production Code and a discussion of the purpose of the Legion of Decency, Quigley presented several examples of films that lowered "traditional morality." Skinner concentrated on demonstrating how the story's theme, plot, and treatment determined a film's moral value.[6]

Reviewers mailed their reports to Looram, who went over them carefully before presenting them to McClafferty. A reviewer who strayed from the Legion guidelines would receive a note in the next mail pointing out where she had gone wrong. When one woman classified a story in which the hero divorces his wife as A–I, Looram noted that it could not be designated suitable for general patronage because the resolution of the story justified divorce and a second marriage. Any serious division over the moral implications of a film was referred to the board of consultors, which McClafferty expanded gradually to include not only priests, physicians, lawyers, and businessmen but also teachers, union leaders, social workers, and theater people.[7]

Despite the fact that the Legion never lost its mistrust of Hollywood, McClafferty developed a successful working relationship with the studios. *Christian Century* claimed that the moviemakers and McClafferty had cut a deal: they would produce nothing that offended the Catholic church as long as the Legion didn't object to monopolistic practices like block-booking. But the church's position on block-booking reflected not so much a quid pro quo as its conviction that it would be easier to wage a single battle in Hollywood than to fight with thousands of individual exhibitors. Consequently, when the National Council of Catholic Women passed a resolution condemning block-booking in 1939, the Legion quietly persuaded the organization to withdraw it. And although the industry would have preferred to see the end of the Legion, its long list of approved pictures proved useful whenever Congress was considering an anti-industry bill. In turn, legislators from heavily Catholic areas like Massachusetts Senator David I. Walsh made it clear that their vote against the Neely anti-block-booking bill hinged on whether the Legion felt that the improved moral tone of the movies made the bill unnecessary.[8]

The Legion's influence was also strengthened by two powerful industry allies, Quigley and Breen, who regularly provided inside information. Although both men were devoted to the church, they were not above using the Legion for their own purposes. Quigley enjoyed being the man to talk to whenever a studio had a problem with the Legion, while Breen knew that enforcing the Code would be much more difficult without the threat of a Catholic boycott in the background. Although Breen worked closely with the Legion during its early years and needed it to keep the producers in line, he resented any second-guessing. Two years into his job, he told *America*'s Father Gerard Donnelly that the Legion had offered him no support and seemed to be waiting for him to make a mistake. But his spirits picked up the next day as he recounted his fights with the producers and the joy of outyelling a Jack Warner or a Sam Goldwyn. Each battle, he told Donnelly, was another chance to do "a real bit of Catholic action [by] regulating the moral thinking of 200 million people."[9]

Breen and the church knew that they needed each other. When Breen became concerned in 1938 that Universal's signing of Danielle Darrieux, who had starred in a French film condemned by the Legion, might signal the beginning of an assault on the Code, he sent Bishop Cantwell a newspaper story and picture of the actress in a sweater and shorts. The bishop dashed off an immediate letter of protest to Will Hays, declaring that he had been under the impression that "the business of undressing in public was a thing of the past." Equally appalling was the news that Darrieux was being paid $100,000 while still learning English and not making any movies, "while millions of our fellow Americans are unemployed." In turn, when the Legion became alarmed by the rumor that Hollywood was considering filming an Upton Sinclair script, all McNicholas had to do was get in touch with Breen, who reassured him that no one was interested in the project.[10]

Meanwhile, Breen's office continued to consolidate its position within the industry. In 1937, the PCA reviewed 2,584 scripts, screened 1,489 films, and rendered 6,477 official opinions. Although tensions often ran high, screenwriter Philip Dunne felt that relations were in no sense adversarial. "After all," he wrote, "they were not the censors. We, the movie makers, had hired them to point out to us the hidden reefs and snags of censorship in various state laws, or the biases of private censorship groups." Similarly, Darryl Zanuck, remembering twenty years of fights with Breen's office, claimed that he had never been prevented from making the type of pictures he wanted to make. Nevertheless, the editing must have tried many a producer's patience. In a *New Yorker* cartoon, as a couple in a movie theater watch "The End" flash over a close-up of the two stars kissing, the woman whispers to her date, "In the book, he kills her."[11]

Although the PCA's alterations were rarely that drastic, the price of screen morality was constant vigilance. Cuts ranged from dropping a sound or a word to rewriting or eliminating a major scene. In its early years, Breen's office erred on the side of caution, cutting anything that might reverse the reforms attained by the Legion's crusade. In *Made for Each Other* (1938), Breen protected the audience's sensibilities by ordering the removal of a belch, a "disgusting, almost obscene sound." The line "hold your hats" also fell on the cutting room floor because it was one of a long list of words or phrases prohibited by the Code, because, according to one of David O. Selznick's assistants, it was the punchline to the first dirty joke Breen ever heard.[12] When the heroine in *Claudia* remarked after receiving a lesson on animal husbandry that "a farm is really a very sexy place," the line had to be eliminated because it suggested an excessive interest in the intimate behavior of the barnyard animals. In response to a shot of Kay Francis milking a cow in *Little Men*, one of Breen's staff told RKO, "At no time should there be any shots of actual milking, and there cannot be any showing of the udders of the cow." The PCA also ordered a long shot of Tom and Huck skinny-dipping in *Tom Sawyer* removed, to the chagrin of David O. Selznick, who grumbled that Mark Twain could hardly be considered "a writer of nude shockers."[13]

The negotiations surrounding Selznick's *Gone with the Wind* illustrate the give and take involved in securing Code approval from the PCA. Breen, who claimed that his office received more unacceptable material from that producer in one year than from any two larger studios, was suspicious of any Selznick script. "He seems to have a weakness," he told Quigley, "for stories of gross illicit sex or cock-eyed marital problems." When the first screenplay for *Gone with the Wind* was submitted, Breen's response on October 14, 1937, consisted of seven pages with fifty specific warnings and suggestions. The protracted negotiations over the next several months included Selznick's battle to keep Rhett Butler's exit line: "Frankly, my dear, I don't give a damn." Anticipating a clash, Selznick had his staff check several magazines, which indicated that even the *Ladies' Home Journal* employed the word "damn" on occasion. Further research uncovered that in a Warner Brothers' short, *The Man Without a Country*, Philip Nolan exclaimed, "I don't give a damn for the United States." Nevertheless, Breen remained adamant, and the Selznick company filed an appeal with the MPPDA's board of directors. Selznick filmed an alternate line for Rhett in case the petition failed. After a two-hour meeting, Will Hays finally agreed to allow Selznick to use "damn," and Rhett was saved from exiting with "Frankly, my dear, I just—don't—care." One of the few who did care, in addition to Breen, was Martin Quigley, who felt that the Hays decision "meant that damage will be done and ground lost after all the tedious and costly efforts of the industry to keep itself in line with American mores."[14]

Another major sticking point was a scene in which the wounded Ashley Wilkes was secretly brought to the parlor of Belle Watling's brothel for medical attention. At first, Breen insisted that the entire episode had to be moved to a more acceptable location. Told by a Selznick assistant that brothels were a reality, he retorted that although he went to the bathroom every morning and didn't deny that such a place existed, he didn't feel it belonged on the screen. As far as he was concerned, the same held true for brothels. Nevertheless, he acquiesced to using Belle's parlor if Selznick promised not to show anything that would "make the profession seem pleasant or exciting," thereby stirring "the lustful emotions of the young."[15]

There was seemingly no end to Selznick's frustrations. The Code prohibited only scenes of actual childbirth, but Breen was uncomfortable about anything that touched on the subject. Always fearful that any hint of discomfort connected to the birth process might dissuade some women from embracing motherhood, Breen insisted that shots of Melanie Wilkes gripping a towel, wincing in pain, and perspiring had to be eliminated. He finally grudgingly allowed Selznick to show a few beads of perspiration on her face and shoot the scene in silhouette.[16]

Much lengthier discussions revolved around how to handle what became known as the "morning-after sequence." After Rhett forcibly carries Scarlett up the stairs, the camera fades out in the traditional Hollywood method for suggesting sexual intimacy. The next shot showed Scarlett still in bed on the following morning, obviously pleased that Rhett had his way with her. Breen objected strongly to Scarlett's "figuratively licking her chops" after having been raped by her husband. Val Lewton, Selznick's contact with the PCA, tried to finesse the problem by assuring Breen that it had been resolved and then showing him the same scene in the hope that he had forgotten what he had originally objected to. Although the stratagem worked with Breen, one of his assistants pointed out the hoax, and the episode was eventually shortened to show less postcoital pleasure. Nevertheless, after the PCA had approved the film, Breen promised Selznick that he would go anywhere in the country to fight the cuts of any local censors.[17]

Breen's office was only the first hurdle a producer had to overcome. The Legion carefully scrutinized every Hollywood release, whether it was a blockbuster like *Gone with the Wind* or a low-budget western. Ironically, Archbishop McNicholas had originally opposed the idea of the Legion's previewing films before release because this would inevitably lead the studios to ask what had to be changed in order to secure a better classification. McNicholas's opposition to negotiating with the studios stemmed from a combination of fear that the producers would get the better of every deal and the hope that public opinion alone would reform the industry.[18]

In the early years of the Legion, the hierarchy also clung to the hope that Catholics might somehow transform movies by becoming the directors and screenwriters of tomorrow. In notes prepared for Bishop Cantwell, Breen suggested an annual award for the best Catholic screenplay, to encourage a "Legion of scriveners." It is important, he told the bishop, "that stories be written by men and women whose instincts are decent and whose thinking is sound." Cantwell thought this was a wonderful idea since, as he told Bishop McNicholas, currently this work was "largely in the hands of Jews and people without any faith." As a result, he declared, Catholic interests suffered in films like *The Crusades*, in which Saladin, instead of the Christians, was the hero. Responding to the challenge, several Catholic colleges considered launching courses in screenwriting in 1936. In the same year, *America* summoned its readers to compete with the "heretics, pagans and infidels" who were making movies. Instead of the usual sex and violence, the magazine maintained that "priests and nuns . . . Catholic husbands and wives . . . altar boys and first communion girls" would provide "sure-fire dramatic material. A Catholic wedding, with a white veiled bride," the writer rhapsodized, "is intensely more dramatic than a ten minute marriage before a Justice of the Peace, wearing a sign-on-the-dotted-line look, chewing a cigar, and surveying a shot-gun in the corner."[19]

But the market for films about altar boys and first communion girls was obviously limited. The Legion's ability to influence filmmaking rested on the studios' fear that negative ratings could hurt them at the box office. Negotiating with producers became an essential part of the Legion's work after the shift to New York, where its reviewers could preview a film before its release. As Moore explained to McNicholas, "We frequently find the producers willing to eliminate . . . a few objectionable lines or a shot or two, that may constitute the reason why a picture, otherwise unobjectionable, would have to be placed in a lower classification." Although a few of the clergy occasionally grumbled about dealing with the devil, a later Legion secretary, Father Patrick Masterson, claimed that without the power to negotiate, the Legion would have become ineffective "because we would have such a large number of C's that it would be meaningless."[20]

Despite the Legion's assertion that it was simply advising Catholics on what films they should avoid, the result was a national classification system that affected what all Americans saw and didn't see on the screen. The required cuts were usually not extensive: a few lines here, a little less cleavage there, and a clear sign that the sinner had been punished usually satisfied the Legion. The real measure of its power was the number of topics and scenes that were never filmed in order to avoid problems with the church. All this naturally raised the question of Catholic control. "What the non-Catholic moviegoers are entitled to decide," declared the *Nation*, "is whether they wish to have their films censored in advance by the Catholic church." Censorship was a sensitive point, and church leaders always rejected the charge. Asserting that only a government body had the power to censor, they argued that they had merely established a consumers' research bureau for Catholics. If producers voluntarily changed their films to earn a better rating, that was their business. Far from stifling people's rights, as Father Masterson put it, the Legion had been formed because the freedom of the screen was imperiled. "Freedom," he declared, "respects the rights of others, among them, the Deity; while license, in abusing freedom's rights, tramples upon the feelings and sentiments of others."[21]

Whether or not it was an agency of censorship, even the Legion's supporters would admit that it was the most powerful pressure group in the film business, relying on the studios' dread of a nationwide Catholic boycott of objectionable films. A study by Robert Janes in 1939 found a significant drop in attendance when condemned films were shown in heavily Catholic neighborhoods in Chicago, but that was in the early years of the Legion campaign, when enthusiasm was at a high point. Whether a critical mass of Catholics would have boycotted the industry over a sustained period of time if Hollywood had chosen to ignore the Legion was never tested. Cardinal Dougherty's experience in Philadelphia suggests that the laity was not as dutiful as Hollywood feared.[22]

Nevertheless, during the first twenty years of the Legion, fear seemed to be the operative word to describe the producers' attitude. The PCA's Geoff Shurlock claimed that Hollywood was so afraid of "the Catholics . . . that there was no room left to be scared of anyone else." The *Literary Digest* agreed, observing, "What scared the movie makers as they had never been scared before was that the Catholic Church, like the American film, is universal [and] the Catholic bishops can make shots which will be heard around the world." While the Legion was in no position to launch a world crusade against the movies, it could inflict a good deal of damage in urban centers. A third of all movie seats in the early 1940s were located in the forty-nine cities with populations greater than 200,000, and most of these were heavily Catholic.[23]

Considering the alternatives, the Legion may not have seemed so bad to some people in the industry. Shurlock pointed out that the bishops began their crusade with a classification system, indicating that there were some pictures they could approve. Many Protestant reformers, he claimed, gave the impression that they didn't like any movies and considered them essentially evil. Legion leaders, on the other hand, had a fondness for films, albeit their kind of films. As Mary Looram put it, "Years of reviewing have not dampened our enthusiasm. . . . We are great movie fans." The industry could also draw some comfort from the Legion's willingness to compromise. Recognizing the costs of reshooting an entire scene, McClafferty often settled for the elimination or replacement of a line or two in order to grant a film a higher rating. The most important evidence that Hollywood could live with the Legion was that weekly attendance rose 9 million to 88 million in 1936, and *Variety* reported that virtually every picture showed handsome profits during the year. Later, the Legion's defenders would never tire of pointing out that Hollywood's "golden years" coincided with the period during which the Legion was at the height of its power. The relation between the Legion and Hollywood was at its best in the three years following the Legion's move to New York. In August 1938, both McNicholas and McClafferty noted that the moral quality of films had improved as a result of the producers' willingness to abide by the Code. Only 32 of 535 films reviewed by the Legion in 1938 were classified as B (morally objectionable in part), and no PCA-approved film was condemned.[24]

The Legion's only difficulty with Hollywood during this period involved the signing of Gypsy Rose Lee to a film contract. The crisis began with an announcement in early 1937 that the burlesque queen would star in Twentieth Century-Fox's *You Can't Have Everything.* Although state legislators periodically filed bills to ban pictures featuring actors and actresses who were divorced or in their eyes led "immoral" lives, the Legion had always judged a film on its merits. And despite the occasional controversy surrounding some star's lifestyle, there was no public support for such legislation. When the *San Francisco News* learned of a proposed bill to prohibit any film that featured divorced stars, it predicted that the bill's passage would limit screen roles to two actors, one actress, plus twelve-year-old Jackie Cooper and Baby LeRoy. Nevertheless, the Legion interpreted the signing of Gypsy Rose Lee as an indication that Fox was trying to groom a new Mae West. Carl Milliken, who had a long relationship with the IFCA, met with Father Edward Moore and Mary Looram, but he indicated that since there were no rules covering the situation, there was little Hays could do. As for Milliken's claim that the actress had participated in only one or two unsavory productions in the past, Moore pointed out that she was "widely . . . and only known as an exemplar of what has most unfortunately become highly publicized under the degrading appellation of the strip tease act." With Joe Breen's secret encouragement, Moore coordinated a letter campaign from Catholic organizations and laypersons, including Al Smith. Joe Schenck, the chairman of Fox's board, claimed that his studio had no intention of exploiting Lee's sensational background and that the decision to award her a contract had been based entirely on her successful screen test. Furthermore, he reminded the Legion, if its efforts to bar her from the screen succeeded, she would be forced to return to burlesque to earn a living.[25]

Hoping to head off an embarrassing confrontation between Fox and the Legion, Will Hays convinced the studio to bill Lee under her birth name, Louise Hovick, to eliminate any suggestion of exploiting her previous career. At Hays's request and backed by Breen's promise to monitor Lee's films carefully, Quigley told McNicholas that there was nothing to be gained by prolonging the protest. As he pointed out, any concerted effort by the industry to keep Lee out could be construed as a criminal conspiracy to prevent her from obtaining employment. With a new name and with no references to her previous work, he concluded, she would be presented to the public as a new performer. From McNicholas's point of view, this was the best of a bad bargain. The advantage evaporated when *Look* and other magazines featured stories about how Gypsy Rose Lee had changed her name to break into the movies.[26]

Much more troublesome were two independently produced films, *Damaged Goods* and *The Birth of a Baby*, in 1938. Breen had rejected *Damaged Goods*, a serious effort to deal with the problem of venereal disease, because the topic was specifically proscribed by the Code. Convinced that this was not the typical exploitation film, the studio sent it to the Legion for approval. Mary Looram commended the filmmakers for handling a difficult subject well and told them she hoped that young adults would see the film. When the Legion's board of consultors raised several easily correctable objections, the distributor was convinced that the film would be classified as A-II. However, the revised film was reviewed by a different group, which argued that passing it would invite other studios to make similar movies. Convinced that he had no choice, McClafferty condemned it as unsuitable for theatrical distribution.[27]

Damaged Goods demonstrated that even a responsible producer could not persuade the Catholic church to reassess its opposition to the use of the movies for sex education. Speaking for the Episcopal Committee, McNicholas declared that the movie theater was neither a clinic nor a doctor's consulting room and urged that sex education be left in the hands of parents. Quigley presented the church's argument more graphically in an editorial in the *Motion Picture Herald*. According to the publisher, offering such a film to the public was comparable to inviting someone to dinner by asking him to "come over and we'll have a lovely time talking of . . . syphilis and gonorrhea."[28]

The condemnation of *Damaged Goods* presented no real problem for the Legion because there was little support for such films in the larger society. A much more difficult decision involved *The Birth of a Baby*, an educational documentary put together by the American Committee for Maternal Welfare and supported by the American Hospital Association, the U.S. Public Health Service, the American Medical Association, the American Association of Obstetricians and Gynecologists, and several state medical societies. Made with the help of five eminent obstetricians and the Cornell University Medical School, the film traced the story of a young woman from the moment she realizes she is pregnant through the actual delivery—a scene that included a brief view of the infant's emerging head. Using the expectant mother's discussions with her doctor, which were accompanied by diagrams, it informed the audience about proper health care, diet, and exercise during pregnancy.

This production could not receive a PCA seal (its passport into the major theaters) because the Code specifically prohibited scenes of childbirth. The filmmakers' only hope of reaching a wider audience was to show it in the independent movie houses. Before that could happen, the film would have to be approved by the relevant local and state censorship boards, which usually frowned on such pictures. Since its creation in 1921, the New York board of censors had consistently rejected any scene showing "a woman in her travail"; it refused to certify *Motherhood* (1926) because the subject was "too sacred to be cheapened in this fashion." Few were surprised when the board denied a permit to *The Birth of a Baby* on July 14, 1937. The producers' appeal was turned down by Frank Graves, the state commissioner of education, who claimed that the film was "indecent, immoral and would tend to corrupt morals." The issue heated up when *Life* published three pages of stills from the movie. A leader of New York state's Knights of Columbus demanded that the magazine recall the issue in the name of human decency. When the publishers refused, the *Life* issue was banned in Pennsylvania and in cities including Boston, Chicago, St. Louis, New Orleans, and Richmond, Virginia.[29]

The National Board of Review and the *New York Times* attacked the New York censors' decision. Citing the country's appalling infant and maternal mortality rates, they both recommended the film strongly. In response the Catholic press launched a campaign spearheaded by *America*, which asked why moviemakers intent on improving public health always concentrated on sexual problems instead of turning out pictures on heart disease and tuberculosis. Monsignor P. M. H. Wynhoven took a separate tack, raising the issue of privacy. Why did doctors order the father-to-be to stand outside the maternity room during the birth of his child, while utter strangers in the movie audience were free to "ogle" the entire birth process? Ignoring the medical credentials of the filmmakers, the *Brooklyn Tablet* lumped them in with common pornographers. Just as termites secretly eat away at a house's foundation, it declared, the "filmites" with their "poison pictures" quietly destroy one's mind. Much of the criticism suggested that the film's opponents either had not seen it or, if they had, saw things nobody else detected. In a fiery speech before his state censorship board, the mayor of Richmond, Virginia, charged that seeing this picture in a theater would "make the minds of the young boys . . . dwell on sex." New Orleans Bishop Joseph F. Rummel claimed that even mature people could be "stimulated in an unwholesome moral way" by the film. The idea that a documentary on childbirth could somehow be titillating appalled the *New Republic*, which noted that the film was "no more an incentive to lust than a plate of lamb kidneys or a motor-car accident." The film's supporters must have derived some satisfaction from the decision of the Virginia Circuit Court, which overturned the state ban. Speaking for the court, the judge declared: "If his mind tends toward obscenity or indecency, he may see it, but if his mind is not so bent he will see something that is educational and wonderful."[30]

Neither Father McClafferty nor Mary Looram found anything wonderful about the film. Both commended the New York censors for keeping from the screen a "subject which all decent minded people regard as sacred, private and personal" and which would be a "threat to public morality." Through the Legion's opposition to any realistic presentation of childbirth on the screen ran the ingrained belief that these films could stimulate an interest in family planning. Dr. Ignatius Byrne reflected the church's position when he charged in the *Brooklyn Tablet* that films like *The Birth of a Baby* traumatized young women, leading them to postpone marriage, thus playing into the hands of the "birth controlists." Claiming that young people were discussing things "that would bring a blush to the cheeks of their mothers," the doctor called for an end to this newfangled fad of talking about sex.[31]

Some states, however, allowed the film to be shown, and this presented the Legion with a dilemma. McClafferty initially favored condemning it along with an explanation of the Legion's action, but he recognized that it would be difficult to defend his decision because there was nothing fundamentally immoral about the film. A priest on the Legion board of consultors offered McClafferty a way out. He admitted in his review not only that was the film educationally valuable but that the subject was handled with "the utmost reverence and delicacy." Nevertheless, he maintained, it would constitute a "moral menace" if shown in theaters. "The young and the evil-minded" would be attracted to it, he argued, out of some expectation that it would be sexually gratifying. What he seemed to be saying was that there was nothing intrinsically wrong with the film; the moral danger lay in the mind of the beholder. The problem with condemning such a film as immoral, he concluded, was that it could expose the Legion to a bitter, and possibly justified attack. The only way out, he said, was to develop a new category—a special classification—for films that did not fit into the regular rating system.[32]

McClafferty hailed the special classification as the perfect device to deal with films that, while not morally offensive, required some explanation to guard against "wrong interpretations or false conclusions." Announcing the Legion's decision to place *The Birth of a Baby* in this new category, McClafferty declared that while "intrinsically . . . moral in theme" and "medically and educationally meritorious," it was not suited to general exhibition "where audiences [were] composed of both sexes and various ages, backgrounds, mentalities and temperaments." Although the separate classification saved the Legion from having to justify a condemnation, most Catholics tended to interpret it as another form of censure. An officer in the Saginaw, Michigan, Saint Vincent de Paul Society happily reported to McClafferty that his threat to file a petition to have *The Birth of a Baby* banned in his city persuaded the Detroit distributor not to show it there.[33]

The specter of Communism colored the church's view about the tragic events unfolding in Spain. The Legion applied the separate classification a second time in 1938 when Walter Wanger released *Blockade*, a tale inspired by the Spanish civil war. The American Catholic hierarchy's support of Franco was virtually unanimous. Among the Catholic press, only the pacifist *Catholic Worker* and *Commonweal* raised questions about the church's position, a stance that McNicholas equated with "turning against Christ." The success of the Communist Popular Front, which enjoyed some liberal support in the mid-1930s, was especially alarming, and the bishops voted at their annual meeting in 1936 to study Communism in the United States in order to formulate a plan for checking its growth. Although Quigley had always couched his public objection to political films in terms of their negative effect on the box office, he warned McNicholas after the meeting that the church now faced a problem as grave as the screen immorality that had originally confronted the Legion: the increased Communist effort to use the movies to realize its goals. Three years later, he claimed that the Communist threat had reached such proportions that the war against "Red propaganda would make the battle for decency seem a skirmish."[34]

Ironically, during the "Red scare" after World War I there had been considerable discussion of using the screen to defeat Bolshevism. Frank Irwin, chair of the National Association of the Motion Picture Industry's executive committee, claimed that if he had been allowed to bolster the Russian army's morale during the war by showing them some films, Lenin would never have been successful. Too late to put his proposition to the test, industry leaders discussed employing "the power of the Motion-Picture screen to spread anti-Red teachings all over the country." NAMPI's Americanism Committee did produce a two-reel anti-Bolshevik film, *Land of Opportunity*, in 1920, but dropped any further projects as the fear of the Bolshevik threat declined.[35]

In the summer of 1936, an alarmed Joe Breen reported that he had detected signs of a concerted effort to inject Communist propaganda into screen stories. Asserting that the American people would not accept any open teaching of Marxism, he predicted that the Hollywood Communists, who he claimed were largely Jewish, would use a more subtle approach. Starting slowly with films vilifying Franco and dealing with world peace, the Communists would dominate the screen unless they were stopped right away. In his letter of resignation, Father Daly had also warned against the growing influence of Communists in Hollywood, pointing out that they had even "slipped a few things by Joe [Breen]" in RKO's version of Maxwell Anderson's *Winterset*, a story inspired by the Sacco and Vanzetti case.[36]

Beginning in March 1938, McClafferty sent a series of lengthy reports to McNicholas summarizing what he claimed was evidence that the Communists were succeeding in their effort to take over Hollywood. The growing number of "leftist leaning" screenwriters included Clifford Odets, John Howard Lawson, and William Dieterle. Even the *Daily Worker*'s decision to publish its own list of the year's best films could be interpreted as one more step in the party's plan to take over the film industry. Equally worrisome, in McClafferty's estimation, was the success of social-message films such as *Dead End*, about slum kids on New York's East Side. It was not simply that pictures dealing with such social problems as poor housing, injustice, and unemployment were on the increase; the Legion head feared that the screenwriters might start offering answers to these problems. "We should not be too surprised to find that . . . these solutions . . . may be not only un-Christian but anti-Christian."[37]

The hierarchy's preoccupation with Communism in the late 1930s led it to minimize the threat of Nazism. As Father Parsons noted, the church opposed the Nazis for political and economic reasons, because they were undemocratic, but it opposed Communism in the name of God. At times, it seemed to treat fascism as a necessary evil that would stop Moscow. Monsignor Fulton J. Sheen explained his support of Franco when he declared: "We cannot breed rats in abundance without being obliged to use rat poison, and so neither can we breed Communists without being obliged to use the poison of fascism."[38]

The film industry remained silent about Hitler until six months before the war, when Warner released *Confessions of a Nazi Spy* in 1939, the first Hollywood film to detail the German threat to America. Karl Lischka of Breen's staff had tried to hold up production, asserting that it was unfair to represent Hitler as "a screaming madman and a bloodthirsty persecutor" in view of his "unchallenged political and social achievements." Although Breen passed the film on the ground that it was based on an actual spy case, McClafferty dismissed it as another example of Communist propaganda. He also complained to McNicholas about the "discourteous" treatment afforded the German director Leni Riefenstahl on her 1938 trip to Hollywood just after Kristallnacht was reported in the American press.[39]

McClafferty was not the only one to suspect Hollywood of leaning to the left. Calling on its members to help the Legion fight subversive activities, the IFCA *Quarterly Bulletin* asked, "Have you ever noticed in motion pictures the present tendency to deplore Hitlerism and all its concomitant atrocities, and to gloss over or even to make light of the work of Stalin?" A month before Pearl Harbor, *America* was still complaining about Hollywood's unfairness. According to a piece in the magazine by John Twoomey, if the studios were more even-handed, Americans might see on their local marquees films like *Confessions of a Communist Spy*, *I Married a Bolshevik*, *Mad Man of Moscow*, and *Night Train from Moscow*. Apparently if it had been left up to Twoomey, Charlie Chaplin would have starred in *The Great Dictator, Stalin*. *America* suggested bitterly that the Legion might have to add a new classification, "class struggle," in order to identify some of Hollywood's latest films properly. While not willing to go that far, the Legion decided that it would no longer classify Russian-made films because their propagandistic content precluded any rating other than C, a classification that would only publicize them.[40]

Consequently, when United Artists released Walter Wanger's *Blockade* in 1938, it touched off a fire storm in Catholic circles. Joe Breen provided some of the fuel by secretly providing McClafferty with an early version of the script. The fact that the film was written by John Howard Lawson and directed by William Dieterle, both of whom had previously been identified by McClafferty as leading Hollywood leftists, was even more frightening to the Legion.[41]

Breen had done his best to depoliticize *Blockade*, approving the script on the condition that nothing—uniforms, flags, locations, or even songs—connect the story to either side in the Spanish civil war. The film starred Henry Fonda as a peasant driven off his land by an invading force. He becomes an officer in the nameless army of volunteers fighting an unidentified foe and meets a spy for the opposition played by Madeleine Carroll. Disillusioned by the horrors of an aerial bombing, she joins forces with him to help bring a supply ship into the harbor to feed the victims of the war. At the close of the film, Fonda's character looks into the camera and expresses his hatred for the modern brand of combat that inflicts so much pain on noncombatants. "It's not war," he exclaims. "War is between soldiers. This is murder. We've got to stop it. Stop the murder of innocent people. The world can stop it. Where's the conscience of the world?"[42]

In spite of Breen's precautions, and as *Life* magazine noted, anyone who read the newspapers "will see in *Blockade* a stern indictment of General Franco's war, a passionate polemic for the humble Spaniards fighting for Republican Spain." News that a special private showing of the film had been arranged for members of Congress shocked McClafferty. He rushed to Cincinnati to discuss the problem with McNicholas, who authorized him to meet with Will Hays to explore what could be done. Hays told the priest that he, too, was worried, explaining that he had always kept in mind the words of Pope Pius XI, who, in a private audience, had emphasized his responsibility to exclude Communist propaganda from the screen. He claimed that the pope had shown him a communication from Stalin to Communist party leaders throughout the world directing them to take control of the film industry wherever they could. Although Hays said he believed that Breen had made a mistake in giving a Production Code seal to *Blockade*, he thought it would be an even greater mistake for the Legion to try to stop it at this point. The best he could offer was to have his office monitor the advertising to prevent references to the current situation like "Come learn the truth about Spain." With the aid of Quigley, McClafferty got Radio City Music Hall to postpone the opening of the film for a week until June 16.[43]

Meanwhile, Quigley met with Walter Wanger, who not only denied any intention to engage in political propaganda but said he was willing to satisfy any reasonable objections the church might have. Wanger agreed to add a foreword to the film written by Quigley, which read: "This story of love and adventure is not intended to treat with or take sides in the conflict of ideas involved in the present Spanish crisis." The Legion's board of consultors felt that Quigley's introduction had failed to counter the Communist propaganda in the picture, but they found themselves in a bind. A condemnation would be seen as based on political factors rather than the moral values the Legion had been formed to defend, while any higher rating could be construed as support for the anti-Franco forces. The consultors finally agreed to McClafferty's suggestion that the film be classified in the special category with the notation: "Many people will regard this picture as containing foreign political propaganda in favor of one side in the present unfortunate struggle in Spain."[44]

The Legion's classification did not prevent Catholic organizations from protesting the film. The more vitriolic Catholic attacks on *Blockade* made it seem as if Walter Wanger had set out to destroy the church single-handedly. One writer blamed Hollywood not only for taking sides in the Spanish civil war but for the war itself. The root cause of the strife, he declared, could be traced back to films like Cecil B. deMille's *Crusades*, which treated the Christian leader as a scoundrel and Saladin as the hero. Apparently emboldened by the film's anti-Christian message, the writer claimed the Communists had butchered thousands of priests in Spain. Father Joseph Luther threatened to obtain an injunction against any Detroit theater that showed the film. If that didn't work, he promised to call down the wrath of God on the film's supporters. The *Brooklyn Tablet* urged a boycott of United Artists and Radio City Music Hall for bringing this "Red fabrication" to the public. Local Knights of Columbus chapters and Catholic Youth Organizations protested the film and set up picket lines in several cities. According to Quigley, demonstrations in New York led to a sharp drop in the first week's receipts at Radio City Music Hall. Although attendance was down in a number of cities, the biggest blow came on the West Coast, where the Fox chain refused to book the film as a regular second-run release. Claiming to have heard from a number of priests asking what all the shouting was about, Breen complained that the Catholic campaign against the film was unfair. Nevertheless, he moved quickly to block the next Wanger project, which was based on Vincent Sheehan's bestseller *Personal History*, the story of an idealistic reporter who, while covering the Spanish civil war, discovers the evils of fascism and the anti-Semitism of the Nazi government. Although Breen felt that the script, written by John Howard Lawson, a co-author of *Blockade* and later one of the Hollywood Ten, did not violate the Code, he warned Wanger that it was bound to cause trouble. Concluding that he had had enough problems with *Blockade*, Wanger quietly shelved the project.[45]

In spite of all this, the Legion continued to be plagued by political films which, although morally acceptable, were deemed inimical to Catholic interests or beliefs. Although the church's action on *Blockade* had frightened Hollywood, its victory was not without cost. Several religious organizations scored the Legion for using its power to block socially significant films; *Box Office* charged that if the Legion had its way, it would be impossible to make any films about the fascist persecution in Spain and China.[46]

Always sensitive to the charge of censorship, McClafferty occasionally approved a film that he felt Catholics would have been better off avoiding. Warner's 1939 production of *Juarez*, which dealt with the Mexican hero's overthrow of Maximilian von Hapsburg, who had been put on the throne by Napoleon III, was the type of film that worried him. Based on Bertita Harding's novel *The Phantom Crown*, which focused on the doomed love affair between Maximilian and his wife, Carlotta, the screenwriters decided to play up the political implications of the story in hope that film audiences would see a parallel between France's nineteenth-century annexation of Mexico and Hitler's designs on Europe. Hearing about Warner's intention to film the story, Father P. J. Dooley of Webster Groves, Missouri, warned the studio that Catholics considered Juarez one of the "arch-villains of history." According to Dooley, the communistic anti-Catholic policy of the present Mexican government was merely a re-enactment of the program begun by Juarez. Hoping for some help, Warner sent the script to Father José Conseco, who urged them to drop the project entirely because Juarez could never be presented as anything "but a hero of anti-clericalism and banditry, religious hatred and Masonic intrigue." Warner had no intention of jeopardizing its heavy investment in the film. Nevertheless, the studio eliminated any hint of Juarez's opposition to the church, even giving it a Catholic touch by adding shots of Carlotta praying at the shrine of the Virgin of Guadalupe and Juarez paying his last respects at the bier of Maximilian in a chapel.[47]

Although Conseco was pleasantly surprised by the results, McClafferty was disturbed by a film that presented a "dishonest and distorted . . . attempt to make a democrat out of a notorious autocrat and persecutor of the church." Although he admitted that there were no violations of decency or morality "as ordinarily understood," he felt that films like *Juarez* embodied "subtle pleas and sympathy for ideas which ultimately would subvert the fundamentals of the Christian philosophy and way of life." Hoping to avoid controversy about what most considered an innocent Hollywood biography, the Legion granted it an A–I rating along with the notation that the "reviewers requested that attention be directed to the fact that Juarez is not to be considered as uniformly reliable in its historical references." Yet David Gordon, who wrote a column for the *Catholic Virginian*, claimed that McClafferty privately agreed with him that *Juarez* was an insult to the church and attacked the film's hero as "a bloodthirsty atheist . . . who hates priests with the hatred of an animalized madman." With a Marxist director and stars like the "radical Paul Muni" and the "red-trained John Garfield," the film, for Gordon, was part of a Communist plot to destroy the church. An enraged Harry Warner wrote to Gordon's bishop, the Reverend Peter Ireton, that William Dieterle, Muni, and Garfield were thinking of suing his paper. Trying to contain the controversy, McNicholas asked McClafferty and Quigley to persuade Gordon to back off, but they failed. Gordon seemed to be, Quigley told a Warner executive after the meeting, "a person . . . of psychopathic tendencies, a small, nervous highly excitable person cocksure in his opinions." Fortunately, McNicholas was finally able to prevail upon Bishop Ireton to muzzle Gordon, and the affair quickly blew over.[48]

Concerned about a political trend in pictures like *Blockade* and *Juarez*, McClafferty talked the problem over with Quigley, who recommended a separate committee to deal with such films in the future. The priest told McNicholas that although the Communists had not given up their efforts to use the screen for propaganda, it would be inadvisable and dangerous for the Legion to lead the struggle against them. Instead, he urged the bishops to set up an independent organization to be called the Catholic Institute of Film Analysis, in which about fifteen members carefully trained in philosophy, history, and current events would evaluate propaganda films in terms of Christian principles of theology and philosophy. But the bishops, who sometimes felt that the movie business was already taking up too much of their time, turned him down. By that time McClafferty found himself engaged in a new test of wills with Hollywood.[49]

EIGHT

The End of the Honeymoon

The honeymoon that followed the Legion's move to New York ended in the late 1930s as the producers started to chafe under the restraints of the Production Code. One sign of the Legion's dissatisfaction was a doubling of the proportion of B films, from 6 percent in 1938 to 11.5 percent by the end of 1941. But the real measure could be found in the Legion's decision for the first time to condemn a film made by a member of the MPPDA. Four films received C ratings between 1939 and 1941: *Yes My Darling Daughter*, *Strange Cargo*, *This Thing Called Love*, and *Two-Faced Woman*. The *Pittsburgh Catholic* warned its readers on August 14, 1940, that now "more than any time since the Legion of Decency was established . . . it is necessary to consult its ratings."[1]

The Legion was not alone in detecting the studios' attempt to spice up their scripts. Of course, Hollywood had learned long ago that it couldn't please all the people all the time. One Buffalo juvenile court judge even found fault with *Boys' Town*, claiming that two boys who came before him had been so impressed with the movie that they had committed a crime in the hope that they would be sent to join Father Flanagan in Omaha. But some responsible film critics supported the Legion's contention that the PCA had eased up on enforcing the Code. The *New York Times'* Bosley Crowther felt that the Hays Office had given the green light to "a lot of frisky business which would have been pulled up short a couple of years ago." Symptomatic of Hollywood's friskiness was an exchange between Ann Sheridan's character and a truck driver who expressed a willingness to finance her "classy chassis" in *They Drive by Night* (1940). Radio commentator Jimmy Fidler warned, "Unless the Hays Office wakes up and does something to stop the imminent cycle of 'naughty' pictures, the net result . . . will give Hollywood its worst headache in years."[2]

Not everyone agreed. The *New York Daily News'* John Chapman conceded that some "naughty stuff" was creeping in, but rather than "old style dirt" it was genuinely witty material. Noting that movies had never before been so much fun, *Mademoiselle* cautioned its readers not to awaken the "moral cops" who would take the screen back two generations. Film columnist Hedda Hopper felt that the industry should loosen the reins even more. "Every now and then it dawns on some old-timer," she said, "that the reason the screen has lost its zip is that it has been practically de-sexed." Much of the blame, she maintained, could be placed at the door of the Legion; if "it ever succeeded in making the pictures 99 percent pure, they'll be classed with knitting and crocheting as far as entertainment value goes."[3]

The producers had been willing to go along with a stricter enforcement of the Code so long as it didn't hurt them at the box office. But the average weekly attendance, which had jumped from 70 million in 1934 to 88 million in 1936, had dropped to 80 million by 1940. Moreover, there was growing concern about the effect the war in Europe would have on overseas markets, which had supplied the American movie industry with about one-third of its revenue for many years. Late in 1939, England restricted currency exports, cutting American film earnings in half. A year later Nazi victories closed off most of the continental European market to American movies.[4]

David O. Selznick was one producer who felt that Joe Breen didn't understand that times had changed. In 1938, he had purchased the rights to Daphne du Maurier's best-seller *Rebecca*, the story of a shy young woman who marries debonair Maxim de Winter, a recent widower. At Manderley, his palatial estate, she is constantly haunted by the ghost of the beautiful Rebecca, the first Mrs. de Winter. When Rebecca's body washes ashore, Maxim confesses to her that he really hated his first wife and after killing her had opened the sea cocks in her boat and cast it adrift in the bay. Breen had balked at several elements in the script, which followed the novel closely. The major sticking point was Maxim's murder of his wife, which she had provoked because she had just found out she had terminal cancer. But an unpunished murder was unacceptable under the Code, so Breen suggested to Selznick that her death should be attributed to some sort of accident. As Selznick complained to his friend Jock Whitney: "*Rebecca* is the story of a man who has murdered his wife, and it now becomes the story of a man who buried a wife who was killed accidentally!" Selznick, who toyed with the idea of taking the Hays Office to court, claimed that he would become a hero in Hollywood for leading the fight against "so insane and inane and outmoded a Code as that under which the industry is now struggling." According to Selznick, "the whole damned Code" had become doubly onerous with the collapse of the foreign market. Faced with declining revenues, Hollywood needed the freedom book publishers and stage producers had in order to survive.[5]

Rebecca's box-office success, followed by the Academy Award for best picture, eventually calmed Selznick. But not every producer had a surefire bestseller to work with, so to boost ticket sales they added a bit of racy dialogue here and a few double entendres there. This convinced Father John McClafferty that the studios were testing the waters to see how far the Legion would bend the Code. In the fall of 1940 Will Hays conferred with the studio heads about the Legion's growing concern that off-color material was making a comeback. Martin Quigley, who seemed to take a perverse delight in needling Breen, attributed part of the problem to poor staffing at the PCA. Breen, who naturally resented the implication that his office was at fault, argued that the call for a renewed crackdown stemmed in part from a desire to protect the young men who were leaving home for the first time in response to the peacetime draft in late 1940. Nevertheless, he admitted to Hays that the number of state censorship bills introduced in early 1941 indicated that they once again had a "legislative censorship epidemic" on their hands. Breen was correct in his belief that his critics had overreacted. In an attempt to circumvent the Code, producers were using unusual marriage situations, such as a trial marriage or a husband or wife, long thought dead, who returns to find the spouse remarried, to introduce suggestive scenes and dialogue. They reasoned that such screenplays would enable them to get away with situations that would be rejected if the couple were unmarried. A string of such films were released between 1939 and 1941: *He Married His Wife*, *My Favorite Wife*, and *Too Many Husbands* all squeaked by with a B rating.[6]

Sophistication was just another word for smut as far as the Legion was concerned. The first film to feel the wrath of the Legion was Warner Brothers' *Yes My Darling Daughter* (1939), which had been staged on Broadway in 1937. The story revolved around the decision by the heroine, played by Priscilla Lane, to talk her reluctant boyfriend into spending a weekend with her before he leaves for a job in Europe so that she can have something to remember him by until he returns. At first her mother opposes the idea, but the situation changes when her daughter discovers that as a radical young feminist her mother had a premarital affair with a Greenwich Village poet. Breen approved the script after Warner agreed to strengthen the mother's objections to the trial marriage and to make it perfectly clear that the young couple did not plan to engage in "any illicit sex" on the weekend trip. In the end, embarrassed to find themselves alone at the cottage, they decide that it would be more daring if he slept on the porch and she inside. Breen, who did not expect any negative reaction from the Legion, was on a cruise when the Legion reviewed the film. *Yes My Darling Daughter* may have been an innocent comedy when it left Hollywood, but by the time the sixteen reviewers and fourteen consultors were through, it had turned into a major assault on the American family. Many were put off by the daughter's crack that her weekend fling was none of her mother's business. Equally objectionable was the mother's negligence in letting her go out of "fear of what her daughter will think of her." Even the grandmother came under fire when she declared, "You know the only thing that puzzles me is why the good Lord invented such beautiful things as the trees and the flowers and the birds and then had to go and invent sex." Even though nothing of consequence happened, reviewers were concerned that the weekend trip could be interpreted as advocating trial marriage as well as conveying the "false idea to young people that it is easy for two people in love to spend the weekend together without sin." Five evaluators were convinced that the star had emasculated her boyfriend by taking the initiative in talking him into going away with her. With so many "serious deficiencies," McClafferty felt that he had to condemn the film.[7]

In order to give the studio a chance to sanitize the story, the Legion held off announcing its decision, but news of the condemnation somehow reached the New York board of censors, which promptly refused to license the film. Irwin Esmond, head of the New York board, was clearly intimidated by the Legion's action because he couldn't point to a specific scene that had caused trouble, just repeat some of the Legion's objections. According to one studio estimate, if the New York decision stood Warner would have to write off 16 percent of the anticipated gross. A threatened nationwide Legion boycott would cut into the remaining profits. The studio felt it had no choice. Working from the Legion's list of objections, Warner cut some 1,300 feet of film amounting to ten minutes of playing time. With almost all the offensive lines eliminated, the Legion reclassified the film as a B, and the New York censors allowed its release. The studio's surrender caused some people to wonder if the New York censors and the Catholic church wielded too much influence. The *Christian Science Monitor* said that one state had laid down the law for the other forty-seven and that a religious organization "representing 21,452,400 people helped decide what three or four times that number should see on the screen." Breen agreed. Although he regularly used the threat of a Legion condemnation to extract concessions from the studios, he resented any criticism of his own decisions. While Breen fumed over the Legion's treatment of *Yes My Darling Daughter*, he was shocked by its next condemnation.[8]

There is no better example of the Legion's sometimes inexplicable standards than its handling of the MGM film *Strange Cargo*. Breen had refused to approve the initial script, which was based on Richard Sale's novel *Not Too Narrow, Not Too Deep*, because it contained too much "illicit sex" and brutality. Satisfied that the studio had met his major objections, he eventually approved the final version, which told of an attempted escape from Devil's Island by several convicts and a bar girl. The escapees are aided by Cambreau, a mysterious figure who seems to possess mystical powers and guides them on their journey. Except for the characters played by Clark Gable and Joan Crawford, the escapees die along the way, making peace with their souls with the help of Cambreau. In the end, transformed by Cambreau's goodness, the convict played by Gable returns to serve out his sentence, secure in the knowledge that Crawford's character will be waiting for him.[9]

Convinced that *Strange Cargo* was a morally inspiring film of redemption, MGM executives were stunned when it ran into trouble with the Legion. Nineteen of the twenty-three reviewers and all fourteen consultors raised serious objections about several specific scenes as well as the overall theme. Considerable criticism was directed toward an episode in which one of the convicts reads to Crawford's character a passage from the Bible used in Catholic liturgy in reference to the Virgin Mary, but it was Cambreau that caused the greatest difficulty. Many felt that audiences were likely to confuse him with Christ, thereby rendering his pronouncements as the word of God. Although McClafferty did not feel the film presented any real danger, he condemned it at the insistence of the priests on the board of consultors. A "flabbergasted" Breen told a member of Hays's staff, "No one seems to know what the C is all about." Breen challenged Father Daniel Lord to figure out what was wrong with the story. Because the Legion's main objection seemed to revolve around Cambreau's role, MGM refused to negotiate any changes, because without this character the film was just one more Devil's Island escape story. Consequently, on March 28, 1940, the Legion announced that it had condemned the film because it presented "a naturalistic concept of religion contrary to the teachings of Christ and the Catholic Church."[10]

The *New York Catholic News* tried to explain the Legion's decision to its readers by conceding that someone who was "fuzzy and foggy" on doctrinal issues might see the film as a "fine portrayal of brotherhood and character formation." But that was not the case, the paper continued, for under the guise of conveying moral and religious lessons it was transmitting heresy.

Hoping to take Breen off the hook, the writer reminded his readers that an occasional slipup was understandable in light of the tremendous volume of screenplays the PCA "sifts, adjusts, and chlorinates." Because McClafferty's heart wasn't in it, the Legion did not coordinate a campaign against the film. Nevertheless, a few local Legion chapters did attempt to block it. *Variety* reported that Catholics in Saint Paul, Minnesota, made hundreds of phone calls to one theater manager, but he refused to back down. The Detroit police commissioner banned the film, and in Providence, the amusements inspector shut it down because of the Legion's classification after it had played for two weeks. But, having experienced only minor difficulties in other cities, MGM ran the film unchanged for six more months.[11]

MGM then told the Legion that it wanted to see what could be done to have it reclassified. The studio's feeler stemmed from the fact that the film had finished its first and second runs and was about to go into the neighborhood theaters, where the Legion had its greatest influence. McClafferty was willing to accept any concession in order to rid himself of a condemnation that no one but the consultors seemed to understand. Consequently, MGM made a few symbolic changes so that the Legion could save face, adding a few shots at the beginning of the film intended to suggest that Cambreau was human, but the studio did little to minimize the mystical qualities that had bothered the consultors. The changes were so small that when an MGM executive was pressed by the *New York Times* to explain what revisions had been made, he said he couldn't remember any off hand. Nevertheless, the Legion announced on October 10 that it was raising the film's classification to A–II, unobjectionable for adults.[12]

With the matter of *Strange Cargo* resolved, the Legion returned to its growing concern about Hollywood's new fascination with nontraditional marriage situations. At first glance, the writers must have viewed *This Thing Called Love* (1941) as a surefire method of slipping a few suggestive lines and some heightened sexual tension into a story without getting into too much trouble with the PCA or the Legion. The twist in the story centered on the heroine's persuading her new husband, played by Melvyn Douglas, that they should live together chastely for three months in order to ensure that they were compatible. The rest of the film revolved around the husband's imaginative efforts to wear down the resolve of his wife, played by Rosalind Russell. His final subterfuge, implying that he might be having an affair with another woman, worked. Marriages may have been made in Heaven, but the studios' sudden interest in offbeat unions didn't fool the press. *Variety* saw it as a "new way of skirting around Mr. Breen's frowns," while *Cue* characterized the film as "skating skillfully along the thin edge of the Hays Office code."[13]

The ice broke on January 24, 1941, when the Legion condemned *This*

Thing Called Love because its depiction of a trial marriage not only conflicted with the concept of matrimony as a permanent union but denied the woman's partner his marital rights. And although the wife eventually abandoned the idea at the film's end, no effort was made to point out that her scheme was wrong. In fact, she jettisoned her plan only out of fear that her husband might be unfaithful. Breen admitted to Lord that his office had been worried about the story, but after negotiating with Columbia off and on for five years, everyone at the PCA was "punch drunk with it" and willing to do anything to get it out of their hair.[14]

Breen initially admitted to McClafferty that if he were a Legion reviewer, he might have been hard pressed to decide between a B and a C. But when he learned that McClafferty had overridden an eight-to-three vote by the Legion's reviewers in favor of a B, he complained to Lord that the priest had unfairly used the film to send a message to the studios to stop exploiting offbeat marital situations as a means of boosting ticket sales. Convinced that it was being scapegoated, Columbia at first dragged its heels, but soon found itself on the defensive. MPPDA counsel Charles Pettijohn, never one to pass up a shot at Breen, told Will Hays that the picture "stinks in general" and "will definitely encourage the introduction of censorship bills." McClafferty's public announcement of the condemnation, on February 5, was accompanied by a thinly veiled hint of a possible boycott of all Columbia pictures. "Decency still pays dividends," he declared; "dirt pays deficits." Unwilling to get caught in the middle, the studio agreed to cut a few objectionable lines, but two viewers who saw the later version declared that they couldn't detect the deletions without consulting the original script. Nonetheless, McClafferty, satisfied that he had made his point, reclassified the film as a B.[15]

The condemnation of *Yes My Darling Daughter* and *This Thing Called Love* reflected the Legion's growing concern that Hollywood was undermining family values. More than half the Legion's B classifications in 1940 resulted from what it termed the pictures' "light treatment of marriage" or divorce. The fact that the leading characters usually remarried before the house lights came on failed to satisfy the Legion, which felt that the introduction of divorce into the story made it more acceptable in the eyes of moviegoers. Despite Breen's growing resentment over the rising number of PCA-approved films found wanting by the Legion, he too was bothered by Hollywood's handling of marriage, divorce, and remarriage, as he told Count Enrico Galeazzi, the most powerful layman at the Vatican. He said to the count that it was almost impossible to come up with a solution because the United States was a "nation of pagans." Things had reached such a low point, he declared, that most Americans no longer professed even what he called a watered-down Protestant version of Christianity. Breen felt, however, that it would be impolitic for the Legion to take on the issue as this would jeopardize its non-Catholic support. The only way to handle the problem, he told the count, was to persuade the European bishops in heavily Catholic countries to lead boycotts of any film that attacked the sanctity of marriage.[16]

Because none of the predominantly Catholic European countries—with the possible exception of Ireland—had anything comparable to the Legion, Breen's plan had no chance of success. Even the general secretary of the Catholic Central Office for Cinema and Radio in Paris admitted that, in view of the apathy within the European branch of the church, the possibility of launching any type of boycott was nil. But Breen refused to give up. He sounded out Quigley on the possibility of clamping down on Hollywood's treatment of divorce and remarriage so as not to give the impression that his office condoned these practices. While Quigley sympathized with Breen's predicament, he advised him that any attempt to introduce such an amendment to the Code would be traced to the church and spark a wave of anti-Catholicism.[17]

Breen's concern that he would somehow be blamed for Hollywood's "divorce mania" came out of his general feeling that no one appreciated the tremendous job he was doing to protect the nation's morals. Father Devlin told a friend that "at times [Breen] felt that he was doing a 'real bit of Catholic action,' but then he would complain about feeling isolated and deserted and vulnerable to any attack the Legion might launch." It was starting to wear him down. "I seem always to be in sort of an internal foment," Breen told Quigley. With his digestion "gone to pot" and frequently vomiting, he predicted an early grave for himself.[18]

The Legion's B classification of Universal's 1941 remake of *Back Street*, starring Charles Boyer and Margaret Sullavan, did nothing to soothe his stomach. He had initially opposed using the same title as the 1932 version of this story of a kept woman but had acquiesced with the proviso that the film avoid glamorizing the mistress's role, one of the problems that had touched off the original Legion campaign. Universal agreed to stress the "dullness and boredom and futility of [her] life," allowing her "no friends . . . in a city of six million." It drew the line, however, at Breen's recommendation that Boyer's character should die when news of the affair surfaced, leaving his mistress to end up as some gambler's "cheap hag."[19]

To Breen's dismay, what the PCA chief viewed as a film filled with minor victories over the producer (transforming the original script into an acceptable story), the Legion discounted as a mere repeat of the earlier version. Defending his action in a long letter to Lord, Breen argued that the film was thoroughly acceptable under the Code because the "sin [was] definitely and affirmatively shown to be wrong." To prove his point, he carefully outlined the differences between the two versions of the film to demonstrate to Lord just how much they differed. Among other things, all physical contact between the two stars had been eliminated along with the mistress's next-door neighbor, a prostitute. Moreover, turning Sullavan's character into a working woman he felt removed all the details that had identified her in the original story as a kept woman. Most important, the new version, in Breen's estimation, "definitely and affirmatively" showed adultery to be wrong. The wife in the original was "mean and narrow-minded, thus suggesting a possible . . . justification for her husband's actions." In the remake, she is shown only once, from the back, boarding a ship bound for Europe. The new film also introduced a new character, played by Frank McHugh, who as the "voice of morality" condemns the affair as wrong. In a measure of punishment, although Universal refused to kill the husband off, he loses his chance to make a speech at a conference which would have given his career a major boost. Breen told Lord he had heard that a number of Legion reviewers had admitted their unfairness in classifying the film as B, but, nevertheless, it went down as one more objectionable film that Breen had let slip by.[20]

In March 1941, frustrated over the wear and tear of the job and what he considered to be constant sniping from the Legion and people like Quigley and Pettijohn, Breen accepted an offer from RKO granting him a major role in studio affairs at $1,700 a week plus $200 for entertainment and $100 for a limousine and chauffeur. Geoff Shurlock, his key aide, agreed to take over the PCA until a replacement was found, but everyone knew that Breen's was a difficult act to follow. Several studio heads had asked RKO to withdraw its offer; meanwhile, the Legion and its supporters looked desperately for a Catholic successor. Shurlock tried his best, but he soon found himself embroiled in the industry's biggest controversy to date with the Legion.[21]

The film was MGM's *Two-Faced Woman* (1941), starring Greta Garbo and Melvyn Douglas. Garbo played a ski instructor who fears that she is losing her New York-based husband to another woman. Posing as her sexier twin sister, Garbo's character travels to the city, where her husband falls in love with what he believes to be a more glamorous version of his wife. All seven PCA staff members who worked on the film passed it without reservations. As one of them pointed out, Garbo's double role was so "obviously farcical" that no one could take it seriously. No one, that is, but the Legion. Once again, Hollywood's attempt to use marriage to develop a titillating story line failed to evade the church's moral radar. Of the twenty-eight people who previewed the film, twenty-one objected to the film's passionate love scenes and "suggestive" dialogue, seventeen disapproved of the low neckline on Garbo's formfitting gown, and ten singled out the film's casual treatment of marriage. Condemnation was clearly in order, and MGM was informed of the Legion's decision in time to make enough changes to avoid public censure.[22]

Two-Faced Woman became a cause célèbre when New York's Archbishop Francis Spellman personally condemned the film as a "near occasion of sin" in a pastoral letter to be read at all masses in his diocese on November 26, 1941. The recent string of condemnations had convinced him that the studios weren't taking the Legion seriously, but his move caught the Legion and McNicholas's committee by surprise. Heretofore, negotiations between the Legion and the studios had taken place behind closed doors. Now, everything was out in the open. Citing Spellman's action, New York Congressman Martin J. Kennedy demanded that Will Hays halt further distribution of the film.[23]

For some, this was one more reminder that the church had no qualms about dictating what could and could not be seen at their favorite movie house. News that the manager of Buffalo's Cataract Theater had agreed to pull the picture at Bishop John Duffy's request touched off a wave of protest letters acknowledging his right to ask Catholics to boycott the film but rejecting his right to prohibit an entire community from seeing it. In a note to the bishop reminding him that he was not a public office holder, one writer suggested that his time might be put to better use stamping out bingo games and gambling at church fairs. Positions quickly polarized. Boston and Springfield, Massachusetts, banned the film entirely, while Chicago and Milwaukee ordered cuts after local newspapers headlined the Legion's condemnation. When the city's amusements inspector canceled the film without having seen it, on the strength of the Legion's condemnation, the *Providence Journal* called for a revamping of the local censorship laws, and the American Civil Liberties Union offered its services to fight the city ban. All this led Dallas film critic John Rosenfield to protest that church policy had been translated into public policy in a number of areas. Angered by the first broad-based assault on the church's influence on the movies, Catholic leaders launched a counterattack. When the *Pinehurst* (N.C.) *Outlook* characterized the actions of the city censors as un-American, Martin Quigley responded that, to the contrary, the censors had acted in the true American spirit of safeguarding minorities against the majority. In fact, the publisher noted, he thought he detected in the *Outlook*'s veiled attack on the Legion the "faint . . . odor of the burning cross and the hooded knight."[24]

Although the film's notoriety led to increased ticket sales in some cities like Rochester, New York, the president of the Association of Theater Owners in Indiana warned Will Hays that unless something was done quickly, the industry could experience the same kinds of losses it suffered in 1934 during the first Legion campaign. Yielding to the growing pressure, MGM announced on December 6 that it would withdraw the film after December 16 and that no new bookings would be made until it had discussed the problems with the Legion.[25]

Working from the Legion's list of objections, MGM eliminated some of the "racy" dialogue in thirty-two scenes. In order to meet the Legion's major complaint—that Douglas's character had committed adultery because he believed he was making love to another woman even though she was his wife—MGM had to bring the actor back to shoot an additional scene on a reconstructed set. In the revised version, he calls his wife's ski lodge only to find out that she has gone to New York. Realizing that the "sister" is really his wife, the star murmurs: "Two can play at that game." On December 13, the *Motion Picture Herald* announced that *Two-Faced Woman* was again on an eastbound train from Hollywood. But before the picture could be cleared, MGM was forced to release a statement, prepared by McClafferty and Quigley and approved by Spellman, that the industry had authorized the PCA to turn down any future screenplays dealing with marital intimacies. Satisfied that it had wrung as many concessions as it could from the studio, the Legion announced on December 18 that it was raising the film's classification to B.[26]

By that point, the Japanese attack on Pearl Harbor had pushed the story to the back pages. Flushed with his victory over MGM, McClafferty felt that Hollywood had learned its lesson and that international events would only reinforce the church's influence. Following a trip to Hollywood shortly after the outbreak of the war, McClafferty reported to McNicholas that the Jewish executives were so fearful of the spread of anti-Semitism that the last thing they wanted to do was to alienate the church. Breen told a *Motion Picture Herald* reporter that he didn't expect the war to raise any issues for movie-makers that were not already covered in the Code. In a sense he was right; the 1945 Code contained the same restrictions adopted in 1930. But the changes unleashed by the war began to weaken its moral underpinnings.[27]

McClafferty worried about who would succeed Breen as head of the PCA. Quigley felt that Breen, who had once declared, "I am the Code," had amassed too much power. Breen's resignation, he told Will Hays, would give him a chance to transform the PCA into a group effort rather than a one-man show. Of course, a more retiring director would leave Quigley as the most influential Catholic layman in the movie business. Whatever changes were made, Quigley, McClafferty, and McNicholas's committee agreed that it was imperative that a Catholic succeed Breen. In fact, upon hearing in March that Breen was stepping down, Quigley and Bishop John Cantwell had urged him to begin training a Catholic as his replacement. Eager to fill what they regarded as the "Catholic position" at the PCA, the clergy and the laity flooded

McNicholas's committee with candidates ranging from congressmen and judges to an NBC vice president who was a nephew of the late Cardinal Mundelein. One priest recommended his cousin, the actor Pedro de Cordoba, "the highest type of Catholic gentleman," whose major qualifications appear to have been his active involvement in church affairs and his fathering of six children. Those without any friends in high places, like Margaret Quill, "an employee of MGM for two years . . . 29, Catholic and single," sent in their own applications. The person who eventually emerged from the pack as the Catholic candidate for the job was Judge Stephen Jackson, a former legal consultant to the New York Catholic Charities and the choice of Quigley and Spellman. Church support immediately transformed Jackson into the frontrunner, and a six-man committee made up of representatives from the major studios interviewed him.[28]

Negotiations stalled in February when it was learned that RKO executives were dissatisfied with Breen's work at the studio and were contemplating releasing him. To allow Breen to save face, the studio would announce that it was making the sacrifice in order to enable him to resume the important post of PCA administrator, where he was needed by the entire industry. Dismayed, McClafferty and Quigley did their best to block his return. It was bad enough, they argued, that he had turned the PCA into his own personal fiefdom, but now his effectiveness would be seriously damaged by his failure at RKO. Breen at first played hard to get, indicating that he wasn't sure if he wanted his old job back, so the committee turned to Jackson and offered him the position. Alarmed that he had overplayed his hand, Breen hinted that he could be persuaded to come back if the conditions were right. The committee promptly asked Jackson if he would be willing to serve as Breen's assistant if he came back. Having somehow convinced himself that Breen wouldn't return, Quigley saw his hope of having his own man in charge of the PCA dashed when the MPPDA announced that Breen had decided to resume his old post on May 15, 1942.[29]

He came back to a Hollywood that was already feeling the impact of the war. As the struggle against Hitler's racist ideology made Americans more aware of their own racism, the film industry took a few hesitant steps to improve its own record. In the spring of 1942, a *Variety* headline promised "Better Breaks for Negroes in H'wood." But there was more promise than delivery. A few films like *In This Our Life* (1942) tried to break with the usual stereotyped portrait of African-Americans, but they ran into serious difficulty in the South. In one exchange that caused trouble in Dixie, Bette Davis was confronted by an African-American law student whom she had falsely accused of being a hit-and-run driver. Mrs. Alonzo Richardson, the Atlanta city censor, ordered several cuts, including the student's assertion that "colored boys don't have a chance anyway," and complained vehemently to Breen about the scene that pitted the word of a "Negro boy" against the lies of a white woman. It was pictures like this, she declared, that accounted for the "increased impertinence of the Negro in spite of all the things done for their own good." The Legion's classification of the film as a B because it implied the acceptability of divorce enraged George Schuyler, publisher of the African-American *Pittsburgh Courier.* Schuyler attacked the Legion for labeling as objectionable the only current film in which a Negro didn't have to "disparage his people by acting as a clown or a cretin." McClafferty responded by stating that the church had always supported racial justice but had no control over the movie industry. "You have influence. No quibbling about it," Schuyler retorted, scoring the Legion for failing to use its power to defeat racism on the screen instead of the "insignificant" things it usually focused on.[30]

But racism was not one of the Legion's priorities. Although the prewar increase in B films seemed to be leveling off, the conflict was raising new issues. Concerned about films that focused on enemy atrocities, McClafferty argued that instead of inciting hatred of the enemy, Hollywood should encourage a loathing of the evil philosophies that motivated the enemy. He also worried that Hollywood was using war films to chip away at the Code's prohibition of profanity. In *Air Force* (1943), an American pilot flying over the ruins of Pearl Harbor exclaims, "Damn 'em. Damn 'em," and, at the end of the film, when American flyers are about to bomb Tokyo, their commander tells them to "give 'em hell." McClafferty asked McNicholas for advice, but all the bishop suggested was writing an article in the Catholic press on movie profanity to build up public opposition.[31]

Far more worrisome was the problem of how to respond to Hollywood's portrayal of the new relationship between the Soviet Union and the United States. Although Russians were now comrades in pictures like *The North Star* (1943) and *Song of Russia* (1944), the war had done nothing to sway the church from its opposition to Communism. Consequently, when Paramount decided to film Ernest Hemingway's novel of the Spanish civil war, *For Whom the Bell Tolls,* the church was just as concerned about the political as the moral deficiencies of the film. The Spanish consul in San Francisco had even asked the church to suppress the film, but Quigley warned McClafferty that any attempt to oppose it on anything other than moral grounds would be "political dynamite." Satisfied that Breen had done his best to clean up the screenplay, and with no mention of Franco or the Republican forces in the story, the Legion quietly classified the film as a B because of its excessive brutality and justification of homicide as well as a "suggestive situation" hinting that the couple played by Gary Cooper and Ingrid Bergman had spent a night in the same sleeping bag.[32]

Another 1943 Hollywood release was even more troublesome because there was not even a suggestive scene in it to justify warning Catholics away. In an attempt to improve the country's attitude toward the Soviet Union, President Franklin D. Roosevelt had encouraged Warner to film Ambassador Joseph Davies's best-selling book *Mission to Moscow*. The film, like the book, portrayed the Soviet Union before the war as a country a lot like the United States and ruled by a benevolent Joseph Stalin, who, instead of purging the country's alleged traitors, gives them their day in court in the Moscow show trials. Even though the film drew a great deal of criticism, not only from the right but also from such well-known socialists as Norman Thomas and Sidney Hook, the Legion felt its hands were tied and reluctantly awarded it an A–II rating—suitable for adults—although it noted that the film failed to refer to the antireligious policy of the Stalin government. In spite of McClafferty's argument that the film did not violate morality and decency "as ordinarily understood," he was flooded with complaints that he had failed to recognize Communist propaganda when he saw it. While unwilling to criticize the Legion openly, *America* labeled the film "Russia through rose-colored glasses, or more accurately, plain red ones." Nevertheless, the bishops again rejected McClafferty's attempt to establish an Institute of Film Analysis to deal with problems that fell outside the Legion's original mandate.[33]

One problem that clearly fell within the Legion's purview was the government's use of movies to contain venereal disease among the armed forces. With penicillin not widely available until 1944, the War Department relied on traditional scare tactics to encourage "syphilophobia" among the troops. But, recognizing the limits of its educational programs, the military broke with its World War I policy and distributed condoms on a widespread basis. Although the government's programs drew fire from a number of groups, the Catholic church played a leading role in condemning what it viewed as a sanctioning of sexual activity. As an editorial in *America* put it, "The War Department holds fast to the pessimistic view that since a majority of . . . young men are determined to indulge regularly in promiscuity, any method which will stave off disease is permissible." Reviving the National War Council's World War I strategy, the Legion joined such groups as the Knights of Columbus and the Catholic War Veterans in denouncing the military's program as "indecent, repulsive, and un-American." One priest claimed that many Catholic soldiers were shocked and occasionally terrified by the Army hygiene films. Bowing to pressure, the military abandoned the more graphic films, but it refused to drop the program.[34]

In the 1940s, however, the church had to contend with a fully developed movie industry, capable of turning out a much wider variety of films. The Legion strongly objected to a film in the March of Time series which included scenes of the government cracking down on prostitution near a military base. Time Incorporated, the series' sponsor, agreed under pressure to eliminate shots of anti–venereal disease posters and pamphlets as well as one of a prophylaxis kit but refused to remove scenes involving the posting of a syphilis quarantine notice, the patrolling of red-light districts, and the arrest of some prostitutes. McClafferty referred the matter to McNicholas and Spellman, who decided that it would be better to compromise than risk a battle with Time.[35]

The Legion, however, was much less willing to yield to small independent producers like University Film Productions, which created *No Greater Sin* (1941), a sincere attempt to deal with the venereal disease problem. With several well-known Hollywood actors in leading roles, it was approved by the New York State censors. Set in a town near an army base, the film relates the story of a young man who discovers he has syphilis shortly before his wedding day. After being "cured" by a quack, he goes through with the marriage, only to learn after his wife becomes pregnant that he has unwittingly infected her. Enraged, he kills the charlatan, but rather than reveal the true story, he pleads guilty and is sentenced to death. His friends help him to tell the truth, which leads to his acquittal. *Variety* felt that, by calling for an open discussion of the problem, the film performed a real public service. Among the groups endorsing the film were the U.S. Public Health Service, the Social Hygiene Society of Washington, and the Federal Council of Churches of Christ. Although the film was a straightforward dramatization of the problem, a number of local theaters unfortunately hyped the film with ad slogans like "*No Greater Sin* Raiding the Sin Dens" and "Girls Luring Men to Their Doom." The posters outside one New York drive-in showed the silhouette of a nude woman with the warning "MANY WILL FAINT! If you can't take it PLEASE DON'T COME ALONE."[36]

The Legion would have preferred that people not come at all, and in spite of the film's many endorsements, the church stuck to its conviction that the theater was not the place for sex education. Far from rendering a service to the public, it argued, such films were progressively destroying the moral order. Consequently, McClafferty became alarmed when he learned that Charles P. Taft, assistant director of Defense Health and Welfare Services and brother of the Ohio senator, was trying to get the PCA to issue the film a certificate. Taft, along with several members of his office, had seen the picture and agreed that it accurately portrayed a problem that was undermining the war effort. McClafferty, who was concerned that Taft's actions might lead to a liberalization of the anti–sex-hygiene section of the Code, tried to enlist McNicholas's aid in getting to Taft, but the bishop wrote back that Charles was not the "solid, well-informed man that his brother . . . is." Later, when the priest reported that Taft had dined in "bad company," with a man who had donated $50,000 to Planned Parenthood, McNicholas responded that it was one more example of his lack of judgment.[37]

When Breen refused to approve the film, its producer threatened to launch an antitrust suit against the MPPDA for refusing to show it in association theaters. As part of a series of concessions made in the wake of the Legion campaign in 1934, the association had agreed to levy a $25,000 fine on any member who sold, distributed, or exhibited any film that had not been approved by the PCA. Convinced that it had a good chance of losing the suit, the association, to Quigley's disgust, rescinded the penalty clause. "Hays lacks the fortitude," he wrote Bishop John O'Hara, and "Hollywood is always interested in money above everything else."[38]

Although the MPPDA's decision had little meaning because most theaters continued to shy away from booking the film, the Legion alerted its diocesan directors that it might turn up in their areas. Fearing that a national attack would promote the film, McClafferty recommended convincing local theater owners not to book it. As Syracuse Bishop Walter A. Foery explained to his priests, "we are compelled to conduct a quiet campaign against the picture since publicity, as you know, would only defeat our purposes." Instead, the bishop suggested that parish-society presidents phone or write the Empire Theater to ask the manager to discontinue showing the film.[39]

The Legion campaign apparently was too low-key for some dioceses. When several Rochester priests protested the lobby posters advertising the film, the manager invited them to a private showing along with several public officials. After the viewing, the priests admitted there was nothing morally objectionable in it. Apparently feeling embarrassed about their original protest, they agreed to endorse the film if it was all right with their bishop. When their request reached the bishop's secretary, who was apparently unaware of the Legion's condemnation, he okayed the idea. The next day the theater displayed a poster in the lobby stating, "A committee of priests have reviewed this picture and find no objection." When word reached McClafferty, he wired the bishop asking him to have the poster removed. Fearing that other priests might make the same mistake, he warned the other dioceses of the Rochester episode. Consequently, when the manager of the Fox-Lincoln

Theater in Springfield, Illinois, offered a similar preview to protesting priests, they politely refused.[40]

In spite of such occasional slipups, the independently produced sex-hygiene films with their limited outlets did not pose any real challenge to the Legion. However, news that Walter Wanger, who had produced *Blockade* and successes including *Stagecoach* and *Foreign Correspondent*, had developed a two-reel film on how venereal disease was hurting the war effort caused an uproar at the Legion office. The idea for the film had come from Lawrence Arnstein, executive secretary of the California Hygiene Association, who had interested Wanger and then Thomas Parran, U.S. Surgeon General and a Catholic, in the project. As Arnstein pointed out to Parran, a film made by Wanger would have a wider appeal than government documentaries on the subject. Viewing it as a chance to make a significant contribution to the war effort, both Wanger and Jean Hersholt, the respected character actor who starred in it, agreed to do it without charge. Entitled *To the People of the United States*, the film began with a statement by the Surgeon General of the navy that venereal disease had "too long been allowed to continue its ravages under the protective cloak of a social taboo." The story centered on a flying fortress that has been grounded because its pilot has contracted VD. Told only that the captain had picked up a germ, one of the crewmen wonders "what little germ could knock out a flying fortress. There isn't a fighter plane in the world that can do it." The captain is treated, but the picture drives home what VD means in terms of hours and effectiveness lost.[41]

Wanger didn't anticipate any difficulty in distributing the film, which would be released in two versions: a longer one for the use of the Public Health Service and a shorter one for theater showings. Because the Production Code didn't apply to government documentaries, there was no need to worry about Breen's office. As for the Legion, Wanger felt that the "constructive and patriotic" appeal of the film, which turned it into a "war and peace effort," would overcome whatever resistance such films usually encountered. Wanger threw himself into the project, even writing the California governor to make sure that, because the film urged viewers to get blood tests, the state would be able to handle the demand. The final script was ready by the spring of 1943 and shown to the Surgeon General's office and to General George C. Marshall and his staff, all of whom congratulated the producer on a job well done. With the enthusiastic support of the Public Health Service, the War Department, and the Office of War Information (OWI), Wanger began production. After testing public reaction in a series of sneak previews, he planned to release the film through the major distributors to be shown as a short along with the usual double feature.[42]

Although Wanger was not concerned about the Legion, news that he planned to release the film in movie houses across the country worried McClafferty. Bishop Francis Keough of Providence, who had replaced McNicholas as chair of the Episcopal Committee in 1943, recommended that he contact bishops Spellman and O'Hara, who supervised the religious work of military chaplains. Both men immediately urged McClafferty to lend the Legion's weight to an "energetic protest" against the showing of a film that they felt would be a "dangerous step backwards." O'Hara, who had seen the film, told McClafferty that it was "insulting to Americans, dangerous to health, and definitely a menace to chastity, since it contains not one word of consideration of the unchastity which is even a greater scourge than the disease it spreads." In a letter of protest to Elmer Davis, head of the OWI, McClafferty conceded that venereal disease posed a real threat to the war effort yet insisted that movie theaters were not the place to deal with the problem. In the absence of Davis, Edward Klauber, the acting director, replied that the OWI had assumed there was no problem with the film because the Surgeon General's review committee included a Catholic priest, Father Alphonse Schwitalla of the Catholic Hospital Association. In view of the Legion protest, however, he offered to hold up the film's release until representatives of the Public Health Service could talk to the Legion. Klauber alerted Wanger that a problem had arisen, but reassured him that the situation could be worked out without public controversy.[43]

Klauber's optimism didn't last long. The chief of the venereal disease division of the Public Health Service and two associates held a private screening in New York for McClafferty and Mary Looram on March 9, 1944. Afterward, McClafferty told them that if the Legion ignored the film, it would clear the way for a flood of similar pictures. Moreover, he argued, information alone wouldn't solve the problem; the health service's own statistics showed an increasing rate of infection among the military, which had been bombarded with information on the subject. In addition, the film entirely omitted any consideration of the moral issue. When the visitors suggested that such a message could easily be included, McClafferty declared that the topic was an improper screen subject. Meanwhile, when Schwitalla, who had sat on the Surgeon General's review committee, asked for a full explanation of his objections, McClafferty sent it in time for the next committee meeting. With McClafferty's letter, Schwitalla convinced the committee to recommend that the film be restricted to health agencies and military posts. In order to avoid any suggestion that the Public Health Service was condoning promiscuity, it also advised the Surgeon General to introduce the film with a statement on the importance of moral standards as a means of reducing venereal disease. Convinced that ignoring the Legion's complaint

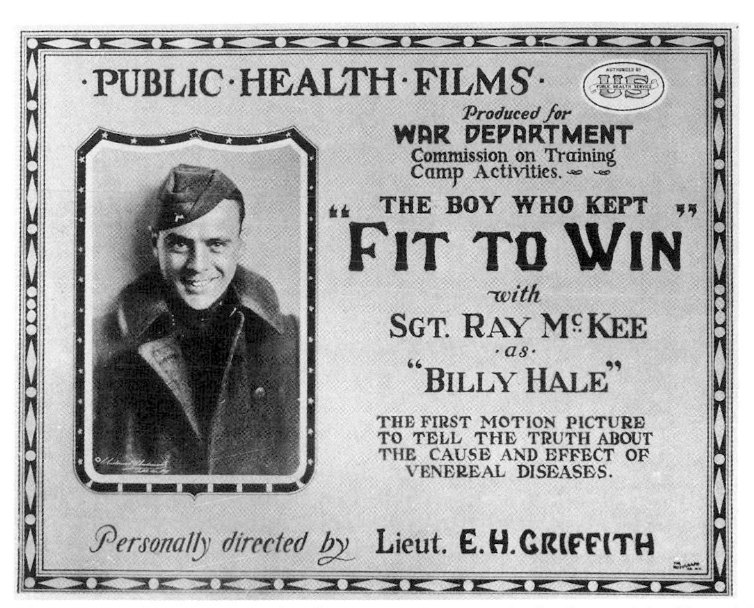

A poster for *Fit to Win* (formerly *Fit to Fight*). The campaign to prevent the distribution of this film and *End of the Road* marked the Catholic church's first significant success in combating objectionable films. (Courtesy of American Social Health Association Records, Social Welfare Archives, University of Minnesota)

Richard Bennett as the doctor and Claire Adams as Mary Lee, the nurse, examine a victim of syphilis in *End of the Road* (1919). The church was especially alarmed by a film on venereal disease directed at a female audience. (Courtesy of the Museum of Modern Art)

Marie Dressler and Polly Moran in *The Callahans and the Murphys* (1927). Branding this film as anti-Catholic and anti-Irish, the church forced MGM to recall it. (Courtesy of the Museum of Modern Art)

Jacqueline Logan as Mary Magdalene in *King of Kings* (1927). Father Lord, objecting to too much sensuality in the film, persuaded Cecil B. deMille to cut 1,500 feet from the Mary Magdalene scenes. (Courtesy of the Museum of Modern Art)

Father Daniel Lord, S.J., a co-author of the Motion Picture Production Code, was one of the prime movers in the formation of the Legion of Decency. (Courtesy of Georgetown University Library)

Father Wilfrid Parsons, S.J., who played a leading role in the creation of the Legion of Decency, was forced to resign his editorship of *America* after he offended Chicago Cardinal George Mundelein. (Courtesy of Georgetown University Library)

Martin Quigley, Cecil B. deMille, and Paramount president Barney Balaban. Quigley enjoyed being the man the studios turned to when they ran into trouble with the Legion of Decency. (Courtesy of Georgetown University Library)

Joyzelle Joyner as Ancaria tries to tempt the Christian virgin played by Elissa Landi in *The Sign of the Cross* (1932). *America* called it "one of the most unpleasant bits of footage ever passed by the Hollywood censors." (Courtesy of the Academy of Motion Picture Arts and Sciences)

Archbishop John Cantwell's attack on Hollywood in 1934 alerted his fellow bishops to the danger of objectionable films. (Courtesy of the Archives of the Archdiocese of Los Angeles)

When Geoff Shurlock (*left*) or Joe Breen passed a film, they knew their decisions were subject to second-guessing by the Legion. (Courtesy of the Academy of Motion Picture Arts and Sciences)

Father John McClafferty served as executive secretary of the Legion of Decency from 1937 to 1947 when the Legion enjoyed its greatest influence in the film industry. (Courtesy of *Catholic New York*)

Will Hays and Mary Looram, head of the IFCA's reviewing staff, which classified films for the Legion of Decency.
(Courtesy of Georgetown University Library)

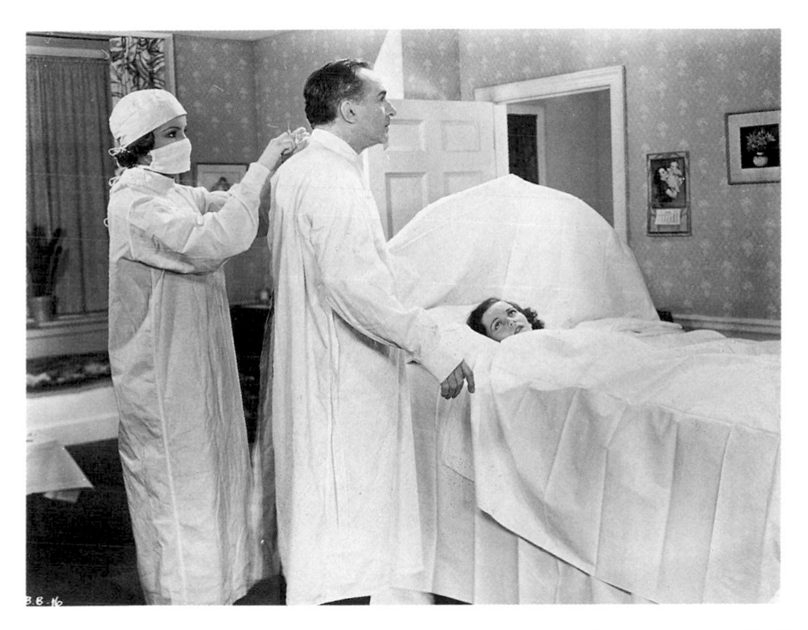

Eleanor King plays a woman who is about to give birth in her home in *The Birth of a Baby* (1937). The church's opposition to showing this film in theaters led the Legion to create a new classification category. (Courtesy of the Museum of Modern Art)

Although Jeffrey Lynn's character slept on the porch while his fiancée, played by Priscilla Lane, slept inside, the Legion, worried that *Yes My Darling Daughter* (1939) might encourage unmarried couples to spend a weekend together, condemned the film. (Courtesy of the Museum of Modern Art)

Concern that audiences might confuse Ian Hunter's character with Jesus led to a Legion condemnation of *Strange Cargo* (1940), also starring Joan Crawford. (Courtesy of the Museum of Modern Art)

Archbishop Francis Spellman of New York personally condemned *Two-Faced Woman* (1941), starring Greta Garbo and Melvyn Douglas. (Courtesy of the Museum of Modern Art)

Jane Russell never wore this blouse in *The Outlaw* (1943), but the Legion had no trouble finding reasons to condemn the film. (Courtesy of the Museum of Modern Art)

Unhappy with the ending in which Pearl, played by Jennifer Jones, and her lover kill each other, the Legion forced David O. Selznick to add an epilogue which alerted the audience to the immoral nature of *Duel in the Sun* (1946). (Courtesy of the Museum of Modern Art)

Linda Darnell and Cornel Wilde in *Forever Amber* (1947). When Twentieth Century-Fox president Spyros Skouras ignored a Legion condemnation of this film, a national boycott forced him to apologize. (Courtesy of the Museum of Modern Art)

Father Chisholm's (Gregory Peck) discussion of the many ways to enter heaven with Philip Ahn as the mandarin caused Catholic consultants three years of trouble trying to get *Keys of the Kingdom* (1944) approved by the Legion. (Courtesy of the Museum of Modern Art)

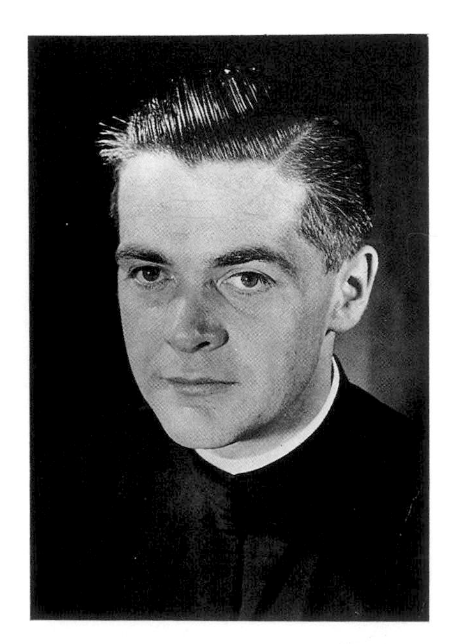

(*above, left*) "Get Father Devlin" was the cry whenever a studio needed a Catholic viewpoint on one of its films. (Courtesy of the Archives of the Archdiocese of Los Angeles)

(*above, right*) As executive secretary of the Legion of Decency and the National Catholic Office for Motion Pictures from 1953 to 1966, Father Thomas Little presided over a gradual liberalization of the church's film classification system. (Courtesy of *Catholic New York*)

(*left*) Father Patrick Sullivan, S.J., executive secretary of the National Catholic Office for Motion Pictures from 1966 to 1980, led the struggle to bring the church's approach to films in line with the spirit of Vatican II. (Courtesy of the Catholic News Service)

Anna Magnani starred in *The Miracle* (1948), a forty-minute Italian movie that led to a U.S. Supreme Court decision limiting the right of states to censor films. (Courtesy of the Museum of Modern Art)

Jimmy Stewart, Betty Hutton, and Charlton Heston in *The Greatest Show on Earth* (1952). The Legion criticized Cecil B. deMille for casting Stewart as a mercy killer and dressing Hutton and the other female performers in "scanty" costumes. (Courtesy of the Museum of Modern Art)

Many Catholics questioned the Legion's condemnation of *The Moon Is Blue* (1953), starring Maggie McNamara and William Holden. (Courtesy of the Museum of Modern Art)

Marcello Mastroianni in the orgy scene in *La Dolce Vita* (1960). Father Sullivan's refusal to condemn this film led Cardinal James McIntyre to prohibit Sullivan from visiting Los Angeles in his official capacity as a representative of the Legion of Decency. (Courtesy of the Museum of Modern Art)

Deborah Kerr about to solve John Kerr's identity problem in *Tea and Sympathy* (1956). (Courtesy of the Museum of Modern Art)

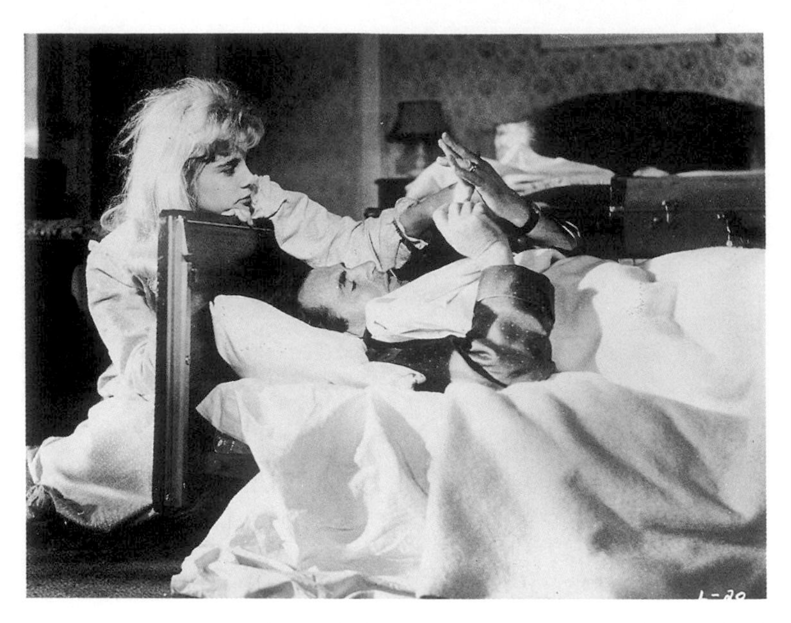

Sue Lyon and James Mason in *Lolita* (1962). The motel scene went through several cuts to satisfy the Production Code Administration and the Legion. (Courtesy of the Museum of Modern Art)

Dean Martin, Ray Walston, and Kim Novak in *Kiss Me Stupid* (1964). In spite of Sullivan's liberalization of the Legion's classification system, he condemned Billy Wilder's film as "morally repulsive." (Courtesy of the Museum of Modern Art)

would threaten the Public Health Service's entire venereal disease program, Parran reluctantly informed Wanger that he had decided against a theatrical release of the film.[44]

Stunned by the Surgeon General's sudden surrender, Wanger asked Francis Harmon, vice-president of the MPPDA's War Activities Committee, for advice. A sympathetic Harmon told him that because he did not construe a sneak preview as a regular public exhibition, he had already made arrangements for several tryouts around the country in the hope that a positive audience response could be used to counter Legion pressure. Wanger was able to arrange showings in several locations with generally favorable results, although six teenagers in Montgomery, Alabama, were put out for disorderly conduct during the screening there. The manager of a theater in Sioux Falls, South Dakota, reported that no exhibitor need fear running it. "It is the first time," he claimed, "that somebody has not jumped down my throat when such a subject matter has been shown." The Sioux Falls PTA even approved the film for children's viewing. Attempts to preview the film, however, were blocked in some cities including Detroit, where the city censor refused to give his permission, and in Lynn, Massachusetts, where the mayor forced its cancellation after receiving a number of complaints. Harmon's strategy of building up popular support for the film was blocked when McClafferty persuaded George Schaefer, head of the War Activities Committee, to halt all further previews.[45]

Unwilling to give up, Wanger asked Parran if he could release the film under Public Health sponsorship to theater owners interested in showing it. But by that point politics had taken precedence. Concerned about an attack on his budget, an embarrassed Parran informed Wanger that it was difficult to explain fully all the factors involved in preventing "this splendid production" from reaching the American public. Reluctant to acknowledge that he had buckled under Legion pressure, Parran told the producer that he had commissioned a study, which would take several months, on the need to integrate moral standards into the Health Service's educational programs.[46]

In a last-ditch effort to build up public support for the film, Wanger issued a press release on April 17, defending his picture and calling attention to a letter of support from the National Council on Freedom from Censorship, which characterized the Legion action as "pressure from intolerant sources." He dismissed the argument that the film violated the Production Code, pointing out that the industry's regulations did not apply to government documentaries. Declaring that he had the greatest respect for "the splendid purposes of the Legion," he took issue with its contention that unchastity was a greater scourge than venereal disease. Hoping to attract bookings, Wanger indicated that prints of the film would be distributed free by the California

Department of Public Health. The anticipated groundswell failed to materialize. The Rialto Theater in New York was the first commercial theater to book the film, on May 5, but few owners followed its lead. With the tide running in his favor, McClafferty decided not to launch a national campaign lest it boost attendance. However, the news of the Rialto engagement prompted him to send a letter to the bishops warning them that the film might be shown in their areas. By the summer of 1944, Wanger had lost the battle. Other than warning their people to avoid the film, even the local Legions ignored the few theaters that decided to book it. When Bishop James Griffin of Springfield, Illinois, turned down an invitation to see the film, he dismissed the idea with what by now had become the church's standard response. "Why," he asked, "if Hollywood was so interested in fighting disease, didn't it make a film about pneumonia?"[47]

In spite of the occasional flap over sex-hygiene films, the Legion's main concern was the effect the war was having on the morality portrayed in Hollywood films. Breen did his best to hold the line, and at times he seemed to be as worried about the changing moral climate as the Legion was. "From where we sit," he wrote McClafferty in March 1944, "it would appear that there has been a near approach to what looks like a complete breakdown in the moral structure of the nation." But Breen worked for the moviemakers, and although he felt that the country was changing for the worse, he recognized that he was going to have to make an accommodation to the new era.[48]

Even the Legion seemed to be willing to let a few movies go, although Preston Sturges's *Miracle of Morgan's Creek* (1943), starring Betty Hutton, may have slipped by under cover of the reviewers' laughter. A movie about a young woman who while drunk becomes pregnant by a soldier she can't remember but whom she thinks she may have married seemed unlikely to pass the Legion reviewers. Desperate to give the baby a name, she marries an old 4–F boyfriend who tries to masquerade as a soldier by wearing a World War I uniform. This leads to their arrest, but the two are saved from the authorities by a miracle: the birth of sextuplets, which turns the mother into a national heroine. The real miracle of *Morgan's Creek* is that the film sailed through Breen's office with so little trouble. Sturges was asked to tone down some of the references to the woman's pregnancy, such as her sister's comment that she's "not the first dumb cluck who got herself in a snarl. . . . What with the war and all there'll probably be millions of them. . . . They say they make the cutest babies." And the Office of War Information's Bureau of Motion Pictures requested that the boyfriend blow the horn of his car to signal his arrival rather than relying on the screech of his brakes and tires, which was contrary to the rubber conservation program. The Legion reviewers objected to the film's casual attitude toward marriage. After all, they pointed out, if Hutton's character hadn't married the original soldier, she was guilty of reckless promiscuity, and if she had, she had committed adultery by marrying her old boyfriend. But they also found the film "very funny," and the Legion ended up giving a B to a picture that was far more risqué than *This Thing Called Love* and *Two-Faced Woman*, which they had condemned on the eve of the war.[49]

The film didn't escape completely unscathed; Hays told Breen that he had received a lot of letters complaining that material like this was contributing to the rise in juvenile delinquency. One Minneapolis father wrote that his son had concluded that Hutton's sextuplets meant that she had slept with six different men in one night. The manager of the Collegian Theater in Ames, Iowa, said that it was bad enough when, a few months earlier, a film that showed teenagers stealing doorknobs had touched off a wave of "knobnappings" in Ames, "but when they start burlesquing things the average good home holds dear—it's dangerous." The PCA decided not to push its luck again. Ten years later, when Paramount discussed a remake with Geoff Shurlock, he turned it down for fear of antagonizing the Legion. Shurlock attributed the original film's good fortune to both Sturges's fast-paced direction, which covered up the "basic sordidness" of the story, and the breakdown of morality during the war.[50]

Although the Legion may have temporarily let down its guard for *The Miracle of Morgan's Creek*, it continued to rail against what it believed was a rising tide of immoral movies. When Hedy Lamarr introduced herself as Tondelaya in the PCA-approved *White Cargo*, the story of a native woman on a rubber plantation who drives men wild with lust, the Legion condemned it until MGM made enough changes to raise it to a B. Nevertheless, McClafferty must have wondered what he had missed when he read MGM's ad claiming that Lamarr was "ravishing, petulant, audacious, forward, shameless, presumptuous, brazen, amorous, virulent, haunting . . . venal, iniquitous, sybaritic, angelic, diabolical, mesmeric—but wonderful."[51]

Breen usually suffered criticism in silence, assuming that second-guessing went with the territory. But when a major effort by his office to purify Stanley Kramer's rendition of W. Somerset Maugham's *The Moon and Sixpence* (1943) failed to satisfy McClafferty, he couldn't contain himself. The film began with Herbert Marshall, who plays Maugham, reading of Charles Strickland's death and deciding to write his biography. Strickland, a middle-aged stockbroker, had walked out on his wife and children and gone to Paris to become a painter. There, he took up with his best friend's wife, only to leave again, causing her to commit suicide. He ends up, like Gauguin, in Tahiti, where he marries a native woman and eventually contracts leprosy. Working feverishly up to the moment of his death, he covers the walls of their hut with murals of the local natives, some in sarongs and others nude. Although the film was shot in black and white, the film's ending was shown in color to underscore the brilliance of his work. Upon his death, his wife honors his wish and burns the hut down. The film ends with the statement that his surviving pictures have since become extremely valuable.

Although the PCA had turned down several treatments of the story by other producers because they appeared to condone adultery, Shurlock had approved the script while Breen was at RKO with the proviso that United Artists should not turn Strickland into a hero. Director Stanley Kramer made enough concessions to get the film approved, but the Legion's stricter reviewers condemned it. McClafferty, who was especially infuriated by the "vile and dirty" plot, outlined his objections to studio president Edward Raftery and Kramer two weeks before the scheduled opening on October 1, 1942. According to McClafferty, the audience would be left with the impression that it was all right for Strickland to desert his family, betray his friend, commit adultery, and cause a suicide because he was a great artist. Equally upsetting was the display of the artist's murals at the end of the film, which he maintained violated the Code's prohibition of nudity.[52]

Eager to avoid a condemnation, Kramer and Raftery agreed to drop the original prologue in favor of: "This is the story of Charles Strickland, painter, whose career has created so much discussion. It is not our purpose to defend him." They also agreed to a new epilogue that provided a moral message: "Such was Strickland. He trod roughshod over obligations as husband and father, over the rights and sensibilities of those who befriended him. Neither the skill of his brush nor the beauty of his canvases could hide the ugliness of his life, an ugliness which finally destroyed him." But both men balked at McClafferty's demand that they get rid of Strickland's murals on the basis that their content violated the Code. Raftery pointed out that because the PCA was the ultimate arbiter of the Code, if his film had violated its regulation on nudity, Shurlock would not have approved it. Moreover, eliminating the paintings would destroy the dramatic climax of the picture. McClafferty suggested that the paintings could be blurred through some sort of device to convey the impression of color and light while disguising the subject matter. Although Raftery rejected the priest's proposal, he promised to substitute some longer shots of the murals, which might make the figures somewhat less well defined, but he warned McClafferty that there was no time to make the changes before the film's opening. Concluding that he had secured as many concessions as he could, McClafferty reclassified the film as a B.[53]

Refusing to let the issue die, McClafferty asked Breen and Will Hays for an explanation. Breen said that he agreed with his staff that the picture was in conformity with the Code. It was certainly "low-toned and sordid and the central character is a repulsive fellow," he admitted, but these defects were compensated by assigning Strickland's role to George Sanders, who usually played "heavies"; this would prevent the audience from identifying with the artist. Breen also rejected McClafferty's contention that the film justified Strickland's immorality, pointing out that not only were his sins shown to be wrong, they were also punished as the artist goes blind and then dies horribly of leprosy. Finally, Breen informed the priest that the PCA had never applied the clause prohibiting nudity to pictures, statues, or other works of art unless they were used as part of a crude joke. He reminded McClafferty that *The Story of the Vatican* in the March of Time series had featured some shots of the paintings in the Sistine Chapel, which included nudes. In any case, he pointed out, the figures in the film's various panels were so crowded together that it was difficult to believe they could stimulate a "lecherous or licentious" reaction. But McClafferty remained adamant; Strickland had not been punished enough for his sins. He neglected to note where he thought the suffering should begin, but the tenor of his remarks suggested that immediately after the opening credits would not have been soon enough. Nor was he satisfied with Breen's attempt to draw a parallel with the Vatican film since those shots were distant and incidental rather than climactic, nor were they highlighted in color. Breen let the priest have the last word, taking some comfort from Father Lord's agreement with him that the film was not morally dangerous.[54]

As a result of the growing number of problems with Hollywood—14.6 percent of the 1942–43 film season's output were classified as B, a new high—Father Patrick Masterson joined the Legion staff as McClafferty's assistant in early 1943, just in time to become involved in the condemnation of another United Artists film, *Lady of Burlesque*, based on Gypsy Rose Lee's mystery, *The G-String Murders*. This was not the first time Lee had run afoul of the Legion. In addition to its abortive attempt to block her movie career, the Legion had classified *Stage Door Canteen* (1943) a B when the producer refused to cut a scene in which she simulated a striptease although she remained fully clothed throughout the entire number.[55]

Lady of Burlesque was produced by Hunt Stromberg, his first independent venture after a long and successful career at MGM. Barbara Stanwyck starred as a burlesque star who, with the help of the show's baggy-pants comic, played by Michael O'Shea, solves a series of backstage murders. Eight Legion reviewers saw the film on April 27, 1943; three felt it deserved a B although it "bordered on a C," while the other five voted to condemn it. Two days later the board of consultors, several of whom wondered if anything could be done to save the film, unanimously classified it as a C. Although United Artists threatened to sue the Maryland board, which banned the film, on the basis that all the other state censors had passed it with few if any cuts, it took a different tack with the Legion. On May 1, the United Artists representative in New York asked McClafferty what could be done to head off the announcement of the condemnation. The priest responded with a long list of objectionable scenes including Stanwyck's shimmying, another dancer's discreet "bump," close-ups of the chorus girls, a number of offensive lines, and several questionable jokes, including an old burlesque routine featuring the use of a hot dog on a string to attract women.[56]

United Artists incorporated several of the Legion's requests in a new version, but not enough to move the consultors, who again voted to condemn the film. Seeking to avoid a public condemnation the studio canceled the film's opening in twenty-two cities, but it was forced to release it in six other locations because of contractual obligations. Meanwhile, at Stromberg's request, Breen traveled to New York to advise him on what other cuts could be made without ruining the film. Stromberg then ordered a second round of changes based on Breen's recommendations, but the new version still didn't satisfy the consultors. With the film showing in several locations, McClafferty couldn't wait any longer and released the condemnation to the press on May 13.[57]

An angry Raftery charged the Legion with using a separate set of standards for his picture and reminding McClafferty of the company's heavy investment in the project. But news that the Montreal censors, who had originally passed it without any changes, had ordered the elimination of some 250 feet in the film after the Legion condemnation brought the studio back to McClafferty for a third round of editing. This time the cuts were more drastic. Several of Stanwyck's dance routines were either eliminated or shortened, and a full-figure shot was substituted for a closeup of her shimmying in order to shift the audience's focus away from any movement of her breasts. The viewers' virtue was also protected by replacing a close shot of the chorus girls with a longer one as well as by eliminating a bump by a featured dancer. The studio also agreed to remove most of the lines the consultors had identified as objectionable. This third round of changes satisfied the Legion, and the film was listed as a B on June 15. Although the Legion had again forced a studio to revise a film, one of its worst fears about the effect of a condemnation on the box office was realized when *Variety* estimated that the resulting notoriety would boost United Artists' gross between 25 and 40 percent.[58]

From the Legion's point of view, Breen's certification of *Lady of Burlesque* was just one more reminder of how much he had changed. In many ways, McClafferty's view of Breen echoed Father Lord's old criticism of Wingate: "there is a straining after gnats and a swallowing of camels." Breen had, for example, made it clear to David O. Selznick that a shot of a woman in bra and panties in *Since You Went Away* (1944) was totally unacceptable: "stockings, bobby socks, a slip or two, pajamas or sun suits, but no intimate garments." Yet Breen did an about-face on three films of James Cain's steamy novels: *Double Indemnity* (1944), *Mildred Pierce* (1945), and *The Postman Always Rings Twice* (1946), which he had previously rejected. *Double Indemnity*, for example, had been turned down in 1935 because of the "general low tone and sordid flavor of the story," which dealt with murder and "an illicit and adulterous sex relationship." Eight years later, Breen approved a new script with the notation that during the passing years "details of crime have become more common and adultery is no longer quite as objectionable." Adultery may have become more acceptable in some quarters, but not at the Legion office. The Legion had entered the war with the belief that its recent series of condemnations on films like *Two-Faced Woman* had taught Hollywood a lesson. It was now far less sanguine about what peace would bring.[59]

NINE

■■■

The Producers Fight Back

Hollywood had enjoyed a good war and anticipated an equally successful peace. The wartime economy, with full employment and higher wages, had translated into steadily rising profits. It looked as though the boom would last forever: in 1946, between 85 and 90 million people crowded America's theaters each week, and revenues reached an all-time high. On top of that, with the end of hostilities, the industry could sell an immense backlog of films that had not been shown in Axis-controlled countries during the conflict and enjoy a second round of profits from the overseas market. But the promise of 1946 soon proved illusory. With 403 million fewer seats sold in the following year, the combined profits of the Big Eight studios fell from $122 million to $89 million. Although television later played a major role in Hollywood's declining revenue, the box-office downturn began well before most families owned a set. Gasoline shortages and a decline in alternative amusements during the war had been a boon for the film industry. Now, as the returning servicemen married, had families, and moved to the suburbs, home entertainment and sports competed with Hollywood for the public's leisure dollars. In

1946, Americans allocated 20 percent of their recreational funds on movies; eleven years later, the film industry's share had shrunk to 7 percent.[1]

The phenomenal growth of television in the 1950s supplied the coup de grâce to whatever hope the industry had of reviving its glory days. As Spyros Skouras, head of Twentieth Century-Fox, told Darryl Zanuck, "We are no longer in a business going through a major readjustment; we are in a business fighting to keep alive." Tony Curtis remembers that when he showed up to take out the winner of a win-a-date-with-Tony contest, the movie magazine photographer avoided shooting the television set in the woman's apartment in order not to advertise the competition. Hollywood tried to fight back with technical innovations like increased use of color, Cinerama, Cinemascope, and 3–D, but nothing seemed to work; the average weekly attendance dropped from a high of 90 million in 1946 to 40 million in 1960.[2]

In 1948 the studios lost an antitrust suit initiated by the Justice Department ten years earlier against Paramount. The decision ordered the Big Eight to divest themselves of their theater holdings and to stop a number of practices, including block-booking. The major studios owned between 60 and 70 percent of the first-run movie houses in the cities, and exhibition revenue accounted for the most profitable part of the motion picture business. Although it would take some companies ten years to complete the divorcement, the court decision meant that the studios could no longer depend on a guaranteed outlet for their films. One of the Paramount decision's first casualties was the low-budget movies that had filled out the second half of double bills in the past.[3]

The studio system was also buffeted by the rising tax rates during World War II. As Thomas Schatz has suggested, the changing tax laws may have played as great a role in undermining the studio system as the government's antitrust suit. As more and more film people in the 90 percent tax bracket discovered that they would be better off substituting profit sharing for the traditional salary arrangement, the studio system with its assembly-line production began to give way to groups of free-lancers who made a separate deal for each film. The rise of individual film companies, in turn, allowed some filmmakers to follow their personal inclinations instead of producing more of the formula films that had dominated the screen for so long. The mass audience of the 1930s passively turned out to see whatever was playing at the local theater. After the war, discrete movie audiences started to emerge, each with its own interests. Sensing that some moviegoers were attracted to more sophisticated fare, independent producers experimented with both social-problem films and more sexually explicit stories that tested the limits of the Code.[4]

The Catholic church viewed all this with rising alarm. Although the Legion never fully trusted the studios to do the right thing, the major producers usually knew how far they could go before getting into trouble. The Legion's job was also made simpler by the fact that there were only eight major studios to deal with. The rise of independents, from 40 in 1945 to about 165 a decade later, complicated its task. In addition, as television came to dominate the family entertainment market, studios became interested in producing the types of film people couldn't get at home. No one was interested in scrapping the Code, but some industry people began to feel that a set of rules laid down in 1930 should be brought up to date. One sign of Hollywood's growing frustration over the Code's constraints was an "ad" that appeared in the *Screen Writer:* "Wanted, an idea: Established writer would like a good updated idea for a motion picture which avoids politics, sex, religion, divorce, double beds, drugs, disease, poverty, liquor, senators, bankers, wealth, cigarettes, congress, race, economics, art, death, crime, childbirth and accidents (whether by airplane or public carrier); also the villain must not be an American, European, South American, African, Asiatic, Australian, New Zealander or Eskimo." A tongue-in-cheek solution proposed by Dore Schary, head of production at MGM, was to buy a country and call it Sylvania; then all the villains could be Sylvanians.[5]

But as far as the Legion was concerned, "modernize" and "up-to-date" were code words for more sex and social-problem films. The move toward bigger-budget pictures with simultaneous openings in a number of theaters hurt the small neighborhood houses, which had specialized in screening films at the end of their run. These were the theaters over which the Legion had always exerted its greatest controls through the pressure of local parish councils. Equally troubling was the retirement of Will Hays in 1945. Quigley and the church leaders had never really trusted Hays, but he was the devil they knew. The devil they didn't know was his replacement, Eric Johnston, former president of the U.S. Chamber of Commerce, who, in his first press interview, remarked that the "Hays job has to be remodeled and changed." Although the Paramount antitrust decision led Johnston to change the association's name from the Motion Picture Producers and Distributors of America to the Motion Picture Association of America (MPAA), the Legion feared that he had more in mind than a simple relabeling.[6]

The Legion continued to be concerned about what it saw as Joe Breen's growing liberalism. A wave of criticism of *The Postman Always Rings Twice* (1946), which *Life* had labeled "a catalog of the seven deadly sins," had caused Breen to crack down temporarily. He stopped Paramount from filming four new stories, including *The Great Gatsby*, and his staff went back to what one producer called their old habit of nit-picking. *Sleep My Love* (1948), in which a young couple's honeymoon is temporarily delayed by an incident on a train, was just the type of thing he was talking about. Under no circumstances, Breen told the director, was there to be any hint that the holdup was a source of sexual frustration for the newlyweds. But after *The Moon and Sixpence* and *Lady of Burlesque*, Father McClafferty and Martin Quigley were convinced that Breen had outlived his usefulness. When Breen asked Los Angeles bishop McGucken to appoint a group of priests to discuss moral values with him and his staff, McClafferty interpreted the move as an attempt to undermine the Legion and persuaded the bishop to turn him down. McClafferty, who preferred to work behind the scenes, went public with his frustrations in a letter to *America* in 1946, pointing out that it was not the Code but the Code administration that was to blame for the rising number of objectionable films.[7]

McClafferty and other defenders of the Code found themselves in an increasingly difficult position. The postwar world was changing rapidly while movies continued to work under a set of rules promulgated when Herbert Hoover was president. The war had sown the seeds of a sexual revolution. The gap between the PCA's view of love and romance, in which married couples slept in separate beds, and reality was underscored by the publication of Alfred Kinsey's studies of American sex habits in 1947. Nevertheless, McClafferty and Quigley did their best to hold the line, arguing that the Code, like the Ten Commandments, was never out of date. Sensing Eric Johnston's discomfort with Breen, who was viewed as a holdover from the Hays regime, they revived their plan to find a replacement. They had failed to get the job for Judge Stephen Jackson after Breen left RKO in 1942, but they were able to persuade Johnston to appoint Jackson to the staff in 1947 as heir apparent. While Breen was on vacation, however, Jackson, who tended to use a prosecutorial style with the producers, made such a botch of things that he destroyed whatever chances he had to move up.[8]

Jackson's appointment caused another problem: several Protestant groups protested the appointment of another Catholic to the PCA. It was not that Breen had failed to protect their interests; he had persuaded Samuel Goldwyn to revise *The Bishop's Wife* (1947), which he said would surely have touched off a major Protestant protest in its original form. In the film, the angel Michael, played by Cary Grant, is sent down to earth to help a bishop whose concern with building a new cathedral alienated not only his parishioners but also his wife, played by Loretta Young. Breen was willing to accept the hint of an infatuation with the angel on the part of the bishop's wife, but he could not condone any scenes that "indicate a kind of sex love . . . including hugging and kissing" between the two stars. But films such as *The Fighting 69th*, *Boys' Town*, *Knute Rockne, All-American*, *The Song of Bernadette*, *The Keys of the Kingdom*, *Going My Way*, and *The Bells of St. Mary's* convinced a number of Protestant leaders that Hollywood had a Catholic bias when it came to making religious pictures. One minister asked at an Albany Baptist conference, "Why are Catholics portrayed on the screen as heroes and Protestant pastors as laughable or weak preachers?" In an effort to gain more leverage, a Protestant Film Council was formed on the West Coast after the war to advise Hollywood on church matters. The council, however, never gained the influence the Legion exerted, a situation that Geoff Shurlock attributed to poor leadership. The studios didn't want "the Catholics running the industry," he said, "but [the Protestants] never showed themselves . . . capable."[9]

Although Hollywood's search for new, more sophisticated themes began to place greater demands on the Legion's time and resources, it was the same shoestring operation that had developed in the 1930s. In 1945, almost half of its $17,000 budget (most of which came from the NCWC) went to printing and mailing the weekly bulletin sent to some three thousand subscribers. When McClafferty requested $1,500 from the Episcopal Committee to attend a Catholic film conference in Rome, it took a herculean effort to raise the funds. The only reason the Legion kept out of the red was the large number of unpaid IFCA volunteers who reviewed the films and took care of its considerable mailings. Local cooperation with the Legion continued to vary from region to region. In Buffalo, the Legion was tightly organized with parishes and student committees in every school ready to spring to action when called on. In some dioceses like Providence, as Bishop Keough noted, "Every recommendation of the *Providence Visitor* regarding the quality of movies is respected and followed by the police authorities." The Boston archdiocese, on the other hand, with no formal organization, did not even submit an annual report to the Legion office in 1946.[10]

The Legion did undertake some organizational changes in the postwar years. Bishop William Scully of Albany succeeded Bishop Keough as chair of the Episcopal Committee on Motion Pictures in November 1946. A year later, McClafferty stepped down as the Legion's executive secretary to become director of Catholic University's School of Social Service. Hollywood's willingness to cooperate during his ten years at the Legion enabled him to help administer the Social Action Division of the Catholic Charities of New York while running the Legion. But the loosening of the reins in the postwar years transformed the Legion assignment into a full-time job. Father Patrick Masterson, who succeeded McClafferty as executive secretary, had served as his assistant before becoming a chaplain during the war. Unlike McClafferty, he not only devoted all his time to Legion affairs but he made sure that Cardinal Spellman provided him with a full-time assistant, Father Thomas Little. Like McClafferty and Masterson, Little had no professional experience with films before joining the Legion. In fact, Little's only previous connection to the movies had been booking films for his fellow students at the North American College in Rome. When he arranged, sight unseen, a showing of *It Happened One Night*, on the strength of its sweep of the Academy Awards, his superiors took him to task for exposing his fellow students to such risqué material.[11]

In spite of Hollywood's attempts to loosen some Code restrictions, the Legion in the postwar years continued to champion self-regulation against a renewed cry for federal censorship from those who felt that pictures like *The Postman Always Rings Twice* went too far. Even opponents of government interference, like the *Dallas Morning News*'s film critic John Rosenfield, warned that the moviemakers were looking for trouble unless they tightened their standards. One sign was the length of screen kisses, up from an average of ten to thirteen feet of film in the 1930s to forty-two feet in the Hedy Lamarr–Paul Henreid film *The Conspirators* (1944). Worse, according to the Dallas reviewer, was Hollywood's increasing tendency to slip in "double meanings and leers," as in the exchange between the two stars of *Adventure* in which Greer Garson suggests, "Let's kill the rooster," and Clark Gable responds, "Oh, no, he's got too much to live for." Nevertheless, whenever any Catholic leaders spoke out in favor of some form of government censorship, the Legion was quick to remind them of the Episcopal Committee's support of self-regulation. When the Ohio bishops discussed filing an amicus curiae brief in favor of their state's censorship law in a case arising out of a reissue of Fritz Lang's *M*, Masterson warned them that such a step threatened the Legion's relationship with the studios, which had proven so successful over the years.[12]

In spite of their being adversaries, the Legion maintained a good working relationship with the producers. Even Walter Wanger, who had run into trouble over *Blockade* and *To the People of the United States*, was able to enlist the Legion in his effort to get his film *Scarlet Street* (1945) past the New York censors, who had denied it a permit. Although the Legion classified the film as a B because of its "suggestive dialogue, costumes and sequences," McClafferty successfully lobbied the board of censor's chairman to approve the film.[13]

Nonetheless, support for the Code and an occasional favor for a producer didn't mean that the Legion went along with Hollywood's liberalization. McClafferty complained to Johnston that each new round of films seemed to have more indecent costuming, "suggestively obscene" dancing, and "lustful kissing," while the compensating moral values that punished evildoing seemed harder to find. One measure of the Legion's displeasure was the rising number of B's, some of which, according to McClafferty, "barely skirt the hazardous limits of the C classification." There were only 48 films on the Legion's B list in 1941, about one-third of which were foreign; four years later, B's totaled 138, only 15 of which were imports. Its list of objectionable films indicates that the Legion was concerned with the same problems that had bedeviled it before the war: Communist influence in the film industry, sex-hygiene films, and divorce and sexual immorality on the screen. The only thing that had changed was that all these themes seemed to be gaining ground in the postwar period. Two months after the end of the war, Father John Devlin, head of the Los Angeles Legion of Decency, wrote McClafferty that the Communists were becoming increasingly active in Hollywood, especially among screenwriters. Their three-stage plan, as he saw it, would first remove all references to God and any attempt to portray spiritual values on the screen. The next step would be to undermine the Legion by constantly equating its efforts with censorship. After that had been accomplished, they would be free to inject Communist doctrine into American movies. According to *America*, the steady stream of message films like *The Best Years of Our Lives* (1946), *Crossfire* (1947), and *Gentleman's Agreement* (1947) were also playing into the hands of the nation's enemies by focusing on the darker side of American life. It took a highly sophisticated detection system to identify the party line in some of these films, but the magazine's editors were clearly up to it. They scored *The Best Years of Our Lives* for a speech by actor Frederic March, "a veteran of more than twenty communist fronts," in which he excoriates a group of bankers for not lending money without collateral to returning servicemen—clearly a step in the Communist effort to destroy the banking system. Similarly, Masterson tried to block a rerelease of *All Quiet on the Western Front* (1930). He admitted that it was relatively innocuous when it was made, but he argued that its antiwar message played into the hands of the Communists, who were intent on weakening the nation's defense system. Convinced of the rising Red tide in Hollywood, most Catholic leaders applauded the House Un-American Activities Committee investigation of the industry, which began in 1947. When Charlie Chaplin was called to testify, the Catholic War Veterans joined the American Legion in a successful boycott of his film *Monsieur Verdoux*.[14]

Occasionally, the witch-hunting backfired. Although the Legion rated *The Farmer's Daughter* (1947) a family film, a few Catholic critics detected a pinkish tinge in the script. The story earned an Academy Award for Loretta Young, who played Katie, a Swedish maid who is elected to Congress on a reform ticket. Nevertheless, Father William A. Nowlin, a specialist on Communist propaganda, argued that Katie's election despite her lack of education or political experience was an excellent argument in favor of Lenin's thesis that "any cook can learn how to run the state." William Mooring, a syndicated film critic for the Catholic press, agreed. Mooring, who had served as Quigley's London correspondent while editing the British trade paper *Bioscope*, had come to America in 1932 as a technical adviser on *Cavalcade*. Having become a Catholic in 1940, he approached anything related to the church with the zeal of a convert. In a column headed "Katie for Communism," Mooring charged that the maid's "humane, progressive" ideas, when coupled with the identification of the opposition as fascist, "clearly establishes Katie's position as Communist." But Mooring had targeted the wrong actress: Young, a devout Catholic, was a close friend of Bishop Manning of Los Angeles, who ordered him to drop the subject.[15]

Another source of continuing concern was Hollywood's casual treatment of divorce. Although the divorce rate was on the rise, the Legion saw no reason for the screen to reinforce the trend. McClafferty had come to suspect Joe Breen's willingness to support Catholic values, but he couldn't fault him in this area. Breen made every effort to persuade the studios to keep divorce out of their stories, but no one seemed to be listening. Twentieth Century-Fox refused to back down, and so the heroine of *Gentleman's Agreement* remained a divorcée; nor could Fox see any reason to turn the divorced Maureen O'Hara into a war widow in *The Miracle on Thirty-Fourth Street* (1947). Although the reviewers praised both films, the Legion slapped them with B's because of their tacit approval of divorce.[16]

Sex-hygiene films also continued to cause trouble in the postwar years. The latest version, *Mom and Dad*, which had been shot in a week, had opened in 1945, telling the story of Joan, a high school student whose parents forced the school committee to fire a teacher for trying to provide his students with sex education. Joan becomes pregnant, and her shame-faced parents, seeing the need for a course on sex hygiene, persuade the school committee to rehire him. The film concluded on a patriotic note with a plea for "clean minds, high moral standards, and good, strong, healthy bodies" followed by a scene showing a group of Boy and Girl Scouts carrying the flag and singing the *Star-Spangled Banner*.[17]

Although the film provided a smattering of sex education—a birth scene and a piece of an Army film on venereal disease were thrown in—it was another effort to turn a profit by exploiting the audience's fascination with a forbidden subject. What was different about this film was the promotional skill of its producer, Howard Kroger Babb, who ballyhooed the picture in each town with a week of advertising hinting at the excitement waiting for anyone who bought a ticket. The first two shows, at 2 P.M. and 7 P.M., were reserved for women. According to Babb's assistant, by the time the 9:30 all-male show rolled around, the men in line were champing at the bit, convinced that they were going to see something much more exciting than what had been delivered to the more delicate female audiences. The carefully orchestrated presentation also included a group of "lovelies in white" who served as ticket takers as well as "nurses" who might be called on to aid anyone who fainted during the presentation.[18]

Anticipating the Legion's reaction, the producer didn't submit the film for review. Consequently, it was not condemned until 1947, when McClafferty received a report on the film from some Legion members who had seen it in St. Louis and Oakland. McClafferty at first treated it as just one more sex-hygiene film, but he hadn't counted on Babb's creativity in securing testimonials. One of the producer's ploys was an "endorsement contest," which offered a series of $10 and $25 prizes, plus a Chevrolet, to the best letter of the year. When Masterson heard that ten priests and two monsignors had won awards, he exploded. One monsignor was forced to refuse the car, and the other priests were ordered to withdraw their letters from the contest. Babb bought a two-page spread in *Box Office* in which he attacked the Legion and listed the names of the priests who "had free minds and were courageous and true Americans enough" to realize the value of his film. The monsignor's recantation was also too late to stop the flood of letters from Catholics asking Masterson if it was true that a priest had proclaimed *Mom and Dad* the year's outstanding educational film. One senses that Babb derived almost as much pleasure from tormenting the church as from the profits that rolled in. When he took out an ad in *Box Office* announcing his latest project—a film entitled *Father Bingo*, heralded as an "exposé of parish gambling halls"—Martin Quigley called to get more information. Babb told him that the film featured a "fast-talking con-man priest" who operates a fixed gambling operation in his church. When the publisher warned him that such a film was bound to be condemned, Babb, who had no intention of making it, hung up before Quigley could hear him laughing.[19]

Irritating as Babb was, the Legion's major anxiety during the postwar period stemmed from the gradual erosion of the Code's rigid restriction regarding sex. Although almost no one wanted to exhibit his films under the burden of a condemnation, producers were much less willing to cooperate with the Legion than they had been in the past. The first serious confrontation took place during the war, when Howard Hughes released *The Outlaw*, a western that offered more sex than shootouts. It starred two unknowns: Jack Beutel as Billy the Kid and Jane Russell, who had never acted before, as Doc Holliday's mistress, Rio. Howard Hawks had been signed to direct it, but after several weeks of arguments, Hughes fired him and put the picture together himself.

The result was a mess. Billy meets Rio, who, realizing that he is the man who killed her brother, takes a shot at him. But Billy throws her down on a haystack and forces himself on her. Later, when Billy is suffering from chills after being wounded by sheriff Pat Garrett, Rio crawls into his bed to warm him. Recovered, Billy sets out to flee, but when he learns that Garrett has killed Doc, he returns, handcuffs the sheriff to a porch, and rides off with Rio. What the plot lacked in coherence was made up by Russell's natural attributes. At times it seemed as though most of the director's ingenuity had gone into devising scenes that would force Russell to lean over for maximum exposure. To whet the public's interest in the film, Hughes hired Russell Birdwell as press agent. Even before filming started, Birdwell, who had masterminded the public search for an actress to play Scarlett O'Hara in *Gone with the Wind*, set out to turn Jane Russell into a new sex symbol. Photographs, including the famous shot of Russell lying on a haystack in an off-the-shoulder blouse (which she never wore in the film), made her one of the most popular pinups during World War II.

Although Hughes, as an independent producer, had no obligation to send the film to the PCA, he needed a seal in order to show the film in major theaters, and Breen, Shurlock, and the other staff members saw it at the end of March 1941. Hughes had ignored all of Shurlock's script suggestions, including cutting Billy's explanation to Doc that he had only borrowed his girl, just as Doc had previously borrowed his horse. When Billy offers to exchange the girl for the horse, Doc growls, "Cattle don't graze after sheep." Even more alarming were the many shots of Rio's breasts straining to escape the confines of her blouse, which seemed to dominate the screen. Breen, who complained to Will Hays that in his ten years in Hollywood he had never seen "anything quite so unacceptable as . . . the breasts of . . . Rio," ordered a number of cuts, including thirty-seven breast shots, but Hughes refused and requested a hearing before the association's appeal board. Birdwell, who represented the producer at the hearing, brought studio stills showing that Hughes was not the only one who had used cleavage to sell a film. He was also accompanied by a mathematician who argued that Russell had exposed a smaller percentage of her bosom than several other actresses in Code-approved films. As no one apparently thought to compare baseline data, the board agreed to grant a seal provided that Hughes made a small number of token cuts.[20]

Breen, who was about to leave for RKO (where cheesecake shots were not unknown), did not make a fuss. Hughes, who decided not to release the film rather than comply with the demands of several state censorship boards for further cuts, tested the waters again by booking the film into a San Francisco theater in February 1943. To advertise the opening, billboards displayed a picture of the sultry Russell reclining on a haystack under the caption: "How would you like to tussle with Russell?" Another ad declared, "*The Outlaw* conclusively proves that sex has not yet been rationed." According to Birdwell, the members of a women's club, who claimed they couldn't believe what they saw, requested a private showing of reel 7 so that they could study Russell more closely. All Birdwell's skill, however, could not hide the film's shortcomings. *Time* declared that it was "a strong candidate for the flopperoo of all time," but Birdwell's campaign led to sellout crowds at the box office. The Legion condemned it, but then, as suddenly as it had appeared, the film was withdrawn without any explanation by Hughes in April 1943.[21]

The film went back into circulation three years later, and this time Birdwell pulled out all the stops. Ads announcing "Not a scene cut" and asking, "What are the TWO reasons for Jane's rise to stardom?" were on one occasion accompanied by a plane that traced the film's title in the sky and then traced two enormous circles with a dot in each one. When the film opened in Los Angeles, the line in front of the theater extended down the block at ten in the morning, and the manager decided not to present the second feature in order to add extra showings. The resulting uproar over Birdwell's campaign led Eric Johnston to withdraw the original PCA seal on the basis of Hughes's violation of the association's advertising code. When a judge upheld the association's right to deny Hughes a seal, an estimated 85 percent of theaters decided not to show it, but Hughes forged ahead, booking it to sellout crowds in independent theaters where state and local censors had not banned it.[22]

Unsure of where and when the film would appear next, McClafferty had to run a state-by-state campaign, which strained the Legion's budget. In Los Angeles, Bishop Cantwell told Catholics that they could not, with a free conscience, attend the picture. Philadelphia's Cardinal Dougherty raised the stakes: the film was off limits to Catholics, any theater showing it would be boycotted, and any newspaper that accepted ads for it would be publicly condemned from the pulpit. In areas with heavy Catholic populations, local officials cooperated. The inspector of amusements in Providence, who could always be counted on, prohibited the film on the strength of the Legion's condemnation. In response, Hughes began to send feelers out to the church in 1946. When Father Devlin, Bishop Cantwell's film adviser, refused to meet with him at his office, Hughes visited the priest at 1 A.M. to see if he could help in getting *The Outlaw* reclassified. Although Devlin told him he had nothing to do with the condemnation process, Hughes asked if a donation to his parish might help. Rebuffed by Devlin, the producer sent Harry Gold as an emissary to visit McClafferty in New York. Charging that the Legion had unfairly scapegoated Hughes, Gold argued that far worse films like *The Postman Always Rings Twice* and *Gilda* had escaped with a B. Sensing that he was not getting anywhere, Gold pointed out that the Legion's action was an unpatriotic slap in the face to a man who had done so much for the war effort.[23]

Although McClafferty refused to reclassify the film, he indicated that the Legion had always been willing in the past to reconsider its decision if modifications were made. He identified several problem areas that would have to be corrected, including Russell's overexposure, suggestive dialogue, and the climax, which allowed a criminal to ride off with his girlfriend while making the sheriff an object of ridicule. Hughes seemed interested. In early April 1946 he promised to curtail Birdwell's advertising campaign. He also stated that he was considering meeting some of McClafferty's demands, including adding an epilogue pointing out that Billy was actually shot by the sheriff. Not sure how to proceed, McClafferty asked Bishop William Scully of Albany for advice. Scully, who believed that reclassification should be limited to the first year of a film's release, was reluctant to enter into further negotiations with Hughes. Noting that the producer had been showing the film for more than four years in about a quarter of the available theaters and thus causing irreparable damage to so many souls, Scully felt that a B rating would only give Hughes a chance to harm a new crop of victims. The only reasonable solution, he suggested, was to take the picture out of the market for a period of time and reissue a cleaned-up version under a new title. Hughes refused to alter the film's title and declared that it would be too costly to make any modifications in the current version. He was willing, however, to revise the ending before any new play dates were scheduled in return for a promise to lift the condemnation. If that was acceptable, he would publicly announce that he had changed the film at the Legion's request. He also promised to clear all his subsequent films with the Legion and to release nothing until he had its unqualified approval.[24]

When the Episcopal Committee met in November, it voted to cut off all further negotiations with Hughes. Still unwilling to give up, Hughes asked Quigley to look at his film and point out what it would take to move the Legion. However, he failed to act on Quigley's suggestions until early in 1948, when he began to negotiate the purchase of RKO. Seeking to rid himself of the Legion problem, he sent Quigley a new print incorporating most of his recommendations and authorized the publisher to act on his behalf in obtaining a reclassification of his film. If the Legion agreed, Hughes offered to issue a statement declaring that he had submitted to its judgment. If the Legion refused, he warned Quigley that he would launch an advertising attack in the press charging the church with acting as an extralegal national censorship board and comparing it to a Georgia lynch mob.[25]

Quigley, who felt that the latest version was acceptable, recommended that the Legion take another look at the film. While Scully's committee was discussing how to handle Hughes, one of Hughes's agents had approached Milwaukee's archbishop and convinced him that the producer was being treated unfairly by the Legion. Miffed by a recent Legion decision to reclassify another condemned film, *Forever Amber*, which he considered much worse, the archbishop was contemplating setting up his own reviewing committee, which would grant *The Outlaw* a B. After a hurried meeting in New York, Masterson reminded the archbishop that although Pope Pius XI's 1936 encyclical on films, *Vigilanti Cura*, clearly stated that a bishop might impose a more severe classification, there was no indication of the power to upgrade a film. Masterson's argument worked, and the church's united front held.

Masterson was just as interested as Hughes in getting rid of the problem. He could understand why some of the bishops were opposed to letting Hughes get away with exploiting the Legion's condemnation for five years and then sell the sanitized version to the rest of society. He also recognized that reclassification could be interpreted as a sign that the Legion had retreated in the face of Hughes's threat. Nonetheless, Masterson recommended that the bishops reopen negotiations. Pointing to the Legion's traditional policy of using reclassification as a means of cleaning up the screen, he argued that it would be unfair to draw the line in this one case. And although he did not want it to appear as though the Legion was bending to pressure, he didn't relish fighting an anti-Legion campaign in the papers. Finally, there was the matter of Hughes's takeover of RKO. "If we refuse to treat with him now," Masterson told the committee, "it would be bad for our relations with him in the future."[26]

With considerable grumbling, the bishops authorized Masterson to contact the producer. On April 27, 1948, Hughes agreed to recall all the prints of *The Outlaw* still in circulation and substitute the version he had sent to Quigley in mid-February. By eliminating Rio's cry of "Let me go!" and Billy's order to "Hold still, lady, or you won't have much dress left," accompanied by the sound of tearing cloth, all signs of the rape disappeared. Hughes also dropped an exchange between Rio and her aunt just before she embarks on her mission of mercy to heal the delirious Billy. When her aunt asks her if she has gone crazy, she responds: "You can bring the minister here in the morning if it'll make you feel better about it. Now get out." The bed-warming scene was shortened to seven seconds of screen time, which eliminated Rio's declaration to Billy, "You're not going to die. I'll get you warm." The cuts reduced the length of the film from 116 minutes to 96. In order to uphold the image of the law, a new ending in which Sheriff Garrett voluntarily agrees to let Billy and Rio go was substituted for the old one, which had left him handcuffed to a post. To underscore the film's new message that crime doesn't pay, Hughes added an epilogue: "So ends our legend of Billy the Kid. The real life story lies hidden in the annals of the untamed West. The best known version is that Billy the Kid was killed by Sheriff Pat Garrett at Fort Sumner, New Mexico, July 13, 1881."[27]

When the Legion's reviewers and consultors gathered in early June to view Hughes's film for the last time, some had seen it as many as twenty times. But even after 147 cuts, the committee was still divided. Several stuck to their original vote for condemnation on the grounds of objectionable costuming and suggestive situations which they felt were degrading to women. But the majority, who voted to reclassify it as a B, did so largely out of fear that since Hughes had finalized the purchase of RKO, he now had an outlet for the film that had been previously limited to the independents. The Legion's decision angered several church leaders. Both Bishop Cantwell and Father Devlin had argued unsuccessfully against reclassification unless the film was retitled, although they were willing to have "The Outlaw" in the subtitle. As far as they were concerned, Masterson's failure to extract that concession amounted to a surrender.[28]

The MPAA voted to give the bowdlerized version a seal, but the Legion's decision was not made publicly because Hughes began to haggle over the wording of his statement in regard to the reclassification, balking at using the word "substantial" to describe the changes that had been made in the original film. He finally settled on a public announcement that Masterson accepted, but because the Legion would not reclassify the film until it had viewed the new ad campaign, it was not until 1949, six years after the original condemnation, that the Legion announced that it had upgraded the film to a B. Still wary of Hughes's promises, the Legion asked its diocesan contacts across the country to monitor the film's advertising. Hughes kept his word, and Masterson breathed a sigh of relief. But to the Legion, *The Outlaw*, a box-office success wherever it had been shown despite the lack of a Code seal and Legion approval, set a dangerous precedent. Legion supporters had to worry how many other producers were wondering if they should follow suit.[29]

There was no better sign of the changing times than the fact that the Legion could no longer count on westerns to contain morally acceptable material. *The Outlaw* could have been dismissed as an aberration if a second such western hadn't found its way onto the Legion's condemned list in 1946. *Duel in the Sun* was based on a novel by Niven Busch that had not been particularly successful, and in an initial studio poll of reaction to the title, most respondents thought it must be a film about a World War II aerial dogfight. Nevertheless, David O. Selznick hoped to turn it into a second *Gone with the Wind.* Yet selling the story to the PCA presented certain difficulties. The novel revolved around Lewt McCanless, the son of a powerful Texas ranch owner, who is attracted to a half-breed servant, Pearl Chavez, whom he rapes and later seduces by promising to marry her. Although he has no intention of honoring his pledge, he guns down a ranch hand and wounds his brother Jesse, who are both interested in her. Enraged by his brutality, Pearl kills Lewt and rides off with Jesse.[30]

The first order of business was to win script approval. Selznick had long felt that the Breen office had held him to a higher standard than other producers. A few months earlier, while working on the script of *Spellbound*, he told an assistant to prepare for a really good row with Breen on their next film. "His criticisms are in many cases absurd," he said, "and many others either contradictions of precedent or a new precedent or completely opposite to what he has permitted others to do. . . . He may act as a petty czar with others but he is not going to do it with me if I have to take the whole damn Code to court." It came as no surprise when Breen's office rejected the initial script of *Duel in the Sun* because of its preoccupation with "illicit sex" and the theme of murder for revenge. The staff singled out several segments, including the rape scene and one suggesting that Pearl sleeps in the nude. They also pointed out that the implication that one of the characters, called the "Sinkiller," was a minister was a clear violation of the Code, which prohibited negative portrayals of the clergy. Equally troublesome was the final scene in which Pearl rides off with Lewt's brother after firing shot after shot into Lewt's body.[31]

In spite of his earlier blustering, Selznick told the PCA that he was open to suggestions on how the story could be saved. He agreed to make a number of changes in the original script, including toning down the rape scene by shortening Pearl's struggle and leaving it to the audience to infer what had happened. In the seduction scene, Pearl would give in to Lewt's advances, but her subsequent attempts to convince him to marry her would show that she was not a tramp. Selznick also promised not to violate the Code by adding dialogue to indicate that the Sinkiller was not an ordained minister. Finally, the revised script ended with Lewt and Pearl shooting each other, followed by Pearl's crawling to die in her dead lover's arms. Breen was still unhappy. "I know that it is more dramatic to have your leading protagonists die in a love embrace in a pool of gore," he wrote, but having them die before they reached each other would be morally more acceptable.[32]

Although the PCA approved the script with the death scene intact, Selznick sensed that Breen still had reservations and invited him and his staff to the set in order to deal with their objections on the spot. It proved to be a wise move because Pearl's sensual dance for Lewt had to be reshot before Breen would give his okay. But Selznick refused to go along with Breen's suggestion that he change the ending to show Pearl making her long climb along the rocks, only to die before reaching Lewt. Breen was unavailable for the final screening; consequently, Geoff Shurlock, who thought it was the best movie he had seen all year, signed off on the film. Selznick, who was worried about second thoughts by Breen, offered to arrange a second showing for him, but Breen said it wasn't necessary in view of his close involvement with the production.[33]

Catholic reaction to the film was quite another matter. Selznick had already made one misstep in his casting of the two leading roles. As Gregory Peck later recalled, Selznick took a kind of "perverse delight" in casting him as Lewt just after he had played a priest in *Keys of the Kingdom* and Jennifer Jones as Pearl following her leading role in *The Song of Bernadette.* "He took two saintly characters," Peck continued, "and made us into kind of sex fiends." Selznick didn't help his situation when he failed to send the Legion a preview print, although no snub was intended. He had wanted to release the film before January 1, 1947, in order to qualify for the Academy Awards, and a strike at the Technicolor lab had left him with just enough prints for the opening in two Los Angeles theaters.[34]

Hedda Hopper's review in the *Los Angeles Times* only added to the church's suspicions. *Duel in the Sun,* she wrote, "is sex rampant. Jennifer Jones is no Bernadette. Gregory Peck . . . is no 'Father Chisolm.' But these two are hotter than a gunman's pistol." The first sign of trouble was a scathing review by William Mooring in the Los Angeles Catholic paper *Tidings* two days after the opening. According to Mooring, the picture was nothing more than plush pornography that flouted the Production Code through its excessive preoccupation with sex. Selznick was taken to task for, among other things, ridiculing a religious figure in the form of the Sinkiller, Jones's indecent costuming, and the "feeble attempt" to punish the two sinners by killing them off at the end of the film. Mooring continued his criticism in the next issue, concluding that Selznick's picture was worse than *The Outlaw.* Protest letters prompted by Mooring's review poured into the Legion from Los Angeles; one was from a Marine who said that although he had been "around," he was "scandalized by the things" he had seen and heard in the film. Alarmed, Bishop John Cantwell informed Los Angeles Catholics that they could not in good conscience see the film until it had been rated by the Legion.[35]

Selznick, who was having an affair with Jones, protested to the editor of *Tidings* about "the callous and diseased mind" which not only had attacked his reputation but had "cast a wicked and wanton slur upon Miss Jones . . . a distinguished artist . . . a Catholic who has received her education in a convent." In view of having won Code approval, Selznick clearly felt victimized by the church's attack, although he had to know that the Legion had no compunction about second-guessing the PCA. Nevertheless, when Selznick's key distributor, Neil Agnew (who was worried about the film), suggested that they ask Martin Quigley to look at it, Selznick agreed. In some ways, Quigley's evaluation was even more disconcerting than Mooring's. Declaring that the film in its present form presented an acute problem for both Selznick and the industry, he warned that it not only would create a wave of censorship throughout the country but would "imperil America's prestige throughout the world." As the controversy over what *Variety* referred to as "lust in the dust" began to grow, Breen sought to put some distance between himself and the picture by claiming that he had been in the hospital when the film received a Code seal. His family tried to help out, telling one priest they thought it was so filthy that it made *The Outlaw* look like *Little Women.*[36]

In view of Quigley's involvement, the Legion held off asking for a preview print in the hope that he could help clean up the film. Masterson was not worried about the delay because *Duel* was playing only in Los Angeles, where Bishop Cantwell had warned his people against seeing it until the Legion had rated it. He was concerned, however, that Mooring's nationally syndicated reviews would create such an uproar that he would be forced to classify it before Quigley had a chance to persuade Selznick to alter the picture. Luckily the Catholic news service agreed at the last minute to delay reprinting Mooring's criticism.[37]

Selznick at first appealed to the other studio heads for support on the ground that the film had been approved by the PCA, but no one wanted to get involved in a fight with the Legion. Especially frustrating was Breen's retreat under church fire. When Masterson confronted him over his negligence, Breen apologized for making a "serious error" and asked for suggestions as to how he could make amends. Deserted by the PCA, which was now pressuring him to deal with the Legion's criticism, Selznick felt he had no choice but to work with Quigley in order to salvage his picture.[38]

The publisher's major objections focused on what he characterized as the excessive sexuality in the film. The first line of attack was the elimination of a number of "suggestive" lines, including Lewt's father's advice that Lewt take his fun where he can find it and a similar comment from Jesse: "Take what you want and when you want it." Recognizing that the entire scene of Lewt's rape of Pearl could not be eliminated because Pearl's subsequent love-hate relationship with Lewt would be incomprehensible without it, Quigley insisted that the sequence be reduced as much as possible. Selznick grudgingly consented, eliminating five shots, including a passionate kiss between the two stars. Quigley also objected to a scene where Lewt implies that he has seen Pearl skinny-dipping. Selznick agreed to cut some of the dialogue but refused to eliminate the entire sequence. He also trimmed Pearl's seductive dance after Lewt promises to announce their engagement. Selznick also made extensive cuts in the "stallion sequence," in which Pearl watches Lewt tame a stallion that had been agitated by a mare in heat. Lines comparing their own passion to that of the animals were cut. Although Quigley was not particularly bothered by the Sinkiller's role, he persuaded Selznick that it would probably be advisable not to refer to him as "padre." In all, Quigley's advice led to thirty-one cuts ranging from a few frames to as much as sixty-five feet of film.[39]

A new print was rushed to the Legion along with Quigley's statement that Selznick's cooperation had led to a substantial improvement in the picture. Nevertheless, Quigley warned the producer, he couldn't guarantee that the Legion would lift its ban and, in light of the film's sordid theme, the best he could hope for was a B. The revised film was shown to the Legion's reviewers and consultors on February 7, after Masterson asked them to be as objective as possible and to disregard the publicity surrounding it. Although most of the viewers were concerned about "the general aura of sex and animality" that characterized the film, they were evenly divided between classifying it as a B or a C. In view of the split, a second viewing was arranged for Bishop Scully, Mary Looram, and another priest, all of whom voted to continue the condemnation. In order not to embarrass Quigley, who had endorsed the new version, the Legion held back on announcing its decision in the hope that Selznick could be persuaded to make another round of cuts, focusing his efforts on the dance and seduction scenes as well as the ending, where Lewt and Pearl not only failed to acknowledge the wrongfulness of their actions but were allowed to triumph in "one last lustful embrace."[40]

Once again several lines disappeared, and Pearl's dance scene was cut by 60 percent, in effect reducing it, in Selznick's words, to "an innocuous schoolgirl dance." In doing so, he felt that he had substantially reduced the quality of the film since it is the dance that fires Lewt to agree to marriage. Lewt must be a schoolboy, he told an assistant, if his initial reluctance was overcome by such a tepid performance. The dance cuts were an especially sore point with the producer, because this sequence had been filmed in the presence of Breen and some of his staff. Moreover, as Jones was not a skilled dancer, the scene had to be repeated a number of times to make it work. At that point, with his picture disappearing before his very eyes, Selznick refused to tinker with the ending despite the Legion's conviction that there was something vaguely wrong about letting the two sinners die in each other's arms.[41]

Selznick's concessions were spurred by the growing protests from the West Coast, where the original print was still playing. Los Angeles Catholic sodality groups announced that they were contemplating a one-month boycott of all films because of the current Hollywood "wave of immoral pictures" like Selznick's, a step that *Variety* called "the most significant Catholic action since the Legion was established" and one that could lead to federal censorship. Although the Legion had not yet made its condemnation public, the news from Los Angeles stirred other Catholic organizations to take steps before it came to their towns. The Houston Catholic Youth Organization asked the mayor to ban "this masterpiece of filth [which] glorifies drunkenness, adultery, rape and other forms of lowest immorality." Father John Sheehy, in charge of chaplains' services in Boston, summed up the feelings of the Catholic opposition when he wrote that the picture was both "incredibly lewd" and a burlesque of religion. According to Sheehy, Selznick had single-handedly destroyed the morality of millions of Americans; he predicted that this would result in "thousands of priests [being] detained years longer in confessionals seeking to dispel the evil images born of witnessing this alleged entertainment."[42]

Selznick canceled an opening in Texas scheduled for February 24, 1946, to give the Legion enough time to review the new version. Nevertheless, encouraged by the news that Eric Johnston had refused the Legion's request that the PCA withdraw its seal, he made it clear to Quigley that he had tried to please the Legion and "remove the blot" from his record, but he warned that if the church was not satisfied with this latest round of cuts, he would release the original nationwide and inform the public of the "raw deal" he had received. The last thing he wanted to do, he said, was to take on the Legion, but if he had to, it would be over the original uncut version. And if the battle hurt the industry, he told Eric Johnston, "it will be because of the complete cowardice of the Code authority and industry leaders in going into hiding."[43]

Meanwhile, the Los Angeles archdiocese, which had led the fight against Selznick, found itself the target of a counterprotest by mid-February. "Thousands of letters" poured in like the one from an "ex-Catholic and a graduate of Holy Cross College," excoriating Cantwell for his "bigotry, intolerance and arrogance," which he claimed was alienating many Catholics who had fought for liberty and democracy in the recent war. Feeling the heat, Bishop Cantwell asked Masterson to look at the original before re-evaluating this latest version in order to appreciate how much Selznick had tried to cooperate. But Masterson, who had Cardinal Spellman's support, pointed out that seeing the original would be a waste of time because the Legion could base its judgment only on the film that was under consideration. The fact that it constituted an improvement over some previous version did not necessarily mean that it should be reclassified. Any other reason, such as trying to avoid anti-Catholic protests, he reminded the bishop, would be contrary to Legion policy.[44]

Sensing that the revised version wasn't going to solve his problems, Quigley told Selznick that his only chance of saving his film was negotiating directly with the Legion. Bitter over what he considered Breen's betrayal, Selznick talked about taking on the church and the entire industry in order to clear his name, but he recognized that with most theaters closed to him because of the Legion's opposition, such a move would spell financial ruin. He asked Neil Agnew to meet with McClafferty and Masterson on February 26. McClafferty suggested that the film's chances of escaping a condemnation would be greatly improved if Selznick followed Breen's original suggestion to conclude the film with Pearl sliding down the hillside in a vain attempt to reach her lover. But Agnew could not sell Selznick on the change. The producer claimed that the Legion was exploiting his willingness to cooperate so that each new set of concessions only spurred them to ask for another round of cuts. He even blamed Agnew for suggesting that Quigley be brought in as a consultant in the first place, for, he claimed, this led Quigley to recommend cuts he would never have asked for in normal circumstances. Now, after he had followed "90 to 95 percent" of Quigley's suggestions, the Legion still wasn't satisfied.[45]

At first Selznick told Agnew that he was prepared to put the film out and let the "chips fall where they may." But he would tell his side of the story in "full-page advertisements, over the radio, with a foreword to the picture, with a trailer and with every other means at my disposal." The result, he warned, would be the destruction of the Code and the onset of federal censorship. Nevertheless, he said, he was willing to go down fighting rather than release an inferior film. But after he got this bravado out of his system, he told Agnew that he was willing to meet with the Legion as long as they would not discuss any further cuts. Quigley prepared McClafferty for the meeting on March 4 with Selznick: "He wavers between this frenzied attitude on one side and a very practicable, sensible, realistic attitude on another." If too many people were present at the meeting, he warned, Selznick would fill the discussion with "violent self-righteous pronouncements." With only Quigley and Masterson present, McClafferty apparently caught Selznick in the right mood, and he agreed to another round of revisions. By this point, Selznick began to complain that he was losing track of all the cuts he had agreed to.[46]

Although Selznick refused to allow any more tinkering with the story, he agreed to add a moral in the form of an introduction written by McClafferty. The prologue's purple prose rivaled that of the studio writers of the day:

> *Duel in the Sun*, two years in the making, a saga of Texas in the 1880s, when primitive passions rode the raw frontier of an expanding nation. Here the forces of evil were in constant conflict with the deeper morality of the hearty pioneers. And here, as in the story we tell, a grim fate lay waiting for the transgressor upon the laws of God and man.
>
> The characters in *Duel in the Sun* are built out of the legends of a colorful era, when a million acres were one man's estate, and another man's life was held as lightly as a woman's virtue.

> The character of the Sinkiller is based upon those bogus unordained evangelists who preyed upon the hungry need for spiritual guidance, and who were recognized as charlatans by the intelligent and God-fearing.[47]

But the ending was still a sticking point for Masterson and McClafferty. After two more days of negotiations, Selznick allowed McClafferty to identify the immorality in the lives of the characters by means of an epilogue following the closing credits. In a strange hybrid of praise and condemnation, the Legion's message was integrated into information about the various awards earned by the cast. Once the picture was over, "Honors" was flashed on the screen along with the statement:

> This theater takes pleasure in calling attention to honors awarded *Duel in the Sun.*
>
> "Jennifer Jones as Pearl Chavez . . . pursued . . . tortured . . . by her own passions, whose moral weakness leads to transgressions against the law of God. . . . Miss Jones, Academy Award winner and four times nominee, has won the *Look* Award and Academy nomination for her portrayal of Pearl.
>
> Gregory Peck as Lewt McCanless . . . untamed . . . Godless . . . whose unbridled recklessness brings down upon him the frustration of his own hopes, and havoc and destruction upon others. . . . Mr. Peck, twice Academy Award nominee, has won the *Look* Award for his portrayal of Lewt.
>
> Miss Lillian Gish as Laura Belle McCanless . . . whose gentle nature cannot cope with the brutal immorality of a crude new world. . . . Miss Gish has won an Academy Award nomination for her portrayal of Laura Belle.[48]

With the prologue and the epilogue serving as moral bookends to the story, McClafferty and Masterson indicated that the film would be reclassified. But because Technicolor film was not in stock at the time of the agreement, the Legion agreed that the epilogue could be printed in either sepia or black and white. Concerned that exhibitors might simply drop the prologue and the epilogue entirely, the Legion pressured Selznick to attach a set of instructions to each film canister explaining that they were an integral part of the film along with directions on the order in which they were to be shown.[49]

What looked good on paper lost something on the screen. McClafferty concluded that the epilogue's lack of color diminished the significance of the message. Moreover, its placement after the film credits instead of at the end of the story meant that many of the audience members would be on their way out by the time the epilogue appeared on the screen. Selznick contacted Quigley, who agreed with him that the priest's belated objections were "immaterial morally and impossible technically." Buttressed by Quigley's support, the producer informed McClafferty that he had honored his part of the bargain and as far as he was concerned the negotiations were over. McClafferty backed down.[50]

But the producer faced one last humiliation. When the Legion agreed to classify the film as a B, McClafferty had promised to release an accompanying statement stressing Selznick's cooperation, but all that materialized was a brief pronouncement grudgingly noting that Selznick had "displayed an awareness of responsibility for the moral and social integrity of motion pictures." For Selznick, the Legion's statement was more of a booby prize than the merit badge he had expected. Not only did it fail to take him off the hook, but its brevity stood in sharp contrast to the lengthy attack to which the film had been exposed. He was enraged to find that Ed Sullivan still thought the film was condemned three weeks after the Legion's announcement. If a major columnist like Sullivan hadn't heard about it, he complained to a friend, it was highly unlikely that the average Catholic knew about it, a situation he attributed to the far greater publicity given to the Legion's condemnation than to the film's reclassification. In an effort to counter whatever damage the Legion's new rating might do, his staff prepared a series of press releases stressing that films like *The Best Years of Our Lives*, *Blue Skies*, *Anna and the King of Siam*, "and other distinguished pictures" had also been classified as a B by the Legion.[51]

Duel in the Sun went into general release on May 1, 1946, four months after the original tryouts in Los Angeles. Although Selznick did his best to block movie houses from offering the usual reduced prices for children because this would open him up to new attacks, several church organizations continued to protest the film, and one bishop condemned it as inappropriate for anyone who was under twenty-one. In spite of Selznick's tribulations, the film earned $10 million in its first year. Nevertheless, as David Thomson has suggested, in light of the film's budget and advertising and distribution costs, it may not have broken even. Selznick, who claimed that the delays caused by the Legion negotiations cost him as much as $5 million, was still fuming three months after the film's release. "Reverend Masterson has not been designated by God as the final word in what is seriously offensive," he charged, "and we are damn sure that the non-Catholics of America, and a goodly percentage of Catholics as well, do not accept him." Quigley was also angry that all his help had not led to additional advertising in his publications, and it is doubtful that Selznick's Christmas gift of a television set changed his mind. Selznick at least learned a lesson. When he completed his next film, *The Paradine Case*, a copy was air-expressed to the Legion as a sign of his willingness to cooperate.[52]

Duel in the Sun turned out to be McClafferty's last shootout with Hollywood. Masterson, who replaced him, had little time to rest before he found himself embroiled in a new controversy with Spyros Skouras, the president of

Twentieth Century-Fox, who had paid $200,000 for the film rights to Kathleen Winsor's sensational novel *Forever Amber*, the story of a young woman who sleeps her way up the social ladder in Restoration England, eventually becoming the mistress of King Charles II. Masterson had already run into difficulty with the Skouras family in connection with the distribution of J. Arthur Rank's *Black Narcissus* (1946), a story about a group of English missionary nuns stationed in the Himalayas. The film, which had been approved by the PCA, highlighted the women's difficulties, which included one nun being driven mad by her sexual frustrations. Despite Rank's decision to identify them in the prologue as "Protestant nuns of the Anglican Church" instead of "Anglo-Catholic nuns" (which was used in the British version), the film was condemned by the Legion because it ignored "the spiritual motivation which is the foundation and safeguard of religious life and it offensively tends to characterize such life as an escape for the abnormal, the neurotic and the frustrated." Hearing that Charles Skouras, Spyros's brother, had booked the film in several of his theaters, Masterson sent him a telegram stating that the Legion was shocked by his action. He dismissed in disbelief Charles's defense that he didn't know about the condemnation. When Charles complained to his close friend Cardinal Spellman about Masterson's attack, the priest was reprimanded for his intemperate language. Quigley tried unsuccessfully to talk Spellman out of sending Charles a letter disavowing Masterson's actions, arguing that it would encourage others to seek his help whenever their films were in trouble.[53]

Although Rank was able to get his film reclassified as A-II by sharply reducing any implication of repressed sexuality among the nuns and coming up with a new ending, Spellman's actions may have given Spyros Skouras a false sense of security. Also, having sunk $5 million into *Forever Amber*, making it the most expensive film in the studio's history, the studio head may have convinced himself that the Legion wouldn't give him too much trouble. He did not invite the Legion to a New York screening on October 8, 1947, and showed *Forever Amber* to the Legion at the last minute. *Theater Facts*, the bulletin of the Associated Theater Owners of Indiana, scored Skouras for delaying the Legion preview, which it branded a "stupid and dangerous maneuver." Breen, who initially characterized the story as "raw stuff, filled on almost every page with details of adultery, illicit sex, crime, perversion, abortion and God only knows what," approved it after almost everything that had made the novel so shocking had been removed. Although the reviewers felt that Fox had cleaned up the film, Masterson wanted to send a message to Hollywood that there would be no relaxation of standards under his stewardship. He saw the film just before its release and promptly notified Fox that unless changes were made, he would condemn it publicly. One week later, with no response from Skouras, Spellman, who obviously felt taken advantage of, publicly condemned *Forever Amber* in a letter to be read at all masses, his first public censure of a film since *Two-Faced Woman* in 1941.[54]

Spellman's announcement coincided with the general release of the film, with more than three thousand bookings secured and extensive advertising. Local Legion directors across the country complained that they had little or no time to contact the theaters in their area. Father Michael O. Driscoll, head of the Legion in Springfield, Illinois, told Masterson that local theater owners had always cooperated in not booking condemned films when given ample notice. He predicted a collapse of the Legion's effectiveness if Skouras's tactics became the norm. The only solution, he believed, was to head off future surprises by persuading Eric Johnston to give the Legion a permanent seat on the PCA.[55]

In a conciliatory gesture, Fox's president invited Masterson to his country home for "golf, lunch, dinner and discussion," but the priest refused. Skouras then agreed to meet Masterson and Mary Looram at the Legion office, where he tried in vain to convince them that *Forever Amber* was not as bad as *Duel in the Sun* or *The Postman Always Rings Twice.* Recognizing that he wasn't making any headway, Skouras warned them that he had no intention of withdrawing the film. If the Legion went ahead with its condemnation, he would issue a press release defending his studio's integrity. Masterson's response—that the bishops would interpret his action as a declaration of war—failed to move Skouras. On October 23, producer William Perlberg announced that he would not alter the film. Pointing out that it had been approved by a Catholic layman, Joe Breen, Perlberg was willing to leave the final decision to the moviegoers, who he noted had flocked to the film on opening day. In an unprecedented attack on the Legion, Skouras the next day branded the church's condemnation as "unfair and harsh" and declared that he too was willing to leave the final decision to the court of public opinion.[56]

"This time the chips are really down," Masterson told Father Devlin. Bishop Scully immediately sent a letter to all the bishops informing them that Skouras had challenged the Legion in the press and the outcome rested on the film's box-office receipts. The bishops and local Legion directors went into high gear. Cardinal Dougherty directed Catholics to stay away for a year from any theater that showed the film. Although Bishop Keough, the former chair of the Episcopal Committee, personally believed that *Forever Amber* should not have been condemned, he banned the film in Providence and successfully pressured local theater owners not to book it in a show of solidarity. "With God's help," he told Bishop Scully, "we can win this time as we have done in the past." In Rochester, New York, Bishop Kearney's call for a Catholic boycott of the film was followed by a directive from the city's safety commissioner ordering theater owners not to show it on the ground that it was "indecent and immoral." When a state Supreme Court justice overturned the ban, Catholic war veterans picketed the theater. Reports of increased Catholic activity poured into the Legion, including four St. Joseph High School students in Rockland, Illinois, who gave up their jobs as ushers rather than work during a showing of the picture.[57]

The results of the campaign were mixed. In Grand Rapids, Michigan, the head of the local Legion was able to get the mayor and city council to block any showing of the film. One Illinois theater put on its marquee: "*Forever Amber* cancelled by protest of the Catholic church." The Legion's classification came too late to affect Buffalo's downtown bookings, but local distributors kept the film out of the neighborhood theaters. In other areas the Legion had to be satisfied with token victories. In Wheeling, West Virginia, the manager of a local chain, while unwilling to stop the film, eliminated specially priced children's tickets and dramatically reduced the size of his newspaper ads. But some, like the owners of the Rockland Theater in Nyack, New York, pointed out that they were not always able to dictate the quality of the films they showed. Although they admitted that *Forever Amber* was not an uplifting story, they believed Fox had done a good job of removing the "trash" from the film. In the final analysis, they said, whose "business judgment" was right—those who canceled the film or those who exhibited it—would be proven at the box office.[58]

Although church leaders were interested in moral judgments and not business judgments, they knew that if the movie was a hit it would deal a serious blow to the Legion. In spite of the film's initial success—it topped all previous attendance records at New York's Roxy Theater and did great business in its opening run around the country—Spyros Skouras was uncomfortable with the negative publicity generated by the Legion campaign. Within a week of *Forever Amber*'s opening, he sent his head of sales and a staff writer to meet with Masterson to see what could be done to get the condemnation lifted. Skouras's initial feeler was dismissed by Masterson as an attempt to string out the negotiations while the studio milked the controversy. Refusing to deal with "low-level people," he demanded that Skouras and Otto Preminger, the director, attend the next meeting. Consequently, Skouras and Preminger, accompanied by Steven Jackson of Breen's office, met on October 27 with Masterson and Mary Looram. Preminger later claimed that Skouras was so frantic by this point that he knelt before Masterson, kissing his hand and begging, "Father, Father, please help," but Masterson's notes on the meeting make no mention of groveling by the Fox president. If anything, he suspected that Skouras was trying to put something over on him by suggesting that he sit down with Preminger and go over the film foot by foot, pointing out what should be cut. Masterson was in a difficult position: his decision to condemn the film stemmed more from a desire to send a message to Hollywood than from any specific objections. Consequently, he turned down the offer, arguing that his complaints had to do more with the nature of the story and its development.[59]

Jackson broke the stalemate a few days later by suggesting a number of cuts aimed at eliminating any suggestion that Amber had slept her way to the top. Consequently, Amber's offer to do "anything, anything" for protection was cut out along with another character's promise that whoever was keeping company with Black Jack would get her reward. There was even a great deal of arguing over the king's dismissal of Amber from the palace with the seemingly innocent declaration that he would undertake provision for her journey, with the studio insisting that Charles was only promising to provide Amber with food for her trip rather than some sexual quid pro quo. Jackson brokered a compromise in which George Sanders, who played the king, would be called back to reread the line, emphasizing the phrase "for your journey."[60]

But none of these cuts met the Legion's original objection to what it characterized as the picture's sordid theme. Fox finally seized on the resolution of last resort: a prologue or epilogue that would serve as a warning label. It had worked for Howard Hughes and David O. Selznick, and it now bailed out Skouras, who tacked on an introduction to show that, although Amber acquired finery and luxury, they did not bring her happiness. Consequently, audiences were introduced to the story with: "This is the tragic story of Amber St. Clare . . . slave to ambition, stranger to virtue . . . fated to find the wealth and power she ruthlessly gained wither to ashes in the fires lit by passions and fed by defiance of the eternal command. . . . The wages of sin is death." At the end of the picture, Amber's lover repeats the lines spoken earlier in the film: "Amber, haven't we caused enough unhappiness? May God have mercy on us both for our sins." In a press release that repudiated his original challenge to the Legion, Skouras declared that he had never intended to question the rights of religious leaders to offer moral guidance to their members or to propose that "the popularity of a motion picture is a true criterion of its moral character." Masterson, who had seen a draft of the statement prior to its release, persuaded Skouras to add that his defiance of the Legion condemnation had hurt him financially.[61]

In spite of Fox's concessions, many of the Legion's reviewers who had been caught up in the campaign against Skouras dismissed the epilogue as a sop that did little to make up for the evil of Amber's life. Although Amber eventually loses her child, some felt that she hadn't been punished enough. As one consultor put it: "She isn't going to the gallows; she isn't subject to poverty; nor to suffering of any kind." Nevertheless, Masterson concluded that the studio had made a good-faith effort and reclassified the film as a B. Neither side was happy: Skouras claimed that the condemnation had cost his studio at least $2 million, and a number of priests wrote to the Legion complaining that the film's notoriety had led to the sale of some 300,000 copies of the novel. But Skouras, like Selznick, did not want to go through it again. Ten years later he told Buddy Adler, his chief of production, to work with the Legion as closely as possible on *Peyton Place* in order to avoid the experience the studio had had with *Forever Amber*.[62]

TEN

"Get Father Devlin"

The Legion's success in forcing producers like David O. Selznick and Spyros Skouras to alter their films represented only part of the church's influence in Hollywood. Working behind the scenes, Catholic consultants labored to shape the image of the church that appeared on the screen. In 1921 a priest had written to the *Ecclesiastical Journal* asking if it would be appropriate for the clergy to play themselves in the movies. The answer was definitely not; "those finer qualities of the true priest" were too subtle to be captured on the screen, and anything Hollywood would try would simply undermine the dignity of the priesthood. Moviemakers, of course, had no qualms about incorporating priests, nuns, ministers, and rabbis into their scripts, and there was no shortage of actors to play the parts. The real problem was ensuring that their portrayal of the clergy didn't end up alienating some religious group. All the various attempts at self-regulation, from the Thirteen Points and the Don'ts and Be Carefuls down to the Production Code, included a pledge not to ridicule the clergy or their beliefs and to make sure that religious ceremonies were handled respectfully.[1]

Father Daniel Lord, who worked with Cecil B. deMille on *King of Kings* in

1927, became the first major Catholic film consultant. The two men kept in touch during the following years, and in spite of the priest's unhappy experience with *The Sign of the Cross*, he gladly served as deMille's sounding board on many religious projects. Consequently, when a friend recommended that the producer consider turning Mary Borden's novel *Mary of Nazareth* into a film in 1934, he immediately sounded out Lord. The priest admitted that he hadn't read the book, but warned deMille that he was on dangerous ground because the story could alienate both "dyed-in-the-wool Protestants, who from Reformation days were taught to distrust the mother of God, and Catholics, to whom she is sacred." Lord was appalled to discover that the book suggested that Mary was the mother of several children. Acting on the priest's advice not to touch this "repugnant" story, the producer immediately dropped all negotiations with Borden's agent.[2]

Nevertheless, the subject continued to intrigue deMille, who enlisted Lord's aid again in the late 1930s in a plan to do a follow-up to *King of Kings*, entitled *Queen of Queens*. On January 9, 1941, he asked Lord to take a look at the uncompleted script to make sure that he was on the right course. Encouraged by Lord's initially positive reaction, deMille sent a copy to Monsignor Fulton J. Sheen, who had gained a great deal of popularity with his radio program, "The Catholic Hour." Sheen said that the script was not only beautifully written but revealed "the spark of a genius" and gave the project his blessing.[3]

The more cautious Lord, who knew from experience deMille's habit of spicing up biblical stories to sell a film, told the producer he wanted to look at subsequent versions of the script to see how he handled such scenes as one marked "the Court of Herod." DeMille planned to use the court as a backdrop for Salome's dance of the seven veils in exchange for the head of John the Baptist. "What in thunder has this to do with the Blessed Virgin?" he asked deMille. Not only was there no indication in the Bible that Mary and Salome had ever met, he noted, but there was no description in it of the dance or, for that matter, of Herod's court. "Whether she danced the dance of the seven veils or Papinta's skirt dance or a Herodian Jitterbug's latest step," he said, "we don't know." When deMille responded that he could understand that some people might resent the appearance of a sensuous dance and a beheading in a picture dealing with the mother of God, Lord responded that he had missed the point. "People can witness murder without being in any way tempted to go out and perform murder." But "dances of passion and scenes of lust are something quite different," he said. "We all know, in strict honesty, that men and women are so biologically constituted that in the presence of [such] scenes they have inevitable reactions." Catholic audiences would be furious, he warned the producer. "They come to see Our Lady, and they get Salome in a dance which was sufficient to whip a man to the point of murder and lust for his own daughter-in-law." It would be especially dangerous for younger audience members, who were more easily influenced by "the hot impact of temptation" and would remember the dance when the Virgin Mary was long forgotten. Lord urged deMille to drop the entire scene and go with "the loveliest single subject connected with woman: the drama of a pure woman who becomes the mother of God." To preface this with Salome, he argued, would be like introducing a movie about Whistler's mother with a dance by Gypsy Rose Lee. Lord never came to grips with the fact that it was the Salomes and not the saints that really interested the producer. Nevertheless, deMille, who didn't want a repeat of the furor surrounding *The Sign of the Cross*, told Lord that his comments had persuaded him to drop the *Queen of Queens* project because it was bound to lose its dramatic effect without the "great black background" of Salome and Herod against which "Mary will stand pure and white as the world's greatest mother."[4]

Although Lord was the best known, he was not the only Catholic movie consultant in the 1920s and early 1930s. In addition to Charles McMahon and Rita McGoldrick, Father Wilfrid Parsons offered a steady stream of advice on a number of scripts, and Monsignor S. J. Peoples served as a technical advisor on *Cradle Song*, the story of a nun who adopts a foundling. But in 1933, Bishop John J. Cantwell announced that because the film industry was situated in his diocese, all Catholic film advising was the proper business of the ordinary of Los Angeles. With this in mind, he asked the president of Loyola University, where many priests stayed when they visited the city, to warn them not to get involved with filmmaking. Cantwell had decided that all technical advising should be placed in the hands of one of his priests. He chose as the official Catholic film adviser the Irish-born Father John Devlin, who had been his personal secretary for five years before becoming pastor of St. Vincent's parish and head of the Los Angeles Legion of Decency. "Get Father Devlin" quickly became the watchword at any studio that was considering making a film touching on the Catholic church. Devlin, who had his own parish to run as well as heading up the diocesan Legion of Decency, regularly reviewed from thirty to fifty scripts each year for everything from big-budget films like *Going My Way* to Red Ryder potboilers at Republic.[5]

Unlike other technical consultants, Devlin did not appear on studio payroll. As Lou Edelman explained to Hal Wallis, head of production at Warner, "There are no charges since it is the duty of the Catholic Archdiocese to look after such matters." Nevertheless, most producers made a contribution to St.

Vincent's whenever Devlin helped them with a script, ranging from the gift of a radio for his work on *The Garden of Allah*, to $50 for *The Great John L*, $675 for *The Miracle of the Bells*, and $2,500 for *Going My Way*.[6]

Occasional articles on "the movie priest" in the Catholic press made Devlin the resident expert on Hollywood for church members across the country. His mail included letters from two aspiring starlets in search of a place to stay and parents checking on their daughter, who had already moved to Hollywood. He also received a steady stream of requests from Catholic extras urging him to use his influence to get them work. He was flooded with "surefire" ideas and scripts, from a priest's story of a coyote hunt to a nun's biography of Saint Adelaide. Trying to let the would-be screenwriters down without hurting their feelings, his stock answer was that any attempt to place a script would compromise his position with the industry. If someone came up with a marketable idea, however, Devlin was the equal of any Hollywood agent. Father Edward Murphy asked Devlin if the $6,000 he had been offered by David O. Selznick for the rights to his script on the life of Mary Magdalene was a fair price. Having heard that Devlin had been able to get $50,000 from a producer for another priest who had come up with a good idea for a movie, he wondered about the apparent discrepancy. Devlin wrote back that the $50,000 had been a donation to a Catholic charity, not payment for a script, and advised him that Selznick's offer was a fair one. But, he told Murphy, he could make some extra money on the deal by insisting that Selznick sign a separate contract making him a technical adviser for the script and the actual production. "Hold out for both jobs," he advised. "They should pay not less than $500 a week in addition to all hotel and transportation expenses."[7]

Still, Devlin's main task (other than his regular priestly duties) was reviewing studio scripts. He claimed in a magazine interview that all the job required "is a thorough knowledge of the moral code given by God and Moses on Mt. Sinai, plus the ability to relate this knowledge to modern trends and changing conditions." Privately, he admitted that it wasn't so easy. Anyone who wanted to take up this line of work, he told Father John McClafferty, should practice the art of evasion. Patience was another prerequisite. But he could be painfully blunt at times. After reading an MGM script for a story about a woman with a split personality, he advised the producer to "consign the script to an incinerator. It would certainly make a good fire."[8]

Although directors and screenwriters feared dealing with Devlin, he maintained a sense of humor. Philip Dunne remembered locking horns with him over his script for *David and Bathsheba*. Unsure of how to handle David's going unpunished for murder and adultery, a clear-cut violation of the Code, the PCA referred the problem to Devlin. The priest, who was more concerned that the story might tarnish the image of a Catholic saint, vetoed the screenplay. Luckily, Darryl Zanuck had received a number of glowing reports on the script from several rabbis, which Dunne presented to Devlin. "Well, what do these prove?" he growled. "Only," said Dunne, "that where King David is concerned, the rabbis think they have a prior claim." The priest glared at him for a moment, then laughed, and approved the script.[9]

Although Devlin was supposed to focus on Hollywood's treatment of the church, he was always sensitive to anything that might defame the Irish. He warned the producer of *The Great John L* against turning the film into a story of good-natured drinkers and brawlers. Similarly, he objected to what he viewed as RKO's attempt to ridicule an "ancient and honorable race" in *Father Malachy's Miracle.* The main interests of the town's inhabitants in the script appeared to be drinking and hurling, which, he complained, turned the Irish national sport into an opportunity for mayhem. Nor was the Legion beyond criticism in this area. When Devlin faulted Father McClafferty for failing to cite the negative Irish stereotypes in *Coney Island* as one reason for classifying it as a B, the priest had to remind him that defending the Irish was not part of the bishops' charge to the Legion.[10]

Because Devlin was in command of the Los Angeles Legion of Decency, he also had no reservations about going beyond his role as technical consultant on Catholic matters to help producers ward off future problems with McClafferty and his successors. Although he was brought in to help Twentieth Century-Fox avoid such mistakes as putting a Gideon Bible in the home of the Irish-Catholic family in *A Tree Grows in Brooklyn* (1945), he also pointed out issues that could lead to a Legion condemnation. Especially dangerous was the role of Aunt Sissy, who, "in plain language," he said, "is a harlot." Characterizing her as a woman with a "cauterized conscience," Devlin declared that references to Sissy's love life like "look kid, all I know is, it can't be wrong, or I couldn't feel like I do about it" were definitely off limits. Worse, according to the priest, the story "glossed over her sins" by making her appear a sympathetic, kindhearted figure. Conversely, he was disappointed in the film's lack of compassion for the mother, who came across as "too hard." She should be the real heroine of the story, he argued. "She, after all, had to put up with a drunken dreamer of a husband, and had to endure hard work in order to feed her family." It was this kind of thing, making sin attractive and virtue unattractive, he warned the studio, that had led to the formation of the Legion of Decency.[11]

Most of Devlin's time was devoted to correcting the minor mistakes that crept into films dealing with Catholic practices. In *The Walls Came Tumbling Down*, a whodunit about the murder of a priest, Devlin pointed out that the victim would not have been using a Protestant Bible, and in a reference to the battle of Jericho where the words were shown in print, the correct Catholic spelling was Josue, not the Protestant Joshua. Similarly, the producer of *The Black Arrow* learned that bishops should be addressed as "My Lord" or "Your Lordship," never as "your reverence." Some of the errors were more glaring, like the priest who blessed himself from right to left instead of touching his left shoulder first. Devlin also dryly noted that the plug of tobacco in the priest's cheek didn't add to the actor's credibility. A bullet's shattering of a holy picture in one film, another studio was informed, would be acceptable only if it hit the background and did not touch Christ's head or heart.[12]

The use of the Catholic sacrament of confession in films was an especially sensitive issue. *Full Confession*, a 1939 RKO film in which a priest urges a murderer who has confessed his sin to him to give himself up to save an innocent man, presented no difficulty. Devlin's reservations, however, forced Warner to remove a scene from *Angels with Dirty Faces* in which the gangster played by Jimmy Cagney is shown confessing to his boyhood friend, a priest.[13]

Alfred Hitchcock's *I Confess* presented a more difficult problem because the entire plot revolved around a priest's duty not to reveal a murderer's confession. Montgomery Clift, playing Father Michael Logan, is accused of the crime because of damaging circumstantial evidence. On learning that Devlin had serious problems with the initial script, the New York Bankers' Trust informed Hitchcock that it would not finance the film until Devlin was satisfied with the story. Although Hitchcock recognized that Logan could not reveal the murderer's confession to the police, Devlin was concerned about two scenes in which the priest might have broken the seal of the confessional. In one, the priest, with the details he had gained from the criminal's disclosure, goes to the site of the murder, which leads the police to suspect him. Devlin felt that by acting on what he had been told, Logan had symbolically breached the walls of the confessional. Devlin was especially bothered by the potential problems arising out of the prosecutor's cross-examination of Logan at the trial. He warned Hitchcock that under no circumstances was the priest to look in the direction of the murderer, who was seated in the courtroom. To do so, he warned, would violate the sacred seal. Devlin was also troubled by Logan's response to the prosecutor's question, did he know who had committed the murder. Initially, the script called for a simple "no," but, as Devlin pointed out, this answer was a lie. Hitchcock satisfied Devlin by having the priest reply, "I cannot answer that." Finally, Devlin took issue with the murderer's actions after he had gone to confession. Concerned that the audience could be led to believe that the act of confession had automatically absolved him of his sins, he advised Hitchcock to insert some dialogue to indicate that penitents are not forgiven unless they are truly contrite.[14]

Hollywood's interest in historical dramas meant that a good deal of Devlin's time was devoted to defending the church's image. Persuading RKO to change the foreword to *The Hunchback of Notre Dame*, which he felt implied that the church had played a role in generating the prejudices and superstitions of the dark ages, was not a problem. Far more troublesome were films that touched on the Inquisition, like *Captain from Castille* (1947). The script was based on a historical novel by Samuel Shellabarger dealing with Cortez's conquest of Mexico. The story opened in Spain, where Diego De Silva, the Grand Inquisitor, has charged Pedro De Vargas with heresy. De Vargas and his family are imprisoned, and his young sister is tortured to death. Fortunately, De Vargas frees himself and his family with the help of a peasant girl who follows him to the New World as part of Cortez's army. De Silva, who travels to Mexico to weed out the heretics in the conquistador's army, demands that De Vargas be turned over to him. Eventually, De Silva is killed by an Aztec prince, which enables De Vargas and the peasant woman who is bearing his child to join Cortez in his attack on Mexico City.[15]

Joseph L. Mankiewicz, who summarized Shellabarger's story for Darryl Zanuck, found it to be not only historically accurate and thrilling but something of a parallel for the Allies' successful invasion of Europe. The film would contrast the birth of a new nation in the West with the feudal society of the old world as represented by De Silva, "Heinrich Himmler out of Torquemada," and his "Nazi" supporters. Devlin took a different slant, viewing the proposed film as a "deliberate attempt to discredit Christianity in general, and the Catholic church in particular." The major problem with the story, he declared, was that it exaggerated some of the evils associated with the Inquisition without giving credit to its noble purpose and "the great good it really accomplished."[16]

Alarmed by Devlin's criticism, Zanuck asked John Tucker Battle, who had worked on the script, how he should proceed. Battle, who agreed with Devlin that the story was certain to antagonize the church, recommended that Zanuck downplay the Inquisition as much as possible. Was it necessary to show heretics burning at the stake, he asked. Wouldn't it be better to have De Vargas's young sister die of torture offscreen, thus eliminating any shots of the rack? Because Hollywood never let the historical record get in the way of a good movie, Battle had no reservations about recommending that Zanuck separate the Catholic church from the Inquisition by removing all religious symbols like crucifixes and rosaries from the scenes connected to the persecution of the De Vargas family. He also suggested eliminating any religious motivation for Cortez's invasion, concentrating instead on his search for adventure and gold. Finally, in order to offset whatever negative images of the church still survived, he advised introducing a friendly priest into the movie who would represent "the true church."[17]

In a story conference based on Battle's critique, Zanuck expressed his concern that acting on all of his recommendations would remove from the picture everything that made the novel a best-seller. He felt that they could satisfy Devlin by adding Battle's "good priest" while minimizing the church's role in the Inquisition by identifying De Silva as the head of its secular arm—meaning that the villain would not appear in clerical robes. Zanuck balked, however, at excising the Inquisition. He even toyed with the idea of giving it another name, but decided to keep it because "inquisitors were just local Ku Klux Klanners, so to speak," an analogy he wisely kept from Devlin. The two changes met most of Devlin's objections, although he tried to persuade the producer to alter a scene in which De Silva, cornered by De Vargas during his escape from prison, swears to God that he will publicly apologize and free his family. Devlin charged that De Vargas's response—that he would be more likely to believe the inquisitor if he renounced his faith in God—was an "act of blasphemy," but by that point Zanuck felt he had done enough to placate the church and left the line in. Satisfied that the studio had gone a long way in meeting Devlin's objections, the Legion classified the film as A–II.[18]

MGM performed a similar screen defrocking of a clerical heavy in its 1948 version of *The Three Musketeers* after Devlin raised objections about the role of the villainous Cardinal Richelieu, who orders a string of assassinations and a diamond theft in order to protect the king. Rumors that MGM had caved in and changed Richelieu into a Protestant minister drew a heated complaint from the general secretary of the Federal Council of Churches. But the studio resolved the problem by transforming Cardinal Richelieu into Duke Richelieu for the film.[19]

Casting saints and priests gave Devlin and the church the most trouble. As one Catholic movie fan commented to Joe Breen when she found out that Twentieth Century-Fox was going to film Franz Werfel's *Song of Bernadette*, the actress "should be an unknown girl, one who never has been associated with any other characterization—no matrimonial comedies, divorces, sarongs, bathing suits, etc.—one whom no breath of scandal has ever touched." Although Jennifer Jones had played in a few minor pictures, *America* was happy with the choice. She is "an exemplary Catholic girl," the magazine informed its readers; "She was Prefect of her Sodality . . . in Tulsa . . . never missed a retreat while in school, and would absolutely not attend movies during Lent." The writer might have changed his tune if he had known that her marriage to Robert Walker was on the rocks and that she had become involved with David O. Selznick, who was married at the time.[20]

Jones's personal life was hidden from the church at the time of her elevation to screen sainthood, but Frank Sinatra had already generated a good deal of negative publicity when he was chosen to play a priest in *Miracle of the Bells* (1948). One irate writer had urged Cardinal Spellman to use his influence to ban Sinatra, "the pal of Luciano, *The Daily Worker* and other rift-raft contacts." The cardinal was so concerned that he asked Los Angeles auxiliary bishop Joseph McGucken whether it might be advisable to persuade RKO to remove Sinatra from the film. McGucken thought Spellman's suggestion was impractical, but he did contact Joe Breen to see if there was anything to the rumors that the actor was involved with the Communist party and had become a notorious philanderer. Breen told McGucken that Sinatra's major problems were excessive drinking and keeping "bad company," especially leftists who had tried to use him as a front for their political objectives. Breen, who was so adept at detecting even the slightest hint of adultery in movie scripts, was apparently less perceptive in real life, assuring McGucken that Sinatra had remained faithful to his wife. McGucken reported this back to the cardinal along with the good news that Sinatra's managers had mapped out an extensive publicity campaign which would include his becoming a benefactor for the Catholic Youth Organization. By the time the film was ready for showing, he assured Spellman, the actor "will be completely rehabilitated in the public mind."[21]

Sinatra may have been no saint, but Joan of Arc was, and therein lay a problem whenever Hollywood contemplated filming the life of the young maid of Orleans who rallies the French army for the dauphin. Her victories lead to the crowning of the dauphin, who eventually betrays her out of fear of her influence. Captured by the English, she is tried by a court headed by Bishop Cauchon and burned at the stake. Fox's Joe Schenck had run into trouble when he looked into putting George Bernard Shaw's anti-clerical play *Saint Joan* on the screen in 1936 and asked Joe Breen for advice. Breen responded that after talking with Devlin and Martin Quigley, who had opposed Cecil B. deMille's silent film *Joan the Woman* (1916), he was convinced that the story was bound to provoke a serious controversy with the church. He agreed to sound out Father William J. Lallou, an expert on Joan of Arc, who taught at St. Charles Seminary in Philadelphia. Pointing out that the film would cost more than a million dollars, Breen told Lallou, "we don't want to go into the thing if we are going to get into trouble with the church." Lallou responded that was exactly what would happen if the story was filmed. It wasn't Shaw's portrayal of Bishop Cauchon that bothered him, he told Breen, as the bishop was generally recognized as a "bad egg" and Rome had reversed the court twenty-five years after Joan's death. The problem with the play, Lallou said, was that it made Joan into a kind of "proto-Protestant" who challenges the "erroneous" teachings of the church with her own views, "whereas she was in all things a most dutiful daughter of the church and a most pious girl." On the basis of this report, Will Hays convinced Schenck to shelve the project unless Shaw agreed to change the story.[22]

Shaw, who had learned of Breen's investigation, lashed out at the MPPDA's collaboration with the Catholic church in a long letter to the editor of the *New York Times*, which touched off a string of denials, including Hays's disingenuous declaration that because the PCA had not received a script, it could not have made any judgments on the story. Father Joseph Daly, the Legion's executive secretary at the time, disclaimed any collusion between the church and the PCA. Dismissing the eighty-year-old playwright as a man in his dotage, he attributed the tirade to Shaw's anti-clericalism and leftist politics. With this much furor before a script had been written, Schenck concluded that the film wasn't worth the trouble, and he quietly dropped the project.[23]

Nevertheless, Hollywood's fascination with Joan of Arc continued. A script by Gabriel Pascal entitled *The Hundred Years' War* was vetoed by Breen in 1943 on the ground that it would alienate the church. Pascal indignantly countered that, with all due respect to Breen's organization, such an important subject could not be treated in the same way as the "literary dilettantism of the so-called scenario screen-writers," but the financing for the film fell apart without the PCA's initial approval.[24]

David O. Selznick, viewing Joan of Arc's story as a great vehicle for Jennifer Jones, commissioned Ben Hecht to come up with a script in 1946. Selznick felt that he could soften the church's opposition to the topic by opening the film with an aerial view of the Vatican while a narrator informed the audience of Joan's canonization. Convinced that he had a winner, he sounded out Martin Quigley, who told him that although Hecht had been a close friend of his since their newspaper days in Chicago, he was worried about whether Hecht would curtail his cynical attitude toward religion and morality. Furthermore, in spite of Father Lallou's view that Bishop Cauchon was an acceptable villain in the eyes of the church, Quigley was still troubled about how it would play on the screen. "While no right-minded person can ask for historical distortion," he told Selznick, "the fact remains that Catholic people are not going to be pleased by a presentation of a Catholic bishop in a despicable light." Selznick felt that he and Hecht had solved the Cauchon problem. While they had no intention of whitewashing the bishop's role, they intended to beef up the part of another priest, Father Massieu, who would emerge "as something of the hero of the piece—a far-sighted cleric who befriended Joan." The producer also said, "We are going even further than the actual historical record," by writing scenes "that would show that Joan had many friends among the clergy and at the Vatican." All in all, he felt there had never been a version of Joan's story told with "such sympathy for the

Catholic viewpoint." But in spite of his initial enthusiasm, Selznick abandoned the project.[25]

But there was always someone waiting in the wings to pick up the story. In 1946, Ingrid Bergman, along with her husband, Peter Lindstrom, and Walter Wanger, decided that Maxwell Anderson's play *Joan of Lorraine*, in which Bergman had starred on the stage, offered the best chance of putting Joan's story on the screen. They formed an independent film company, the Sierra Corporation, and Wanger sounded out the Bankers' Trust of New York, but the film's financing was put on hold while it was cleared with Cardinal Spellman. Unsure how to respond, the cardinal checked with Bishop Cantwell's office to make sure that the film would not run into any difficulties.[26]

Bishop McGucken, who handled the matter for Cantwell, felt that the best way to guarantee the movie's acceptability would be to find a priest knowledgeable in French history and the life of Joan to oversee the project. Breen came up with three clergymen to work with Father Devlin: Father Lallou, who had worked on the Shaw script in 1936; Father Andrew Snoeck, a moral theologian at the Jesuit University at Louvain, Belgium; and Father Paul Donceur, editor of the French Jesuit weekly *Etude*, an expert on Joan's life. Devlin, who felt that he could have handled the film by himself, complained to Masterson that the project suffered from a surfeit of technical advisers. He was especially concerned about Donceur. When the French priest arrived, in August 1947, Devlin presented "in very accurate French" that while he was interested in accuracy, his main concern was that the film should "carefully and sympathetically" convey a Catholic viewpoint. Devlin's message apparently lost something in the translation. When Donceur was interviewed by the *New York Times* Hollywood reporter about how to deal with the problem of depicting clergymen as villains, a direct contravention of the Production Code, he dismissed the question by noting that this was a matter for the Legion of Decency and Breen's office to handle. "I am here as a historical adviser," he told the reporter, "and historically there is no doubt about the bishops and other clerics who condemned St. Joan. They were deeply in error, and Cauchon . . . was an ambitious and venal tool of the English." Masterson, anguished by this "hot potato" of a film, asked Devlin to "drop a word to the wise in his shell-like ear," but Devlin wrote back, "the historian in Father Donceur refused to be dominated."[27]

A month later, still troubled, Masterson suggested to Devlin that they might have to go to Bishop Cantwell or Donceur's superior and have him placed under Devlin's jurisdiction. "After all," he said, "history is one thing, movies another." Masterson sent a copy of the script to Quigley, who was able to work out a satisfactory compromise. The film would show Cauchon in all his villainy, but it would make it clear to the audience that the bishop and the other ecclesiastical judges did not represent the church when they rejected Joan's plea. To reinforce this point, Walter Wanger took Quigley's advice—based on David O. Selznick's idea—and the film began with a shot of St. Peter's in 1920 during Joan's canonization ceremony while an offscreen voice proclaimed her enrollment as a saint of the church. Although Devlin, Masterson, and the church were satisfied with the results, *Joan of Arc* was a box-office disaster. The Knights of Columbus magazine did its best to resuscitate the film, arguing that Catholics had a stake in supporting Wanger's film. If it failed, *Columbia* warned its readers, there wouldn't be another, and the story of Joan would be left to "the New York Communists to hiss and laugh at."[28]

In spite of Hollywood's fascination with Joan of Arc, producers almost reluctantly took on scripts about saints, which had to be handled with kid gloves, often making the resulting product devoid of the dramatic conflict that made for a good story. Not so with priests; screenwriters were enthralled by these mysterious men, who had taken vows of celibacy and who could, if necessary, sing a song or put on boxing gloves. As Darryl Zanuck explained to his writers, the ideal religious film had to have a "miracle of faith where God's hand reaches out when all is lost" leavened with some "good Catholic humor . . . witty in a down-to-earth way." Protestant ministers must have felt that it would take a miracle to get a movie about one of their own made; the screen seemed to be filled with inspiring Father Flanagans, fighting Father Dunnes, and singing Father O'Malleys.[29]

Devlin had no objection to Hollywood's propensity for Catholic characters when it came to making a religious film, but every time a priest or nun appeared in a script this meant more work for him. His first major assignment as a technical adviser on a clerical film came when David O. Selznick decided to produce *The Garden of Allah* in 1935. Robert Hinchens's 1904 novel had been filmed in 1927 with the cooperation of some clerical consultants arranged by the IFCA's Rita McGoldrick. Selznick's treatment not only was the first sound version, but was to be filmed in Technicolor and to star Charles Boyer and Marlene Dietrich. The original Selznick script told the story of Boris Androvsky, a Trappist monk who breaks his vows and leaves his Algerian monastery. Meanwhile, Domini Enfilden has gone to the desert to seek spiritual solace after the death of her father. They meet when Boris saves her after a sensuous dance erupts into a riot. The two are married and go off on their honeymoon, but Boris's constant moodiness reflects his guilt for what he has done. When someone recognizes him, he tells Domini of his deception. After he explains that he has rediscovered his love of God through his love for her, they decide that he must return to the monastery. Domini accompanies him to the door but doesn't tell him that she is carrying his child, who will be her only comfort in the years to come.[30]

Selznick cleared the script with Breen and Quigley, although both warned him to be prepared for trouble. Breen had tested the waters by soliciting the opinions of four priests: Monsignor Joseph Corrigan, the rector of St. Charles Seminary in Philadelphia, Father Wilfrid Parsons, Father Edward Schwegler, and Devlin. The only optimistic note came from Parsons, who said the film might be saved if Boris was turned into a young man who was studying for the priesthood but had not yet been ordained. Father Schwegler summed up the feelings of the others when he pointed out that there were two major problems with the story. "Catholics simply shrink away from this sort of thing on the screen," he told Breen. It wasn't that such relationships never occurred, he said, but that didn't alter the fact "that to the ordinary simple Catholic, the thought of a priest having carnal relations with a woman is sacrilegious." After all, he said, "We cannot get too logical about religious feelings." Equally troublesome was the message that Boris owes his repentance primarily to his love for Domini.[31]

Breen, who liked the story, was not discouraged. After canvassing a number of prominent Catholic writers, he encouraged Selznick to go forward with the film. Devlin had no choice but to remove as many objectionable aspects of the story as possible. Surprisingly, he rejected Breen's suggestion that Boris not be a priest because, he correctly pointed out, this would rob the picture of its drama. But Domini's pregnancy, which had been part of the 1927 silent version, was out of the question. Both Breen and Willis Goldbeck, the associate producer, didn't believe Catholics would be offended, but the priest argued that because Boris was still a priest in the eyes of God, the marriage was not a true marriage and therefore the child would be illegitimate. Ending the film on this note, he told Selznick, would mean that some Catholics who viewed the child as a reminder of the priest's sin would leave the theater on a sour note.[32]

Devlin followed the production from beginning to end, observing some of the filming and reviewing the daily rushes. His greatest battle came over the last major scene, in which Boris and Domini are waiting for the carriage that will take him back to the monastery. For more than a month, Devlin pressured Breen to get Selznick to revise the exchange between the two in which Boris tries to find meaning in their relationship. The problem stemmed from Boris's unwillingness to accept Domini's suggestion not to think of her once he returns to the monastery. Instead he tells her that he will remember her for the rest of his life, declaring: "Since I have been able to pray again, I have told God that I am thankful that I have loved you. And, in knowing your love, I have known him." Devlin objected to this exchange because he read it as a speech of thanks to God for allowing him to sin. Breen tried to break the deadlock by substituting "And God, in His infinite mercy, will forgive me for having loved you" for the unacceptable line. Conceding that the original speech did not violate the Code, he told Selznick that he was acting "unofficially" in an effort to appease Devlin's "dogmatic viewpoint." If the change didn't make any difference to Selznick, he suggested that he use it "and thus free me of Father Devlin's wrath." With expenses mounting rapidly, Selznick accepted the substitution. Devlin also bought it with one small alteration. Because Boris could not know that "God, in His infinite mercy," would forgive him, the line had to be changed to "I have begged God to forgive me, but in knowing your love, I have known Him." When Selznick told his assistant Val Lewton that he was still worried about Devlin, Lewton wisely suggested that he arrange to have Devlin see the final cut at the same time that it was shown to the PCA. "Breen is good at talking Devlin into the proper attitude," he told his boss. At the joint screening, the priest argued that Boris should promise not to think about Domini once he reenters the monastery, but Breen persuaded him not to make an issue out of it.[33]

One of the stresses connected with Devlin's job was waiting to see how other Catholics would respond to his films. Fortunately, in this case, there was little criticism in American Catholic circles. The Legion gave *The Garden of Allah* an A–II rating, and *America* thought it was "the finest thing yet done in Technicolor." The only difficulty came in Italy, where the Vatican's rejection of the film led to its being banned throughout the country. Selznick was willing to cut and dub part of the picture to make it appear that Boris had left the monastery before he took his vows, but for reasons that were never clear, the Vatican refused to budge. All Selznick's Rome representative could tell him was that when the head of the Vatican censors' board was asked what the problem was, he had exclaimed, "Why in the world do these producers insist on putting priests on the screen?"[34]

But insist they did, and each one brought its special problems. The script for Warner's *The Fighting 69th* (1940), a patriotic recounting of the role of Father Francis Duffy and New York's Rainbow Division in World War I, worried Father McClafferty. He urged Devlin to get the studio to minimize Duffy's militarism, but because neither the Code nor the Legion's mission gave him any leverage, the film turned out to be as much a plea for military preparedness as it was a story of World War I. Devlin also had little success in getting Warner to tone down Duffy's "religious indifferentism," the belief that all religions are equally valid. As he complained to McClafferty, producers were always trying to put "expressions of tolerance in the mouth of the character of a priest," like "all religions are good, we're all going to Heaven by different routes" and "it doesn't matter what your religion is so long as you have some religion." It's difficult to explain the Catholic view of tolerance to them, he told McClafferty; "the best we can do is to have such expressions removed." Sometimes it was a difficult sell. In one case, Devlin asked Republic to prevent a priest in *That Brennan Girl* (1946) from saying "all religions are good" because this presented a misconceived idea of tolerance. "We must tolerate others," he explained to the studio, "but we do not have to tolerate their opinions, particularly when they are wrong." A bewildered executive responded that everyone felt the remark was "an effective encouragement of that religious tolerance that is so strongly necessary in the world today."[35]

Even the immensely successful *Going My Way* stirred up strife within the church. Bing Crosby starred as the singing Father O'Malley, who is sent to bail out the financially troubled Saint Dominic's, under its aging pastor Father Fitzgibbon, played by Barry Fitzgerald. Devlin did his best to interject some spiritual values into the film while trying to tone down what Breen termed the "undignified conduct" of O'Malley, but Paramount wisely ignored his advice. In spite of Devlin's careful monitoring of the film, rumors circulated in Catholic circles that the story had O'Malley getting involved with an old girlfriend, played by opera star Risë Stevens. Los Angeles's auxiliary bishop Joseph McGucken asked Breen for information on the alleged "sex angle." Breen, who had asked Paramount to make sure that Crosby and Stevens didn't appear alone together in any scenes, reassured the bishop that there was nothing to worry about.[36]

The film swept the 1944 Academy Awards and prompted one cardinal to say that it did more for the Catholic church than a dozen bishops could have accomplished in a year. But, not every Catholic was satisfied. Father Paul J. Glenn of St. Charles Seminary in Columbus, Ohio, took issue with the Legion's A–I classification and wrote a scathing review in the *Pittsburgh Catholic*, denouncing the film as "un-Catholic throughout" and in some spots "anti-Catholic." Glenn ridiculed the film for failing to show the two priests at prayer or saying mass; their priestly duties seemed to consist of doing social work among the poor. According to O'Malley, he didn't even have time to meditate. All the audience saw of Barry Fitzgerald's portrayal of Father Fitzgibbon, the priest maintained, was a "doddering old man . . . slightly mercenary and tricky, who had done nothing for forty-five years." Glenn was especially troubled by a scene like the one in which O'Malley and Fitzgibbon share a nightcap before the priest sings an Irish lullaby to put the pastor to sleep. Viewers could only conclude, Glenn declared, "that to be Catholic is to be Irish, and to be Irish is to be a whiskey drinker." Glenn's review touched off a heated exchange of letters over the next several weeks in the Pittsburgh paper. Although most of the correspondence questioned the advisability of one Catholic authority challenging the wisdom of the Legion, a number of writers supported Glenn. Referring to the exchange between Fitzgibbon and O'Malley, one writer declared that any priest should be denounced who "would put a glass of whiskey to the lips of any young person, lay or clerical." When some readers wondered how such a scene slipped by the technical consultant, the editor tried to absolve Devlin by pointing out that his job was very taxing; "that's why some things get past him." But when Pope Pius XII later discussed the film with Mervyn LeRoy, he asked the director, "Don't you love that scene where the priest takes a little drink?"[37]

Keys of the Kingdom, the story of a Scottish priest who volunteers for missionary work in China, best illustrates the potential problems of building a movie around the life of a priest. The script was based on A. J. Cronin's 1941 best-seller, which told the story of a simple nonconformist priest, Father Francis Chisolm, who devotes his life to God while warding off his narrow-minded and self-serving clerical colleagues, who have lost sight of the true meaning of the church. The story opens in 1938 with Father Chisolm nervously awaiting a visit from the bishop's secretary, Monsignor Sleeth. Chisolm has been serving as a priest in his native parish for some twelve months after having lived for thirty-five years in China. Although Bishop Mealey was a boyhood friend, he has sent his "elegant" emissary to prod Chisolm to retire. When the old priest asks why, Sleeth tells him that the bishop had received some disturbing news about his sermons. "Here is an incredible remark you made during Holy Week. 'Atheists may not all go to hell. I knew one who didn't.' . . . And good gracious, this atrocity: 'Christ was a perfect man, but Confucius had a better sense of humor!'"[38]

His two best friends from boyhood are Anselm Mealey, who is headed for the priesthood, and Willie Tulloch, an atheist. Chisolm is torn between his love for his half-cousin Nora and a life dedicated to God, but his decision is made for him when Nora commits suicide after becoming pregnant by another boy while he is away at college. At the San Morales Seminary in Spain, he is as miserable as Mealey is successful. Chisolm's brand of liberal theology alienates almost everyone on the staff with declarations like "religious belief is such an accident of birth God can't have set an exclusive value on it" (p. 58). Frustrated by his life at the seminary, Chisolm takes a long walk one day to clear his thoughts, only to find that he has gone too far and is forced to spend an innocent night in the cottage of a prostitute, who bathes his blistered feet before he returns to complete his studies.

During an early assignment as a priest, with the help of Willie Tulloch, he exposes a faked miracle that had taken in his unsuspecting pastor. A former headmaster, now a bishop, encourages him to go to China, where he finds his true vocation. Interested only in sincere converts, he kicks out the two native "rice Christians" who have been working in the rundown mission at Pai-tan in exchange for a comfortable living. Eventually he is joined by a group of nuns headed by the aristocratic Mother Superior Veronica, which leads to a conflict between his ascetic life style and her haughty ways. In the midst of a pestilence that sweeps the area, Willie Tulloch arrives as the head of a medical relief expedition. In the course of saving others, Willie is stricken. As he is dying, he tells his friend the priest that he still can't believe in God, but the priest insists that God believes in him.

Some time later, the local mandarin, Mr. Chia, whose son was saved by Chisolm, offers to force out two American Methodist missionaries, but the priest rejects the offer, pointing out that "there are many gates to heaven. We enter by one, these new preachers by another" (p. 235). Chisolm's last great trial comes when, faced with the destruction of his mission by a local warlord, he helps the opposition blow up his cannon. At the end of the story, Monsignor Sleeth is ready to depart with a scathing report for the bishop. When Sleeth accuses Chisolm of having a very slight regard for "Holy Church," Chisolm responds: "On the contrary . . . perhaps there are other mothers. And perhaps even some poor solitary pilgrims who stumble home alone" (p. 341). That night, the monsignor suddenly realizes that Chisolm is the best hope of the church. After tearing up his report, he falls on his knees, pleading, "Oh, Lord . . . Let me learn something from this old man" (p. 343).

David O. Selznick had taken an option on the book before it was published on the strength of Cronin's success with *The Citadel.* In May 1941, hoping to head off problems with the church, he arranged a private meeting with Father Devlin. He didn't know that the priest, who had read the novel before publication, had already talked two other studios out of purchasing the rights to it. Selznick had expected a list of the usual minor technical errors. Instead, Devlin told him that he should have thrown out the book, but because he had purchased it, the story would have to undergo a major revision before it reached the screen. Stunned by the priest's vehement reaction, Selznick asked him what was wrong. Claiming that he didn't have time to list all the book's deficiencies, Devlin quickly identified several trouble spots. Most of them stemmed from Chisolm's "extreme broad-mindedness" as exemplified by his notion that "we are all going to Heaven by different gates" as well as the priest's failure to try to convert the atheist Willie Tulloch. Finally, Devlin was concerned that the story gave the impression "that everyone including all people in the Catholic Church are out of step with the exception of the hero, Francis."[39]

Breen, who had been given a forty-seven-page synopsis, was no more encouraging. He felt that some of the story's priests came dangerously close to violating the Code's prohibition against negative clerical portrayals. Then there was the book's treatment of the fake "miracle." He noted that no priest would endorse such an event before a proper ecclesiastical examination had taken place. As if Selznick didn't have enough trouble dealing with Devlin,

Breen warned him that the producer was likely to have "a heck of a time" with Protestants if he didn't handle the Methodist missionaries carefully, and he could also expect to hear from the Chinese government if he didn't present China in a favorable light.[40]

Alarmed by these generally negative reactions, Selznick sounded out a number of Catholics, including studio counsel Daniel O'Shea and playwright Myles Connelly. Although everyone thought the book would make a great picture, most agreed with Devlin and Breen that there were too many religious "heavies" in the story. All agreed with Breen that "the miracle" was worrisome, especially the possibility that people who didn't believe in miracles might use this incident to demonstrate how easily the church could be duped on such matters. The group unanimously recommended that Selznick sign Father Wilfrid Parsons as a technical consultant on the project. The producer readily agreed, but Myles Connelly had to urge Parsons to take the job, telling him that it would be great publicity for Catholic University, where he was teaching, as well as earning the school some money. Ironically, in view of the fact that Parsons's involvement with the film would stretch over the next three years, Connelly told him that all of the problems could be cleaned up in a week at the most if he came out to Hollywood. Moreover, he wouldn't have to worry about Chisolm's missionary career because a second adviser, Father Albert O'Hara, who had served in China, would deal with that topic. The rest, "when to tip the biretta, etc.," could be handled by Devlin. Once Parsons agreed, Connelly, acting on Selznick's behalf, obtained Bishop Cantwell's agreement to let the two Jesuits work in his diocese. The bishop's only proviso was that they work with Devlin, who would be the church's contact when the film went into production.[41]

Meanwhile, reviews of the novel in the Catholic press indicated that Selznick was going to need all the help he could get. *Commonweal* accused Cronin of stacking the deck with too many unattractive priests, and *Catholic World* charged him with implying that organized religion was futile. Although *America* liked the book, it worried that Father Chisolm in his attempts "to be all things to all men" frequently gave the impression that he was tinged with "religious indifferentism." Father Frank Gartland, writing in the *Catholic Students' Bulletin*, warned his readers that rather than treating tolerance as a virtue, they "must be intolerant . . . of error." Similarly, the editor of "The Answer Box" in the missionary journal the *Far East* explained to his readers that tolerance of their neighbors didn't necessarily mean that they had to countenance their ideas. The heaviest broadside came in a lengthy critique by Father Edward Wuenschel, who claimed in the *American Ecclesiastical Review* that the story's hero sounded more like a Protestant minister than a Catholic priest. His fundamental error, the priest declared, was to ignore church dogma that "she is the divinely appointed guardian of the one true religion. 'Many gates to Heaven' and 'solitary pilgrims stumbling home alone' may form a sort of 'Rotarian fraternalism,'" he concluded, but they had no place within the teachings of the one, true church.[42]

Selznick had already met with Cronin to discuss how to counter some of the early Catholic criticism when the Wuenschel review appeared. The producer was so upset by the attack that he told Parsons he wanted to take it up with him piece by piece as soon as the priest reached Hollywood. When Parsons arrived, in late January 1942, he read in *Tidings* that he had been brought out to serve as Devlin's assistant on the picture. Daniel O'Shea convinced him that the announcement was merely a technical way of handling the situation and that he would arrange a meeting with Devlin. Unfortunately, Parsons failed to touch base with Devlin, which created a good deal of tension between the two priests.[43]

When Parsons finally met with Selznick, a script prepared with Cronin's help did little to meet the objections that Devlin and the others had raised. As Parsons saw it, the problem of turning *Keys of the Kingdom* into an acceptable script was twofold. First, the original thesis of the book—"a false idea, dogmatic tolerance"—had to be transformed into a "straight story of a holy man of humility, patience and charity." The second challenge was to eliminate "the false statements of dogmatic tolerance with which it was reeking, and when that was not possible, to turn them into innocuous statements of permissible personal civil tolerance." Parsons also talked with Cronin during his thirteen-day stay in Hollywood. The novelist told him that he had no intention of having Father Chisolm preach religious indifferentism, which he agreed would be heresy.[44]

Parsons found Selznick eager to cooperate. Several minor technical issues such as having Chisolm sign his letter "yours in Christ" instead of "your devoted brother in J. C." were easily resolved. Selznick also agreed to find a new name for Chisolm's seminary as San Morales meant "without morals." Parsons also talked Selznick out of launching a contest for the best design for the nuns' habits, pointing out that this might make the picture more glamorous but less realistic. At Parsons's insistence, Selznick promised to make it clear that Chisolm was not the father of Nora's child, perhaps by adding a bit of dialogue to indicate that he had not been home for more than a year. Nor did the producer have any problem adding a few lines so that the audience would understand that the night Chisolm spent in the Spanish prostitute's cottage was innocent, but he balked at eliminating the scene. Parsons argued that if it stayed, he should eliminate the shot of the woman washing Francis's feet because the Mary Magdalene metaphor was in bad taste. Resolving the issue of too many clerical heavies in the story proved to be more complicated.

Selznick initially rejected Parsons's suggestion that some of the less attractive priests should be eliminated or made less objectionable, claiming that the conflicts provided the story with much of its drama. However, he agreed to make Chisolm's first pastor appear less bigoted and mercenary.[45]

The problem that would haunt Parsons until the completion of the film was how to deal with Chisolm's open-mindedness. One way out, Parsons suggested, was to portray Chisolm's tolerance as personal and not dogmatic. His rebelliousness had to be shown to be a rejection not of church doctrine but of those people who are intolerant in their relationships with others. Parsons supplied Selznick with a number of statements from a standard Catholic work on tolerance to be inserted into the film. Already sensing that what had seemed like a simple consulting job could get him into trouble with the church, Parsons advised Selznick to stick as closely as possible to the text "so that if we are challenged, we can refer to the original." But, as he soon discovered, the devil was in the details. Instead of Chisolm's line "Creed is such an accident of birth that God does not place exclusive value on it," Parsons suggested: "Surely, sir, the church recognizes that a man is not going to be damned just because of an accident of birth." Unhappy with Parsons's proposal, Barbara Keon, Selznick's script assistant, recommended replacing it with a line from another section of the novel, which Parsons felt was not an improvement. Unable to come up with a compromise, Parsons and Selznick added the line to their steadily growing list of differences to be resolved at a later date.[46]

Another sticking point was Chisolm's conversation with the mandarin about the "many gates to heaven." Parsons tried to get Selznick to eliminate the line, but when the producer dug in his heels, he looked for something that would retain the thought without implying that the members of all religions had an equal chance of entering heaven. A possible solution, he suggested, was to have Chisolm reject the mandarin's offer to expel the Methodist missionaries, declaring that he would "use no force. If my preaching can't stand up against theirs, etc." Barbara Keon thought it would be better to have him simply state, "We're not the only good people in the world. There are other good people—millions of them. In this country, neither you nor I have the right to close them up." Sensing that neither substitution served their purpose, Parsons suggested a long-winded speech that might have passed for a Sunday sermon. Selznick, who had watched the original simple exchange grow into a theological treatise, told Parsons that he had seen nothing that was any better than the "many gates" metaphor. They added the issue to the list.[47]

The other major issue revolved around Willie Tulloch's death as an unrepentant atheist. Selznick was willing to let Chisolm make an effort to get him to accept God. In response to Willie's dying declaration that he still couldn't believe in the Almighty, Selznick suggested having the priest say: "But, Willie, God is good. . . . He believes in you." Then, when Willie replied, "Don't delude yourself, I'm not repentant," Chisolm would tell him, "All human suffering is an act of repentance." Parsons felt they were moving in the right direction, but because the church didn't equate involuntary suffering with penance, he recommended that Francis should inform his old friend, "God can take your suffering as an act of repentance, if you will." By the end of his 1942 trip, Parsons had suggested changes in 118 passages in the script and had rewritten six scenes. Selznick, who had received a crash course in Catholic theology, asked him to return the following summer to assist in the shooting of the film. When Parsons returned to Washington, however, he was alarmed by a warning from his superior in the Jesuit order not to let his name or the Society be used as a defense against future criticism that could lead to both becoming the object of "justifiable censure." Unless he could get Selznick to "eliminate all indifferentism and off-color Catholicism with which Father Chisolm is saturated," Parsons was to sever his relations with the project.[48]

Meanwhile, Selznick was having problems finding a star to play Father Chisolm. More than twenty Hollywood actors were considered for the role, including Henry Fonda, Joseph Cotten, Alan Ladd, and Edward G. Robinson. Robert Young was so eager to get the part that he supplied Selznick with stills showing how, with the aid of makeup, he could play both the young and the old Chisolm. Singer Rudy Vallee, who thought the story was about a Protestant minister, was politely told that he was "unsuitable" for the part. At one point, Selznick toyed with the idea of having a real priest, like Fulton J. Sheen, play the part. And in a grand if misguided ecumenical gesture, he even considered casting a Protestant minister who had some acting experience as the priest. After deciding on Van Heflin, only to lose him to the draft, Selznick gave the role to Gregory Peck.[49]

By that point, the producer was having second thoughts about going into production on the film. After his success with *Gone with the Wind* and *Rebecca*, Selznick had increasingly become a packager of movie projects and an agent who rented out the services of such actresses as Joan Fontaine and Ingrid Bergman and director Alfred Hitchcock, who were under contract to him. On November 16, 1942, Selznick announced that he had sold several films to Twentieth Century-Fox including *Jane Eyre*, *Claudia*, and *Keys of the Kingdom*, along with the loan of several actors, including Peck.[50]

In taking over the *Keys of the Kingdom*, Fox took on the task of trying to please the Office of War Information's Bureau of Motion Pictures while heading off any trouble with the Catholic church. The bureau, which monitored, among other things, Hollywood's treatment of America's allies on the screen, was worried about the portrayal of the Chinese in the film. The studio had little difficulty satisfying most of the government's concerns, although it wisely ignored one agency criticism that would have caused an irreparable breach with the Catholic church. A reviewer, apparently imbued with the OWI's distaste for colonialism, suggested eliminating the missionary phase of the story, since in her view religious imperialism was just as bad as any political imperialism. "The Catholic church appears as the villain in the piece," she said. "It invades a foreign land—forces its way . . . by taking advantage of the people's miserable living conditions to offer rice and medical care in exchange for souls." Recognizing that there would be no story without Chisolm's missionary work, the bureau didn't press the point and gave the studio high marks for its cooperation. An agency review of the final film reported that all the Chinese in the picture were "shown to be clean, brave, and intelligent [except for] one dishonest couple." The bureau representative made an extensive tour of the set and reported approvingly that not only was there no squalor in the village of Pai-tan when Chisolm first arrives, when he leaves, thirty years later, the houses had been upgraded to "neat little brick places with a considerable feeling of civilization about them." In fact, as adviser Father Albert O'Hara dryly added, the village looked much better than anything he had seen as a missionary in China.[51]

By the fall of 1943, with the bureau's objections out of the way, the studio turned to the more complex Catholic situation. Convinced that Father O'Hara had no influence with the American hierarchy, the studio signed on Parsons as technical adviser, with the agreement that he would receive $500 in expenses with an additional $3,000 going to his order. By the time he received the new script, several changes had been made. Producer Darryl Zanuck, who felt the story was too long, had decided to cut out the scenes of the plague and move Willie Tulloch's death into the Chinese civil war. When an assistant asked if there might be some criticism over fiddling with a well-known novel, Zanuck told him there was nothing to worry about. "In *Grapes of Wrath*, we took out one of the most important elements of the book, the starvation, and yet people talked about how true it was to the novel. In *How Green Was My Valley*, we left out the strikes and there was no criticism." Zanuck also decided against Selznick's recommendation that another of his contract actresses, Ingrid Bergman, play Mother Veronica. Some consideration had been given to enlarging the part to fit an actress of Bergman's stature, but Nunnally Johnson, one of the film's directors, had convinced Zanuck that this would not only change the story too much but would add to the "popular suspicion in some quarters that Father Chisolm was engaged in an amorous relationship with Mother Veronica, which is an aspect of the story which frightens Catholics to death."[52]

When Parsons returned to Hollywood in January 1944, he faced the same list of issues that had been unresolved when Selznick pulled out. Troubled by a rumor that Father Devlin thought he had not been firm enough with the producer, Parsons contacted the priest, who assured him that he had no reservations about his work on the film. The misunderstanding, however, stirred up Parsons's own insecurities. To protect himself from any future church criticism, he reminded studio executives that he had been hired only to point out those pitfalls that might cause trouble with the church; the execution of these suggestions was their responsibility.[53]

The new script revealed a fresh problem. Even without Bergman, Parsons had become concerned about the handling of Chisolm's relationship with Mother Veronica. Zanuck's casual remark that when a man and a woman take an immediate dislike to each other at the beginning of a film, it usually signals that they will eventually fall in love only added to his worries. He strongly advised eliminating Tulloch's comment to Chisolm when he first meets Mother Veronica that it must be pleasant to spend his days with such a fine-looking woman. He also cautioned the studio that after the two had resolved their problems, their relationship could be "affectionate but casual: she could even mother him a bit . . . but it is important that there be no sexual implications in the scene."[54]

Parsons was also concerned that audiences might read some illicit sexual relationship into Chisolm's overnight stay in the prostitute's cottage and recommended that some third party, perhaps a maid, be present. Fortunately for Parsons, when director Nunnally Johnson, whose previous idea of a lengthy script was 125 pages, began to winnow the 200 pages he had inherited, one of the first scenes to go was the episode at the cottage. The shortening of the script solved another of Parsons's major objections: the existence of "too many Catholic heavies" in the story. Johnson eliminated seven of the fourteen priests in Cronin's novel, including the pastor who had fallen for the fake miracle. Parsons was also able to persuade the writers to rehabilitate Bishop Mealey, transforming him from a conceited, self-centered individual into more of a "bustling, practical go-getter."[55]

But Chisolm's tolerance remained the central problem. Some minor issues were resolved without much difficulty. Father O'Hara had argued that Chisolm's assertion that "Christ was a perfect man, but Confucius had a better sense of humor" was a contradiction in terms because Christ would have had a perfect sense of humor. However, when pressed by producer Joe Mankiewicz, he had to admit that he couldn't think of any humorous passages in the Bible. Parsons and Mankiewicz finally settled on changing the focus from Christ and Confucius to their followers: Chisolm could maintain that "a good Christian is a good man, but I found Confucists had a better sense of humor."[56]

The circumstances of Willie Tulloch's death continued to disturb Parsons, especially Chisolm's statement in his sermon that "atheists may not all go to hell. I knew one who didn't." O'Hara had already pointed out that it would be impossible for Chisolm to make such a statement "since only canonized saints are said with certainty to have gone to heaven." Mankiewicz suggested that the issue could be solved by having Chisolm say, "Not all atheists are damned. I know one who probably wasn't." Mankiewicz finally accepted Parsons's version: "Not all atheists are godless men—I knew one who I hope may now be in heaven." The death scene itself was another source of contention. Mankiewicz rejected Parsons's suggestion that Chisolm should make some effort to get Willie to accept God. It was too flat, he told the priest: "There should be greater conflict in Francis because he wants to save his friend if he can, but still he can't urge him to accept a faith which he knows he doesn't believe in." Father O'Hara had pointed out that in a case like this, where the dying person might have a certain amount of good will toward the faith, a priest might do more harm than good by trying to force him to accept God. Parsons rewrote the scene so that after stating that he still couldn't believe in God, Willie asks Chisolm, "Are you mad at me?" "Of course not," he responds. "Are you disappointed that I won't let you save me?" Willie inquires. "Your salvation will be your doing—not mine," Chisolm answers. "Wouldn't it be fun, if just by chance we could meet again?" And with his last words, Willie murmurs: "I never loved you as much as I do now because you haven't tried to bully me into heaven."[57]

By January 1944, Zanuck and Mankiewicz had agreed to thirty-seven of Parsons's suggestions, but they still didn't have a final script. The writers had revised the "many gates to heaven" exchange between Chisolm and the mandarin to read "Each of us *chooses* his own road to the Kingdom of Heaven. Though I *believe* another's to be wrong, I still have no right to *deny* him his choice." Parsons admitted that this was better than the original, but he was still worried that it could be misunderstood. He extracted a small concession from Mankiewicz so that Chisolm would say: "Each of us *travels* his own road to the Kingdom of Heaven. Though I *know* another's to be wrong, still I have no right to *interfere* with his choice." Even more worrisome was a new exchange between Chisolm and the mandarin over the right of the two Methodists to do their missionary work in Pai-Tan. In place of the "many gates" metaphor, the writers had substituted what became known as the "parable of the berries" in which Chisolm explains to the Mandarin why they should not be harassed. "I always remember," the priest declares, "that when I was a little boy and went berry-picking, I always resented other little boys who found the same bushes I did and who insisted on picking the berries. I knew that I had no more right to the berries than they." Once again, Mankiewicz insisted on retaining the scene, but after a good deal of haggling, Parsons was able to rework the final line into, "I knew that they had the same right to the berries as I," which he felt was more positive.[58]

By June 1944, Parsons had worked his way through three different scripts since the beginning of the year. He had done his best to redeem Chisolm. The rest was in Mankiewicz's hands. Devlin, who was to oversee the shooting of the film, reported to Parsons that all the really objectionable scenes had been eliminated except for the "different roads to heaven" and the parable of the berries. He admitted that the script was much better than the book, but he felt that it lacked something to make it a truly great film. Father O'Hara attributed Devlin's comments to sour grapes over his subordinate role in the production, but Parsons wasn't quite sure how to interpret his letter. And would Catholic critics recognize that he had done his best, or would they focus on whatever vestiges of Chisolm's religious indifferentism had survived?[59]

His worst fears were realized when he learned that the Legion was contemplating classifying the film as a B, objectionable in part. The troublesome points were Chisolm's tolerance and a new issue that neither Parsons nor O'Hara had anticipated: the priest's role in blowing up the war lord's cannon, which resulted in the deaths of some soldiers. Concerned about his own reputation, Parsons tried to show Father McClafferty at the Legion how he had taken Chisolm's statement out of the realm of religious indifferentism. The priest's statement that "each of us travels his own road to . . . heaven" had no doctrinal implications, and Chisolm's second line, that although he knew "another's to be wrong, still I have no right to interfere," referred to the social right of the Methodists not to be persecuted for their religious beliefs. Similarly, Parsons stated, their right to pick the berries was a civil right. As Parsons reminded McClafferty, Chisolm's friendly attitude toward the two Methodists was the practice of Catholic missionaries throughout the world.[60]

He conceded that those in the audience who had read the book might ignore the changes, but, he argued, that was not the fault of the film. He couldn't understand the Legion's concern about the destruction of the cannon; Chisolm was justified in destroying the weapon in order to save the mission and had not intended to kill anyone. A similar example could be found in the war, he argued, where the legitimate bombing of a military target could result in the death of innocent civilians. He concluded, "at the time of the Boxer Rebellion in China, the missionaries everywhere manned the walls of besieged cities and fought off the attackers with guns; and this, at the order of their bishops." He argued that Twentieth Century-Fox had furnished the Catholic foreign missions with "a couple of million dollars' worth of propaganda." In the face of that, what was the harm in a "couple of blemishes that pass in a flash?"[61]

While awaiting the response of Bishop Keough, head of the Episcopal Committee on Motion Pictures, Parsons told a studio executive that he still had a responsibility for the film now that he had reverted to his primary role as Catholic priest. His main concern, he said, for himself, the church, and the studio, was to avoid an attack from the Catholic press. Consequently, he again asked that the "different roads" and berries parables be removed from the film. Fox agreed to make one last concession and took out the "different roads" line but refused to drop the berries parable, which provided the only rational explanation for the mandarin's decision not to force the Methodists out.[62]

Fortunately for Parsons, the Catholic reaction to the film was largely positive, with a few scattered criticisms. *America*, *Commonweal*, and *Catholic World* praised the film, noting that it was a marked improvement over the novel. Meanwhile, Father Urban Nagle, speaking at a Catholic book fair in Seattle, warned his audience that the film contained two heresies. A priest in St. Michael's, Vermont, wrote to Parsons that one penitent had felt compelled to go to confession after seeing *The Keys of the Kingdom*, and a woman told Devlin that she was "flabbergasted" to learn that two Jesuits had served as advisers on the film. But Parsons's reputation escaped damage. Convinced that he had done his best, the Legion of Decency classified *Keys of the Kingdom* as A–I, suitable for general audiences, although McClafferty couldn't resist adding a notation that the film "contains statements by the leading character, the priest, which are susceptible to meaning not in accordance with Catholic doctrine."[63]

ELEVEN

An Unwelcome *Miracle*

At the mid-century mark, the Legion seemed as powerful as ever. With new churches going up in the suburbs, increasing enrollments in seminaries and convents, and church attendance at an all-time high, the Legion appeared to have little to worry about. Critics like Arthur Schlesinger, Jr., complained that the movies were being filmed according to ground rules set by a minority religious faith, and the *Saturday Review* likened the Legion to a sort of secret police, but no one in the industry dared to take on the church. N. Peter Ravthon, a participant in *Life* magazine's 1949 "movie roundtable," acknowledged: "Among all the pressure groups the Legion of Decency is the one with the teeth—the group that can hurt your picture very much." That the only criticism of the Legion came from the one roundtable participant who insisted on anonymity indicates how much fear it still inspired. "I think it is evil for a minority group to stop a majority from seeing a film," he said, but "the Legion holds the whip hand over Hollywood and nothing can be done about it."[1]

If Hollywood was afraid to confront the Legion directly, it had no reservations about chipping away at the Code's restrictions in an effort to win back the fans it had lost to television. Sensing the changing mood, Joe Breen had held a meeting with several priests early in 1946 in which they agreed to maintain a united front against any attempt to introduce such controversial topics as rape, homosexuality, and abortion to the screen. Although the Code did not specifically prohibit films dealing with abortion (it hadn't drawn the censors' attention when the regulations were originally devised), Breen had routinely rejected even the slightest hint of it. But the times were changing, and MGM took aim at the taboo in *The Doctor and the Girl*, the story of a young doctor whose sister dies while undergoing an abortion. When Breen rejected the script in the spring of 1949, the studio filed an appeal with MPAA president Eric Johnston, claiming that *The Doctor and the Girl* should be allowed as long as the subject was handled tastefully. Instead of backing Breen, Johnston directed him to work out some sort of a solution. Breen argued that abortion had come up for discussion close to five hundred times in twenty years and had always been rejected. Nevertheless, his warning that any compromise would serve as a green light for the other studios was ignored, and he had to negotiate with MGM. The studio's substitution of an "illegal operation" for what had previously been identified as an abortion satisfied the PCA and the Legion, which gave the film an A–II rating.[2]

Breen's prediction soon proved correct. Within a month of *The Doctor and the Girl*'s release, Warner Brothers submitted the script for *Beyond the Forest*. The story starred Bette Davis as Rosa Moline, who is dissatisfied with her life in Loyalton, Wisconsin, as the wife of a country doctor, played by Joseph Cotten. She falls in love with a vacationing millionaire who she hopes will take her to Chicago, but instead of a one-way ticket to the big city, the affair results in an unwanted pregnancy. Still hoping to escape, Rosa defiantly pats her stomach and taunts her husband with the news that she is pregnant by another man. Convinced that her lover will take care of her if she can only get rid of the child, she goes to an abortionist's office, where the only other woman in the waiting room is incongruously knitting baby clothes. Her husband, who wants the baby, arrives before Rosa can see the abortionist and tries to take her home. Undeterred, she persuades him to stop the car and hurls herself over an embankment in a desperate attempt to rid herself of the child. She awakes in the hospital operating room with a smile on her face: the baby is dead, and she can leave Loyalton forever. But her luck runs out; burning up from peritonitis, she staggers out of bed, hoping to catch the train for Chicago. As the train pulls out, the camera reveals Rosa dead at the side of the track with one hand reaching out in a last desperate effort to make it to the Windy City.[3]

Breen had assigned the film to Jack Vizzard, who had joined the PCA after dropping out of a Jesuit seminary. Vizzard reworked the abortion scenes, persuading the studio to identify the abortionist as a "psychological consultant." Remembering Johnston's lack of support in *The Doctor and the Girl* and fearing an appeal to the MPAA's board of directors, Breen reluctantly granted the film a seal of approval. But Father Patrick Masterson was in no mood for compromises. After all, he worked for a far greater power than Johnston. He informed Warner that the film would be condemned in its present form. When the studio failed to respond, the priest released the condemnation. Warner was flooded with the usual letters of complaint following a Legion ban, including one from a group of Catholic high school students who asked, "Why are you offering our people moral filth that makes them animal like and leads them to the depths of hell?"[4]

Masterson suspected that Warner planned to ride out the condemnation while the film was in its first run and then negotiate some cuts to obtain a B for its appearance in neighborhood theaters, where the Legion had its greatest strength. But scathing reviews led a number of theaters to use the Legion condemnation as a convenient excuse to discontinue the film. At first, Warner indicated that it was willing to make only a few token cuts. But as cancellations poured in, the studio's mood changed. As one executive put it, "Every hour the 'C' rating stood, Warners was losing playdates by the gross." Because the film had been approved by the PCA, Jack Warner asked Breen to intercede on the studio's behalf with the Legion. He dispatched Vizzard to New York to negotiate whatever changes it would take to ensure the film a B, but Masterson, who had been growing increasingly disenchanted with Breen's office, wasn't particularly happy about dealing with an ex-seminarian who had approved what the priest felt was a totally evil picture.[5]

Nevertheless, Vizzard was able to get the film reclassified. Several scenes, including one in which a glass of water drips on what Masterson felt was too much Davis cleavage, were cut, but most of Vizzard's week was spent correcting "the abortion problem." Four years earlier, both Breen and the Legion had failed to make an issue of a similar incident in the A–II film *Leave Her to Heaven*, in which Gene Tierney had induced a miscarriage by throwing herself down the stairs. Masterson was determined not to make the same mistake. Out went the scene in which Davis patted her stomach along with the shot of the woman knitting in the waiting room. The psychological consultant's office, which the PCA had introduced in order to erase any hint of an abortion, was still too close to home for the Legion, so it was transformed into a lawyer's office. The operating-room scene where Davis learns that she has lost her baby as a result of the fall was also cut in the hope that her jump over the embankment would be viewed as an attempt at suicide rather than abortion. Finally, in what was becoming the standard penance in films condemned by the Legion, Warner agreed to add a prologue informing the audience: "This is the story of evil. Evil is headstrong—is puffed up. For our soul's sake it is salutary for us to view it, in all its naked ugliness, once in a while. Thus may we know how those who deliver themselves over to it end up like the scorpion, in a mad fury stinging themselves to eternal death."[6]

Still smarting over the Legion's frosty reception, Vizzard reported to Breen that Masterson and Little had become overzealous in their "sex-snooping," which he attributed to their isolation and youth. Breen sent Martin Quigley a copy of the report in the hope that the priests might back off a little, but his ploy backfired. After chiding Vizzard for switching his role "from that of a person seeking to preserve right moral standards on the screen to that of an attorney for the defense," the publisher told Breen that the problem was not raised standards at the Legion office but lowered ones at the PCA. Breen, who was in the midst of another abortion battle with Paramount over *A Place in the Sun*, a remake of *An American Tragedy*, defended himself by blaming the scripts, which he claimed were worse than anything since 1934. "There is some sinister force at work hereabouts," he told Quigley. "I just can't put my finger on it, but I am satisfied in my own mind that this condition, which has come about in recent months, did not just 'happen.' There is an African in the woodpile!"[7]

Breen was correct in sensing that things were happening in Hollywood. But it wasn't some sinister conspiracy; the studios were trying to give people what they couldn't find on television in order to survive. Abortion was just one of the many problems confronting Breen at this point. News in early 1950 that Warner Brothers would adapt Tennessee Williams's Pulitzer Prize-winning play, *A Streetcar Named Desire*, left Hollywood wondering how the studio expected to get a story that included homosexuality, nymphomania, and rape past the PCA. "For the first time," said Geoff Shurlock, "we were confronted with a picture that was obviously not family entertainment. Before then we had considered *Anna Karenina* a big deal. *Streetcar* broke the barrier."[8] In the play, the neurotic Blanche DuBois visits her pregnant sister, Stella, who is married to Stanley Kowalski. Stanley, who can't stand Blanche's airs, learns that her husband had committed suicide because of his homosexuality and that Blanche, who has had a long series of sexual relationships, had been fired from her teaching position for having seduced one of her young students. While Stella is in the hospital having their baby, a drunken Stanley rapes Blanche, causing her to have a mental breakdown. In spite of all this, Stanley is able to coax Stella back into his arms at the end of the play.

Noting that the Code absolutely forbade "sex perversion," Breen's office recommended that something other than homosexuality be found as the cause of Blanche's husband's suicide. Breen also felt that Blanche's "neurotic attitude toward sex, and particularly [her] sex attraction for young boys," also bordered on perversion. Instead of lusting after "gross sex," he suggested that she could be presented in a more traditional framework as a woman searching for romance and security. As for the rape scene, two alternatives were offered that Breen felt would make Stella's return to Stanley at the end of the movie more understandable. One possibility would allow Stanley to prove to Stella that Blanche's charge of rape was false and stemmed from her hatred of him. The other option, which Shurlock and Vizzard favored, would be to have the already disturbed Blanche imagine that the rape had occurred.[9]

Director Elia Kazan had no problem with cleaning up Blanche's background, but both he and Williams balked at eliminating the rape. Without it, the movie lost its meaning, which was, Williams argued, the "ravishment of the tender, the sensitive, the delicate by the savage and brutal forces of modern society." Eventually they compromised. Breen would accept the rape if it were done "by suggestion and delicacy" while Kazan, in turn, agreed to change the ending to supply "compensating moral values." In the revised version, Stanley would be punished for violating Blanche by losing his wife's love. In the last scene, Stella rejects Stanley's attempt to woo her back, picks up her baby, and leaves their apartment, murmuring: "We're not going back in there. Not this time. We're never going back." Stanley vainly screams "Stellaaaaa!" as the picture ends with his wife listening impassively from a neighbor's apartment.[10]

Breen kept his fingers crossed when Warner sent the film to the Legion, hoping that the sixty-eight changes he had ordered would be enough to satisfy Father Patrick Masterson. The Legion may have been willing to accept the view, as it had in the *Beyond the Forest* prologue, that "it is salutary . . . to view . . . naked ugliness once in a while," but it was unwilling to make a habit of it. To Masterson, this particular streetcar was powered by sex from beginning to end, making it a completely undesirable vehicle. According to the priest, when Stella tries to explain to Blanche why she put up with such a boorish husband, it is clearly her physical satisfaction that keeps her in the marriage. News that the Legion had condemned the film was hard enough for Warner to take; even more alarming was Masterson's warning that it would take more than a few simple cuts to save it.[11]

Panicked, the studio postponed the opening rather than risk whatever damage the condemnation might wreak at the box office. Once again, Warner authorized Jack Vizzard to act as its intermediary with the Legion, but when he failed to win over Masterson, the studio called on Martin Quigley to save the picture. Quigley, who had not seen the film, went with Vizzard to the studio's New York projection room. As Vizzard later recalled: "His face wore the ashen look of a man who had seen IT. He flicked his dull agate eyes at me and painfully drew a cigarette from a silver case, while he let words and emotions roll through his mind. When he had finally fit the cigarette into a long holder, he lit it, inhaled with slow deliberation, and uttered his verdict. 'Jack,' he declared, 'I tell you, this fellow Kazan is the type who will one day blow his brains out.' "[12]

Meanwhile, Kazan, who suspected that something was up, tried unsuccessfully to find out what was happening to his picture. When he learned that Warner had dispatched a cutter to New York to work under Quigley's direction, he pleaded with a studio executive not to let anyone meddle with the "guts" of his picture. Although he was assured that there was nothing to worry about, the cutter was snipping away. Twelve cuts later, four minutes of film had been eliminated. Some deletions made little sense: reducing "I would like to kiss you on the mouth" to "I want to kiss you." Kazan was especially angered by the elimination of close-ups of Stella's face in another scene because Quigley felt they displayed a "carnal" desire for her husband.[13]

Quigley's cuts may have incensed Kazan, but they won a B from the Legion. In a futile effort to exhibit his film intact, Kazan asked Warner to release both his version and Quigley's in New York; if the church was worried, it could station priests in the lobby to take down the names of any Catholic who tried to see the original. He also made a serious effort to get his own version shown at the Venice Film Festival, but Warner was unwilling to risk the ire of the church. A bitter Kazan later recalled: "It was at that time that I became aware of the similarity of the Catholic church to the Communist Party; particularly in the 'underground' nature of their operations." But what amazed him most was the absolute self-assurance of Quigley, "the gluttonous Pope of Fiftieth Street." "He had no doubt about what he had done," Kazan exclaimed. "He felt he'd saved *Streetcar* for Warners." There was no question in Jack Warner's mind that he had done the right thing. A few years later, when another Kazan film, *A Face in the Crowd* (1957), ran into trouble with the Legion, he secretly called Quigley in again to suggest what should be eliminated. Without telling Kazan that Quigley had already seen the film, he suggested that the director solicit his advice. Knowing from experience that the film would be cut with or without his participation, Kazan met with Quigley and worked out enough changes to avoid another confrontation with the Legion.[14]

The willingness of a major studio such as Warner Brothers to knuckle under suggested that the Legion was still a powerful presence in the 1950s. But forces were taking shape that would gradually undermine its influence. While Quigley was recutting *Streetcar* in the summer of 1951, a controversy surrounding a hitherto obscure Italian film was about to hand the Legion its first serious defeat. Although British films enjoyed a small but solid market in America in the early 1950s, most foreign-language films were restricted to some three hundred art theaters in large cities. Not subject to the Production Code and having to pass only a customs inspection to guard against obscenity, these movies were free to be more sophisticated and sexually explicit. The French director Jean Renoir, who had chafed under the Code restrictions during an enforced stay in Hollywood during World War II, touched on the differences between Hollywood and European films when he bade farewell to Darryl Zanuck with "Goodbye. . . . It certainly has been a pleasure working at Sixteenth Century-Fox."[15]

The freedom enjoyed by foreign producers began to bother their American counterparts, who felt that in an era of declining movie attendance they were being forced to make pictures with one arm tied behind their backs. "It seems unfair," David O. Selznick wrote Quigley, "that native producers are denied what all the authorities permit foreign producers. Neither censorship boards, nor the Code authorities, nor the Catholic [and] Protestant Church . . . seems to bother about their product either at home or abroad." Selznick's conviction that the Catholic church had followed a policy of benign neglect when it came to foreign films was not entirely accurate. In October 1945 Quigley had secured an audience with the pope to enlist his help in an abortive effort to get the French film industry, which the Legion saw as the main source of objectionable films, to establish a set of regulations similar to the Production Code.[16]

A few months later Father McClafferty went to a meeting of the Office Catholique International du Cinéma (OCIC) in Rome to try to persuade European Catholics to "clean up" the foreign films that were beginning to find their way to the United States. The OCIC (unlike the Legion, which was controlled by the hierarchy) was a private organization sanctioned by the Vatican. As such, it occasionally published articles in its magazine *International Film Review* critical of the Code and recommended films that the Legion had campaigned against. A major problem as the Legion saw it was that the OCIC went beyond moral evaluations of films, commenting on their artistic and technical qualities as well—the same approach that had caused so much trouble for Father Daly during the Legion's first year. The OCIC, in turn, had quietly let it be known that it did not agree with the Legion's classification system. However, in deference to the American hierarchy, the directors of the various European equivalents of the Legion who were members of the OCIC, did not issue English translations of their reviews.[17]

The Legion tried to avoid any open conflict, which might suggest that Catholic moral judgments were not universal when it came to the movies. It narrowly missed an embarrassing situation in 1951 when it found out just in time that *God Needs Men*, which it was considering condemning, had just been awarded a prize by the OCIC. But its luck ran out when it condemned Marcel

Pagnol's *Letters from My Windmill*, a light-hearted movie with stories about a priest who succumbs to gluttony and a brother in a poor monastery who discovers a formula for a popular liqueur. The film had won kudos from the Centrale Catholique du Cinéma, and 4,500 priests and nuns attended a special screening in Paris and "enjoyed it immensely." When the *New York Post* picked up the story, Masterson's assistant, Father Thomas Little, tried to explain the disparity by arguing that "the receptivity of a picture in one country might not be the same as the receptivity in another country." But as *Commonweal* pointed out, Little had touched on a major problem in censorship: the difficulty of attempting to judge the effect of a film on its audience. After all, the differences he found to exist between American and French audiences could just as easily exist within a particular country. The editorial concluded by suggesting that the Legion's condemnation did an injustice to those Americans "who could discern in this film the poetry, humor, and charm that . . . 4,500 French priests and nuns have found."[18]

Although the Legion regularly condemned a number of foreign films, it rarely publicized its actions other than to include the films in its classification lists. Without the leverage they enjoyed with the American studios, the Legion had opted for a policy of malign neglect. In view of the limited audience for such fare, it felt that campaigns like those directed against *Duel in the Sun* and *Forever Amber* would only prolong a film's stay and boost its box-office receipts. The superior artistry of some European films had begun to capture the attention of movie critics, however. When the National Board of Review placed four foreign imports on its list of the ten best pictures of 1949, Martin Quigley accused the board of "intellectual menopause," charging it with ignoring the needs of the American film industry by favoring films "from the unhappy foreign left, dripping with the bitter juices of the complaining art of a defeated world." Despite Quigley's carping, some foreign films were graduating from the art theater circuit and moving into larger houses, forcing the Legion to take a more aggressive stance. It had quietly condemned *Bitter Rice*, a tale of Italian harvesters, starring the voluptuous Sylvana Mangano, on October 12, 1950, but when Father Little discovered that it was receiving much wider distribution than that usually accorded foreign language films, he warned local Legion directors that it might be booked in their area. Convinced that a national campaign would only add to its success, he recommended they take whatever action they deemed appropriate for their locale.[19]

The response varied from diocese to diocese. In Harrisburg, Pennsylvania, the threat of a permanent ban against the Colonial Theater forced the owner to pull the picture, and objections from the Albany Legion of Decency led the police chief to stop it after a half-hour at the Ritz Theater. In Buffalo,

Father Edward Schwegler ignored its run at the small downtown Mercury Theater, but he "got it withdrawn in every instance" when the distributor tried to move it into the neighborhood houses. Most dioceses decided to ignore *Bitter Rice* in the hope that it would disappear after a week or two, but by February 1951, it had already played for six months in New York, three in Detroit, and twenty-five theaters had booked it in Chicago. Despite Charles Skouras's policy of not showing condemned films, his West Coast chain of Fox theaters exhibited it in a number of cities. Sensing it had a hit and hoping to expand into a wider market, Lux Film, the American distributor, decided to see what it would take to get the Legion to lift its ban. Several rounds of cuts were made, totaling 673 feet of film, but this wasn't enough to move the Legion. The movie's "sensuous dance scenes," abortion, suicide, and suggestive lines made Little, who coordinated the Legion's response, believe that all the cutting in the world couldn't correct the film. Martin Quigley told one of Lux's directors that the film violated "every standard of decency applicable to public entertainment."[20]

Pressed by both the Italian government and the original distributors for American dollars, the Lux Film directors told Little that their jobs were in jeopardy and that they could not guarantee that their successors would be as cooperative as they had been. Little refused to back down. On August 28, Lux presented a new version with additional cuts. Gone was a shot of Mangano reclining on a cot, which one of the Lux directors considered "undoubtedly the most beautiful and artistic photograph of Sylvana in the film." The distributors also agreed to eliminate a number of "suggestive" lines, including one woman's claim that she had seen more soldiers than a retired army general. The only remaining major problem, an abortion, was handled by a change in subtitles which turned it into a miscarriage. This time, the alterations satisfied Little, and the film was reclassified as a B.[21]

The Legion didn't reject every foreign film, but the uproar over Roberto Rossellini's *Stromboli* (1949) must have made Father Masterson wish it had. Two days after its reviewers had classified it as A-II, news broke that Ingrid Bergman, pregnant by Rossellini, had decided to abandon her husband, Dr. Peter Lindstrom, and their daughter. The Legion office was immediately deluged with telegrams and letters demanding that it revise its rating and condemn the film. In an attempt to relieve the growing pressure on the Legion, Quigley launched his own investigation into Bergman's husband. A rumor that he had been previously married, if confirmed, could mean that his marriage to Bergman was invalid and would put the star in a better light, but the story proved groundless. Masterson was shocked to learn that Father Felix Morlion, a Dominican priest close to Rossellini and Bergman, had praised the star for having the courage to accept the responsibilities of motherhood, which he said would bring the two closer to God. When Materson learned that Morlion was planning a trip to New York, he contacted Cardinal Spellman, who was able to keep him out of the country.[22]

As long as distributors were content to book foreign films in the small, independent art theaters, they didn't pose a problem for the PCA. The critical success of *The Bicycle Thief* (1948), however, prompted its distributor, Joe Burstyn, to ask the PCA for a seal in order to expand its bookings. Breen refused, citing two unacceptable scenes: one in which a boy, with his back to the camera, relieves himself against a wall, and the other in which his father chases the thief through a bordello while the fully clothed female inhabitants were having their Sunday meal. Bosley Crowther of the *New York Times* summed up the feelings of many critics when he declared that the Breen office had lost touch with reality. And the editor of the MPAA's own advertising bulletin recommended *The Bicycle Thief* as "a picture for everyone," while three of the association's five chains decided to book it in their theaters. A few Catholic organizations supported Breen. The Knights of Columbus objected to the film because it "glorified a thief," which *Commonweal* dryly remarked was "a surprising way to sum up that remarkable film." Even the Legion, which automatically condemned any film Breen turned down, classified it as a B. Masterson and Little understood Breen's fear that this could open the floodgates to a series of toilet jokes, but they felt that neither this nor the run through the brothel posed a danger to morality. The final blow came when it received the Academy Award for the best foreign film of 1949.[23]

No one in the audience that night could have anticipated that two years later a court case involving another foreign film, *The Miracle*, would extend to the film industry the First Amendment privileges it had been denied since the 1915 *Mutual* decision, which sanctioned prior censorship of movies. In the midst of the *Forever Amber* campaign, Bishop Keough had predicted correctly that the courts would soon have to take a stand on censorship. He was mistaken, however, in believing that the church would be on the winning side.[24]

The origins of the *Miracle* case can be traced to Joe Burstyn, who had brought *The Bicycle Thief* to the American screen. Burstyn, who tended to focus his energies on one foreign film project at a time, had another one ready for 1950: *The Ways of Love*, a trilogy that included Jean Renoir's *A Day in the Country*, Marcel Pagnol's *Jofroi*, and Roberto Rossellini's *Miracle*. Mary Looram had seen Burstyn speaking with Rossellini at the Venice Film Festival in 1948 and had unsuccessfully tried to talk him out of buying his movie. Nevertheless, *The Miracle* was licensed without any deletions by the New York State board of censors on March 2, 1949, but the forty-minute film was never exhibited independently. Nor did the censors have any trouble with it when it came before them again on November 28, 1950, as part of the trilogy. Ironically, the only piece that worried them was *A Day in the Country*, which was held over for further discussion. Nonetheless, the board approved *The Ways of Love* two days later, and the film opened at the Paris Theater on December 12.[25]

There was no reason to expect trouble, especially over *The Miracle*, which had received the censors' blessings on two separate occasions. The Rossellini film told the story of a deranged peasant woman who is seduced by a wandering stranger she mistakenly believes is Saint Joseph. The first scene ends with a voice-over saying: "Joseph . . . fear not to take unto thee Mary thy wife: for that which is conceived in her is of the Holy Ghost." When she learns she is pregnant, the woman treats it as a miracle, which leads her neighbors to mock and taunt her before throwing her out of town. In the final scene, she goes to a shed behind an abandoned mountain church and gives birth to what she believes to be the Christ child.[26]

Reviews of *The Miracle* were mixed: some critics found it boring while Bosley Crowther of the *New York Times*, who thought it was "overpowering and provocative," predicted that it would "certainly cause a lot of stir." Crowther was correct about its eventual impact. The trilogy did poorly in its opening week and probably would have quietly closed its run at the Paris had it not been for Edward T. McClafferty, the city's commissioner of licenses and a former state commander of the Catholic War Veterans. McClafferty, who found the film "blasphemous," closed its run to prevent an assault on the religious beliefs of "hundreds of thousands" of New Yorkers. A series of court appeals by Burstyn led to a lifting of McClafferty's ban on December 29, followed by a decision on January 5 that the commissioner had exceeded his powers when he closed a film that had been licensed by the official state censorship board. Not even the legendary Russell Birdwell could have created as much publicity as McClafferty's move had. *The Ways of Love* began to play to packed audiences.[27]

Ordinarily, the Legion would have handled it without any fanfare, but the controversy forced its hand. Masterson condemned *The Miracle* as "sacrilegious and blasphemous." Monsignor Walter Kellerberg, chancellor of the New York archdiocese, denounced it as an "open insult to the faith of millions throughout the world" and warned the faithful to stay away. Martin Quigley joined the campaign with an editorial in his *Motion Picture Herald.* Communists and fellow-travelers applauded every time someone bought a ticket to see the picture, he declared, because they knew that religion was an essential bulwark against the Red threat. His assertion that Rossellini and the film's star, Anna Magnani, were active leftists and that the logical birthplace of the film was the Soviet Union helped transform the Legion's condemnation into a crusade.[28]

The campaign reached a fever pitch when, for the third time in his career, Cardinal Spellman issued a letter denouncing a film to be read at all masses at St. Patrick's Cathedral. Condemning it as "a vicious insult to Italian womanhood," he charged on January 7 that "only a perverted mind could so represent so noble a race of women." Spellman's assertion that the picture should have been entitled "Woman Further Defamed" was a swipe at Rossellini for "ruining" Bergman, who had won Catholic hearts playing a nun in *The Bells of St. Mary's.* Claiming that the film had been condemned by the Vatican, Spellman concluded with a call to all people with a sense of decency to unite with him against the efforts of the "minions of Moscow" to "enslave this land of liberty." Although Spellman was wrong about the Vatican condemnation—*L'Osservatore Romano* had declared that there were passages in the film of "undoubted cinematic distinction"—the time for rational discussion was over. Several priests who had seen the film and found it a profoundly religious experience tried to get the Cardinal to reconsider. But Spellman was not a man who took advice graciously. "The film is filth," he told them, and that was the end of the discussion.[29]

The battle lines were now drawn. Catholic war veterans set up picket lines outside the Paris Theater the afternoon the Cardinal's letter was read. Those who wished to see the film were confronted with protesters carrying signs denouncing the film as "blasphemous" and "an insult to every decent woman and her mother." On the following Sunday, the veterans were joined by more than a thousand Holy Name men with placards warning, "This is the kind of picture the Communists want" and "Don't be a Communist—All the Communists are inside." Passersby and filmgoers alike were handed pamphlets containing a series of questions and answers in catechism form explaining why they should avoid the film. Counter-pickets took up positions outside the theater, and several Protestant ministers, while recognizing the freedom of those who wished to protest the film, argued that they had no right to impose their will on others. Reverend Karl Chworowsky of the Flatbush Unitarian Church in Brooklyn took Spellman to task for his arrogant assumption that all decent Americans were on his side and urged his congregation to see the film and make up their own minds. But minds were snapping shut across the city. Bomb threats to the Paris Theater were followed by warnings that St. Patrick's would be blown up. After clearing the theater in response to one threat, the fire department decided that its practice of allowing standees had violated the city's fire laws and fined the owners $100. In a further effort to harass the owners, the fire commissioner accused them of bribing fire inspectors, a charge that was eventually dropped after an investigation.[30]

When the New York Film Critics voted *The Ways of Love* the best foreign film of 1950, Catholics saw it as a slap in the face. The awards were slated to be given out at the Radio City Music Hall on January 28, but Martin Quigley called the manager, warning him that his hosting of the awards could lead to a boycott of his theater. The ceremony was moved to the Rainbow Room of the RCA Building.[31]

Although the State Supreme Court had enjoined the city's licensing commissioner from interfering with the picture, it had left open the possibility that opponents of *The Miracle* could ask the state board of censors to reverse its decision and revoke the film's license. Targeted by a letter campaign accusing them of playing into the hands of the Communists, the censors began desperately searching for some way to get off the hook. Dr. Hugh Flick, head of the censorship board, argued that Cardinal Spellman's condemnation in combination with the film's showing during the Christmas season were grounds for reopening the case. Armed with these new "insights," a committee reviewed the film on January 15 and declared unanimously that it was indeed sacrilegious. One month later, the state board accepted the committee report and voted to revoke the film's license.[32]

Meanwhile, *The Miracle*'s success in New York had generated a great deal of interest among Los Angeles art theaters. Convinced that the New York diocese's public confrontation had boosted box-office receipts, Father Devlin recommended that Bishop James Francis McIntyre, Cantwell's successor, refrain from openly attacking the film. Instead, Devlin advised him to pressure the local theater owners by sending a letter opposing the film signed by a number of people whose names carried weight in the film industry. Acting on behalf of McIntyre, Mendel Silverburg, an attorney for the film industry and president of the Los Angeles Community Council, persuaded most local exhibitors not to book it. Noting that the controversy in New York could only hurt the community, McIntyre also wrote to the editors of all the city papers asking them not to play up the story if any theater showed the film. In return, he promised not to denounce the film publicly. The bishop's plan worked; when one theater decided to show the film in March, the lack of notoriety hurt box-office receipts.[33]

Catholic opposition to *The Miracle*, however, was far from unanimous. For the first time, a few Catholic publications criticized the church's strong-arm tactics of picketing and raised questions about its right to dictate what non-Catholics could and could not see. "We are burdened with an ancient siege complex," declared a *Commonweal* editorial, so that "a movie coming from a Catholic country . . . can send our blood pressure boiling and our picket lines parading." Hinting at a concern that was beginning to trouble some Catholic leaders, the editorialist wondered if, by threatening rather than persuading, the church may have made non-Catholics "feel as if they were being treated like children by an alien force that didn't give two cents for their personal liberty." Others wondered just what standards the Legion used to make its decisions. Frank Getlein, the movie reviewer for the Davenport (Iowa) *Catholic Messenger*, claimed that the theater that originally exhibited *The Ways of Love* in New York had consistently showed better and more intrinsically Catholic films than "the gaudy palaces specializing in wholesome and harmless, odorless, colorless, tasteless, lifeless native American fare." Church leaders, however, were in no mood for constructive criticism. The piece cost Getlein his job at Fairfield University, a Catholic College in Connecticut. Similarly, William Clancy, a young English teacher at the University of Notre Dame, was fired for writing an article entitled "The Catholic as Philistine," in which he characterized the campaign against *The Miracle* as "semi-ecclesiastic McCarthyism."[34]

In October, the New York Court of Appeals in a five-to-two decision upheld the state board's right to bar Burstyn's film because it was sacrilegious. The Legion's satisfaction, however, was short-lived. Arguments were heard by the United States Supreme Court in April 1952, and for the first time a movie was shown to the justices as a body, although three refused to view it. Justice Minton, who did see it, said that if he "paid anything to see that film it would have been too much." But the justices' job was to decide on the constitutional, not the artistic, merits of showing the film. On May 26, 1952, the Supreme Court unanimously reversed the New York Court's ruling. Justice Tom Clark, who wrote the opinion, noted that the *Mutual* decision that had denied motion pictures First Amendment protection was "out of harmony" with the court's present views. Clark made it clear that this protection did not mean that the industry had "absolute freedom to exhibit every motion picture of every kind at all times and places." Nevertheless, he declared, "We hold . . . that a state may not ban a film on the basis of a censor's conclusion that it is 'sacrilegious.'"[35]

The Legion and its supporters were stunned by the decision. Syndicated Catholic film critic William Mooring likened the jubilation at a luncheon held by the International Motion Picture Organization in honor of Burstyn to Hitler's dance at the railroad car in Compiegne after the fall of France. An editorial in the *Albany Evangelist* termed the decision a victory "for the forces of paganistic secularism" and "tragic in its implication." *America* agreed, declaring that the Court had "just about emptied our law of respect for Almighty God." *Commonweal* was the only major Catholic journal to support the decision, declaring that the Court had done the right thing in rejecting the state's right to play theologian. Although the Court did not eliminate film censorship in the *Miracle* case, it made it clear that the state had "a heavy burden" to demonstrate that the situation justified prior restraint. Over the next five years the Court would expand on its decision, striking down a number of state and municipal standards including "prejudicial to the best interests of the people," "harmful," "immoral or tended to corrupt morals," "cruel, obscene, indecent or immoral, or such as tend to debase or corrupt morals," and "immoral and obscene."[36]

Despite its disappointment in the Court's *Miracle* decision, the Legion refused to become embroiled in the struggle to maintain state censorship. When Ohio's Bishop Michael J. Ready filed an amicus curiae brief in a case involving that state's banning of the German film *M*, Masterson reminded him that the church had never officially supported political censorship. Furthermore, Masterson argued, the film was a weak peg on which to hang the forces of movie morality because the Legion had classified it as a B. But the real danger, he warned, was the possibility that the bishop's stance could be interpreted as a sign that the Legion had been seriously weakened by the Court's decisions and had lost faith in the Code. Nevertheless, the courts' critical view of state censorship placed a greater burden on pressure groups like the Legion. "Now, the only effective bulwark against pictures which are immoral, short of being obscene," declared the National Council of Catholic Men, "is public opinion, manifested through such organizations as the Legion of Decency." Unfortunately for the Legion, it could no longer count on the support it had once generated.[37]

Part of the difficulty stemmed from the growing independence of a better educated laity, but the Legion didn't help itself by the type of films it singled out for criticism. Cecil B. deMille's *The Greatest Show on Earth* (1952) seemed an unlikely Legion target. The film, which chronicled the lives of several circus performers, drew much of its excitement from the danger associated with the daring high-wire acts. Sebastian, an aerialist played by Cornel Wilde, is a ladies' man who becomes the circus's star act before injuring himself when he performs without a net. A subplot revolves around a former surgeon who once performed a mercy killing and is now hiding from the law disguised as Buttons the Clown. When one of the entertainers, jealous of his girlfriend's infatuation with Sebastian, wrecks their train, the circus boss is pinned under a car. Buttons, played by Jimmy Stewart, performs an on-the-spot operation saving the boss's life and is spotted by the police and led away in handcuffs. In true Hollywood "on with the show" spirit, the performers pull themselves together and give "the greatest show on earth" in the next town.

DeMille was informed that the Legion had three major objections to his film. One problem in a film that would probably draw a large number of children was the "carnal, lustful" characterization of Sebastian, who, the Legion reviewers claimed, was "depicted as so physically irresistible that the virtue of the circus girls are in peril the moment they caught his fancy." Masterson and Little, who worked on the film, were also concerned about the female costumes, which they felt left nothing to the imagination. But it was Buttons the Clown that caused the greatest concern. Masterson claimed that this was the first introduction into an important American film of a sympathetic character who commits a mercy killing, made all the more disturbing by the fact that the character was played by the popular Jimmy Stewart, who heretofore had always played positive role models. "Youth and poorly instructed adults could only conclude," he told deMille, "that mercy killing is not so bad or a nice clown would not have done it." Reminding deMille that one of his previous pictures, *The Sign of the Cross*, had played a major role in the formation of the Legion, both priests warned him that this film could run into similar trouble when nuns and priests across the nation protested his sordid treatment of circus life.[38]

Donald Hayne, deMille's right-hand man, drafted a response to Little. It was clear from the start that there would be no concessions. Hayne, who had obtained a copy of a pamphlet in which Father Masterson had characterized the work of the Legion's executive secretary as "priestly work," derisively scribbled in the margin of his draft: "like the Inquisition." DeMille pointed out that the movie's characterization of Sebastian as "a gay charmer who apparently made rather light of the affections of numerous young women" was an integral part of the story and quite outside the priest's "province as a moralist." Moreover, he continued, "I cannot by any stretch of the imagination conceive that the soul of any human being, young or old, could be corrupted" by any of Sebastian's dialogue. And as for the costuming, deMille reminded Little that they were the same outfits worn by performers in the Ringling Brothers and Barnum & Bailey circus, which was blessed every year by a Catholic priest. "I suppose," he conceded, "that there are a few individuals so morbidly prurient that looking at someone dressed in a circus costume might constitute a moral danger for them." Those "unfortunate persons," he declared, "should go to see a psychiatrist rather than *The Greatest Show on Earth*."[39]

The Legion's contention that the film condoned euthanasia was rejected out of hand. Not only did Buttons suffer for his crime throughout the picture, deMille pointed out, but he is shown being taken off in handcuffs at the story's end. Finally, he concluded: "If your objection is not that Buttons was a sinner, but that he is treated sympathetically in spite of the crime . . . for which he pays the full penalty, I can only say in all humility [a difficult task for deMille], that I am honored to share that reproach with Another who was accused of being a friend of sinners." Little responded that he, too, subscribed to the principle "hate the sin and love the sinner," but, he noted, the Legion would be remiss if it approved a film that would move the audience to condone Buttons's "evil act." He agreed with the producer that circus costumes in their usual environment were not suggestive, but they became a problem in camera close-ups. When deMille made it clear that he would not back down, the Legion classified the film as a B, placing it off limits for children after deciding that it couldn't justify a condemnation.[40]

Masterson and Little knew they could never enlist the laity in a campaign against a B film. *Commonweal* refused to advertise it, but *Extension* magazine published a positive review by William Mooring. When Father John McGrath, director of the Springfield, Illinois, Catholic Youth Organization, asked Monsignor J. B. Lux, managing editor of the magazine, to retract Mooring's recommendation, Lux arranged for a private screening of the film for four monsignors and several laypeople. Their evaluations were unanimous: it was, indeed the greatest show on earth. Characterizing the Legion's concern about euthanasia as "sheer nonsense," Lux declared that the viewer could gather that Buttons had committed such a crime only by piecing together two or three hints during the show. Because several adults in his audience were uncertain about the clown's crime, he was sure that a child would not understand why Buttons was arrested. The costuming was ordinary circus costuming, he argued, and "if this justifies the banning of this picture, then all circuses must be rated a 'B' and no Catholic child could ever attend one." What really worried him was that by objecting to such an innocent film, the Legion would undermine its influence in the minds of the Catholic people. "We won't retract the review," he told Bishop McGrath, "for we are not behind the iron curtain and we have a right to disagree [with] the Legion."[41]

With no support from the church, Masterson and Little suggested to Paramount that a few technical changes in the film could lead to a higher classification. Knowing that the two priests were on their own—someone had sent him a copy of Lux's letter to McGrath—deMille refused to help them save face. "I don't know whether it is proper to tell a [priest] to go to hell," he said to Frank Freeman, Paramount's production head, "but since these [two] will probably finish near there anyway, it needs no comment from me." Despite his frustrations with the Legion, deMille had no interest in escalating the conflict. When questioned about a story in the Masonic journal *New Age* about the "sinister hand of Rome in the movies," he denied that the church had tried to influence his films.[42]

Some independent theater owners were also challenging the Legion's right to tell them how to run their business. When Little informed the Brandt theater chain that he was contemplating implementing a boycott unless it stopped showing *The Seven Deadly Sins* (1952), which had been condemned by the Legion, the owner sent the priest a blistering letter. "I have no objection to the Legion [advising] the people of yours or of any other faith as to what you consider morally objectionable," he told Little, "but I resent the implied threat of a boycott as being totally irreligious, immoral or un-American."[43]

No longer able to count on the cooperation of everyone in the industry, the Legion might have been wiser to approach its next challenge with greater caution. *The Moon Is Blue*, produced and directed by Otto Preminger for United Artists, was based on a popular comedy by F. Hugh Herbert. The film's plot revolved around the unsuccessful efforts of a young architect and a middle-aged rake to seduce a woman named Patty O'Neil, played by Maggie McNamara. Although Patty is not opposed to heavy necking, she makes it clear that she intends to remain a virgin until marriage. But her declaration that "lots of girls don't mind being seduced" and her resentment of the architect's accusation that she is a professional virgin suggest that there may be more than meets the ear. According to the architect, anyone who advertises her virginity so much must be interested in selling it. But Patty protects her virtue and becomes engaged to the architect at the end of the story.

Geoff Shurlock, who was assigned the job of monitoring the film, liked it, but his argument that goodness wins out because McNamara gets her man without compromising her principles failed to sway Joe Breen. Only a week before, Breen had approved the controversial *From Here to Eternity*, despite the adulterous relationship between the characters played by Burt Lancaster and Deborah Kerr. Moreover, everyone knew that the soldiers in the film who paid money to talk with women in the Congress Club's private rooms were buying more than conversation. Nevertheless, Breen somehow felt that the introduction of words like "virgin," "seduce," and "pregnant" made *The Moon Is Blue* much more dangerous. He also singled out the phrase "You are shallow, cynical, selfish, immoral, and I like you," because under the Code it was not possible for a person to be both immoral and likable. The real cause of Breen's ire may have been Preminger's unwillingness to negotiate any changes, but whatever the reason, he refused to grant the film a seal. Breen was supported by Quigley, who told United Artists that the film's treatment of "free love" violated the section of the Code that declared that "pictures shall not infer that low forms of sex relationship are the accepted or common thing." Unless the film was revised, Quigley warned, the Legion would condemn it.[44]

United Artists appealed Breen's decision to the MPAA board, which seemed receptive, but a last-minute attack by Loews's elderly president, Nicholas Schenck, saved Breen. "I wouldn't let my daughter see it," he told the other members. "It's true that the girl is not seduced in the time she spends with the boy, but other girls in a similar situation might get closer to the flame." Unwilling to undertake the "drastic rewriting" demanded by Breen, Preminger and the studio heads decided to release the film in June 1953 without a seal. In order to do so, United Artists had to resign from the MPAA because upholding the Code was a condition of membership.[45]

Legion reviewers felt that the film deserved a B, but Masterson and Little overruled them and condemned it for essentially political reasons. Because Martin Quigley's credibility could be damaged if the film received a higher classification after he had told United Artists it would be condemned, he pressured Masterson and Cardinal Spellman to ensure a Legion condemnation. It was one thing to break with the PCA over a foreign film like *The Bicycle Thief*, which had a limited run, but in the case of a major studio production such division could be the beginning of the end of the Code.[46]

According to Father Thomas Little, who took over the Legion after Father Masterson's sudden death a week before the premiere of *The Moon Is Blue*, it had been rejected because of its sympathetic portrayal of seduction. Because the heroine remained a virgin to the end, Little could present only a slippery-slope situation in which she is well on her way to damnation as the picture ends. "Inferentially she is a fool," Little declared. "Dramatically this is presented first by smoking, second by drinking and thirdly when she succumbs and knocks on Holden's bedroom door. At this point the moral degeneration is accomplished." The fact that nothing happened in the bedroom and the couple become engaged without any sacrifice of her virtue apparently were immaterial.[47]

Whatever reservations Little had about his decision, he did his best to rally the Legion's supporters. Both Cardinal Spellman and Bishop McIntyre labeled attendance at the film "a near occasion of sin." Bishops were provided by the Legion with a sermon to distribute to their priests, noting that over the years the church's objection to immoral movies had been felt where it counted. "Decency means dollars," Little argued. "Dirt means deficit." A number of dioceses swung into line. An El Paso priest reported to the Legion that he had "put the hate" on the local chain that had exhibited the picture. In Poughkeepsie, New York, Father Michael O'Shea presented the city council with a petition signed by 4,125 people in an unsuccessful effort to get it to adopt an ordinance prohibiting the showing of immoral films like *The Moon Is Blue*. Upon learning of the Legion's action, the San Francisco Junior Chamber of Commerce canceled its sponsorship of the premiere of the film "in the interest of good taste." In Jersey City, the police seized two prints of the film and arrested the theater manager. When he showed a reserve print after his release, he was threatened by some local hoods. Deciding that he had made enough sacrifices for artistic freedom, he wisely handed over his last print. "There must be dozens of houses of prostitution, gambling halls [along with] burlesque houses within walking distance of the theater," fumed a United Artists branch manager, while people "are prevented from enjoying a wholesome comedy." The film was also banned in Kansas, Ohio, and Maryland, but with *The Miracle* as a precedent, United Artists fought and won all ten state and local efforts to censor it. The Maryland judge who heard the case was bewildered by the state's action. It is "a light comedy," he noted in his opinion, "telling a tale of wide-eyed, brash, puppy-like innocence routing or converting to its side the forces of evil it encounters."[48]

The controversy dealt a severe blow to Breen's image. Claiming that the PCA had ceased to have teeth, *Variety* pointed out that a few years earlier, the lack of a seal automatically meant no play dates in 3,000 theaters affiliated with the major studios. In fact, the paper argued, without the publicity generated by the PCA and the Legion, *The Moon Is Blue* would not have been so successful.[49]

In the long run, *The Moon Is Blue* proved much more troublesome than *The Miracle*. The latter case had crippled the state censorship boards, but the church had never relied on government agencies to control Hollywood. The Preminger picture, on the other hand, signified a major turning point for the Legion. Father Little had to admit that the condemnation had clearly boosted ticket sales, and the Legion could no longer count on the automatic support it had once commanded. *Commonweal*'s stance was that the film was hardly the best case on which to make a stand in defense of the Code. The movie critic for *St. Joseph's Magazine*, not realizing that the film had been condemned, recommended it. With United Artists seeking to capitalize on this endorsement, local Legion directors told their members that the reviewer had subsequently recanted and bowed to the Legion's judgment.[50]

For the first time a significant number of Catholics, laity as well as clergy, complained about a Legion condemnation. Many later recalled that its handling of the film made them lose faith in the Legion's judgment. Nor was it just the liberal laity that refused to fall in line. Father Ferdinand Falque of the Sacred Heart Church in Staples, Minnesota, had dropped into a local theater to see "how bad a movie can get." Preminger's film turned out to be the best picture he had seen since Frank Capra's 1936 film *Mr. Deeds Goes to Town*. Characterizing *The Moon Is Blue* as a marvelous argument against promiscuity, he told Little he couldn't understand how such a film had been condemned when "so many slushy and truly promiscuous plots" slipped past the Legion. While Little could do nothing more than to urge Father Falque to accept the Legion's decisions, other Catholic critics did not fare so well. When George Shaefer, the producer's representative, criticized the Legion's attack, he was asked to resign from the New York archdiocese's Communion Breakfast Committee.[51]

Some municipal officials no longer responded to Legion demands as they once had. In 1951 Providence had banned a rerelease of Marlene Dietrich's *Blue Angel* on the strength of a Legion condemnation. "If the Legion of Decency condemns a picture," a city official said, "we'll condemn a picture. We go along with the Legion and we'll continue to go along with it." But when the city amusements inspector recommended banning *The Moon Is Blue,* he found the city authorities unwilling to cooperate. "Well can I recall," he told Bishop McVinney, "that if any clergy from any faith opposed a license or spoke or wrote a letter against any condition that they thought was wrong, the greatest respect was shown to them." A number of Catholics who saw this and other films like *The Greatest Show on Earth* wondered if the Legion was out of touch with the times in its evaluations. The real danger was that the millions of Catholics who saw these films might begin to doubt the reasonableness of the church's other decisions.[52]

TWELVE

Waning Powers

Although the Legion had risked some of its credibility in shoring up the Production Code Administration, Father Thomas Little felt that Joe Breen had failed to show his gratitude by cracking down on the studios after the *Moon Is Blue* case. If anything, he and Father Paul Hayes, his new assistant, became increasingly disenchanted with Breen's performance. The relationship between the Legion and Breen hit an all-time low in 1953, when Little took Breen to task on several films: the dancing in *Let's Do It Again* was "definitely off the reservation"; Rita Hayworth's numbers in *Miss Sadie Thompson* were little more than a series of "bumps and grinds"; and Cyd Charisse's movements in *Singin' in the Rain* were definitely "suggestive." All this, in combination with a kissing sequence in *The Wicked Woman*, "the likes of which hasn't been seen in some time," and a "navel shot" in another, convinced him that Breen had thrown in the towel. In fact, the PCA director was tired. He had had a lung removed in 1951, and the twenty years of battles with producers and directors had taken a toll. In February 1954 he quietly told MPAA president Eric Johnston that he intended to retire in the fall.[1]

Nevertheless, Breen had one last fight in him, which would enlist the

Legion in their last joint battle against their old nemesis, Howard Hughes. RKO had been in trouble ever since Hughes's takeover in 1947, losing more than $20 million in five years. Desperate for a hit, Hughes cast Jane Russell as a young heiress who disguises herself as a poor young model in order to find a husband in *The French Line*. The story was thin, but the film included several song and dance numbers that would highlight Russell's obvious attractions in the new 3-D format. There was the usual trouble with any Hughes script: Breen wouldn't approve any gags based on the Kinsey Report or any "toilet humor." He was also worried about the costuming of Russell. When he saw the finished product, which included a performance by the star in a brief costume with a bare midriff, he told Hughes he would not issue a certificate unless substantial changes were made in the film.[2]

Hughes, who had been through it all before with *The Outlaw*, ignored Breen and opened the film in Saint Louis on December 29, 1953. The film was accompanied by the usual Hughes ads: "J. R. in 3-D. That's all, brother!" and "Jane Russell in 3 Dimensions—and what dimensions!" But this time the stakes were higher. Hughes had not belonged to the Motion Picture Association of America when he exhibited *The Outlaw*. But no member studio had released a film without a seal since the PCA was formed in 1934. Breen immediately levied a $25,000 fine on Hughes—the only form of punishment available, yet one that was hardly a threat to the millionaire.[3]

Breen sent Jack Vizzard to Saint Louis, ostensibly to see the premiere but with instructions to contact Archbishop Joseph Ritter. After the two men worked out a press statement denouncing Hughes for selecting Saint Louis as the film's opening site, Ritter asked Vizzard what he thought of his issuing a pastoral letter forbidding all Catholics under his jurisdiction to see the film under pain of mortal sin. "I think it's a good idea," Vizzard responded, but later he wondered if he should be part of such a decision. But he comforted himself with the thought that it was a "bit much" to assume "that the eternal fate of a human being [would] be connected to Jane Russell's mammaries."[4]

Nevertheless, when the owners of the Fox Theater refused to cancel the film, an angry Ritter issued a pastoral letter to be read at all masses on January 3 forbidding Catholics from seeing it. Because Hughes had not sent a copy of the film to the Legion, Father Little asked Ritter to send a delegation to the Fox Theater to appraise the film. On the strength of their evaluation, Little sent a telegram to Hughes informing him that the Legion viewed the film as "gravely and grossly offensive to decency and morality" and warning him that it would issue a condemnation unless the film was withdrawn immediately. Little's telegram drew an immediate response from RKO complaining that the Legion had condemned the film without seeing it. Little fired back that the advertising for the film in conjunction with the fact that it had not received a

PCA seal was enough for him. He gave the studio a January 5 deadline, at which time he would announce its condemnation unless something was done to correct the film. RKO made a conciliatory gesture, sending a print of the film along with a studio cutter to New York. On January 6, Little, Father Paul Hayes, Mary Looram, and six reviewers saw the film and voted unanimously to condemn it on the basis of some suggestive lines, Russell's costuming, and several of her dance routines. Little issued an ultimatum: there would be no negotiations on the rest of the picture until the final dance sequence was eliminated. Hughes was given twenty-four hours to respond.[5]

On January 8, Hughes informed the Legion that the film was being resubmitted to Breen's office and would be pulled as soon as he could make an accommodation with the owners of the Fox Theater. Although Hughes had failed to meet his demands, Little held off announcing the condemnation in order to give him a chance to make amends. The understanding was that Hughes would resubmit his film to the PCA and that the Legion would reevaluate the new version. Cardinal Francis Spellman, who had discussed the matter with Breen, threatened to upset the negotiations when he learned that the producer of the film was Edward Grainger, a graduate of St. Francis Xavier and Fordham University. Breen talked the cardinal out of making a public statement, although he admitted that it was a sad state of affairs that he now had to worry about movies made by the alumni of Catholic colleges as well as the liberal Ivy League schools. Mary Looram and Martin Quigley talked to Breen about the Legion's objections, but the PCA director needed no bracing. If he was going to retire at the end of the year, he was going to go out with one last victory. On January 16, Breen notified Hughes that he had turned down his latest version. Miffed, Hughes informed the Legion the following day that he had had enough; he would not withdraw the picture from Saint Louis, nor would he make any substantial changes to meet its objections.[6]

James Grainger, president of RKO and the producer's father, told Little that although the decision to break off negotiations was made by Hughes alone, he agreed that the Legion was being unfair in this case. He pointed out that Hughes, who had given $100 million to charity, deserved better. Much of the problem, he told the priest, stemmed from a personal feud between Hughes and Breen, abetted by Breen's staff of "small-fries," who were inclined to throw their weight around to compensate for their limited salaries. Reminding Little that "overexposure" was acceptable in Catholic countries like Italy and France, he wondered if perhaps the Legion had become too puritanical. Whatever the case, cutting the last dance sequence, as the Legion demanded, was impossible as it would cost $250,000 to make the necessary changes. This was hardly an argument likely to win Little over. Declaring that no cost was too high when it came to matters of morality, he reminded Grainger that Hughes had already received a billion dollars worth of free publicity from the controversy.[7]

With no further word from RKO, the Legion issued its condemnation to the press on January 18. In view of the Supreme Court's decision on the same day overturning both a New York state ban on the French film *La Ronde* and Ohio's refusal to license *M,* Little knew that the fight against *The French Line* was going to be an uphill battle. As Father Paul Hayes noted in *Pastoral Life,* "Never before was the Legion of Decency so urgently necessary for our moral survival." Knowing that Hughes planned to put his film into general release in late February, Little urged the bishops to press their local theaters not to book it. In Springfield, Illinois, Father Michael Owen Driscoll, head of the local Legion chapter, told the pastors in his diocese that unless *The French Line* were stopped, the standards of decency that had been upheld in the film industry over the past two decades would be seriously weakened. Driscoll personally contacted all the downtown Springfield theater managers while the pastors worked on the theater owners in their parishes to head off any future bookings. But unlike earlier cases, when the Legion had relied on a display of public support, Driscoll cautioned the pastors to avoid newspaper publicity or sensational action, which would only sell more tickets. Most other diocesan Legions adopted a similar strategy. *Variety*'s story of the Legion's campaign featured an interview with George Mackenna, manager of Buffalo's Lafayette Theater, who said that the thousands of letters and telephone calls he had received included some of "the most vulgar and obscene and immoral language ever uttered."[8]

In spite of the recent decisions stripping down ambiguous state censorship standards, the Supreme Court had not eliminated the right to reject a film on the ground of obscenity. Citing the same dance sequence that the Legion had singled out, New York, Pennsylvania, Kansas, and a number of municipalities refused to license *The French Line.* As the Providence amusement inspector explained to his supervisor: "All the clothes she has on is a G string and a small rhinestone harness covering on her bosom. . . . In her dance in this costume she manages, through some physical manner, to rotate her bosom which is uncovered to allow one to see the apex of her breasts." Although Hughes had refused to deal with Breen and the Legion, he had to cut the dance sequence in order to show the film in a number of areas. Several major chains, including RKO Theaters (which was divorced from RKO Pictures), refused to book it. Many theaters that did show it tried to placate the Legion by posting signs outside the lobby advising their Catholic patrons that the film had been condemned. But not every owner was willing to cooperate. The owner of the Park Theater in Orchard Park, New York, announced that he had originally intended not to book the film because the rent was too high, but "blackmail" from the Legion of Decency informing him that if he did, all Catholics would be ordered to boycott his theater for six months caused him to change his mind. "We guarantee you," he informed the public, "that if you are corrupted by this picture we will pay your reform school tuition."[9]

Although Joe Breen may have derived some pleasure from taking one last swipe at Howard Hughes, the Legion didn't. Father Little couldn't help reminding Breen that the famous dance in *The French Line* was the conclusion to a long string of infractions that the PCA had ignored. Even more discouraging was the news supplied by Martin Quigley that the Hughes film, made at a cost estimated at $1.5 million, was expected to gross some $3 million domestically and $2 million abroad. In his annual report to the bishops, Little admitted that part of the film's success was due to the large number of Catholics who ignored the Legion's condemnation.[10]

The Legion had little time to worry about Hughes. Will Hays died in 1954, the same year that Joe Breen retired. It was one more measure of the Legion's declining influence that its Catholic candidate to replace Breen, Jack Vizzard, failed to beat out Geoff Shurlock, an Episcopalian. At first glance, Shurlock, who had been with the PCA since the early 1930s, offered little in the way of change. Nevertheless, although a loyal supporter of Breen, Shurlock had taken a more liberal view of the Code than his boss on several occasions—most notably in the case of *The Moon Is Blue*. If Breen had disappointed the Legion in recent years, Shurlock's takeover promised an even more strained relationship. Within a few months of Shurlock's appointment, Father Little accused him of permitting the showing of an unprecedented number of immoral pictures. In 1955, Shurlock's first full year in office, 33 percent of Hollywood films received a B rating, up 11 percent over the previous year. And although the percentage dipped the next year, Little declared that the films in this category were far worse than in past years. Having already filed more complaints with the major studios by August 1956 than in any previous year, Little met with Eric Johnston to complain about a string of "blatant violations of decency" in films dealing with "impotency, sterility, breakdown of parental morality, excess brutality, [and] indirect incest."[11]

The Legion was still able to get the studios to make many requested cuts, but the negotiations were more protracted and the final result seemed less satisfactory. RKO's *Son of Sinbad* (1955) was an Arabian Nights fantasy with harem girls playing the part of the forty thieves, featuring dances by the burlesque star Lily St. Cyr, who, unlike Gypsy Rose Lee, had kept her stage name. Breen had denied the film a seal two years earlier, but Shurlock approved it with a few minor changes. The Legion condemnation of the film was especially harsh. Noting that it posed a serious threat to Christian morality because of its "continuing violation of the virtue of purity" and its "grossly salacious dances," Little charged that it was a good example of why juvenile delinquency was on the rise. But RKO milked the film's notoriety for several months before it made enough cuts to get it reclassified as a B.[12]

Faced with a shrinking general audience, few producers, with the exception of Hughes, were willing to risk condemnation. Consequently, the Legion boasted of a string of victories as late as 1957. Producer Robert Aldrich was forced to make thirty changes, including dropping the entire ending of *Kiss Me Deadly* (1955), in order to escape condemnation, and Paramount had to eliminate all the "cleavage shots" in *Anything Goes* (1956). United Artists was able to avoid a condemnation by making some dialogue changes and adding a prologue and epilogue to *Captain's Paradise* (1953), the story of a captain with wives in two separate ports. Aspiring bigamists were warned at the beginning of the film, "The hero Captain Henry St. James never existed. The whole saga is in fact a fairy story," and the film's final scene was followed by: "We have to conclude this is a fairy tale. It never happened. It couldn't happen. If it has ever occurred to you as a possibility, forget it. There are all kinds of laws divine and human against it, to say nothing of the scandal."[13]

Most of Little's triumphs, however, consisted of petty changes. As a result of his efforts, Virginia Grey contemplated a separation instead of a divorce in *All That Heaven Allows* (1955), and Dan Dailey told Jayne Mansfield in *The Wayward Bus* (1957) that she was "fabulously" attractive instead of "physically" attractive. Warner agreed to remove a line from *The High and the Mighty* (1954) asking, "Does that answer your question, Mister, or do you feel like a bored priest hidin' behind a curtain?" And when the Legion declared that it was implicit that a dancer who runs up a staircase pursued by the villain in *Oklahoma* (1955) was heading for a brothel, the scene was reshot to establish that it was, in fact, a gambling hall. Even though the makers of *Oklahoma* viewed the film as family entertainment, they refused to make all the requested changes that would have moved it from a B to an A-II rating. It was becoming increasingly clear that the studios felt that a B no longer did any damage at the box office. When MGM and United Artists introduced a new clause in their contracts with independent producers requiring them to deliver the film with no worse than a B rating, *Variety* noted that this was the first known instance where producers had been forced to meet any censorial standards other than those imposed by the Production Code. But it was small consolation for Father Little, who cringed every time a studio claimed that a B film had been "approved by the Legion."[14]

Like the PCA, the Legion's power had to be measured in part by the amount of material producers avoided in order to prevent any trouble with the church. Producer Julius Blaustein claimed that a number of his colleagues censored themselves in advance, knowing that the Legion would object to certain themes. Consequently, he said, "Divorce never can be shown as a solution to a domestic problem. Thus a major factor in the life of the United States can never be shown in the movies."[15]

Although Blaustein was concerned about too much Legion power, church leaders were increasingly worried about its declining influence. In 1955, Little attributed the "revolution in cinema morals" to the industry's increased reliance on bestsellers and plays for its stories, recent Supreme Court decisions in *The Miracle* and *La Ronde* cases, and the financial success of some condemned movies, which, he sadly admitted, would not have been possible without Catholic support at the box office. The following year, the Episcopal Committee on Motion Pictures launched a new campaign to counteract the growing apathy among church members. Local Legion directors dutifully cranked out a few extra warnings about the new wave of film immorality, but with no noticeable effect. As a result, Little found himself in a more difficult position than his predecessors. Unable to count on the PCA to hold the line, he also wondered about the support he could muster among his own constituency.[16]

Four films released in 1955 and 1956—*Battle Cry*, *Storm Center*, *Tea and Sympathy*, and *Baby Doll*—confirmed Little's suspicions that Shurlock's takeover would make his job tougher. *Battle Cry*, which was approved before Breen's retirement, was a good example of what Little viewed as Hollywood's increasing inclination to return to the bad old pre-Code days when it used sex to sell films. Based on the Leon Uris best-seller, the film focused on a group of young Marines in training prior to the invasion of Saipan. Danny Forrester, one of the young warriors, becomes involved with Elaine Yarborough, a married USO worker, until a phone call to his childhood sweetheart back home rekindles his old love. His colonel, a hard-nosed military officer with a heart of gold, senses the boy's difficulties and arranges a weekend pass. Danny and his girlfriend go out on a picnic at a beach, and after staying out all night return the next morning married.

The project ran into trouble at the start when two Warner representatives tried to get the Defense Department and the Marine Corps to cooperate in filming the story. The Marine spokesman, who had read the novel, argued that the film would hurt their recruiting effort, especially Forrester's relationship with the USO worker, which showed an idealistic eighteen-year-old, the type of youth they hoped to attract, "humping a married woman twice his age." No mother, he concluded, would let her son join the Marines after seeing the picture. After transforming Danny's affair into a teenage infatuation and approving the use of the word "hell" by the colonel in a battle scene, the PCA passed the picture. By the time the Legion screened it, Shurlock had taken over. When the reviewers turned in a negative report, Father Little and Mary Looram saw the film and decided to send a message to Shurlock.[17] While objecting to the general "low moral tone" and the "sexual and sensuous" treatment of the story, they focused on two episodes: one involving a group of Marines out on the town, and the beach scene with Danny and his girlfriend. Unless changes were made, Little told Warner, he would have to issue a condemnation.

The studio agreed to make some alterations, including eliminating a line that the Legion argued indicated that a woman at a bar was soliciting. It refused, however, to cut a shot of a second Marine tossing two dollar bills on a countertop in front of another woman, which the Legion interpreted as the beginning of another sexual transaction. When Warner insisted that the gesture was meant to represent a free-spending Marine out on the town, Little let it slide. In the beach scene, after the couple embrace, the camera panned up to the sky, which Little insisted was a traditional Hollywood device indicating that a sexual encounter was taking place offscreen. At first, the studio claimed that it was unfair to have a movie condemned on the basis of what Little imagined happened offscreen. After considerable discussion, Martin Quigley persuaded the studio to cut the scene immediately after the embrace. Although Little awarded the film a B, he singled out *Battle Cry* in his annual report to illustrate the PCA's growing laxness.[18]

Shurlock also ran into trouble with the Legion over an old problem: how to handle politically controversial films. The church had long feared that the screen could be used to spread Communist propaganda. The advent of the Cold War coupled with the industry's growing interest in social-problem films had rekindled the Legion's concern about the "red menace" in Hollywood. Leading the charge was the Catholic syndicated columnist William Mooring, who detected evidence of Communist influence in films that the most zealous patriot failed to see. Even an anti-Communist film like *Steel Helmet* (1953) erred by showing a Korean prisoner of war taunting an African-American GI about racism in America. "True, he gave the Red an answer," Mooring conceded, "but the sum effect was to remind the audience about our failings." Seemingly innocent films like *Asphalt Jungle* (1950), *White Heat* (1949), and *Born Yesterday* (1950) apparently also served the "crooked purposes of the Soviet Union" by focusing on the ugliness and decadence of American life. Mooring's attack on *Born Yesterday* because of its depiction of corruption in government and big business, which even the conservative Quigley thought was unwarranted, led to picketing by Catholic war veterans in several cities. And according to Mooring, the unwillingness of the local congregation to come to the aid of Gary Cooper in *High Noon* masked a more sinister objective: the Communist effort to prove that religion is an opiate that prevents people from working against social injustice.[19]

Since the bishops' committee had rejected Father John McClafferty's repeated efforts to establish a Catholic Institute of Film Analysis to deal with the political implications of such movies, the Legion remained the church's only bulwark against what it perceived to be the leftist tendencies of some filmmakers. But because the Legion's classification system had been established to deal with immorality, it continued to run into trouble when it attempted to take on these issues, as in the case of *Storm Center*, which starred Bette Davis as the widow of a World War I soldier who devoted her life to a small-town library. The plot focused on the librarian's refusal to remove a book entitled *The Communist Dream* from the shelves because she believes that any reader would recognize it as propaganda. Accused of being a Communist dupe, she is fired from her job and is ostracized by most of the community. One of her few friends is a boy who is confused about the growing criticism of someone he looked up to. He sneaks into the library and accidentally sets it on fire. This shocks the town back to its senses, and Davis is invited to begin the rebuilding process.

The idea for the story had been kicking around for several years. When President Eisenhower warned against the dangers of book burning in a 1953 speech at Dartmouth College, Daniel Taradash, co-author of the script, thought the time might be right for such a film. Taradash had no difficulty with the PCA, whose only concern was whether the boy's actions might lead children to play with matches. At the Legion, however, reviewers split over how to classify the film. A Newark, New Jersey, librarian applauded the story for its willingness to show how values can be imperiled by fear, but other reviewers felt that it presented a biased account of censorship, which could harm an unsophisticated audience. As one reviewer put it, the film's assumption that readers would not be influenced by Communist propaganda ignored the effect of original sin. "Intellectual freedom has a place within the moral order," he concluded, "but it is subordinate to higher and ultimate values."[20]

In spite of their fears, most of the reviewers felt they had to classify the film as A-II because it was morally unobjectionable. But Little, who had been warned by Mooring that Taradash was a leftist, believed that the film presented a "one-sided presentation of book burning" and placed it in the separate classification category. In announcing his decision, he wrote: "The highly propagandistic nature of this controversial film (book burning, anti-Communism, civil liberties) offers a warped, over-simplified and strongly emotional solution to a complex problem of American life. Its specious arguments tend seriously to be misleading and misrepresentative by reason of an inept and distorted presentation." Most of the Catholic press supported

Little's decision. Father John Sheerin, writing in the *New World*, charged that a librarian must have a sense of responsibility for the good of the community. It was "preposterous," he declared, to say, as Davis's character did in the film, that Communism is a "political heresy and that Communist books should be shelved alongside other books on political heresy." She was wrong: "Communism is far more than a heresy, it is a conspiracy to overthrow the American government." *Commonweal* was again the only major Catholic publication to take the Legion to task for ignoring its original mandate by rejecting the film on political rather than moral grounds.[21]

Taradash accused the Legion of political censorship and urged the industry to ignore its criticism. Hollywood, which usually avoided any public criticism of the Legion, agreed. The Motion Picture Industry Council, which was made up of various elements in the business including producers and the Screen Actors Guild and headed by Lou Greenspan, a former editor of *Variety*, condemned the Legion's handling of *Storm Center*. Although the council recognized the Legion's right to offer religious counsel, it accused the Catholic group of going beyond normal spiritual advice and engaging in "a form of censorship with the purpose of dictating and controlling the content of motion pictures contrary to American principles of freedom of thought and expression." Even more startling was the decision of the MPAA to defend the film. A special brochure prepared by its Community Relations Department featured a quote from Eisenhower's book burning speech: "Don't think you are going to conceal faults by concealing evidence that they ever existed." For the first time, Jack Vizzard began to hear comments from industry people that the Legion was getting "too big for its pants."[22]

The Legion hadn't changed, argued Little in his defense; Hollywood's constant quest for more shocking material along with its willingness to adapt Broadway plays was the problem. In the summer of 1954, he took the unusual step of complaining to Dore Schary, head of production at MGM, about his studio's purchase of the rights to Robert Anderson's 1953 hit play *Tea and Sympathy*. The play chronicled the struggle of a young boy at a prep school who is concerned that he may be a homosexual. He gets no support from his father or his headmaster, who want to "make a man" out of him, while his fellow students tease him unmercifully. His only friend is the headmaster's wife who feels that he needs more than the traditional tea and sympathy expected of her. After an argument with her husband, she goes to the boy. Taking his hand, she says, "years from now . . . when you talk about this . . . and you will . . . be kind." By giving herself to him, she enables him to realize he is not a homosexual.[23]

Little and Breen, who was still PCA director, had been alerted to the dangers of the play by Martin Quigley. They faced a major problem, he warned them, if a studio decided to film it. He thought that the homosexuality angle could be glossed over, but he couldn't see how Breen could pass it if "the wife's solution to the boy's problem is an essential part of the story." Breen's job was complicated by Anderson's initial insistence that there be no tampering with the play's essential elements. The boy's problems had to spring from the charge of homosexuality he declared; portraying him as just a "sissy" would rob the story of its dramatic tension. Even more important, Anderson identified it as a sine qua non that the resolution of the boy's difficulties comes from the wife's giving herself to him sexually. It would be unacceptable, he said, if she merely offers him her support.[24]

Little's complaints about the homosexuality theme and the story's "glorification of adultery" went to the heart of the plot, but Schary assured him that they could be worked out. The issue of the boy's sexual identity would be resolved by presenting him as someone his classmates brand as "sister-boy" because he is something of a loner who can sew and play tennis (a game for "sissies"), and wants to become a folk singer when he leaves school. A voice of morality would be introduced to indicate that what the headmaster's wife did was wrong: the boy, now a successful author who has written a novel about their affair, would return to the campus and find an unmailed letter she had written to him after leaving her husband, expressing her guilt over what had happened. Geoff Shurlock, who handled the negotiations with MGM, was still not satisfied. As far as he was concerned, the affair's awakening of the boy's manhood appeared to justify the adulterous act. After negotiations dragged on through the spring and summer of 1955, Shurlock gave in and approved the script.[25]

In August 1956 the finished film arrived in New York for a Legion review, and the studio found itself in a new battle. Little informed MGM that the story was unacceptable and that unless changes were made, he would be forced to go public with the condemnation. The main problem revolved around the letter containing the wife's recognition of the error of her ways. The priest was especially troubled that no one appeared to have suffered from what was, no matter how much the writer tried to gloss over it, adultery. Nor was the wife's confession enough because the letter failed to point out the boy's responsibility for the affair.[26]

Still convinced that the problem could be easily resolved, Schary responded that the studio would locate Deborah Kerr, who played the wife, and come up with a different ending. Two weeks later, Little received a recording of the new version in which the wife indicates their joint responsibility for what she and the boy had done. "I just read your . . . novel about us," she tells him. "I came out rather like a saint, but I think that is not the whole picture, not even the true picture. You have rationalized the wrong we did." Reminding him that actions always have consequences, she tells him that their brief affair ruined her husband's life. Miffed that he had not been consulted about the rewrite, Little declared that the new version was still too weak. The word *wrong*, he argued, was too elastic to sum up what they had done; something stronger was needed to "pinpoint the gravity of adultery." MGM should have shown him the revised letter before having Kerr record it, he said, but it would just have to be done again. Convinced that he had leaned over backward to accommodate Little, Schary indicated that he was considering risking a condemnation.[27]

Nevertheless on August 28, Schary dispatched Charles Reagan, an MGM vice-president, to meet with Little, Mary Looram, and Martin Quigley to break the impasse. At Reagan's suggestion, Quigley agreed to rewrite the wife's letter, which would indicate the serious nature of the sin that had been committed by both the woman and the boy. If MGM accepted the Quigley version, Little told Reagan, the film would be upgraded to a B. Reagan assured him that he was personally opposed to marketing a condemned film, and he was positive that the studio would go along with the change.[28]

However, when Dore Schary and producer Pandro Berman refused to budge, Little told Reagan that he had no choice but to go ahead and announce the condemnation. Reagan, who had learned that Radio City Music Hall would not show the film if it were condemned, made one last stab at heading off a breach by having Robert Anderson, who had written the screenplay, meet with the Legion people on September 4 to discuss the two versions of the letter. The discussion seemed to have expanded beyond the issue of the wife's letter. Quigley told Anderson that the film was a clear-cut violation of the Code's prohibition against depicting "sex perversion." The playwright denied that there was any suggestion that the boy was a homosexual: he was just not "one of the boys." He also pointed out that those who had seen a preview were not aware that adultery had taken place. Moreover, if Quigley wanted to discuss obscenity, he should look at films like *Battle Cry*, which glorified war. *Tea and Sympathy*, in contrast, taught a moral lesson, "namely, to understand your fellow man and be tolerant." That was the problem, countered Quigley, "because the evil is so smoked up" that it masked the immoral nature of the film's message. Anderson stormed out, telling Quigley that he was sick of the whole affair and was leaving it in MGM's hands.[29]

Fearing that a condemnation could lead to a public relations fiasco along the lines of *The Moon Is Blue*, Little decided that the decision was too big to be made alone. A showing of the revised version of the film to forty new reviewers, including sixteen priests and Bishop Scully, yielded ratings that ranged from A-II to C. The next day, Scully told the Legion staff he was not convinced that the film should be condemned. After all, the boy seemed to be an "off-beat character," and the wife's letter did express her contrition and remorse. Quigley had gone out on a limb in the negotiations with MGM and now the bishop was sawing it off. He failed to convince Scully that the studio would eventually back down, and the film was awarded a B. Little correctly sensed that the Legion would have had difficulty mustering meaningful support for a boycott of *Tea and Sympathy*. MGM, which had not encountered any serious problems with the church since *Two-Faced Woman* (1941), was willing to risk a confrontation—one more sign that the Legion was losing its grip on Hollywood.[30]

There was still life in the Legion, as Warner Brothers learned when it chanced a condemnation later in 1956. Elia Kazan, who had directed *A Streetcar Named Desire*, convinced the studio to film another Tennessee Williams story, entitled *Baby Doll.* Kazan reflected the thoughts of many moviemakers when he wrote to Jack Warner that with fewer and fewer people willing to leave their television sets, the industry was fighting for its life and had to come up with exceptional stories and "really unusual treatment." When Warner gave him the green light, Kazan, remembering how the studio had let Martin Quigley edit *Streetcar*, made sure he had final-cut approval. If Kazan wanted to give people something they couldn't see on their television, he had the right story. Karl Malden played the much older cotton gin owner Archie, who marries nineteen-year-old Baby Doll with the understanding that the union will not be consummated until she is twenty. Meanwhile, Archie, jealous of the owner of another local cotton gin, played by Eli Wallach, decides to burn down his business. Eager to find out if Archie did it, his rival seduces Baby Doll while sitting on a swing outside her house. Although Wallach never kisses her, Jack Vizzard, who monitored the film for the PCA, was convinced that the swing scene was "as 'raw' as had been attempted in American pictures."[31]

The PCA ordered thirty changes, but Kazan was told by a Warner executive to treat them "seriously but not literally." When the film was completed, Vizzard still harbored serious reservations about the swing scene, along with a shot of Wallach's character sleeping alone in Baby Doll's crib, which he felt signified that he and Baby Doll had slept together. After a good deal of arguing, Kazan convinced Vizzard that any tampering with the encounter on the swing would ruin the film. He kidded Vizzard out of his concern about the crib scene, pointing out that it was physically impossible for any sexual activity to take place in such a limited area. In the end, Kazan's threat to take legal action convinced the PCA to approve the film. The Code was already on shaky ground; a lawsuit could topple it.[32]

The Catholic church was not so cooperative. Citing a *Variety* review that the film made "some of the 'sexy' pix of the past seem like child's play,"

America insisted that its "thinly disguised smut" was a clear violation of the Code. Quigley agreed, declaring that the picture had broken all three general principles of the Code by lowering the audience's moral principles, disregarding "correct standards of life," and undermining natural and human law. *America* and Quigley's reactions were expected, but Kazan received an unexpected blast from *Time* magazine, which claimed that *Baby Doll* was "just possibly the dirtiest American-made motion picture that has ever been legally exhibited." When Kazan indicated that he was not interested in bargaining for a better rating, the Legion condemned his film, declaring that "the subject matter dwells almost without variation . . . upon carnal suggestiveness [with] . . . an unmitigated emphasis on lust." Convinced that if *Baby Doll* was successful, it would signal the collapse of the Code, Quigley and Little persuaded Cardinal Spellman to denounce the film publicly.[33]

Spellman's previous condemnations of *Two-Faced Woman*, *Forever Amber*, and *The Moon Is Blue* had all come in the form of a letter read by priests at Sunday mass. When he denounced *Baby Doll* on Sunday, December 16, 1956, in St. Patrick's Cathedral, it was the first time Spellman had personally condemned a film from the pulpit. The gravity of the move was underscored by the fact that the last time he had climbed the pulpit stairs, it was to condemn the jailing of Cardinal Mindzenty by the Hungarian Communists in February 1949. He told the congregation that he was "anguished" to learn of the imminent release of a film that "has been responsibly judged to be evil in concept and which is certain to exert an immoral and corrupting influence on those who see it." The cardinal hadn't seen *Baby Doll*. As a leading critic of censorship, Edward de Grazia, has remarked, Justice Potter Stewart asserted that he knew pornography when he saw it; Spellman "knew it even when he did not see it." But the cardinal maintained that one didn't have to contract an illness to know what it was. He also dismissed the suggestion that his action would contribute to the film's success. "If this be the case," he retorted, "it will be an indictment of those who defy God's law and contribute to the corruption of America." Spellman's condemnation was as significant for what it left out as for what it contained. The typed announcement, which had been drafted by Quigley, had warned Catholics to refrain from patronizing the film "under the pain of mortal sin." Although the average Catholic believed that viewing a condemned film was a mortal sin, there had never been an official church pronouncement to that effect. For Quigley, such a declaration would help shore up the Code, but the Cardinal didn't follow the publisher's text, warning his people to avoid the film "under the pain of sin," but failing to define the nature of the sin.[34]

Baby Doll quickly became a test of the Legion's power. "If the action of Warner Brothers . . . turns out to be successful," Syracuse's Bishop Walter

Foery wrote one of his priests, "future action on our part will be extremely difficult." Bishops across the country joined in the campaign to make sure that Warner didn't win. *Time*'s charge that *Baby Doll* represented an unprecedented exploration in sensuality strengthened the Legion's hand. Pickets and mail campaigns were launched against theater owners who decided to book it. All three Connecticut bishops issued an unprecedented joint statement warning their people to avoid the film, and Bishop Scully was one of several prelates who placed a six-month attendance ban on theaters that showed it in his diocese. "I have a large family, six children and nine grand-children," wrote the owner of a Buffalo restaurant chain to the city's Center Theater. "If you do not discontinue showing this picture, I will tell my children, family, friends . . . and 488 employees . . . not to patronize your theater for at least six months." The Old Colony Advertising Company in Rhode Island refused to promote the film. Another major advertiser, John Donnelly & Sons of Boston, convinced the Outdoor Advertising Association of America not to print posters for it.[35]

All this activity demonstrated that the Legion could still occasionally rally the faithful, but the American Civil Liberties Union denounced its six-month boycott as "contrary to the spirit of free expression in the First Amendment." Indicating a growing willingness on the part of other religious leaders to criticize the Legion, several Protestant clergymen, including Bishop James Pike, dean of the Cathedral of St. John the Divine in New York, disparaged Spellman's campaign as "the efforts of a minority group to impose its wishes on the city." Several movie chains defied the Legion and booked the film. Robert J. O'Donnell, the Catholic head of the Interstate Circuit, which dominated the Southwest, claimed that although he had misgivings about the film, he couldn't break his contract with Warner. Sam Pinanski, owner of a Massachusetts chain, said he saw no reason he shouldn't book the film since it had been approved by the PCA.[36]

Not all the criticism came from outside the church. Writing in *Commonweal*, John Cogley supported Spellman's right to warn Catholics against seeing *Baby Doll*, but he was disturbed by the use of "naked economic pressure." Likening such coercion to measures used by the Inquisition, he argued that the church should limit itself to changing the hearts and minds of people through moral suasion. Foreshadowing an idea that would take hold during the Second Vatican Council, he declared that living in a pluralistic society involved self-restraint by all the religious institutions in the country, including the Catholic church. Vatican II, however, was still several years away. Cogley had disagreed with past Legion decisions, but the conviction that they were engaged in a life-or-death struggle caused the anti–*Baby Doll* forces to worry about any Catholic defection. "The greatest hurt we are suffering,"

Quigley complained to Bishop Scully, "is what is written and spoken by various persons who identify themselves as Catholics." When British Jesuit John Burke, the head of the Catholic Film Institute, praised the film as "a powerful denunciation of social and racial intolerance and as such is something for thoughtful people to see," it was too much for Cardinal Spellman. According to Burke, "the long arm of clerical vengeance reached across the Atlantic," and in the name of church unity, a British cardinal had Burke removed from his post.[37]

Still, many owners shied away from the film. Four months after its release, *Baby Doll* had played in only 2,320 theaters, well under the 7,000 to 8,000 bookings of a major Warner production. Kazan later admitted that the Legion's attack had hurt him. "There'd be one good week," he recalled, "then a quick slide down. I never made a profit." Kazan's loss, of course, was seen as the Legion's gain. A jubilant Quigley wrote Spellman that Ben Kalmenson, executive vice-president at Warner, told him that they had received truckloads of letters denouncing the studio. "It was a terrible experience for our company," he said, "and we never want to go through it again."[38]

When the Legion warned Warner that it was about to condemn another of its pictures following the *Baby Doll* campaign, the studio canceled all its bookings and asked what it had to do to make things right. "I doubt that they would have done it," Quigley told Spellman, "prior to *Baby Doll*." Warner wasn't alone. Quigley told the cardinal that one of his informants had indicated that another company, which originally had dug in its heels, suddenly was ready to negotiate away a threatened condemnation. It would be eight years before another major studio dared to lock horns with the Legion.[39]

But caution didn't mean capitulation. Hollywood producers felt they could not afford to stop making more mature films in an effort to recapture some of the audience they had lost to television. If anything, *Baby Doll* illustrated how an outmoded Code could be used against them by someone like Quigley. The idea of revising the Code had first surfaced in a serious way in 1949 when Eric Johnston suggested that it might be responsible for declining box-office receipts. Johnston's offhand comment evoked a blistering response from Breen, who advised him to examine the 1931 to 1934 files to see the trouble that had stemmed from the studios' attempt to "jazz up" their films to counter declining attendance during that period. Citing a *Variety* list of the sixty-four "all-time top grossers," Breen pointed out that all but two, *Duel in the Sun* and *Forever Amber*, were in conformity with the Code. Even so, three months later, in a roundtable discussion for *Life* magazine, a number of Hollywood producers and directors called for modernizing the Code. As participant Robert Rossen noted: "We have a new audience, an audience that has grown up out of the war and been in contact with greater realities." To many, the regulations drafted during the first year of the Great Depression seemed out of date in the postwar era.[40]

The Code had, in fact, undergone a few modifications since 1930. On September 11, 1946, without any publicity or previous notification to the board of directors, the MPAA amended the section of the Code that prohibited any presentation of the illegal drug traffic on the screen. The change had come at the request of Columbia, which had been urged by Harry Anslinger, head of the Federal Bureau of Narcotics, to make *To the Ends of the Earth* (1948) to dramatize its fight against the international drug trade. Instead of the original blanket proscription, the amendment prohibited portraying the drug traffic in such a way as to stimulate curiosity about drugs and showing the use of illegal drugs or their effects. Upon learning of the change, Martin Quigley sent telegrams to the Legion and the bishops' committee urging them to fight the revision. Father John McClafferty, who headed the campaign, asked all dioceses to send protest letters to Eric Johnston. Claiming that the new amendment would lead to a wave of drug pictures, McClafferty warned that they would spawn a plague of dangerous experimentations that could only increase the nation's addiction rate. Dismissing the notion that the Narcotics Bureau needed to publicize its work, he warned that such a film could very well disclose the agency's operations to such an extent as to "forewarn and forearm" the suppliers.[41]

While the Legion worked to overturn the amendment, it scrutinized all films for any attempt to slip drugs into the plot. Father Patrick Masterson even challenged a Hopalong Cassidy film in which a boy is induced to commit a crime after drinking a cup of tea prepared for him by the villain. Breen was able to obtain Archbishop McIntyre's help in persuading the priest to drop the issue. Pointing out that Eric Johnston might be persuaded to back down, McIntyre suggested to Bishop Scully that using a Hopalong Cassidy film in the battle could boomerang by putting the Legion in a ridiculous light. However, Masterson got United Artists to make a change in a scene in *Sleep My Love* (1948) in which the character played by Don Ameche had been secretly administering a drug to his wife in order to make her receptive to hypnotic directions. The studio agreed to substitute sleeping pills for the drug, and the Legion approved the film. Meanwhile, Legion pressure had begun to pay off. Federal Narcotics Bureau head Harry Anslinger, convinced that his role in helping to put *To the Ends of the Earth* on the screen had been a mistake, proposed that the industry do everything possible to keep from the screen even a discussion of the drug problem. In March 1951, the association voted to eliminate the 1946 amendment and return to the total ban of the topic.[42]

A clearly antiquated part of the Code was the section that prohibited films from dealing with miscegenation. Quigley had always argued that it didn't belong in the Code, but Will Hays had originally inserted it into the regulations to placate theater owners in the South. The war caused Hays to have second thoughts, and he asked Mortimer Adler, author and editor of the Great Books of the Western World series, to look into the matter in the fall of 1942. Adler, who pointed out that miscegenation was listed in the section of the Code that also prohibited sex perversion and other types of sexual obscenity, agreed with Hays that it was neither perverse nor obscene. Nevertheless, Adler cautioned him to go slow because of the strong objection to miscegenation in large sections of the country. After all, he reminded Hays, the industry was devoted to entertainment, not social reform. Adler suggested that if the industry wanted do something for African-Americans, it could make a picture about a black hero like Booker T. Washington.[43]

Ten years later, Hollywood was still wrestling with the subject. When Breen, who believed that the miscegenation clause not only cast an unfair reflection on African-Americans but was "unworthy" of the film industry, asked Quigley for advice, he suggested moving the topic from the forbidden list to the category of subjects that were to "be treated within the careful limits of good taste." But this placed it under the heading of "repellent subjects," a category that required the "tasteful" treatment of such items as hangings, third-degree interrogation methods, and the sale of women. In a compromise, miscegenation was moved to the new category of "special subjects" that should be treated with good taste. The dropping of the ban in combination with the Court's restrictions on censorship meant that within a few years the Virginia Censorship Board would be flooded with protests about films like *Island in the Sun* (1957), which dealt with an interracial relationship.[44]

Although the association also dropped a number of words and phrases from its list of forbidden profanity, including "alley-cat," "fanny," "hold your hat," "tom-cat" (applied to a man), "traveling salesmen," and "farmer's daughter jokes," the Code critics remained unimpressed. The Theater Owners of America and producer Sam Goldwyn, who was one of the original signers of the Code, joined the rising chorus of movie people calling for a more radical update. Most producers were tired of coming up with creative solutions to satisfy the Code, especially when it was costing them money. The continued drop in weekly movie attendance, to 46,000 in 1955 from 60,000 in 1950, convinced the owners that they had to do something. The success of movies like *The Moon Is Blue* and *The French Line* meant that the most important arbiter of the industry's future, the audience, was voting with its box-office dollars in favor of liberalization.[45]

Still, there were those within the industry who defended the Code. Darryl

Zanuck, pointing to the successful adaptations of *From Here to Eternity* and *A Streetcar Named Desire*, challenged anyone to name ten best-selling novels or stage plays that could not be put on the screen because of Breen's office. In his *Newsweek* column, Raymond Moley, an old friend of Will Hays, shuddered to think of what the movies would have become without the Code. The industry needed orderly limitations, he declared. "And in truth," he continued, "those limitations are what compel the artist to his utmost efforts." Quigley, of course, continued to support the Code. "Declaring the Code out of date," he proclaimed, "is like arguing that the Ten Commandments are out of date and need revision." In an article entitled "Scummies Gun for Production Code," columnist William Mooring accused the Code's critics of playing into the hands of "Hollywood Reds."[46]

Nonetheless, the Catholic front that had solidly supported the Code during the 1930s was no longer as united as it once had been. *America* favored maintaining the ethical underpinnings of the Code but argued that removing extraneous rules and regulations dealing with the treatment of drug addiction and liquor, the use of the flag, and the prohibition of words like "damn" and "hell" would not damage its moral force. *Commonweal* added that it would be impolitic to block the revisions because the Code was going to be rewritten with or without Catholic support. To campaign blindly against the revision, it declared, would only ensure that Catholics would have no role at the bargaining table.[47]

Even the Legion expected some change. When the PCA refused to grant a seal to Otto Preminger's *Man with the Golden Arm* (1956) because of its gritty depiction of drug addiction, the Legion decided not to support it. Twenty-five reviewers saw the film, and their ratings ranged from condemnation to A-II, with the majority voting to classify it as B. Fathers Thomas Little and Paul Hayes and Mary Looram agreed that although the picture was "no lily," the public would not support a C rating. It was clear, Little told Bishop Scully, that the MPAA would soon revise this section of the Code. He pointed out to the bishop that although Twentieth Century-Fox had voted with other members of the appeals board to support the PCA's decision, it too must have anticipated reform because it had brought the rights to another drug story, *A Hatful of Rain*. But the Legion's treatment of *The Man with the Golden Arm* suggested that it also was changing. Eight years earlier, it had worried about a suspicious cup of tea in a Hopalong Cassidy film; now it refused to condemn the most candid film on addiction to date.[48]

The success of the Preminger film was one more example of the moviegoing public's willingness to ignore the lack of a seal. *Variety* and the Legion both interpreted the major circuit's willingness to book the film—the first time that Loews theaters had shown a non-seal picture—as a sign that the church was more powerful than the PCA. But the theater owners were already chafing under the PCA's restrictions, and the Legion's decision had merely given them an excuse to book a film that would sell tickets.[49]

On December 11, 1956, Eric Johnston announced that the Code had been revised. The result, he said, was to prove once again that it was "intended to be—and has been—a flexible living document—not a dead hand laid on artistic and creative endeavor." Nudity, sex perversion, open-mouth kissing, and venereal disease were still forbidden subjects, but many of the old prohibitions against depicting drugs, prostitution, and abortion were removed. Abortion, which previously had been labeled as not a proper subject for motion pictures, had become a topic to be "discouraged" and "never be more than suggested, and when referred to, shall be condemned." Although Johnston maintained that the new Code was "simpler and more precise," it raised the question, among others, of what constituted a suggestion of an abortion. Clearly, the real meaning of the new Code could be determined only by analyzing how it worked in practice. Cardinal Spellman was not optimistic. One thing hadn't changed, he said ominously; there was still a need "to watch the watchers."[50]

THIRTEEN

The Jesuits to the Rescue

While the Legion was worrying about the growing liberalization of the film industry, the Catholic church was about to embark on a process of modernization that led to the Second Vatican Council. As the reform movement took shape, questions were raised about the role of the Legion within a changing church. Where once the Legion's major challenge was to hold the line in Hollywood, its supporters began to wonder if it could even hold the line within the church. A new generation of better-educated Catholics valued pluralism and rejected the parochialism of the past. Priests in the new suburban churches were forging a relationship with the laity that differed from the more authoritarian one that had existed in the insular prewar parishes. A growing number of Catholics, who felt they were better able to judge the moral implications of films than their parents, wondered if the Legion had outlived its usefulness. Edward Fisher spoke for many of the new breed of Catholics in *Ave Maria* when he charged that those who supported censorship often underrated the intelligence of others. Fisher's remarks were stimulated by a meeting of the Catholic Press Association at which a participant had read a letter from a mother who often woke up at 3 A.M. worried about "the smut that would be in the world when her children grew up." Far from applauding—the response such a remark would have received a decade earlier—everyone in the audience, Fisher claimed, recognized that the letter was the "product of an unbalanced mind."[1]

Within the church, one of the more progressive voices belonged to Father John Courtney Murray, who served as editor of *Theological Studies* and religion editor of *America.* Murray had been arguing for some time that in a pluralistic society each minority group had the right to direct its own members, but no group had the right to impose its own religious or moral standards on others. Concerned about the damage Murray might do to the Legion, Father Thomas Little sought the advice of Father Francis Connell, dean of the School of Sacred Theology at Catholic University and first president of the Catholic Theological Society of America. Connell dismissed Murray's thesis out of hand, declaring that, in spite of its minority status, the Catholic church as the one true church had not only the right but the duty to demand that the government impose its moral standards on its citizens. The apostles were a minority group, he told Little, "but they had the right to tell any Ruler of the Earth . . . that he must abolish any type of theatrical production they deemed harmful to morality."[2]

But doubts about the Legion persisted. Frank Getlein, in *The Art of the Movies,* charged that Catholics who reduced movie evaluations to holding a "sexual geiger counter against decolletage and double entendres . . . write off art, demean sex and betray religion." Similarly, John Fitzgerald, in *Our Sunday Visitor,* blasted the Catholic "listing mentality," which viewed the arts not as opportunities to grow but as possible occasions of sin. Others like Monsignor Francis Lally, editor of the *Boston Pilot,* suggested that organizations like the Legion raised suspicions in the minds of many about Catholic views on religious liberty and church-state separation. Quigley, who had been defending the Legion against outside assaults for close to a quarter century, was shocked by the attacks from within the church. What possible good, he asked Cardinal Samuel Stritch, could come of John Courtney Murray's "curious arguments" that Catholics in a pluralistic society are under "some strange obligation to be quite tolerant of anything their neighbor seems to want."[3]

One of the first areas to feel the effect of all this was the pledge Catholics took each year at Sunday mass. Although the original version had undergone a few minor alterations, its objective had always been to discourage the production and exhibition of objectionable films. Catholics promised not only to avoid immoral motion pictures but also to stay away from any theaters that showed them. The boycott was the Legion's ultimate weapon, because, as Little declared, "the economic pinch must be tangibly and concretely felt." By the mid-1950s, however, critics wondered if the annual pledge had become a meaningless exercise for many of those who took it. Father Gerald Kelly, a Jesuit at St. Mary's College in Kansas, suggested to Little that, instead of the "herd action" of the public commitment, a printed pledge could be made privately in the sanctuary of one's heart. At the same time, Archbishop Richard J. Cushing of Boston was urging his priests to administer the pledge in a more positive framework and to avoid excessively emotional attacks on films, which would cause more harm than good.[4]

Quigley warned Cardinal Francis Spellman that if the liberal trend continued, it would destroy the Legion. A growing number of Catholics were ignoring the Legion, he said, and attending condemned films such as *The Moon Is Blue* and *The French Line.* The fault, Quigley believed, lay in the church's failure to instruct the laity properly about its moral obligations. More and more priests, he claimed, were telling their parishioners that the pledge was optional. He had heard Father Joseph Moffitt, an assistant dean at Georgetown University, tell the congregation at a mass that the pledge was voluntary and that those who did not wish to take it could stand with the others but not say the words. What was especially startling was his declaration that although Catholics should avoid going to condemned films to satisfy their curiosity, it was not a sin to see such films.[5]

Father Moffitt's relaxed view symbolized a general shift in attitude toward the Legion's classification system. Although neither the pope nor the bishops had ever obligated Catholics to follow the Legion's decisions, there was a general impression among the laity in the early years that anyone who knowingly saw a condemned film had committed a mortal sin. Everyone knew that an A–I film was good for the entire family and that there was something wrong with a B picture, but it was unclear if seeing one of the latter constituted a sin. Many priests were unsure of the fine distinctions among the four categories. Father Francis Connell tried to help them advise their parishioners in 1946 in the *American Ecclesiastical Review.* An A–I anyone could see without harm. C's, in contrast, according to Connell, were to be avoided by all persons on pain of mortal sin. For Connell, the major questions centered on the A–II and B classifications. One issue that often came up was whether children should be allowed to view A–II films like *A Tree Grows in Brooklyn.* Although Connell felt that most children would be bored by these stories, he cautioned against letting them attend because of the chance that they could stir up their curiosity about such topics as "conjugal relations, marital infidelity, and pregnancy." Whether or not adolescents should be allowed to view A–II films was more complex. Citing a study by Brother Urban Fleece, supplied by Joe Breen, Connell noted that 43 percent of Catholic high school boys admitted that the movies gave them the "wrong ideas about sex, love and petting." Admitting that mere chronological age should not be the determining factor, Connell concluded that, as a general principle, eighteen was the point at which most young people would not be harmed by an A–II film.[6]

The most perplexing moral problem, according to Connell, was how to treat B films. This category was so broad that it contained everything from *The Doughgirls*, a wartime farce that ran into trouble because it included the acceptability of divorce, to *Duel in the Sun*, with its "immodestly suggestive sequences [and] glorification of illicit love." All this was compounded by the fact that a particular picture might be a "proximate occasion of sin to one person, whereas to another it would be only a remote occasion or no occasion at all." For example, he pointed out, someone with a good grasp of the church's teachings could see without harm a film in which divorce was portrayed as justifiable, while a less educated viewer might wonder if perhaps the church's stand on divorce was too strict. Similarly, some elderly people could "witness a representation of passionate love-making without any other emotion than a feeling of disgust, while the same scene might incite grave temptations in adolescents." But this didn't mean that some Catholics were free to pick and choose. A well-educated Catholic, who might not be harmed by a B film, had to weigh the chances that his or her attendance might encourage others, who could be placed in grave moral danger by the same picture. Consequently, a priest could never attend a B picture publicly because even though he would not suffer any spiritual harm, it could lead his parishioners to argue, "if it's all right for [him] to see this picture, it is certainly all right for me to do so."[7]

But, writing in a clerical journal, Father Connell was obviously preaching to the converted. It is doubtful even in 1946 that many seventeen-year-olds avoided *A Tree Grows in Brooklyn* or that their parents stayed away from films like *The Doughgirls*. Nevertheless, a significant number of Catholics thought twice about seeing a movie that the Legion had singled out as especially harmful. A decade or so later, church leaders were beginning to wonder how many were doing even that. A National Catholic Welfare Conference study of 1956 suggested that Catholics were not abiding by the Legion's rulings. Although he didn't question its accuracy, Frank Hall, the NCWC director, decided not to publish this "definitely embarrassing" news because it might encourage the studios to take greater liberties. Nevertheless, "the widespread apathy and indifference" of many Catholics had become a regular topic at the annual meetings of the Episcopal Committee on Motion Pictures. According to a Legion inquiry, even most teenagers in Catholic schools were patronizing any and every film short of those actually condemned. Nor was apathy limited to the laity. Father Little complained to the bishops that 50 percent of the diocesan Legion directors had not filed their annual reports. "If the National Office had 100 percent cooperation," he declared, "*The Moon Is Blue* would not have grossed $4,000,000."[8]

Hoping to reach the faithful, pamphlets like "Poison! Believe the Label" tried to translate Father Connell's discussion into simpler language. Likening the Legion to the Pure Food and Drug Administration, the authors pointed out that just as the poisoner couldn't fool the government experts, the movie producer couldn't fool the church experts. In effect, they declared, the Legion, like the government, put labels on films: A–I, "Harmless"; A–II, "Harmless for Grown-ups—Not Good for Children"; B, "Contains Small Doses of Poison"; and C, "Deadly Poison." Sensing the need to shock the public into action, some of the pamphlets revived the vitriolic attacks that had characterized the Legion campaign of the early 1930s. The cover of one put out by the Philadelphia Legion pictured the neighborhood theater as an octopus with tentacles labeled "murder," "suicide," "nudity," "sex," and "brutality" reaching out to crush the moral life out of movie audiences. "A Catholic who goes to any movie . . . without first knowing what kind of picture it is," the authors noted, "is as crazy as a deep sea diver who goes down without an octopus knife." Recognizing the changing mood within the church, the pamphlet was filled with advice on how parishioners should respond to Catholic friends who ignored the Legion's recommendations. Catholic civil libertarians, who talked about freedom of expression, had to be advised that they were free to sin, but the penalty was hell. The biggest challenge came from those Catholics who maintained that movies didn't affect them. But "can a he-man view feminine indecencies," the authors asked, "without one single passing bad thought or emotion?" These were dangerous times, they declared, and "fighting for public decency is a job for men, not for their womenfolk or children." But, as it turned out, there was still a role for women: in a vintage 1950s piece, the Newark archdiocesan paper informed its readers that Father Paul Hayes had taken advantage of women's "love of talking on the phone" to establish a Legion of Decency hot line to provide ratings for any pictures playing in the area.[9]

Catholic moviegoers weren't the only ones expected to follow the Legion's decisions. William Mooring declared that Catholics who had a voice in the Academy Award selections should be prohibited from voting for *A Streetcar Named Desire* or any other B-rated film. Demands like this made Walter Kerr, the *New York Tribune* drama critic and a member of Catholic University's drama department, wonder if the church was censoring the art as well as the immorality out of movies. The church, he declared, seems to say: "I don't care what the quality of the art work is, so long as its content is innocuous, or perhaps favorably disposed in our direction. . . . A film featuring a Saint is a film of majestic technical excellence. A film showing a nun driving a jeep is a superbly made comedy. A film embracing a jolly priest, a self-sacrificing Catholic mother and an anti-Communist message must be defended."[10]

It was one thing to question the Legion's aesthetic judgment, and quite another to challenge its authority. In an article in *Cross-Currents*, Erwin Geissman, an assistant professor at Fordham University, rejected as simplistic the notion that it was a sin to attend any motion picture condemned by the Legion. Geissman's article brought a swift response from Quigley, who called for his dismissal. Suggesting that Father Little bring the matter to the attention of Fordham's president, Quigley noted, "It seems to me that this is rather a dangerous post for a 'liberal,' influencing, as he must, untold thousands." Father Gerard Dennen accused Geissman of being a "self-styled intellectual" who had no right to interfere in theological matters. Moreover, Dennen pointed out, there was nothing to debate, because Father Gerald A. Kelly had reaffirmed Father Connell's contention that it would be a mortal sin to attend a condemned film. Liberals and conservative theologians might differ on some matters, he said, but they were united on the danger of attending a movie that had been placed off limits.[11]

Ironically, Kelly had rethought his original piece by the time of the Geissman affair. "There is a vast difference," he wrote Little, "between saying some obligation exists and trying to weigh that obligation in terms of mortal and venial sin." Nor was Kelly as certain as Connell was about the impact of B-rated films. The problem, according to Kelly, was that this category lumped together two kinds of pictures: those which had "sensuous sequences," and those with objectionable themes, like divorce, suicide, and mercy killings. While conceding that it was probably best to avoid sensuous films because it was difficult to arm oneself against their moral dangers, he felt that the average Catholic would not be harmed by seeing, say, a film dealing with divorce. Moreover, since the only thing wrong with a great film like *The Best Years of Our Lives* was that it painted a positive picture of divorce, the church, to be consistent, should urge the laity to quit reading newspapers that reported marital breakups.[12]

In September 1957, Kelly and a fellow Jesuit, Father John Ford, wrote a new article on the subject for *Theological Studies*. They reminded their readers that official ecclesiastical documents had deliberately avoided definitive statements that attendance at any category of films was mortally sinful. While recommending a general policy of avoiding B's and C's, Kelly and Ford declared that one could not rule out attendance at all such films. The fact that several definitions had been attached to B films before 1936, they argued, should make one cautious about formulating any general statement concerning the morality of viewing them. Focusing so much attention on the degree of sinfulness of movies, they warned, could undo much of the good the Legion had accomplished. A sweeping declaration that condemned films are "always, or almost always, the occasion for mortal sin" went too far. "It would be much more in keeping with sound theology," they argued, "to say that they would involve the proximate danger of serious sin for many people, especially young people, and that any more specific statement would require a knowledge of the film itself and of its prospective audience." In a cautionary note aimed at the recent outpouring of pamphlets like "Poison! Believe the Label," the two Jesuits warned that it would be an error to follow the lead of the bishops who had established the Legion. Their purpose, they noted, "was not to teach in the quiet, clear method of the catechism, but to arouse people to take an active part in the Legion of Decency crusade." They had occasionally resorted to "oratorical exaggerations," but it would be a mistake to continue that style. After all, they reasoned, the old cry that "one hour in the darkness of a movie theater is sufficient to destroy the good effects of many years of Catholic education" was "just as much a indictment of Catholic education as it is a condemnation of the movie industry."[13]

Alarmed by what he viewed as a concerted Jesuit attack on the Legion, (Kelly, Ford, Murray, and Moffitt were all members of the Society), Quigley suggested to Cardinal Spellman that he appoint one of their ranks to the Legion in the hope that loyalty would quiet their criticism. At the cardinal's request, Father Thomas Henneberry, the superior of the New York province, recommended a thirty-seven-year-old priest, Father Patrick Sullivan, who had received a doctorate of sacred theology from the Gregorian University in Rome and had been a professor of dogmatic theology at the Jesuit seminary in Woodstock, Maryland, since 1954. Father Sullivan arrived in New York in September 1957 to replace Father Paul Hayes as Little's assistant. His fresh view of its proper role in a changing society would have a far-reaching influence on the Legion. Where Father Hayes had staunchly defended the Legion, Sullivan shared some of John Courtney Murray's concerns about the right of the church to impose its morality on non-Catholics. Sullivan, an early ecumenist, had reservations about the church's right in a pluralistic society to dictate the type of picture that Hollywood turned out. Given the Legion's mandate, however, he felt that something could be done to identify morally sound but more mature films for those Catholics who were hungering for more than mass entertainment. He also thought, given the changes in the laity, condemnations of films like *The Moon Is Blue* not only raised questions about the Legion's judgment but also could in the long run undermine the church's credibility on more serious moral issues.[14]

Quigley was impressed with the appointment. Sullivan told him that he came to New York with no specific plan other than "an enthusiastic selling" of the Legion to his fellow Jesuits. He also tried to smooth over a breach between Quigley and Father John Ford over the publisher's criticism of the Kelly-Ford article in *Theological Studies.* Quigley had interpreted the priest's unfavorable response as an example of the Jesuits' lack of cooperation, but Sullivan pointed out that although most of Quigley's criticisms were concerned with the historical section of their article, Father Ford had interpreted them as a challenge to his competence as a moral theologian. The solution, Sullivan told Quigley, would not be found in a campaign to preserve the Legion in its present form. In order to survive, it would have to come to grips with the growing criticism that it was too negative in its approach. Sullivan received an unexpected boost from Pope Pius XII's encyclical *Miranda Prorsus* (Remarkable Technical Inventions), which was issued on September 8, a week after he arrived at the Legion. Although the papal message was an essentially conservative one—it noted, among other obligations, the state's need to censor films, to establish a Catholic rating system in every country, and to forbid Catholic theater owners to show films contrary to Catholic morality—it contained one positive note. Noting that much good could be accomplished by the media, the pope urged Catholics to make sure that "the applause and approval of the general public will not be wanting as a prize for really worthwhile films."[15]

The pope's call for a more positive approach touched on an issue that had long bothered Hollywood. In an article in the *Motion Picture Exhibitor* entitled "All Knock and No Boost," Jay Emanuel complained that a number of morally worthwhile films had died because of a lack of Catholic support. Instead, he said, the Legion seemed to revel in reminding people of the industry's past sins. A case in point was the Legion's October 1957 list, which contained eighty-five condemnations, including such oldies as *Ecstasy* (1936–37) and *No Greater Sin* (1940–41). By pairing this cumulative list of preponderantly foreign films with the 1957 slate of eighty-eight A–I pictures, the Legion led the casual observer to conclude that a great proportion of the industry's product was immoral.[16]

While conservatives like Father Connell interpreted the encyclical as a reaffirmation of the Legion's traditional approach, Sullivan saw it as a means of forging a new and more productive role for the Legion. "I would have kept my peace for a year in order to learn something about the movie industry," he told Quigley, but the pope's declaration had added "urgency to the situation." As Sullivan later recalled, *Miranda Prorsus* was an opportunity to put the bishops' "feet to the fire" to get them to support his reform efforts. Although Sullivan was nominally Father Little's assistant, the Episcopal Committee expected him to revitalize the Legion. Quigley had his first inkling that he might have made a mistake in trying to forge a link with the Jesuits when the bishops adopted a new statement on censorship, which he suspected had been written by Sullivan and Father Harold Gardiner. What alarmed Quigley was the bishops' declaration that "While good taste cannot supply the norm for moral judgment on literature and art, yet it must be admitted that good taste will inevitably narrow the field of what is morally objectionable." Symbolizing their desire for a more positive approach to the movies, the bishops also decided to break with the past and have the Legion recommend films in the A–I category that not only reinforced Christian values but were artistically and dramatically worthwhile. To Quigley, it sounded a lot like the return of the Golden Seal awards, which had contributed to Father Joseph Daly's departure in 1936.[17]

But the major news was the bishops' decision to try to deal with the B-rated films, which they had come to believe were the Achilles heel of the Legion system. The box-office success of the last three musicals exhibited at New York's Radio City Music Hall in 1957 in spite of their B ratings—*Silk Stockings*, *The Pajama Game*, and *Les Girls*—made it clear that more and more Catholics were ignoring the Legion. Father Sullivan initially felt that the problem stemmed from the fact that the category had become a catch-all for pictures ranging from the "light B films," those that were almost approved for an A–II rating but might present a danger to adolescents, to the "heavy B's," those that had narrowly escaped condemnation. The difficulty, as he perceived it, was that college-educated Catholics, in their search for adult entertainment, began by attending "light B films" and ended up by questioning the competence of the Legion in the whole area of B films. In fact, an increasing number of diocesan Legion directors had urged dividing the category into B–I and B–II to reflect these differences.[18]

The solution the bishops agreed to at their annual meeting in November 1957 was the establishment of a new adult category, A–III. The new divisions would correspond to the pope's classification of films in *Miranda Prorsus:* A–I, "those which can be seen by all"; A–II, can be seen "by the young"; A–III, can be seen "by adults"; B, "those . . . which can be a moral danger to spectators"; and C, "those which are entirely bad and harmful." Under the new system, a film like *Man of a Thousand Faces* (1957), a biography of actor Lon Chaney, which had been classified as a B because it reflected the acceptability of divorce, would be elevated to A–III because it would have little effect on mature Catholics. The bishops naively hoped that with the B category now reserved for films that were truly objectionable, B's would become as scarce as C's. Twentieth Century-Fox's reaction to the new system suggested that the bishops might be on the right track. The studio volunteered to present any questionable pictures in rough form to the Legion to ensure an A–I, A–II, or A–III rating, with the result that forty-four of the next forty-eight Fox films to be rated were placed in one of these categories. The bishops could also point to the fact that the percentage of B films dropped from 33 percent in 1957 to 19 percent the following year. This was more smoke and mirrors than real reform; if the A–III category hadn't been created, the percentage of B's would actually have gone up that year.[19]

Some conservative Catholics also wondered if a lot of the remaining B's would have been C's in Father McClafferty's day. An *America* review of Twentieth Century-Fox's remake of *A Farewell to Arms* noted that "the celluloid fairly crackle[d] with sex" and contained an objectionable obstetrical scene which "casts revolting and sinister light on childbirth and motherhood." The reviewer concluded that, compared to the remake, the 1932 version, which had aroused so much criticism, looked like "a church picnic." The Legion still gave the film a B, clearly accommodating its standards to the changes in Hollywood.[20]

Nevertheless, it almost condemned *Some Like It Hot* (1959), in which the characters played by Jack Lemmon and Tony Curtis masquerade as female musicians in order to escape the mob. Father Little told Shurlock that, in addition to the dialogue, which was filled with double entendres and "outright smut," the subject matter—"transvestism with its clear implications of homosexuality and lesbianism"—constituted a serious breach of the Code. Noting that no one else had questioned the morality or good taste of the film, Shurlock pointed out that cross-dressing was standard theatrical fare dating back to *As You Like It* and *Twelfth Night*.[21]

The new A–III category first sparked doubts about the Legion's new course. Loyalists wrote in asking how films like *Peyton Place* (1957), based on Grace Metalious's novel about sexual scandals in a small New England town, could be recommended for adult viewing. Father Sullivan tried his best, explaining to one woman that the producer had removed the objectionable parts of the novel. In fact, he wrote, "I know of no picture in recent times that contains such exemplary speeches, e.g., the difference between love and lust, the proper role of the educator in our society, the function of sex hygiene belonging to the parent, the rebuke to abortion as being an offense against God and the law." Sullivan's letter may have placated some critics, but not Quigley. Within a month of the bishops' November 1957 meeting, the publisher sharply attacked the expanded rating system. If B films were unsuitable fare for Catholics, he asked Chicago's Cardinal Samuel A. Stritch, how did relabeling some of them as A–III make them any less objectionable? If adults needed mature material, they could stay home and read a book. In January 1959 he warned Bishop Scully that his recommendation that a Jesuit be added to the Legion staff had clearly backfired. Declaring that Sullivan suffered from inexperience and a "mass of academic notions," he warned the bishop that his reforms, if left unchecked, could pose a serious threat to the Legion's status and influence. What was especially dangerous about the A–III category, he claimed, was the tendency to use it to pass off sordid and suggestive films as adult fare. Each new A–III film seemed to him to represent a deeper break with the past. The Legion could recommend the French film *Rocco and His Brothers*, he told Little, "but until hell freezes over, I will maintain that the [rape] scene is 'objectionable.'" Nowhere were Sullivan's reforms more welcome, he claimed, than in Hollywood, where producers who had been held in check by the Legion interpreted them as a sign that the church no longer cared.[22]

Sullivan recognized that some Catholics were confused by the new A–III rating. In an effort to deal with films that were "legitimate morally, although some elements were beyond the capacity of some adults," he made more use of the separate classification category. It had been used sparingly in the past to cover films like *Blockade*, *The Birth of a Baby*, *Storm Center*, and *Martin Luther*, which the Legion felt were not morally offensive in themselves but required some explanation in order to help the laity avoid false conclusions.[23]

The first film to benefit from the expanded use of the separate classification was Otto Preminger's *Anatomy of a Murder* (1959), the story of a small-town lawyer's successful defense of an army officer who murdered the man who raped his wife. After a lengthy struggle with the PCA, it was approved. Acceding to Shurlock's requests, Preminger eliminated the term "knocked up," changed "male sperm" to "evidence," and sharply reduced the number of references to "rape" and "panties." The director refused, however, to substitute "violation" for "penetration" in a courtroom discussion of what constitutes rape. Jack Vizzard did his best to persuade Preminger, asking him to "imagine these sexual details coming over the loud speakers of a public theater with a mixed audience." In a response that looked like a Supreme Court brief, the director cited everything from court decisions to *Black's Law Dictionary* to prove that "penetration" was the accepted standard for rape. It was only after he argued that the picture would be ridiculed by the law profession if he used any other term that Vizzard approved it.[24]

Preminger was still not out of the woods. The Chicago police chief, a Catholic, wanted to make five additional cuts in his film but told the director he would settle for one: the elimination of the word "contraceptive," which he said, he wouldn't want his eighteen-year-old daughter to hear in a movie. Preminger refused, and the chief denied him a license. But the days of arbitrary censorship were ending, and an Illinois court judge overruled the chief. The Legion, on the other hand, had no difficulty with the film. Recognizing that it might be shocking to "sensitive" or "impressionable" people, it declared that it was not an immoral film in theme or treatment and placed it in the separate category. Quigley was astounded by what he saw as Sullivan's misuse of the classification, which had been devised for an entirely different problem. And even though he and William Mooring had once feuded over the critic's characterization of *Born Yesterday* as pro-Communist, the two men now agreed that the Legion was going to hell in a handbasket carried by Sullivan and his "liberalistic colleagues." Mooring claimed that Preminger was delighted with the separate classification because he had been prepared to alter his film to get it past the Legion.[25]

It seemed at times to Quigley and Mooring that their world was turning upside down. Even Bing Crosby, who once had only to don a clerical collar to win nearly every Catholic viewer's heart, ran into trouble when he played the pastor of an actors' church in *Say One for Me* (1959). Quigley, who had served as a consultant on the film, was convinced that Twentieth Century-Fox had a winner. Yet the Crosby film received a series of bad reviews. Nowhere was the criticism greater than in some Catholic circles. *America* branded it "cheap, sentimental, meretricious and . . . basically immoral [for] suggesting that if you throw an aura of religion around artistic tripe, anything will be excused." Other Catholic reviewers blasted it as "puerile," "a globe of treacle," and "a shocking piece of mush." Mooring complained that the Catholic press had treated it more harshly than *Baby Doll*. And Crosby couldn't understand why he had received a pat on the back for playing a lush in *Country Girl* and "a left to the jaw" for playing a priest in *Say One for Me*. What did Catholics want from Hollywood, Mooring asked, "morally decent entertainment appealing to a variety of tastes . . . or a heavy diet of art for art's sake?"[26]

Suddenly Last Summer (1959), the film version of the Tennessee Williams play, was more grist for the conservative Catholic mill. In the movie, a wealthy widow uses herself as bait in order to attract young men for her homosexual son. When the son travels to Spain with his cousin, played by Elizabeth Taylor, as substitute for his ailing mother, he returns to the hunt until a group of poor and hungry beach boys strike back in an attack which ends in their devouring his body. As one critic put it, where else, "for a single admission," could you get "a practicing homosexual, a psychotic heroine, a procuress-mother [and] a cannibalistic orgy"? If there ever had been a picture that seemed ripe for condemnation, this was it. But Geoff Shurlock, whose objections had been overruled by the MPAA's Appeals Board, warned Sullivan and Little that condemning the film would only add to the PCA's woes. If the Legion decided to condemn it, he pleaded with Little to place the blame where it belonged: at the door of the Appeals Board, not the PCA. While admitting that the film violated the Code's prohibition against "sex perversion," the Legion characterized it as a moral treatment of a serious subject that was intended for mature audiences and tucked it into the special category.[27]

The Legion's announcement touched off a flood of criticism. "Who intended it for a mature audience?" asked one writer. "Certainly not Columbia Pictures. No motion picture company in its right business mind would attempt to limit pictures to an audience in any way." Others asked, with 50 percent of movie audiences typically made up of adolescents and children, who was going to monitor the theaters to ensure that only mature people saw it? Hollywood gossip columnist Hedda Hopper fueled the flames by claiming that, when she explained the story to a bank president who had seen the film and not understood the story, he was shocked, noting that a number of youngsters had been in the audience. What is the Legion doing about this, she queried; "it doesn't seem to be functioning any more." Nor could Sullivan find much support in the Catholic press. Even *America* found the film unacceptable, though in deference to their fellow Jesuit, the editors directed their criticism at the PCA for granting it a seal. Bishop James McNulty of Paterson, New Jersey, who had succeeded Bishop Scully as chair of the Episcopal Committee, was not so kind. He reminded Sullivan that the Legion office was not designed for an intellectual elite and that its decisions had to be aimed at the average Catholic, not just college graduates.[28]

The bishop's admonition presented Sullivan with a dilemma. Any effort to return to the more rigid standards of the past would risk losing whatever influence the Legion had over the growing number of independent-minded Catholics. But because they, in turn, wanted liberalization to proceed at a faster pace, they offered Sullivan little support. In a sense, he was the victim of the paradox that accompanies any revolution. Some Catholics who had patiently lived under the old authoritarian Legion without a murmur now criticized the conservatism of the new Legion, although it was steering a more liberal course. Meanwhile, every new separate classification added to the ranks of the conservative coalition that opposed his program.

Each passing year found Sullivan spending more time patiently answering complaints about the Legion's relaxed standards. How to handle the loose coalition of his critics that coalesced within a year of his appointment was a much more difficult task. The opposition of Cardinal James Francis McIntyre, Cantwell's successor, was especially troubling as it undermined the Legion's close working relationship with the Los Angeles diocese, which had existed since the beginning of the church's film campaign. There was little Sullivan could have done to salvage the situation. McIntyre, an archconservative, was suspicious of any hint of liberalism within the church. In his eyes, the Legion's approval of *On the Beach* (1959), a film about the aftermath of a nuclear war, was another example of its failure to do its job. Convinced that the film was part of a Soviet plot to get the United States to disarm unilaterally, he had asked Bishop McNulty to use his contacts in the FBI to determine just how many Communist sympathizers were involved in making the film. When the bishop reported that the bureau could not find any traces of Soviet influence, McIntyre said he was not surprised since the Reds were so good at working behind the scenes in Hollywood. McIntyre didn't need to contact the FBI to determine who was behind the Legion's lurch to the left. Sullivan had already made an enemy of the cardinal when the Legion added the Mexican-made film *Adam and Eve* to the growing list of separately classified films. McIntyre, who had attacked it as "irreverent and a veritable caricature of the first chapter of Genesis," had already persuaded a local distributor not to show it. Now he had to explain how the Legion could characterize the same picture as a "reverent presentation of the origin of man."[29]

What finally pushed McIntyre into the Quigley-Mooring camp was the Legion's decision to place *King of Kings* (1961) and *La Dolce Vita* (1960) in the separate classification category. Starring young and handsome Jeffrey Hunter, *King of Kings* had been derisively referred to in some circles as "I was a teen-aged Jesus," but it would have earned an A–I rating in the old days. McIntyre, who had planned to use the Los Angeles premiere as part of a fund-raiser, was stunned to learn of the pairing of the two films and canceled the opening. The Legion's treatment of *King of Kings* reflected the changes Sullivan had instituted in its staff. As the old IFCA reviewers left, they were replaced by a more sophisticated mix of reviewers consisting of business people, film teachers, movie reviewers, academics, and graduate students. While finding nothing immoral about the film, several reviewers commented on its theological, scriptural, and historical inaccuracies as well as its "hackneyed pietism." Unable to give the film a positive recommendation, Sullivan felt the only thing to do with it was to classify it separately, with a warning that it could lead to "wrong interpretations and false conclusions" by less sophisticated Catholics.[30]

The slap at *King of Kings* was bad enough in itself, but when *La Dolce Vita* appeared on the same list, it was too much for McIntyre. The Fellini film, which opened with a statue of Christ being carried over the city by a helicopter, took the audience on a tour of decadent Rome. The principal guide, played by Marcello Mastroianni, engages in a number of overnight affairs, including a menage à trois with a bored heiress and a prostitute and an orgy with a divorcée. Add the voluptuous Anita Ekberg, a fake "miracle," two suicides—a failed attempt by Mastroianni's mistress and a successful effort by his friend after murdering his two children—and the film easily broke all the old Legion's rules. Sullivan had seen the film in Milan and was impressed by the director's artistry. Nevertheless, he recognized that it was not going to be a hit with the Ladies' Sodality or the Holy Name. The ninety-five reviewers who saw the film included diocesan priests, seminary professors, eight film critics, the editor of a large Catholic publishing house, a judge, a television producer, and a few IFCA holdovers. Their votes reflected the subjective nature of movie evaluations: twenty-three recommended an A–III rating, twenty-two favored a B, twenty-two voted to condemn it, and twenty-eight, including fourteen priests, thought it deserved the separate classification. Putting the best light on the results in his letter to Bishop McNulty, Sullivan pointed out that seventy-three of the ninety-five reviewers, including thirty-eight of the forty-four priests, had voted against condemnation.[31]

The decision to classify the film separately was not simply a matter of counting votes. As Sullivan explained to McNulty, the recent court rulings on censorship meant that it was going to be shown no matter what the Legion did. Moreover, the early reviews by both secular and religious critics reaffirmed the judgment of the seventy-three Legion reviewers that the film was morally sound and worth seeing. "Only ignorance or lack of charity," Sullivan maintained, "could lead one to accept the conclusion that all of these . . . critics were being deceived or were being socially irresponsible." A Legion condemnation would receive little support in influential circles, he believed, and was doomed to failure. The best course of action, he concluded, was to limit the way the film was exhibited so that it would not reach "the masses." With McNulty's support, Sullivan suggested to the distributor, Astor Pictures, that a separate classification might be awarded if he could be sure that the film would be shown only to mature audiences. Eager to avoid a condemnation, Astor entered into an agreement with the Legion that the film would be advertised as limited to those over eighteen. To target it to a more sophisticated audience, the company consented to using subtitles instead of the dubbed version that had been shown in England. In order to underscore the moral and artistic value of the picture, the distributor also promised not to exploit the more sordid aspects of the film and to furnish the Legion with sample advertising.[32]

With the Astor Pictures agreement in hand, the Legion announced that it had awarded *La Dolce Vita* a separate classification. Warning that it could pose serious moral problems for "the immature and intellectually passive viewer," the announcement made it clear that, unlike most movies, the Fellini film had something important to say. Thematically, it was "a bitter attack upon the debauchery and degradation of a hedonistic society of leisure and abundance." Conceding that the filmmaker had used some highly sensational subject matter to make his point, the Legion noted that the shocking scenes were never exploited. "On the contrary, their shock value is intended to generate a salutary recognition of evil as evil and sin as sin."[33]

The Legion's treatment of *La Dolce Vita* garnered isolated Catholic support. The movie critic for the *Davenport Messenger* commented that in the past, Catholics had seemed to believe that there were only two kinds of films: "'clean' ones, preferably featuring a singing priest and produced either by Leo McCarey or Walt Disney; and 'dirty' ones, which for some reason appeal to Protestants, Jews and secularists." As he pointed out, ten years before "*La Dolce Vita* would have been condemned, but times had changed for the better, thanks to a more enlightened Legion."[34]

For Quigley, the case was one more example of the "phony sophistication and shocking lack of common sense" that pervaded that "jungle of amateurism" at Legion headquarters. Father John Devlin, who had been dispatched by Cardinal McIntyre to see the film, reported that he considered the assignment a three-hour penance. Claiming that he had tried to be objective, he could only conclude that it was a "sick picture . . . disgustingly degrading and degradingly disgusting." The only ones to benefit, he predicted, would be the Communists, as the film portrayed the decadence of the idle rich while church representatives moved helplessly in and out of the film. Quigley was right, Devlin told the cardinal; it was impossible to figure out what standards the Legion was following in its evaluations. Others, fearing the worst, felt they knew the answer. According to one magazine, the Legion's handling of *La Dolce Vita* was a clear sign that Communists had infiltrated the Catholic church. McIntyre telephoned Father Little to complain about the Legion's new policy, but the thought of classifying a picture of the life of Christ and one of a Roman orgy in the same category was too much for him, and he hung up abruptly before losing his temper. Still fuming, he let it be known that Sullivan would not be welcome in Los Angeles in his official capacity as the Legion's assistant secretary. McIntyre was not the only church leader dismayed by Sullivan's handling of the Fellini film. Archbishop Karl Alter of Cincinnati exercised a rarely used prerogative which enabled local prelates to apply a more severe standard than the Legion's and condemned the movie in his archdiocese. Even Bishop Scully, who had sympathized with Sullivan's efforts to develop a more positive Legion policy, publicly urged his people to pass up the film for the good of their souls, although he stopped short of condemning it.[35]

Meanwhile, Sullivan and Little were kept busy answering a flood of complaints. *La Dolce Vita* threatened the organization with its first serious split since Quigley and Parsons's battle with the Chicago Legion a quarter century before. In a letter addressed to Bishop McNulty and circulated to several other prelates and sympathetic Catholic editors as well as the Vatican, Quigley denounced *La Dolce Vita* as the most immoral and sacrilegious film he had seen in his nearly forty-six years in the business. He had talked Twentieth Century-Fox, Columbia, and major distributors James Mulvey and Joseph E. Levine out of handling the American rights to *La Dolce Vita* on the basis that the Legion was sure to condemn it. But as in the case of *Tea and Sympathy*, he had been proven wrong because of a "Jesuit clique," seemingly more interested in wooing the American Civil Liberties Union than in protecting the innocent against immoral filmmakers. Unless the Legion reversed its course, he warned, it would deal a death blow to the Code and the cause of movie morality, to which he had devoted his life. Worse, the attack had come not "from over the ramparts of the enemy, but from within the Household itself."[36]

Quigley was no doubt sincere, but he also had his own agenda. His inability to control Sullivan threatened to undermine his reputation as the man the producers would see in order to overcome any difficulties with the Legion. It was not simply a matter of ego; the studios' forced divestiture of their movie houses under the terms of the 1948 Paramount court decision had altered the industry's method of advertising. As a result, Quigley Publications began to run into trouble during the 1950s. Declining revenues forced the publisher to name his son, Martin Quigley, Jr., editor in chief in 1956. Although Quigley remained president and publisher until his death, the move enabled him to spend more time as a consultant to moviemakers facing problems with the PCA or the Legion. Using his fees to prop up his publishing business, his interest in the Legion was now as much a matter of money as of morality. The usually politically astute Quigley seemed not to have realized that in railing against Sullivan and his supporters, he ran the risk of a counterattack. The opposition to *La Dolce Vita* by McIntyre, Alter, Scully, and other bishops may have nurtured his hope that Sullivan could be stopped, but it may have blinded him to his own vulnerabilities.[37]

The seeming contradiction between Quigley the moral reformer, who wanted to clean up the movies, and Quigley the publisher, who advertised Hollywood's wares in his magazines, had long been a potential trouble spot. Father Daniel Lord had noted that it must have been difficult for an "honorable and religious man" to be "the medium through which the tainted product reached the men who would retail it." The issue had first surfaced in 1954 when the *Catholic Times* of Columbus, Ohio, charged that the ads in the *Motion Picture Herald* constituted a flagrant violation of decency. Arguing that the publisher couldn't have it both ways, the paper pointed to an ad for *Wicked Woman* featuring a curvaceous actress in a tight off-the-shoulder dress along with the promise that the film generated "as much heat as the screen will allow." The Columbus paper accused Quigley of being in the same class as "the pimp and the panderer." The attack was reinforced by the *New World*, which charged that "the champion of decency offends against decency" in his advertising. Noting that Quigley had recently taken Hollywood to task for a rash of sexually charged films, the paper asked him why he didn't begin the cleanup with his own magazine. Especially troubling were his magazine's ads for the condemned *French Line*, which trumpeted: Jane Russell "tosses herself—I do mean 'tosses'—into her famous dance." Equally embarrassing was a headline in the *Catholic Transcript:* "Martin Quigley Is Rapped for Running Lurid Movie Ads."[38]

Quigley first suspected that William Mooring was behind the sudden onslaught, in reprisal for his criticism of the reviewer's characterization of *Born Yesterday* as Communist propaganda, but Cardinal McIntyre assured the publisher that the critic was not to blame. Eager to clear himself, Quigley sent a copy of the ads to Father Francis Connell at Catholic University, asking for his advice. In his defense, he noted that he could not survive in the highly competitive publishing business if he turned down ads for B- and C-rated films. If he followed such a course, the ads would still appear, but in another journal. Moreover, he piously added, if he were forced out of business, it would curtail his ability to do so much good within the industry. To his relief Connell agreed, noting that Quigley was not unlike the Catholic newspaper editor who accepts ads inviting attendance at the local Protestant church. He was also heartened by the support of Cardinal Spellman, who directed Father John T. McClafferty, the former head of the Legion, to write to the editors of the *Catholic Times* and the *New World* praising Quigley and explaining that as a businessman he was not always in a position to force studios to shape their ads to conform to his personal standards. With the help of his friends, Quigley weathered the attack, but it left a scab that could be easily picked in the future.[39]

A more serious problem involved the many enemies Quigley had accumulated over the years, not the least of whom was Father John Courtney Murray, whom he had criticized for his "strange notions" about the role of the church in a pluralistic society. Others who harbored their own special grudges, like Geoff Shurlock and Jack Vizzard, had long resented the publisher's complaints about lax Code enforcement. When Vizzard met with Murray early in 1957 on his way to a meeting with Bishop Scully, Murray had suggested that he tell the bishop, then chair of the Episcopal Committee, that Quigley was boasting that he was the dog that wagged the Legion's tail. Murray's ploy worked. Scully hotly denied that Quigley ran the Legion, but he indicated to Vizzard that the publisher had often made its job more difficult. The Albany bishop resented Quigley's complaints to Cardinal Stritch and other members of the hierarchy about Scully's role in derailing the publisher's effort to get the Legion to condemn *Tea and Sympathy*. Convinced that Hollywood's view of Quigley's influence could be damaging, Scully quietly advised Father Little to begin to dispel the notion that Quigley spoke for the Legion.[40]

The campaign against Quigley picked up momentum in the following months. When Bishop McNulty took over the Episcopal Committee, he was provided with an internal memorandum that contained a blistering attack against the publisher. Admitting that Quigley was sincerely dedicated to the cause of movie morality, the author pointed out that his financial interests had been greatly enhanced by his reputation as the Mr. Fix-it of any film condemned by the Legion. "It is our opinion," he continued, "that the man has intentions savoring of a form of megalomania and unless he personally can make all the important decisions of this office he will be unhappy to his dying day." Furthermore, in his desperate effort to recapture his lost prestige and power, Quigley had fostered the canard that a Jesuit clique had taken over the Legion. Quigley had come to McNulty shortly after his takeover of the Episcopal Committee to complain about the Jesuit cabal that was subverting the Legion. After investigating his charges, McNulty concluded not only that they were groundless but that all of Quigley's statements had to be treated with great caution. Consequently, when the publisher renewed his attack during the *La Dolce Vita* controversy, the bishop quickly dismissed his criticism as "unadulterated nonsense."[41]

Sullivan widened the wedge between Quigley and the Legion by encouraging Little, who like his predecessors had relied on the publisher's advice, to follow a more independent course. Sullivan pointed out that since Quigley had been serving as a paid consultant to the studios, his close relationship with the Legion presented a possible conflict of interest. Quigley had often invited Little and members of the hierarchy to lunch at the Plaza Hotel's Oak Room, a restaurant frequented by many movie executives. Sullivan persuaded the priest to refuse further invitations, pointing out that the publisher was using these occasions to underscore his influence with the Legion.[42]

Quigley realized that Sullivan and his supporters had decided to launch a counteroffensive when they revived the question of Quigley's responsibility for the ads that appeared in the *Motion Picture Herald*. Little resurrected the issue when he criticized the promotion for *Babette Goes to War* (1959), which dwelled on the physical charms of its star, Brigitte Bardot. Pointing to a revealing picture of Bardot, Little asked tartly, "Is this an ad for a movie, or an ad for bras?" Little had requested five copies of the ad from the magazine's circulation department, planning to send them to the bishops on the Episcopal Committee. Hoping to control the damage, Quigley sent a copy of his correspondence with Little to the committee members along with a reminder that Father Connell had cleared him of any wrongdoing. Meanwhile, he quietly advised his son to refuse any ads for *Les Liaisons Dangereuses*, which had just been condemned by the Legion.[43]

This latest flap over his advertising policy should have warned Quigley that if he were going to challenge the Legion leadership, he should make sure that his own record was spotless. Nevertheless, while claiming that the Legion had lost its moral compass by failing to condemn pictures like *Suddenly Last Summer* and *La Dolce Vita*, Quigley signed on as a consultant for one of the most controversial movie projects of the day: James Harris and Stanley Kubrick's effort to film Vladimir Nabokov's novel *Lolita*. After failing to secure backing from United Artists, Warner, and Columbia, Harris and Kubrick finally struck a deal with Seven Arts, a television production company, to finance the project, with MGM acting as the distributor.[44]

This was typical of what was happening in the film industry. The major studios were becoming distributors rather than producers of films; they had made only fourteen of the ninety-eight pictures released in the first half of 1960. Some studios had also created subsidiaries that enabled them to get around Shurlock, as only MPAA member companies were subject to the Code. Columbia had recently gone this route, releasing *And God Created Woman* (1956), starring Brigitte Bardot, through its art film subsidiary, Kingsley-International. Within a few months, it became the biggest foreign moneymaker up to that time. In fact, some movie houses proudly included the Legion condemnation in their ads in order to attract customers. Recognizing that the threat of a Legion boycott was losing its impact, Monsignor James Ling, pastor of St. Agnes Church in Lake Placid, New York, tried unsuccessfully to persuade the local theater owner to cancel the film in exchange for $350.[45]

The Episcopal Committee had scored the growing number of subsidiaries and independent filmmakers at the bishops' annual meeting in November 1960. Although Quigley must have known that he was opening himself to criticism for working on the *Lolita* project, an unlikely ally, *Commonweal*, proclaimed the book "brilliant" and placed it on its list of recommended gifts for Christmas. Forgetting his past admonitions against adapting sophisticated material to the screen, Quigley rationalized that because someone would eventually make the film, he was the best choice to "take this notorious story out of the gutter."[46]

Quigley's job was to help secure a Production Code seal for the film and get it past the Legion. Although Kubrick had reportedly said that the Code "didn't make much difference any more," everyone involved in the project wanted a seal to ensure as wide a distribution as possible. Quigley faced a formidable task: making acceptable the story of Humbert Humbert, who marries his landlady in order to be close to his real love, her twelve-year-old daughter. After the mother is conveniently killed, Humbert takes Lolita out of her summer camp and into a motel bed. By the time Quigley read the script, Harris and Kubrick, in cooperation with Nabokov, who wrote the script, had already made a number of changes to make the story more palatable, including boosting Lolita's age from twelve to fifteen.[47]

Working at a distance—the film was shot in London for financial reasons as well as to keep Shurlock at bay—Quigley did his best. "You have in *Lolita* a sensational piece of material," he told Harris and Kubrick; "you don't need to rely on prurient, suggestive and shocking material" to turn it into a hit. Moreover, if the two men would take his advice, some of which, he recognized, they might "gag over," they would have not only a success but a picture, "at least with respect to recently prevailing standards," they could be proud of. He then proceeded to red-line all the double entendres in the script, such as Lolita's declaration that her sweater was virgin wool, which had prompted the comment: "The only thing about you that is, kiddo." He also objected to gags about feeling as "limp as a noodle" and an "unacceptable dirty joke" about Lolita needing to have her cavity filled. Harris and Kubrick assured him that they were playing the story for comedy and not sex and that everything would work out. References to limp noodles would be tastefully handled, and the cavity joke would be shot several different ways, one of which would show Lolita tapping her teeth to make it clear which cavity was being filled, as back ups if the censors objected.[48]

The seduction scene, however, bothered Quigley most. After perfunctorily noting that Humbert's affair with Lolita was forbidden by the Code's prohibition against perversion, he conceded that it was an integral part of the picture. Quigley's solution was to accomplish as much of the scene as possible through suggestion. Kubrick had already made a major concession by agreeing to shoot it with Lolita dressed in a heavy flannel, long-sleeved, high-necked, full-length nightgown and with Humbert in not only pajamas but a bathrobe as well. Quigley had initially suggested that the seduction take place somewhere other than the motel bed, but he agreed with Harris that it would probably be more offensive if they implied that it happened on the floor. He told Kubrick that the seduction would go a lot easier if the audience could be convinced that Humbert had developed "a wholesome and dedicated love" for Lolita. But the director had no intention of turning the story into *A Date with Judy*. Instead, when Humbert asks Lolita in the motel room what she wants to do, she suggests that they play some games. When he asks what type of games, she whispers to him while sticking her tongue in his ear. Then, kneeling above the reclining Humbert, she eyes him expectantly as the scene fades out.[49]

Quigley was appalled. There were a million ways of accomplishing the seduction, he sputtered, "other than demonstrating to millions of teen-agers around the world this notorious device for arousing sexual passion in a person." It fell in the same category, he said, as "the tongue-in-mouth business," banned by the Code but gradually finding its way into more pictures in recent years, to the detriment of millions of young people, in Quigley's view. "All of this goes double, or even triple, for the tongue-in-ear device," which, he claimed, constituted an even greater threat to American youth. Sensing that Kubrick was not going to be won over by this argument, he warned him that this single episode would earn the picture a Legion condemnation. However, Harris and Kubrick, who were filming while some of Quigley's recommendations were still in the mail, were determined to make their own picture. In light of the changing Hollywood climate and the Legion's recent liberalization, they reasoned, the film had a good chance of squeaking by the PCA and landing in the Legion's separate classification category.[50]

Yet Shurlock and Vizzard couldn't pass up the opportunity to take a few shots at the man who for years had chided them about their lax enforcement of the Code. When he first heard that Quigley had signed on as a consultant, Shurlock had asked him how he felt about shepherding a notorious film past the system he had created. Quigley pointed out that the film was going to be made anyway and asked, "Would you just want to turn the producers loose, to make it their way? Or would you rather settle for a silk purse from a sow's ear?" Upon hearing this, Shurlock's old resentment about the publisher's constant sniping came to the fore: "For God's sake, Martin, now you're talking just like us. This's what we've been saying over the years, and you've sneered at us for it. . . . Now that you're suddenly on the other side of the fence, it's all right." Hanging up, he told Vizzard: "The pious prick. . . . Well, when he comes to us with that picture, it had better be clean or I'm going to rub his nose in it."[51]

When the time came to screen the film, Shurlock had to admit privately that it was a marked improvement over the book and that a seal rejection would be overturned easily on appeal. Nevertheless, it was a good chance to make Quigley, who attended the review, squirm a little. The staff kicked around several possible sticking points just to keep him on edge, finally settling on the seduction, which was resolved by shortening the scene. When Shurlock went to call Harris to tell him what they had decided, Quigley tried to stop him so that he could be the bearer of the good news. "Are you paying for the certificate?" Shurlock acidly asked. "If not, then my responsibility is to the producer." The film had passed, but it was an uncomfortable afternoon for the father of the Code who would have gladly consigned the film to the eternal fires a decade ago. Wearied by the ordeal, he took to bed for several days.[52]

Quigley still needed the approval of Sullivan and Little, who had been under constant attack from Quigley for three years. Quigley's battle with Sullivan had been kept within church circles, so that Harris and Kubrick had every reason to believe that he was still the man who could win over the Legion. The two priests had received complaints about the film since the day it was announced, including one from a woman in San Antonio urging them to help free Sue Lyons, (the actress who played Lolita) who, she claimed, had been sold to Stanley Kubrick by her parents. The film was screened by fifty-three Legion reviewers, eighteen of whom were priests: nine favored an A–III classification, fourteen a B, twenty-six a condemnation, and four the separate classification. The staff was also divided, with Little in favor of condemnation, Mary Looram a B rating, and Sullivan the separate classification as a means of controlling distribution although he felt that the film was intrinsically worthy of condemnation. A separate showing was arranged for Bishop McNulty, who added his vote in favor of condemnation. Little's letter to Harris and Kubrick was much harsher than the vote warranted. Their film was, he said, two and a half hours of "bad taste, revolting material and sexual depravity." Equally reprehensible was their willingness to corrupt a fourteen-year-old girl (Sue Lyons) to make money from a picture.[53]

Seeking to head off a public announcement of the condemnation, David Stillman of Seven Arts informed Bishop McNulty (in a letter that the Legion staff believed was written by Quigley) that it was withdrawing *Lolita* from the review process. In view of the Legion's granting a separate classification to pictures of such "prurient and sensational character" as *La Dolce Vita* and *Suddenly Last Summer*, he wrote, the public would interpret the Legion's condemnation as a sign that the film was obscene. The withdrawal of the film would return it to the status of a "private, unpublished work," and any Legion action could lead to a lawsuit. Stillman, who accused the Legion of condemning the novel *Lolita* and not the film in an effort to counter the furor surrounding *La Dolce Vita*, also implied Harris and Kubrick's movie was the victim of a vendetta. "We have been unable to discover a single case," he told McNulty, "in which you, personally, chose to view a film which was up for classification, and then to fix its classification."[54]

Under McNulty's direction, Little pointed out that Stillman had displayed an appalling lack of respect for the bishop. Reminding him of the reasons for the condemnation, he declared that McNulty had seen the film only at the staff's request after an overwhelming vote in favor of condemnation. With the Legion digging in its heels, Quigley tried to get Cardinal Spellman to intercede. Conceding that the resulting product left a lot to be desired, Quigley argued that it did not deserve a condemnation in view of the many truly objectionable films that had recently received relatively favorable classifications from the Legion. Claiming incorrectly that the majority of the reviewers had voted for an A–III or B classification, he could only conclude that the Legion's condemnation was an effort to blacken his reputation.[55]

When Father Little supplied him with a breakdown of the reviewers' votes, the cardinal backed off. Meanwhile, David G. Baird, a friend and benefactor of the cardinal, asked to meet with Little. Claiming that he personally had no financial interest in the film, he told the priest that he had been asked by the Boston bank that had financed the film to facilitate a reclassification. Baird indicated that he personally thought that the film was objectionable and had arranged a showing for a group of religious leaders, who agreed with him. Nevertheless, he contended, condemnation would quadruple box-office returns in the United States, an argument that, if true, would make one wonder why its backers were seeking a better rating. Baird asked Little to arrange for a review of an amended version, suggesting that if the vote was still in favor of condemnation the Legion might refrain from publicly announcing its decision in order to cut down on the notoriety. Little did not object to a second viewing, but he pointed out that his request for secrecy flew in the face of the Legion's obligation to those who looked to it for guidance.[56]

The rescreening for the Legion revealed that Seven Arts had made only a few minor changes. Negotiations continued for two months, mainly over the seduction scene. After the company agreed to reduce the scene to a minimum, with a fade-out just after Lolita begins to whisper in Humbert's ear, cutting off any hint of the games to come, the Legion granted it the separate classification. Sullivan, who had always favored this step as a means of exerting some control over the film's distribution, extracted several additional concessions. Seven Arts agreed that the exhibitors' contracts would include a clause limiting the film to viewers over eighteen; the press book would be submitted to the Legion for approval; and, finally, there would be no tie-in between the movie and the paperback sale of the novel.[57]

It had been a long ordeal for everyone. Quigley turned down Kubrick's invitation to the premiere, stating that the film had worn him out. Kubrick and Nabokov both felt that too much of the story had been left on the cutting room floor. The *New York Times* responded to the movie ad slogan, "How did they ever make a movie of *Lolita?*" with, "They didn't."[58]

Nevertheless, *Lolita* was one more reminder of how rapidly times were changing. With all the talk of "nymphet" seduction and in view of three forthcoming pictures—*The Best Man*, *Advise and Consent*, and *The Children's Hour*, all of which touched on homosexuality—the MPAA voted to liberalize its prohibition against "sex perversion." Once forbidden, "sex aberration" could now be discussed as long as it was done with "care, discretion and restraint." But not only the Code had undergone change. Sullivan noted that "ten to fifteen years ago, the Legion would hardly have accepted *Lolita* even on an adults only basis." Little agreed, adding that audiences were now more mature and consequently, ready for *Lolita*. The lawyer Ephraim London, who had represented exhibitors and distributors in cases involving *The Miracle* and *Lady Chatterley's Lover*, had a different slant. "It is not so much the audiences which have grown up," he said, "as the Legion, and I applaud it for this."[59]

FOURTEEN

End of the Road

Having survived his ordeal over *Lolita,* Martin Quigley, who was now seventy-one, decided to make one last effort to turn back the clock. He had met Bishop Karl Alter of Cincinnati, who had condemned *La Dolce Vita,* on a plane back from Rome that summer and was encouraged by the bishop's declaration that Quigley was in a far better position to judge films for the average Catholic moviegoer than the current Legion staff, which seemed overly concerned about the needs of a more sophisticated audience. Quigley worked on Alter during the months before the bishops' annual conference in November 1961. The Legion started to lose its way, he told Alter, with the appointment of Father Patrick Sullivan, who had subordinated moral standards to cultural and artistic considerations. Concerned with the needs of an "intelligentsia," the staff had forgotten that its principal purpose was providing moral guidance for young and less sophisticated moviegoers. The outcome of all this was a rating system based on the premise that any theme or subject, including sexual perversion, was acceptable adult fare as long as it was treated in good taste. This insanity, he claimed, had even affected segments of the Catholic press, whose film critics were promoting and approving "the ugliest subjects which have appeared in the history of the screen"—films like *Suddenly Last Summer* and *La Dolce Vita*. All this had, in turn, affected the Code. He admitted that, given the changes in society, it may have been impossible for the Legion to hold the line, but Sullivan didn't have to back down completely. "At a time when a stiffening-up was required, the Legion offered only a softening down." A case in point, he declared, was its refusal to condemn *Suddenly Last Summer*. The Legion's willingness to accept a picture based on homosexuality, he maintained, had encouraged the industry to strike at the Code's prohibition of "sex perversion."[1]

For a moment, it looked as though Quigley might be on the verge of a comeback. Alter shared Quigley's view of the Legion's "liberalistic opinions" and promised to do something about it. That same day, the bishop wrote to the general secretary of the National Catholic Welfare Conference asking him to put the matter of the Legion's ratings on the next agenda. But Quigley knew that Sullivan's removal alone would not turn the Legion around. Recognizing that many Catholics were simply ignoring its evaluations, liberal as they were, he realized that something also had to be done to bring the laity back in line. The answer, he suggested to Cardinal Francis Spellman, was to give the ratings the force of ecclesiastical law and consequently make them binding under the pain of mortal sin. Meanwhile, Bishop McNulty responded to Alter's complaints to the NCWC general secretary, saying that the publisher's problems with the Legion began when "he tried to derive more prestige, power and profit than he was entitled to." Moreover, he had investigated Quigley's "obsession with 'The Jesuit Conspiracy' to control the Catholic Communications Media in America" and concluded that it was unfounded. The real basis of Quigley's charges, he intimated, was his fear that his declining influence with the Legion would hurt his pocketbook. According to McNulty, the publisher had submitted a bill of $5,000 to each of the major studios for his consulting services in the spring of 1959. "The damaging interpretation being placed on these facts by Industry people," the bishop claimed, "is that Mr. Quigley has been remunerated for his supposed role of 'intermediary with the Legion of Decency.'"[2]

The November meeting underscored Quigley's isolation. Where once he could pick up the phone and talk to Archbishop McNicholas, he now had to wait anxiously to hear what had transpired. McNulty's counterattack persuaded Alter to drop the matter. Cardinals McIntyre and Spellman did bring up the matter of *La Dolce Vita* and *King of Kings* receiving the same rating, which prompted the bishops to insist that future judgments be made on moral rather than artistic standards. Nevertheless, the bishops, sensing a need to close ranks, publicly endorsed the Legion's policies. "It is difficult indeed to understand why, in the face of clear evidence of the disastrous consequences," a shocked Quigley complained to Alter, "no appropriate remedial action has been taken."[3]

Quigley had clearly been beaten. Even Alter distanced himself. "I wasn't at the meeting that discussed the Legion," he told Quigley coldly, suggesting that if he wanted to find out what had happened, he should write to the secretary of the NCWC. Quigley must have wondered how his campaign had collapsed so quickly. He had failed to consider that his role in *Lolita* had left him open to attack. Bishop McNulty had blasted Quigley's hypocrisy in attacking Sullivan and Little while serving as a consultant on a movie about a pedophile. Quigley's criticism of the Legion in recent years had also alienated some of the bishops on the Episcopal Committee, including Scully. Nor had his suggestion about giving the Legion's classifications the force of church law helped his cause. Sullivan had convinced Cardinal Spellman that the bishops' conference had no right to supplant papal authority and that any effort to do so would be an embarrassment.[4]

Quigley was simply out of step with the times. Within a year, Pope John XXIII summoned the world's bishops to Rome for an ecumenical council, popularly known as Vatican II. Latin was phased out of the liturgy and the altar turned so that the priest faced the congregation. Church statements on the liturgy, ecumenism, the role of the laity, and religious liberty adopted over the next four years lessened the isolation and self-righteousness that had characterized much of its view of the non-Catholic world. When the Second Vatican Council adopted a "Declaration of Religious Freedom" in 1965, which was written in part by John Courtney Murray, the church for the first time accepted the twin principles of separation of church and state and religious liberty. What Quigley had once referred to as "the curious arguments" of Father Murray were now part of the Catholic mainstream. Eventually, the council would redefine the church as a whole, viewing it as the people of God instead of in terms of its hierarchy.[5]

Although no one in 1961 could have anticipated the course the council would take, change was already in the air. The previous year, Father Gustave Weigel, S.J., had told a group of Catholic laymen: "The world is new. The situation of 1960 is revolutionary. It is quite unlike the world of 1900. Consequently, the relationship of the action of the laity and hierarchy must be seen in the light of the new world." Returning the Legion to what it had been in an earlier age was an effort doomed to failure.[6]

One small measure of the changing mood within the church was the replacement of the old pledge. The first revision, written by Sullivan, was presented to the bishops in 1959 as a means of incorporating the call in *Miranda Prorsus* for a more positive approach to motion pictures. Instead of the promise to "condemn indecent and immoral pictures," the new one would "promote by word and deed what is morally and artistically good in entertainment." And where the laity once promised to "unite with all those who protest against . . . indecent pictures," they now pledged to work against such films, "especially by [their] good example and always in a responsible and civic-minded manner." Picket lines and pressure tactics were clearly on the way out. The conservative forces, led by Cardinal McIntyre, were still strong enough, however, to hand Sullivan a temporary setback. The motion to adopt the new pledge was defeated 93 to 60. Quigley naturally applauded the bishops' stand, terming Sullivan's effort a "long and fuzzy harangue having to do with culture in the movies" and an "emasculation" of Archbishop McNicholas's original pledge that would have left the laity confused and bewildered.[7]

Over the next few years, several bishops tried out the new pledge in their own dioceses. Citing the work of the Vatican Council, Little brought the matter up again in late 1963. "The pledge, during the past ten years," he said, "has become an object of criticism, dissatisfaction, indifference, and even hostility. In these ecumenical times, it is branded as a pathetic anachronism by our laity [and] creates the image of the church as a patroness of boycotts." When a survey indicated that only three dioceses favored retaining the old pledge, Sullivan's recommendation was adopted the next year, but by that time it didn't make much difference. Some bishops, like John Wright of Pittsburgh, were no longer administering any pledge while others, including John Dearden of Detroit, simply included it in the diocesan bulletin. Within a few years, the pledge had faded into memory, the only reference to it coming in an occasional letter from some local Legion director asking Father Sullivan whatever happened to it.[8]

The old IFCA reviewers were also fading away. In 1962, Quigley complained to Bishop John J. Krol, the new chair of the Episcopal Committee, that they had been reduced to "virtual ineffectiveness." Quigley's last shot at the liberal forces came in a letter to Krol and Scully, wondering why the church hadn't done something to stop Moira Walsh, the film reviewer for *America*. He had long disliked her commentaries, which he had characterized as strangely secular. He once complained that her critique of *The Left Hand of God* was something that one would have expected to find in a journal representing the "viewpoint of the pagan, cynical, irresponsible left." Walsh's latest transgression was a positive review in *America* of the British film *A Taste of Honey*, which Quigley felt epitomized what was wrong with the Legion. "Is it right," he asked, "for a Catholic agency . . . to recommend for the leisure hours of Catholic men and women entertainment subjects ladened with homosexuality, illegitimacy and promiscuity?" The identical responses of the two bishops suggested that a third party had drafted both letters. Citing the bishops' 1957 statement that good taste would inevitably reduce the number of objectionable pictures, they included a copy of an editorial from the *Davenport Messenger* praising the Legion's newfound maturity. Reminding Quigley that Walsh did not speak for the Legion, the bishops curtly suggested that it would be more effective if he directed his complaints to the reviewer herself.[9]

Sometime later that year it dawned on Quigley that he not only had lost the battle but was in danger of losing his consulting business as well. He had signed a contract with New World Films in December to edit *Of Love and Desire*, the story of an affair between an employee and the nymphomaniac half-sister of his boss, who is also in love with her. According to his contract, Quigley would receive $10,000 for his work plus $15,000 if the film received a Code certificate and avoided a Legion condemnation. Whatever his private feelings about Sullivan and Little, he had no interest in repeating his experience with *Lolita*. On January 23, 1963, he went to the Legion office and declared that he had decided to submit to the "voice of authority" with regard to its policy and administration. Two days later, he happily reported back to New World that its film would be awarded a separate classification after three minor changes had been made.[10]

The termination of his campaign against the Legion revived some of Quigley's old self-confidence. A few months later, after shepherding *Cleopatra* through the Code approval process, he was with Little and Sullivan in Fox's preview room in New York. During a break in the discussion, as a lavish cart of food and drinks was wheeled into the room, he suggested to Sullivan that if *Cleopatra* received an A–III, he might be able to persuade Cardinal McIntyre to drop his interdiction against Sullivan in Los Angeles. But Sullivan wasn't interested, and Quigley had to be satisfied with a B.[11]

One of Quigley's last consulting jobs was for Otto Preminger's *The Cardinal*, which chronicled the trials and tribulations of the fictional Father Stephen Fermoyle, the son of a Boston streetcar driver, who rises to the highest ranks of the Catholic church. At times Fermoyle seemed to be a one-man church, advising Al Smith in the 1928 election, being horsewhipped by a Klansman while on an assignment in the South, and helping to construct Vatican policy on Hitler and Mussolini. All that, despite the fact his own personal problems of making a life-or-death decision about his unmarried sister's difficult pregnancy and falling in love with a beautiful Italian countess.

Walter Wanger had first broached the idea of adapting Henry Morton Robinson's best-selling novel to the screen in 1950 but bowed out when he learned that Cardinal Spellman was opposed to the project. Spellman, who came from Massachusetts and had spent time in Rome, claimed that the film would damage the church, but the real source of his resistance was his fear that audiences would identify him as the subject of the story. Although nothing of the kind had happened in his own family, he was especially concerned about the priest's choice between the life of his sister and that of her baby. His opposition also dissuaded Louis B. Mayer and Spyros Skouras from pursuing their interest in doing the picture.[12]

Columbia Pictures decided to try a fresh approach in 1956. Every effort was made to distinguish Fermoyle from Spellman: locating the cardinal in Philadelphia rather than Boston and eliminating one of his two sisters, so that there would be no resemblance to the Spellman family. But when word of the script reached the cardinal, he immediately contacted his lawyers, who informed him of a recent libel case against MGM which could be used to scare Columbia off.[13]

The studio decided that it wasn't worth the trouble, so the project went back on the shelf for six years, until Otto Preminger became interested in it. When the president of Columbia told him he was afraid that Spellman's opposition would hurt the picture, Preminger pointed out that the entire church had thrown its weight against *The Moon Is Blue* and had failed. Nevertheless, Spellman's campaign against the project made it difficult to locate a church where some interior shots could be filmed until a pastor in Bridgeport, Connecticut, let Preminger film there. The cardinal's opposition forced Preminger to hire an ex-priest and Quigley as his technical advisers. They made the usual minor technical corrections: priests didn't carry wine with them except in the wilderness; it was "holy oil" and not "oil stock"; Fermoyle was far more likely to read his breviary than the *New Republic* in his quiet moments; and "Jeez, a profane corruption of Jesus" was out of order in a Catholic classroom.[14]

The Cardinal cleared the PCA with no difficulty, but the Legion office was just a stone's throw away from St. Patrick's Cathedral, and Little and Sullivan didn't want any missiles hurled in their direction. Preminger sidestepped the Legion by persuading Boston's Cardinal Cushing to host the world premiere of the movie, with all the proceeds going to diocesan charities. The producer had arranged a private screening for Cushing, who liked it so much that he wrote a rave review in the *Pilot*. As Quigley noted to Preminger: "I would not, of course, venture to suggest that Cardinal Cushing has missed his vocation, but I would say if he should decide to take up film reviewing professionally I would predict a promising future for him." By reprinting the *Pilot* review in an advertisement in the *New York Times*, Preminger threw the Legion on the defensive, forcing it to square its evaluation with Cushing's. Word that the Legion had picked up on Cushing's statement that the picture "will be best appreciated by mature movie-goers" in order to limit it to adult viewing prompted a quick response from Columbia Pictures. J. Raymond Bell, a studio publicist, pointed out to Little that he had taken Cushing's statement out of context because the cardinal had stated not only that the picture had something for everyone, but that many youngsters could derive a great deal from seeing it.[15]

When the Legion finally classified the film as A–III, it made every effort to avoid any apparent conflict with the text of Cushing's review. Ordinarily the Legion did not issue an explanation for A–III ratings, but it felt a lengthy rationale necessary in this case. Conceding that the film was "absorbing entertainment," the Legion declared that it was necessary to evaluate it more closely, at least for immature and uninformed viewers. The Legion singled out several problems with the film, beginning with the hero's refusal to allow a doctor to perform a craniotomy on his sister's child, which would have sacrificed the infant in order to save the mother's life. The scene presented the audience with "a stacked deck," the Legion claimed. It also objected to Father Fermoyle's declaration that although he didn't question church law, he could have pretended he didn't know about it if he were a layman at the time. His response suggested a double standard, the Legion charged—namely, that priests have to obey the church's rules, but the laity was free to ignore it when they confronted a moral dilemma. The Legion also complained that the film gave the impression that Fermoyle had become a priest only because of his parents' pressure, ignoring the spiritual dimensions of a vocation. Equally troublesome was his emotional involvement with a young woman while on a two-year leave of absence from the priesthood, which the Legion felt could confuse immature viewers.[16]

By this point, one had to wonder if an A–I, A–II, or B rating of *The Cardinal* would have made any difference. By 1964, thirty years after the birth of the Legion and the PCA, it looked as though both organizations had reached the end of the road. Shurlock and his staff were administering a Code that was fast becoming an anachronism. And *America* could laud the Legion for giving moviegoers an "intelligent and discriminating guide," but in reality it seemed to be fine-tuning an instrument to which fewer and fewer people were listening. That year, the Legion created an A–IV classification, which it claimed was not a new category but a substitution for the controversial separate classification it had used in the case of a number of recent films such as *Freud, Divorce Italian Style, The Sky Above and the Mud Below,* and *Advise and Consent.* In contrast to A–III, which required a maturity of judgment and a basic understanding of Christian values, A–IV was given to films which, "while not morally offensive in themselves," required some explanation as a protection against false conclusions. *Time* dubbed the new classification "the thinking man's category," but some people wondered if the only difference between an A–IV and a condemnation was the artistic quality of the film. In the final analysis, both Sullivan and Little knew, one could separate the A and B classifications into any number of subdivisions, but most Catholics simply divided the Legion ratings into condemned and not-condemned.[17]

Hollywood responded in kind, showing little interest in producing A–I-rated films. Of the 270 films classified by the Legion in 1964, only 52 were found acceptable for family viewing, the lowest number of A–I's in its thirty-year history. All that really mattered for the studios and for those independents seeking a national distribution was to trim just enough to escape whatever effect a C still might have at the box office.[18]

Despite Quigley's criticism, the Legion occasionally did say "enough." Warner ran into trouble over *Splendor in the Grass* (1961). Sullivan informed the studio that in view of the script's lack of any redeeming features, several scenes were unacceptable. Especially troublesome was a parking sequence suggesting "mass fornication" and a shot of the heroine kneeling before her boyfriend telling him she would do anything he wanted. The studio told Sullivan it was willing to alter the film, but its contract with director Elia Kazan gave him final-cut approval. Warner's Ben Kalmenson said he was thinking of asking Martin Quigley "to talk some sense" into Kazan as he had done in the case of *A Streetcar Named Desire*, but Sullivan said that he preferred an intermediary from the PCA. In the end, Jack Vizzard was given the assignment and persuaded the director to make enough changes to secure a B classification for the film.[19]

While Sullivan was wrapping up the problems connected to *Splendor in the Grass*, he told Kalmenson that the Legion was especially concerned about the studio's next project, *The Chapman Report*, a story about a Kinsey-like study of the sexual behavior of four suburban women. His fears were confirmed when he and Little previewed the film; both felt it gave the impression that extramarital affairs were the norm. Although the studio refused Little's suggestion—to add a fifth case which would show "a healthy . . . marriage-oriented sexual relationship"—it agreed to beef up the role of the one doctor in the story who questioned the survey's validity. It was enough to earn the film a B.[20]

There were still movies that the Legion wouldn't approve. Universal ran into serious difficulty over *The Private Lives of Adam and Eve*, which had cleared the PCA. When the Legion advised producer Albert Zugsmith that the film would be condemned because of its "blatant violations of Judeo-Christian standards of decency" and its "blasphemous and sacrilegious presentation of man's sex life," he said he was ready to make any changes to get a better rating. As it turned out, the Legion's objections were so pervasive that in the end Zugsmith decided to shelve the film. No studio, in fact, had risked releasing a condemned film since Warner's trouble with *Baby Doll* in 1956.

For their part, Sullivan and Little seemed to be willing to cut the studios as much slack as possible. Although eleven reviewers had voted to condemn *Irma La Douce* (1963), as opposed to eight favoring a B and three an A–III, the film was awarded a B. After the script for *Tom Jones* (1963) had been rejected by Geoff Shurlock, the film was made anyway. Apparently convinced that he could secure better treatment there, a company executive showed it to the Legion's reviewers first—a wise move. Characterizing the film as an "earthy satire" about eighteenth-century English manners and morals, the Legion gave it an A–IV. When it finally arrived at the PCA, Shurlock simply waved it through, declaring that he wasn't going to be "holier than the Pope."[21]

In view of all this, Billy Wilder and I. A. L. Diamond, who had produced *Irma La Douce*, didn't anticipate any problems as they prepared to show *Kiss Me Stupid* (1964) to the PCA and the Legion. The movie starred Dean Martin as Dino, a popular singer who is forced to stop in the little town of Climax on his way back to Los Angeles. There he is recognized by the gas station operator, who, along with Orville, the local piano teacher, is a would-be songwriter. Hoping to persuade Dino to use one of their songs, the gas station operator sabotages his car, forcing him to spend the night at the piano teacher's home. Orville, who is married to Zelda, the prettiest woman in town, is insanely jealous, a condition elevated by Dino's revelation that he gets headaches if he doesn't have sex at least once a day. In order to get Zelda out of Dino's clutches, Orville picks a fight with her just before they are about to go to bed on their fifth anniversary. Needing someone to satisfy Dino, he convinces Polly, a prostitute at a local club (played by Kim Novak), to substitute for his wife. Dino will get to bed Polly, and Orville will get a song contract. But Orville's jealousy is apparently free-flowing, and he kicks Dino out after he makes a pass at Polly. Meanwhile, the distraught Zelda gets drunk at the nightclub and is put to bed in Polly's trailer. Feeling a headache coming on, Dino ends up in the trailer and spends the night with Zelda. A few months later, the reconciled couple hear Dino singing one of Orville's songs on his television show. When Orville wonders how he obtained the song, his wife smiles and says, "Kiss me stupid."

Jack Vizzard likened Shurlock's announcement that he was going to pass the film to "the sound of hammers on casket nails." "As is?" one of the reviewers asked. "If dogs want to return to their vomit," Shurlock responded, "I'm not going to try to stop them." Sullivan and Little had leaned over backward to give Hollywood a chance to make mature movies, but this one was as sophisticated as a second-rate burlesque show. Father Little protested to United Artists that what was billed as a situation comedy turned out to be a sordid piece of realism. He furnished the studio with a list of offensive material, including the seduction scenes involving Dino and Polly, her low-cut costumes, and jokes involving religion. But the major difficulty was the thematic resolution of the plot, which rested on swapping sex for a song contract, thereby "glamorizing infidelity."[22]

Billy Wilder told the studio that he was genuinely stunned by the Legion's attitude. It seemed to him that *Kiss Me Stupid* was a much milder comedy than his *Irma La Douce*, *Some Like It Hot*, and *The Apartment*. Nevertheless, after reviewing the Legion's list of detailed objections, he told Father Little that he would make a few alterations as a sign of good faith. The removal of the off-scene sound of bedsprings after Orville and Zelda go to bed was no problem, and a reference to an incident in the organ loft "last Palm Sunday" could be modified by substituting "Thanksgiving." The best he could do was eliminate a few other lines because the sets had been torn down and Kim Novak was in England shooting another picture. The trailer episode could be redone as it involved a small set, and Dean Martin and Felicia Farr, who played Zelda, were still available. Making it clear that the two do not go to bed, Wilder felt, would resolve the Legion's major objection that the film glorified infidelity.[23]

Little responded that he was happy about Wilder's concessions, but that they didn't go far enough to avoid a condemnation. There were ten "sine qua non" changes that had to be made, including shortening the seduction scenes, shadowing some of the more revealing shots of Novak's cleavage, and eliminating several objectionable lines. One line that Little insisted had to go was Zelda's reference to her wedding day: "Who ever heard of a groom playing the organ at his own wedding?" Wilder claimed he couldn't understand how anyone could read anything improper into that line, but Little insisted that it had an unacceptable double meaning. An equally objectionable play on words, according to Little, involved an exchange between Orville and Polly about the piano teacher's house. "You'll like it," he says. "It's not very big, but it's clean." "What is?" she responds. No matter what the words said, Little declared, it was clear that Orville wasn't talking about his house. Little was willing to make one compromise. He had originally demanded the removal of Dino's remark that he wanted to go out to the garden to see Zelda's parsley. Noting that several female reviewers felt there was something particularly suggestive in the use of parsley, he said that he was willing to substitute any other vegetable.[24]

When United Artists refused to meet Little's demands, noting that it would be impossible to bring Novak back for reshooting, the Legion announced that it had condemned the film. In a lengthy explanation of its decision, it noted that satires like Wilder's *The Apartment* were a salutary method of exposing human weakness, but in *Kiss Me Stupid* he had produced something that was "aesthetically as well as morally repulsive. Crude and suggestive dialogue, a leering treatment of marital and extra-marital sex, a prurient preoccupation with lechery compound the film's bald condonation of immorality." In the press release accompanying the announcement, the Legion also took a shot at the PCA. Noting with astonishment that a film "so patently indecent and immoral" could have received a Code seal, Little declared: "It is difficult to understand how such approval is not the final betrayal of the trust which has been placed by so many in the organized industry's self-regulation." Martin Quigley, Jr., agreed. The passing of *Kiss Me Stupid,* he wrote, marked the end of the Code; "it could be blown away by a gentle zephyr." As it turned out, it was Wilder's film that was blown away at the box office. Protests caused cancellation of the film in several towns, but its failure was ultimately due to a host of negative reviews, like the one in *Time,* which characterized it as something "that seems to have scraped its blue-black humor off the floor of a honky-tonk club." Nevertheless, *Kiss Me Stupid*'s lack of success led Paramount to bow to the Legion's request to cut five minutes from *The Amorous Adventures of Moll Flanders* (1965).[25]

The *New York Times* film critic, Bosley Crowther, agreed that the Wilder film deserved to be condemned, but there was little support for the Legion's rejection of *The Pawnbroker* in 1965. At first glance, it appeared to be just the type of serious film that Sullivan had hoped to encourage by his creation of the A–IV category: a story about a Holocaust victim whose wife and children had died in the concentration camps. Shurlock, who personally admired the film, had withheld approval because it contained two nude scenes: a fleeting glimpse of the pawnbroker's wife in the camp, and one in which a prostitute shows her breasts to him in his shop in order to get a better deal. The producers appealed to the MPAA Code Review Board, which was put in the middle. If it supported Shurlock, Allied Artists would simply release the film intact through a subsidiary. If it overruled him, a precedent would have been set. Also, Ely Landau, the film's associate producer, was threatening to launch an antitrust action against the association. It might take more than the "zephyr" of Martin Quigley, Jr., to blow away the Code, but a lawsuit would do it, and the studios had nothing to put in its place. After four hours of deliberation, the review board granted *The Pawnbroker* a "special exemption" provided that the producer cut the length of the nude scenes. Landau eliminated a few token frames, and Shurlock dutifully passed it.[26]

The film posed a dilemma for the Legion. Sullivan and Little recognized its artistic quality, but the Episcopal Committee had recently mandated that nudity in any film would automatically result in condemnation. According to the Legion, the bishops' policy had forced the producers to eliminate nude shots from thirty-four films in 1964 and 1965. But, armed with a Production Code seal, Allied Artists released *The Pawnbroker* in New York on April 20, 1965. Three weeks later, the Legion reluctantly announced that it had decided to condemn the film, not because the picture was in itself obscene, but because of its categorical opposition to nudity in motion pictures. It was, said *Variety*, perhaps the mildest Legion condemnation ever made.[27]

The Legion's decision opened it up to widespread criticism. Judith Stone, writing in *Ramparts*, asked how the Legion could be taken seriously when it condemned "one of the few significant moral films made by Hollywood." Joe Mankiewicz ridiculed the Legion's argument that the dangerous precedent set by the film outweighed its artistic value. If Fellini wanted to film *Oedipus Rex*, he scoffed, that shouldn't set a precedent for a wave of "quickie, tasteless tantalizers called 'My Son, My Lover' or 'Daddy Does It Best.'" And *Newsweek* wondered how the Legion could talk about maintaining high standards in the movie industry when it condemned films like *The Pawnbroker*, *Breathless*, *Jules and Jim*, and *Saturday Night and Sunday Morning* while placing *The Earth Dies Screaming* and *Godzilla* on its A–I list.[28]

The Pawnbroker's critical success was an additional indictment of the Legion: Rod Steiger was nominated for an Academy Award for best actor, the film was chosen to represent the United States at the 1965 Berlin Film Festival, and Philip T. Hartung, *Commonweal*'s film critic, included it on his list of the ten best movies of the year. Even the bishops, at their annual meeting in November 1965, noted that the widespread Catholic criticism of the Legion's condemnation of *The Pawnbroker* was a source of real anxiety. A year later, the two offending scenes were eliminated in an effort to improve the disappointing box-office receipts, and *The Pawnbroker* was reclassified as A–IV.[29]

But the Legion of Decency didn't make the announcement. On December 8, 1965, Archbishop John J. Krol of Philadelphia, chairman of the Episcopal Committee, had announced that the Legion's name had been changed to the National Catholic Office for Motion Pictures (NCOMP). Although *Time* praised the Legion for dropping its "arrogant and muscular name," Krol warned that the new title should not be interpreted as a sign that the church was no longer concerned about decency in motion pictures. The creation of an office *for* motion pictures was meant to emphasize the positive approach to films that the Legion had pursued over the previous several years.[30]

The change also marked the end of an era. Martin Quigley had died in 1964, and Joe Breen followed him the week of Krol's announcement. Declaring that the PCA had made a mistake back in 1953, Geoff Shurlock quietly gave *The Moon Is Blue* a seal of approval, and no one seemed to care. Moreover, state censorship boards like the New York Motion Picture Department, which were the raison d'être for the Code, were fast disappearing. Early in 1965, the Supreme Court's invalidation of the Maryland law that required the approval of the Board of Censorship before a film could be shown to the public signaled the end of state regulation. The Virginia board of censors had been losing decision after decision in the early 1960s. In one of its last cases, involving labeling a Scandinavian film as "obscene," a member had been asked to supply the court with her standard for obscenity. "It's what offends me," she answered. And when questioned about whether she had kept informed about the leading court decisions in the field of censorship, she replied engagingly: "I try not to confuse myself with anything like that." Recognizing that distributors were bypassing the board in the wake of the Maryland decision, the Virginia legislature abolished it a few months later.[31]

The church and its members had also changed. Vatican II, with its endorsement of freedom of religion and conscience, put an end to the sin of indifferentism that had bedeviled Father Wilfrid Parsons in dealing with the producers of *Keys of the Kingdom.* The laity was moving at a faster pace. The election of John F. Kennedy as president marked the end of ghetto Catholicism and the feeling that Catholics were a minority group living in a hostile society. They were now solidly anchored in the middle class, and within a few years a Carnegie Report on higher education would indicate that Catholics were attending college at a higher rate than Protestants.[32]

Father Little, who had almost condemned *The Greatest Show on Earth*, had also changed. Shortly after the formation of NCOMP, he declared the Legion, with its reputation as a "stubborn, antiquarian, unrealistic defender of Catholic movie goers" and its militaristic theater picketing and boycotts, was out of harmony with a post–Vatican II approach to a pluralistic society. There was a need to respond to the new generation of Catholics, who, because of their higher level of education, were better equipped to cope with the content of films than their parents were. And Little admitted to Jack Vizzard that he himself had changed. When he was young, he said, everything had appeared to him as "stark blacks and whites," but as he grew older, "issues seemed less simple and more complex, and assumed various shades of gray." And despite *The Pawnbroker* controversy, the Legion's willingness to accept such sensitive subjects as unwed pregnancy in *The L-Shaped Room* and infidelity in *Juliet of the Spirits* indicated that it had developed a much more sophisticated approach to films in its last years.[33]

Not everyone was happy with what had happened to the Legion or, for that matter, the church. A group of conservative Catholics put together a book of *National Review* essays under the title *What in the Name of God Is Going on in the Catholic Church?* One woman wrote to Father Little wondering if the new name of the Legion signified that the church had decided, "If you can't whip them, join them." Father Paul Hayes, who had been replaced by Sullivan as Little's assistant, felt that the bishops could have done a better job in holding the line, although he conceded that the laity was much less willing to listen to the Legion than their parents had been. William Mooring, recognizing that he was hopelessly outnumbered, blamed it all on the "ultra-sophisticated" Legion staff led by Sullivan, who, he declared, had an "un-Catholic tolerance for immoral movies." But even he had unconsciously loosened up a bit over the years. Back in 1936, Mooring had praised the PCA for its work on *These Three*, based on Lillian Hellman's play *The Children's Hour*, which dealt with two teachers accused of lesbianism. Breen had forced Sam Goldwyn to change the script by substituting a heterosexual triangle for the original plot. Yet when Mooring saw the 1961 remake, which included a scene of the two teachers embracing, he acclaimed it as a marked improvement over the previous version.[34]

Anyone visiting the NCOMP office in its first few years might have wondered what had really changed. Father Little continued as the nominal head of the new agency while Sullivan ran it on a day-to-day basis, and the reviewers used the old Legion classification system. The faithful still occasionally wrote in asking for guidance, such as the owner of a small theater who wanted to know if it was a sin to show movies that had been condemned by NCOMP. The studios continued to negotiate with NCOMP in order to avoid a condemnation, although they showed increasing reluctance to make any meaningful cuts. United Artists was even willing to risk a condemnation of its film of Mary McCarthy's novel *The Group* (1966), until Ralph Hetzel, the acting head of the MPAA following Eric Johnston's death in 1963, intervened at NCOMP's request. But one had to wonder what sort of moral calibrations went into the decision to rescue a film from condemnation. Although NCOMP had identified fourteen separate objections, the removal of a hand on a covered breast, the elimination of another hand touching a woman's thigh, and the reduction in the number of times a husband hits his wife were enough to secure a B.[35]

NCOMP also pushed Hollywood to adopt the age classification system that the bishops, at Sullivan's suggestion, had first recommended at their annual meeting in 1960 because of the growing ineffectiveness of the Code. Because no rating system, including the Legion's, was capable of reviewing every movie, Sullivan reasoned that only the film industry had the means to provide parents with the information they needed to protect their children. In an effort to encourage the industry to move in this direction, the Legion had decided against condemning films like *La Dolce Vita*, *Lolita*, and *Elmer Gantry* because their distributors had voluntarily advertised them as "adults only" pictures. Most producers, however, were reluctant to endorse the scheme because it meant excluding a portion of the audience before the film was released. The industry had flirted with the concept during the panic arising out of the Legion campaign of 1934, when Warner had talked about classifying its pictures A for adults and F for family, but it had gladly dropped the idea after the establishment of the PCA appeared to satisfy its critics. The idea was no more palatable in the early 1960s, when ticket sales were less than half what they had been in the 1930s. In 1959, the MPAA had prepared a kit for theater owners and distributors to fight any legislative move toward age classification, including sample protest letters. Sullivan unsuccessfully lobbied Eric Johnston and industry leaders to adopt the idea. In addition to fearing its effect on the box office, Twentieth Century-Fox president Spyros Skouras warned Sullivan that such a system would be followed by a deluge of sex films that would give the industry a black eye.[36]

In 1962, Hollywood's reluctance to accept an age-classification standard prompted the bishops to call for legislation to allow states to establish some system that would aid parents in choosing films for their children. Rejecting Johnston's argument that self-regulation was still the best guarantor of film morality, the bishops pointed out that fewer than 200 of the 798 films licensed in New York State for public exhibition that year had a Code seal. In spite of the church's support, the MPAA beat back all the classification bills proposed in 1962 and 1963.[37]

Sullivan refused to let the issue die. The catalyst for change proved to be Warner's purchase of the rights to Edward Albee's *Who's Afraid of Virginia Woolf?* in March 1964. Geoff Shurlock, who had seen the play a few months earlier, had said that he hoped no one would bring the script to him as he wouldn't want to be the one "to butcher it." Nevertheless, when he was presented with the shooting script in October 1965, he felt he had no choice under the Code than to reject it because of its "blunt sexual references" and "coarse and sometimes vulgar language." In spite of Shurlock's warning, the studio went ahead, filming on a closed set. The PCA finally saw the film on May 2, 1966. Although Shurlock rejected it, he recommended that Warner take it to the MPAA Code Review Board in the hope it might grant it an exception, as it had done in the case of *The Pawnbroker*.[38]

While the appeal was pending, the studio, in what Spyros Skouras later characterized as the "most clever trick in the history of censorship," decided to take the film to NCOMP. Jumping at Sullivan's suggestion that some sort of age restriction would make the Legion's reviewers more receptive, Jack Warner announced that he would insist that the film be shown to "adults only." The film was seen by eighty-five reviewers, whose votes ranged from A–II to condemnation, with the largest number, forty-three voters, favoring an A–IV rating. A breakdown of the vote revealed a sharp difference between the old IFCA members and the consultants who had been chosen largely by Father Sullivan. Only 10 percent of the sixty-six consultants were in favor of condemnation, in contrast to 58 percent of the remaining IFCA reviewers. In an obvious effort to gain the greatest impact, NCOMP held off announcing its decision to award the film an A–IV rating until June 9, the day before Warner's appeal came before the review board.[39]

By that point, the association had a new president, Jack Valenti, a former special assistant to Lyndon Johnson, who had none of his predecessor's deep-seated opposition to age classification. Valenti had been able to persuade Warner to throw a sop to the board by eliminating two phrases: "screw you" and "frigging." Citing the high quality of the picture, the age limitation, and NCOMP's A–IV rating, Valenti recommended exempting the film from the Code. Spyros Skouras led the fight against passage, arguing that "God damn," "son of a bitch," and "hump the hostess" should all be removed before anyone could think of passing the film. But, in spite of his impassioned plea, all the other board members voted to grant it an exemption. Martin Quigley, Jr., in an editorial in the *Motion Picture Herald*, announced that the Code was dead and its replacement was waiting in the wings. As the *Hollywood Reporter* had predicted, Warner's decision to insist that an "adults only" clause be included in all exhibition contracts for *Who's Afraid of Virginia Woolf?* literally "forced the movie industry into classification."[40]

Church pressure had created the PCA in 1934, and, thirty-two years later, the church played a major role in hastening its demise. The decision to award *Who's Afraid of Virginia Woolf?* an A–IV rating touched off the biggest outpouring of protest letters in the history of the Legion and NCOMP. Twenty-one "outraged Catholic laymen" in La Jolla, California, petitioned the hierarchy to get rid of the "NCOMPetents." Martin Quigley, Jr., wrote to Cardinal Spellman asking him to intervene before NCOMP did any more harm. Noting that the provisions forbidding blasphemy, profanity, and obscenity had been written in 1929, he challenged Spellman to explain what had transpired over the subsequent thirty-seven years to make them acceptable screen fare. Sullivan spent the summer answering more than a thousand letters of complaint. One irate writer grumbled that he had heard that someone had tried to justify NCOMP's evaluation of *Who's Afraid of Virginia Woolf?* by equating it to the present acceptability of bikinis as compared to the beachwear of a generation before. "Having indisputable knowledge of the sins against purity engendered in several acquaintances by immodest beach dress," he declared, he was no more ready to accept the notion that current films were any less dangerous. Sullivan patiently explained to all complainants that the film's A–IV rating was by no means a recommendation and that, given the type of movies turned out by Hollywood, securing an "adults only" limitation from Warner was a positive step for NCOMP. A letter to Bishop Michael Hyde of Wilmington, Delaware, best summed up the changes Sullivan had introduced. *Who's Afraid of Virginia Woolf?* was admittedly controversial, he explained, but it did endeavor to make "a moral statement about our times consistent with a

Christian viewpoint on life." This did not mean, he went on, that "the artist is expected to play the role of a successor to the Apostles; . . . his statement will rather derive from a naturally human reflection on life, which in spite of its imperfections . . . will often be valid." And then, in something that would have shocked the creators of the Legion, he noted that, so far as adults were concerned, the A–IV classification could not have been clearer. "Beyond providing them with exact prudent guidance, we cannot intrude upon what is alone their right and obligation, namely, the exercise of individual responsibility in conscience."[41]

The review board's passage of *Who's Afraid of Virginia Woolf?* had demonstrated that the Code standard requiring a simple approval or disapproval of a film no longer fit the broad variety of movies Hollywood was producing. A few weeks after the board passed *Who's Afraid of Virginia Woolf?* Jack Valenti previewed revised industry regulations that were an abbreviated version of the old Code, easing restrictions on a number of areas including drugs, profanity, nudity, and abortion. With association members still leery about an age restriction system, the new document was a stopgap measure, authorizing Shurlock to identify certain pictures as "suggested for mature audiences."[42]

Speaking for the Episcopal Committee, Archbishop Krol applauded the industry's hesitant step in the direction of age classification. He wanted to make it clear that the church not only shared the MPAA's interest in artistic excellence but recognized that "mature audiences must not be bound to a level of entertainment fit (from a moral point of view) only for children." It would be hard to imagine McNicholas's original committee issuing such a statement, let alone Krol's affirmation of the church's dedication to the Bill of Rights, "no part of which is more important to the American people than that freedom of utterance which includes artistic expression."[43]

The industry might have stayed with the revised Code a little longer if it had not been for two 1968 Supreme Court decisions. In *Interstate v. Dallas*, the Court struck down the city's age classification system because it was too vague, but the justices' opinion suggested that a more tightly drawn law might be acceptable. On the same day, in *Ginsburg v. New York*, the justices ruled that the state could prohibit the sale of material to young people that would not be considered obscene if adults were to read it. The two decisions opened the door for state and city governments to establish their own age-classification systems, which meant that the industry would face the same potential problem it had confronted in the pre-Code days: how to deal with a variety of standards across the country. The answer was an industrywide age classification.[44]

Using the standards of the revised 1966 Code, the new system, which went into effect on November 1, 1968, established four classifications: G, for general audiences; M, contains mature material for which parental discretion was advised; R, no one under 16 admitted unless accompanied by an adult; and X, no Code seal of approval and no one under 16 admitted. The rating system marked the end of the Production Code Administration, which was replaced by the Code and Rating Administration (CARA). With the adoption of the new rating system, Geoff Shurlock retired. He had been involved with the Code almost from the beginning, and in many ways his job had been far tougher than Joe Breen's because he had to administer the Code after it lost the power and respect it once enjoyed. He was replaced by Eugene Dougherty, the senior member of the PCA staff, who had served under both Breen and Shurlock. He was a Catholic, but the appointment did not win the Catholic cheers that had accompanied Breen's appointment in 1934. Father Little, declaring that he wanted "to die in the Stations of the Cross, not looking at Gina Lollobrigida," also decided to call it quits.[45]

Consistent with the church's effort after Vatican II to expand the role of the laity, Sullivan, who took over NCOMP, appointed Richard Hirsch, the former associate editor of the interfaith publication *Guideposts*, as his assistant, the first layman to hold that position. Henry Herx, who had been involved in Catholic film education programs in Chicago, was brought in to edit the *Catholic Film Newsletter*, which provided subscribers with sophisticated reviews of the major films of the day in contrast to the simple black and white Legion listings. Two other changes further underscored NCOMP's break with the past. The IFCA, which had been relegated to a minor role in the reviewing process, quietly severed its relationship with NCOMP in 1969. A year later, Mary Looram retired after thirty-four years with the Legion and then NCOMP's executive committee.[46]

Father Sullivan had high hopes for the new rating system, which reflected the change that had begun to take shape during the Legion's last years. The *Catholic Film Newsletter* welcomed it as a means of allowing the industry to produce films that dealt with mature subjects. "We have come to a point in history when all human experience is the field for the artist's insight," the *Newsletter* declared. "There are no closed gates, no taboos in subject matter." *Darling* (1965), a story about the empty lives of the English jet set starring Julie Christie as a woman who flits from one affair to another, received NCOMP's prize for best film for mature audiences along with *Sound of Music*, which topped the general audience category. The award touched off a series of protests from Catholics, who couldn't understand, as one writer put it, how a film that exploited "adultery, self-indulgence, homosexuality, sex-aberration, promiscuity, irresponsibility, illegal abortion, disbelief in marriage, verbal profanities and obscenities plus many more despicable ideas" could garner anything but a condemnation.[47]

Subjects that in the past had aroused the church's ire were no longer an issue. *M,* which the Ohio bishops had once tried to block through court action, was now hailed as a classic in the *Catholic Film Newsletter.* Much of the old defensiveness had also faded. NCOMP awarded an A–II to the latest version of *The Three Musketeers* even though Richelieu, who had been disguised as a duke in the 1948 version, had been restored to his rightful position of cardinal. And ten years after *Storm Center* was placed in a separate classification because of its handling of book burning, *Fahrenheit 451,* which dealt with a similar theme, was awarded an A–II. Despite its frank language and theme, *Boys in the Band* received an A–IV because it offered an insight into the lives of homosexuals. *Alfie,* a film about a cynical womanizer whose selfishness leads one of his lovers to abort their child, received a similar rating because it was "a serious film which develops the unmistakable theme that to be human, an individual must accept responsibility for all his actions." And despite CARA's X rating, NCOMP gave *Midnight Cowboy* an A–IV because by exploring "the dark shadows of the human heart" it illustrated "the loneliness and alienation of our times."[48]

NCOMP had tried to hold the line on nudity, but a series of embarrassing decisions forced it to revise its policy. Twentieth Century-Fox complained when the threat of a condemnation forced it to snip a three-and-a-half-second strip of film from *Caprice* because the bottom half of actress Irene Tsu's bikini was dislodged by her dive into a swimming pool. The studio pointed out that *Ulysses* had received an A–IV despite the exposure of the bare bottoms of two of the male actors. Father Sullivan's response—that "a brief shot of a male derriere is not going to present a problem to a normal individual," but exposure of the female rear is "pruriently stimulating"—probably reflected a male bias more than any fixed moral principle. One frustrated Catholic, who demanded to know how Sullivan knew that rear-view male nudity was not stimulating to women, charged that NCOMP's decision was based on a "medieval, unchristian double standard" that was making a laughing stock out of the church. Sullivan had reluctantly placed *Blow Up,* which had been refused the seal, on the condemned list because of director Michelangelo Antonioni's unwillingness to eliminate nude scenes. Nevertheless, he indicated privately that Catholics could see an artistic film like *Blow Up* "without any scandal to themselves or others so long as they are serious about their purpose." NCOMP's handling of James Michener's *Hawaii* only added to the confusion. Although the young native women who swam and paddled out to greet the missionary's ship were bare-breasted, NCOMP awarded the film an A–III. Sullivan's defense to Archbishop Krol, that the nudity was an essential part of presenting the primitive conditions of the Hawaiians, raised more questions than it answered. One could think of a number of plots in which nudity played an essential role, and producers were doing just that.[49]

America urged NCOMP to rethink its policy, which the magazine's editors felt was based on faulty criteria. "The real problem," they declared, "is not whether there is nudity in a given film, but whether the film as a whole is likely to corrupt the adult viewer." In his annual report to the bishops in 1967, Sullivan noted his concern about the growing number of complaints from Catholic sources about NCOMP's "blanket condemnation of nude treatment" in films. Two years later, recognizing the need for a more flexible policy, the Episcopal Committee dropped the automatic condemnation of any films involving nudity.[50]

How far NCOMP had come (or fallen, in the eyes of its critics) was illustrated best in its handling of films involving priests and nuns. Where once the idea of Father O'Malley alone in a room with a woman in *Going My Way* set off alarms at the Legion office, NCOMP had no difficulty awarding an A–IV rating to the story of a priest who had a love affair with a young Protestant woman in *Act of the Heart* (1970). In 1957, the PCA had handled *Heaven Knows Mr. Allison*, the story of a nun and a Marine marooned in wartime on a Pacific island, with kid gloves. Although it was rare to send a PCA representative on location, Catholic films were an exception, and Jack Vizzard was sent to Encenada, Mexico, armed with a long list of Father Devlin's objections, to make sure that there was no hint of scandal in the story. Ten years later, *Nasty Habits*, a satire on convent life in which helmeted nuns play football while a sister embraces her clerical lover in full view of the abbess's window, had no trouble getting an A–IV.[51]

In many ways, Sullivan's job was far more difficult than his predecessors'. In the black and white world of Fathers McClafferty and Masterson, the Legion's policy was to shoot on sight anything that crossed the moral line. But distinguishing among the various shades of gray that were coming out of Hollywood during the 1960s and 1970s was a real challenge. Noting that NCOMP was still trying to enforce the Legion's rating system while trying to be relevant to an expanding film form and a new generation of sophisticated Catholic moviegoers, *Commonweal* suggested that Sullivan may have embarked on a schizophrenic course. Others simply called for a revamping of the rating system. *America*, which thought that NCOMP was slicing morality too thin with its six categories, recommended some pruning. One survey indicated that even the NCOMP reviewers had their own reservations about the system. Several favored the creation of a new category called "harmless trash" so they could stop including low-quality releases among their A–I classifications.[52]

Sullivan began to entertain the idea of putting an end to condemnations. It was now clear that a C brought attention to some films that would otherwise have faded quietly. Furthermore, the negative publicity attached to NCOMP when it condemned a film overshadowed in the public mind the more positive work it was doing. One Catholic paper, for instance, had devoted much more space to the condemnation of *Blow Up* than it did to NCOMP's 1967 best picture awards.[53]

For the moment, the industry's new rating system bothered Sullivan most. He had hoped that it would encourage more mature films while protecting young people, but he was quickly disappointed. Fitting the "notorious" films of the past into CARA's classification scheme sometimes raised eyebrows, but everyone recognized that standards had changed. No one at NCOMP questioned the board's decision to place *The Outlaw* in the G category along with Walt Disney's children's classics. After all, NCOMP had moved *Gone with the Wind* from a B to A–II a few years earlier. Awarding *Kiss Me Stupid* a G rating hurt, however, because the film had been condemned relatively recently, with Sullivan's approval. But the real problem was CARA's treatment of current films. At times it seemed to Sullivan to be the industry's lapdog rather than its watchdog. He was shocked when it backed down in the face of MGM's threat to quit the MPAA in December 1970 unless the R rating for its multi-million-dollar film *Ryan's Daughter* was changed to a G. Skouras's warning that an age classification system would open the door to more objectionable films came back to haunt him. As NCOMP's newsletter noted, the new freedom, which was meant to encourage greater artistry, had been translated into "now that the kiddies are protected . . . anything goes."[54]

Each end-of-year report painted an increasingly dismal picture. Taking a page from Jane Addams's early attempt to reach out to the neighborhood children of Hull House, two Detroit priests tried unsuccessfully to run a theater showing only family films. "There seems to be some feeling among the producers," the *Catholic Film Newsletter* noted, "that a G rating is a handicap rather than a help at the box office." Frustrated over what it viewed as CARA's failure to protect young moviegoers, NCOMP joined the Broadcasting and Film Commission of the National Council of Churches in announcing its withdrawal of support for the motion picture industry rating system in May 1971.[55]

No one in the industry seemed to care. At a time when more than half of all U.S. Catholic women reported practicing birth control, a much more serious sin in the eyes of the church than attending a condemned film, it was hard to believe that the laity was paying much attention to NCOMP's evaluations. Where once the threat of a Legion condemnation could bring the movie moguls to heel, news that NCOMP had condemned 20 percent of the films it reviewed in 1971 caused hardly a ripple within the industry. Once CARA was in place, producers worried about X ratings, but they were no longer interested in negotiating their way out of a condemnation. MGM was the last studio to employ a contact man to deal with NCOMP, and he disappeared when the studio left the movie business in the early 1970s.[56]

Nor was there a great deal of interest in NCOMP within the church. A few conservative Catholics longed for the good old days of the Legion, but for the most part NCOMP's ratings attracted little attention. At Creighton University, a Jesuit school, the faculty and students invited Otto Preminger to the campus to screen his latest film, *Hurry Sundown*, which had been condemned by NCOMP. Nor did John E. Fitzgerald, film critic for *Our Sunday Visitor*, give it a vote of confidence when he included two condemned films, *Clockwork Orange* and *The Last Picture Show*, in his 1971 ten-best list. By 1980, with a dwindling number of subscribers, the bishops decided that they could no longer afford to subsidize NCOMP. In a farewell editorial in the *Newsletter*, Father Sullivan informed his readers that the September 1 film evaluations would be the last. Since the first ratings, issued in January 1936, some 16,251 feature films had been previewed and classified. For much of that time, the Catholic church had played a major role in determining what Americans saw at the movies. "As everyone knows," Sullivan wistfully concluded, "Catholics had 'clout' in those days and because of that clout, motion pictures were a family entertainment."[57]

EPILOGUE

■■■

The decision to discontinue NCOMP did not mean the Catholic church had turned its back on the movies. The United States Catholic Conference still issues film ratings that are distributed to diocesan newspapers across the country. A glance at the reviews, which are put together by Henry Herx and his colleague Gerri Pare, suggests a certain continuity with the Legion of Decency and the NCOMP era. The old A–I through A–IV categories have survived, although the B and C ratings were replaced in 1982 by an O for "morally offensive which is reserved for films with excessive violence or graphic sexuality."

A new movie crusade began to emerge in the wake of the Catholic church's decision to terminate NCOMP. Individual church leaders like Philadelphia's Archbishop John Foley occasionally lash out at Hollywood "sleaze," and a number of Catholics, including Monsignor Paul Hayes, who served as Father Little's assistant in the Legion in the 1950s, are involved in interfaith endeavors like Morality in Media. In spite of their efforts, there is no indication that the Catholic church has any intention of reviving anything like the Legion of Decency in the 1990s. Much of the energy for the current campaign to clean up the screen comes from Christian fundamentalist groups like the Reverend Donald Wildmon's American Family Association. Its full-page ad in the *New York Times* every two months urges readers to fill out and mail a petition to the boards of directors of the various entertainment companies asking them to put a halt to the "sex, violence, filth and profanity" in the media.[1]

The best organized fundamentalist film reform effort is Ted Baehr's Christian Film and Television Commission, which resembles the Legion of Decency in many ways. In addition to asking its supporters to take an oath of decency, the commission issues a biweekly *Movieguide* advertised as a "family [formerly biblical] guide to movies and entertainment." Baehr, like the creators of the Legion, has developed a classification system, although he assesses both the artistic and moral quality of the latest releases. Entertainment ratings range from poor (one star) to excellent (four stars), while the moral evaluations are more complex, measuring eight levels from "evil: intentional blasphemy, evil &/or gross immorality" (–4) to "exemplary: no questionable elements whatsoever" (+4).

The *Movieguide*'s dual rating system is not without its problems. As Father Daly found out in the 1930s, reconciling the artistic and moral qualities of a particular film can create a dilemma for moviegoers. *The Shawshank Redemption* (1994), a movie about friendship and survival in a maximum security prison, was awarded four stars but a –3 rating because of its "violence, foul language and implied homosexual acts" along with its notion that "salvation lies within" and not with God. Readers of the *Movieguide* are also supplied with the names and addresses of the heads of the production companies for all the listed films, a tactic Father Daniel Lord introduced in 1934.[2]

A survey of *Movieguide*'s ratings for the first nine months of 1994 indicates that Hollywood has a long way to go to please Baehr. More than 60 percent of the films reviewed during that period fell into the lowest three categories: evil, bad, or extreme caution. Some of the rankings are surprising. The widely acclaimed *Schindler's List* received four stars, but it carried an extreme caution warning because of the "extensive nudity in concentration camp scenes . . . graphic sex scenes between unmarried individuals . . . [and] 19 obscenities, 8 profanities and several vulgarities."[3]

In keeping with its fundamentalist orientation, many of *Movieguide*'s reviews are punctuated with biblical references. A warning label is attached to *Mrs. Doubtfire* because of Robin Williams's disguise as an English nanny. As the reviewer notes, the film is funny if you "disregard the admonition in Deuteronomy 22:5: 'A woman must not wear men's clothing, nor a man wear women's clothing, for the Lord your God detests anyone who does this.'" *Philadelphia*, for which Tom Hanks won an Academy Award for playing a lawyer terminated by his firm after being diagnosed with AIDS, also received a biblical blast. The magazine concedes that the film poignantly argues that AIDS victims should not suffer discrimination, but it rejects the idea that homosexuality is "'just another lifestyle.'" The review reminded readers that it is "wrong and abhorrent to God and moral individuals (Romans 1:20ff)."[4]

Another parallel to the earlier Catholic crusade is Baehr's effort to persuade film and television executives to adopt a set of regulations that sounds remarkably like the old Production Code. "Evil, sin, crime and wrong-doing are not to be justified." The revised version would also prohibit, among other things, the demeaning of religion, detailed and protracted acts of violence, police dying at the hands of criminals, and sex scenes violating "common standards of decency, including sex perversion or any inference of it."[5]

Perhaps remembering the role that Bishop John J. Cantwell had played in the campaign to establish the original PCA, Baehr in early 1992 tried to persuade Cardinal Roger Mahony of Los Angeles to join him in a call for a new regulatory system. The cardinal seemed supportive at first, noting that a new code might help rectify the media's assault on morality, but he quickly backed off after a number of industry leaders criticized the plan. In a pastoral letter released in September, he rejected the idea of a return to the days of Breen's office, calling instead for voluntary efforts by producers to reduce the amount of sex and violence in films. In spite of the cardinal's continuing refusal to join the new movie crusade, Baehr remained undaunted. In an ad that appeared in the *Washington Times* in the fall of 1994, he continued to urge the cardinal to promote his code. Mahony's declaration that he had no wish to dictate what moviegoers can see is just one more indication of how much the Los Angeles archdiocese has changed since the days of Bishop Cantwell and Cardinal McIntyre. Although the cardinal made it clear that he had no intention of absolving anyone from individual moral responsibility, he declared that moviegoers must decide what to see "in the solitude of [their] own well formed conscience." In the final analysis, he concluded, just as people in a democracy get the kind of government they deserve, "the viewing public gets the kind of motion pictures it will support." If anything, the cardinal sounded much more like McIntyre's nemesis, Father Patrick Sullivan, who had responded to the criticism of his handling of *Who's Afraid of Virginia Woolf?* in a similar fashion, asserting that in the end the decision to see the film was a matter of individual conscience.[6]

No film better illustrates the contrasting approaches of Catholic and fundamentalist leaders in combatting objectionable films than their respective responses to Martin Scorsese's *The Last Temptation of Christ*, based on the novel by Nikos Kazantzakis. A passion play, *The Last Temptation of Christ* depicts Jesus wrestling with his divine mission as he imagines making love to

Mary Magdalene and becoming a parent. Although fundamentalist protests forced Paramount to withdraw support in 1983, Scorsese, after a five-year struggle, made the film with the help of Universal for less than $7 million. News that Universal was about to release the film in the summer of 1988 touched off a public demonstration of 7,500 chanting picketers outside of its studio led by Wildmon, who threatened a four-year boycott of any theater that showed it. Although the Reverend Bill Bright, president of the Campus Crusade for Christ, failed to persuade Universal to turn the film over to him so that it could be destroyed, the public protests forced General Cinema, the nation's fourth largest chain, not to book it. Threats of violence caused the police to search the bags of anyone entering Washington's Odeon Theater, although the only potential weapon they found was a soda can that the embarrassed film critic for WRC-TV carried in his briefcase.[7]

Catholic church leaders had learned from the Legion's experience that demonstrations often backfired, so when the United States Catholic Conference rated *The Last Temptation of Christ* morally objectionable, it did not call upon the laity to join in the protests. Instead, San Francisco's Archbishop John Quinn labeled picketing counterproductive and Richard Hirsch, the secretary of the Catholic Conference's communication department, suggested that priests might do more harm than good by preaching against the film from the pulpit. They had a point: the notoriety stemming from Wildmon's campaign gave a film intended for a small audience an invaluable amount of free publicity including an appearance on the cover of *Time*. According to the *New York Times*, long lines and sold-out theaters accompanied its opening in nine selected cities.[8]

Scorsese and Universal even garnered some Catholic support for their film. Father Andrew Greeley maintained that its critics subscribed to a third-century heresy called Docetism—the notion that Jesus was not really human. "Those who would exclude the poignancy and joy of erotic desire from the life of Jesus," he declared, "wish to deny Him his full humanity." Voicing his faith in Lew Wasserman, head of MCA (which owned Universal), Cardinal Mahony decried the anti-Semitism that had crept into some of the protests. Although he did not single anyone out, he clearly had in mind the 500,000 flyers sent out by Wildmon characterizing Universal as "a company whose decision-making body is dominated by non-Christians," an accusation that would not have troubled Bishop Cantwell.[9]

Although *The Last Temptation of Christ* was controversial, Hollywood has learned after a century of continuous criticism that it is hard to make a movie that doesn't offend some group. Films like *Rising Sun* (1993) have alienated Japanese-Americans, whereas *Falling Down* (1993) created a wave of Korean-American protests. Gays have also expressed their unhappiness over the inclusion of a murderous transvestite in Orion's *The Silence of the Lambs* (1991). They are not the only ones to attack Hollywood's perceived insensitivity. Charging that the films presented disabled people as maladjusted, the advocacy group Barrier Busters demonstrated outside the 1993 Academy Awards presentation over the Oscar nominations for *Scent of a Woman* and *Passion Fish*. Others concerned about the debilitating effects of Hollywood stereotypes include Wiccan Worshipers, who deplored the industry's tendency to discredit witches in films like *Hocus Pocus*. Nor are animated films safe from attack. Charges of racist insensitivity in *Aladdin* (1992) forced Disney Studios to make a substitution in the video version for the line in a song about a land "where they cut off your ears if they don't like your face." Another Disney success, *The Lion King* (1994), has taken several hits, including charges of racism because of the jive-talking hyenas who some claim stigmatize urban blacks, homophobia arising out of the villain's "effeminate" gestures, and sexism because the victims' only hope in the story is to "find a male lion who can save them."[10]

It is difficult to imagine how one would put together a new motion picture code that would accommodate the concerns of the Christian Film and Television Commission as well as the many interest groups who are unhappy about their portrayal on the screen. The experience of the Legion demonstrates how difficult it is for even a tightly organized group to decide what is immoral or too violent. In their later years, the Legion's reviewers often disagreed among themselves over pictures like *La Dolce Vita*, where their votes were evenly distributed among the A–III, B, separate classification, and condemnation categories.

For reasons they have never been able to spell out, it is has always been an article of faith among movie reformers that Hollywood has resisted meeting the need for family movies. Despite Jean Harlow's and Mae West's popularity, Father Lord insisted that college students hungered for stories about wholesome and clean national heroes like Charles Lindbergh, Bobby Jones, Babe Ruth, and Al Smith instead of the "degenerates, libertines, prostitutes and unfaithful husbands and wives" that filled the screen in the early 1930s. Similarly, Michael Medved, PBS television critic and author of *Hollywood vs. America: Popular Culture and the War on Traditional Values*, claims that much of the industry's box-office troubles stem from its failure to turn out the kind of uplifting films associated with director Frank Capra. As proof, he notes that average weekly attendance dropped from 90 million in 1948 to 18.9 million in 1991. But, Medved slides over the fact that the greatest drop, to 44 million, came between 1948 and 1953 when Capra was still around. One of Medved's favorite Capra films, *Mr. Smith Goes to Washington*, was almost blocked by Joe Breen because it showed a U.S. Senate filled with corrupt politicians controlled by lobbyists. Moreover, a recent poll conducted by the Gallup Organization for *Variety* showed that moviegoers were least likely to attend a G-rated film (6 percent) while the largest number (39 percent) preferred R-rated films.[11]

Implicit in much of the criticism of today's movie reformers who talk in glowing terms of Hollywood's golden age is that the movies of yesterday were superior to today's screen fare. However, for every *Citizen Kane* there were hundreds of films that would not have challenged the intelligence of the average twelve-year-old. With the Legion and Joe Breen looking over their shoulders, the moviemakers of yesterday tried to show life as it should be, not as it was—a world where social problems were easily solved. As soon as Bing Crosby showed up at the local parish house, juvenile delinquents became choirboys, miserly businessmen turned into philanthropists, and young couples abandoned whatever thoughts they had about premarital sex.

While there is nothing wrong with a little nostalgia, public policy based on films that were shot through rose-colored filters can be a dangerous thing. When Speaker of the House Newt Gingrich initially came under fire for his idea of placing problem children in orphanages, he cited the 1938 movie *Boys' Town* for his supporting data, not an actual group home. And those who hope to solve today's social problems by censoring movies should remember that any number of "scientific" reports like the 1933 Payne Studies also concluded that the movie theater had become a school for crime. Movie reformers and nostalgia seekers alike might be advised to remember an event that occurred during the picketing of *The Last Temptation of Christ* in New York when in response to a protester's placard charging "blasphemy," a man in the ticket line waved a sign that said, "It's only a movie."[12]

Molly Ivins likes to tell a story about John Henry Faulk. When he was seven, his mother sent him and his six-year-old friend Boots to get a chicken snake out of the hen house. They found the snake, but it frightened them so much they bolted out of the hen house, doing considerable damage to themselves in the process. When they reported back, Mrs. Faulk said, "Boys, boys, boys, what is wrong with you? You know perfectly well that a chicken snake will not hurt you." Boots, the first one to get his voice back, replied, "Yes, ma'am, but there are some things that will scare you so bad that you will hurt yourself."[13]

That is the problem with censorship. We can be so frightened of "evil" films that we look for a Legion of Decency or a Joe Breen to save us from ourselves. The Catholic church has realized the futility of a motion picture policy based on codes—which suggests that perhaps we can learn from the mistakes of the past.

NOTES

The following abbreviations appear in the notes.

AAB	Archives of the Archdiocese of Boston
AALA	Archives of the Archdiocese of Los Angeles
AAP	Archives of the Archdiocese of Providence
AMPAS	Academy of Motion Picture Arts and Sciences
DOS	David O. Selznick Archive
IFCA-CUA	International Federation of Catholic Alumnae Collection
KC	Knights of Columbus Archives
LDA	National Legion of Decency Archives
NBR	National Board of Review of Motion Pictures Collection
NCWC-CUA	National Catholic Welfare Conference Archives, Catholic University of America
NCWC-NCCB	National Catholic Welfare Conference Archives, National Catholic Conference of Bishops, Catholic University of America
NYMPD	Motion Picture Division of the New York State Archives
OWI	Office of War Information, Bureau of Motion Pictures
PCA	Production Code Administration Archives
WHP	Will H. Hays Papers
WW	Walter Wanger Papers

INTRODUCTION

1. *Life*, June 27, 1949.
2. *Christianity Today*, April 27, 1992.

CHAPTER 1. IN SEARCH OF CENSORS

1. Nye, *Unembarrassed Muse*, p. 364. Rosenzweig, *Eight Hours*, p. 196.
2. Czitrom, "Politics of Performance," p. 530. Brownlow, *Behind the Mask of Innocence*, p. xvii; Nye, *Unembarrassed Muse*, p. 372. Uricchio and Pearson, *Reframing Culture*.
3. Rosenzweig, *Eight Hours*, p. 191; Herbert A. Jump, pamphlet entitled "The Religious Possibilities of the Motion Picture" (New Britain, Conn., no date).
4. McCarthy, "Nickel Vice and Virtue," p. 43.
5. Foner, "A Martyr to His Cause," pp. 104–105; Ross, "Struggles for the Screen," p. 340.
6. *New York Times*, July 7, 1911. *The Mormon Maid* file, NBR.
7. Getlein and Gardiner, *Art of the Movies*, pp. 89–90. Lynes, *Lively Audience*, pp. 36–37. De Grazia and Newman, *Banned Films*, pp. 9–10. Brownlow, *Behind the Mask of Innocence*, p. 4.
8. Addams, *Spirit of Youth*, pp. 75–80. *Moving Picture World*, April 27, 1907. Boller and Davis, *Hollywood Anecdotes*, p. 181. Nye, *Unembarrassed Muse*, p. 373. National Board of Censorship Report, Sept. 17, 1915, NBR.
9. *Views and Films Index*, 1, Sept. 22, 1906, p. 3.
10. McCarthy, *Nickel Vice and Virtue*, p. 45; Jowett, "Moral Responsibility and Commercial Entertainment," p. 4. De Grazia and Newman, *Banned Films*, p. 9. Randall, *Censorship of the Movies*, p. 12. Jowett, "Moral Responsibility and Commercial Entertainment," p. 4.
11. *New York Times*, Dec. 24, 1908. Czitrom, "Politics of Performance," p. 537. Jowett, *Film*, p. 113.
12. Bowser, *Transformation of Cinema*, pp. 49–50; Brownlow, *Behind the Mask of Innocence*, pp. 5–6.
13. William Gaynor to Frederic C. Howe, Dec. 24, 1912; Gaynor to Rev. J. W. Moore, July 10, 1912; Gaynor to Rhinelander Waldo, Apr. 12, 1911; Mayor William Gaynor Papers, New York Municipal Archives and Research Center.
14. *Harper's Weekly*, Jan. 23, 1915, p. 87. Bowser, *Transformation of Cinema*, p. 50.
15. Fisher, "Film Censorship and Progressive Reform," p. 144. G. R. Radley to National Board of Review of Motion Pictures, May 23, 1916, Controversial Films file, NBR.
16. Courtland Smith to Will Hays, July 2, 1924, WHP. *Moving Picture World*, April 28, 1913. Jowett, "'A Capacity for Evil'" pp. 62–63.
17. Jowett, *Film*, p. 117. Maryland State Board of Motion Picture Censors annual report, 1920–21, p. 6, Maryland State Archives, Annapolis. *Exhibitor's Herald*, Feb. 1, 1919, Dec. 15, 1917, May 11, June 29, 1918.
18. Rosenzweig, *Eight Hours*, p. 205. De Grazia and Newman, *Banned Films*, p. 14. Brownlow, *Behind the Mask of Innocence*, p. 9.
19. Brownlow, *Behind the Mask of Innocence*, p. xviii.
20. *Catholic Messenger*, May 10, 17, 31, 1907, Feb. 11, 1910. Rosenzweig, *Eight Hours*, pp. 205–207.
21. *Pilot*, Sept. 2, 1916, March 17, 1917. Keyser and Keyser, *Hollywood and the Catholic Church*, pp. 19–20. *America*, Jan. 4, 1913. McAvoy, *History of the Catholic Church*, p. 362.
22. Jowett, *Film*, p. 69. O'Brien, *Public Catholicism*, pp. 128–129, 153. Fogarty, "Public Patriotism," pp. 1–48.

23. Brandt, *No Magic Bullet*, pp. 62, 73.
24. Williams, *American Catholics in the War*, pp. 170–171.
25. Brandt, *No Magic Bullet*, p. 112; Rev. John J. Burke to Newton D. Baker, June 12, 1918, Executive Secretary files, NCWC-CUA. Lee A. Stone to Rev. John J. Burke, Aug. 21, 1918, NCWC-CUA.
26. Thomas D. Eliot letter, Nov. 27, 1917; "Comments on Pamphlet 'Venereal Disease,'" no date; NCWC-CUA.
27. Brandt, *No Magic Bullet*, pp. 68–69; Kuhn, *Cinema, Censorship, and Sexuality*, p. 52.
28. Malcolm L. McBride to Walter G. Hooke, June 18, 1918; Hooke to John P. Peters, July 12, 1918; Peters to Frederick H. Whitin, June 27, 1918; NCWC-CUA. Rev. John J. Burke to Major William F. Snow, July 27, 1918; NCWC-CUA.
29. Brandt, *No Magic Bullet*, pp. 80–81; Hobson, *Uneasy Virtue*, p. 175.
30. *End of the Road* is in the Motion Picture Division of the National Archives (RG200). Brandt, *No Magic Bullet*, p. 83; Kuhn, *Cinema, Censorship, and Sexuality*, p. 52. Francis P. Sloan to Edward H. Griffith, Nov. 13, 1918, NCWC-CUA.
31. Rev. John J. Burke to Raymond Fosdick, Oct. 12, 1918, NCWC-CUA.
32. William F. Snow to Raymond Fosdick, Oct. 26, 1918; Fosdick to Rev. John J. Burke, Oct. 29, 1918; NCWC-CUA.
33. Brownlow, *Behind the Mask of Innocence*, p. 517, N. 161.
34. Lashley and Watson, *A Psychological Study of Motion Pictures*, p. 8. Brownlow, *Behind the Mask of Innocence*, pp. 61–62.
35. *End of the Road* file, March 7, 1919; *Open Your Eyes* file, no date; NBR.
36. *Moving Picture World*, April 12, 1919. *Exhibitor's Herald*, May 10, 31, Nov. 8, 1919.
37. *Exhibitor's Herald*, June 14, 1919. *Moving Picture World*, Jan. 4, 1919. Campbell, *Reel America and World War I*, pp. 118–119. Brownlow, *Behind the Mask of Innocence*, p. 68.
38. Charles I. Denechud to "Dear Sir," Jan. 1, 1919, NCWC-CUA.
39. John F. Gilbert to Rev. John J. Burke, Feb. 28, 1919; Burke to Gilbert, March 29, 1919; Gilbert to Burke, April 22, 1919; NCWC-CUA. Brownlow, *Behind the Mask of Innocence*, p. 62.
40. John B. Peters to William F. Snow, June 25, 1919, NCWC-CUA.
41. Rev. John J. Burke to Mr. Gilchrist, May 2, 1919, NCWC-CUA.
42. Judge Kapper's decision can be found in NCWC-CUA.
43. "Fit to Win," June 1919, NCWC-CUA. Brownlow, *Behind the Mask of Innocence*, p. 62. Rupert Blue to National Board of Review, Aug. 15, 1919; National Board of Review decision, no date, NBR. *New York Herald*, Aug. 4, 1919.
44. Fogarty, *Patterns of Episcopal Leadership*, p. 215. Fogarty, "Public Patriotism," p. 30. McShane, *"Sufficiently Radical" Catholicism*, pp. 85–88. O'Brien, *Public Catholicism*, pp. 154–155. Dumenil, "The Tribal Twenties," pp. 7, 8, 32. *NCWC Bulletin* 2, Nov. 1920.
45. Bishop John Murray to Rev. John J. Burke, June 8, 1928, NCWC-CUA.
46. *NCWC Bulletin* 1, Oct. 1919, pp. 23–24; *NCWC Bulletin* 4, Jan. 1923, p. 12. An Ursuline Religious, "Movies and the Young," attached to letter from Francis Sullivan to Rev. George W. Mundelein, June 22, 1918, Mundelein Papers.
47. Karl K. Kitchen, excerpt, no date, KC. *Brooklyn Tablet*, April 9, 1921.
48. Rev. Edward J. Garesche, S. J., "Pastors and the Censorship of Movies," *Ecclesiastical Review* 60, March 1919, pp. 257, 259. *Brooklyn Tablet*, Jan. 29, May 10, June 14, Sept. 23, 1922. *NCWC Bulletin* 2, February 1921, p. 18. *New York Times*, Jan. 19, 1924.
49. *NCWC Bulletin* 18, Dec. 1926, p. 9. *Moving Picture World*, May 21, 1921, p. 258. MPPDA release "To Catholic Editors," June 10, 1926; Rev. John B. Kelly to Will Hays, April 29, 1925; WHP.

50. Minutes of the NCWC Administrative Board, April 15, 1926; Michael Williams to Rev. John J. Burke, Sept. 3, 1919; NCWC-CUA.
51. *NCWC Bulletin* 1, Oct. 1919, pp. 23–24.
52. Charles McMahon to Bishop William T. Russell, Nov. 29, 1919, NCWC-CUA. *NCWC Bulletin* 1, Aug. 1919, p. 12. Charles McMahon, report, June 8, 1921; "Address to be delivered previous to the showing of the NCWC film," no date; McMahon to Rev. John J. Burke, Nov. 25, 1919; Ed Murtaugh to Marie Murtaugh, Sept. 25, 1919; NCWC-CUA.
53. Charles McMahon to Rev. John J. Burke, Oct. 19, 1922, NCWC-CUA.

CHAPTER 2. WHEN IRISH EYES WEREN'T SMILING

1. Rosenbloom, "Between Reform and Regulation," p. 320. Jowett, *Film*, p. 155. *Exhibitor's Herald*, May 24, May 31, 1919.
2. *Baltimore Sun*, Oct. 24, 1920.
3. Jowett, *Film*, pp. 130, 157–158.
4. *Variety*, April 18, 1921.
5. Jowett, *Film*, p. 158. "Form Letter," Jan. 1, 1925, WHP. Wexman, "Suffering and Suffrage," p. 58.
6. *Exhibitor's Herald*, Aug. 27, 1921. *Variety*, Aug. 19, 1921.
7. William Jennings Bryan to Will Hays, March 7, 1923, WHP. *New York Times*, Dec. 25, 26, 1921.
8. Unidentified magazine clipping, Feb. 10, 1923, WHP.
9. *Exhibitor's Herald*, Oct. 1, 1921. *Moving Picture World*, Sept. 24, 1921. Sklar, *Movie-Made America*, p. 79.
10. *Boston Globe*, Nov. 4, 1922. Goodwin, *Fitzgeralds and Kennedys*, p. 341. Jack Connolly to Will Hays, July 12, 1922; unsigned letter to Hays, Oct. 5, 1922; WHP. John M. Casey to Wilton Barrett, Oct. 17, 31, 1922, NBR.
11. Moley, *Hays Office*, p. 54. Courtland Smith, personal and confidential report to Will Hays, Sept. 29, 1922, WHP.
12. *Pilot*, May 13, 1922. *Variety*, Sept. 1, 1922.
13. *NCWC Bulletin* 2, Feb. 1921, p. 19; March 1921, pp. 23–24. Charles McMahon to Rev. John J. Burke, Dec. 23, 1920; Burke to McMahon, Dec. 28, 1929; NCWC-CUA.
14. *Pilot*, May 13, 1922. B. Preston Clarke to Robert T. O'Brien, Oct. 2, 1922, Massachusetts file, NBR. "A New Era in Motion Picture Management," *NCWC Bulletin* 4, July 1922, p. 13. Jack Connolly to Will Hays, July 12, 1922, WHP. Charles McMahon to Rev. John J. Burke, Oct. 19, 1922, NCWC-CUA.
15. Jowett, *Film*, p. 167. *Variety*, Oct. 28, 1953. Leff and Simmons, *Dame in the Kimono*, pp. 4–7. Koszarski, *An Evening's Entertainment*, p. 201. Secretary of the Virginia Division of Motion Picture Censorship to Oscar Michaux, March 12, 1925; see list of banned films, no date; Virginia State Archives, Richmond.
16. "Report on State Censorship," Jan. 23, 1925, WHP. *Exhibitor's Herald* and *Moving Picture World*, Aug. 25, 1928. *Variety*, March 7, 1928.
17. Chair of the Campaign Committee to Hal Roach, April 26, 1919, Hal Roach Collection, USC. Charles Pettijohn to Will Hays, Feb. 10, 1927; Fred Beetson to Will Hays, Feb. 18, 28, 1925; WHP.
18. Public Relations Committee, "The Plan," Feb. 1924; Fred Beetson to Will Hays, March 16, 1928, WHP.

19. Jowett, *Film*, p. 175.
20. Moley, *Hays Office*, pp. 57–58. Will Hays to Hal Roach, May 26, 1926, Roach Collection, USC.
21. Maltby, "'To Prevent the Prevalent Type of Book,'" pp. 557, 562. Maurice McKenzie to Will Hays, April 24, 1926, WHP.
22. "The Motion Picture Situation and the Need for Federal Regulation of the Industry," 1925; report beginning "My Dear Mr. . . . ," Jan. 7, 1925, WHP.
23. *Exhibitor's Herald*, July 16, 1923.
24. Charles McMahon to Rev. John J. Burke, Oct. 19, 1922, Feb. 15, 1923; McMahon to Msgr. Ready, April 9, 1940; McMahon to Burke, April 19, 1923; Burke to McMahon, April 28, 1923; NCWC-CUA.
25. Charles McMahon to Msgr. Ready, April 9, 1940; McMahon to Rev. John J. Burke, Nov. 25, 1919; NCWC-CUA. *NCWC Bulletin* 6, Sept. 1924, pp. 12–13; Jan. 1925, p. 8.
26. *NCWC Bulletin* 6, Sept. 1924, p. 13, Apr. 1925, p. 8.
27. Rev. Placid Schmid to Rev. John J. Burke, Feb. 19, 1925; Burke to Schmid, Feb. 24, 1925; NCWC-CUA. *NCWC Bulletin* 6, Jan. 1925, p. 8.
28. *Quarterly Bulletin* 3, March 1920, pp. 35–37. Rita McGoldrick, report, Nov. 12, 1927, *America* Archives, Georgetown University, Washington, D.C.
29. Wilton Barrett to Rita McGoldrick, June 20, 1926, NBR.
30. R. H. Cochrane to Will Hays, Jan. 22, 1923; Carl Laemmle to Hays, Jan. 13, 1923; WHP. *NCWC Bulletin* 6, June 1924, p. 13. Rita McGoldrick to Rev. Edward J. Cahill, Dec. 4, 1926, Mundelein Papers.
31. Fred Beetson, report, Jan. 28, 1926, Hal Roach Collection. Carl Milliken to Rita McGoldrick, April 7, 1927; Milliken to McGoldrick, May 16, 1927, Oct. 19, 1927; *America* Archives.
32. Rita McGoldrick, report, Nov. 12, 1927, *America* Archives. *Texas 100 Percent American*, Oct. 6, 1922. George Lockwood to Will Hays, April 13, 1926, WHP.
33. Proceedings of the stockholders' meeting, June 16, 1924; Jason Joy to Will Hays, Jan. 13, 1926; WHP.
34. *Quarterly Review* 9, Jan. 1926, p. 26. President's annual report, March 18, 1927, WHP. Charles McMahon to Pat Scanlan, Jan. 25, 1926, NCWC-CUA. Jowett, "'A Capacity for Evil,'" pp. 74–75. Carl Milliken to Will Hays, Nov. 16, 1926, WHP.
35. Will Hays, annual report, March 1926, WHP.
36. Garesche, "Parish Priest and Moving Pictures," pp. 470–471.
37. *Harrison's Reports*, Aug. 10, 1929. John M. Casey to Wilton Wilcox, July 26, 31, 1927, NBR. See Walsh, "*The Callahans and the Murphys*," pp. 33–45.
38. *Los Angeles Times*, June 17, 19, 1927. Schatz, *Genius of the System*, p. 51.
39. The film of *The Callahans and the Murphys* no longer exists. Various versions of the script can be found in PCA; MGM Files, Special Collections, USC; and Motion Picture Division, NYMPD.
40. Marion, *Off with Their Heads*, p. 157. A list of the cuts made by the state boards can be found in *The Callahans and the Murphys* file, NYMPD. *Selected Guide Magazine* 11, July 1927, p. 12; Wilton Wilcox to John M. Casey, July 28, 1927, NBR.
41. *Los Angeles Times*, June 16, 1927. *Variety*, July 13, 1927. *Film Daily*, July 24, 1927. *Los Angeles Record*, quoted in *Motion Picture News*, July 7, 1927. Sherwood review in Audrey Chamberlain scrapbooks, vol. 19, p. 118, AMPAS.
42. *Tidings*, July 15, 1927.
43. Marion, *Off with Their Heads*, p. 159.

44. Eddie Mannix to Mr. Horan, July 14, 1927, *The Callahans and the Murphys* file, PCA.
45. Fred Beetson to Darryl Zanuck, June 29, 1927, *Irish Hearts* file, Warner Collection, USC. Jason Joy to Will Hays, July 25, 1927, *The Callahans and the Murphys* file, PCA.
46. Jason Joy to Will Hays, July 22, 1927; unsigned to W. D. Kelly, July 19, 1927; Eddie Mannix telegram, July 22, 1927, *The Callahans and the Murphys* file, PCA. Carl Milliken to Rita McGoldrick, Oct. 7, 1927, NCWC-CUA.
47. Charles McMahon to Carl Milliken, July 25, 1927, NCWC-CUA. McMahon, news release, July 25, 1927, *The Callahans and the Murphys* file, PCA. Jason Joy to Eddie Mannix, Aug. 8, 1927, NBR. Joy to Will Hays, Aug. 26, 1925, WHP.
48. John M. Casey to Wilton Wilcox, July 26, 31, 1927, NBR. W. D. Kelly to resident managers, July 26, 1927; Kelly to James Wingate, Aug. 8, 1927, *The Callahans and the Murphys* file, NYMPD. A description of the cuts ordered by the New York censors can be found in Eddie Mannix to Jason Joy, July 23, 1927, *The Callahans and the Murphys* file, NYMPD.
49. Carl Milliken to Jason Joy, Oct. 6, 1927, *The Callahans and the Murphys* file, PCA. *Milwaukee Journal*, Aug. 26, 1927.
50. William A. Orr to James Wingate, Aug. 5, 1927, *The Callahans and the Murphys* file, NYMPD. *Gaelic American*, July 30, 1927.
51. Charles McMahon to Rev. John J. Burke, Aug. 4, 1927; McMahon to Charles F. Dolle, July 25, 1927; NCWC-CUA.
52. Eddie Mannix to Frank J. Barry, July 15, 1927; William A. Orr to Will Hays, Aug. 23, 1927; *The Callahans and the Murphys* file, PCA. Orr to James Wingate, Aug. 5, 1927, *The Callahans and the Murphys* file, NYMPD.
53. *Irish World and Independent Liberator*, Aug. 13, 1927. *Gaelic American*, Sept. 3, 1927. *Baltimore Catholic Review*, Sept. 2, 1927.
54. *Irish World and Independent Liberator*, undated clipping, NBR. *Gaelic American*, Sept. 3, 1927. *Moving Picture World*, Oct. 8, 1927, pp. 339–340. *Irish World and Independent Liberator*, July 30, Aug. 27, 1927. *Gaelic American*, Aug. 6, 1927.
55. *New York Times*, Aug. 25, 26, 27, Sept. 6, 1927. *Bronx Home News*, Aug. 29, 1927. *New York Daily News*, Sept. 1, 1927. *Gaelic American*, Sept. 3, 1927. Unidentified trade paper clipping, *The Callahans and the Murphys* file, Motion Picture Division, Museum of Modern Art, New York. *Life*, quoted in *Exhibitor's Herald*, Oct. 15, 1927.
56. *Gaelic American*, Sept. 17, 1927.
57. *Gaelic American*, Sept. 10, 24, 1927. *Irish World and Independent Liberator*, Aug. 13, 1927.
58. Carl Milliken to Jason Joy, Aug. 26, 1927, *The Callahans and the Murphys* file, PCA. *Gaelic American*, Aug. 13, 1927. *Exhibitor's Herald*, July 6, 13, 20, Aug. 20, Sept. 3, 17, 1927. *Exhibitor's Daily*, Aug. 13, 1927. *San Bernadino* (Calif.) *Sun*, Oct. 5, 1927.
59. Camden R. McAttee to Hinckle C. Hays, Sept. 13, 1927, Will Hays Collection, Indiana State Library, Indianapolis. *Tidings*, July 29, Nov. 11, 1927. *New York Times*, Sept. 2, 7, 10, 17, 1927. *Gaelic American*, Aug. 20, Sept. 3, 10, 1927. *Morning Telegraph*, Aug. 27, 1927. James Wingate to W. D. Kelly, Sept. 6, 1927, *The Callahans and the Murphys* file, NYMPD.
60. James Wingate to John T. Kelly, Sept. 12, 1927, *The Callahans and the Murphys* file, NYMPD. *New York Times*, Oct. 24, 1927. *Variety*, Nov. 2, 1927.
61. *Catholic Standard and Times*, Nov. 5, 1927. *New York Times*, Nov. 19, 1927. *Gaelic American*, Nov. 10, 17, 24, 1927, Jan. 7, 14, 28, 1928. *Exhibitor's Herald* and *Moving Picture World*, Jan. 7, March 24, 1928.
62. Unsigned note, Nov. 22, 1927, WHP.
63. NCWC news release, Aug. 8, 1927, NCWC-CUA. *Motion Picture News*, Sept. 7, Nov. 11, 1927.

Exhibitor's Herald, July 23, Aug. 6, 1927. *Exhibitor's Daily*, Aug. 13, 1927. James J. Barrett to James Wingate, Aug. 24, 1927, *The Callahans and the Murphys* file, NYMPD.

64. Albert Howson to James Wingate, July 5, 1927; Howson to "All branch managers," July 28, 1927, *Irish Hearts* file, NYMPD. Jason Joy memorandum, Aug. 16, 1927; Carl Milliken to Joy, Oct. 6, 1927, *The Callahans and the Murphys* file, PCA. First Division Pictures to Motion Picture Commission, Nov. 16, 1927, *Finnigan's Ball* file, NYMPD. *Mother Machree* advertisement, *Exhibitor's Herald*, March 24, 1928.
65. Assistant Secretary, Public Relations Committee, to Jason Joy, Dec. 23, 1927, *The Callahans and the Murphys* file, AMPAS. Joy to Will Hays, Feb. 4, 1928, WHP.

CHAPTER 3. A NEW MORAL CODE

1. *New York Times*, May 21, 1926. Marquis, *Hopes and Ashes*, p. 51. Walker, *Shattered Silents*, p. 6.
2. Walker, *Shattered Silents*, p. 58. Allen and Gomery, *Film History, Theory, and Practice*, pp. 195–196. Jenkins, "'Shall We Make It for New York or for Distribution?'" p. 38.
3. *Variety*, July 21, 1929.
4. Jowett, *Film*, pp. 466–467. Jason Joy, annual report, 1929, AMPAS.
5. Inglis, *Freedom of the Movies*, p. 117. Jason Joy to Will Hays, Feb. 4, 1928, WHP. Shenton, *Public Relations of the Motion Picture Industry*, pp. 126–127.
6. Black, "Hollywood Censored," p. 170. Jason Joy to Will Hays, May 19, 1928, WHP. Joy, annual report, 1928, AMPAS.
7. Carl Laemmle to Irving Thalberg, no date; R. H. Cochrane to Will Hays, April 5, 1927, WHP.
8. *Variety*, July 24, 1929. R. H. Cochrane to Will Hays, April 5, 1927; Harry Warner to Hays, Sept. 24, 1929, WHP.
9. *Churchman*, Sept. 7, 1929, p. 9. Arthur deBra to Carl Milliken, Jan. 23, 1930, WHP. Will Hays, speech, Sept. 26, 1929, WHP. *Roanoke News*, June 21, 1929.
10. Will Hays, President's Report, June 20, 1928; Hays, President's Report, Jan.–March, 1929, WHP.
11. Memorandum to Hays, June 13, 1928; Jason Joy to Will Hays, Jan. 3, 1928; WHP. Rita McGoldrick to Carl Milliken, Oct. 12, 1927; Rev. Francis Talbot to McGoldrick, Nov. 28, 1927, *America* Archives.
12. Carl Milliken, press release, Dec. 16, 1928, WHP. Rita McGoldrick, report, Nov. 27, 1928, *America* Archives. *Quarterly Bulletin* 12, Dec. 1929, p. 17.
13. Rita McGoldrick, "For Your Confidential Information," Nov. 17, 1930, Lord Papers. Gordon White to McGoldrick, Feb. 19, 1931; McGoldrick to Joe Brandt, Nov. 7, 1929; IFCA-CUA. *America*, Nov. 24, 1928.
14. Rita McGoldrick to Mrs. James Sheeran, Dec. 29, 1929, IFCA-CUA.
15. Philip Burke, "Our Celluloid Teachers," *Columbia*, December 1930. Rev. J. Russell Hughes to Pat Scanlan, Sept. 24, 1937, Parsons Papers. Fox Movietone reviews, Jan. 4, 1929; Rita McGoldrick to Edward Percy Howard, Jan. 9, 1929; McGoldrick to Mrs. Antonio Gonzales, Jan. 18, 1929; Cardinal Hayes Papers, Archives of the Archdiocese of New York.
16. Rita McGoldrick, report, Nov. 17, 1930, Lord Papers. *Quarterly Bulletin* 12, June 1929, p. 38. Carl E. Milliken, "Memo for Mr. Platten," no date, WHP.
17. Maltby, "*King of Kings*," p. 209. McDonough, *Men Astutely Trained*, pp. 86–88, 169.
18. *Variety*, Oct. 13, 1926.

19. Rev. Daniel Lord, report attached to letter from Rev. Joseph Husslein, Jr., to Rev. John J. Burke, April 26, 1927, NCWC-CUA. Keyser and Keyser, *Hollywood and the Catholic Church*, p. 22.
20. Rev. Daniel Lord, report, attached to letter from Husslein to Burke, April 26, 1927, NCWC-CUA.
21. Ibid.; Lord to Burke, no date, NCWC-CUA. Lord to Rev. Wilfrid Parsons, April 12, 1927, *America* Archives.
22. Rev. Joseph Husslein, Jr., to Rev. John J. Burke, April 26, 1927, NCWC-CUA.
23. Cecil B. deMille to Rev. Daniel Lord, May 7, 1927; deMille to Lord, March 17, 1927, Cecil B. deMille Collection, Harold B. Lee Library, Brigham Young University. Lord to Rev. John J. Burke, attached to letter from Rev. Joseph Husslein to Burke, Apr. 26, 1927, NCWC-CUA. Alfred M. Cohen to Carl Milliken, Dec. 21, 1927; Public Relations Committee report, 1927, WHP.
24. Rita McGoldrick to "Journée de Cinéma," June 29, 1932, *America* Magazine Archives. Carl Milliken, report, Sept. 19, 1928, WHP.
25. Rev. Daniel Lord to Rev. Wilfrid Parsons, April 27, 1927, *America* Archives. Maltby, "*King of Kings*," p. 211.
26. Jason Joy, memorandum, Aug. 16, 1927; Carl Milliken to Joy, Oct. 6, 1927; Joy to Will Hays, Nov. 12, 1929; Cardinal Hayes speech quoted Oct. 25, 1929; WHP.
27. Fogarty, "Public Patriotism," p. 32. Fogarty, *Patterns of Episcopal Leadership*, p. 206. Charles Byrne to Msgr. Sheil, June 16, 1926, Mundelein Papers.
28. *New York Times*, Dec. 8, 1965. Doran, "Mr. Breen Confronts the Dragons," pp. 327–330. *America*, Aug. 8, 1934.
29. Leff and Simmons, *Dame in the Kimono*, p. 8. Charles Pettijohn to Will Hays, Feb. 28, 1929, WHP.
30. Maltby, "The Production Code and the Hays Office," p. 46. *Exhibitor's Herald*, April 7, 1917, March 1, 1919. Martin Quigley to Gabriel Hess, Feb. 12, 1919, NBR. *Exhibitor's Herald World*, June 1, 1929.
31. Francis Sullivan to Rev. George Mundelein, June 22, 1918, Mundelein Papers. *New World*, June 7, 1918. *Moving Picture World*, May 31, 1919. Doran, "Mr. Breen Confronts the Dragon," p. 327. Frank J. Wilstach to Jason Joy, April 2, 1929, *Trial of Mary Dugan* file, PCA.
32. Charles C. Pettijohn to Will Hays, Nov. 5, 1926, WHP.
33. *NCWC Bulletin*, 2, April 1921, p. 29. Rev. FitzGeorge Dinneen to Cardinal Mundelein, July 30, 1929; W. R. Sheehan to Mundelein, May 28, 1924, Mundelein Papers. Rev. FitzGeorge Dinneen to Cardinal Mundelein, July 30, 1929; Chicago Exhibitors' Association to Mundelein, June 22, 1929, Mundelein Papers.
34. Rev. FitzGeorge Dinneen to Cardinal Mundelein, July 30, 1929, Mundelein Papers. *New World*, Oct. 11, 1929.
35. Jason Joy to Will Hays, Nov. 12, 1929, WHP.
36. Stephen Vaughn, "Morality and Entertainment," p. 41. Wilfrid Parsons to Joe Breen, Oct. 4, 1932, Parsons Papers. *Harrison's Reports*, Jan. 25, 1930. Martin Quigley to Pat Scanlan, Sept. 1, 1926, Quigley Papers.
37. Doran, "Mr. Breen Confronts the Dragon," p. 327. Lord, *Played by Ear*, p. 275. Rev. Daniel Lord to Martin Quigley, Dec. 7, 1929, Lord Papers.
38. Wilfrid Parsons, "Authorship of Movie Code," *America*, May 26, 1956. Martin Quigley, "Statement of Origin, Development, and Introduction to the Industry of the *Motion Picture Production Code*," July 18, 1946, Quigley Papers. Martin Quigley, "The Motion Picture Production Code," *America*, March 10, 1956.

39. Vaughn, "Morality and Entertainment," pp. 57–60.
40. Vaughn, "Financiers, Movie Producers, and the Church," p. 203.
41. Vaughn, "Financiers, Movie Producers, and the Church," p. 214.
42. Martin Quigley to Raymond Moley, March 14, 1945, Ramsaye Collection.
43. Rev. Wilfrid Parsons to Martin Quigley, March 27, 1930, Quigley Papers.
44. Martin Quigley to Rev. Daniel Lord, March 6, 1930, Lord Papers. Rev. Wilfrid Parsons to Quigley, March 27, 1930, Quigley Papers. Jowett, *Film*, p. 241.
45. *Kalamazoo Gazette*, Oct. 6, 1929. "This Is What They're Saying," MPPDA report, April 12, 14, 1930, WHP. *New Britain Herald*, April 2, 1930.
46. *Atlanta Constitution*, April 3, 1930. *Boston Traveler*, April 2, 1930. *Baltimore Sun*, April 12, 1930. *Dallas Morning News*, April 13, 1930. Rev. Wilfrid Parsons to Martin Quigley, March 27, 1930. "This Is What They're Saying," MPPDA report, April 14, 1930, WHP.
47. Wilton Barrett, no date, NBR. *Time*, June 29, 1931.
48. *Exhibitors' Herald World*, June 14, 1930.
49. Rev. Wilfrid Parsons to Rev. Francis Talbot, April 3, 1930, Parsons Papers. *Commonweal*, April 16, 1930. *Columbia*, February, June, 1931.
50. Martin Quigley to Cardinal McNicholas, no date, Quigley Papers. Joe Breen to Rev. Wilfrid Parsons, June 12, 1931, *America* Archives. Rita McGoldrick, radio broadcast, April 30, 1930, *America* Archives.
51. Martin Quigley to Joe Breen, June 5, 1930; Breen to Quigley, Oct. 7, 22, 30, Nov. 25, 1930, WHP. Breen to Quigley, June 21, 1930, Quigley Papers. Breen to Rev. Wilfrid Parsons, June 12, 1931, Parsons Papers. *Motion Picture Herald*, Aug. 22, 1931.
52. *America*, April 19, 1930. Rev. Wilfrid Parsons to Cardinal Hayes, July 17, 1930, *America* Archives. Martin Quigley to Rev. Daniel Lord, Feb. 28, March 1, 1930, Lord Papers. Rev. Wilfrid Parsons to Rev. Francis Talbot, April 3, 1930, Parsons Papers.
53. Rev. Daniel Lord to Martin Quigley, Feb. 14, 1930; Quigley to Lord, Feb. 14, 28, 1930; Lord to Quigley, March 17, 1930, Quigley Papers. Rev. Wilfrid Parsons to Quigley, March 27, 1930, Parsons Papers. Parsons to Rev. Francis Talbot, April 30, 1930, *America* Archives.
54. C. C. Pettijohn to Quigley, March 19, 1930, Quigley Papers. Rev. FitzGeorge Dinneen to Cardinal Mundelein, no date, Mundelein Papers. Rev. Wilfrid Parsons to Rev. Francis Talbot, April 3, 1930, *America* Archives.
55. Joseph Breen to Martin Quigley, June 21, 1930; Quigley to Pat Scanlan, Aug. 4, 1936, Quigley Papers. Rev. Daniel Lord to Cardinal Mundelein, May 24, 1930, Mundelein Papers. *America*, Nov. 1, 1930.
56. Rev. Wilfrid Parsons to Rev. Francis Talbot, April 3, 1930, *America* Magazine Archives.
57. Jowett, *Film*, p. 247. Rev. Wilfrid Parsons to Will Hays, December 5, 1931, *America* Magazine Archives. *Catholic Review*, Nov. 21, 1930.

CHAPTER 4. DISILLUSION

1. Rev. Daniel Lord to Cardinal George Mundelein, May 14, 1931, Mundelein Papers. Will Hays to H. L. Clarke, Aug. 19, 1931, WHP.
2. Doran, "Mr. Breen Confronts the Dragon," p. 327. Glenn Griswold to Glendon Allvine, Aug. 25, 1931, *Bad Girl* file, PCA. Martin Quigley to Joe Breen, March 3, 1931; J. K., memorandum to Will Hays, Aug. 5, 1932, WHP.
3. E. J. Montaigne to B. P. Schulberg, Dec. 23, 1930, DOS. Katherine K. Vandervoort to Carl Milliken, Nov. 18, 1938, *Frankenstein* file, PCA.
4. *Motion Picture Herald*, April 4, 1931. Jason Joy, annual report, April 29, 1931, AMPAS. *Brooklyn*

Tablet, Jan. 9, 1935. Rita McGoldrick, radio report, NBR. IFCA, "Statement of Policy and Procedure," 1931, IFCA-CUA.

5. Maltby, "Censorship and Adaptation," pp. 559–560, 564. Jason Joy to Maurice McKenzie, Sept. 19, 1930, *An American Tragedy* file, PCA. B. P. Schulberg to Jesse Lasky, June 2, 1930, Dreiser Papers.
6. Lamar Trotti, "Note on *An American Tragedy,*" no date; Mark Larkin to Jason Joy, Jan. 21, 1931; Will Hays to B. P. Schulberg, April 25, 1931; Joy, memorandum, May 18, 1931; John Wilson to Will Hays, May 25, 1931; Hays to Wilson, May 26, 1931; Hays to Jesse Lasky, July 15, 1931; *An American Tragedy* file, PCA.
7. Theodore Dreiser, draft of article, "What Are America's Powerful Motion Picture Companies Doing?" Dreiser Papers.
8. Jason Joy, annual report, March 1, 1932, AMPAS. Lamar Trotti to Joy, Oct. 28, 1931, *Are These Our Children?* file, PCA.
9. Rev. Daniel Lord to Martin Quigley, April 30, 1930. Lord to Cardinal Mundelein, May 14, 1931, Mundelein Papers. Lord, report, "The Code—One Year Later," April 23, 1931, Lord Papers.
10. Ibid. *Motion Picture Herald*, April 25, 1931. Schatz, *Genius of the System*, p. 159. Izod, *Hollywood and the Box Office*, p. 96.
11. *Motion Picture Herald*, Feb. 7, 1931. Rev. Wilfrid Parsons to Carl Milliken, June 23, 1931, *America* Archives.
12. Lamar Trotti to Will Hays, April 14, 1931, WHP. Leff and Simmons, *Dame in the Kimono,* p. 15. James Wingate to First National Pictures, Dec. 8, 1930, NYMPD.
13. Shadoian, *Dreams and Dead Ends*, ch. 1. Clarens, *Crime Movies*, pp. 57–61. Lord, report, "The Code—One Year Later," April 23, 1931, Lord Papers. Donald Ewing to Maurice McKenzie, April 22, 1931, *Little Caesar* file, PCA.
14. *Time*, Aug. 10, 1931. Clarens, *Crime Movies*, p. 89. Black, "Hollywood Censored," n23, pp. 187–188.
15. August Vollmer to Will Hays, April 20, 1931, WHP. *Harrison's Reports*, April 13, 1935. Maltby, "'Baby Face,'" p. 30.
16. Jason Joy to Joe Breen, Dec. 15, 1931, *Possessed* file, PCA. Cecil B. deMille to Rev. Daniel Lord, Jan. 13, 1933, deMille Collection. Lord, report, "The Code—One Year Later," April 23, 1931, Lord Papers.
17. See Jacobs, *Wages of Sin.* Lamar Trotti to Jason Joy, Oct. 22, 1931, *Possessed* file, PCA.
18. Lamar Trotti to Jason Joy, Oct. 22, 1931; Joy to Will Hays, Dec. 13, 1931, *Possessed* file, PCA.
19. Bergman, *We're in the Money*, pp. 52–53. Lamar Trotti to Will Hays, Aug. 1, 1931, *Possessed* file, PCA; Trotti to Jason Joy, July 23, 1931, *Back Street* file, PCA. Maltby, "'Baby Face,'" pp. 31–33. *San Francisco Chronicle*, May 24, 1993.
20. Mrs. Alonzo Richardson to Hays Office, Dec. 3, 1931, *Possessed* file, PCA. *Christian Century*, Jan. 27, 1932. Jason Joy, report, Feb. 4, 1931, WHP.
21. *Motion Picture Herald*, Dec. 19, 1931. *Harrison's Reports*, Jan. 30, 1932.
22. Leff and Simmons, *Dame in the Kimono*, pp. 23, 296. Wall. "Interviews with Geoffrey Shurlock," oral history, L. B. Mayer Library, American Film Institute, Los Angeles, 1970, p. 92. Carl Milliken to Will Hays, June 25, 1932; Martin Quigley to Hays, Aug. 4, 1932; William Randoph Hearst to Hays, Jan. 2, 1931; WHP. Leff and Simmons, *Dame in the Kimono*, pp. 297–298.
23. Darryl Zanuck to James Wingate, March 29, 1933, *Mary Stevens, M.D.*, file, PCA.
24. Leff and Simmons, *Dame in the Kimono*, pp. 27–29.

25. Leff and Simmons, *Dame in the Kimono*, pp. 30–31. *New Haven Register* clipping, no date, Ramsaye Collection. *Motion Picture Herald*, Jan. 6, 1934.
26. Jowett, "Moral Responsibility and Commercial Entertainment," p. 11.
27. Jowett, *Film*, pp. 220–226. Powers, *G-Men*, p. 67. Forman, *Our Movie-Made Children*, pp. 213, 225. *Philadelphia Public Ledger*, June 6, 1933.
28. Will Hays to B. B. Kahane, July 31, 1933, Lord Papers. Maltby, "'Baby Face,'" pp. 39–40. Leff and Simmons, *Dame in the Kimono*, pp. 37–38.
29. Rev. Daniel Lord to Will Hays, Feb. 20, 1933, Lord Papers. Alice Winter to Will Hays, July 10, Nov. 21, 1933, WHP. Hays to Russell Hollman, June 13, 1933, *Song of Songs* file, PCA. Rev. Daniel Lord to Joe Breen, July 27, 1933; Breen to Martin Quigley, Aug. 1, 1933, Lord Papers.
30. Annual Conference of Bishops, 1932, NCWC-CUA. Rev. FitzGeorge Dinneen to Rev. Wilfrid Parsons, Dec. 14, 1932, *America* Archives. Lally, *Catholic Church in a Changing America*, p. 48. O'Brien, *American Catholics and Social Reform*, p. 46.
31. *America*, April 8, June 27, 1933. Rev. Wilfrid Parsons to Rev. FitzGeorge Dinneen, Aug. 14, 1933, Parsons Papers.
32. *America*, Oct. 29, 1932, May 20, 1933.
33. Rev. Daniel Lord to Cecil B. deMille, no date; deMille to Lord, Feb. 24, 1932; Lord to deMille, Feb. 26, 1932; deMille Collection.
34. Rev. Daniel Lord to Cecil B. deMille, April 10, 1932, deMille Collection. Lord to Martin Quigley, Jan. 28, 1933; James Wingate to Will Hays, no date; Jason Joy to Harold Hurley, Aug. 1, 1932; *Sign of the Cross* file, PCA.
35. Carl Milliken to Jason Joy, Oct. 7, 1932, *Sign of the Cross* file, PCA. Rev. Daniel Lord to Cecil B. deMille, Nov. 26, 1932, Lord to deMille, no date, deMille Collection.
36. *America*, Dec. 17, 1932. *Michigan Catholic*, Feb. 23, 1933. *Our Sunday Visitor*, March 5, 1933.
37. Cecil B. deMille to Elsa Junker, Feb. 6, 1933; Richard Dana Skinner to deMille, no date; deMille Collection. *Motion Picture Herald*, Aug. 11, 1934.
38. *Catholic Action of the South*, Feb. 18, 1932. Rev. Thomas Little to Rev. Michael Driscoll, July 28, 1953, Quigley Papers. Rev. Wilfrid Parsons to Rev. Daniel Lord, Jan. 23; Lord to Parsons, Feb. 1, 1933, Parsons Papers.
39. *Buffalo Catholic Union and Times*, Aug. 24, 1933.
40. *Columbia*, Dec. 30, 1930. *New York Catholic News*, June 3, July 8, 1933. *Catholic Union and Times*, Aug. 10, 1933. *Harrison's Reports*, April 1, May 27, 1933.
41. Rev. FitzGeorge Dinneen to Rev. Wilfrid Parsons, Jan. 1, 1932. Joe Breen to Martin Quigley, Aug. 1, 1933, Quigley Papers.
42. Fogarty, *Patterns of Episcopal Leadership*, p. xxxvi. Davis, *City of Quartz*, p. 330. Bishop Cantwell to Rev. Michael J. Mullins, Feb. 24, 1932, AALA. Extract of Martin Quigley letter to Rev. Daniel Lord, Aug. 15, 1933, Lord Papers.
43. Joe Breen to Will Hays, Nov. 9, 1930, Aug. 29, 1931, WHP.
44. Carl Laemmle to Rev. M. J. Foley, Jan. 7, 1931; Joe Breen to Maurice McKenzie, Jan. 14, 1931, WHP. Rev. Daniel Lord to Luke Hart, Feb. 19, 1931, KC. Joseph Breen to Rev. Joseph V. McGucken, May 28, 1931, AALA.
45. Joe Breen to James Wingate, May 5, 1933; James Fisher, memorandum for Wingate, May 27, 1933; B. B. Kahane to Will Hays, June 27, 1933; Kahane to Hays, July 10, 1933; Hays to Kahane, July 5, 27, 1933; Joe Breen to Hays, Aug. 26, 1933, *Ann Vickers* file, PCA.
46. Rev. Wilfrid Parsons to Joe Breen, Oct. 4, 1932; Breen to Parsons, Oct. 10, 1932, Parsons

Papers. Breen to Martin Quigley, May 1, 1932; Rev. Daniel Lord to Quigley, Jan. 28, 1933, Quigley Papers. Breen to Rev. FitzGeorge Dinneen, April 1, 1934, Lord Papers.

47. Joe Breen to Will Hays, Aug. 29, 1931, WHP. Breen to Rev. Wilfrid Parsons, Oct. 10, 1932, Parsons Papers. Breen to Martin Quigley, May 1, 1932, Quigley Papers.

48. Joe Breen to Rev. Wilfrid Parsons, Oct. 10, 1932, Parsons Papers. Bishop Cantwell to Cardinal Dougherty, Dec. 29, 1933, AALA. Cantwell to Joseph Scott, July 14, 1933, NCWC-NCCB. Joe Breen to Martin Quigley, Aug. 1, 1933; extract, Quigley letter to Lord, Aug. 15, 1933, Lord Papers.

49. Rev. Daniel Lord, "Movies Betray America," (pamphlet). Joe Breen to Martin Quigley, Aug. 1, 1933, Lord Papers. Bishop Cantwell to Archbishop McNicholas, July 17, 1933, AALA.

50. Joe Breen to Martin Quigley, Aug. 4, 1933, Lord Papers. Joseph Scott to Bishop Cantwell, Aug. 2, 1933, AALA.

51. Bishop Cantwell to Rev. John J. Burke, July 20, 1933; Cantwell to Archbishop McNicholas, Aug. 14, 1933; Joe Breen to Cantwell, Aug. 9, 25, 1933; Cantwell to Patrick Casey, Aug. 29, 1933, AALA. Rev. Wilfrid Parsons to Rev. FitzGeorge Dinneen, Aug. 14, 1933, Parsons Papers. Breen to Martin Quigley, Aug. 1, 1933, Lord Papers. Dinneen to Parsons, July 12, 1933; Parsons to Breen, Aug. 25, 1933; Parsons Papers.

52. Rev. Wilfrid Parsons to Rev. Daniel Lord, Aug. 23, 1933. Parsons to Arthur D. Maguire, June 22, 1934; Parsons to Rev. M. J. Ahern, Aug. 10, 1934; Parsons Papers. Facey, *The Legion of Decency*, pp. 44–45.

53. Martin Quigley to Archbishop McNicholas, Oct. 4, 1933, NCWC-NCCB. Kirk Russell, reports, Oct. 13, 18, 30, 1933. Joe Breen to Archbishop McNicholas, Oct. 27, 1933; John E. Morris to Dr. Thomas Purcell, Oct. 23, 1933, NCWC-NCCB. Rev. Daniel Lord to Rev. Wilfrid Parsons, Oct. 14, 1933. Lord to Breen, Oct. 30, 1933, Lord Papers.

54. Joe Breen to Archbishop McNicholas, Oct. 27, 1933, NCWC-NCCB. Breen to Rev. Wilfrid Parsons, Nov. 4, 1933, Parsons Papers.

55. Bishop Cantwell, "Report to the Bishops," AALA.

56. Bishop Cantwell to Archbishop McNicholas, Dec. 28, 1933. O'Brien, *Public Catholicism*, p. 178. Wall, "Interviews with Geoffrey Shurlock," pp. 96–97.

57. *Variety*, Feb. 20, 1934. Leff and Simmons, *Dame in the Kimono*, p. 44. Joe Breen to Rev. FitzGeorge Dinneen, March 17, 1934, Lord Papers. Will Hays to J. Robert Rubin, Jan. 4, 1934, *Men in White* file, PCA. Breen to J. J. Warner, Feb. 27, 1934; I. Auster to Breen, March 5, 1934; Breen, memorandum, April 10, 1934; *Doctor Monica* file, PCA.

58. Martin Quigley to Archbishop McNicholas, March 20, 1934, Parsons Papers. Joe Breen, memorandum, Aug. 3, 1933, April 10, 1934, *Tarzan and His Mate* file, PCA.

59. Joe Breen to Harry Zehner, May 7, 1934, *Affairs of a Gentleman* file, PCA. Cantwell, "Priests and the Motion Picture Industry," p. 146. Weber, "John J. Cantwell and the Legion of Decency," pp. 237–247. Archbishop McNicholas to Cantwell, Dec. 4, 1933, NCWC-NCCB. Rev. FitzGeorge Dinneen to Rev. Wilfrid Parsons, March 8, 1934, Parsons Papers. McNicholas to "All Bishops," Feb. 7, 1934, AALA.

60. *Variety*, Nov. 7, 1933. *Hollywood Reporter*, March 12, 1933.

61. Solomon Goldman to Hon. Newton Baker, May 11, 1934; Carleton Hayes to Bishop Cantwell, May 15, 1934; Cantwell to Hayes, May 19, 1934, NCWC-CUA.

62. *Tidings*, Jan. 5, 26, 1934. *Monitor*, Jan. 27, 1934. *Boston Globe*, Dec. 31, 1934. F. W. Allport, report, March 5, 1934, WHP.

63. *Ave Maria*, April 14, 1933, p. 473. Noll, "Can Catholics Really Clean Up the Movies?" p. 371. Rev. James Gillis, editorial, *Catholic Citizen*, Feb. 24, 1934. *Buffalo Times*, May 23,

1934. Mary G. Hawks, confidential report on Cinema Congress in Rome, April 19, 1934, NCWC-CUA.

64. Assistant Secretary to Archbishop McNicholas, March 8, 1934, NCWC-NCCB. Joe Breen to Rev. FitzGeorge Dinneen, March 30, 1934, Lord Papers. "Notes on the Motion Pictures," no date, AALA. McNicholas to Rev. Blessing, May 16, 1934, AAP.
65. Sparr, *To Promote, Defend, and Redeem*, p. 15. *Ecclesiastical Review* 91, Sept. 1934, p. 285; 90, April 1934, p. 366.
66. *Ecclesiastical Review* 91, Sept. 1934, p. 285. *America*, Aug. 29, 1936. *Catholic Standard*, Nov. 10, 1933. *Pilot*, July 28, 1934.
67. Rev. Wilfrid Parsons to Rev. FitzGeorge Dinneen, March 13, 1934, Parsons Papers. Weber, "John J. Cantwell and the Legion of Decency," p. 239. *St. Louis Star Times*, June 11, 1934. *Michigan Catholic*, June 7, 1934. Joe Breen to Archbishop McNicholas, March 17, 1934. Bishop Cantwell to Cardinal O'Connell, April 17, 1934; O'Connell to Cantwell, April 27, 1934, AALA.
68. Bishop Noll to Archbishop McNicholas, March 12, 1934, NCWC-NCCB. Rev. Wilfrid Parsons to Rev. FitzGeorge Dinneen, March 13, 1934. *Harrison's Reports*, March 10, 1934. Noll, "Can Catholics Really Clean Up the Movies?" p. 367. *Fall River Herald News*, March 12, 1934.
69. Facey, *Legion of Decency*, pp. 144–145. "Meetings of the Episcopal Committee," no date, NCWC-NCCB. *America*, March 24, 1934. Facey, *Legion of Decency*, p. 50. Unsigned letter to Rev. McGucken, Oct. 18, 1934, AALA.
70. Bishop Joseph Schrembs to pastors, no date, Archives of the Archdiocese of Cleveland. Inglis, *Freedom of the Movies*, p. 123. McLaughlin, "A Study of the National Catholic Office for Motion Pictures," p. 41. Cardinal Hayes to Archbishop McNicholas, July 18, 1934, NCWC-NCCB.
71. Bishop Scher to manager, Warner Brothers Theater, Fresno, Calif., Feb. 14, 1934; Miss R. Hemington to Scher, Feb. 26, 1934, AALA. Charles Skouras to Fox managers, no date, AALA. Bishop Cantwell to Archbishop McNicholas, March 1, 1934, NCWC-NCCB.
72. Martin Quigley to Bishop McNicholas, March 20, 1934, Parsons Papers. Joe Breen to Rev. FitzGeorge Dinneen, March 17, 30, 1934, Lord Papers. Bishop Cantwell, cover letter, May 10, 1934, AALA.
73. *Variety*, April 10, 1934.

CHAPTER 5. A CATHOLIC CRUSADE

1. Bishop Gorman to Archbishop McNicholas, Feb. 12, 1934, NCWC-NCCB. *Variety*, Dec. 5, 1933.
2. Bishop Cantwell to Bishop Noll, Feb. 12, 1934; Cantwell to Rev. Krauss, June 8, 1934, Cantwell to Archbishop McNicholas, Dec. 28, 1933, AALA.
3. *Baltimore Catholic Review*, April 17, 1931. Bishop Curley to Archbishop McNicholas, March 2, 1934, Archives of the Archdiocese of Baltimore.
4. Bishop Curley to Arthur Maguire, Nov. 29, 1933, Archives of the Archdiocese of Baltimore. *St. Paul Catholic Bulletin*, Nov. 20, 1930. E. E. B. to Sue Breen, no date, *Hips Hips Hooray* file, PCA. *Michigan Catholic*, Jan. 18, March 29, May 10, 1934. Arthur Maguire, notes of the Detroit Council of Catholic Organizations meeting, May 18, 1934, AALA.
5. *Michigan Catholic*, Jan. 18, March 29, 1934.
6. George Trendle to Arthur Maguire, May 8, 1934; Maguire to Trendle, May 11, 1934, NCWC-NCCB.

7. F. W. Allport to Will Hays, May 15, 1934, WHP. *Queen's Work*, May, June 1934. *Harrison's Reports*, July 14, 1934. Leff and Simmons, *Dame in the Kimono*, p. 48; *Queen's Work*, May 1934.
8. *Queen's Work*, June 1934. *Variety*, June 5, 22, 1934. *New World*, May 24, 1934. *Albany Knickerbocker*, no date, NCWC-NCCB.
9. Martin Quigley to Archbishop McNicholas, June 6, 1934, Quigley Papers. Bishop Cantwell to McNicholas, June 8, 1934, NCWC-NCCB.
10. Joe Breen to Archbishop McNicholas, May 22, 1934; Martin Quigley to McNicholas, June 4, 1934, NCWC-NCCB. Breen to Rev. Daniel Lord, May 23, 1934, Lord Papers. Quigley to McNicholas, June 11, 1934, NCWC-NCCB. Lord to Rev. Wilfrid Parsons, Aug. 20, 1934, Parsons Papers. Lord, *Played by Ear*, p. 299.
11. Arthur Maguire to Bishop John Noll, May 29, 1934, AALA. Rev. Wilfrid Parsons to Francis S. Mosely, June 14, 1934, Parsons Papers. *Variety*, May 1, 1934.
12. Joe Breen to Carl Milliken, Oct. 28, 1930; Breen to Bishop Cantwell, Oct. 17, 1930, WHP. Martin Quigley to Rev. Wilfrid Parsons, Sept. 14, 1933; Rev. R. M. Kelley to Parsons, Nov. 27, 1932, Parsons Papers. Archbishop McNicholas to Rev. Amleto Cicognani, June 10, 1934; Bishop Cantwell to McNicholas, April 21, 1934, NCWC-NCCB. Bishop Boyle to Mrs. Philip Brennan, March 5, 1934, AALA.
13. Arthur Maguire to Bishop Noll, May 29, 1934; Rev. Daniel Lord to Archbishop McNicholas, May 31, 1934, NCWC-NCCB. Maguire to Bishop Cantwell, May 19, 1934, AALA. Lord to Martin Quigley, no date, Quigley Papers.
14. Bishop Cantwell to Archbishop McNicholas, April 24, 1934, NCWC-NCCB. Bishop Gallagher, "Letter to be read at all the masses," April 30, 1934; McNicholas to Cantwell, May 20, 1934, NCWC-NCCB. McNicholas to Bishop Schrembs, May 5, 1934; Schrembs, "Letter to be read at all the masses," June 7, 1934, Archives of the Archdiocese of Cleveland.
15. *Cleveland Plain Dealer*, June 18, 1934. *New York Times*, June 18, 1934.
16. Archbishop McNicholas to Joe Breen, May 15, 1934; Martin Quigley to McNicholas, May 18, 1934, NCWC-NCCB. *New World*, June 8, 1934.
17. Rev. Wilfrid Parsons to Father Provincial, June 14, 1934; Rev. Russell Sullivan to Parsons, June 16, 1934, Parsons Papers.
18. Facey, *Legion of Decency*, p. 54. Joe Breen to Msgr. Lamb, no date, Archives of the Archdiocese of Philadelphia.
19. Facey, *Legion of Decency*, pp. 59, 151. Telephone interviews with Dr. Margaret Reher and Rev. Hugh Nolan, March 30, 1990. Cardinal Dougherty, "Statement to be read at all the masses," June 10, 1934, Archives of the Archdiocese of Philadelphia. *Catholic Standard and Times*, June 22, 1934. Facey, *Legion of Decency*, p. 34. *Variety*, May 22, 1934. F. W. Allport, reports, May 5, 11, 21, 29, June 22, 1934, WHP.
20. *Los Angeles Times*, June 10, 11, 1934. *Box Office*, April 5, 1934. *Cleveland Plain Dealer*, June 10, 1934. *Variety*, June 5, 12, 1934.
21. Lord, report, "The Code—One Year Later," April 23, 1931, Lord Papers. *Variety*, Aug. 7, 1934. F. W. Allport, memorandum, Oct. 29, 1934, WHP. Martin Quigley to Joe Breen, March 30, 1934, Quigley Papers.
22. Martin Quigley to Archbishop McNicholas, May 29, 1934; Joe Breen to McNicholas, June 7, 1934; Rev. FitzGeorge Dinneen to Archbishop McNicholas, June 5, 1934; Dinneen to Quigley, June 9, 1934, NCWC-NCCB.
23. Rev. FitzGeorge Dinneen to Archbishop McNicholas, June 9, 1934; McNicholas to Dinneen, July 7, 1934; NCWC-NCCB. Rev. Wilfrid Parsons to Rev. Daniel Lord, Aug. 23, 1934, Parsons Papers.
24. Martin Quigley to Archbishop McNicholas, June 9, 1934, NCWC-NCCB. Rev. FitzGeorge

Dinneen to Rev. Daniel Lord, June 27, 1934, Lord Papers. De Grazia and Newman, *Banned Films*, p. 43.

25. Martin Quigley to Rev. Wilfrid Parsons, Aug. 27, 1934; Parsons to Lord, Sept. 19, 1934, Parsons Papers. Hays, *Memoirs*, p. 453.
26. Rev. FitzGeorge Dinneen to Rev. Daniel Lord, June 27, 1934, Lord Papers.
27. Rev. FitzGeorge Dinneen to "The sisters," July 2, 1934, Quigley Papers. *Variety*, July 13, 1934.
28. Leff and Simmons, *Dame in the Kimono*, pp. 53, 57, 63. *Variety*, June 19, 1934. Doran, "Mr. Breen Confronts the Dragon," pp. 327–330. *Terre Haute Star*, July 17, 1934. Martin Carmody to Luke Hart, July 9, 1938, KC. Joe Breen to Rev. Daniel Lord, Dec. 5, 1937, Lord Papers. Arthur Maguire to Anthony Beck, May 1, 1934, NCWC-NCCB.
29. Rev. Daniel Lord to Bishop Noll, April 5, 1935, Lord Papers. *Michigan Catholic*, July 26, 1934. *New World*, Aug. 10, 1934. Rev. FitzGeorge Dinneen to Joe Breen, Aug. 6, 1934, NCWC-NCCB.
30. Vizzard, *See No Evil*, p. 51. Wall, "Interviews with Geoffrey Shurlock," pp. 130, 132.
31. Joe Breen, annual report, 1934, AMPAS. Vizzard, *See No Evil*, 94.
32. Joe Breen, annual report, 1935, AMPAS. Black, "Hollywood Censored," pp. 178–180.
33. Joe Breen to Martin Quigley, Aug. 23, 1935, Quigley Papers. Breen to Rev. Edward Schwegler, no date, *Barbary Coast* file, PCA. Jacobs, *Wages of Sin*, pp. 120–125. David O. Selznick to Joe Breen, March 7, 1935; Selznick, story comment, Aug. 19, 1935, *Man with a Load of Mischief* file, DOS.
34. Frederick James Smith, "Hollywood's New Purity Tapemeasure," *Liberty*, Aug. 15, 1935, p. 45. David O. Selznick, story comment, Aug. 19, 1935, *Man with a Load of Mischief* file, DOS. Black, "Hollywood Censored," p. 184. Walsh, "Films We Never Saw," p. 565.
35. Walsh, "Films We Never Saw," pp. 566–568.
36. Black, "Hollywood Censored," p. 184. Joe Breen to Walter Wanger, Nov. 22, 1934, *President Vanishes* file, PCA.
37. Joe Breen to Vincent Hart, July 28, 1934, *Gay Bride* file, PCA.
38. See *Merry Widow* file, PCA. Dooley, *From Scarface to Scarlett*, pp. 466–467.
39. Martin Quigley to Joe Breen, Oct. 12, 1934, Quigley Papers. Quigley to Archbishop McNicholas, Oct. 16, 30, 1934, NCWC-NCCB. Joe Breen to Will Hays, Oct. 22, 1934, WHP.
40. Will Hays, memorandum, Nov. 1, 1934, WHP. Martin Quigley to Archbishop McNicholas, Oct. 16, 1934, NCWC-NCCB.
41. Martin Quigley to Rev. Wilfrid Parsons, March 3, 1935, Parsons Papers.
42. *Dallas Morning News*, May 20, 1935. *Dallas Times Herald*, June 5, 1934. *New York Times*, Sept. 9, 1934. Ferrell Emmett Long to Joe Breen, Sept. 27, 1934, Quigley Papers.
43. F. W. Allport to Will Hays, July 6, 26, Aug. 10, 1934; Roy Howard to Hays, June 29, 1934, WHP. *Cleveland Plain Dealer*, June 29, 1934.
44. Facey, *Legion of Decency*, p. 57.
45. Archbishop McNicholas to Bishop Boyle, Aug. 12, 1934; McNicholas to Martin Quigley, Aug. 12, 1934; Boyle to McNicholas, Aug. 17, 1934; NCWC-NCCB. *Catholic News*, Jan. 11, 1935.
46. McGrath, "Catholic Action's Big Opportunity," pp. 280–287. *Our Sunday Visitor*, July 8, 1934. Archbishop McNicholas to Cardinal Hayes, June 23, 1934, Sept. 2, 1934, NCWC-NCCB. *New York Daily News*, July 16, 1934. Black, "Hollywood Censored," p. 177.
47. *Our Sunday Visitor*, July 8, 1934. *New World*, Oct. 19, 1934.
48. *Michigan Catholic*, Aug. 23, 1934. *Time*, Dec. 12, 1934. F. W. Allport, report, Oct. 30, 1934, WHP. Lupton A. Wilkinson, memorandum to J. J. McCarthy, Aug. 8, 1934, Quigley Papers.

49. Herman G. Weinberg to Vincent dePaul Fitzpatrick, Jan. 26, 1935, Archives of the Archdiocese of Baltimore.
50. *Michigan Catholic*, Dec. 20, 1934. *New World*, Aug. 3, Oct. 5, 1934.
51. Facey, *Legion of Decency*, pp. 84, 152, 156. Lupton A. Wilkinson, "Memorandum for J. J. McCarthy," July 31, 1934; Lupton A. Wilkinson, memoranda to J. J. McCarthy, Aug. 3, 5, 14, 1934, Quigley Papers.
52. Lupton A. Wilkinson, memoranda to J. J. McCarthy, Aug. 12, 14, 29, Sept. 4, 6, 1934, Quigley Papers.
53. Lupton A. Wilkinson, memoranda to J. J. McCarthy, Aug. 14, 29, Sept. 4, 6, 1934, Quigley Papers.
54. Archbishop McNicholas to Bishop Boyle, Dec. 31, 1934, NCWC-NCCB. Cardinal William O'Connell, "The Scandal of the World," *Columbia*, July 1934, p. 4. *Boston Pilot*, July 28, 1934. Rev. M. J. Ahern to Rev. Wilfrid Parsons, Aug. 18, 1934, Parsons Papers. *New York Herald Tribune*, July 23, 1934. Joseph Kirby to McNicholas, July 18, 1934, NCWC-NCCB.
55. Martin Quigley to Cardinal O'Connell, Aug. 1, 1934, Quigley Papers. *Boston Daily Record*, July 27, 1934.
56. Martin Quigley to Archbishop McNicholas, Aug. 1, 1934, NCWC-NCCB. Rev. Wilfrid Parsons to Joe Breen, Aug. 21, 1934; Parsons to Rev. M. J. Ahern, Aug. 10, 1934, Parsons Papers.
57. Bishop Francis Spellman to Martin Quigley, July 31, 1934; Quigley to Cardinal O'Connell, Aug. 1, 1934, Quigley Papers. *Boston Herald*, Aug. 2, 1934. Martin Quigley to Archbishop McNicholas, Jan. 23, 1935, NCWC-NCCB. Rev. Daniel Lord to Rev. FitzGeorge Dinneen, March 28, 1935, Lord Papers.
58. *America*, Aug. 4, 1934.
59. *Philadelphia Inquirer*, July 4, 1934. "An open letter to Bishop Dougherty," no date; "Statement by Motion Picture Theater Operators of Philadelphia," no date; Quigley Papers.
60. *Catholic Standard and Times*, July 6, 13, Aug. 17, 1934.
61. Lupton A. Wilkinson, memorandum to J. J. McCarthy, Aug. 3, 1934; Martin Quigley to Will Hays, March 15, 1935, Quigley Papers. Wall, "Interviews with Geoffrey Shurlock," p. 98.
62. Vizzard, *See No Evil*, p. 49. Cardinal Dougherty to H. M. Warner, no date, Quigley Papers. Will Hays to Dougherty, Oct. 5, 1934; Dougherty to Hays, Oct. 8, 1934; NCWC-NCCB.
63. Lupton A. Wilkinson, memorandum to J. J. McCarthy, Aug. 22, 1934. Martin Quigley to Rev. Amleto Cicognani, Oct. 11, 1934; Cicognani to Quigley, Oct. 18, 1934; Quigley Papers.
64. *Catholic Standard and Times*, Oct. 12, 1934, Jan. 4, 1935. Martin Quigley to Cardinal Dougherty, Dec. 24, 1934, NCWC-NCCB.

CHAPTER 6. BATTLE OF THE BISHOPS

1. Rev. Joseph A. Luther to Rev. Wilfrid Parsons, Dec. 30, 1934, Parsons Papers.
2. *Buffalo Catholic Union and Times*, July 19, Aug. 2, Sept. 6, 1934. *Hollywood Reporter*, July 16, 1935.
3. *Pittsburgh Catholic*, July 12, Sept. 27, 1934.
4. R. Dana Skinner to Arthur Maguire, Dec. 14, 1933, Archives of the Archdiocese of Baltimore. *Catholic Standard and Times*, Sept. 21, 1934.
5. Rev. Amleto Cicognani to Archbishop McNicholas, June 8, 1934, NCWC-NCCB.
6. Archbishop McNicholas to Rev. FitzGeorge Dinneen, July 7, 1934, NCWC-NCCB. Dinneen to Rev. Daniel Lord, June 27, 1934, Lord Papers. Dinneen to Martin Quigley, July 4, 1934, Quigley Papers. *New World*, July 6, 13, 1934. Joe Breen to Will Hays, April 10, 1934, *Affairs of Cellini* file, PCA.

7. Rev. FitzGeorge Dinneen to Archbishop McNicholas, Aug. 7, 1934; McNicholas to Rev. FitzGeorge Dinneen, Aug. 12, 1934; NCWC-NCCB.
8. Martin Quigley to Rev. Samuel K. Wilson, Aug. 29, 1934, Quigley Papers. Carl Milliken to Will Hays, Nov. 9, 1934, WHP.
9. *Daily Mirror*, July 9, 1934. *Birmingham News*, Aug. 29, 1934. *New York Times*, Dec. 16, 1934. *Waterbury American*, Aug. 8, 1934.
10. Facey, *Legion of Decency*, p. 175. *Time*, Dec. 31, 1934.
11. Bishop Boyle to Archbishop McNicholas, Jan. 2, 1935, NCWC-NCCB.
12. *New World*, July 13, 1934. F. W. Allport, report, WHP. Boyle, "The Legion of Decency," p. 369. "Some Observations on the League of Decency," no date, Archives of the Archdiocese of Cleveland.
13. For protest letters and Paul O'Brien's responses, see United Artists Collection. *Our Sunday Visitor*, Aug. 12, 1934.
14. Paul D. O'Brien to United Artists Corp., Aug. 29, 1934; O'Brien to W. G. Ripley, Nov. 9, 1934; United Artists Collection. Martin Quigley to Rev. Edward Schwegler, March 29, 1935, Quigley Papers.
15. Martin Quigley to Will Hays, Feb. 28, 1935, WHP. Quigley to Rev. Edward Gorman, Feb. 2, 1935; Gorman to Archbishop McNicholas, June 10, 1935, NCWC-NCCB.
16. W. H. Erbb to Rev. Edward Gorman, May 14, 1935; Gorman to Erbb, May 15, 1935; Martin Quigley to George Schaefer, May 29, July 1, 1935; Quigley Papers. Joe Breen to Pat Scanlan, April 24, 1935, Parsons Papers.
17. Rev. Edward Schwegler to Martin Quigley, July 26, 1935, Quigley Papers. Schwegler to parish pastors, May 23, 1935, Archives of the Archdiocese of Buffalo. *Buffalo Catholic Union and Times*, Aug. 1, 1935.
18. *New York Herald Tribune*, Dec. 16, 1934. Community Service Department, MPPDA, annual report, NBR. F. W. Allport, report, Aug. 10, 14, 1934, WHP. Rev. Wilfrid Parsons to Rev. Daniel Lord, Aug. 23, 1934, Parsons Papers.
19. Joe Breen to Will Hays, June 25, 1934, WHP. *Commonweal*, Aug. 31, 1934. *America*, Aug. 10, 1934. Breen to Merian C. Cooper, March 27, 1934, *Vergie Winters* file, Theater Arts Collection, University of California, Los Angeles. Breen, notice for files, May 23, 1934, PCA. Rev. Wilfrid Parsons to Breen, Aug. 21, 1934; Parsons Papers.
20. Rev. Wilfrid Parsons to Rev. Daniel Lord, Sept. 19, 1934, Parsons Papers. *America*, Dec. 9, 1934.
21. Martin Quigley to Rev. FitzGeorge Dinneen, July 6, 1934; Dinneen to Quigley, July 9, 1934; Quigley to Archbishop McNicholas, July 11, 1934, Aug. 17, 1934, NCWC-NCCB. Rev. Wilfrid Parsons to Rev. Daniel Lord, Sept. 13, 1934, Parsons Papers.
22. Rev. Wilfrid Parsons to Rev. Daniel Lord, Sept. 19, 1934; Lord to Parsons, Sept. 14, 1934; Parsons to Rev. FitzGeorge Dinneen, Aug. 20, 31, Sept. 14, 1934; Parsons Papers.
23. Martin Quigley to Archbishop McNicholas, Dec. 31, 1934; McNicholas to Quigley, Jan. 15, 1935; NCWC-NCCB. Rev. FitzGeorge Dinneen to Rev. Wilfrid Parsons, Aug. 24, 1934, Quigley Papers. Parsons to Rev. Daniel Lord, Sept. 19, 1934, Parsons Papers.
24. Martin Quigley to Archbishop McNicholas, Oct. 30, 1934; McNicholas to Cardinal Hayes, Oct. 15, 1934; Cardinal Dougherty to McNicholas, Oct. 25, 1934; McNicholas to Cardinal Hayes, Oct. 15, 1934; NCWC-NCCB.
25. Avella, *Confident Church*, p. 113. Cardinal Mundelein to Archbishop McNicholas, Nov. 9, 1934, Mundelein Papers. Rev. Daniel Lord to Rev. FitzGeorge Dinneen, no date, Lord Papers. Cardinal Dougherty to McNicholas, Nov. 6, 1934, NCWC-NCCB.
26. Annual Conference of Bishops, Nov. 14, 1934, NCWC-NCCB. Cardinal Mundelein to Archbishop McNicholas, Nov. 9, 1934, Mundelein Papers.

27. Bishop Boyle to Archbishop McNicholas, Jan. 2, 1935, Annual Conference of Bishops, Nov. 14, 1934, NCWC-NCCB.
28. *New York Times*, Dec. 8, 16, 1934. Rev. FitzGeorge Dinneen to Rev. Daniel Lord, Nov. 23, 1934, Lord Papers. *New World*, Dec. 7, 1934, Feb. 1, 1935. Rev. George McCarthy, *Manual of Handy Reference*, no date, *America* Archives.
29. Bishop Boyle to Archbishop McNicholas, Jan. 1, 1935, NCWC-NCCB. Rev. John Devlin to Bishop Cantwell, Dec. 7, 1934; Cantwell to McNicholas, Dec. 19, 1934, AALA. The four pictures were *Lime House Blues*, *Men of the Night*, *The Firebird*, and *Hat, Coat, and Glove*. Devlin to Cantwell, no date, AALA. Joe Breen to Martin Quigley, Jan. 22, 1935, Parsons Papers. Quigley to McNicholas, Jan. 18, 1935; Devlin to Cantwell, Oct. 11, 1934; NCWC-NCCB.
30. Rev. Wilfrid Parsons to Rev. Daniel Lord, Sept. 13, 1934, Parsons Papers. *America*, Dec. 29, 1934. Rev. FitzGeorge Dinneen to Father LeBuffe, Dec. 30, 1934, Lord Papers. Parsons to Rev. J. Francis McIntyre, Dec. 10, 1934, Quigley Papers.
31. Rev. FitzGeorge Dinneen to Rev. Daniel Lord, Dec. 4, 1934, Lord Papers. Cardinal Mundelein to Rev. Amleto Cicognani, Feb. 16, 1935, Mundelein Papers. Rev. Joseph Luther to Rev. Wilfrid Parsons, Dec. 30, 1934, Parsons Papers.
32. Martin Quigley, "Notes on a Program of Action for the New York Archdiocesan Council of the Legion of Decency," Jan. 2, 1935, Quigley Papers.
33. Rev. Wilfrid Parsons to Martin Quigley, Feb. 6, 8, 1935, Parsons Papers. *Catholic News*, Feb. 9, 1935.
34. Martin Quigley to Rev. J. Francis McIntyre, Dec. 12, 1934; Quigley to Archbishop McNicholas, Jan. 12, 1935; Quigley to Bishop Francis Spellman, Jan. 16, 1935; Quigley Papers.
35. *New World*, Aug. 9, Sept. 6, 1935. Rev. John Devlin, "Note on Anna Karenina," no date, AALA. H. P., "Memo for Mr. B," *Anna Karenina* file, PCA. *Catholic News*, Aug. 24, 1935. Joe Breen, annual report, 1935, AMPAS.
36. Joe Breen to Rev. Edward Schwegler, Sept. 3, 1935; Schwegler to Breen, no date; *The Informer* file; Breen to Will Hays, Oct. 18, 1935, *Barbary Coast* file, PCA.
37. *New World*, May 17, 1935. Mary Looram to Mrs. Thomas Hearn, Aug. 2, 1935; Joe Breen to Will Hays, Oct. 7, 1935, AALA. *Catholic News*, Aug. 24, 1935. Rev. Daniel Lord to Rev. FitzGeorge Dinneen, May 21, 1935; Dinneen to Lord, May 22, 1935, Lord Papers.
38. Rev. John Devlin to Bishop Cantwell, Oct. 11, 1935, AALA. Rev. Wilfrid Parsons to P. S. Harrison, Feb. 21, 1935, Parsons Papers.
39. Rev. Daniel Lord to Bishop John Noll, April 5, 1935, Lord Papers. Rev. Joseph Luther to Parsons, Jan. 2, 1935, Parsons Papers. Arthur Maguire, "An Epistle from a Layman to the American Hierarchy," NCWC-NCCB. Rev. FitzGeorge Dinneen to Lord, Nov. 9, 1935, Lord Papers. Martin Quigley to Archbishop McNicholas, Nov. 22, 1935; McNicholas to Quigley, Dec. 8, 1935, NCWC-NCCB.
40. Rev. FitzGeorge Dinneen to Archbishop McNicholas, Feb. 19, 1935; Rev. Daniel Lord, Nov. 4, 9, 1935; Lord Papers. Dinneen to Joe Breen, June 5, 1935, Quigley Papers.
41. Rev. Daniel Lord to Rev. FitzGeorge Dinneen, Nov. 13, 1935, Lord Papers. Martin Quigley to Lord, Sept. 23, 1936; Lord to Quigley, Sept. 23, 1936; Quigley to Pat Scanlan, Sept. 23, 1936; Quigley Papers.
42. Martin Quigley to Rev. Edward Moore, Nov. 26, 1935, Quigley Papers.
43. Mary Looram to Mrs. Thomas Hearn, Aug. 2, 1935, AALA. Rev. FitzGeorge Dinneen to Rev. Daniel Lord, Nov. 9, 1935. Martin Quigley to Bishop McNicholas, Oct. 16, 1935; Moore,

memorandum to Bishop Donahue, Dec. 14, 1935, NCWC-NCCB. Annual Conference of Bishops, Nov. 13, 1935, NCWC-NCCB.

44. Martin Quigley to Rev. Edward Moore, Nov. 26, 1935, Quigley Papers.
45. Rev. Edward Moore, memorandum to Bishop Donahue, Dec. 14, 1935, NCWC-NCCB. McLaughlin, "A Study of the National Catholic Office for Motion Pictures," p. 38. Martin Quigley to Archbishop McNicholas, Dec. 12, 1935; Moore, "Memorandum to His Excellency," Dec. 2, 1935, NCWC-NCCB. Rev. Wilfrid Parsons to Quigley, no date, Parsons Papers. Bishop Curley to Vincent dePaul Fitzpatrick, Jan. 9, 1936, Archives of the Archdiocese of Baltimore.
46. Archbishop McNicholas to Bishop Boyle, Jan. 1, 1936; McNicholas to Cardinal Hayes, Jan. 1, 1936; McNicholas to Amleto Cicognani, Jan. 1, 1936; NCWC-NCCB.
47. Bishop Mooney to Cardinal Mundelein, Nov. 27, 1935, Mundelein Papers. Rev. Edward Moore to Archbishop McNicholas, Jan. 18, 1936, NCWC-NCCB. Gardiner, *Catholic Viewpoint on Censorship*, p. 88.
48. Connell, "How Should Priests Direct People," p. 253. Facey, *Legion of Decency*, p. 162. *Buffalo Catholic Union and Times*, Jan. 2, 1936. *America*, March 14, 1936. *The Sign Post*, March 1949, pp. 34–35. Response of Bishop McGucken, Dec. 28, 1947, AALA.
49. Martin Quigley, draft of news release, Jan. 24, 1936, Quigley Papers. *Catholic News*, Feb. 1, 1936. *Buffalo Catholic Union and Times*, Feb. 6, 1936. Resolution of the Detroit Council of Catholic Organizations, Jan. 1, 1936, AALA. Rev. Edward Moore to Archbishop McNicholas, Jan. 16, 1936, Quigley Papers.
50. Rev. Wilfrid Parsons to Martin Quigley, May 24, 1956, Quigley Papers.
51. Rev. Francis Talbot, "Report to Rome," no date, *America* Archives. Rev. John Devlin to Bishop Cantwell, Oct. 11, 1935, NCWC-NCCB. *America*, July 27, 1935.
52. *New World*, Sept. 20, 1935. Joe Breen to Martin Quigley, March 1, 1935, Quigley Papers. Breen to Will Hays, April 10, 1934, *Affairs of Cellini* file, PCA. Leff and Simmons, *Dame in the Kimono*, pp. 59–61.
53. Joe Breen to S. J. Briskin, Feb. 10, 1937, *Ann Vickers* file, PCA. Leff and Simmons, *Dame in the Kimono*, p. 60. Carl Milliken to Will Hays, June 17, 1935, *Cock of the Air* file, PCA.
54. *Catholic News*, Feb. 1, 1936. Archbishop McNicholas to Rev. John J. Burke, March 13, 1936, NCWC-NCCB.
55. Martin Quigley to Archbishop McNicholas, March 24, 1936, Quigley Papers. Facey, *Legion of Decency*, pp. 139–140. Bishop Mooney to McNicholas, March 31, 1936, NCWC-NCCB.
56. Martin Quigley to Archbishop McNicholas, March 19, 1936, NCWC-NCCB. *Hollywood Reporter*, March 2, 1936.
57. Martin Quigley to Archbishop McNicholas, March 19, 1936, NCWC-NCCB. Curry, "Mae West As Censored Commodity," pp. 61–62. Joe Breen to Will Hays, Dec. 31, 1935, *Klondike Annie* file, PCA. McNicholas to Rev. Edward Moore, March 5, 1936, NCWC-NCCB.
58. Rev. Edward Moore to Archbishop McNicholas, March 6, 1936, NCWC-NCCB. *New York Evening Journal*, March 2, 1936. Rev. John Devlin to Rev. Joseph Daly, March 4, 1936; Daly to McNicholas, March 7, 1936; NCWC-NCCB. Joe Breen to Martin Quigley, no date, Quigley Papers.
59. Archbishop McNicholas to Rev. Edward Moore, March 5, 1936; press release attached to letter from Moore to McNicholas, March 6, 1936; NCWC-NCCB.
60. Martin Quigley to Archbishop McNicholas, March 19, 1936, NCWC-NCCB. Pete Harrison to Archbishop McNicholas, March 28, 1936, NCWC-NCCB.
61. Martin Quigley to Archbishop McNicholas, April 13, 1936, NCWC-NCCB.

62. Martin Quigley to Archbishop McNicholas, March 24, 1936; Quigley to McNicholas, Sept. 14, 1936; NCWC-NCCB. Quigley to E. Traslosheros, Jan. 30, 1939, Quigley Papers. Quigley to McNicholas, April 13, Sept. 21, 1936; "Special Estimate of Pictures Reviewed in September 14, 21, 1936," attached to Quigley to McNicholas, Sept. 14, 21, 1936; NCWC-NCCB.
63. Martin Quigley to Archbishop McNicholas, Sept. 14, 21, 1936, NCWC-NCCB.
64. *Harrison's Reports*, Oct. 20, 1936.
65. Archbishop McNicholas to Martin Quigley, July 17, 1936, NCWC-NCCB. Martin Quigley to Archbishop McNicholas, July 21, 1936, NCWC-NCCB.
66. Martin Quigley to Archbishop McNicholas, April 13, 1936, Sept. 25, 1936; McNicholas to Rev. Edward Moore, Nov. 11, 1936; NCWC-NCCB. Rev. Wilfrid Parsons to Quigley, no date, Parsons Papers.

CHAPTER 7. SUCCESS

1. Rev. Edward Moore to Archbishop McNicholas, Dec. 11, 1936, NCWC-NCCB. Personal interview with Monsignor McClafferty, April 20, 1990.
2. Rev. John McClafferty to director, Providence Legion of Decency, May 8, 1939; McClafferty to Bishop Keough, Dec. 15, 1944; "Observer" to Bishop Keough, no date; AAP. Msgr. J. Carroll McCormick to McClafferty, Oct. 9, 1942, Archives of the Archdiocese of Philadelphia.
3. Rev. John McClafferty to Bishop Keough, May 23, 1941, AAP. Rev. Edward Schwegler to Bishop John Duffy, Oct. 5, 1943, Legion of Decency file, Archives of the Archdiocese of Buffalo.
4. DeGrazia and Newman, *Banned Films*, p. 44. Personal interviews with Martin Quigley, Jr., April 19, 1990, and Msgr. John McClafferty, April 20, 1990.
5. Archbishop McNicholas to Rev. Edward Moore, April 19, 1937; Moore to McNicholas, April 26, May 14, 1937, NCWC-NCCB.
6. *America*, Oct. 6, 1934. Mary Looram, "Report of the Motion Picture Bureau, 1934–1936," AALA. Facey, *Legion of Decency*, pp. 87–88.
7. Mary Looram to Mrs. Deveraux, Aug. 3, 1937, AALA. Personal interview with Msgr. Paul J. Hayes, April 1, 1991. Rev. Edward Moore to Archbishop McNicholas, Feb. 1, 1937; NCWC-NCCB.
8. Jowett, *Film*, p. 283. Archbishop McNicholas to Cardinal O'Connell, Nov. 16, 1938, AAB. "Resolutions of National Council of Catholic Women on the Movies," attachment to May 29, 1940, letter; Bishop Cantwell to McNicholas, July 15, 1939; NCWC-NCCB. C. C. Pettijohn, "Testimony in opposition to H.R. 6472," 1936, Mundelein Papers.
9. Rev. Gerard Donnelly to Rev. Wilfrid Parsons, no date, Parsons Papers.
10. Wall, "Interviews with Geoffrey Shurlock," p. 110. Bishop Cantwell to Will Hays, April 11, 1938, AALA.
11. Black, "Hollywood Censored," p. 185. Dunne, "Blast It All," p. 8. Darryl Zanuck to Jerry Wald, Feb. 23, 1954, *The Robe* file, PCA. *New York Times*, Jan. 28, 1990, section 7, p. 36.
12. Finlay McDermid to Steve Trilling, Feb. 3, 1954, *Battle Cry* file, PCA. Val Lewton to Barbara Keon, Jan. 12, 1939, DOS.
13. Barbara Keon to Mr. Kern, Dec. 19, 1939; Joe Breen to Val Lewton, March 27, 1941; David O. Selznick to Lewton, June 7, 1937; DOS.
14. Joe Breen to Martin Quigley, April 23, 1940, Quigley Papers. Val Lewton to David O.

Selznick, Sept. 19, 1938, DOS. Miller, "'Frankly, My Dear,'" pp. 17, 23, 25, 27. Selznick to John Hay Whitney, Oct. 20, 1939, DOS. Leff and Simmons, *Dame in the Kimono*, p. 106.

15. Val Lewton to David O. Selznick, April 7, 1939, DOS.
16. Miller, "Frankly My Dear," p. 20.
17. Leff and Simmons, *Dame in the Kimono*, pp. 93–94. Miller, "Frankly My Dear," pp. 20–22. Val Lewton to David O. Selznick, Sept. 19, 1939; Selznick to Lowell Calvert, Dec. 7, 1939; DOS.
18. Archbishop McNicholas to Amleto Cicognani, June 11, 1936, AALA.
19. Joe Breen, "Notes for Bishop Cantwell," Sept. 1, 1936; Cantwell to Archbishop McNicholas, Sept. 1, 1936; NCWC-NCCB. Breen to Cantwell, Dec. 10, 1943, AALA. Breen to David O. Selznick, Sept. 29, 1936, DOS. *America*, Dec. 5, 1936.
20. Rev. Edward Moore to Archbishop McNicholas, Dec. 11, 1936, NCWC-NCCB. Rev. Patrick Masterson to Rev. Michael O'Shea, Dec. 2, 1947, LDA.
21. Jowett, "Moral Responsibility and Commercial Entertainment," p. 17. *Nation*, July 11, 1936. Gardiner, *Catholic Viewpoint on Censorship*, p. 83. *Film Daily*, May 18, 1948.
22. See Janes, "The Legion of Decency and the Motion Picture Industry," passim.
23. Wall, "Interviews with Geoffrey Shurlock," p. 110. *Literary Digest*, July 7, 1934. Schatz, *Genius of the System*, p. 298.
24. Wall, "Interviews with Geoffrey Shurlock," pp. 119, 356. *Film Daily*, May 18, 1948. Personal interview with Father John McClafferty, April 20, 1990. *New York Times*, Jan. 3, 1936. *Variety*, Jan. 6, 1936. *Motion Picture Herald*, April 13, 1940.
25. *San Francisco News*, March 12, 1934. Rev. Edward Moore to Archbishop McNicholas, April 12, 1937; Moore to Will Hays, April 12, 1937; Moore to McNicholas, April 16, 1937; Joseph Schenck to Mary Looram, May 7, 1937; NCWC-NCCB.
26. Martin Quigley to Archbishop McNicholas, May 11, 1937, NCWC-NCCB. *Look*, Aug. 2, 1938.
27. *New York Times*, Aug. 21, 22, 1938. Joe Breen to Will Hays, June 25, 1937, *Damaged Goods* file, PCA. Albert Donovan to Sam Cummings, Jan. 7, 1941; Donovan to Rev. John McClafferty, Jan. 23, 1941; *Damaged Goods* file, LDA.
28. Statement by Archbishop McNicholas, Sept. 9, 1941, AALA. *Motion Picture Herald*, March 26, 1938.
29. Cuts in *Motherhood* in the file for *The Forgotten Village*, NYMPD. "In the matter of the appeal relating to . . . *Birth of a Baby*," no date, *Birth of a Baby* file, NYMPD.
30. *America*, Jan. 1, 1937. *New World*, Dec. 13, 1940. *Brooklyn Tablet*, April 23, 1938. *Life*, April 11, 1938. *Motion Picture Herald*, April 16, 1938. *New York Times*, March 17, 1938. *Special Pictures Corp. v. Div. of Motion Picture Censorship*, Sept. 19, 1938, *Birth of a Baby* file, Virginia Division of Motion Picture Censorship. *Catholic Action* 20 May 1938, p. 7. *New Republic*, March 27, 1938.
31. *America*, Jan. 1, 1937. *Brooklyn Tablet*, April 23, 1938.
32. Rev. Edward Plover, report, no date, *Birth of a Baby* file, LDA.
33. William Mooring, draft of "It Started with the *Birth of a Baby*," April 1, 1960, Quigley Papers. Legion of Decency statement, *Birth of a Baby* file, PCA. Fernando J. Bory to Rev. John McClafferty, May 24, 1938, *Birth of a Baby* file, LDA.
34. Hennesey, *American Catholics*, p. 272. Bishop Alter to diocesan social action directors, May 21, 1937, Archives of the Archdiocese of Detroit. Martin Quigley, notes for Bishop McNicholas, Nov. 27, 1936, NCWC-NCCB. Quigley to Joe Breen, Jan. 10, 1939, Quigley Papers.
35. Ross, "Struggles for the Screen," p. 348. *Exhibitor's Herald*, April 12, 1919.

36. Joe Breen to Count Galeazzi, attached to letter from Breen to Lord, Dec. 5, 1937, Lord Papers. Rev. Joseph Daly to Rev. John Devlin, Nov. 21, 1936, AALA.
37. Rev. John McClafferty, memorandum, March 29, 1938, attached to letter from McClafferty to Archbishop McNicholas, April 30, 1938, NCWC-NCCB.
38. O'Brien, *Renewal of American Catholicism*, pp. 125–126. Sayre, *Running Time*, p. 206.
39. Karl Lischka, memorandum, no date, *Confessions of a Nazi Spy* file, PCA. Rev. John McClafferty, report, June 6, 1939, Quigley Papers.
40. *Quarterly Bulletin*, March 1941. *America*, October 25, 1941. *America*, Dec. 17, 1938. Mary Looram, "Report of the Motion Picture Bureau, 1936–1938," Quigley Papers.
41. Rev. John McClafferty to Archbishop McNicholas, March 29, 1938, NCWC-NCCB.
42. Dick, *Star-Spangled Screen*, pp. 17–19.
43. *Life*, June 13, 1938. Rev. John McClafferty to Archbishop McNicholas, June 8, 1938; Will Hays to Rev. John McClafferty, June 11, 1938; Martin Quigley to Archbishop McNicholas, June 10, 1938; NCWC-NCCB.
44. Rev. John McClafferty to Archbishop McNicholas, June 11, 1938; McClafferty to McNicholas, June 15, 1938; NCWC-NCCB.
45. Untitled, undated magazine clipping, AAP. *Brooklyn Tablet*, June 18, 1938. *Film Survey*, Aug. 8, 1938. Rev. John McClafferty to Archbishop McNicholas, June 29, 1938, NCWC-NCCB. *Nation*, July 9, 1938. Joe Breen to Rev. Daniel Lord, Sept. 18, 1938, Lord Papers. Koppes and Black, *Hollywood Goes to War*, pp. 26–27.
46. *Box Office*, Aug. 15, 1938. "Report of the Motion Picture Committee to the Ohio Pastors' Convention, 1939," Ramsaye Collection.
47. Roddick, *New Deal in Entertainment*, pp. 190–195. Rev. Jose Conseco, review of script, no date, *Juarez* file, PCA. H. M. Warner to Bishop Peter Ireton, June 20, 1939, NCWC-NCCB.
48. Rev. Jose Conseco to Joe Breen, Sept. 23, 1938, *Juarez* file, PCA. Rev. John McClafferty to Archbishop McNicholas, June 6, 1939; McClafferty to Bishop Peter Ireton, July 5, 1939; NCWC-NCCB. *Catholic Virginian*, June 1939. H. M. Warner to Ireton, June 20, 1939; Martin Quigley to Charles Einfeld, June 13, 1939; NCWC-NCCB.
49. Phelan, *National Catholic Office for Motion Pictures*, p. 108. Rev. John McClafferty to Archbishop McNicholas, June 5, 1939, NCWC-NCCB.

CHAPTER 8. THE END OF THE HONEYMOON

1. Facey, *Legion of Decency*, p. 164. *Pittsburgh Catholic*, Aug. 15, 1940.
2. *Buffalo News*, May 17, 1940. *New York Times*, Aug. 4, 1940. *South Bend* (Ind.) *Tribune*, July 23, 1940.
3. *New York Daily News*, Sept. 3, 1940. *Mademoiselle*, Nov. 1940.
4. Jowett, *Film*, p. 475. Izod, *Hollywood and the Box Office*, p. 112. Leff and Simmons, *Dame in the Kimono*, pp. 81–82. Rev. John McClafferty to Bishop Schrembs, July 8, 1940, Archives of the Archdiocese of Cleveland.
5. Leff, *Hitchcock and Selznick*, pp. 37, 53. David O. Selznick to J. W. Whitney, Sept. 6, 1939, DOS.
6. *New York Telegraph*, Nov. 21, 1940. *Motion Picture Herald*, Nov. 23, 1940. Joe Breen to Will Hays, Feb. 17, 1941, *Primrose Path* file, PCA.
7. Joe Breen to Harry Warner, Sept. 19, 1938, *Yes My Darling Daughter* file, Warner Brothers Collection-USC. Facey, *Legion of Decency*, pp. 107–109.
8. Francis Harmon to Joe Breen, Feb. 18, 1939. *Yes My Darling Daughter* file, Warner Brothers

Collection-USC. *New York State Exhibitor*, Feb. 22, 1939. Facey, *Legion of Decency*, pp. 107–108. *Christian Science Monitor*, March 10, 1939.

9. Joe Breen to Rev. Daniel Lord, March 1, 1941, Lord Papers. Personal interview with Father McClafferty, April 20, 1990. Joe Breen to L. B. Mayer, June 5, 1939, *Strange Cargo* file, PCA.
10. Facey, *Legion of Decency*, p. 105. Joe Breen to Francis Harmon, April 4, 1940; Harmon to Breen, March 15, 1940; *Strange Cargo* file, PCA. Breen to Rev. Daniel Lord, May 4, 1940, Lord Papers.
11. *Catholic News*, April 27, 1940. *Variety*, June 12, 1940. *Strange Cargo* file, PCA.
12. *New York Times*, Oct. 7, 1940.
13. *Variety*, Dec. 25, 1940. *Cue*, Feb. 14, 1941. Facey, *Legion of Decency*, pp. 103–104.
14. Facey, *Legion of Decency*, p. 104. Joe Breen to Rev. Daniel Lord, March 1, 1941, Lord Papers.
15. Joe Breen to Rev. Daniel Lord, March 1, 1941, Lord Papers. C. C. Pettijohn, memorandum, Feb. 17, 1941, *Turnabout* file, PCA. Rev. John McClafferty, files, Feb. 5, 1941, *Yes My Darling Daughter* file, LDA. Estelle Harcourt and Martha Addams to Carl Milliken, March 18, 1941, Quigley Papers.
16. Joe Breen to Rev. Daniel Lord, March 1, 1941; Breen to Count Galeazzi attached to letter from Breen to Lord, Dec. 5, 1937; Lord Papers.
17. Joe Breen to Martin Quigley, June 22, 1940; Quigley to Breen, July 3, 1940; report of Abbe Stourn, July 15, 1937; Quigley Papers.
18. Rev. John Devlin to Rev. Gerard Donnelly, no date, NCWC-NCCB. Joe Breen to Martin Quigley, Sept. 23, 1937, Quigley Papers.
19. Joe Breen, memorandum for the files, Feb. 1, 1938; Breen to Maurice Pivar, Oct. 24, 1940; *Back Street* file, PCA. Jacobs, *Wages of Sin*, p. 131.
20. Joe Breen to Rev. Daniel Lord, March 1, 1941, Lord Papers.
21. Joe Breen to Martin Quigley, Sept. 25, 1937, Quigley Papers. Leff and Simmons, *Dame in the Kimono*, pp. 115, 120.
22. Production Code Report, no date, *Two-Faced Woman* file, PCA. Facey, *Legion of Decency*, p. 103.
23. Cooney, *American Pope*, pp. 108–109. Archbishop Spellman to Archbishop Cantwell, Nov. 29, 1941, AALA. *Motion Picture Herald*, Dec. 6, 1941.
24. John A. Merrill to Bishop John Duffy, Dec. 4, 1941; Ernest Brown to Duffy, Dec. 5, 1941; Archives of the Archdiocese of Buffalo. *Film Daily*, Dec. 2, 1941. *Dallas Morning News*, Dec. 3, 1941. Martin Quigley to Robert Harlow, Dec. 22, 1941, Quigley Papers.
25. *Film Daily*, Dec. 2, 1941. Roy E. Harrold to Will Hays, Dec. 5, 1941, *Two-Faced Woman* file, PCA.
26. W. D. Kelly to Irwin Esmond, *Two-Faced Woman* file, NYMPD. Rev. John McClafferty to Archbishop McNicholas, Dec. 16, 1941, NCWC-NCCB.
27. Rev. John McClafferty to Archbishop McNicholas, March 6, 1942, NCWC-NCCB. Doherty, *Projections of War*, pp. 37–38.
28. Vizzard, *See No Evil*, p. 103. Rev. John McClafferty to Archbishop McNicholas, March 28, June 3, 1941; Rev. J. T. McDermitt to Bishop Noll, June 1, 1941; McClafferty to McNicholas, Sept. 17, 1941; Rev. Joseph McGucken to McNicholas, Sept. 21, 1941; McNicholas to McClafferty, Nov. 2, 1941; Margaret Quill to Bishop Spellman, Jan. 27, 1942; McClafferty to McNicholas, March 12, 1942; NCWC-NCCB.
29. Rev. John McClafferty to Archbishop McNicholas, Feb. 2, 1942, March 12, April 1, 1942, NCWC-NCCB.
30. Cripps, *Slow Fade to Black*, pp. 369–371. Mrs. Alonzo Richardson to Joe Breen, June 6, 1942,

In This Our Life file, PCA. George Schuyler, press summary of *In This Our Life*, June 19, 1942; Schuyler to Rev. John McClafferty, June 30, July 18, Aug. 6, 1942, Quigley Papers.

31. Facey, *Legion of Decency*, p. 164. "Trends in Films," AAP. *Motion Picture Herald*, Sept. 8, 1943. Rev. John McClafferty to Archbishop McNicholas, Jan. 27, 1943; McNicholas to McClafferty, Feb. 7, 1943; NCWC-NCCB.
32. F. de Amat to Bishop Noll, June 12, 1942; Rev. John McClafferty to Archbishop McNicholas, July 13, 1942; NCWC-NCCB.
33. Koppes and Black, *Hollywood Goes to War*, p. 191. *America*, May 15, 1943. Unsigned letter to Rev. John McClafferty, May 15, 1943, *Mission to Moscow* file, LDA. Rev. John McClafferty to McNicholas, June 28, 1943, NCWC-NCCB. Minutes of the Episcopal Committee meeting, November 1943, AAP.
34. Brandt, *No Magic Bullet*, pp. 161–165. *America*, Sept. 20, 1941. Rev. Michael Harding to Rev. Thomas Collins, May 3, 1944, AAP.
35. Rev. John McClafferty to Martin Quigley, Dec. 4, 1942, Quigley Papers.
36. *Variety*, June 17, 1941. *No Greater Sin* file, NYMPD.
37. *America*, Oct. 18, 1941. Charles P. Taft to George Schaefer, Dec. 15, 1941; Rev. John McClafferty to Archbishop McNicholas, Jan. 15, Feb. 1, 1943; McNicholas to McClafferty, Jan. 31, 1942, Feb. 7, 1943; NCWC-NCCB.
38. Rev. John McClafferty to Archbishop McNicholas, Jan. 9, 1942, NCWC-NCCB. Martin Quigley to Bishop O'Hara, Jan. 7, 1942, Quigley Papers.
39. Bishop Foery to parish priests, Nov. 10, 1941, Archives of the Archdiocese of Syracuse.
40. Bishop Kearny to Rev. John McClafferty, Jan. 20, 1941; Rev. Michael Owen Driscoll to Rev. John McClafferty, June 26, 1942; Quigley Papers.
41. Lawrence Arnstein to Dr. Thomas Parran, Dec. 10, 1942; script for *Silent Enemy* (original title of the film); WW.
42. Walter Wanger to Dr. Halverson, Nov. 1, 1943; Wanger to Dr. R. A. Vonderlehr, March 16, 1943; Wanger to Gov. Earl Warren, Jan. 4, 1943; Gen. George C. Marshall, memorandum, no date, WW. Rev. John McClafferty to bishops Keough and Spellman, Feb. 2, 1944, AAP.
43. Bishop O'Hara to Rev. John McClafferty, Feb. 29, 1944; McClafferty to Elmer Davis, March 2, 1944; Edward Klauber to Walter Wanger, March 3, 1944; WW. Klauber to McClafferty, March 2, 1944, AAP.
44. Rev. John McClafferty to Dr. J. R. Heller, March 10, 1944; McClafferty to Bishop Keough, March 13, 1944; Rev. Alphonse Schwitalla to McClafferty, March 15, 1944; AAP. Dr. Thomas Parran to Walter Wanger, March 16, 1944, WW.
45. Reports from sneak previews received March 15, 1944; Francis Harmon to Walter Wanger, March 16, 1944; WW. Rev. John McClafferty to Bishop Keough, March 22, 1944, AAP.
46. Walter Wanger to Dr. Thomas Parran, March 31, 1944; Parran to Wanger, March 31, 1944; WW.
47. Walter Wanger, press release, April 17, 1944, WW. Rev. John McClafferty to Bishop Keough, May 10, 1944, AAP. *Variety*, Dec. 13, 1944.
48. Joe Breen to Rev. John McClafferty, March 6, 1944, NCWC-NCCB.
49. Joe Breen to Luigi Luraschi, Oct. 21, 1942; Luraschi to Preston Sturges, Oct. 16, 1942; Russell Holman to Luraschi, Oct. 5, 1943; Sturges Papers.
50. Carl Milliken to Joe Breen, March 7, 1944; Geoff Shurlock, memorandum for the files, Dec. 1, 1955; *Miracle of Morgan's Creek* file, PCA.
51. *Motion Picture Herald*, Nov. 7, 1942.
52. Production Code Administration to Stanley Kramer, Oct. 3, 1941; memorandum, Oct. 9,

1941; *Moon and Sixpence* file, PCA. Rev. John McClafferty to Archbishop McNicholas, Sept. 22, 1942, NCWC-NCCB.

53. Rev. John McClafferty to Archbishop McNicholas, Sept. 22, 1942, NCWC-NCCB.
54. Joe Breen to Rev. John McClafferty, Oct. 2, 1942; McClafferty to Breen, Oct. 21, 1942; *Moon and Sixpence* file, PCA. Breen to Rev. Daniel Lord, Jan. 26, 1943, Lord Papers.
55. *Variety*, July 21, 1943.
56. Rev. Patrick Masterson, memorandum, May 1, 1943, George Mitchell to Rev. John McClafferty, May 1, 1943; *Lady of Burlesque* file, LDA.
57. Rev. Patrick Masterson, memoranda, May 12, 18, 1943, *Lady of Burlesque* file, LDA.
58. Helen Conversano, memorandum, May 14, 1943; Rev. Patrick Masterson, May 18, 1943, *Lady of Burlesque* file, LDA. Rev. John McClafferty to Rev. Collins, June 12, 1943, AAP.
59. Mrs. McDonell to David O. Selznick, Sept. 17, 1943, DOS. Schumach, *Face on the Cutting Room Floor*, p. 63. Leff and Simmons, *Dame in the Kimono*, pp. 127–128.

CHAPTER 9. THE PRODUCERS FIGHT BACK

1. Izod, *Hollywood and the Box Office*, pp. 113, 119, 134–138. Jowett, "Moral Responsibility and Commercial Education," p. 19.
2. Spyros Skouras to Darryl Zanuck, June 9, 1952, Skouras Papers. *New York Times*, Dec. 19, 1993, section 7.
3. Jowett, *Film*, p. 345. Izod, *Hollywood and the Box Office*, pp. 122–123.
4. Schatz, *Genius of the System*, pp. 299–300. Gans, "The Rise of the Problem Film," pp. 327–330.
5. Izod, *Hollywood and the Box Office*, p. 126. *Life*, June 1949.
6. Jowett, *Film*, p. 398.
7. Leff and Simmons, *Dame in the Kimono*, p. 136. Joe Breen to Ralph Cohn, May 23, 1947, *Sleep My Love* file, PCA. Bishop McGucken to Rev. John Devlin, Jan. 23, 1946; Rev. John McClafferty to Devlin, Feb. 19, 1946; AALA. *America*, July 14, 23, 1946.
8. Leff and Simmons, *Dame in the Kimono*, p. 169. Wall, "Interviews with Geoffrey Shurlock," p. 212.
9. Martin Quigley to Rev. Wilfrid Parsons, April 15, 1947, Quigley Papers. Joe Breen, memorandum, *The Bishop's Wife* file, PCA. Rev. John Devlin to Bishop Cantwell, no date, AALA. Protestant Film Council Archives, Good News Communications, Atlanta, Georgia. Wall, "Interviews with Geoffrey Shurlock," pp. 116, 119.
10. Legion of Decency 1945 budget; Bishop Keough to Rev. John McClafferty, Oct. 2, 1946; AAP. Msgr. Walter Furlong to Rev. Patrick Masterson, Oct. 7, 1948, AAB.
11. Personal interview with Msgr. Paul J. Hayes, April 11, 1991.
12. *Dallas Morning News*, July 7, 1945. R. J. O'Donnell to Joe Breen, Feb. 13, 1946, WW. Rev. John McClafferty to Bishop Keough, Dec. 3, 1945, AAP. Rev. Patrick Masterson to Bishop Ready, Jan. 13, 1953, Quigley Papers.
13. Budd Rogers to Walter Wanger, Jan. 7, 1946; Wanger to Ed Life, Jan. 4, 1946; WW. Acting director to O. J. Silverthorne, Feb. 1, 1946, *Scarlet Street* file, NYMPD.
14. Rev. John McClafferty to Eric Johnston, April 9, 1946, Archives of the Archdiocese of Philadelphia. *America*, Nov. 23, 1946. Rev. John Devlin, annual report, Oct. 28, 1946, LDA. Devlin to McClafferty, Oct. 17, 1945, AALA. *America*, Dec. 9, 1950, Jan. 13, May 12, Oct. 20, 1951. Rev. Patrick Masterson to Bishop O'Connor, Dec. 15, 1949, Quigley Papers. Izod, *Hollywood and the Box Office*, p. 132.
15. *America*, Feb. 17, 1951. *Tidings*, May 2, 1947. Helen Ferguson to Loretta Young, May 16, 1947, AALA.

16. Leff and Simmons, *Dame in the Kimono*, p. 143. *Nation*, May 8, 1948. *Brooklyn Tablet*, Jan. 31, 1948.
17. White, "Mom and Dad," pp. 252–256.
18. Ibid. Friedman, *A Youth in Babylon*, p. 34.
19. White, "Mom and Dad," pp. 254–255. Rev. John McClafferty to Rev. John Devlin, Feb. 3, 1948, AALA. See *Mom and Dad* file, LDA. Friedman, *A Youth in Babylon*, pp. 38–39.
20. Skinner, "Tussle with Russell," pp. 6, 8. Leff and Simmons, *Dame in the Kimono*, pp. 112–113, 118. Corliss, "The Legion of Decency," p. 39.
21. Leff and Simmons, *Dame in the Kimono*, pp. 124–125. Skinner, "Tussle with Russell," p. 9. Copy of *Outlaw* ad in the *San Francisco Examiner*, Feb. 17, 1943, AAP.
22. Skinner, "Tussle with Russell," p. 9. Shumach, *The Face on the Cutting-Room Floor*, p. 60. Leff and Simmons, *Dame in the Kimono*, pp. 136–139.
23. Cardinal Dougherty to William Annenberg, Oct. 29, 1947, Archives of the Archdiocese of Philadelphia. Rev. John Devlin, annual report, Oct. 28, 1946, AALA. William F. McTernan to Bishop Keough, Sept. 20, 1946; McClafferty to Keough, Aug. 19, 1946; AAP. Personal interview with Msgr. Francis Weber, March 18, 1988. McClafferty, memorandum, *The Outlaw* file, LDA.
24. Bishop Scully to Bishop Cantwell, April 5, 1947, AALA. Scully to Bishop Keough, April 5, 1947, AAP. Scully to Cantwell, April 5, 1947, AALA. Personal interview with Msgr. John McClafferty, April 20, 1990. Summary of telephone conversation between Rev. Patrick Masterson and Howard Hughes, June 17, 1947; Masterson to Bishop Scully, July 2, 1947; *The Outlaw* file, LDA.
25. Bishop Scully to Rev. Patrick Masterson, July 11, 1947; Howard Hughes to Martin Quigley, Feb. 16, 1948; Quigley to Bishop Scully, Feb. 19, 1948; *The Outlaw* file, LDA.
26. Martin Quigley to Bishop Scully, Feb. 20, 1948; Rev. Patrick Masterson to Scully, Jan. 23, 1948; Scully to Masterson, Feb. 4, 1948; *The Outlaw* file, LDA. Masterson to Scully, Feb. 25, 1948, Archives of the Archdiocese of Baltimore.
27. Howard Hughes to Rev. Patrick Masterson, April 27, 1948; Masterson, memorandum, July 23, 1948; *The Outlaw* file, LDA.
28. Rev. Patrick Masterson to Bishop Scully, June 7, 1948; Bishop Cantwell to Scully, June 22, 1948; AALA.
29. Rev. Patrick Masterson to Bishop Scully, July 23, Oct. 19, 1948, *The Outlaw* file, LDA. Jowett, *Film*, p. 397. Rev. Thomas Little to Msgr. Furlong, AAB.
30. Haver, *David O. Selznick's Hollywood*, p. 353. Thomson, *Showman*, p. 449.
31. David O. Selznick to Mrs. McDonell, May 20, 1944, *Spellbound* file, DOS. Joe Breen to William Gordon, Aug. 2, 1944; Geoff Shurlock to Breen, Aug. 8, 1944; *Duel in the Sun* file, DOS.
32. Joe Breen to David O. Selznick, Feb. 27, 1945, *Duel in the Sun* file, DOS.
33. Thomson, *Showman*, p. 469. Hal Kern to David O. Selznick, Dec. 11, 1946, *Duel in the Sun* file, DOS.
34. Gregory Peck interview, the Oral History Collection on the Performing Arts, Southern Methodist University, Dallas, Texas. James Stewart to Neil Agnew, Dec. 28, 1946; Stewart, memorandum for the files, Dec. 29, 1946; *Duel in the Sun* file, DOS.
35. Thomson, *Showman*, p. 469. *Tidings*, Jan. 3, 10, 17, 1947. Rev. John Randall to Rev. Patrick Masterson, no date, *Duel in the Sun* file, LDA.
36. Haver, *David O. Selznick's Hollywood*, p. 366. David O. Selznick to Martin Quigley, Jan. 6, 1947, *Duel in the Sun* file, DOS. Quigley to Selznick, Jan. 10, 1947; Rev. John Randall to Rev.

Patrick Masterson, Jan. 10, 1947; Quigley to Masterson, Jan. 21, 1947; *Duel in the Sun* file, LDA.

37. Rev. Patrick Masterson to Bishop Scully, Jan. 22, 1947, *Duel in the Sun* file, LDA.
38. Martin Quigley to Rev. Patrick Masterson, Feb. 22, 1947, *Duel in the Sun* file, LDA.
39. Martin Quigley, "Proposed cuts," Feb. 3, 1947; David O. Selznick to Neil Agnew, Feb. 3, 1947; *Duel in the Sun* file, DOS.
40. Martin Quigley to Rev. Patrick Masterson, Feb. 3, 1947; Quigley to David O. Selznick, Jan. 27, 1947; Masterson, files, Feb. 11, 18, 1947; *Duel in the Sun* file, LDA.
41. David O. Selznick to Neil Agnew, no date, attached to letter from Martin Quigley to Rev. Patrick Masterson, Feb. 24, 1947, *Duel in the Sun* file, LDA.
42. *Variety*, Feb. 5, 1947. Resolution of the Houston CYO, Feb. 9, 1947, DOS. Rev. John Sheehy to Rev. John McClafferty, April 3, 1947, AAB.
43. David O. Selznick to Neil Agnew, no date, attached to letter from Martin Quigley to Rev. Patrick Masterson, Feb. 24, 1947, *Duel in the Sun* file, LDA.
44. Rev. Patrick Masterson, files, Feb. 21, 1947, *Duel in the Sun* file, LDA.
45. Ibid., Feb. 27, 1947. David O. Selznick to Neil Agnew, Feb. 28, 1947, *Duel in the Sun* file, LDA.
46. Ibid. Martin Quigley to Rev. John McClafferty, Feb. 27, 1947; Rev. Patrick Masterson, files, no date; *Duel in the Sun* file, LDA. David O. Selznick to Jim Stewart, March 27, 1947, *Duel in the Sun* file, DOS.
47. Ibid.
48. Ibid.
49. Lee, "Pending Catholicization," p. 86.
50. Martin Quigley to David O. Selznick, April 11, 1947; James Stewart to Rev. John McClafferty, April 14, 1947, *Duel in the Sun* file, DOS.
51. *Tidings*, March 21, 1947. David O. Selznick to Paul MacNamara, April 26, 1947, *Duel in the Sun* file, DOS. *Tidings*, May 16, 1947.
52. J. R. Striegel to Rev. John Devlin, May 16, 1947, AALA. Rev. John McClafferty to Rev. John Sheehy, April 8, 1947, AAB. Thomson, *Showman*, pp. 472–473. David O. Selznick to Paul MacNamara, April 26, Sept. 9, Nov. 4, 1947, *Duel in the Sun* file, DOS. Selznick to Neil Agnew, Oct. 30, 1947; Selznick to Martin Quigley, Dec. 20, 1947; Milton Kusell to C. Barker, Dec. 14, 1947; *The Paradine Case* file, DOS.
53. *New York Times*, July 27, 1947. Martin Quigley to Bishop Scully, Oct. 9, 1947; Cardinal Spellman to Charles Skouras, Oct. 3, 1947; Quigley Papers.
54. Leff and Simmons, *Dame in the Kimono*, p. 128. Davis, *City of Quartz*, p. 96. Rev. Patrick Masterson to Bishop Scully, Oct. 24, 1947. *New York Times*, Oct. 23, 1947. *Theater Facts*, Oct. 28, 1947.
55. Rev. Michael O. Driscoll to Rev. Patrick Masterson, Oct. 22, 1947, *Forever Amber* file, LDA.
56. Rev. Patrick Masterson to Bishop Scully, Oct. 24, 1947, *Forever Amber* file, LDA. *New York Times*, Oct. 24, 25, 1947.
57. Rev. Patrick Masterson to Rev. John Devlin, Oct. 27, 1947; *National Register* clipping, no date; *Forever Amber* file, LDA. Bishop Keough to William McTernan, Oct. 20, 1947, AAP. Keough to Scully, Nov. 1, 1947, AALA. Rev. Cletus Benjamin to Masterson, Oct. 31, 1947, Archives of the Archdiocese of Philadelphia. Scully, "To all bishops," Oct. 28, 1947, AALA. *New York Times*, Oct. 30, 31, 1947.
58. *National Register* clipping, no date; Rev. John Daly to Rev. Patrick Masterson, Nov. 4, 1947; Bishop O'Hara to Bishop Scully, Nov. 3, 1947; Rev. Masterson to Cardinal Spellman, Nov. 6,

1947; George Skouras to Thomas J. Smith, Oct. 29, 1947; *Forever Amber* file, LDA. *New York Times*, Nov. 22, 1947.

59. Davis, *Hollywood Beauty*, p. 104. Rev. Patrick Masterson to Bishop Scully, Oct. 27, 1947; Masterson to Cardinal Spellman, Oct. 29, 1947; *Forever Amber* file; LDA. Preminger, *Autobiography*, p. 127. Masterson to Spellman, Oct. 29, 1947, *Forever Amber* file, LDA.
60. Steven Jackson to Rev. Patrick Masterson, Nov. 6, 1947, *Forever Amber* file, LDA.
61. Ibid. *New York Times*, Nov. 5, 1947. Spyros Skouras to Father Masterson, no date, *Forever Amber* file, LDA.
62. Reviewers' evaluations, Nov. 26, 1947; Rev. Patrick Masterson to Rev. Leo Griffin, Feb. 6, 1948; *Forever Amber* file, LDA. Rev. John Devlin to Masterson, Oct. 28, 1948, AALA. Spyros Skouras to Buddy Adler, June 10, 1957, Skouras Papers.

CHAPTER 10. "GET FATHER DEVLIN"

1. *Ecclesiastical Review* 65, Dec. 1921, pp. 629–630.
2. D. W. Nye to Cecil B. deMille, Oct. 14, 1933; Rev. Daniel Lord to deMille, no date, Jan. 11, 1934. Jeff Lazarus to deMille, Jan. 16, 1934, deMille Collection.
3. Cecil B. deMille to Rev. Daniel Lord, Jan. 9, 1941; William deMille to C. deMille, May 21, 1941; Msgr. Fulton J. Sheen to C. deMille, March 26, 1941; deMille Collection.
4. Cecil B. deMille to Rev. Daniel Lord, May 28, 1941; Lord to deMille, June 2, 1941; deMille to Lord, Aug. 12, 1942; deMille Collection.
5. Bishop Cantwell to Rev. Hugh Duce, Sept. 26, 1933, AALA. Information on Devlin supplied by Msgr. Francis J. Weber, head of the AALA. *America*, Dec. 16, 1929.
6. Lou Edelman to Hal Wallis, Dec. 12, 1939, *The Fighting 69th* file, Warner Brothers Collection, USC. B. F. Grillo to Rev. John Devlin, June 11, 1946; notation on *Miracle of the Bells*, Sept. 21, 1947; AALA.
7. Letters are in the Father John Devlin file in the AALA. Rev. Edward Murphy to Devlin, Dec. 26, 1944; Devlin to Murphy, Jan. 6, 17, 1945; AALA.
8. *Columbia*, August 1942. Rev. John Devlin to Rev. John McClafferty, no date, Quigley Papers. Vizzard, *See No Evil*, p. 80. Devlin to Al Block, Nov. 4, 1944, AALA.
9. Dunne, "Blast It All," p. 10.
10. Rev. John Devlin to F. R. Masterly, June 23, 1944; Devlin to William Gordon, Jan. 11, 1945; Rev. John McClafferty to Devlin, July 6, 1943; AALA.
11. Rev. John Devlin to Clarence Hutson, May 4, 1944, AALA.
12. Rev. John Devlin to Al Cohen, Dec. 18, 1945; Msgr. Joseph Brennan to Jack Fier, no date; Devlin to B. B. Kahane, July 27, 1947; AALA. *Columbia*, August 1942.
13. Joe Breen to Jack Warner, June 24, 1938, *Angels with Dirty Faces* file, PCA.
14. Jack Vizzard to Martin Quigley, April 18, 1952, *I Confess* file, PCA. *Columbia*, August 1942. Geoff Shurlock, memorandum for files, April 10, 1952; Joe Breen to Alfred Hitchcock, July 24, Aug. 6, 1952; *I Confess* file, PCA.
15. Bishop Cantwell to Rev. John Devlin, no date, AALA. Mary Looram, IFCA "Report of the Chairman, 1936–1938," Quigley Papers.
16. Joseph L. Mankiewicz to Darryl Zanuck, no date, *Captain from Castille* file, Twentieth Century-Fox Collection, UCLA. Rev. John Devlin to Clarence Hutson, Dec. 14, 1944, AALA.
17. John Tucker Battle to Darryl Zanuck, Jan. 19, 1945, *Captain from Castille* file, Theatre Arts Collection, UCLA.
18. "Conference with Mr. Zanuck," Jan. 19, 20, Feb. 16, 1945, Twentieth Century-Fox Collection, USC. Rev. John Devlin to Jason Joy, Nov. 19, 1946, AALA.

19. Rev. John Devlin to Al Block, Feb. 20, 1947, AALA. Joe Breen to Louis B. Mayer, Dec. 16, 1947; Francis Harmon to Breen, no date; *Three Musketeers* file, PCA.
20. Florence Rounds to Joe Breen, Aug. 16, 1942, *Song of Bernadette* file, PCA. *America*, Jan. 2, 1943. Thomson, *Showman*, p. 396.
21. John J. McNulty, "To whom it may concern," April 10, 1947, *Miracle of the Bells* file, LDA. Bishop McGucken to Joe Breen, May 7, 1947, *Miracle of the Bells* file, PCA. McGucken to Bishop McIntyre, May 13, 1947, AALA.
22. Joe Breen to Rev. William Lallou, July 1, 1936; Will Hays to Joseph M. Schenck, July 18, 19, 1936; Lallou to Breen, July 6, 1936; Hays to Schenck, July 19, 1936; *Joan of Arc* file, PCA.
23. *New York Times*, Sept. 14, 15, 18, 1936.
24. Francis Harmon, memorandum, April 4, 1941; Joe Breen to Wolfgang Reinhardt, March 11, 1943; Gabriel Pascal to Breen, June 15, 1943; *Joan of Arc* file, PCA.
25. Martin Quigley to David O. Selznick, Oct. 4, 1946; Selznick to Quigley, Oct. 19, 1946; *Joan of Arc* file, LDA.
26. Bishop McIntyre to Bishop McGucken, April 15, 1947, AALA. Bernstein, *Walter Wanger*, pp. 237–246.
27. Bishop McGucken to Bishop McIntyre, May 13, 1947, AALA. Joe Breen to Giovanni Pagnamenta, Aug. 9, 1947; Rev. John Devlin to Rev. Patrick Masterson, Aug. 13, 1947; Masterson to Rev. John Devlin, Aug. 11, 1947; Devlin to Masterson, Aug. 13, 1947; *Joan of Arc* file, LDA.
28. Rev. Patrick Masterson to Rev. John Duffy, Sept. 4, 1947, LDA. Rev. Paul Donceur and Rev. William Lallou, "Summary of Joan of Arc," no date, *Joan of Arc* file, PCA. Martin Quigley to Rev. John Devlin, Sept. 16, 1947, AALA. Bernstein, *Walter Wanger*, pp. 243–244. *Columbia*, February 1949.
29. Darryl Zanuck, memorandum, Sept. 20, 1952, *The Gun and the Cross* file, Twentieth Century-Fox Collection, UCLA.
30. Summary in *Garden of Allah* file, PCA.
31. Joe Breen to David O. Selznick, Feb. 18, 1935, DOS. Martin Quigley to Breen, March 1, 1935; Msgr. Joseph Corrigan to Breen, Feb. 11, 1935; Rev. Wilfrid Parsons to Breen, Feb. 9, 1935; Rev. Edward Schwegler to Breen, Feb. 11, 1935; *Garden of Allah* file, PCA.
32. Joe Breen to David O. Selznick, Feb. 18, 1935, *Garden of Allah* file, PCA. Willis Goldbeck to Selznick, March 21, 1936, *Garden of Allah* file, DOS. Miller, "'Frankly, My Dear,'" p. 13.
33. Joe Breen to David O. Selznick, May 11, June 13, 1936, *Garden of Allah* file, DOS. Thomson, *Showman*, pp. 221–222. Val Lewton to Selznick, Oct. 8, 9, 1936, *Garden of Allah* file, DOS.
34. *America*, Nov. 28, 1936. Martin Quigley to Rev. Wilfrid Parsons, Nov. 10, 1936, Parsons Papers. *Motion Picture Herald*, Nov. 7, 1936. David O. Selznick to Lowell Calvert, May 20, 1937; G. Archibald to Calvert, April 28, 1937; *Garden of Allah* file, DOS.
35. Rev. John McClafferty to Msgr. McIntyre, Aug. 21, 1939, *The Fighting 69th* file, Warner Brothers Collection, USC. Rev. John Devlin to McClafferty, Oct. 17, 1945; Stephen Goodman to Devlin, Sept. 28, 1945; Devlin to Goodman, Oct. 8, 1945; AALA.
36. Bishop McGucken to Joe Breen, Aug. 19, 1943; Breen to McGucken, Aug. 20, 1943; Breen to Luigi Luraschi, Aug. 12, 1943; *Going My Way* file, PCA.
37. Richards, *Visions of Yesterday*, p. 260. *Pittsburgh Catholic*, July 27, Aug. 3, 10, 17, 1944. Keyser and Keyser, *Hollywood and the Catholic Church*, p. 93.
38. Cronin, *Keys of the Kingdom*, p. 8. Subsequent references appear parenthetically in the text.
39. "Notes on interview with Father John J. Devlin," no date, *Keys of the Kingdom* file, DOS.
40. Report from Joe Breen, no date, *Keys of the Kingdom* file, DOS. Breen to David O. Selznick, July 15, 1942, *Keys of the Kingdom* file, PCA.

41. Daniel O'Shea to David O. Selznick, Aug. 13, 1941, *Keys of the Kingdom* file, DOS. Myles Connelly to Rev. Wilfrid Parsons, Sept. 12, 1941, Parsons Papers.
42. *Commonweal*, Aug. 1, 1941. *Catholic World*, August 1941. *America*, July 26, 1941. *Catholic Students' Bulletin*, undated clipping, Parsons Papers. *Far East*, February 1942. Wuenschel, "Keys of the Kingdom," pp. 10–26.
43. "Outline . . . compiled from conferences between Dr. Cronin and Mr. Selznick," Sept. 8, 11, 1941, *Keys of the Kingdom* file, DOS. Rev. Wilfrid Parsons, diary, Jan. 29, Feb. 2, 1942; Parsons to Daniel O'Shea, Jan. 31, 1942; Parsons Papers. Rev. John Devlin to Rev. John McClafferty, Feb. 28, 1942, AALA. Parsons, memorandum on *The Keys* . . ., no date, Parsons Papers.
44. Rev. Wilfrid Parsons to "Father Assistant," April 4, 1942, Parsons Papers.
45. Notes on conferences between David O. Selznick and Father Parsons, Jan. 20–Feb. 6, 1942; Parsons Papers.
46. Rev. Wilfrid Parsons to "Father Assistant," April 4, 1942; Parsons to Daniel O'Shea, Nov. 7, 1941; 1942 conference notes; Barbara Keon to Rev. Wilfrid Parsons, Feb. 5, 1942, Parsons Papers.
47. 1942 notes on conferences between David O. Selznick and Father Parsons, Jan. 20–Feb. 6, 1942, Parsons Papers.
48. Rev. Vincent L. Keelan to Rev. Wilfrid Parsons, April 1, 1942; Parsons to "Father Assistant," April 4, 1942; Parsons Papers.
49. David O. Selznick to Jim Stewart, March 27, 1942; Robert Young to Selznick, April 8, 1942; Selznick to Rudy Vallee, Feb. 10, 1942; Whitney Bolton to Selznick, Jan. 6, April 25, 1942; Daniel O'Shea to Selznick, June 3, 1942; *Keys of the Kingdom* file, DOS.
50. Schatz, *Genius of the System*, pp. 322–330.
51. T. K. Chang to Joe Breen, Feb. 23, 1942, *Keys of the Kingdom* file, PCA. For a complete discussion of the relation of the Office of War Information to the film, see Black, "Keys of the Kingdom," pp. 434–446. Peg Fenwick, memorandum, Jan. 6, 1943, *Keys of the Kingdom* file, OWI Archives.
52. OWI Review, Dec. 12, 1944; William S. Cunningham to Randolph Sailer, April 13, 1944; *Keys of the Kingdom* file, OWI Archives. Jason Joy to Rev. Wilfrid Parsons, Oct. 19, 1943, Parsons Papers. Conference with Joseph L. Mankiewicz, Dec. 21, 1943, *Keys of the Kingdom* file, Twentieth Century-Fox Collection, UCLA.
53. Nunnally Johnson to Darryl Zanuck, June 17, 1943, Johnson Papers.
54. Rev. Wilfrid Parsons to Jason Joy, Feb. 6, 1944; Parsons to Rev. John Devlin, Feb. 7, 1944; Devlin to Parsons, Feb. 15, 1944; Parsons Papers.
55. Conference with Joseph L. Mankiewicz Sept. 2, 1943, *Keys of the Kingdom* file, Twentieth Century-Fox Collection, UCLA. Rev. Wilfrid Parsons, notes, Jan. 3, 1944; Parsons, memorandum, Jan. 28, 1944; Parsons Papers. Nunnally Johnson to Darryl Zanuck, June 17, 1943, Johnson Papers.
56. *Columbia*, July, 1944. Rev. Wilfrid Parsons, notes, Jan. 3, 1944, Parsons Papers.
57. Conference with Joseph L. Mankiewicz, Sept. 2, 1943, *Keys of the Kingdom* file, Twentieth Century-Fox Collection, UCLA.
58. Ibid. Rev. Wilfrid Parsons, memorandum on *Keys of the Kingdom*, no date, AAP.
59. Rev. Wilfrid Parsons, memorandum on *Keys of the Kingdom*, no date, AAP.
60. Rev. John Devlin to Rev. Wilfrid Parsons, Sept. 28, 1944, AALA. Rev. Albert O'Hara to Parsons, Jan. 15, 1944, Parsons Papers.
61. Rev. Wilfrid Parsons, memorandum on *Keys of the Kingdom*, no date; Rev. John McClafferty to Bishop Keough, Dec. 15, 1944; Parsons, memorandum on *Keys of the Kingdom*, no date, AAP.

62. Rev. Wilfrid Parsons, memorandum on *Keys of the Kingdom*, no date, AAP.
63. *America*, Jan. 13, 1945. *Commonweal*, Jan. 5, 1945. *Catholic World*, February 1945. Rev. Wilfrid Parsons to Tom Connors, Dec. 6, 1944; Rev. V. B. Maloney to Parsons, March 20, 1945; Rev. John Devlin to Parsons, May 25, 1945; Parsons Papers. *Catholic Northwest Progress*, Nov. 31, 1947.

CHAPTER 11. AN UNWELCOME *MIRACLE*

1. Hennesey, *American Catholics*, p. 287. *Saturday Review*, Feb. 20, 1949. *Life*, June 27, 1949.
2. Rev. John Devlin to Rev. John McClafferty, March 14, 1946, AALA. Joe Breen to Eric Johnston, April 15, 1945, *Doctor and the Girl* file, PCA. Leff and Simmons, *Dame in the Kimono*, pp. 168–170.
3. Jack Vizzard, memorandum for the files, Nov. 14, 1949, *Beyond the Forest* file, PCA. Stine, *Bette Davis, Mother Goddam*, pp. 228–229.
4. Rev. Patrick Masterson to Jack Warner, Oct. 26, 1949; Rev. Michael O'Shea to Masterson, Nov. 29, 1949; Evilyn Copenhauer to Warner Brothers, Nov. 1, 1949; *Beyond the Forest* file, PCA.
5. Rev. Patrick Masterson, memorandum, Oct. 28, 1949, *Beyond the Forest* file, LDA. Leff and Simmons, *Dame in the Kimono*, p. 170. Jack Vizzard, memorandum for the files, Nov. 14, 1949, *Beyond the Forest* file, PCA.
6. Joe Breen to Jason Joy, March 2, 1945, *Leave Her to Heaven* file, PCA. Albert Howson to Rev. Patrick Masterson, Nov. 8, 17, 1949; Jack Vizzard, memorandum for the files, Nov. 14, 1949; *Beyond the Forest* file, PCA.
7. Martin Quigley to Joe Breen, Nov. 23, 1949; Breen to Quigley, Nov. 29, 1949; *Beyond the Forest* file, PCA. Rev. Patrick Masterson, memorandum to Bishop Scully, Dec. 13, 1949, *Beyond the Forest* file, LDA.
8. Joe Breen to Luigi Luraschi, Sept. 30, 1949, Nov. 1, 14, 1949, *A Place in the Sun* file, PCA. Rev. Patrick Masterson, memorandum to Bishop Scully, Dec. 13, 1949, *Beyond the Forest* file, LDA. Leff and Simmons, *Dame in the Kimono*, p. 177.
9. Joe Breen to Jack Warner, April 28, 1950, *A Streetcar Named Desire* file, PCA. Schumach, *The Face on the Cutting Room Floor*, p. 72.
10. Joe Breen to Jack Warner, Aug. 24, 1950; Elia Kazan to Warner, Oct. 19, 1950; *A Streetcar Named Desire* file, PCA. Leff and Simmons, *Dame in the Kimono*, pp. 174–175. Schumach, *The Face on the Cutting Room Floor*, pp. 75–76.
11. Albert Howson to Jack Vizzard, July 11, 1951, *A Streetcar Named Desire* file, Warner Brothers-USC. Pauly, *American Odyssey*, p. 131.
12. Vizzard, *See No Evil*, p. 177.
13. Elia Kazan to Steve Trilling, July 27, 1951, *A Streetcar Named Desire* file, Warner Brothers Collection, USC.
14. Kazan, *A Life*, pp. 435–438. Rev. Paul Hayes, memoranda, May 10, 16, 1957, *A Face in the Crowd* file, LDA.
15. Izod, *Hollywood and the Box Office*, pp. 147–148. Leff and Simmons, *Dame in the Kimono*, p. 148. Leslie Halliwell, *Halliwell's Filmgoers and Video Viewer's Companion*, 9th ed. (New York, 1990), p. 1189.
16. David O. Selznick to Martin Quigley, no date, DOS. Rev. John McClafferty to Bishop Keough, Oct. 29, 1945, AAP.
17. Cardinal Stritch to Bishop Cushing, Sept. 3, 1946, AAB. Rev. Patrick Masterson to Bishop Scully, Feb. 19, 1952, Quigley Papers. *Variety*, Sept. 28, 1957.

18. *Variety*, Sept. 28, 1957, Dec. 26, 1956. *Commonweal*, Feb. 3, 1956.
19. *Motion Picture Herald*, Dec. 24, 1949. Rev. Thomas Little, memorandum to Diocesan Directors, March 9, 1951, *Bitter Rice* file, LDA.
20. *Tidings*, March 16, 1951. *New York Times*, Feb. 8, 1951. Rev. Edward Schwegler to Bishop Burke, July 28, 1952, Archives of the Archdiocese of Buffalo. *New York Times*, Feb. 8, 1951. Rev. Thomas Little, files, June 19, 1951; Martin Quigley to E. R. Zorgniotti, July 31, 1951; *Bitter Rice* file, LDA.
21. Entire list of cuts attached to letter from Clare Catalano to Rev. Patrick Masterson, Aug. 28, 1951, *Bitter Rice* file, LDA.
22. Rev. Patrick Masterson to Bishop Scully, Feb. 21, 1950; Mary Looram to Miss V. Bradford, March 23, 1950; Joe Breen to Martin Quigley, March 22, 1950; Rev. F. A. Morlion to Breen, Jan. 26, 1950; Quigley to Rev. Patrick Masterson, Feb. 3, 1950; Masterson to Cardinal Spellman, Feb. 3, 1950; *Stromboli* file, LDA.
23. Leff and Simmons, *Dame in the Kimono*, pp. 148, 153–155. Rev. Thomas Little to William Mooring, Jan. 28, 1954, *French Line* file, LDA. *Commonweal*, March 2, 1951.
24. Bishop Keough to Bishop Scully, Nov. 1, 1947, *Forever Amber* file, LDA.
25. Westin, *The Miracle Case*, pp. 7–8. Hugh Flick to James Allen, Jan. 10, 1951, *The Miracle* file, NYMPD.
26. Westin, *The Miracle Case*, p. 4.
27. Ibid. Hugh Flick, to James Allen, Jan. 10, 1951, *The Miracle* file, NYMPD.
28. *New York Times*, Dec. 31, 1950. *Motion Picture Herald*, Jan. 6, 1951.
29. *New York Times*, Jan. 8, 1951. De Grazia and Newman, *Banned Films*, p. 79. Cooney, *The American Pope*, p. 198.
30. *New York Times*, Jan. 8, 15, 1951. *Churchman*, Feb. 1, 1951. *Variety*, Jan. 24, 1951. *New York Times*, Jan. 28, 1951.
31. *New York Times*, Jan. 23, 1951.
32. For the letters on the film, see *The Miracle* file, NYMPD. Hugh Flick to Dr. James Allen, Jan. 10, 1951, *The Miracle* file, NYMPD.
33. Rev. Joseph McGucken to Bishop McIntyre, Jan. 11, 1951; McIntyre, "To editors of the papers," Jan. 30, 1951; AALA. *New York Times*, March 12, 1951.
34. *Commonweal*, March 2, 1951. Cooney, *The American Pope*, pp. 198–199. *Commonweal*, March 16, 1951.
35. De Grazia, *Girls Lean Back*, p. 81. Westin, *The Miracle Case*, pp. 30–31.
36. *Brooklyn Tablet*, June 28, 1952. Jowett, *Film*, p. 408. *America*, June 14, 1952. Westin, *The Miracle Case*, p. 33. Randall, *Censorship of the Movies*, pp. 51–52.
37. Rev. Patrick Masterson to Bishop Ready, Jan. 23, 1953, Quigley Papers. Jowett, *Film*, p. 408.
38. Rev. Patrick Masterson to Cecil B. deMille, Dec. 11, 1951; Rev. Thomas Little to Rev. Michael Driscoll, July 28, 1953; Quigley Papers.
39. Donald Hayne's notation is to the pamphlet "Reason and Purpose of the Legion of Decency"; Cecil B. deMille to Rev. Thomas Little, Dec. 26, 1951, deMille Collection.
40. Ibid. Rev. Thomas Little to Cecil B. deMille, Jan. 4, 1951, deMille Collection.
41. Msgr. J. B. Lux to Rev. John McGrath, April 7, 1952, deMille Collection.
42. Y. F. Freeman to Cecil B. deMille; deMille to Freeman, June 19, 1952; deMille Collection. *Providence Visitor*, June 25, 1953.
43. Rev. Thomas Little to Harry Brandt, Oct. 15, 1953; Brandt to Little, Nov. 12, 1953; Quigley Papers.
44. Vizzard, *See No Evil*, pp. 152–155. Leff and Simmons, *Dame in the Kimono*, pp. 193–195. Personal interview with Rev. Patrick Sullivan, April 19, 1990.

45. Leff and Simmons, *Dame in the Kimono*, pp. 193, 197. Balio, *United Artists: The Company Built by the Stars*, p. 66.
46. Leff and Simmons, *Dame in the Kimono*, p. 199. Personal interview with Rev. Patrick Sullivan, April 19, 1990.
47. Rev. Thomas Little to Rev. Albert Bauman, July 7, 1953, LDA.
48. *New York Times*, June 25, 1953. *Tidings*, July 3, 1953. Legion of Decency to all bishops, Nov. 26, 1954, AAB. *Variety*, Oct. 28, 1953. Rev. H. D. Buchanan to Rev. Patrick Masterson, July 24, 1953, *Moon Is Blue* file, LDA. Robert Seoane to management of the McLean Theater, July 8, 1953, Virginia Division of Motion Picture Censorship. Balio, *United Artists: The Company Built by the Stars*, pp. 68–69. Vizzard, *See No Evil*, p. 157.
49. *Variety*, Sept. 16, Aug. 17, 1953.
50. Rev. Thomas Little, National Legion of Decency annual report, 1954; Rev. Albert Bauman to Rev. Thomas Little, July 15, 1953; Rev. Edward Schwegler to parish priests, Sept. 10, 1953; NCWC-NCCB. *Commonweal*, June 17, 1953.
51. Rev. Ferdinand Falque to Rev. Patrick Masterson, Aug. 28, 1953; Falque to Rev. Thomas Little, Sept. 5, 1953; George Schaefer to Patrick Fagan, Dec. 2, 1953; Little to Cardinal Spellman, Dec. 10, 1953; *Moon Is Blue* file, LDA.
52. *New York Times*, Feb. 22, 1951. William F. McTernan to Bishop McVinney, Oct. 16, 1953, AAP. Personal interview with Rev. Patrick Sullivan, April 19, 1990. Rev. Ferdinand Falque to Rev. Thomas Little, Sept. 5, 1953, *Moon Is Blue* file, LDA.

CHAPTER 12. WANING POWERS

1. Rev. Thomas Little to Martin Quigley, Feb. 1, 1954, Quigley Papers.
2. Gardner, *The Censorship Papers*, pp. 13–14.
3. Leff and Simmons, *Dame in the Kimono*, pp. 202; 206.
4. Vizzard, *See No Evil*, pp. 206–207.
5. Rev. Thomas Little, memorandum for the files, Jan. 8, 1954, *French Line* file, LDA.
6. Ibid. Mary Looram, memorandum for the files, Jan. 11, 1954; Rev. Thomas Little, confidential report, Jan. 18, 1954; *French Line* file, LDA.
7. Mary Looram, memorandum for the files, Jan. 11, 1954; Rev. Thomas Little, confidential report, memorandum for the files, Jan. 18, 1954; *French Line* file, LDA.
8. *Pastoral Life*, May–June 1954. Rev. Michael Driscoll to "Reverend Dear Father," Feb. 15, 1954, *French Line* file, LDA. *Variety*, May 12, 1954.
9. Ibid. Lt. William McTernan to John Murphy, *French Line* file, NYMPD. Leff and Simmons, *Dame in the Kimono*, p. 210. Ad in Religious News Service photo, *French Line* file, LDA. *Orchard Park Penny Saver*, Dec. 2, 1954, Archives of the Archdiocese of Buffalo.
10. Rev. Thomas Little to Joe Breen, Feb. 1, 1954; Little to Bishop Scully, Sept. 23, 1954; *French Line* file, LDA. Scully quote from undated note in Archives of the Archdiocese of Buffalo. National Legion of Decency annual report, 1954, NCWC-NCCB.
11. *America*, May 28, 1955. Legion of Decency annual report, 1955, Archives of the Archdiocese of Buffalo. Legion of Decency annual report, 1956, AAB.
12. *Variety*, May 5, 1955.
13. *Variety*, June 24, 1955. *Los Angeles Times*, June 12, 1955. Legion of Decency annual report, 1954, NCWC-NCCB.
14. Frank McCarthy to Rev. Thomas Little, May 7, 1957. Legion of Decency annual report, 1956, AAB. National Legion of Decency annual report, 1954, NCWC-NCCB. *Variety*, Feb. 24, 1955.

15. *Hollywood Citizen News*, July 21, 1956.
16. *Brooklyn Tablet*, Sept. 3, 1955. Rev. Robert Sennott to Rev. Thomas Little, Oct. 5, 1956, AAB.
17. R. R. Christ to Henry Blanke and Leon Uris, Oct. 19, 1953, *Battle Cry* file; Joe Breen to Eric Johnston, Sept. 10, 1954; Warner Brothers Collection, USC. Rev. Thomas Little, files, Jan. 10, 1955, *Battle Cry* file, LDA.
18. Rev. Thomas Little, files, Jan. 10, 1955, *Battle Cry* file, LDA. Legion of Decency annual report, 1955, Archives of the Archdiocese of Buffalo.
19. Koppes and Black, *Hollywood Goes to War*, p. 27. *Tidings*, Jan. 26, 1953, Feb. 9, 1951, May 8, 1953.
20. *New York Times*, Oct. 14, 1956. Rev. Thomas Little, memorandum, June 1, 1956; reviewers' comments; *Storm Center* file, LDA.
21. Rev. Thomas Little, memorandum, June 1, 1956. Legion of Decency annual report, 1956, AAB. *New World*, Sept. 14, 1956. *Commonweal*, Aug. 3, 1956.
22. Vizzard, *See No Evil*, p. 226. Arthur DeBra, special brochure issued by MPAA, July 1956, *Storm Center* file, PCA.
23. Rev. Thomas Little to Dore Schary, July 22, 1954, Quigley Papers.
24. Martin Quigley to Joe Breen, Oct. 12, 1953; memorandum for the files, Oct. 29, 1953; *Tea and Sympathy* file, PCA.
25. Dore Schary to Rev. Thomas Little, July 27, 1954, Quigley Papers. Little to Nicholas Schenck, Sept. 27, 1955, *Tea and Sympathy* file, LDA. Geoff Shurlock, memorandum for the files, Nov. 10, 1953, April 6, 29, 1955, *Tea and Sympathy* file, PCA. Simmons, "The Production Code under New Management," p. 8.
26. Rev. Thomas Little, files, Aug. 14, 23, 1956, *Tea and Sympathy* file, LDA.
27. Ibid.
28. Ibid., Aug. 29, 1956.
29. Ibid., Sept. 5, Sept. 7, 1956.
30. Ibid., Sept. 14, 1956.
31. Gadge Kazan to Jack Warner, Nov. 15, 1955, *Baby Doll* file, Warner Brothers Collection, USC. Vizzard, *See No Evil*, p. 206.
32. Vizzard, *See No Evil*, pp. 207–208. Bishop Scully to Jack Vizzard, April 15, 1957, Archives of the Archdiocese of Albany.
33. *America*, Dec. 29, 1956. Vizzard, *See No Evil*, p. 209. *Time*, Dec. 24, 1956.
34. *New York Times*, Dec. 17, 24, 1956. Cooney, *American Pope*, p. 202. De Grazia, *Girls Lean Back*, p. 407. Martin Quigley to Cardinal Spellman, Dec. 14, 1956, Quigley Papers. *New York Times*, Dec. 24, 1956.
35. O'Brien, *Faith and Friendship*, p. 293. Information on boycotts in *Baby Doll* file, LDA. Papers relating to restaurant chain protest in Archives of the Archdiocese of Buffalo. *Providence Visitor*, Jan. 3, 1957. John Donnelly to Rev. Thomas Little, *Baby Doll* file, LDA.
36. Giglio, "The Decade of *The Miracle*," p. 218. Vizzard, *See No Evil*, p. 209. Martin Quigley to Bishop Scully, Jan. 2, 1957, Quigley Papers. Undated *Variety* clipping, *Baby Doll* file, LDA.
37. *Commonweal*, Jan. 11, Feb. 1, 1957. Martin Quigley to Bishop Scully, Jan. 2, 1957, Quigley Papers. Vizzard, *See No Evil*, pp. 209–210.
38. Martin Quigley to Cardinal Spellman, April 30, 1957, Quigley Papers. Kazan, *A Life*, p. 564.
39. Martin Quigley to Cardinal Spellman, April 26, 30, May 2, 1947, Quigley Papers.
40. Joe Breen to Eric Johnston, March 18, 1949, Quigley Papers. *Life*, June 27, 1949.
41. Rev. Patrick Masterson to Bishop Scully, May 13, 1948; Martin Quigley to Masterson, May 17, 1948; Martin Quigley to Burke Walsh, Sept. 12, 1946; Rev. Patrick Masterson to Bishop

Scully, May 13, 1948; Quigley Papers. Rev. John McClafferty to Rev. Cletus Benjamin, Dec. 6, 1946, Archives of the Archdiocese of Philadelphia.

42. Archbishop McIntyre to Bishop Scully, May 7, 1948; Rev. Patrick Masterson to Bishop Scully, May 13, 1948; Joe Breen to Martin Quigley, Nov. 30, 1950; Quigley Papers.
43. Joe Breen to Eric Johnston, July 14, 1952, Quigley Papers. Mortimer Adler to Will Hays, Nov. 1, 1942, WHP.
44. Joe Breen to Eric Johnston, July 14, 1952; Martin Quigley to Breen, June 24, 1952; Quigley Papers. *Island in the Sun* file, Virginia State Archives.
45. Joe Breen, confidential report, Nov. 30, 1950; Breen, "Recommended changes," no date; Quigley Papers. Jowett, *Film*, appendix 7, p. 475.
46. Darryl Zanuck to Jerry Wald, Feb. 23, 1954, *The Robe* file, PCA. *Newsweek*, Jan. 7, 1957. *Motion Picture Herald*, Jan. 2, 1954. *Tidings*, March 13, 1953.
47. *America*, March 9, 1956. *Commonweal*, Feb. 19, 1954.
48. Rev. Thomas Little to Bishop Scully, Dec. 21, 1955, *Man with the Golden Arm* file, LDA.
49. Legion of Decency annual report, 1956, AAB. *New York Times*, Dec. 16, 1956. *Variety*, Aug. 22, 1956. *Catholic Standard*, Jan. 27, 1956.
50. MPAA news release, Dec. 11, 1956, LDA. *New York Times*, Dec. 12, 1956. *Newsweek*, Jan. 7, 1957.

CHAPTER 13. THE JESUITS TO THE RESCUE

1. *Ave Maria*, Feb. 4, 1951.
2. O'Brien, *Public Catholicism*, p. 225. Murray, *We Hold These Truths*, p. 168. Rev. Thomas Little to Rev. Francis Connell, June 28, 1956; Connell to Little, July 18, 1956; Quigley Papers. Reher, *Catholic Intellectual Life in America*, p. 128.
3. Getlein and Gardiner, *The Art of the Movies*, p. 99. *Our Sunday Visitor*, May 21, 1961. O'Brien, *Public Catholicism*, p. 207. Lally, "Points of Abrasion," pp. 78–82. Martin Quigley to Cardinal Stritch, Dec. 31, 1957, Quigley Papers.
4. Rev. Thomas Little to William Mooring, Jan. 28, 1954, *The French Line* file, LDA. Rev. Gerald Kelly to Little, Sept. 25, 1954, Quigley Papers. Bishop Cushing, "To all priests," Dec. 28, 1954, AAB.
5. Martin Quigley to Cardinal Spellman, Aug. 1, 1956, Quigley Papers.
6. Connell, "How Should Priests Direct People," pp. 253, 249, 250. Bishop Cantwell to Rev. Francis J. Connell, Feb. 2, 1946, AALA.
7. Connell, "How Should Priests Direct People," pp. 244, 249.
8. Frank Hall to Msgr. Carroll, Jan. 14, 1957; Rev. Thomas Little, National Legion of Decency annual reports, 1954, 1960; NCWC-NCCB. Annual Conference of Bishops, November 1960, Archives of the Archdiocese of Baltimore.
9. Paul Edwards, "Poison! Believe the Label," no date, pamphlet no. 264, Catholic Information Society. Paul Edwards was the pseudonym of two brothers: Father Edward and Father Paul Hayes. Philadelphia Legion Pamphlet in the AAP. *Advocate*, May 10, 1958.
10. William Mooring, *Tidings*, Feb. 1, 1952. Walter Kerr, "Catholics and Hollywood," *Commonweal*, Dec. 19, 1952, pp. 275–277.
11. Martin Quigley to Rev. Thomas Little, Jan. 14, 1954, Quigley Papers. Geissman, "All is God," pp. 1–5. Rev. Gerard Dennen to Erwin Geissman, Jan. 14, 1954, Quigley Papers.
12. Rev. Gerald Kelly to Rev. Thomas Little, Sept. 25, 1954, Quigley Papers.
13. Kelly and Ford, "The Legion of Decency," pp. 417–419, 426, 424, 412–413.

14. Personal interviews with Father Patrick Sullivan, April 19, 1990, April 12, 1991.
15. Rev. Patrick Sullivan to Martin Quigley, Oct. 29, 1957, Quigley Papers. Pius XII, *Miranda Prorsus*, pp. 21–26.
16. *Motion Picture Exhibitor*, Oct. 23, 1957.
17. Connell, "Pope Pius XII and the Legion of Decency," pp. 392–399. Personal interview with Father Patrick Sullivan, April 12, 1991. Bishop Krol to Martin Quigley, June 11, 1962; Quigley to Bishop Scully, June 13, 1962; Annual Conference of Bishops, Nov. 12, 1957; Quigley papers.
18. Annual Conference of Bishops, Nov. 12, 1957, Quigley Papers. Episcopal Committee Report, Nov. 14, 1956, Archives of the Archdiocese of Albany.
19. Ibid. Annual Conference of Bishops, Nov. 11, 1958, Quigley Papers. National Catholic Office for Motion Pictures, *Films 1969–1970*, (1970).
20. *America*, Jan. 18, 1958. T. M. Manos to Spyros Skouras, Jan. 16, 1959, Skouras Papers.
21. Rev. Thomas Little to Geoffrey Shurlock, March 5, 1959; Shurlock to Little, March 18, 1959; LDA.
22. Rev. Patrick Sullivan to Anita Hart, July 8, 1958, *Peyton Place* file, LDA. Martin Quigley to Cardinal Stritch, Nov. 31, 1957; Quigley to Bishop Scully, Jan. 21, 1958; Quigley to Rev. Thomas Little, June 26, 1961; Quigley, memorandum, Jan. 13, 1961; Quigley Papers.
23. Personal interview with Father Patrick Sullivan, April 12, 1991.
24. Geoffrey Shurlock to Otto Preminger, Dec. 8, 1958, Aug. 30, 1959; Preminger to Shurlock, Feb. 25, April 29, 1959; *Anatomy of a Murder* file, PCA.
25. Preminger, *An Autobiography*, p. 188. Legion of Decency, annual report, 1959, LDA. Martin Quigley to William Mooring, July 20, 1959; Rev. Thomas Little to Mooring, March 29, 1960; Mooring to Little, March 30, 1960; Quigley Papers. *Tidings*, March 25, 1960.
26. Martin Quigley to William Mooring, July 27, 1959; Mooring, "Hollywood Focus," July 24, 1959; Quigley Papers.
27. Fragment of undated review in Quigley Papers. Rev. Thomas Little, files, *Suddenly Last Summer* file, LDA.
28. Mary B. Healy to Rev. Thomas Little, no date, LDA. *Brooklyn Tablet*, Dec. 12, 1959. *New York Sunday News*, April 3, 1960. *America*, Jan. 9, 1960. Bishop McNulty to Cardinal McIntyre, Dec. 15, 1959, AALA.
29. See May 8, 10, 1951, *Hoodlum Priest* file, LDA. Rev. John Devlin to Cardinal McIntyre, Nov. 9, 1959; Bishop McNulty to McIntyre, Jan. 12, 1960; McIntyre to McNulty, Jan. 19, 1960; McIntyre to Rev. Thomas Little, no date; AALA.
30. Rev. Thomas Little, files, Sept. 15, 1961; Reviewers' evaluations; Rev. Patrick Sullivan to Sister Annella, Sept. 21, 1961, *King of Kings* file, LDA. Personal interview with Father Patrick Sullivan, April 12, 1991.
31. Personal interview with Father Patrick Sullivan, Jan. 31, 1992. Rev. Patrick Sullivan, memorandum to Bishop McNulty, May 24, 1961, *La Dolce Vita* file, LDA.
32. Rev. Patrick Sullivan, memorandum to Bishop McNulty, May 24, 1961, *La Dolce Vita* file, LDA. Geoff Shurlock to Joseph G. Besch, April 13, 1962, *La Dolce Vita* file, PCA. A. Tarell to Rev. Thomas Little, April 28, 1961; *La Dolce Vita* file, LDA.
33. *Variety*, May 19, 1961.
34. *Davenport Messenger* review reprinted in *Catholic Assent*, June 7, 1962.
35. Martin Quigley to Patrick Scanlan, Nov. 16, 1959, Quigley Papers. Rev. John Devlin to Cardinal McIntyre, May 5, 1961, Jan. 11, 1962, AALA. *Limelight*, July 27, 1961. Rev. Thomas Little, files, Sept. 25, 1961, *King of Kings* file, LDA. Little to David Maguire, Sept. 19, 1961;

Bishop Scully, "Statement on La Dolce Vita," Oct. 3, 1961, *La Dolce Vita* file, LDA. Personal interview with Father Sullivan, April 19, 1990.

36. Martin Quigley to Bishop McNulty, May 5, 1961; Quigley to McNulty, May 17, 1961; Quigley Papers.
37. Information on Quigley Publications' financial difficulties supplied by Martin Quigley, Jr., personal interview, April 19, 1990.
38. Lord, *Played by Ear*, p. 281. *Catholic Times*, April 9, 1954. Undated *New World* clippings in Quigley Papers. *Catholic Transcript*, April 15, 1954.
39. Martin Quigley to Rev. Francis Connell, May 21, 1954; Connell to Quigley, May 30, 1954; Rev. John McClafferty to editor of *Catholic Times*, April 22, 1954; Quigley Papers.
40. Vizzard, *See No Evil*, pp. 257–258. Bishop Scully to Jack Vizzard, April 15, 1957, Archives of the Archdiocese of Albany. Joe Breen to Martin Quigley, Feb. 21, 1957; Quigley to Cardinal Stritch, Dec. 31, 1957; Quigley Papers.
41. Unsigned, undated memorandum, LDA. Bishop McNulty to Martin Quigley, May 17, 1961, Quigley Papers.
42. Personal interviews with Father Patrick Sullivan, April 19, 1990, Jan. 31, 1992.
43. Rev. Thomas Little to Martin Quigley, March 7, 9, 1960, Quigley Papers. Quigley to Little, March 8, 14, 1960; Quigley to Martin Quigley, Jr., Nov. 17, 1961; Quigley Papers.
44. Leff and Simmons, *Dame in the Kimono*, pp. 222–224.
45. Leff and Simmons, *Dame in the Kimono*, p. 222. Movie advertisement; Msgr. James Ling, news release, July 28, 1958; *And God Created Woman* file, LDA.
46. Annual Conference of Bishops, November 1960, NCWC-NCCB. *Commonweal*, Oct. 24, Dec. 5, 1958. Leff and Simmons, *Dame in the Kimono*, p. 230.
47. Leff and Simmons, *Dame in the Kimono*, p. 222.
48. Martin Quigley to Stanley Kubrick and James Harris, Nov. 30, 1960, Quigley Papers. Leff and Simmons, *Dame in the Kimono*, p. 224. Harris to Quigley, Dec. 14, 19, 1960, Quigley Papers.
49. Martin Quigley to James Harris, Dec. 19, 1960; Harris to Quigley, Jan. 30, 1961; Quigley Papers. Leff and Simmons, *Dame in the Kimono*, p. 230.
50. Martin Quigley to James Harris, Dec. 19, 1960, Quigley Papers.
51. Vizzard, *See No Evil*, p. 267.
52. Vizzard, *See No Evil*, pp. 270–271.
53. Elliot Hyman to Martin Quigley, Aug. 1, 1961, Quigley Papers. Letter of complaint, Dec. 9, 1960, *Lolita* file, LDA. Rev. Thomas Little, memorandum to Cardinal Spellman, Oct. 20, 1961; Little to David Stillman, Oct. 16, 1961; *Lolita* file, LDA.
54. David Stillman to Bishop McNulty, Oct. 13, 1961, *Lolita* file, LDA.
55. Rev. Thomas Little to David Stillman, Oct. 16, 1961, *Lolita* file, LDA. Martin Quigley to Cardinal Spellman, Oct. 20, 1961, Quigley Papers.
56. Rev. Thomas Little, files, Oct. 26, 1961; Little to David Baird, Oct. 26, 1961; *Lolita* file, LDA.
57. Elliot Hyman to Rev. Thomas Little, Feb. 6, 1961; Little, "Conference re *Lolita*—Feb. 6th—4 P.M."; *Lolita* file, LDA.
58. Leff and Simmons, *Dame in the Kimono*, pp. 238, 316.
59. Leff and Simmons, *Dame in the Kimono*, pp. 235, 238. *New York Herald Tribune*, July 15, 1962.

CHAPTER 14. END OF THE ROAD

1. Bishop Alter to Martin Quigley, July 3, 1961; Quigley to Alter, Sept. 26, 1961; Quigley Papers.

2. Bishop Alter to Martin Quigley, Oct. 3, 1961, Quigley Papers. Alter to Msgr. Paul Tanner, Oct. 3, 1961, NCWC-NCCB. Personal interview with Father Patrick Sullivan, April 12, 1991. Bishop McNulty to Tanner, Oct. 12, 1961, NCWC-NCCB.
3. Msgr. Paul Tanner to Bishop McNulty, Oct. 30, 1961; minutes of the Administrative Board of the NCWC, Nov. 13, 14, 1961, NCWC-NCCB. Martin Quigley to Bishop Alter, Dec. 29, 1961, Quigley Papers.
4. Bishop Alter to Martin Quigley, Jan. 2, 1962, Quigley Papers. Bishop McNulty to Msgr. Paul Tanner, Oct. 26, 1961, NCWC-NCCB. Personal interview with Father Patrick Sullivan, April 19, 1990, April 12, 1991.
5. O'Brien, *Public Catholicism*, p. 235. Allitt, *Catholic Intellectuals and Conservative Politics*, p. 10.
6. McAvoy, *A History of the Catholic Church*, p. 460. Cogley, *Catholic America*, p. 117.
7. Annual Conference of Bishops, November 1959, Archives of the Archdiocese of Baltimore. Martin Quigley to Father John Devlin, Dec. 4, 1959, Quigley Papers.
8. Rev. Thomas Little to the bishops, Nov. 27, 1963, AAP. Personal interview with Father Patrick Sullivan, April 19, 1990. Annual Conference of Bishops, Nov. 12, 1964, NCWC-NCCB.
9. Martin Quigley to Bishop Scully, Nov. 25, 1949, *Beyond the Forest* file, LDA. Quigley to Bishop Krol, June 7, 1962; Quigley to Rev. Thomas Little, Sept. 21, 1955; Quigley Papers. *America*, Sept. 24, 1955. Krol to Quigley, June 11, 1962; Quigley Papers. Bishop Scully to Quigley, June 13, 1962, Archives of the Archdiocese of Albany.
10. Martin Quigley to New World Films, Dec. 3, 1962; Quigley to Darryl Zanuck, Jan. 25, 1963; Quigley Papers. Rev. Thomas Little, files, Jan. 23, 1963, *The Cardinal* file, LDA.
11. Personal interview with Father Patrick Sullivan, Jan. 31, 1992.
12. Rev. Patrick Masterson to Martin Quigley, Feb. 24, 28, 1950, *The Cardinal* file, LDA.
13. Michael Blankfort to Harry Cohn, Oct. 2, 1956; Hodges et al. to Cardinal Spellman, Oct. 15, 1956; *The Cardinal* file, LDA.
14. Preminger, *An Autobiography*, pp. 213, 214. Martin Quigley to Preminger, Nov. 20, 1962, Quigley Papers.
15. *Boston Pilot*, Sept. 14, 1963. Martin Quigley to Otto Preminger, Sept. 17, 1963, Quigley Papers. J. Raymond Bell to Rev. Thomas Little, Oct. 8, 1963, *The Cardinal* file, LDA.
16. Rev. Thomas Little to Bishop Krol, Oct. 31, 1963, *The Cardinal* file, LDA. "Grounds for A–3 rating of *The Cardinal*," no date, LDA.
17. *America*, May 9, 1964. *Time*, Dec. 3, 1965. Phelan, "National Catholic Office for Motion Pictures," p. 299.
18. *Tidings*, March 25, 1960.
19. Rev. Patrick Sullivan, files, May 23, 1961; Rev. Thomas Little, files, June 22, 1961; *Splendor in the Grass* file, LDA.
20. Rev. Patrick Sullivan to Rev. Thomas Little, July 11, 1961, *Splendor in the Grass* file, LDA. Little, files, May 28, 1962, *The Chapman Report* file, LDA.
21. Rev. Thomas Little to Cardinal McIntyre, March 28, 1960, LDA. *Box-Office*, Dec. 14, 1964. Phelan, "National Catholic Office for Motion Pictures," pp. 189–190. Vizzard, *See No Evil*, pp. 302–303.
22. Vizzard, *See No Evil*, pp. 303–304. Rev. Thomas Little to David Picker, Oct. 25, 1964, *Kiss Me Stupid* file, LDA.
23. Billy Wilder to Robert Benjamin, Nov. 6, 1964, *Kiss Me Stupid* file, LDA.
24. Robert Benjamin to Billy Wilder, Nov. 9, 1964, Diamond Papers.
25. *Variety*, Dec. 9, 1964. Vizzard, *See No Evil*, p. 304. *Motion Picture Daily*, Dec. 8, 1964. Balio, *United Artists: The Company that Changed the Film Industry*, p. 183.

26. *Los Angeles Examiner and Herald American*, Dec. 27, 1964. Leff and Simmons, *Dame in the Kimono*, pp. 252–253.
27. *America*, Dec. 11, 1965. Leff and Simmons, *Dame in the Kimono*, pp. 251–253.
28. Stone, "The Legion of Decency," *Newsweek*, Dec. 28, 1964.
29. Phelan, "National Catholic Office for Motion Pictures," p. 95. Legion of Decency annual report, 1965, NCWC-NCCB.
30. *Time*, Dec. 3, 1965. Phelan, "National Catholic Office for Motion Pictures," p. 95. NCOMP, press release, Dec. 8, 1965, LDA.
31. *Richmond News-Leader*, March 1, 1965. *Richmond Times Dispatch*, May 20, 1965.
32. Dolan, *The American Catholic Experience*, p. 426.
33. McLaughlin, "Study of the National Catholic Office for Motion Pictures," p. 91. *America*, Dec. 11, 1965. Vizzard, *See No Evil*, p. 264.
34. O'Brien, *The Renewal of American Catholicism*, p. 155. Mrs. Van C. Newkirk to Rev. Thomas Little, Feb. 28, 1966, *Darling* file, LDA. Personal interview with Msgr. Paul Hayes, April 11, 1991. *Brooklyn Tablet*, Jan. 6, 1962, Aug. 26, 1965. *Tidings*, March 19, 1943.
35. Jerry Gutzweiler to Rev. Patrick Sullivan, April 17, 1967, *Hurry Sundown* file, LDA. Summary, Feb. 24, 1966; David Picker to Rev. Thomas Little, March 2, 1966; *The Group* file, LDA.
36. McLaughlin, "Study of the National Catholic Office for Motion Pictures," p. 134. *Variety*, Aug. 7, 28, 1934. F. W. Allport, report, Oct. 29, 1934, WHP. Age classification kit in Interstate Theater Collection, Dallas Public Library. Personal interview with Father Patrick Sullivan, April 12, 1991.
37. *Variety*, Dec. 5, 1962. Eric Johnston to Spyros Skouras, April 10, 1963, Skouras Papers.
38. Leff, "A Test of American Film Censorship," pp. 213–219.
39. Leff, "A Test of American Film Censorship," pp. 223–224.
40. Transcript of Production Code Review Board, June 15, 1966, Skouras Papers. Leff, "A Test of American Film Censorship," pp. 219, 224–227.
41. Vizzard, *See No Evil*, p. 323. Martin Quigley, Jr., to Cardinal Spellman, June 27, 1966; letters of complaint; Rev. Patrick Sullivan to Bishop Hyde, June 16, 1966; *Who's Afraid of Virginia Woolf?* file, LDA.
42. Leff and Simmons, *Dame in the Kimono*, pp. 264–265.
43. Phelan, "National Catholic Office for Motion Pictures," p. 102.
44. Jowett, "Moral Responsibility and Commercial Entertainment," pp. 25, 26.
45. Leff and Simmons, *Dame in the Kimono*, p. 274.
46. Personal interview with Henry Herx, Dec. 15, 1993.
47. *Catholic Film Newsletter*, Aug. 15, 1969. Mrs. Van C. Newkirk to Rev. Thomas Little, Feb. 28, 1966, *Darling* file, LDA.
48. *Catholic Film Newsletter*, Aug. 15, 1969, Aug. 15, 1970. Phelan, "National Catholic Office for Motion Pictures," p. 254.
49. *Time*, April 28, 1967. John T. Murphy to Rev. Patrick Sullivan, April 27, 1967, *Caprice* file, LDA. McLaughlin, "Study of the National Catholic Office for Motion Pictures," p. 132. *America*, June 15, 1968. Rev. Patrick Sullivan to Archbishop Krol, Oct. 14, 1966, *Hawaii* file, LDA.
50. *America*, June 15, 1968, April 19, 1969. McLaughlin, "Study of the National Catholic Office for Motion Pictures," p. 131.
51. *Catholic Film Newsletter*, March 30, 1974, Aug. 30, 1974. *Film and Broadcasting Review*, April 1, 1977. Wall, "Interviews with Geoffrey Shurlock," p. 312. Vizzard, *See No Evil*, p. 231.
52. *Commonweal*, May 23, 1969. *America*, April 19, 1969. Phelan, "National Catholic Office for Motion Pictures," p. 300.

53. *America*, Nov. 11, 1967.
54. *America*, May 29, 1971. Skinner, "Tussle with Russell," p. 11. Leff and Simmons, *Dame in the Kimono*, p. 273. *Catholic Film Newsletter*, Feb. 29, 1972.
55. *Catholic Film Newsletter*, Sept. 30, 1970. *Film and Broadcasting Review*, Feb. 1, 1980.
56. Dolan, *The American Catholic Experience*, p. 435. *Variety*, Jan. 27, 1972. Personal interview with Henry Herx, Dec. 15, 1993.
57. *Variety*, April 26, 1967, March 8, 1972. *Film and Broadcasting Review*, Sept. 1, 1980.

EPILOGUE

1. *New York Times*, Jan. 10, 1993.
2. *Movieguide*, October A, 1994.
3. *Movieguide*, September A, 1994.
4. Ibid.
5. *Family Voice*, October 1992. *Boston Globe*, Feb. 8, 1992.
6. *Daily Variety*, May 4, 1992. Cardinal Mahony, "Film Makers, Film Viewers: Their Challenges and Opportunities," Sept. 30, 1992, p. 4, courtesy of the Archdiocese of Los Angeles. *Washington Times*, Sept. 20, 1994.
7. *New York Times*, Aug. 12, July 21, Aug. 13, 1988.
8. *New York Times*, Aug. 12, 13, 1988.
9. *New York Times*, July 21, Aug. 14, 1988.
10. *Boston Globe*, July 25, 1993. Associated Press, July 19, 1994. *Movieguide*, Aug. A, 1994.
11. Rev. Daniel Lord, "The Code—One Year Later," April 23, 1931, Lord Papers. Medved, *Hollywood vs. America*, pp. 52, 277. Gardner, *Censorship Papers*, pp. 100–101. *Variety*, Sept. 12, 1994.
12. *New York Times*, Aug. 13, 1988.
13. Molly Ivins, "Take No Bull," *Boston Phoenix*, June 25, 1993.

BIBLIOGRAPHY

■■■

ARCHIVAL COLLECTIONS

American Antiquarian Society, Worcester, Mass.
American Film Institute, Los Angeles
America Archives, Special Collections Division, Georgetown University Archives, Washington, D.C.
Archives of the Archdioceses of Albany, Baltimore, Boston, Buffalo, Cleveland, Detroit, Los Angeles, New York, Philadelphia, Providence, San Francisco, and Syracuse
Audrey Chamberlain Scrapbook, Margaret Herrick Library, Academy of Motion Picture Arts and Sciences, Los Angeles
Cecil B. deMille Collection, Harold B. Lee Library, Brigham Young University, Provo, Utah
I. A. Diamond Papers, Special Collections, University of Wisconsin, Madison
Theodore Dreiser Papers, University of Pennsylvania
Will H. Hays Papers, Indiana State Library, Indianapolis. Microfilm edition, University Publications of America
International Federation of Catholic Alumnae Collection, Catholic University of America, Washington, D.C.

Interstate Theater Collection, Dallas Public Library
Nunnally Johnson Papers, Special Collections, Mugar Library, Boston University
Knights of Columbus Archives, New Haven, Conn.
Daniel A. Lord Papers, Jesuit Missouri Province Archives, Missouri Province of Society of Jesus, Saint Louis
Maryland State Board of Motion Picture Censors, Maryland State Archives, Annapolis
MGM Files, Doheny Library, School of Cinema and Television Collection, University of Southern California, Los Angeles
Motion Picture Division, Museum of Modern Art, New York
Motion Picture Division of the New York State Archives, Albany
Motion Picture Division, National Archives, Washington, D.C.
George Cardinal Mundelein Papers, Archives of the Archdiocese of Chicago
National Board of Review of Motion Pictures Collection, New York City Public Library, New York, N.Y.
National Catholic Welfare Conference Archives, Catholic University of America
National Catholic Welfare Conference Collection, United States Conference of Catholic Bishops, Catholic University of America, Washington, D.C.
National Legion of Decency Archives, United States Catholic Conference Communications Department, New York, N.Y.
New York Municipal Archives and Research Center, New York, N.Y.
Office of War Information Archives, Motion Picture Division, Washington National Records, Suitland, Md.
Oral History Collection, Southern Methodist University, Dallas
Wilfrid Parsons Papers, Special Collections Division, Georgetown University Library, Washington, D.C.
Production Code Administration Archives, Margaret Herrick Library, Academy of Motion Picture Arts and Sciences, Los Angeles
Protestant Film Council Archives, Good News Communications, Atlanta, Ga.
Martin P. Quigley Papers, Special Collections Division, Georgetown University Library, Washington, D.C.
Terry Ramsaye Collection, Special Collections Division, Georgetown University Library, Washington, D.C.
Hal Roach Collection, Hollywood Museum Collection, Doheny Library, School of Cinema and Television Collection, University of Southern California
David O. Selznick Archive, Harold Ransom Humanities Research Center, University of Texas, Austin
Spyros Skouras Papers, Special Collections, Stanford University
Preston Sturges Papers, Special Collections, University of California, Los Angeles
Twentieth Century-Fox Collection, Doheny Library, School of Cinema and Television Collection, University of Southern California
Twentieth Century-Fox Collection, Theater Arts Collection, University of California, Los Angeles
United Artists Collection, Special Collections, University of Wisconsin, Madison

Virginia Division of Motion Picture Censorship, Virginia State Archives, Richmond
Walter Wanger Papers, Special Collections, University of Wisconsin, Madison
Warner Brothers Collection, Doheny Library, School of Cinema and Television Collection, University of Southern California

BOOKS AND ARTICLES

Addams, Jane. *The Spirit of Youth and the City Streets* (New York: Macmillan, 1909).

Allen, Robert C., and Douglas Gomery. *Film History, Theory, and Practice* (New York: Alfred A. Knopf, 1985).

Allitt, Patrick. *Catholic Intellectuals and Conservative Politics in America, 1950–1985* (Ithaca: Cornell University Press, 1993).

Avella, Steven M. *The Confident Church* (Notre Dame, Ind.: University of Notre Dame Press, 1992).

Balio, Tino. *United Artists: The Company Built by the Stars* (Madison: University of Wisconsin Press, 1976).

———. *United Artists: The Company That Changed the Film Industry* (Madison: University of Wisconsin Press, 1987).

Basinger, Jeanine. *A Woman's View: How Hollywood Spoke to Women, 1930–1960* (New York: Alfred A. Knopf, 1993).

Bell, Daniel. "Religion in the Sixties," in Patrick H. McNamara, ed., *Religion American Style* (New York: Harper and Row, 1974), 170–177.

Bergman, Andrew. *We're in the Money: Depression America and Its Films* (New York: Harper & Row, 1972).

Bernstein, Mathew. *Walter Wanger: Hollywood Independent* (Berkeley: University of California Press, 1994).

Black, Gregory D. *Hollywood Censored: Morality Codes, Catholics, and the Movies* (New York: Cambridge University Press, 1994).

———. "Hollywood Censored: The Production Code Administration and the Hollywood Film Industry, 1930–1940," *Film History* 3 (1989), 167–189.

———. "Keys of the Kingdom: Entertainment or Propaganda?" *South Atlantic Quarterly* 75 (1976), 434–446.

———. "Movies, Politics and Censorship: The Production Code Administration: Political Censorship of Film Content," *Journal of Policy History* 3 (1991), 95–129.

Blanshard, Paul. *American Freedom and Catholic Power* (Boston: Beacon Press, 1949).

Boller, Paul F., and Ronald L. Davis. *Hollywood Anecdotes* (New York: Ballantine, 1987).

Bordwell, David, Janet Staiger, and Kristin Thompson. *The Classical Hollywood Cinema: Film Style and Mode of Production to 1960* (New York: Columbia University Press, 1960).

Bowser, Eileen. *The Transformation of Cinema, 1907–1915* (New York: Charles Scribner's Sons, 1990).

Boyle, Hugh C. "The Legion of Decency: A Permanent Campaign," *Ecclesiastical Review* 90 (October 1934), 367–370.

Brandt, Allan M. *No Magic Bullet: A Social History of Venereal Disease in the United States Since 1880* (New York: Oxford University Press, 1987).

Brownlow, Kevin. *Behind the Mask of Innocence* (New York: Alfred A. Knopf, 1990).

Campbell, Craig W. *Reel America and World War I* (Jefferson, N.C.: McFarland, 1985).

Cantwell, John J. "Priests and the Motion Picture Industry," *Ecclesiastical Review* 90 (February 1934), 136–146.

Clarens, Carlos. *Crime Movies* (New York: W. W. Norton, 1979).

Cogley, John. *Catholic America* (New York: Dial Press, 1973).

Connell, Francis J. "How Should Priests Direct People Regarding Movies?" *American Ecclesiastical Review* 114 (1946), 241–253.

———. "Pope Pius XII and the Legion of Decency," *American Ecclesiastical Review* 137 (1957), 392–399.

Cooney, John C. *The American Pope* (New York: Times Books, 1984).

Corliss, Richard. "The Legion of Decency," *Film Comment* 4 (Summer 1969), 24–61.

Couvares, Francis G. "Hollywood Censorship and American Culture," *American Quarterly* 44 (December 1992), 509–524.

———. "Hollywood, Main Street, and the Church: Trying to Censor Movies Before the Production Code," *American Quarterly* 44 (December 1992), 584–616.

Cripps, Thomas. *Making Movies Black: The Hollywood Message Movie from World War II to the Civil Rights Era* (New York: Oxford University Press, 1993).

———. *Slow Fade to Black* (New York: Oxford University Press, 1977).

Cronin, A. J. *The Keys of the Kingdom* (Boston: Little, Brown, 1941).

Crosby, Donald F. "Boston's Catholics and the Spanish Civil War: 1936–1939," *New England Quarterly* 44 (March 1971), 82–100.

Curry, Ramona. "Mae West As a Censored Commodity: The Case of Klondike Annie," *Cinema Journal* 31 (Fall 1991), 57–84.

Czitrom, Daniel. "The Politics of Performance: From Theater Licensing to Movie Censorship in Turn-of-the-Century New York," *American Quarterly* 44 (December 1992), 525–553.

Davis, Mike. *City of Quartz* (New York: Verso, 1990).

Davis, Ronald. *Hollywood Beauty: Linda Darnell and the American Dream* (Norman: University of Oklahoma Press, 1991).

DeGrazia, Edward. *Girls Lean Back Everywhere: The Law of Obscenity and the Assault on Genius* (New York: Random House, 1992).

DeGrazia, Edward, and Roger K. Newman. *Banned Films: Movies, Censors, and the First Amendment* (New York: R. R. Bowker, 1982).

Dick, Bernard F. *Radical Innocence: A Critical Study of the Hollywood Ten* (Lexington: University Press of Kentucky, 1989).

———. *The Star-Spangled Screen: The American World War II Film* (Lexington: University Press of Kentucky, 1985).

Doherty, Theodore. *Projections of War: Hollywood, American Culture, and World War II* (New York: Columbia University Press, 1993).

Dolan, Jay P. *The American Catholic Experience* (Garden City, N.Y.: Doubleday, 1985).

Dooley, Roger. *From Scarface to Scarlett: American Films in the 1930s* (New York: Harcourt Brace Jovanovich, 1979).

Doran, Daniel E. "Mr. Breen Confronts the Dragons," *The Sign* 21 (January 1942), 327–330.

Draper, Ellen. "'Controversy Has Probably Destroyed Forever the Context': *The Miracle* and Movie Censorship in America in the Fifties," *Velvet Light Trap* 25 (Spring 1990), 69–79.

Dumenil, Lynn. "The Tribal Twenties: The Catholic Response to Anti-Catholicism," Charles and Margaret Hall Cushwa Center for the Study of American Catholicism Working Paper Series 19 (Spring 1988), 1–42.

Dunne, Philip. "Blast It All," *Harvard Magazine* (September–October 1987), 9–10.

Facey, Paul W. *The Legion of Decency: A Sociological Analysis of the Emergence and Development of a Social Pressure Group* (New York: Arno Press, 1974).

Farber, Stephen. *The Movie Rating Game* (Washington, D.C.: Public Affairs Press, 1972).

Feldman, Charles M. *The National Board of Censorship of Motion Pictures, 1909–1922* (New York: Arno Press, 1977).

Fisher, James Terence. *The Catholic Counterculture in America, 1933–1962* (Chapel Hill: University of North Carolina Press, 1989).

Fisher, Robert. "Film Censorship and Progressive Reform," *Journal of Popular Film* 4 (1975), 143–156.

Fogarty, Gerald P. *Patterns of Episcopal Leadership* (New York: Macmillan, 1989).

———. "Public Patriotism and Private Politics: The Tradition of American Catholicism," *U.S. Catholic Historian* 4 (1984), 1–48.

Foner, Philip S. "A Martyr to His Cause: The Scenario of the First Labor Film in the United States," *Labor History* 24 (1983), 103–111.

Forman, Henry James. *Our Movie-Made Children* (New York: Macmillan, 1933).

Friedman, David F. *A Youth in Babylon* (Buffalo, N.Y.: Prometheus, 1990).

Friedrich, Otto. *City of Nets: Portrait of Hollywood in the 1940s* (New York: Harper & Row, 1986).

Gabler, Neal. *An Empire of Their Own: How the Jews Invented Hollywood* (New York: Crown, 1988).

Gans, Herbert. "The Rise of the Problem Film: An Analysis of Changes in Hollywood Films and the American Audience," *Social Problems* 11 (Spring 1964), 327–336.

Gardiner, Harold C. *Catholic Viewpoint on Censorship* (Garden City, N.Y.: Hanover House, 1958).

Gardner, Gerald. *The Censorship Papers: Movie Censorship Letters from the Hays Office* (New York: Dodd, Mead, 1987).

Garesche, Edward. "The Parish Priest and Moving-Pictures," *Ecclesiastical Review* 83 (May 1927), 465–478.

———. "Pastors and Censorship of Movies," *Ecclesiastical Review* 60 (March 1919), 256–266.

Geissman, Erwin. "All Is God," *Cross Currents* 4 (Fall 1953), 1–5.

Getlein, Frank, and Harold Gardiner. *The Art of the Movies* (New York: Sheed and Ward, 1962).
Giglio, Ernest D. "The Decade of the Miracle, 1952–1962: A Study in the Censorship of the American Motion Picture." Ph.D. diss., Syracuse University, 1964.
Gomery, Douglas. *The Hollywood Studio System: House Style in the Golden Age of the Movies* (New York: St. Martin's Press, 1986).
Goodwin, Doris Kearns. *The Fitzgeralds and the Kennedys* (New York: Simon and Shuster, 1987).
Halsey, William M. *The Survival of American Innocence: Catholicism in an Era of Disillusionment, 1920–1940* (Notre Dame, Ind.: University of Notre Dame Press, 1980).
Haskell, Molly. *From Reverence to Rape: The Treatment of Women in the Movies* (New York: Holt, Rinehart & Winston, 1974).
Haver, Ronald. *David O. Selznick's Hollywood* (New York: Alfred A. Knopf, 1980).
Hays, Will. *Memoirs of Will H. Hays* (Garden City, N.Y.: Doubleday, 1955).
Hennesey, James J. *American Catholics: A History of the Roman Catholic Community in the United States* (New York: Oxford University Press, 1981).
Hobson, Barbara Meil. *Uneasy Virtue: The Politics of Prostitution and American Reform Tradition* (New York: Basic Books, 1987).
Inglis, Ruth. *Freedom of the Movies: A Report on Self-Regulation* (Chicago: University of Chicago Press, 1947).
Izod, John. *Hollywood and the Box Office, 1895–1986* (New York: Columbia University Press, 1988).
Jacobs, Lea. *The Wages of Sin: Censorship and the Fallen Woman Film, 1928–1942* (Madison: University of Wisconsin Press, 1991).
Janes, Robert W. "The Legion of Decency and the Motion Picture Industry." M.A. thesis, University of Chicago, 1939.
Jenkins, Henry, III. "'Shall We Make It for New York or for Distribution?' Eddie Cantor, Whoopee, and Regional Resistance to the Talkies," *Cinema Journal* 29 (Spring 1980), 32–52.
Johnson, Charles, and Al Antczak, "Padre of the Films," *Catholic Digest* (September 1942), 24–27.
Jowett, Garth. "'A Capacity for Evil': The 1915 Supreme Court *Mutual* Decision," *Historical Journal of Film, Radio and Television* 9 (1989), 59–78.
———. *Film, the Democratic Art* (Boston: Focal Press, 1976).
———. "Moral Responsibility and Commercial Entertainment: Social Control in the United States Film Industry, 1907–1968," *Historical Journal of Film, Radio and Television* 10 (1990), 3–31.
Kazan, Elia. *A Life* (New York: Alfred A. Knopf, 1988).
Kelly, Gerald, and John Ford. "The Legion of Decency," *Theological Studies* 18 (September 1957), 387–433.
Keyser, Les, and Barbara Keyser. *Hollywood and the Catholic Church: The Image of Roman Catholicism in the American Movies* (Chicago: Loyola University Press, 1984).

Koppes, Clayton R., and Gregory D. Black. *Hollywood Goes to War: How Politics, Profits, and Propaganda Shaped World War II Movies* (New York: Free Press, 1987).

Koszarski, Richard. *An Evening's Entertainment: The Age of the Silent Feature Picture, 1915–1928* (New York: Charles Scribner's Sons, 1990).

Kuhn, Annette. *Cinema, Censorship, and Sexuality, 1909–1925* (New York: Routledge, 1988).

Lally, Francis J. *The Catholic Church in a Changing America* (Boston: Little, Brown, 1962).

———. "Points of Abrasion," *Atlantic* 210 (August 1962), 78–82.

Lashley, Karl S., and John B. Watson. *A Psychological Study of Motion Pictures in Relation to Venereal Disease Campaigns* (Washington, D.C.: U.S. Interdepartmental Social Hygiene Board, 1922).

Lee, Stephen C. "Pending Catholicization: The Legion of Decency, *Duel in the Sun*, and the Threat of Censorship." M.A. thesis, University of Texas at Austin, 1985.

Leff, Leonard J. "A Test of American Film Censorship: *Who's Afraid of Virginia Woolf?* (1966)." In Peter Rollins, ed., *Hollywood As Historian* (Lexington: University Press of Kentucky, 1983), 211–229.

———. *Hitchcock and Selznick: The Rich and Strange Collaboration of Alfred Hitchcock and David O. Selznick in Hollywood* (New York: Weidenfeld & Nicolson, 1987).

Leff, Leonard J., and Jerold L. Simmons. *The Dame in the Kimono: Hollywood, Censorship, and the Production Code from the 1920s to the 1960s* (New York: Grove Weidenfeld, 1990).

Lord, Daniel. *Played by Ear* (Chicago: Loyola University Press, 1955).

Lynes, Russell. *The Lively Audience: A Social History of the Visual and Performing Arts in America, 1890–1950* (New York: Harper & Row, 1985).

McAvoy, Thomas T. *A History of the Catholic Church in the United States* (Notre Dame, Ind.: University of Notre Dame Press, 1969).

McCarthy, Kathleen D. "Nickel Vice and Virtue: Movie Censorship in Chicago, 1907–1915," *Journal of Popular Film* 5 (1976), 37–55.

McDonough, Peter. *Men Astutely Trained: A History of the Jesuits in the American Century* (New York: Free Press, 1992).

McGilligan, Patrick. *George Cukor: A Double Life* (New York: St. Martin's Press, 1991).

McGrath, Owen A. "Catholic Action's Big Opportunity," *Ecclesiastical Review* 91 (September 1934), 280–287.

McLaughlin, Mary. "A Study of the National Catholic Office for Motion Pictures." Ph.D. diss., University of Wisconsin, 1974.

McNicholas, John T. "The Episcopal Committee and the Problem of Evil Motion Pictures," *Ecclesiastical Review* 90 (August 1934), 113–119.

McShane, Joseph M. *"Sufficiently Radical" Catholicism, Progressivism, and the Bishops' Program of 1919* (Washington, D.C.: Catholic University Press, 1986).

Maltby, Richard. "'Baby Face,' or How Joe Breen Made Barbara Stanwyck Atone for Causing the Wall Street Crash," *Screen* 27 (1986), 22–45.

———. "*The King of Kings* and the Czar of All the Rushes: The Propriety of the Christ Story," *Screen* 31 (Summer 1990), 188–213.

———. "'To Prevent the Prevalent Type of Book': Censorship and Adaptation in Hollywood, 1924–1934," *American Quarterly* 44 (December 1992), 554–616.

———. "The Production Code and the Hays Office." In Tino Balio, ed., *Grand Design: Hollywood as a Modern Business Enterprise, 1930–1939* (New York: Charles Scribner's Sons, 1993), 37–72.

Marion, Frances. *Off with Their Heads: A Serio-Comic Tale of Hollywood* (New York: Macmillan, 1972).

Marquis, Alice Goldfarb. *Hope and Ashes: The Birth of Modern Times* (New York: Free Press, 1986).

Medved, Michael. *Hollywood vs. America: Popular Culture and the War on Traditional Values* (New York: HarperCollins, 1992).

Miller, John M. "'Frankly, My Dear, I Just—Don't—Care': Val Lewton and Censorship at Selznick International Pictures," *Library Chronicle of the University of Texas at Austin* 36 (1986), 10–31.

Moley, Raymond. *The Hays Office* (New York: Bobbs-Merrill, 1945).

Murray, John Courtney. *We Hold These Truths: Catholic Reflections on the American Proposition* (Garden City, N.Y.: Sheed and Ward, 1960).

Musser, Charles. *The Emergence of Cinema: The American Screen to 1907* (New York: Charles Scribner's Sons, 1990).

Nash, Jay R., and Stanley R. Ross, eds. *The Motion Picture Guide* (Chicago: Cinebooks, 1985–1987).

Noll, John F. "Can Catholics Really Reform the Movies?" *Ecclesiastical Review* 90 (April 1934), 366–372.

Nye, Russel. *The Unembarrassed Muse: The Popular Arts in America* (New York: Dial Press, 1970).

O'Brien, David. *American Catholics and Social Reform* (New York: Oxford University Press, 1968).

———. *Faith and Friendship: Catholicism in the Diocese of Syracuse* (Syracuse, N.Y.: Office for Communications, Catholic Diocese of Syracuse, 1987).

———. *Public Catholicism* (New York: Macmillan, 1989).

———. *The Renewal of American Catholicism* (New York: Oxford University Press, 1972).

Pauly, Thomas H. *An American Odyssey: Elia Kazan and American Culture* (Philadelphia: Temple University Press, 1983).

Phelan, James Martin. "The National Catholic Office for Motion Pictures: An Investigation of the Policy and Practice of Film Classification." Ph.D. diss., New York University, 1968.

Pius XI. *Vigilanti Cura: Encyclical Letter on Motion Pictures* (Washington, D.C.: National Catholic Welfare Conference, 1936).

Pius XII. *Miranda Prorsus: Encyclical Letter on Motion Pictures, Radio, and Television* (Washington, D.C.: National Catholic Welfare Conference, 1957).

Powers, Richard Gid. *G-Men: Hoover's FBI in American Popular Culture* (Carbondale: Southern Illinois University Press, 1983).
Preminger, Otto. *An Autobiography* (New York: Bantam, 1977).
Quigley, Martin. *Decency in Motion Pictures* (New York: Macmillan, 1937).
Ramsaye, Terry. *A Million and One Nights: A History of the Motion Pictures through 1925* (New York: Simon and Schuster, 1926).
Randall, Richard. *Censorship of the Movies* (Madison: University of Wisconsin Press, 1968).
Reher, Margaret. *Catholic Intellectual Life in America* (New York: Macmillan, 1989).
Richard, Alfred C., Jr. *Censorship and Hollywood's Hispanic Image: An Interpretive Filmography, 1936–1955* (Westport, Conn.: Greenwood Press, 1994).
———. *Contemporary Hollywood's Negative Hispanic Image: An Interpretive Filmography, 1956–1993* (Westport, Conn.: Greenwood Press, 1993).
———. *The Hispanic Image on the Silver Screen: An Interpretive Filmography: From Silents into Sounds, 1898–1935* (Westport, Conn.: Greenwood Press, 1992).
Richards, Jeffrey. *Visions of Yesterday* (London: Routledge, 1973).
Roddick, Nick. *A New Deal in Entertainment: Warner Brothers in the 1930s* (London: British Film Institute, 1983).
Roffman, Peter, and Jim Purdy. *The Hollywood Social Problem Film: Madness, Despair, and Politics from the Depression to the Fifties* (Bloomington: Indiana University Press, 1981).
Rosen, Marjorie. *Popcorn Venus: Women, Movies, and the American Dream* (New York: Coward, McCann & Geohegan, 1973).
Rosenbloom, Nancy J. "Between Reform and Regulation: The Struggle Over Film Censorship in Progressive America, 1909–1922," *Film History* 1 (1987), 307–325.
Rosenzweig, Roy. *Eight Hours for What We Will: Workers and Leisure in an Industrial City, 1870–1920* (New York: Cambridge University Press, 1983).
Ross, Steven J. "Struggles for the Screen: Workers, Radicals, and the Political Uses of the Silent Screen," *American Historical Review* 96 (April 1991), 333–367.
Sayre, Nora. *Running Time: Films of the Cold War* (New York: Dial Press, 1982).
Schatz, Thomas. *The Genius of the System: Hollywood Filmmaking in the Studio Era* (New York: Pantheon, 1988).
Schumach, Murray. *The Face on the Cutting Room Floor: The Story of Movie and Television Censorship* (New York: William Morrow, 1964).
Schwegler, Edward. "A Legion of Decency Program," *American Ecclesiastical Review* 125 (July 1951), 107–119.
Shadoian, Jack. *Dreams and Dead Ends: The American Gangster/Crime Film* (Cambridge, Mass.: MIT Press, 1979).
Sheerin, John B. *Never Look Back: The Career and Concerns of John J. Burke* (New York: Paulist Press, 1975).
Shenton, Herbert. *The Public Relations of the Motion Picture Industry* (New York: Department of Research and Education, Federal Council of the Churches of Christ in America, 1931).

Simmons, Jerold. "The Production Code under New Management: Geoffrey Shurlock, *The Bad Seed*, and *Tea and Sympathy*," *Journal of Popular Film and Television* 22 (Spring 1994), 3–10.

Skinner, James M. *The Cross and the Cinema: The Legion of Decency and the National Catholic Office for Motion Pictures, 1933–1970* (Westport, Conn.: Greenwood Press, 1993).

———. "The Tussle with Russell: The Outlaw as a Landmark in American Film Censorship," *North Dakota Quarterly* 46 (Winter 1981), 5–12.

Sklar, Robert. *Movie-Made America: How the Movies Changed American Life* (New York: Vintage Books, 1975).

Sloan, Kay. *The Loud Silents: Origins of the Social Problem Film* (Urbana: University of Illinois Press, 1988).

Sparr, Arnold. *To Promote, Defend, and Redeem: The Catholic Literary Revival and the Cultural Transformation of American Catholicism* (Westport, Conn.: Greenwood Press, 1990).

Stine, Whitney. *Bette Davis, Mother Goddam* (New York: Berkeley, 1974).

Stone, Judy. "The Legion of Decency: What's Nude," *Ramparts* 4 (September 1965), 43–55.

Thomson, David. *Showman: The Life of David O. Selznick* (New York: Alfred A. Knopf, 1992).

Uricchio, William, and Roberta E. Pearson. *Reframing Culture* (Princeton, N.J.: Princeton University Press, 1993).

Vaughn, Stephen. "Financiers, Movie Producers, and the Church: Economic Origins of the Production Code," *Current Research in Film* 4 (1988), 201–217.

———. "Morality and Entertainment: The Origins of the Motion Picture Production Code," *Journal of American History* 77 (June 1990), 39–65.

———. *Ronald Reagan in Hollywood: Movies and Politics* (New York: Cambridge University Press, 1994).

Vizzard, Jack. *See No Evil: Life Inside a Hollywood Censor* (New York: Simon and Shuster, 1970).

Walker, Alexander. *The Shattered Silents: How the Talkies Came To Stay* (London: Harrap, 1978).

Wall, James M. "Interviews with Geoffrey Shurlock," Oral History, Louis B. Mayer Library, American Film Institute, Los Angeles, 1970.

Walsh, Francis R. "*The Callahans and the Murphys* (MGM, 1927): A Case Study of Irish-American and Catholic Church Censorship," *Historical Journal of Film, Radio, and Television* 10 (1990), 33–45.

———. "The Films We Never Saw: American Movies View Organized Labor, 1934–1954," *Labor History* 27 (Fall 1986), 564–580.

Weber, Francis J. "John J. Cantwell and the Legion of Decency," *American Ecclesiastical Review* 151 (October 1964), 237–247.

Westin, Alan F. *The Miracle Case: The Supreme Court and the Movies* (Tuscaloosa: University of Alabama Press, 1961).

Wexman, Virginia Wright. "Suffering and Suffrage: Birth, the Female Body, and

Women's Choices in D. W. Griffith's *Way Down East*," *Velvet Light Trap* 29 (Spring 1992), 53–65.
White, Suzanne. "*Mom and Dad* (1944): Venereal Disease, 'Exploitation,'" *Bulletin of the History of Medicine* 62 (1988), 252–270.
Wilk, Max. *The Wit and Wisdom of Hollywood* (New York: Atheneum, 1971).
Williams, Michael. *American Catholics in the War* (New York: Macmillan, 1921).
Wuenschel, Edward. "The Keys of the Kingdom," *American Ecclesiastical Review* 106 (January 1942), 10–26.

INDEX

■■■

D0341002

The Dow Jones-Irwin Guide to
MODERN PORTFOLIO THEORY

The Dow Jones-Irwin Guide to MODERN PORTFOLIO THEORY

ROBERT L. HAGIN
Vice President—Director of Quantitative Research
Kidder, Peabody & Co., Incorporated

DOW JONES-IRWIN
Homewood, Illinois 60430

Some material in this book is adapted from *The New Science of Investing* and from *The Dow Jones-Irwin Guide to Common Stocks.*

ISBN 0-256-02379-4 paperbound

ISBN 0-87094-181-X hardbound
Library of Congress Catalog Card No. 79–51785

Printed in the United States of America

4 5 6 7 8 9 0 K 6 5 4 3 2

To Susie

Preface

Modern portfolio theory (MPT)—which enables investment managers to classify, estimate, and then control the sources of investment *risk* and *return*—is revolutionizing traditional approaches to investment management. This book explains the evolution, meaning, and practical significance of MPT—sometimes referred to as the "new investment technology" or "modern investment theory."

The goal of the book is to provide a complete, accurate, and *easily understandable* explanation of MPT. The occasionally formidable math has been replaced by verbal explanations and easily understood diagrams. Technical definitions and equations are presented in footnotes for readers interested in such details. For the average reader, however, technical details have been kept to the barest minimum, and no special knowledge or educational level is assumed. The result is an accurate, yet easily understood, presentation of the subject matter of an advanced investments course.

The book is written for two broad groups of people—those who use professional investment management services and those who provide such services. The knowledge of MPT gained here should be helpful to pension plan sponsors, trustees, attorneys, and accountants, who are responsible for the selection and monitoring of professional investment managers. Similarly, the book is intended to give investment professionals a better understanding of the elements of MPT so that they can evaluate its usefulness to their clients.

Part One explains the three forms of the efficient market hypothesis and the theoretical foundation of MPT. Part Two

explains additional building blocks: Risk, performance, expected returns, and diversification. Part Three develops the structure of MPT. Part Four describes tests of the theory, as well as the major extensions and applications.

Many people have contributed to the growth, interest, development, and practical use of MPT. Some of these contributors are acknowledged throughout the text, but references to numerous others have been omitted because of space limitations. My thanks to all of those who have shared their thoughts on this exciting subject both publicly through published articles and in personal conversations.

I would like to extend special thanks to Stefanie O'Keefe, who edited the manuscript; to Renee Romagnole, who assisted me with the research and typing; and to Laurel Mehl, who through the resources of the information center at the Girard Bank assisted with the bibliographic material.

Readers wishing to address comments, criticisms, and inquiries to the author are encouraged to do so. Every effort will be made to draft an individual reply to such letters. Correspondence should be addressed to:

Robert L. Hagin
Vice President
Director of Quantitative Research
Kidder, Peabody Co., Incorporated
10 Hanover Square
New York, NY 10005

Contents

PART III: MPT: CONCEPTUAL FOUNDATION

PART IV: MPT: TESTS, EXTENSIONS, AND APPLICATIONS

INTRODUCTION

Chapter 1
The changing investment environment

Chapter 1

The changing investment environment

The investments profession is in the midst of a philosophical revolution. The "battle statistics" in this revolution are startling. Enormous sums of the new, or transferred, pension monies are being given to practitioners who use elements of modern portfolio theory (or, as it is coming to be known, MPT).

In the face of evermore stringent laws governing the deployment of pension funds, it is safe to assume that the decision to employ these MPT practitioners is not made casually. In fact, given the size and resources of the companies which employ pension managers with MPT expertise, it is clear that the decision is being made by some of the investment profession's most astute and well-educated clients. This increased use of MPT raises many questions—both outside and inside the professional investment management community.

Outside the professional investment community, there are hundreds of thousands of people with varying degrees of responsibility for the selection and monitoring of investment managers. These individuals are becoming increasingly aware of MPT and need to answer many questions. Will MPT provide better results? Is it imprudent *not* to employ an MPT-based approach? Inside the investment profession, in addition to questions regarding the usefulness and prudence of MPT, there is one more: Can firms compete effectively without an MPT-based approach?

The purpose of this book is not only to explain MPT but also to contrast MPT-based investment techniques with other investment philosophies. This comparative examination will answer the above questions as well as equip the reader to distinguish between true and pseudopractitioners, who are attempting merely to relable their old products "MPT."

A RAPIDLY CHANGING WORLD

We live in a rapidly changing world. In 1946, Presper Eckert and John Mauchly built ENIAC—the forerunner of today's electronic digital computers. With its 18,000 vacuum tubes, ENIAC weighed 30 tons, occupied 1,500 square feet, and could not operate without large-scale specialized power sources and air conditioning. Today, computer microprocessors are so small that it would take 40 such processors to cover a standard postage stamp. More importantly, when powered by energy cells the size of a shirt button, modern microprocessors possess more computing power than the early room-size computers.

In October 1957, the USSR announced to a stunned world that it had launched an earth-orbiting satellite—Sputnik I. In 1969, Neil Armstrong set foot on the surface of the moon and, after space walks by other members of the crew, returned safely to earth.

In 1952, Harry Markowitz [185][1] published a paper succinctly entitled "Portfolio Selection." This paper was the catalyst in an unbroken stream of ideas—both pre- and post-Markowitz—which have found practical application in what is now called *modern portfolio theory*, or more typically, MPT.

INVESTING: SIMPLE OR COMPLEX?

Investing is at one and the same time both simple and complex. The simplicity of stock market investing was aptly summarized by Andrew Tobias when he wrote,

> . . . there are just two ways a stock can go: up or down. There are just two emotions that tug in those opposite directions: greed and fear. There are just two ways to make money in a stock: dividends and capital gains. And there are just two kinds of investors in the market: the "public," like you and me; and the "institutions," like bank trust departments and mutual funds and insurance companies. It's the amateurs against the professionals, and it's not clear who has the advantage." [267, p. 68]

From this perspective, investing is very simple. Anyone with enough money can purchase a share of common stock. Further, because of the long-term underlying growth of the economy, the odds are good that this share of stock will prove

[1] Bracketed numbers refer to bibliography at end of book.

to be a good investment. In fact, research which will be discussed later has shown that roughly three out of four randomly selected investments, held for randomly chosen lengths of time, have been profitable!

Such "success" is often attributed to the "process" used to select the investment. Conversely, if the investment proves to be a poor selection, such "failure" is often attributed to the fact that the "market" was bad. Such investors explain their successes by saying, "XYZ Widget went up because it was a good *company*," and rationalize their failures by saying, "ABC Devices went down because of the *market*."

An important but subtle factor is at work in such explanations of investment performance. First, these investors are aware of the distinction between risk and return. Second, they recognize the important distinction between security- and market-related *sources* of risk and return.

Meaningful explanations of investment performance require explicit statements of *risk* and *return* which, in turn, each break down into security- and market-related components. This is the linchpin of MPT—the classification, estimation, and control of the sources of both risk and return.

A useful way to consider investment alternatives is to think of the *risk-reward spectrum* shown in Figure 1–1. Investing is

FIGURE 1–1: Risk-reward spectrum

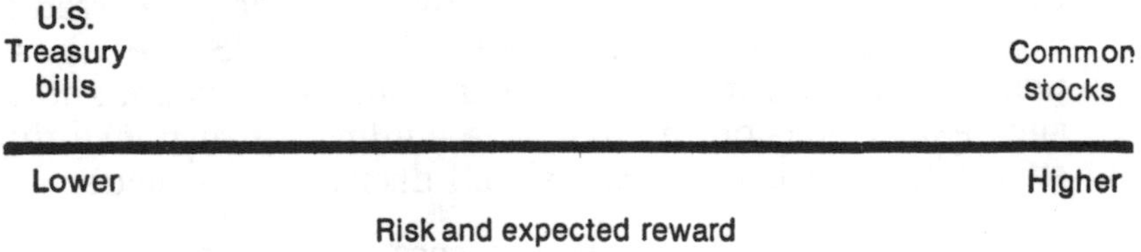

U.S. Treasury bills	Common stocks
Lower	Higher

Risk and expected reward

subjecting a sum with a certain present value to risk, in hopes of obtaining an uncertain future reward. The left-hand end of the spectrum represents the lowest risk investment. Probably the lowest risk instrument available is a short-term interest-bearing obligation of the U.S. Treasury. Here the investment risk (defined as the deviation between the actual and the expected rewards) is very low.

Moving to the right on the risk-reward spectrum increases both risk and expected reward. That is, by selecting any investment other than U.S. Treasury bills, an investor increases the expected return. Concomitantly, however, as is true of

common stock investments, higher anticipated rewards go hand in hand with increases in the deviations (risk) between the "expected" and "actual" results.

Thus, when pairs of reasonable investment alternatives are compared across the risk-reward spectrum, greater risks and larger "expected" returns will always go together. In fact, popular terms such as *investing, speculating,* and *gambling* came into use to describe progressively higher levels of both risk and expected (but, by definition, progressively uncertain) reward. Although this important gradation of risk and reward has been built into our everyday vocabulary, traditional forms of investment management are severely deficient in the quantification of the relationship between risk and expected return.

Modern portfolio theory can be thought of as magnifying and refining the relationship between risk and reward which is depicted by the risk-reward spectrum. More specifically, MPT provides the ability to classify, estimate, and hence control, both the types and amounts of risk and expected return.

ERISA

Although elements of modern portfolio theory have been around for a long time, the current revolution was "sparked" in late 1974. In that year, Congress enacted the Employee Retirement Income Security Act—now commonly referred to as ERISA. In a nutshell, Section 404(a)(1) of ERISA requires that persons engaged in the administration, supervision, and management of pension monies have a *fiduciary responsibility* to ensure that all investment-related decisions are made:

1. With the care, skill, prudence and diligence . . . that a prudent man . . . *familiar with such matters* [italics added] would use . . . ,
2. By *diversifying the investments . . . so as to minimize risk* [italics added]. . . .

If this law is extended to all fiduciary and trust relationships under which individuals have responsibility for other people's investments (and, after all, there is nothing unique about a trustee's fiduciary responsibility for a pension account), it is clear that the law now virtually mandates two significant changes in traditional investment practices.

The first deals with the age-old "prudent man" issue. Note that ERISA demands "a prudent man . . . *familiar with such matters.*" Thus, the general interpretation is that ERISA does

not require a prudent man but a prudent "expert." While it is admittedly difficult to define an expert and it is clearly within the province of experts to disagree, many people who now manage other people's money could not meet this test. A well-meaning family friend who is a part-time student of investments would likely not qualify as a prudent expert. Similarly, a group of physicians which collectively manage their staff's pension fund would probably be unable to satisfy this criterion. As a result, all of the admittedly sincere, honest, hardworking people who at one time were charged with the management of trust investments now have a *new responsibility—the selection and monitoring of a prudent "expert."*

The second change mandated by ERISA is the requirement that investments must be *diversified* "so as to minimize risk." MPT could be defined as "the control of risk through diversification." Thus, much as the concept of a prudent expert has replaced that of the prudent man, *the notion of a prudent portfolio has replaced the concept of a prudent investment.* Practically speaking, this means that investments must be analyzed—and managed—within the context of an overall risk-controlled portfolio.

From this perspective, it is easy to see why a tidal wave of demand is forming for MPT practitioners. Faced with evermore stringent legal requirements, persons who are charged with the prudent selection and monitoring of professional investment managers cannot treat this responsibility lightly. Furthermore, the *law now requires* that pension monies be managed by prudent experts who "diversify the investments within portfolios so as to minimize risk." Broadly speaking, this is MPT!

MPT OVERVIEW

Historically, the investment profession has focused on "classical" forms (those that do not quantify risk) of security analysis. It was widely believed that investment selections which were made through a combination of this analysis and hard, honest work would yield handsome rewards. For some 20 years, a generally rising market provided little test of this belief. Further, the generally favorable results obscured the need, until relatively recently, to focus on the relationship between the potential risks, as well as the potential rewards, of investing. In short, conscious efforts to deal explicitly with the dimension of risk did not enter the picture.

The investment results of the last ten years have now shown that information derived from classical security analysis is neither complete nor infallible. In fact, in the face of MPT, "traditional" forms of investment management which do not incorporate the explicit estimation and control of risk stand, along with ENIAC and Sputnik I, as relics of another era.

Concise definitions of MPT are difficult—if not outright dangerous. As used here, MPT is intended to emcompass *all notions of modern investment and portfolio theory.* Hence, terms such as new investment technology (NIT) and modern investment theory (MIT) can be regarded as synonomous with MPT.

Four types of MPT-based applications are shown in Figure 1–2. Starting with the foundation, MPT can be thought of as

FIGURE 1–2: Four types of MPT-based applications

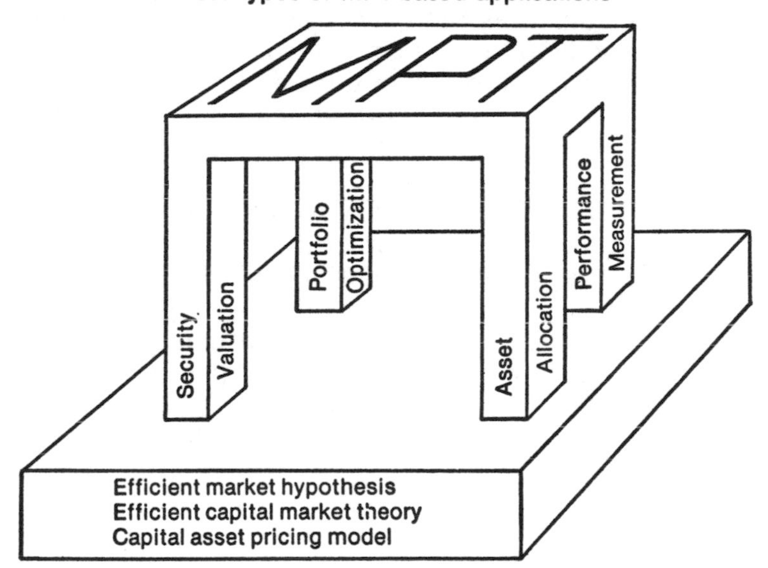

the theoretical constructs that have spawned applications for security valuation, portfolio optimization, asset allocation, and performance measurement. Viewed from this perspective, it is clear that MPT rests on the theoretical foundation of such concepts as the efficient market hypothesis, efficient capital market theory, and the capital asset pricing model. Thus, the first step in evaluating MPT must begin with an essential part of its foundation—the efficient market hypothesis.

PART ONE

THE EFFICIENT MARKET HYPOTHESIS

Chapter 2

Forms of the efficient market hypothesis

An *efficient capital market* is an arena in which many participants, with similar investment objectives and access to the same information, actively compete. The stock market—with numerous profit-motivated professional and private investors continually searching for misvalued securities—certainly provides such a setting. Profit-motivated investors do have strikingly similar objectives. Each prefers a high rate of return to a low one, certainty to uncertainty, low risk to high risk, and so forth. Furthermore, securities law provides that both parties to a transaction must have access to the same material facts.

The efficient market hypothesis asserts that it would be impossible consistently to outperform the market—which reflects the composite judgment of millions of participants—in an environment characterized by many competing investors, each with similar objectives and equal access to the same information. In the context of this hypothesis, "efficient" means that the market is capable of quickly digesting new information on the economy, an industry, or the value of an enterprise and accurately impounding it into securities prices. In such markets participants can expect to earn no more, nor less, than a fair return for the risks undertaken.

In an efficient market, for example, news of an earnings increase would be quickly and accurately assessed by the combined actions of literally millions of investors and immediately reflected in the price of the stock. The purported result of this efficiency is that whether you buy the stock before, during, or after the earnings news, or whether another stock is purchased, only a fair market rate of return can be expected—commensurate with the risk of owning whatever security is bought.

THE FORMS OF THE EFFICIENT MARKET HYPOTHESIS

The efficient market hypothesis does not by any means deny the profitability of investing. It merely states that the rewards obtainable from investing in highly competitive markets will be fair, on the average, for the risks involved. Importantly, however, the three forms of the efficient market hypothesis hold that acting on publicly available information cannot improve one's performance beyond the market's assessment of a fair rate of return.

The *weak form* of the efficient market hypothesis describes a market in which historical price data are efficiently digested and, therefore, are useless for predicting subsequent stock price changes. This is distinguished from a *semistrong form* under which all publicly available information is assumed to be fully discounted in current securities prices. Finally, the *strong form* describes a market in which not even those with privileged information can obtain superior investment results.

If the stock market efficiently digests all available information, as the progressively stronger forms of the hypothesis imply, there is little justification for seeking extraordinary gains from investing. However, this does not lessen the importance of investing. It merely changes the underlying investment philosophy of a prudent and knowledgeable investor from that of trying to beat the other person to one of seeking a rate of return that is consistent with the level of risk accepted.

Thus, rather than being the all-encompassing specter of gloom which some people assume it to be, the efficient market hypothesis in its various forms provides a useful benchmark. From its perspective, researchers can determine how "efficiently" or "inefficiently" information is processed. It is thus possible to scrutinize the market's ability to impound various kinds of information into securities prices. Most importantly, if research can determine which information is efficiently processed, investors can avoid analyzing this useless, fully discounted information—the first step in the successful and prudent application of MPT techniques!

TWO USEFUL ASSOCIATIONS

The following chapters in Part One review the conclusions of the many tests of the three forms of the efficient market hypothesis (weak, semistrong, and strong). However, before

these findings are presented, it should prove useful to discuss the association between two forms of the efficient market hypothesis and two popular (although highly suspect) approaches to investment analysis—fundamental and technical.

Fundamental investment analysts base their predictions of stock price behavior on factors which are "fundamental" or internal to a company, its industry, or the economy (for example, earnings, products, management, competition, consumer spending, and so on). A market fundamentalist might issue a purchase recommendation for a company which has consistently shown year-to-year earnings increases and is in an industry that he or she believes will grow faster than the economy.

Technical analysts, by contrast, hold that all such fundamental factors are reflected in the market behavior of the stock. Thus, to a pure technician, all data of importance are internal to the stock market, and future stock price movements can be predicted from the diligent study of historical stock market information (for example, changes in stock prices and trading volume). A market technician might, therefore, base a buy recommendation on a certain pattern of recent price and volume changes.

Under the weak form of the efficient market hypothesis, information on historical price trends is of no value for the prediction of either the magnitude or direction of subsequent price changes. As such, the weak form is directly opposed to the basic premise of technical analysis. Similarly, the semistrong form of the efficient market hypothesis holds that all publicly available information (as well as forecasts developed from such data) is of no value in the prediction of future prices. Thus, the semistrong form of the hypothesis is diametrically opposed to the concept of fundamental analysis.

Chapters 3 through 5 discuss research findings on the weak form of the hypothesis. Chapters 6 through 11 then examine the value of traditional forms of fundamental analysis within the context of the semistrong form of the efficient market hypothesis. Chapter 12 addresses the subject of inside information and the strong form of the hypothesis. The conclusions reached in Chapters 3 through 12 are summarized in Chapter 13.

Chapter 3

Early research

According to the weak form of the efficient market hypothesis, historical price and volume changes cannot be used to predict either the direction or magnitude of subsequent price changes. Historically known as the *random-walk model* of stock prices, this highly important countertheory to technical analysis has received much attention. Numerous university researchers, investment practitioners, and students of the stock market have devoted countless hours to developing and testing this model.

Remarkably, however, some members of the investment community have failed to assimilate these findings into their decision making. The sad result is that certain segments of the financial community still base investment decisions on analysis for which there is no theoretical or empirical justification!

THE WEAK FORM—DEFINITION AND MEANING

The weak form of the efficient market hypothesis or, as it was referred to for many years, the random-walk model, states that the pattern of recent changes in the price of a stock provides no useful information for predicting the next price movement. In early works, the random-walk model was described by means of an analogy to a "drunkard's walk," the pattern of whose steps cannot be forecast with any accuracy—either in size or direction. Similarly, the random-walk issue boils down to one basic question: Is historical price information on a stock useful in predicting future price movements of that stock? Those who support the random-walk model answer this question with an emphatic no!

It was unfortunate that the word "random" was first used in connection with the description of this model. The *Webster's New Collegiate Dictionary* lists the following synonyms for

random: haphazard, casual, and desultory. These words carry the implication of "happening by accident," "at the mercy of chance," "working without intention or purpose," and "ungoverned by a method or system." It should be emphasized that the random-walk model does not imply that changes in stock prices "just happen by accident." Indeed, the forces of supply and demand, most often converging on the floor of the stock exchange, cause price changes. As such, stock price levels are determined by the well-defined economics of a competitive marketplace. This is not a random or chance process.

Many researchers have tested the model by studying the movements of actual stock prices. If such studies are unable to discern repetitive price patterns (which can be used for prediction), the researcher must, by default, accept the weak form of the efficient market hypothesis and conclude that stock price changes cannot be forecast from prior price information.

Before turning to this research, it is important to remember that the random-walk model does not "assume" anything—it is a description of the way prices move. While "efficient" or "competitive" markets might explain what we observe, their existence, or lack thereof, does not alter the assertion of the random-walk model that price changes occur without trends or patterns. Also, the random-walk model does not deny the possibility of "experts" (or lucky dart throwers) being able to achieve higher than average returns. The random-walk model simply states that investors should not try to predict future price movements from historical price information! Now let's examine the work which has been done to test this assertion.

BACHELIER AND SLUTSKY

The random-walk model dates back to one of the first academic studies of speculative price behavior. In 1900, Louis Bachelier [10], a brilliant French mathematics student studying under the distinguished mathematician, H. Poincaré, formulated and tested the random-walk model of stock price behavior in his doctoral dissertation.

Bachelier's dissertation is an amazing document even today. Not only did he discover one of the most significant phenomena of the stock market—over 75 years ago—but his research was filled with other landmark contributions as well. In fact, the equation Bachelier used to describe the random walk was

identical to that developed by Albert Einstein, five years later, to describe Brownian motion.[1]

Bachelier's dissertation bears on modern stock market research in two significant ways. First, it provided an explicit statement of the random-walk model. Second, Bachelier's tests of actual security prices corresponded closely to those predicted by the random-walk model. In short, the prices he studied did not move in meaningful trends, waves, or patterns. Thus, Bachelier showed that recent historical price data were useless for predicting future price changes. Either because Bachelier's work ran so counter to intuition or because it took an "Einstein" to understand it, his research findings fell into obscurity until they were rediscovered in 1960.[2]

An important lesson to be learned from Bachelier's work is that a person with an intellect comparable to Einstein's could spend years studying the stock market and could develop a model that was to spark intellectual excitement 60 years later, but could not succeed in changing the investment behavior of his period. Apparently, in 1900, scientists quietly applauded Bachelier's achievements but made little effort to bridge the gap between theory and practice. Hopefully, we have learned an important lesson from the case of Bachelier.

A number of other studies performed early in this century raised doubts over the usefulness of historical price data in predicting price movements. The work of the Russian economist Eugene Slutsky [258] in 1927 is recognized as an independent rebirth of the random-walk model. Slutsky, who was not aware of Bachelier's work, showed that randomly generated price changes resemble actual stock price movements and seem to exhibit cycles and other pattterns. Unfortunately, ten years passed before Slutsky's work was translated into English, and even in 1937, it did not spark the intellectual interest of either academicians or investment practitioners.

[1] Named after Robert Brown, the Scottish botanist who first observed the phenomenon, Brownian motion is the name given to the random movement of microscopic particles that are suspended in liquids or gases. This motion is caused by the collision of such particles with surrounding molecules and is of great interest to physicists. In 1905, Albert Einstein presented the renowned paper in which he "discovered" the mathematical equation that describes the phenomenon of Brownian motion. Einstein reportedly regarded this discovery as one of his greatest contributions. Yet, Einstein died not knowing that Bachelier, five years earlier, had discovered the same equation could be used to describe the random behavior of stock prices!

[2] The first modern-day reference to Bachelier's work was published by Alexander [1] in 1961.

THE ERA OF DISREPUTE

Although market technicians proliferated during the boom preceding the 1929 stock market crash, there were no rigorous attempts to establish the validity of technical analysis during this period. Following the 1929 debacle, virtually all enthusiasm for investment advice evaporated during what was known as Wall Street's "era of disrepute." Memories of Black Tuesday, stock manipulation by investment pools, and suicides persisted. Nor could the public forget the corruption exemplified by Richard Whitney, scion of the wealthy Whitney family and former president of the New York Stock Exchange, who was jailed for misusing company funds. Wall Street bore the stigma of these events for almost two decades, and both the general public and qualified researchers had little to do with the market. In fact, only two research studies that made material contributions to the science of investments were reported in the United States between 1930 and 1959.

WORKING AND COWLES—SOLE U.S. CONTRIBUTORS FOR THREE DECADES

In 1934, Holbrook Working [288] of Stanford University demonstrated that even artificially generated series of price changes form apparent trends and patterns. He later offered charts of simulated as well as real price changes and challenged readers to distinguish between the real and the artificial series. [289] Working's studies unfortunately lacked both the mathematical rigor and empirical evidence needed to attract the attention of qualified researchers.

In 1937, two distinguished researchers, Alfred Cowles and Herbert Jones [54] of the Cowles Commission (now Foundation) for Research in Economics, gave authoritative support to the case for technical analysis when they reported that stock prices indeed moved in predictable trends. As it happened, these findings were withdrawn in 1960 after an error in the analysis was discovered. For more than two decades, however, the widespread belief that Cowles had put the random-walk theory to rest deterred would-be U.S. researchers from further examination of the subject. As a result, another 15 years passed until someone again questioned the basic tenet of technical analysis: stock prices move in discernible patterns.

KENDALL—SERIAL CORRELATION

While the seeds sown by early researchers lay dormant in the United States, Maurice Kendall [145] at the London School of Economics made significant advances in the study of the random-walk model. In 1953, Kendall found, to his surprise, that stock price changes behaved almost as if they had been generated by a suitably designed roulette wheel. That is, each outcome was statistically independent of past history.

Using periods of 1, 2, 4, 8, and 16 weeks, Kendall reported that when price changes were observed at fairly close intervals, the random fluctuations from one price to the next were large enough to swamp any systematic patterns or trends which might have existed. He concluded that, ". . . there is no hope of being able to predict movements on the exchange for a week ahead without extraneous [that is, something besides price] information." [145, p. 16]

In contrast to the widely quoted (but later shown to be erroneous) research by Cowles and Jones, Kendall's 1953 work was published in the rather obscure *Journal of the Royal Statistical Society* and received little attention. So, while there was scattered evidence challenging the theory, prior to 1959 no one seriously questioned the doctrine of technical stock market analysis.

ROBERTS AND OSBORNE—THE SEED OF CONTROVERSY

In 1959, a widely read paper by Harry Roberts [220] of the University of Chicago and another study by M. F. M. Osborne [209], and astronomer at the U.S. Naval Research Laboratory in Washington, D.C., plus the discovery of Bachelier's 60-year-old dissertation by Professor Paul Samuelson and others at the Massachusetts Institute of Technology, kindled interest in using computers to study the random-walk model.

After placing the earlier work of Holbrook Working and Maurice Kendall in the context of the random-walk model, Roberts showed that a series of randomly generated price changes would very closely resemble actual stock data. Noting that this chance behavior produced patterns, Roberts was the first modern author to conclude that "probably all the classical patterns of technical analysis can be generated artificially by a suitable roulette wheel or random-number table." [220, p. 10]

Osborne's paper developed the hypothesis that the subjective perception of profit is the same for a price change from $10 to $11 as one from $100 to $110. This means that one should study price changes in logarithmic form, which Osborne showed did conform to the random-walk model. These widely read papers thus planted the seed of the random-walk controversy in the United States!

WORKING AND ALEXANDER—FALSE PRICE CORRELATIONS DETECTED

Additional cornerstone research was reported in 1960 and 1961 by Working [290] and Sidney Alexander [1], respectively. Each author discovered on an independent basis that research employing weekly or monthly stock price averages could show erroneous correlations which would not appear if unaveraged prices were used.

This finding was extremely important because in 1937, Cowles and Jones, both respected researchers, had reported that historical price movements could be used to predict monthly price changes—a study which, as mentioned before, provided weighty empirical support for technical analysis. When Cowles realized that data composed of averages could produce his original results as a statistical artifact, he withdrew his earlier findings (in an article published concurrently with Working's [53]). In the 1960 article Cowles concluded that there was no evidence that historical month-to-month price data could be used to predict the direction of price changes in subsequent months!

Chapter 4

More rigorous tests

Working's 1960 discovery that studies of average prices could show fallacious period-to-period correlation, together with Cowles' admission that his 1937 investigation suffered from this statistical bias, combined to open up new avenues for research. Furthermore, the ever-increasing availability of electronic computers and the introduction of high-level programming languages such as FORTRAN provided the long-needed tools for detailed statistical analysis. A careful research study was now warranted to show whether or not the random-walk model was indeed a tenable representation of price movements in modern capital markets.

THE "DIFFERENCING INTERVAL" ISSUE

The random-walk model states that "any price change is independent of the sequence of previous price changes." It is essential to understand that "price change" implies a period-to-period measurement. For example, one can test the validity of the random-walk model for daily (day-to-day) price changes, monthly (month-to-month) price changes, or any other interval.

This span between price observations is called the *differencing interval*. Daily price quotations in newspapers represent a one-market day differencing interval. Similarly, the quotations in the financial weekly *Barron's* show a one-week differencing interval.

Since the random-walk model is concerned with how prices change from period to period, the differencing interval must be specified when discussing the model. Differencing intervals can vary from the shortest possible interval (consecutive transactions shown on the ticker tape) to extremely long intervals of

a year or more. Also, instead of reflecting fixed time periods, differencing intervals can be defined by the occurrence of particular events, such as a new price high, the formation of a certain pattern, and so on.

Thus, the object of research is not simply to test the validity of the random-walk model. Instead, research must ask, "Is the model valid for some particular differencing interval?" That is, is the relationship between day-to-day price changes random? What about the week-to-week and month-to-month comparisons as well?

The early random-walk experiments by Kendall and Osborne were criticized for assuming fixed differencing intervals. Their research had shown that a series of price changes, measured at fixed one-week or one-month intervals, could not be used to predict future price movements. But suppose a prediction scheme relied on certain "events" such as large price swings or specific chart patterns, which can occur at variable time intervals?

Variable-time models seek to reveal complicated patterns of price behavior which fixed-time models will not detect. Myriad variable-time models have been developed, but they all monitor a continuous series of price changes in search of some extraordinary "event." One common variable-time model forms the basis for "point-and-figure" charting. This method of technical analysis is based on recording the "event" of a stock's price moving by some predetermined amount. Chartists employing this technique plot xs and os for stocks which rise or fall, respectively, by a specified amount, often $1 per share.

An exhaustive analysis of the infinite number of possible variable-time models would be an impossible undertaking. Fortunately, a single premise does underlie all technical prediction methods. This premise is that the market repeats itself in patterns and that historical information about price movements is therefore useful for prediction. Consequently, the commonly used techniques of technical analysis—be they fixed- or variable-time models—can be classified and explicitly tested against the random-walk model.

ALEXANDER—TESTING OF FILTER TECHNIQUES

In 1961, Sidney Alexander [1] of M.I.T. reported the first scientific investigation of a variable-time model of stock price behavior. Alexander tested what is known as a "filter tech-

nique."[1] He contended that if the filter technique could show above-average profits, this return would be indicative of non-random price movements. Alexander evaluated his filter technique with Kendall's [145] data and reported that it was more successful than a buy-and-hold strategy, although brokerage commissions would have had a significant impact on profitability. Alexander's results are summarized in Table 4–1.

TABLE 4–1: Comparative profitability of the filter technique, 1928–1961

		Terminal capital as multiple of initial capital		
Filter size	*Number of transactions*	*If no commissions*	*With commissions*	*Buy and hold*
1.0%	1,730	41.3	0.0	5.1
4.0	418	10.7	0.0	5.1
8.2	142	14.8	0.9	5.1
12.5	88	4.0	0.7	5.1
17.0	54	2.1	0.7	5.1
21.7	32	6.4	3.4	5.1
29.5	20	5.3	3.6	5.1
34.6	16	4.8	3.5	5.1
40.0	12	6.2	5.0	5.1
45.6	8	10.6	9.2	5.1

Source: After Alexander [1].

Thus, although Alexander found some "statistical" evidence which contradicted the random-walk model, he concluded his investigation by saying, "I should advise any reader who is interested in practical results . . . and . . . [who] must pay commissions, to turn to some other source for advice on how to beat [the] buy and hold [strategy]." [1, pp. 351–52]

[1] Filter techniques are based on the assumption that trends exist in stock prices but that these patterns are obscured by insignificant fluctuations, or market "noise." The filter precept is utilized to justify a procedure whereby all price changes smaller than a specified size are ignored. The remaining data are then examined. A typical filter rule might be: If the stock price advances 5 percent (signaling a breakout), buy and hold the stock until it declines by 5 percent (signaling the start of a reversal). At that time, sell the stock held and sell short an equal amount until the stock again moves up 5 percent. Under such a rule, all moves of less than 5 percent are ignored. Filter techniques seek to discover "significant moves" by studying price changes of a given magnitude, irrespective of the length of time between them. In short, the filter technique substitutes the dimension of the "move" for the dimension of "time." This precept is the basis of the point-and-figure chart technique (cf., Cohen [42] and [43]), the rationale for the so-called Dow theory (cf., Alexander [1]), and many other forms of technical analysis.

It should also be emphasized that while one might find a grain of support for technical analysis in Alexander's results, Paul Cootner [50] has noted a procedural error in Alexander's computations. Another problem is that Alexander did not state his conclusions in terms of statistical confidence. Thus, the likelihood of obtaining similar research results purely by chance, or a "dart board" selection, is not known.

HOUTHAKKER—COMMODITY FUTURES

In another 1961 paper, Harvard economist Hendrik Houthakker [125] similarly reported that a variable-time decision rule yielded superior returns when applied to commodity futures. Houthakker advanced the hypothesis (cf., Darvas [59]) that changes in prices are characterized by long "runs" (that is, a series of price changes in the same direction). If this hypothesis were correct, standing sell orders, called "stop orders," could be used by a speculator to liquidate his or her position when adverse runs were encountered. Conversely, a standing sell order would not be triggered when favorable runs were being experienced.

Thus, if a trader wished to limit losses to, say, 5 percent, a stop order could be placed to sell when the stock's price dropped to 95 percent of the purchase price. If price fluctuations were not random, and if a price drop were likely to lead to a further decline, such a trading policy would reduce losses without affecting upward runs of profits. Hence, average profit would increase. Houthakker's test of his trading rule on wheat and corn futures proved quite successful and led him to say, "I feel that . . . [the results] . . . indicate the existence of patterns of price behavior that would not be present if price changes were random." [125, p. 168]

HAGIN—NO EVIDENCE IN SUPPORT OF TECHNICAL ANALYSIS

Aside from Houthakker's surprising results with commodity futures, numerous experiments with variable-time decision rules by other researchers have not turned up any evidence in support of technical analysis. This author's (see Hagin [116]) own experiments in the early 1960s tested numerous fixed- and variable-time decision rules against a four-year file of daily data on 790 actively traded stocks. Several hundred tests of decision rules based on moving averages, filters, thresholds,

consistently found no *evidence in support of technical analysis!*

COOTNER AND MOORE—ACCELERATION OF THE DEBATE

By 1962, the academic debate on the validity of the random-walk model had picked up momentum, although the issue was still almost unknown on Wall Street. Cootner's research focused attention on a common source of confusion in random-walk research—the differencing interval. The random-walk model, it will be remembered, states that "future" price changes cannot be predicted from "past" price movements. Cootner's research emphasized that there is not one random-walk model, but rather one for every definition of "past" and "future." Thus, when Cootner defined "past" and "future" as "one week," his test of the random-walk model indicated that price changes were random. But when "past" was defined as 14 weeks, the random-walk model was not valid!

Thus, as the debate intensified, it seemed that predictions based upon the more distant past might be useful. But, in the race for "hot new information," it appeared that information on recent price changes is worthless!

Further evidence that studying weekly price changes is futile came from Arnold Moore's 1962 doctoral dissertation at the University of Chicago. Moore's research [196] validated the random-walk model for weekly price changes with a sample of 33 representative stocks listed on the New York Stock Exchange.

THE DEFINITIVE STUDIES OF THE MID-1960s

Eugene Fama's 1965 doctoral dissertation [68] also at the University of Chicago, was regarded as the definitive study of the random walk during the mid-1960s. A number of tests were used to examine the validity of the model; data included daily to 16-day differencing intervals for the 30 stocks in the Dow Jones Industrial Average—spanning periods from five to seven years. The results of one of these tests is shown in Table 4–2. Following his exhaustive study, Fama found no evidence of trends in stock prices for any differencing interval he tested.

TABLE 4–2: Runs of consecutive price changes in same direction: Actual versus expected for each Dow Jones industrial company

	Daily changes		*4-Day changes*		*9-Day changes*		*16-Day changes*	
Stock	*Actual*	*Expected*	*Actual*	*Expected*	*Actual*	*Expected*	*Actual*	*Expected*
Allied Chemical	683	713	160	162	71	71	39	39
Alcoa	601	671	151	154	61	67	41	39
American Can	730	756	169	172	71	73	48	44
AT&T	657	688	165	156	66	70	34	37
American Tobacco	700	747	178	173	69	73	41	41
Anaconda	635	680	166	160	68	66	36	38
Bethlehem Steel	709	720	163	159	80	72	41	42
Chrysler	927	932	223	222	100	97	54	54
DuPont	672	695	160	162	78	72	43	39
Eastman Kodak	678	679	154	160	70	70	43	40
General Electric	918	956	225	225	101	97	51	52
General Foods	799	825	185	191	81	76	43	41
General Motors	832	868	202	205	83	86	44	47
Goodyear	681	672	151	158	60	65	36	36
Int'l. Harvester	720	713	159	164	84	73	40	38
Int'l. Nickel	704	713	163	164	68	71	34	38
Int'l. Paper	762	826	190	194	80	83	51	47
Johns Manville	685	699	173	160	64	69	39	40
Owens Illinois	713	743	171	169	69	73	36	39
Procter & Gamble	826	859	180	191	66	81	40	43
Sears	700	748	167	173	66	71	40	35
Standard Oil (Cal.)	972	979	237	228	97	99	59	54
Standard Oil (N.J.)	688	704	159	159	69	69	29	37
Swift & Co.	878	878	209	197	85	84	50	48
Texaco	600	654	143	155	57	63	29	36
Union Carbide	595	621	142	151	67	67	36	35
United Aircraft	661	699	172	161	77	68	45	40
U.S. Steel	651	662	162	158	65	70	37	41
Westinghouse	829	826	198	193	87	84	41	46
Woolworth	847	868	193	199	78	81	48	48
Averages	735	760	176	176	75	75	42	42

Source: After Fama [77].

The conclusion: Information on stock price changes over any or all days of a given 16-day period is useless!

Subsequently, Fama and Marshall Blume [76] conducted a thorough analysis of the filter technique. They employed a variety of filter sizes in an effort to determine the "best" size. Their conclusion was that none of the approaches tested would have been more profitable (after commissions) than a buy-and-hold strategy. On another front, James Van Horne and George G. C. Parker [277] studied "breakouts" from moving

averages. Again, in no case was the profitability (after commissions) of a buy-and-hold strategy surpassed.

LEVY—AN IMPORTANT DISTINCTION

In 1966, Robert Levy's doctoral dissertation at the American University in Washington, D.C., was described by *Fortune* magazine as a "decisive refutation of the random walk." [293, p. 160] This characterization was erroneous, however, as two facts had been overlooked. First, there are any number of random-walk models—each with an explicit definition of what is "past." Second, research dating back to Cowles [54] in the 1930s, and to Cootner [48] in the early 1960s, has correctly shown that when stock price changes are studied over long differencing intervals, discernible trends do appear.

Levy [160] reported that stocks exhibiting higher than average price changes in any six-month period also tended to show higher than average price changes during the next six months. Random price behavior should have resulted in only average movements for the second six-month period. This phenomenon has been called *relative strength*, or *relative strength continuation*.

Thus, Levy reported that stocks with relatively above- (or below-) average price performance in the "past" six months tended to maintain above- (or below-) average performance in the "next" six months. This phenomenon is not new, however, nor does it refute the random-walk model. Levy's findings were perfectly consistent with other research. As long ago as 1937, Cowles reported that, "taking one year as the unit of measurement . . . the tendency is very pronounced for stocks which have exceeded the median in one year to exceed it also in the year following." [54, p. 285][2]

Furthermore, a careful study of Levy's work by Michael Jensen [131] revealed that Levy had overstated the returns earned from his relative strength trading rules (see [161] and [162]). When correct rate of return calculations are used, none of Levy's "profitable" trading rules showed greater returns, after transaction costs, than those available from the correct buy-and-hold returns. The conclusion: Levy found evidence of a well-known, subtle form of long-term, nonrandom behavior

---

[2] It should be noted that while Cowles' article had a statistical error (referred to earlier) which invalidated the apparent predictability of monthly prices, the error did not invalidate his conclusions with regard to one-year relative strength.

which, nonetheless, cannot be used to beat average market returns!

To verify this conclusion, Jensen and George Benington [137] tested two of Levy's "better" decision rules on 200 individual securities over successive five-year time intervals from 1931 to 1965. Jensen and Benington concluded that after allowance for transaction costs, Levy's trading rules, on the average, were not significantly more profitable than the buy-and-hold policy.

NIEDERHOFFER AND OSBORNE—THE OTHER END OF THE DIFFERENCING INTERVAL

Victor Niederhoffer, individually [203, 204] and with Osborne [206], studied the other end of the differencing interval time spectrum—successive transactions on the ticker tape. Research on this smallest possible differencing interval provides striking evidence of dependence between successive stock transactions.

Niederhoffer and Osborne reported that successive transactions display several nonrandom properties:

1. There is a general tendency for prices to reverse between trades.
2. Following two changes in the same direction, the chances of continuing in that direction are greater than after changes in opposite directions.
3. Price reversals occur more frequently just above and below integers. [206, p. 194]

Unfortunately, these short-term and small-percentage dependencies, although consistent, are eclipsed by transaction costs and consequently provide no basis for successful trading strategies.

SUMMARY

The preceding two chapters have examined historical milestones in the development of the weak form of the efficient market hypothesis. This research illustrates how the renaissance of investing knowledge has been accompanied by progressively more rigorous, and more probing, computer-based investigations. In addition, the conclusion reaffirmed by each investigation is that no research yet discussed has refuted the random-walk model, given a differencing interval of between 1 and 16 days.

Chapter 5

Definitive tests: Weak form

By the mid-1960s, the body of evidence in support of the random-walk model was growing but still rested on possibly incomplete tests and limited test data. It might be argued, for example, that the statistical tools (serial correlation, run tests, and so on) used to study stock price behavior were inadequate to detect the complicated patterns (for example, head and shoulders) which, according to some chartist's (cf., Jiler [139]), serve as predictors.

Similarly, test data tended to be confined to only a few stocks. Fama's [68] data base, for example, consisted of daily prices for only the 30 stocks of the Dow Jones Industrial Average. Furthermore, although early research on the random-walk model neglected trading volume, many technicians contended that volume was a necessary adjunct to historical price data.

Also, early studies of the random-walk model searched almost exclusively for patterns that were present throughout the data. It was quite possible, however, that a test which looked at all price data might indicate randomness, while a test examining only a portion of the price changes (for example, "large changes") would show predictable patterns.

As a result, during the mid-1960s it was not known whether the findings obtained from these limited tests on limited empirical data could be substantiated for a much larger sample of stocks, studied over various intervals. It was unknown, for example, whether or not a systematic investigation of chart patterns would reveal a potential tocl for forecasting that went undetected by traditional statistical analysis. Further, it was not known whether industry or price-range differences might invalidate the random-walk description of stock price behavior.

By the mid-1960s, then, the early shortcomings of the research on the random-walk model could be summarized as follows:

1. The random-walk model had not been tested on enough stocks over a long enough period of time.
2. Research on the random-walk model was incomplete because it did not include trading volume information, which was seen by some as a necessary adjunct to historical price data.
3. Random-walk research was too limited because it was designed almost exclusively to detect patterns present throughout the entire time period.
4. The statistical techniques used to confirm the random-walk model might be unable to detect the complicated visual or graphic relationships discovered by chartists.

ALL ACTIVELY TRADED STOCKS

To overcome the foregoing limitations, this author (see Hagin [116]) studied the daily prices and volume for 790 actively traded stocks on the New York and American Stock Exchanges over several three-year periods. The first research question was: Does the random-walk model hold for all actively traded stocks? A large variety of computer programs and statistical tests yielded quite conclusive findings: There was no systematic behavior in stock prices that could be used for profitable prediction when the data were studied with differencing intervals of between 1 and 16 days. Further, there were no systematic differences that would allow profitable prediction when the findings were cross-tabulated by stock price range, stock exchange, or industry.

In summary, this author's research, based on an exhaustive investigation of fixed-time stock price dependencies utilizing traditional statistical tools, found no evidence that profitable prediction schemes can be developed from recent historical price data. In other words, knowledge of a stock's price behavior during any 16-day period provides no useful information for predicting the direction of future price changes.

PRICES AND VOLUME?

Is it true, as many technicians contend, that the combination of price *and* trading volume data is what provides useful pre-

dictive information? To answer this question, this author (see Hagin [116]) studied the possibility that price changes can be predicted from the simultaneous interaction of preceding price and volume changes. The study employed a computer-readable file of prices and volumes on 790 stocks, and while the details of the research are beyond the scope of this book (they are available in [116]), the results are significant for anyone who invests: Knowledge of preceding volume changes,[1] even coupled with information on preceding price changes, does not improve one's ability to predict the direction of the next price change.

In sum, these results reaffirm previous findings that short-term (defined as less than 40 days in this study) stock price changes exhibit random, and hence unpredictable, patterns. Further, the introduction of the preceding period's trading volume data does not provide even a slight improvement in the ability to predict the direction of future period-to-period stock price changes.

BREAKOUTS?

There is conclusive evidence that data on the direction of short-term (within 40 days) price and volume changes cannot be used to predict the direction of subsequent price changes. This conclusion was reached by studying historical market data over fixed-time intervals. Most stock market technicians do not purport to predict price changes solely from fixed-time models, however. They contend that situations occasionally arise which foreshadow certain kinds of predictable price behavior. Thus, technicians typically characterize the stock market by a variable-time or event-triggered model. This author (see Hagin [116]) has conducted exhaustive tests of the premises underlying such variable-time models. For example, do relatively large daily price changes precede predictable events?

There are several conflicting viewpoints on how stock prices behave after large price changes. On the one hand, some investors contend that steep advances or declines are typically followed by reversals—brought about either by profit taking at the high price or by bargain hunters attracted to the lower

[1] It should be noted that "information" concerning various relative and absolute volume levels was also tested and that none of these schemes invalidated the above conclusions.

price. On the other hand, there are investors who believe that large price increases signal "breakouts" which are apt to continue. If both kinds of investors participate in the market, one group's actions would tend to offset those of the other group. Large price changes, then, might be followed by movements which are typical of those generated by a random process.

Benoit Mandelbrot [182] suggested yet another model. He submitted that any large price change might tend to be followed by further large changes, either up or down. Fama has provided the following rationale for this model:

> . . . this type of dependence hinges on the nature of the information process in a world of uncertainty . . . when important, new information comes into the market, it cannot always be evaluated precisely. Sometimes the immediate price change caused by the new information will be too large, which will set in motion forces to produce a reaction. In other cases the immediate price change will not fully discount the information, and impetus will be created to move the price again in the same direction. [68, p. 85]

Fama tested this hypothesis on ten stocks and found only slight evidence of large changes being followed by further large changes. Furthermore, such successive price changes were unpredictable in direction. The same results have been substantiated by this author (Hagin) in a study of 790 stocks over a four-year period. That is, there is some evidence that "large" price changes occur in succession, but the direction of the change is random. This result interests economists but is of little value to investors, who are obviously interested in the direction of the subsequent price movement.

In addition, numerous other hypotheses have been formulated by this author to test the usefulness of coupling trading volume information, such as "volume shocks," with data on large price changes. In summary, there was no evidence that the occurrence of any special price or volume situation over the short run (less than 40 days) has any predictive value.

CHART PATTERNS?

There are two kinds of chartists: bar chartists (cf., Edwards and Magee [62] and Jiler [139]) and point-and-figure chartists (cf., Cohen [42], [43]). Bar charting is a fixed-time model, while point-and-figure charting is a variable-time model. Both types plot price on the vertical scale. On bar charts, the horizontal

scale is uniformly divided into fixed-time periods. One point-and-figure charts, the units on the horizontal scale indicate reversals in the direction of stock prices and occur at variable-time intervals.

Once the stock's historical record has been charted, the technical analyst visually studies the configuration for predictive signals. While it is unlikely, it must be conceded that chartists might be able to pick out extremely complex patterns that the traditional statistical tests used by researchers are unable to isolate.

The validity of basing predictions of stock price movements on chart patterns can, however, be tested rigorously by an unconventional use of a computer. Such investigation is possible because all charting theories rest on a single premise: They assume that visually detectable price patterns have repeating characteristics. This premise has also been rigorously tested by this author (Hagin). It is again beyond the scope of this book to discuss such research on chart patterns in detail.[2] Rather, a brief summary of the two methodological approaches and the general findings should be sufficient.

The first research approach was to simulate a chartist's vision. Chartists look for specific kinds of patterns, such as head and shoulders, saucer bottoms, and triple tops. During the first phase of this research, a computer was used to search the price history of each of 790 stocks for specified patterns that are purported by chartists to serve as predictors.

The computer was instructed to "look for" the computerized equivalent of what a chartist hopes to find visually. Next, the occurrence of any of these patterns was recorded, and the stock's succeeding price behavior was noted. Finally, a statistical analysis was conducted to determine whether these patterns indeed preceded certain kinds of price performance. The investigation was unable to detect any evidence that the commonly used chart patterns were forerunners of certain price changes.

Under the second research approach, the computer attempted to derive original predictive patterns from the data. The computer was first instructed to group charts on the basis of the price behavior following the chart. For example, one classification consisted of all chart patterns which appeared before dramatic price increases. Then each group of patterns

---

[2] Some of this author's early work on computerized detection and classification of chart patterns is reported in [116].

was studied for similarities. Again, this research offered no evidence that predictable stock price movements follow visually detectable chart patterns.

DOESN'T TECHNICAL ANALYSIS WORK SOMETIMES?

For some readers, the evidence presented here may seem to contradict their personal experience. Such people "know" that technical schemes which are based on historical price and volume work. But do they? The answer is quite clear. There is absolutely no evidence that information on the price and volume movements of a stock over the recent past will aid in predicting the future price behavior of that stock.

Yet, many practitioners persist in using this kind of technical analysis. They must occasionally consider themselves successful; otherwise, they would abandon the technique. Success in the stock market, however, must be gauged against a realistic benchmark. One could expect a certain level of performance even if technical analysis is indeed useless. Stated another way, the benchmark for comparing investment performance should be the rate of return one would expect from unskilled stock selection.

Suppose that instead of basing investment decisions on the results of elaborate technical analysis, an investor selected stocks by throwing darts at the financial page of a newspaper. Further, suppose transaction dates were chosen by throwing darts at a calendar. What investment returns would be achieved from such random selection processes?

The work of Lawrence Fisher and James Lorie [91] has revealed that the median rate of return from random investment in common stocks was 9.8 percent compounded annually during the period from 1926 to 1960. Also, using random holding periods averaging several years, they found that 78 percent of such transactions were profitable.

These findings become especially interesting when you consider that technicians generally claim to be accurate only some of the time. For example, Edmund W. Tabell, regarded as the dean of chartists until his death in 1965, said that he was right only about 70 percent of the time. Admittedly, the longer a position is held, the more likely it is to become profitable, and Tabell made no statement as to how long or short a period it took for him to be "right." Also, the total annual rate of return

is usually more important than the percentage of individual purchases with profitable outcomes.

Nevertheless, until proven otherwise, it must be concluded that people who credit their success to technical analysis have not, in fact, benefited from it in any way. They have merely obtained normal results, as could be achieved from random investment.

SO WHERE DO WE STAND?

Academic research, which has no vested interest in the matter, is in overwhelming agreement—technical market prediction schemes based on price and volume movements over the preceding 40 days appear to be useless. Some market practitioners will react to this statement by asserting that they use such technical analysis only occasionally. This is ridiculous! The evidence is overwhelming that such analysis should never be employed.

Why, then, does this kind of technical analysis persist? Why does the investing public support advisory services which rely on charts? Isn't it strange that hospital patients who will trust their lives to a computer's ability to read their electrocardiograms will not listen when told that the same pattern detection techniques cannot discern any useful patterns in historical stock price data?

In spite of this research, "technical" jargon remains an integral part of Wall Street's vocabulary. Financial pages make frequent references to events such as a "technical correction," even though few commentators agree on its definition or occurrence. Unfortunately, most of this gobbledygook appears to serve the purpose of the psychiatrist's inkblot—to project meaning into nothing.

Yet, in spite of its thoroughness, the research summarized here is subject to several provisos. First, it should be emphasized that technical analysis, as discussed here, refers to the study of recent (within 40 days) price and/or volume information. Second, direct investigative comparisons against the actual work of technicians are difficult because these practitioners usually interpret basic price data with the help of "necessarily secret" formulas to calculate relative strengths, moving and geometric averages (see James [130]), ratio lines, trend forecasts, and the like. Third, prediction schemes under the rubric of "technical analysis" are by no means limited to

the study of price and volume information. Hence, our analysis of the technical point of view will not be complete until we examine the usefulness of such nonprice technical indicators as splits and odd-lot transactions in Chapters 10 and 11.

In spite of these provisos, several definitive statements can be made about technical analysis. William Sharpe has said that "many regard technicians as the lunatic fringe of the investment world. Descriptions of their activities are felt to be a suitable subject for anthropologists, but inappropriate in a book intended for a serious investor." [252, p. 489] The evidence clearly supports this view. It is doubtful that the tea leaves left behind by today's stock market can foretell tomorrow's tracings. For now, an important "don't" of prudent investing is: Do not use technical analysis based on recent historical price or volume information.

This does not mean, of course, that practitioners who use 'elements" of technical analysis have disappeared from the investment scene. Unfortunately, while it is virtually impossible to find either theoretical or empirical evidence in support of technical analysis, the technical gobbledygook of "trends, resistence, strength, and patterns" has obvious marketing appeal to naïve investors. Thus, a situation exists in which a stock selection technique that has been so thoroughly researched—and debunked—that it would no longer be a fitting subject for an investments seminar at any leading business school can nonetheless form the basis for an investment management approach just a few blocks away. Unquestionably, employing such analysis is *illogical.* What constitutes *imprudence* is a matter which, in the final analysis, must be decided by the courts.

Chapter 6

Usefulness of information

The semistrong form of the efficient market hypothesis focuses on how rapidly and how efficiently market prices adjust to new publicly available information. We have seen that the weak form of the hypothesis (that is, the random-walk model) has been the subject of inquiry for many years. In fact, given the duration of the controversy over the weak form and the wealth of evidence in its support, it is fair to say that its validity is now generally recognized by both academic researchers and astute professional investors.

This chapter moves from the weak form of the efficient market hypothesis (which focuses on the usefulness of historical price and volume information) to the semistrong form of the hypothesis (which deals with the usefulness of all publicly available information). Since the semistrong version of the hypothesis is a relatively new concept (compared with the old weak-form random-walk model), the subject has, to date, received far less attention in the financial literature.

Basically, the semistrong form of the hypothesis states that if the market is truly efficient in both disseminating and processing publicly available information, any value that this information might have to a recipient is destroyed by the competitive forces of the market. Thus, to achieve consistently above-average risk-adjusted investment performance, an investor must know: (1) that certain kinds of *information* (2) will, with known *probabilities,* (3) influence certain investment *instruments* (4) in certain investment *markets,* (5) in known *directions,* (6) by approximate *magnitudes,* and he or she must (7) *act on the information before other investors.*

If this cannot be done, and the semistrong form of the efficient market hypothesis is a valid description of the stock market, investment analysis becomes an expensive exercise in wishful

thinking! The fact that more than 100,000 professional security analysts, brokers, and portfolio managers—plus approximately 25 million U.S. residents who directly own shares of common stock—are all trying to do the same thing makes this a very competitive endeavor.

KINDS OF INFORMATION

Several kinds of information can precipitate price movements of various instruments in various markets. Three broad categories of such data are:

1. *Economy-related information.* General economic news typically affects the market as a whole. On days when several hundred stocks reach new lows while only a few achieve new highs, it is clear that even the stocks of well-managed companies in growing industries cannot withstand a bear (downward) market.
2. *Industry-related information.* Instead of affecting the general economy, news sometimes only has an impact on a single industry. For example, news that dry breakfast cereals contained little or no nutritional value had an adverse effect on all breakfast cereal manufacturers; publicity over the potential health hazards of cyclamates and saccharine have affected only users of those products; an industrywide strike would affect only the firms in that or related industries, and so on.
3. *Company-related information.* Announcements regarding a company's earnings, dividends, forthcoming stock splits, patents, merger offers, new discoveries, and so forth—with little or no bearing on an entire industry or the general economy—can still prompt a change in the price of a firm's stock.

If one is going to attempt to predict price movements, a logical first step is to determine the relative importance of each of these three basic kinds of information before turning to the question of how efficient the market is at impounding the various kinds of information into the price of a stock. For example, if the relative importance of information related to a company, an industry, and the economy is about equal (and the market is equally inefficient across each information category), it might behoove analysts to allocate their research efforts to these three areas equally. Similarly, if 80 percent of the fluctuations of a stock's price are associated with market

and industry factors, it would be inappropriate for an analyst to concentrate on company-related information. In such a situation, the relative importance of company-related information would be swamped by the effect of market swings.

WHAT CAUSES PRICE CHANGES?

Benjamin King [149], in his doctoral dissertation at the University of Chicago, sought to determine the relative importance of these underlying causes of price movements: the market, the basic industry (such as metals), the industry subgroup (such as nonferrous metals), and the company. After studying 403 consecutive months of data (1927–60) for 63 NYSE stocks, King reported that:

1. There is a strong tendency for stocks to move with the overall market.
2. Stock price comovements correspond closely to industry classifications.
3. Only a minor proportion of overall price movements can be attributed to company-related factors.

King's research is startling in its consistency. First, his findings parallel earlier but less comprehensive results reported by Granger and Morgenstern [111] and by Godfrey, Granger, and Morgenstern [108]. Second, King's market and industry comovements were remarkably consistent, especially after consideration of the industry changes which doubtless occurred over the more than 33 years spanned by his study. In the most recent period he examined (1952–60), King showed that, on the average, price changes were attributable to the investing public's reaction to four discernible components in the following proportions:

1. The market as a whole 31%
2. The basic industry 12%
3. The industry subgroup (or other common factors) . 37%
4. The particular company 20%

On the average, 31 percent of a stock's price movement was ascribable to general economic factors influencing the market as a whole. About half of the movement was traceable to the influence of a firm's basic industry and its industry subgroup—12 percent and 37 percent, respectively. After these market and industry comovements were accounted for,

only a scant 20 percent of the total price movement could be attributed to individual-company developments!

These aggregate figures do not present the entire picture which King developed. There were some interesting differences within the composite averages. These are summarized in Table 6–1 using King's most recent data.

TABLE 6–1: Classification of price comovements by industry membership

	Percentage movement explained by:			
Industry membership	*Overall market*	*Basic industry*	*Industry subgroup*	*Individual company*
Railroads	47	8	26	19
Metals	46	8	31	15
Petroleum	37	20	28	15
Utilities	23	14	41	22
Retail stores	23	8	42	27
Tobacco	9	17	49	25
Average	31	12	37	20

Source: Derived from data in King [149].

These data show that the shares of railroads, metal companies, and petroleum firms rank highest in overall market dependence, with the stocks of tobacco firms being relatively insensitive to overall market swings. The industry columns confirm King's statement that the "general adherence to the pattern of industry comovement is ineluctable . . . the strongest industry effects are those for petroleums, utilities, and tobaccos—the weakest for metals, [retail] stores, and rails." [149, pp. 203–4]

King's research is important for three reasons. First, he showed that, on the average, roughly one third of a stock's movement can be traced to general market swings. Second, and very important, there are clear industry differences. In the tobacco industry, for example, King could attribute only 9 percent of stock price variations to general market swings. Third, this relationship between stock swings and market swings appears to be consistent over time.

King's research was expanded and updated in 1968 by Marshall Blume [28] in his doctoral dissertation at the University of Chicago. Blume, who studied 251 securities, confirmed that certain stocks had a tendency to move with the market and that this relationship persisted over time.

INFORMATION HIERARCHY

The semistrong form of the efficient market hypothesis encompasses all publicly available information. A more useful classification of "all" information can be distilled by:

1. Specifying the investment "instrument" (for example, common stock).
2. Defining the "market" (for example, the NYSE).
3. Tabulating the kinds of "information" that might affect the value of this instrument at each of the four levels of the information hierarchy.

This procedure is illustrated in Figure 6–1.

FIGURE 6–1: The investment analysis function

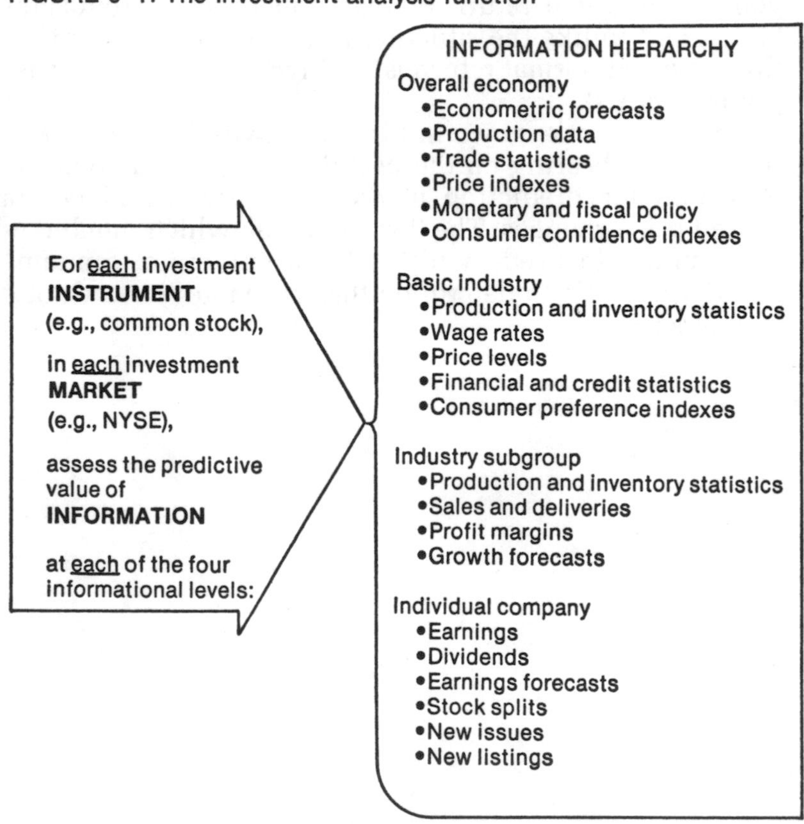

When possibly useful information is placed in the perspective of Figure 6–1 for specific investment vehicles in specific

markets, one can assess how efficiently information is processed at each hierarchical level. If the news is quickly and accurately impounded into the security's price, the market would be deemed economically "efficient" in terms of the impact of that information on that instrument. But, if for some reason the market does not fully react to a certain kind of news, or reacts slowly, the discovery of this economic "inefficiency" will permit one to profit in excess of a fair rate of return.

It should be reiterated, however, that one does not have to discover market inefficiencies to profit from investments. An efficient market is one in which everyone can expect a "fair return" for assuming risk. If such a market is efficient at digesting earnings information, for instance, investors acting on such information could not increase their expected profits beyond a fair-game return or reap "abnormal" profits. Importantly, and unlike the situation in Las Vegas or Atlantic City, this expected normal return is positive—the reward for assuming market risk.

The framework shown in Figure 6–1 will be used to explain the research bearing on the usefulness of various types of information for predicting market-, industry-, and company-caused price changes. The first topic—on which much modern research has focused—will be the usefulness of fundamental security analysis to determine the comparative worth of common stocks.

Chapter 7

Fundamental security analysis

Investing is to forego present spending in exchange for expected future benefits. Since today's stock price is a known quantity, investing entails a certain sacrifice for an uncertain future benefit. These uncertain future returns depend on a firm's earning power, which will determine the extent of its future divided distributions and, to varying degrees, the future selling price of the company's stock.

A wealth of evidence shows that stock prices tend to move together, reflecting investor expectations about the overall economy or various industry segments. However, in spite of these comovements, companies are fundamentally different. Clearly, profit expectations differ among firms, as do the risks associated with these various profit expectations.

Recognizing these obvious differences, thousands of security analysts study publicly available information in an effort to discover over- and undervalued companies. On the other hand, the semistrong form of the efficient market hypothesis holds that such analysis cannot accurately discern over- or undervalued securities. Specifically, this form of the hypothesis maintains that any and all publicly available information is efficiently reflected in the price of the underlying stock.

If this is true, the use of such information for fundamental security analysis is a rather expensive waste of time. To examine this important controversy, we will first describe the process of fundamental security analysis.

FUNDAMENTAL SECURITY ANALYSIS

When buying common stock, an investor acquires the legal right to share in the company's future earnings through dividends. A cornerstone of fundamental security analysis is that a

share of common stock is worth the present value of the future income its owner will receive. Since the income from dividends will be received in the future, the discounted present value[1] of this stream of income can reflect both rates of return and risk.

A popular, and much simpler, way to think about the price of a share of stock is in terms of its price-earnings ratio. A P/E, as it is generally called, is simply the ratio of a stock's current price to its annual earnings. Thus, by using the price-earnings ratio, a stock can be described as selling at five times earnings, ten times earnings, and so on.

The analyst faced with the task of assigning some measure of value to a security thus has two alternatives. The first is to calculate the present value of the security from estimates of the future stream of income that the owner will receive. This, in turn, requires an estimate of an appropriate discount rate, which in turn is derived from estimates of required future risk-adjusted rates of return. In view of the theoretical, as well as practical, complexity of this estimation procedure (which MPT has now minimized), analysts have traditionally opted for the much simpler second alternative—valuation based on price-earnings ratios.

PRICE-EARNINGS RATIOS

Fundamental analysis based on price-earnings ratios is conceptually very simple. It calls for

1. Estimating a stock's earnings per share for the next year or so.
2. Estimating the price-earnings ratio that is expected to prevail when the estimated earnings are reported.
3. Multiplying the estimated future earnings per share by the estimated price-earnings ratio to obtain the estimated future price.

To examine the usefulness of this approach, we must determine

1. The degree to which security prices are related to differences in price-earnings ratios.
2. The degree to which security prices are related to earnings.

[1] The concept of present value is explained in Chapter 30.

THE RELATIONSHIP OF PRICES TO MARKET-LEVEL FACTORS

The average price-earnings ratios for the Dow Jones Industrials over the 1961–78 period are shown in Figure 7–1. As illustrated, since 1961, the P/E for the Dow Jones Industrials

FIGURE 7–1: Price-earnings ratios for the Dow Jones 30 industrials, 1961–1978

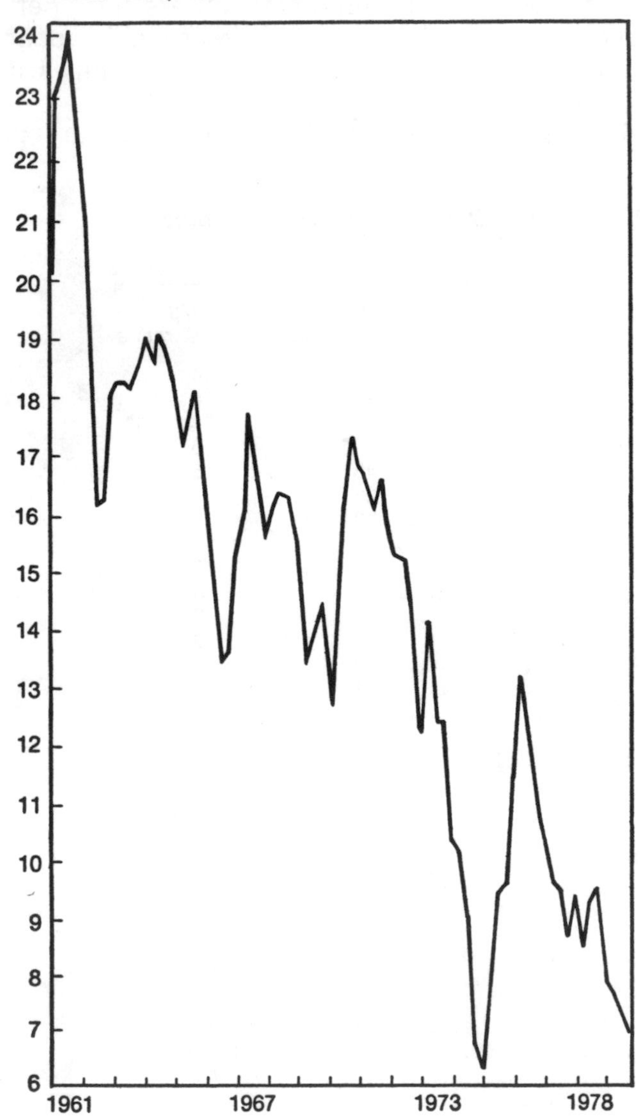

has averaged about 14 and has ranged from less than 7 to over 24 times.

To provide a real-world forecasting exercise, cover the right-hand portion of Figure 7–1 so that only the P/E ratio for the first part of 1961 is visible. Then slowly uncover the P/Es for the succeeding years—while trying to guess both the direction and magnitude of each year-to-year change. This exercise clearly demonstrates that even if *earnings* for the Dow Jones Industrials could be forecast with complete accuracy, the future price level could not be predicted unless the "perfect" earnings forecast was combined with a "reasonably accurate" estimate of the P/E ratio that would prevail when the earnings were announced.

Table 7–1 shows a representative list of company price-

TABLE 7–1: P/E ratios for 30 large companies on February 6, 1973 and January 8, 1979

Company	*1973 P/E ratios*	*1979 P/E ratios*
Aetna Life & Casualty	11	4
AT&T	11	8
Avon Products	60	14
Chase Manhattan	12	6
Coca-Cola	45	15
Delta Airlines	22	6
duPont	20	9
Eastman Kodak	46	13
Exxon	13	9
Ford	8	3
General Electric	24	9
General Foods	12	8
General Motors	10	5
Gulf Oil	11	7
IBM	39	16
IT&T	13	7
McDonnell Douglas	10	9
Mobil Oil	12	7
Philip Morris	27	11
Polaroid	78	16
Procter & Gamble	31	14
Safeway	11	9
Sears, Roebuck	29	8
Tenneco	11	7
Texaco	12	9
Texas Utilities	16	7
Union Carbide	13	6
U.S. Steel	10	13
Weyerhaeuser	21	9
Xerox	48	10

Sources: *The Wall Street Journal,* February 5, 1973 and January 5, 1979.

earnings ratios as of February 6, 1973 (the market's most recent high) and January 8, 1979. Note that the 1973 P/Es range from a high of 78 for Polaroid to a low of 8 for the Ford Motor Company. This means that in early 1973 the market valuation of earnings for Polaroid was almost *ten times* the multiple of Ford Motor Company stock.

The variations in P/Es reflect investors' assessments of the prospects for growth and/or certainty in the earnings and dividends of the market as a whole as well as individual companies. Notice that in early 1973 the outlook for oil companies was remarkably consistent across the groups as represented by the P/Es for Exxon (13), Gulf Oil (11), Mobil Oil (12), and Texaco (12). By early 1979, the overall level of the market had fallen (as reflected by generally lower P/Es). Yet, in spite of the broad decline in stock multiples, the *relationships* between P/Es—such as those of the oil companies Exxon (9), Gulf Oil (7), Mobil Oil (7), and Texaco (9)—remained relatively stable. When relative shifts in P/Es do occur, it is because investors anticipate differing growth rates and/or degrees of uncertainty in forecasted dividends and earnings of individual stocks.

THE RELATIONSHIP OF STOCK PRICE TO EARNINGS FACTORS

One of the first widely read studies of earnings growth rates and P/E ratios was published in 1963 by Volkert Whitbeck and Manown Kisor at the Bank of New York. After examining historical growth rates, Whitbeck and Kisor concluded that, "as investors, we buy common stocks not simply for records prior to purchase, but, more fundamentally, for what we anticipate from them after our commitment." [285, p. 337]

The conclusion reached by Whitbeck and Kisor was that differences in expected growth rates explain about 60 percent of the differences in normal P/E ratios. Similarly, John Cragg, of the University of British Columbia, reported that anticipated growth in earnings explained, on the average, 67 percent of the differences in P/E ratios (see [55, p. 79]).

Richard Crowell [56], in his doctoral dissertation at M.I.T., studied the relationship between expected earnings and P/E ratios in different industries. Of the 12 industries analyzed, Crowell demonstrated that at one extreme, 69 percent of the differences in P/E ratios for bank stocks could be explained by differences in anticipated growth rates; at the other extreme, only 5 percent of the differences in the P/E ratios accorded steel stocks could be traced to expected growth differences.

Further research relating earnings to stock prices was reported by Philip Brown and Ray Ball.[38] Stock price changes of selected companies were adjusted to eliminate the movements attributable to swings in the general market. These "nonmarket" stock price changes were then analyzed for 12 months before, and 6 months after, the date of each company's earnings announcement. They found that where actual earnings exceeded the forecast amounts, the price of the stock had typically risen during the preceding 12-month period, with the rise faltering in the 6-month period after the actual earnings announcement. This tendency is depicted in Figure 7–2, where 0 on the horizontal scale denotes the official earnings announcement date.

FIGURE 7–2: Average price movement during months preceding and succeeding the earnings announcement of stocks of companies producing unexpectedly good earnings

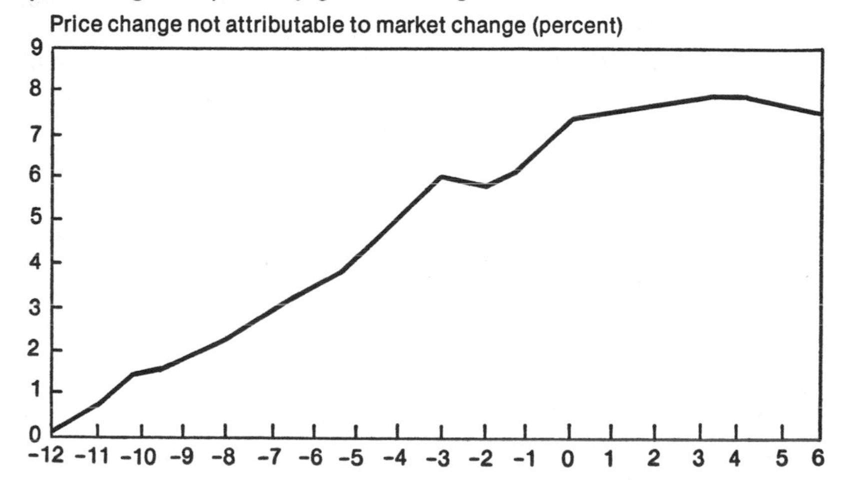

Source: After Brown and Ball [38].

Brown and Ball also reported that price movements during the months both preceding and following unexpectedly poor earnings announcements showed declines. Figure 7–3 traces the average price movement when actual earnings were below the forecast level.

The information portrayed in Figures 7–2 and 7–3, which show what typically happens to a stock's price in the months that precede and follow an unexpected earnings performance,

FIGURE 7–3: Average price movement during months preceding and succeeding the earnings announcement of stocks of companies producing unexpectedly bad earnings

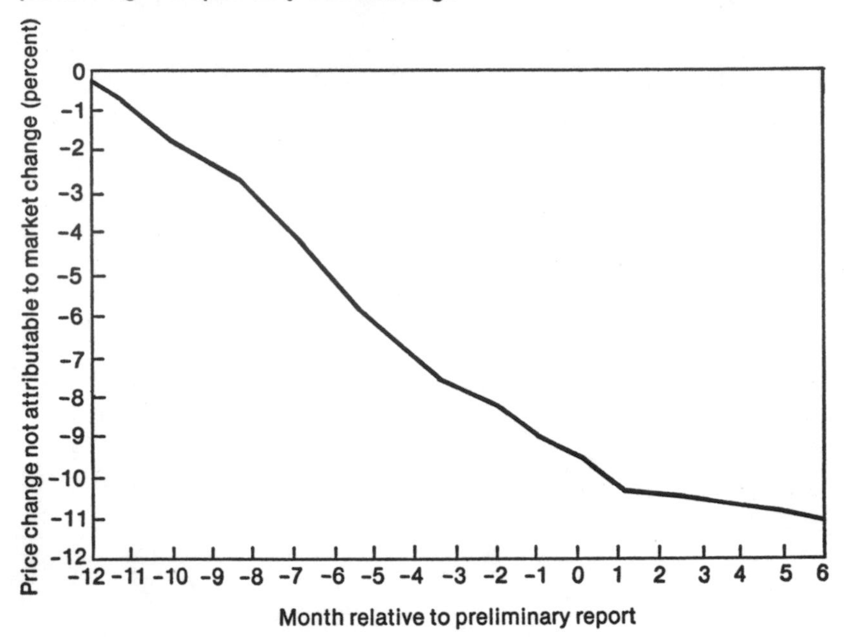

Source: After Brown and Ball [38].

is very revealing. *Note that by the time earnings were announced, the market had almost fully anticipated the contents of the report.*

This research indicates that on the average, stock prices react well in advance, and over time, to the reported annual earnings of companies. Further, the process by which the market anticipates this future earnings stream is both continuous and accurate. The market action, derived from the aggregate decisions of millions of investors, is remarkably efficient at anticipating published earnings announcements.

Chapter 8

Earnings forecasts

There is a strong, albeit not perfect, relationship between stock prices and earnings. The research of Whitbeck and Kisor, Cragg, and Crowell has shown that differences in P/E ratios are only partially explained by differences in anticipated earnings growth. Brown and Ball have shown that on the average, the price change in response to an earnings change is gradual and extends over many months while the actual earnings are being realized. These studies can be capsulized by saying that *there is a partial relationship between stock prices and earnings.*

The question remains: If an investor had the ability to forecast earnings with complete accuracy, could such information be used to predict stock price changes? Henry Latané and Donald Tuttle, at the University of North Carolina, answered this question by comparing changes in earnings with changes in the corresponding stock's price for 48 companies over a 14-year period. They found large year-to-year differences in the proportion of price changes that could be explained by changes in earnings, ranging from 64.5 percent to 0.8 percent. *The correlations were all positive,* however. That is, stock price gains were generally associated with increases in company earnings. Likewise, price declines were, on the whole, accompanied by decreases in company earnings.

In some years, this tendency was almost eliminated by market factors, while in others the influence of earnings on prices was quite strong. Over the entire 14-year period studied, Latané and Tuttle reported that only 17.4 percent of all price variations could be explained by earnings changes. This is a surprisingly small proportion. Nonetheless, Latané and Tuttle concluded that "perfect knowledge of future earnings would be of great value in selecting stocks." [156, p. 347]

Richard Brealey has expanded the work of Latané and Tuttle to determine just how much benefit could be realized if

one had perfect knowledge of future earnings. Commenting on their research, Brealey states that "the average annual price appreciation of the 48 stocks was 12.2 percent. If, however, at the beginning of each year, an investor had been able to select from this group, stocks of those 8 companies (out of the 48 studied) that were to show the greatest proportion of earnings increase, his average annual profit would have been 30.4 percent." [34, p. 85]

Thus, two conclusions are well supported in the research literature. First, P/E ratios reflect, to some degree, the anticipated growth in company earnings. Second, if one could accurately estimate future earnings, an investment strategy that would provide above-average returns could most certainly be devised. The term *one*, however, is more than literary impartiality. Indeed, if many individuals could predict future earnings accurately, one's profitable strategy would succumb to an efficient capital market.

If accurate earnings forecasts can provide investors with above-average performance, the important question becomes, "Can changes in earnings be predicted?"

CAN CHANGES IN EARNINGS BE PREDICTED?

There is good reason to expect companies with consistently strong earnings records to continue to be capable of producing good earnings in the future. Similarly, companies with low profitability in the past *intuitively* seem likely to have similar difficulties in the future. Some of the super-growth stocks of the past, such as Avon Products, IBM, Polaroid, and Xerox, enjoyed a certain monopolistic advantage in rapidly expanding markets, enabling them to post consistently good results. It therefore seems reasonable that companies with satisfied customers and large, successful investments in product development, personnel, and plant and equipment should have a competitive advantage that is likely to persist.

It is important to remember, however, that if a company continues to outgrow the economy, it will eventually become the economy! The old adage that "trees do not grow to the sky" is apt. It is reasonable to expect that as companies become progressively larger, their growth rates will approach that of the overall economy. Therefore, the "model" for a growth stock should assume that growth will be above average for a number of years and thereafter will approximately parallel that of the economy.

Nonetheless, is there any evidence that over the short run, say year to year, earnings records persist? Richard Brealey [34] sought to answer this question by studying the earnings changes of approximately 700 industrial companies over a 14-year period. Contrary to what intuition would suggest, Brealey found that year-to-year earnings changes do *not* tend to be in the same direction! Based on separate classifications for 62 different industries, Brealey could not find any evidence that period-to-period earnings changes occur with discernible patterns or trends.

Similar findings have been reported by Joseph Murphy, Jr., who studied the earnings of 344 companies in 12 industries over 38 different time periods. Murphy, who conducted his research at the University of Minnesota, reported that "there appears to be little significant correlation between relative rates of growth of earnings per share in one period and relative growth in earnings per share in the next period." [199, p. 73]

Thus, a company which has achieved a consistent pattern of earnings growth does not have a better than average chance to sustain such growth into the future. In the context of investment theory, this means that *period-to-period earnings changes behave in accordance with a random-walk model.*

Intelligent discussion of the random-walk model, when applied to either price or earnings changes, must include the time span over which one attempts to make predictions. Random-walk research on price movements has shown, for example, that recent price and volume changes do not provide predictive information. Conversely, however, we have seen that long-term price movements are not random.

To determine whether or not changes in earnings can be described by the random-walk model, two questions must be answered. First, are long-term earnings changes, such as long-term price changes, predictable from past results? Second, can earnings be forecast from information other than historical performance?

LONG-TERM TRENDS IN EARNINGS?

John Lintner and Robert Glauber [171] of Harvard have studied the earnings of 323 companies over varying periods of time (up to five years) in an attempt to discern predictive patterns. Somewhat surprisingly, while there is evidence of long-term patterns in price movements, Lintner and Glauber were unable

to detect consistent patterns in long-run earnings which could be used to produce above-average investment results.

Manown Kisor and Van Messner [151] studied earnings changes over six-month intervals. They first showed that if they could calculate the direction of earnings changes six months into the future, irrespective of the magnitude of the change, they could outperform the market. But based on a sample of 813 industrial companies, they found only one pattern that could be used to predict the direction of subsequent earnings changes. The pattern, which they called "increased momentum in relative earnings," is characterized by acceleration in the rate of change in a company's earnings relative to the earnings performance of the general market.

Thus, Kisor and Messner showed that when the momentum of a company's relative earnings accelerates, the likelihood of some increase in earnings for that company over the subsequent six months is significantly better than it is for the universe of companies whose shares make up the market as a whole. Consequently, there is evidence that a company whose earnings gains substantially outpace those of the market in one six-month period will continue to show positive earnings growth in the succeeding six months.

The Kisor-Messner findings tend to parallel Levy's [160] and this author's [116] evidence that stocks which advance in price substantially faster than the market in any six-month period tend to show slightly above-average price appreciation in the following six-month period. However, with the exception of a six-month pattern characterized by accelerated earnings growth, *there is overwhelming evidence that future earnings changes cannot be forecast from past movements.*

The research summarized here concludes that apart from the possible exception which has been noted, neither the direction nor magnitude of earnings changes can be predicted from historical patterns. But does anyone really *try* to predict earnings from historical patterns? The answer is a resounding yes!

There is considerable evidence that individual investors, as well as Wall Street professionals, rely heavily on historical results to predict future earnings. John Cragg and Burton Malkiel [55] have studied earnings estimates made by professionals who specialize in bank trust management, investment banking, mutual fund management, general brokerage, and the investment advisory business. The remarkable conclusion of the Cragg-Malkiel study was that when these experts were asked to forecast earnings, the overwhelming tendency of the

group was to base their predictions on recent changes in historical earnings.

Even more startling was the fact that the predictions of the top analysts were ". . . no better than the simplest strategy of the naïve investor—who simply believes the company growth will parallel changes in gross national product." [256, p. 43] Thus, many people base earnings projections on apparently useless historical earnings data—in the face of evidence which shows that (with one minor exception) *the study of changing patterns of earnings is worthless!*

This research, it should be emphasized, does not mean that earnings cannot be predicted from information other than past earnings. Thus, a vital question is, "Can earnings be forecast from such things as balance sheet items, sales estimates, computerized cash-flow simulations, and so forth?" To answer this question, we must first define what is meant by "earnings."

EARNINGS

The concept of corporate earnings would seem to be simple enough. Since the securities legislation of 1933, certified public accounting (CPA) firms have been required to attest to the authenticity of earnings reported by publicly owned companies. These accounting statements have traditionally been prepared within the broad guidelines of so-called generally accepted accounting principles (popularly referred to as GAAP, pronounced gap).

But because of the accounting profession's belief that its rules should not impinge on management's flexibility, some latitude is allowed within the realm of "accepted" principles. As a result, companies which appear to be similar based on size, common products, and so forth, can, from an operating point of view, elect to manage their assets quite differently.

The accounting for these differences can cause substantial variations in reported earnings among different companies. More important, however, is the fact that under the "generally accepted" guidelines, even identical operating decisions can be accounted for differently. One airline, for example, might depreciate its airplanes over 12 years, while another might employ an 18-year schedule.

This flexibility has given rise to the allegation that companies will take advantage of this flexibility to "smooth" reported period-to-period earnings comparisons. Evidence from Barry Cushing's [57] doctoral dissertation at Michigan State

University supports this belief. But there is also substantial evidence that for all the confusion such accounting variations generate among the public and for all the grief they cause corporate officers and their CPAs, *the market is remarkably efficient at properly reflecting the true worth of a company.*

Robert Kaplan and Richard Roll [142], who studied the impact on securities prices of elective changes in investment credit or depreciation accounting, had difficulty discerning any statistical significant price effects. Their research is evidence of the market's efficiency at incorporating all publicly available information into the price of a stock.

EARNINGS AND THE ECONOMY

The sensitivity of corporate earnings to the economic climate of particular industries has been studied by both Richard Brealey [35] and Brown and Ball [38]. Brealey found that in some industries less than half of a particular firm's earnings changes were attributable to differences between it and competitor companies. Industries which exhibited a strong tendency to parallel the economy included the auto, department store, nonferrous metal, paper, rubber, and clothing segments. Overall, Brealey found that the impact of the general economy on the earnings of a firm is not only significant but also fairly consistent. He concluded that an understanding of the implications of major economic events should be of considerable value to those attempting to forecast earnings changes.

THE DEFICIENCY OF FUNDAMENTAL ANALYSIS

The most popular approach to valuation entails (*a*) estimating a stock's future earnings per share, (*b*) estimating the future price-earnings ratio, and (*c*) multiplying the two numbers to obtain the expected future value of the stock. While the technique is appealing in its simplicity, its application has several shortcomings. First, large percentages of corporate earnings reflect the state of the economy and the health of a company's industry. Conversely, the expertise of the individual company accounts for a *minor* portion of its earnings and the price performance of its stock. Thus, while it is conceivable that information on economy-, industry-, and company-related factors could be combined to develop reliable earnings estimates, the methodology is not well suited for the comparative valuation of a universe of securities.

Second, even if this type of analysis is used to develop a probabilistic range of earnings estimates, the methodology does not lend itself to explicit estimates of risk—the crux of MPT. Third, an investor who could forecast future P/E ratios would realize superior rates of return on that basis alone. Thus, linking unreliable estimates of the second variable in the forecasting equation—the future P/E ratio—to even reliable earnings estimates is comparable to using a rubber band to measure distance.

In spite of the case against the traditional forms of fundamental analysis, it will always have its disciples. These people generally recognize the late Benjamin Graham—who (with David Dodd and Sidney Cottle) wrote the classic book *Security Analysis* [109]—as the father of fundamental security analysis. This author (Hagin) had the pleasure of knowing Benjamin Graham, first as a graduate student and later on as a friend. For those who blindly use these techniques, the following quotation stands as a solemn memorial to the professional stature and intellectual integrity of a truly great man.

> . . . I am no longer an advocate of elaborate techniques of security analysis in order to find superior value opportunities. This was a rewarding activity, say, 40 years ago, when *Graham and Dodd* was first published; but the situation has changed . . . [today] I doubt whether such extensive efforts will generate sufficiently superior selections to justify their cost. . . . I'm on the side of the "efficient market" school of thought. . . .
>
> Benjamin Graham, 1976 [292, p. 20].

Chapter 9

Dividends

The rate of return on an investment depends on two factors: capital appreciation and dividend income. To many investors, however, dividend income is something for widows or orphans. But as Richard Brealey has emphasized, "if in 1926 a tax-exempt investor had purchased an equal amount of all New York Stock Exchange equities, and if he had reinvested all subsequent dividends he would have found that by the end of 40 years his capital had multiplied 35 times" (after Fisher and Lorie [91]). Without dividends, "the value of his portfolio would have increased by a factor of only six." [34, p. 4] This would hardly seem to be an advantage sought only by widows and orphans.

While an investor can elect to buy either a high- or a low-dividend payout stock, dividend decisions are made by company management. Basically, a company can do two things with its aftertax earnings. They can be distributed to stockholders as dividends, or they can be retained and reinvested, or plowed back, into the company. It is important to remember, however, that dividends received by a shareholder are included in the shareholder's taxable income. Retained earnings, by contrast, represent an automatic plow back of earnings which, if distributed to stockholders, would be taxed *before* being reinvested. Further, after earnings are distributed to stockholders, and then taxed, they generally cannot be reinvested without an underwriting or brokerage commission.

DIVIDEND-REINVESTMENT PROGRAMS

One way to reinvest dividends without incurring brokerage commissions is to utilize one of the automatic *dividend-reinvestment programs* now offered by over 600 major corporations. AT&T, the largest publicly held U.S. company, insti-

tuted a dividend-reinvestment program in 1973. While it should be emphasized that AT&T is an extremely public-minded company, individual investors' overwhelming response to the program is, in the words of Warren Buffett, "out of *Alice in Wonderland.*" [40, p. 266]

In 1978, AT&T paid out more than $3.0 billion in cash dividends to the nearly 3 million owners of its common stock. By the end of the year, almost one out of every four stockholders had reinvested a total of $786 million in additional shares supplied directly by the company. This means that AT&T got back 26.7 percent of the money it paid out in dividends by means of what analysts call *disguised payouts*.

Generally speaking, an investor seeking dividend reinvestment has three alternatives. An investor might purchase very low- or zero-dividend payout stocks; reinvestment is truly automatic, and the investor avoids the twin burdens of dividend taxation and reinvestment transaction charges. Alternatively, an investor can participate in an automatic dividend-reinvestment program. With this plan, the investor avoids reinvestment transaction charges and can frequently purchase new stock at a 5 percent discount, although income taxes must be paid on the amount of the dividend. Under the third alternative, an investor can reinvest dividends merely by purchasing additional shares in the open market. In this situation, reinvestment expenses and taxes must be paid.

The real "price" of the automatic dividend-reinvestment alternative for tax-paying investors can be best appreciated by comparing two admittedly extreme situations. In the first case, suppose that in 1978 AT&T, instead of declaring a dividend, merely reinvested the $3.0 billion. In the second situation, suppose that AT&T declared a $3.0 billion dividend and every shareholder signed up for the dividend reinvestment plan.

Under the second program, AT&T would notify each stockholder, as well as the IRS, that the "dividend" had been paid, and the company would supply each investor with the equivalent dollar value of shares of AT&T stock. Shareholders would be required to pay income taxes on the portion of the retained earnings which management had declared as "dividends." If shareholders tax rates averaged 30 percent and the "dividends" totaled $3.0 billion, the IRS would collect $900 million from reinvesting shareholders.

In each situation the company ends up in the same cash position and each investor retains the same proportionate interest in the company. In the latter case, however, the inves-

tors end up paying $900 million to the IRS. In this situation, again quoting Warren Buffett, "imagine the joy of shareholders in such circumstances, if the directors were then to double the dividend." [40, p. 267] Such action would double the shareholder's tax bill while all other consequences would remain the same.

DIVIDEND INFORMATION

Research on dividend information has focused on two important decision-making areas:

1. Should you buy a high- or a low-dividend stock?
2. Can news of dividend changes be used to select stocks with above-average returns?

High- versus low-payout stocks. The percentage of a company's total earnings that is distributed as dividends is called the "dividend payout ratio." Typically, a rapidly growing company will retain all or most of its earnings to finance expansion. Similarly, companies with sufficient plant and equipment to meet the demand of their customers have modest expansion needs and can distribute a large fraction of their profits as dividends.

The importance of the dividend payout ratio lies in the fact that the timing and rates of taxes on dividends differ from those on capital gains. Dividends are taxed currently as part of income, while long-term capital gains (assets held more than one year) are subject to taxation only upon sale of the appreciated asset and at rates which are generally half those on income. As a result, for the average investor, *after taxes, a dollar of dividends is worth significantly less than a dollar of capital gains.*

We could therefore reasonably assume that low-dividend payout stocks are relatively more attractive for any investor subject to taxes. It follows, then, that in an efficient market made up only of tax-paying investors, the price of a low-dividend stock would include a premium for this advantage. This conclusion, that *low-dividend stocks are worth more* to tax-paying investors, is counter to one of the age-old tenets of fundamental security analysis. Authors such as Graham, Dodd, and Cottle [109] have long held that the market's pricing mechanisms overwhelmingly favor liberal dividends.

Clearly, however, if the prices of low-dividend stocks were

bid up by tax-paying investors, tax-exempt investors would capitalize on this "temporary" inefficiency and, through their actions, restore the market to an "efficient," fairly priced, state. Not surprisingly, therefore, the actual evidence indicates that there are no substantial differences between the values placed by the market on dividends and those accorded capital gains (see Brealey [35, pp. 4–21]).

While certain kinds of valuation models (discussed in Chapter 28) add the yield "dimension" to a stock's other characteristics, on the average, the market seems to have struck a balance between the traditional belief that liberal dividends are overpriced and the logic that because of differential taxation, cash payouts should receive a lower valuation.

This means that on the average, the investor pays roughly the same price for a dollar of future dividends that is paid for a dollar of future capital gains. But since dividends are taxed at a higher rate, they are worth proportionately less. Hence, for tax-paying investors, there appears to be a slight unadjusted *penalty for owning high-dividend stocks.*

Dividend announcements. Several researchers have examined the rationale which underlies how a firm decides on the percentage of earnings to distribute as dividends versus the amount to be retained by the company. For a variety of reasons, this research shows that the most significant factor in the decision is the amount of earnings which management feels "should" be distributed. To the astonishment of many people, it appears that notions of an "appropriate," or "target," dividend tend to dominate this decision process.

In turn, it appears that the target dividend level is guided by management's desire to establish a pattern of stable dividend growth. This reluctance to change the level applies to both dividend increases and decreases. Dividend reductions are typically viewed as a last resort, while the hesitancy to increase a dividend is attributed to the fear that a higher dividend implies a commitment to continue at that level. Paul Darling [58] has supported this conclusion by showing that the levels of dividends paid between 1930 and 1955 could not be explained by variations in earnings, but instead corresponded to management's optimism about the future.

Here, then, is an important point to consider in examining the usefulness of dividend announcements. Studies that have relied on interviews with corporate management [165], and others which have studied dividend histories [75], conclude

that firms do not make dividend changes without thorough assessment of the future. Decreases take place largely because firms have little choice other than to cut the payout. Increases, in addition to reflecting high current earnings, reflect management's optimism that the new dividend level can be sustained. It follows, then, that if dividend changes reflect management's opinion about the future, and if managers can correctly assess the future, dividend changes should serve as barometers of a firm's future prosperity.

This possibility raises two questions. The first, and most obvious, is whether or not dividend changes portend future changes in earnings. If they do, the next question is whether or not the stock's price reflects the fact that prosperity or difficulty lies ahead, by the time the news of the dividend change is available.

To answer the first question, whether or not dividend changes portend future changes in earnings, Joseph Murphy [200] studied the relationship between dividend changes and the subsequent earnings of 244 companies between 1950 and 1965. While the association between dividend changes and subsequent earnings was not as strong as one would like, Murphy was able to conclude that dividend changes tend to reflect the usually accurate assessment by management of future earnings.

Another study of the relationship between dividend announcements and subsequent changes in both earnings and stock prices was made by Richardson Pettit [212] at the Wharton School of Finance and Commerce. Pettit studied the impact of dividend announcements on the subsequent earnings and price performance of 625 companies over four and one-half years. He found that dividend announcements were closely associated with subsequent price performance and that the effect was generally proportionate to the magnitude of the dividend change.

In terms of the market's efficiency, Pettit concluded that the "market's judgment concerning the information implicit in the [dividend] announcement is reflected almost completely as of the end of the announcement month." [212, p. 38] It can be concluded, therefore, that *news of a dividend change contains useful information that is not immediately reflected in the price of the stock*—evidence that the semistrong form of the efficient market hypothesis is not a valid description of the market in this regard.

SUMMARY

Two conclusions can be made regarding dividends. First, contrary to the thinking of many seasoned market professionals, as well as noted authors such as Benjamin Graham, there is evidence that high-dividend payout stocks provide the tax-paying investor with a somewhat lower rate of return than low-payout stocks of comparable risk. Second, presumably because corporations do not alter their dividends casually, dividend changes do mirror management's largely correct assessment of a firm's future earnings trends.

Chapter 10

Company information

The semistrong form of the efficient market hypothesis holds that all publicly available information—not just historical price and volume data—is already reflected in the prices of various investment vehicles. A definitive test of this hypothesis would require the study of all kinds of information, bearing on all types of investment instruments, in every capital market. Fortunately, however, the most popular investment vehicles are those stocks listed on the New York Stock Exchange (NYSE) and the American Stock Exchange (AMEX).

Further, of the four main kinds of information—that is, on the overall economy, a basic industry, an industry subgroup, and a company—many analysts concentrate on company-related data. These people claim that the specificity of company-related information makes this the most predictable level in the information hierarchy. But those who support the efficient market hypothesis argue that the constant scrutiny of company-related information by millions of investors destroys its value to any individual.

This chapter summarizes the research on three kinds of company-related information—stock splits, new listings, and professional opinions.

STOCK SPLITS

The average investor has more misconceptions about stock splits than any other event. A stock split is a decision by the management of a firm to increase (often double) the number of shares of stock outstanding. Many people fail to understand that even though the company has decided to issue more shares, everything else about the company remains unchanged. For instance, following a two-for-one stock split, the

price of each new share should be exactly one half the price of an old share and earnings per share, exactly one half their original level.

After a split, each shareholder has exactly enough additional shares to compensate for the lower price. The total worth of each person's holdings, and of the firm's securities, is unchanged. An investor's pieces of paper represent precisely the same proportion of ownership as before the split. In the classic words of A. Wilfred May, one of Wall Street's elder statesmen, "a pie does not grow through its slicing!" [187, p. 5]

Some people contend that the lower price per share brought about by a stock split will "broaden the market" for the company's shares and that the lower price will, in turn, stimulate investment demand. There is no merit to this contention, however, unless one is referring to those investors who could not afford to buy a *single* share at the former price. But, the argument runs, a split lowers the price of 100 share purchase, and investors prefer to buy stock in round lots because they carry lower commission rates. The problem with this reasoning is that while commissions on some trades are lower after a split, the increased volumes of trading at the lower share prices that result from stock splits typically generate higher commissions for the same dollar amount of business.

A final reason some people might give for interpreting splits favorably hinges on the so-called self-fulfilling prophecy. In the stock market, if enough people believe something will happen, their actions will make it happen—despite the fact that the logic underlying their belief is defective. Thus, even though there is no theoretical reason to expect the value of one's holdings to increase because of a stock split, if splits are seen as expressions of progress or management optimism, they might become self-fulfilling predictions.

The first widely read articles on splits were published by C. Austin Barker in the *Harvard Business Review* in 1956. In his first article, Barker concluded that "contrary to the general belief, stock splits do not automatically produce a lasting price gain." [14, p. 101] In his second article he concluded that ". . . split-ups produced no lasting real gains . . . whether . . . in a normal market or in an outstanding bull market." [15, p. 551]

More recent studies of splits have shown that companies announcing stock splits have generally experienced a price improvement in the months before the announcement of the split, but that after the announcement no significant improvement remained.

The most extensive study of stock splits was conducted by Eugene Fama et al. [79], who monitored the behavior of 940 stocks for the 30 months before and after stock splits. The relative performance (that is, with market comovements removed) of a portfolio consisting of these stocks is shown in Figure 10–1. It is important to note that information on the

FIGURE 10–1: Relative pre- and post-split performance of 940 stocks

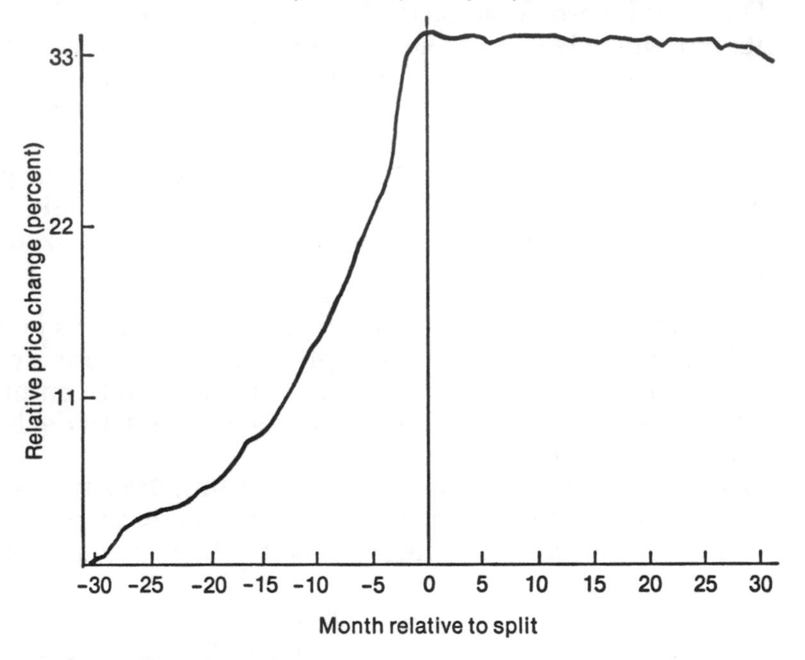

Source: Fama, Fisher, Jensen, and Roll [79].

splits was not available until immediately before the splits occurred (designated by 0 on the horizontal scale of Figure 10–1)—the point at which the relative price growth *stops*. Those who believe that news of impending splits is useful should note that on the average, for two and one-half years after each split, *the relative price remained within 1 percentage point of the split price.*

This research, plus other evidence reported by Hausman, West, and Largay [121], indicates that splits are a *consequence*, and not a *cause*, of rising stock prices. Thus, it can be concluded that there is no evidence to support buying stocks on news of impending splits. Such information is apparently useless!

NEW LISTINGS

To be eligible for listing on the NYSE, a company must have a minimum of $2.5 million in annual pretax earnings, $16 million in net tangible assets, and $14.5 million in publicly held common stock representing at least 1 million shares spread among 2,000 round-lot shareholders. Needless to say, not all companies can meet these criteria.

One could reason that the decision to list on the NYSE represents the pinnacle of management optimism. In line with this train of thought, news that a company has applied for NYSE listing might indicate that its shares offer an opportunity for above-average future rates of return.

Numerous researchers [79, 177, 276] have examined the pre- and post-listing behavior of stocks traded on the NYSE. The consistent pattern which emerged may be summarized as follows:

1. *Pre-listing.* Over a period from three to six months before the application date to the application date, these stocks performed significantly better than the market. Such price advances are doubtless a factor in the subsequent decision to list a security.
2. *During listing.* During the time spanning the application date, the approval date, and the listing date, these stocks continue to show significantly better than average price appreciation.
3. *Post-listing.* Whether the period measured is one day, one month, or one, three, or five years from the listing date, the rate of return for these stocks is, on average, *below that for the general market.*

Based on these studies, *stocks which have recently moved their trading to the NYSE do not, on the average, represent a likely source of above-average returns.*

PROFESSIONAL INVESTMENT RECOMMENDATIONS

Consistently superior investment analysis must meet three rather severe tests:

1. The analysis must be correct.
2. The "market" must realize that the analysis was correct in "time."
3. The analysis must not be widely used.

One of this author's acquaintances once confided that he had developed a sophisticated technique for selecting undervalued securities. His problem was that the market did not have the benefit of his careful analysis and his favored securities remained "undervalued."

At the other extreme, it is possible that regardless of the underlying "correctness" of an investment recommendation, the publicized opinion of a respected professional could precipitate dramatic price changes. Such stock market opinions could, in fact, become self-fulfilling predictions. If this is so, it might be a useful investment strategy to respond quickly to the recommendations of widely circulated advisory services.

Researchers have long been intrigued by the possibility that advisory services either make forecasts which turn out to be correct or, alternatively, issue forecasts which cause market shifts which, in turn, render the forecasts correct. As long ago as 1933, Alfred Cowles studied the forecasting ability of 16 financial services, 20 insurance companies, and 25 financial publications. Cowles concluded that the 16 financial services underperformed the market by 1.43 percent per annum, the 20 insurance companies underperformed by 1.20 percent, while the 25 financial publications underperformed by 4 percent per annum. [52]

Several modern studies have measured the market's response to published investment advice. In 1958, Robert Ferber, at the University of Illinois, studied the price movements related to recommendations of four major advisory services. After removing market and industry comovements, Ferber found that "in the very short run, stock market service recommendations tend to influence the prices of approximately two-thirds of the stocks in the direction indicated. . . ." [85, p. 94] By the end of the first week after publication, the average profit attainable from this information was 1.1 percent. However, after this very short-run adjustment, Ferber found no evidence of a longer run impact. Ferber also concluded that the short-run price adjustments were *caused* by the recommendation, and not *predicted* by them. He based this conclusion on ". . . the failure of the recommended stocks . . . to outpace the market . . . in the week or two immediately preceding the recommendation." [85, p. 94]

Other studies by Ruff [235] and Stoffels [264] confirm the general conclusion that professional recommendations accurately foretell future price changes and that there is a measurable short-term price adjustment to reflect the "news." Further

evidence by Colker [47] indicates that stocks recommended by advisory services and brokerage houses tend to outperform representative market averages over the following year. It can be concluded, therefore, that *widely distributed professional opinions can to some degree presage short-term and (to a lesser extent) long-term relative price changes.*

SUMMARY

Several conclusions are possible from the examination of information on splits, new listings and professional investment recommendations. First, to the chagrin of many advocates, stock splits typically signal the *end* of price growth and *not* its continuation! Second, new listings do not offer the potential for better-than-average rates of return. Third, professional opinions can *cause* price movements. Since such publicly available information apparently is not efficiently assimilated into stock prices, *the semistrong form of the efficient market hypothesis is not valid* in this regard.

Chapter 11

Market information

This chapter examines the usefulness of information about new issues, secondary distributions, block trades, odd-lot transactions, short-interest positions, and odd-lot short sales.

NEW ISSUES

The new issue market channels investment capital into companies. The creation of a new issue requires three steps: origination, underwriting, and distribution. Origination includes the negotiations between investment banking firms and the issuing corporation to determine price and assure compliance with legalities. Underwriting refers to the purchase or guaranteed sale of the issue by participating investment banking firms. Finally, distribution involves the sale of the shares to the public and the public's financial intermediaries.

In these transactions, the underwriter has a "two-hat" role of trying to obtain the "highest" offering price for the issuing company while, at the same time, ensuring that the offering price will be "low" enough to enable the issue to be fully subscribed. If the shares offered are priced above what the market is willing to pay, the underwriter guaranteeing the sale at the offering price can sustain large losses. Thus, one could reason that to play it safe, underwriters will tend to underprice new issues.

Such underpricing was alleged in a 1963 Securities and Exchange Commission (SEC) study and later refuted by Professor George Stigler at the University of Chicago. In a pointed article criticizing the SEC, Stigler [263] showed that between 1923 and 1955 the relative long-term performance of new issues was consistently below that of the market.

In a contradictory study on the post-offering behavior of seasoned new issues between 1953 and 1963, Irwin Friend et

al. reported ". . . no evidence of any penalty or premium associated with new issues. . . ." [104, p. 492] Still another contradictory study by Frank Reilly and Kenneth Hatfield, at the University of Kansas, traced the relative appreciation of 53 new issues between 1963 and 1965 for a week, a month, or a year after their respective offerings. All tests showed superior results for investors in new issues. [219, p. 80]

Results paralleling those of Reilly and Hatfield were reported by Dennis Logue in his doctoral dissertation at Cornell in 1971. Logue studied 250 new issues marketed between 1965 and 1969 and reported that "on the average, the risk-adjusted rates of return of new issues bought at the offerings were significantly greater than they sould be in an efficient market no matter if the holding period is two weeks, three months, or one year." [172]

Still different results were reported in a recent study by John McDonald and A. K. Fisher [176] at Stanford University. They examined the post-offering performance of 142 unseasoned new issues during 1969 and 1970. Their findings showed extremely large positive returns if measured one week after the offerings. However, the end of the first week to the end of the first year, 51 weeks later, they found that average returns were negative. McDonald and Fisher also showed that the size of the price change in the first week was unrelated to future performance.

Hence, studies on the performance of new issues over different time periods appear contradictory. To resolve these differences, it might be useful to examine only measures of "risk-adjusted" performance. Specifically, it would be valuable to know: (*a*) the comparative level of risk that is inherent in the new issue market and (*b*) the prevailing "price of risk" (i.e., the "character" of the market) in each of the time periods studied. These topics are discussed in subsequent chapters.

SECONDARY DISTRIBUTIONS

Any offering of stock after its new issue offering is termed a "secondary." When a secondary distribution is so large in size that it might swamp the exchange's auction process, the offering is generally organized off the floor of the exchange. The sellers are typically institutional investors or the trusts of families of the company's founders. The reasons for such sales are as varied as the reasons for any sale. But the fact that these sellers consist of knowledgeable investors, who are sometimes presumed to have superior information—in combination with

the fact that *they* are disposing of their shares—is viewed by many as a "sell signal."

A detailed study of secondary distributions has been made by Myron Scholes [236] at the University of Chicago. By tracing the average relative performance (that is, with market comovements removed) for 345 stocks from 26 days before the offerings to 14 days after, Scholes found that secondary distributions were followed by an abrupt drop in market price of approximately 2 percent.

To study the long-term consequences of secondary offerings, Scholes traced the monthly performance of 1,207 stocks for 18 months preceding and following the sales. Here Scholes found that the market, on the average, interprets a secondary distribution as a signal that "something" is wrong with the stock. Further, when Scholes classified the relative pre- and post-secondary distribution performance by the kind of seller, he found some interesting differences. These are shown in Figure 11–1.

These data indicate that individuals typically sell after a substantial price rise (relative to the market). Further, the market does not react to the "news" embodied in individuals' sales. While firms and officers also frequently sell their own stock after a substantial rise, the market clearly interprets this "information" as a signal to sell and adjusts relative share

FIGURE 11–1: Comparative performance of secondaries by type of seller

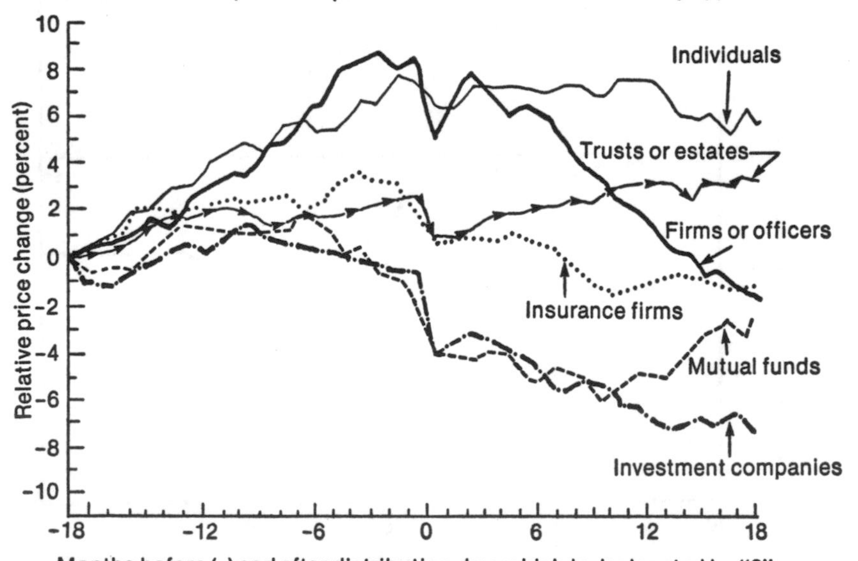

Source: Scholes [236].

prices downward. Whether or not from the herd (or if you prefer, "heard") effect, when mutual funds and investment companies sell, this information has lead to a further mark-down in share prices.

Thus, whether superior analysis or self-fulfilling prophecies were responsible, Scholes found that stocks sold by mutual funds and investment companies were destined to exhibit relatively poor performance. The price drops that are observed after large secondary distributions may be the result either of the sellers' wisdom or of the market's assumption of their wisdom, but the result remains the same—large secondary distributions, on the average, precede price declines.

BLOCK TRADES

Alan Kraus and Hans Stoll [155] have studied the price behavior of stocks before and after block trades. (A block trade is

FIGURE 11–2: Relative price performance for 1,121 blocks on minus ticks

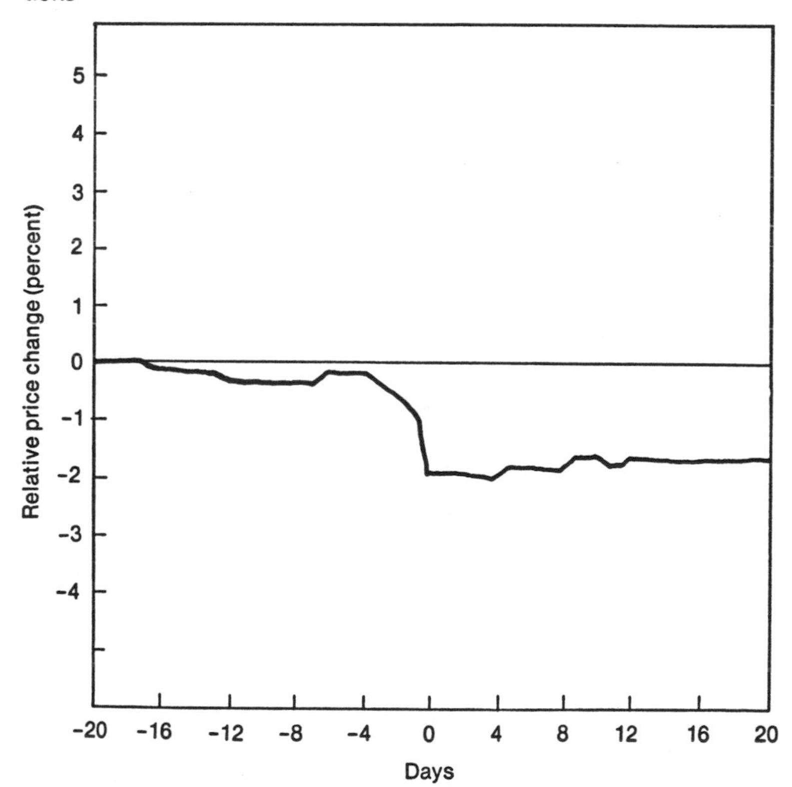

Source: Kraus and Stoll [155].

a transaction of 10,000 shares or more.) They reasoned that block trades occurring on minus ticks might portend further selling pressure. (A minus tick means that the transaction was at a lower price than the immediately preceding transaction.) Similarly, they proposed that a block trade occurring on plus ticks might presage further demand.

To test these possibilities, Kraus and Stoll studied 2,199 block trades on the NYSE from July 1968 to September 1969. The results of the study for 20 days before and after each block trade (adjusted for the movement of the market) are shown in Figures 11–2 and 11–3.

FIGURE 11–3: Relative price performance for 345 blocks on plus ticks

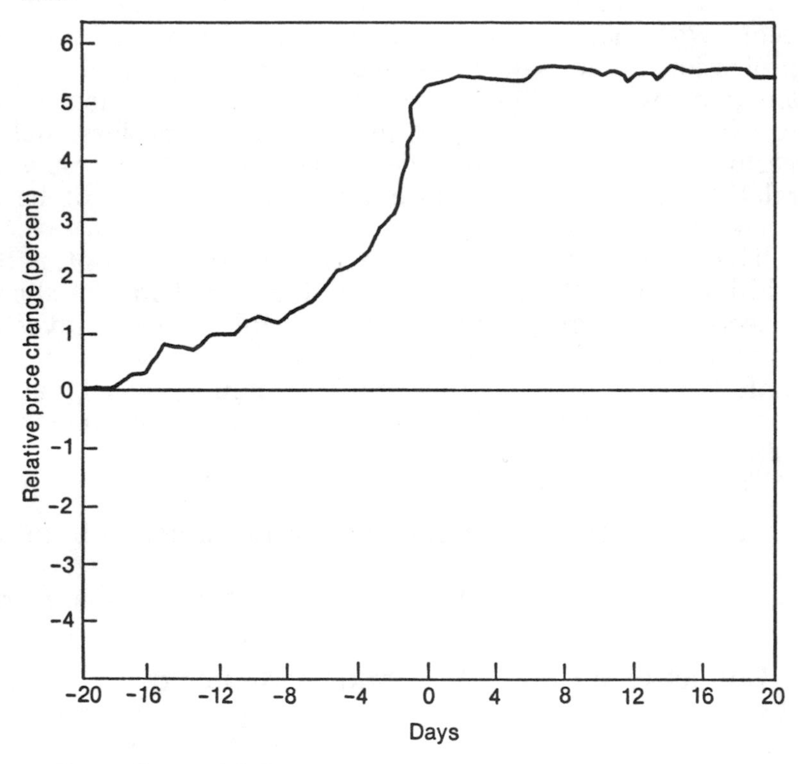

Source: Kraus and Stoll [155].

Figure 11–2 summarizes their findings for minus ticks. Notice that the prices on day zero (the day of the trade) averaged 2 percent below the prices of a day earlier. This figure vividly illustrates the validity of the semistrong form of the efficient market hypothesis. By the time the information was

publicly available (day zero), the price adjustment was complete.

Figure 11–3, showing the average performance preceding and following block trades on plus ticks, presents a similar picture of the market's efficiency. Throughout the 20-day period preceding the day that the block trade occurred, average prices made a significant upward adjustment. This adjustment process was complete, however, by the time the news of the block trade became publicly available.

ODD-LOT TRANSACTIONS

If asked to rank various classes of investors in terms of their "closeness" to important information, one would probably begin with management insiders, closely followed by market professionals. In last place would probably be the small amateur investor. Given such a ranking, there is a temptation to expect the informed, presumably skillful, professional investors to attain above-average rates of return. Conversely, the relatively unskilled and uninformed amateurs might be expected to show below-average returns.

The so-called odd-lot theory is based on the assumption that odd-lot trading (transactions involving less than 100 shares) reflects the sentiments of small, presumably amateur, investors and that these odd-lot investors are consistently below-average performers. If this is so, this simplistic notion goes, by acting contrary to the odd-lot investor one can obtain above-average returns.

This raises two questions:

1. Is the performance of odd-lot investors different from that of round-lot investors?
2. Can odd-lot information be used to forecast share price movements?

Odd-lot versus round-lot market performance. D. J. Klein [153], at Michigan State University, compared the rates of return on the 20 most sold and most bought odd-lot stocks. Regardless of the period measured, the odd-lotters' purchases yielded lower rates of return than did the stocks they sold. This conclusion was subsequently confirmed by Stanley Kaish [141]. The studies of such performance differences have not been as numerous or as definitive as one would like, and there is some countervailing evidence, but the research leans toward the conclusion that odd-lot investors are relatively unsuccessful.

Odd-lot trading rules. Unfortunately, a big step in logic is required to move from modest evidence that odd-lot investors as a group achieve below-average performance, to the use of information about their trading activities to develop a market strategy. Nonetheless, some people believe that useful trading rules can be developed from odd-lot statistics. The problem is that the strategies based on odd-lot statistics [see 146, 147] which have performed well have been "fined tuned" on historical data. But without some reason why odd-lot sale/purchase ratios should work, there is neither empirical nor theoretical justification for their use.

SHORT-INTEREST POSITIONS

One contrary opinion approach to stock selection and market timing is based on short-interest statistics. Short sales are made by people who expect the market to go down. In a regular securities transaction, shares are bought first and sold later. In a short transaction, the sale comes first, the purchase later. A short sale is effected by borrowing stock through a broker and selling it at the current market price. The proceeds of the sale are then held as collateral for the loan of the stock. To close out the short position, the borrowed stock must be replaced. This is done by buying[1] an equivalent number of shares at the then current market price. If a short sale is made at $100 and the short can later be covered by buying the stock at $90, there will be a $10 per share profit (before any intervening interest on the loan and repayment of any dividend income).

Market technicians know that each short position must eventually be closed out with a purchase. Hence, they reason, an increase in outstanding short interest represents an increase in potential demand, which serves as a downside cushion for the stock. Conversely, followers of this system believe that a reduction in short interest reflects a decline in latent demand and makes the market for the stock weak.

To assess the usefulness of short-interest information, it is necessary to answer three basic questions:

1. Do short-interest traders consistently attain above-average performance?

[1] Short sales "against the box" are not replaced by market purchases. The term "against the box" means the sale is made against stock held in a safe-deposit box. For a full description of this trading strategy and when it might be used, see Cohen, Zinbarg, and Zeikel [44].

2. Can short-interest statistics be used to forecast general market movements?
3. Can short-interest statistics be used to predict the movements of individual stocks?

Performance of short-interest traders. A *trader* is a short-term, in-and-out speculator. Most short sellers are traders, as evidenced by SEC statistics showing that most short positions are held for only about two weeks. In view of the fact that short sellers (*a*) receive no dividends, (*b*) pay interest on the borrowed stock, and (*c*) must deal with the difficulties inherent in predicting short-term price movements, one would expect short sellers to do *worse than the average* investor.

Not surprisingly, studies of short-interest transactions [189] have concluded that on the average, short sellers have absolutely no market timing ability and, as a result, incur large losses. Their poor performance does not, however, bear on the question of whether such behavior serves as a market predictor. Regardless of their success or failure, the asserted cushioning effect resulting from short-interest profit taking in a price decline is a separate issue.

Short-interest market indicators. According to several researchers [see 35, 187], the aggregate level of short interest is not correlated with market levels. But because the level of short interest fluctuates with the market's overall volume, a better relative measure of this activity is the ratio of short interest to average daily volume. Tests of this measure indicate that there is a slight correlation between the short-interest ratio and the market [see 35, 119, 238, 239]—as predicted by proponents of short-interest indicators. There is no evidence, however, that such information can be translated into a profitable trading strategy.

Short-interest stock indicators. To test the usefulness of short-interest statistics for predicting the movement of individual stocks, Randall D. Smith [260] studied the performance of portfolios of NYSE and AMEX stocks that were selected according to the short-interest statistics. Smith found that the portfolios picked on this basis favored extremely volatile stocks. This is easily explained by the proclivity of the short-interest trader for quick action. A portfolio of such stocks would also be expected to amplify the market's movement. Indeed, Smith found that the stocks selected by using short-interest statistics as a guide showed wide fluctuations in prof-

its and losses. But the overall performance of stocks picked on the basis of the short-interest statistics was in line with that of randomly chosen stocks with similar risk.

ODD-LOT SHORT SALES

Many people who believe that both odd-lot transactions and short sales are plausible indicators reason that together—in other words, odd-lot short sales—they provide a useful, but quite different, indicator. The reasoning behind this indicator is based on the assumption that small investors are usually not short sellers. When the small investors do move to the short side, it is because they feel strongly that the market is going down. If the little guy is always wrong, this clear indication of small-investor pessimism is interpreted as a sure sign that a market bottom is near.

The conclusion that small investors do not obtain dependable advice (or if they do, shun it in favor of intuition) is further buttressed by the fact that odd-lot investors, with remarkable consistency, do sell short at market lows. Manown Kisor and

TABLE 11–1: Relation between levels of odd-lot short-sales ratio and changes in market index over subsequent month, 1960–1969

Odd-lot short-sales ratio	*Number of occurrences*	*Percentage of occasions that market rose*	*Average market change (by percent)*
0.0–1.0	1,222	56.1	0.2
1.0–2.0	652	71.0	1.1
2.0–3.0	181	63.0	0.4
3.0–4.0	65	67.7	1.8
4.0–5.0	43	72.1	2.3
5.0–6.0	35	88.6	3.3
Greater than 6.0	50	96.0	6.1

Source: Kisor and Niederhoffer [152].

Victor Niederhoffer [152] documented this phenomenon by contrasting the odd-lot short-sales ratio with the general level of the market between 1960 and 1969. Their results, reproduced in Table 11–1, show that the "little guy" who sold short consistently misjudged the market during that period.

SUMMARY

The research reported in this chapter leads to the general conclusion that the market is efficient. While it appears that the new issue market has not provided abnormally high, or low, risk-adjusted returns, there is evidence that secondary distributions by "knowledgeable" sellers preceed price declines. Conversely, block trades provide a classical illustration of market efficiency—by the time the information is publicly available, the price adjustment is complete. The studies of odd-lot transactions and short sales, both individually and together, tend to support the belief that both short-sellers and small (odd-lot) investors have below average performance. Nonetheless, the case for using trading schemes based on these statistics is far from persuasive.

In short, the evidence supports the semistrong form of an "almost" efficient market. That is, while careful analysis of historical data can, from time to time, reveal selected inefficiencies, there is no evidence that these inefficiencies can be translated into investment strategies that will provide above-average performance.

Chapter 12

Inside information

Under the strong form of the efficient market hypothesis, even investors with privileged information cannot use it to produce consistently superior investment performance. This chapter examines that assertion.

INSIDERS

Insiders (i.e., exchange specialists, substantial owners, directors, and corporate officers) are required to report their security dealings to the SEC. Relatives of these insiders, various employees, and banks which might have access to the same confidential information are not subject to SEC monitoring. Obviously, it would be extremely difficult to monitor the stock transactions of every insider's friends and relatives. So, to protect against the possibility of abuse by secretly informed outsiders, the law considers any individual who trades on the basis of nonpublic information to be a de facto insider.

In one landmark case concerning the use of nonpublic information, it was alleged that Merrill Lynch had advised certain institutional clients that Douglas Aircraft would soon report disappointing earnings. The SEC hearing examiner, Warren E. Blair, used the term "tippees" to refer to persons who, through a corporate insider, came into the possession of confidential information. He held that it was the responsibility of a tippee receiving "material inside information" from insiders either to disclose the information publicly or to refrain from trading on it.

The SEC has subsequently reaffirmed that acting on a tip is a violation of the law if there is reason to believe that the information was not made public. In fact, the SEC has ruled that people who use information which innocently comes into their

possession are in violation of the law if they have reason to know that the information was intended to be confidential. The law is thus explicit: *all parties to securities transactions must have access to the same material facts.*

The significance of the preceding point cannot be overemphasized. This rule obligates all publicly owned companies to ensure that disclosed changes in material facts are widely disseminated. If information is disclosed to one analyst, it must be made available to all analysts. This constructively limits all investment research to the gathering and analysis of publicly available facts.

The law notwithstanding, the prospective buyer of a share of stock faces two groups of people who have access to confidential information. First, the management of the company knows, or certainly should know, more about that company than the average investor. Second, when a purchase order reaches the floor of a stock exchange, the specialist in that stock is privy to nonpublic information on pending buy and sell orders at specific prices.

Thus, four important questions are:

1. Do management insiders profit from their privileged information?
2. Do specialists profit from their privileged information?
3. Do the actions of management insiders provide investors with useful information?
4. Do the actions of specialists provide investors with useful information?

MANAGEMENT INSIDERS

Of all groups, management insiders are in the best position to foresee the future of their companies. This does not mean that insiders use such information for personal profit. There are two deterrents to such insider transactions. First, there is the moral obligation of corporate officers to honor their fiduciary responsibilities. Second, certain SEC restrictions (preventing short-term gains, for example) constrain those who might otherwise neglect their moral and fiduciary obligations.

Nonetheless, insiders can and do make fully disclosed purchases and sales of their companies' stock. After a clerical and printing delay of about one month, a complete record of these transactions is available in the *Official Summary of Security Transactions and Holdings.*

Several researchers have attempted to find out whether management insiders display better than average foresight in their company-related investment decisions. Donald Rogoff [221] studied the relationship between insider trades and subsequent stock performance in his doctoral dissertation at Michigan State University. Based on a sample of 98 companies between 1957 and 1960, Rogoff found that in 162 cases of predominant insider buying, the stock outperformed the market during the next six months in 102 cases and underperformed the market in only 54 cases. Of 210 instances of predominant insider selling, 112 sales preceded relative declines, while 98 were followed by relative gains.

In a study of insider activity during 1963–64, James Lorie and Victor Niederhoffer [175], at the University of Chicago, found that predominant insider buying preceded 36 advances, compared with 19 declines. Of the 124 instances of predominant selling, 81 sales were followed by declines and 43 preceded advances.

Shannon Pratt and C. W. DeVere [215] took the issue of insider trading a step further and studied the profitability of 52,000 insider transactions between 1960 and 1966. They defined an "insider consensus" as three or more buys or sells, respectively, with none of the opposite transaction. The average relative stock performance following such insider activity is shown in Figure 12–1.

Notice that one year after a consensus of insider sales, those stocks showed an average positive return of 9.6 percent. This is a respectable rate of return and reflects the general market uptrend during the period covered by the study. The results following insider buying, however, are almost too good to be true. Stocks bought by three or more insiders during one month had appreciated 27.1 percent a year later. Further, there was an obvious long-run difference between the performance of the two groups. Clearly, the information depicted in Figure 12–1 does not support the strong form of the efficient market hypothesis.

It should also be asked whether the publicly available knowledge of insider activities is useful to outsiders seeking above-average returns. Studies on the usefulness of the published reports of insider activities are encouraging. Pratt and DeVere found that imitating insiders' actions even one or two months after the record of their actions was published provided above-average performance.

It is not really surprising that management insiders are bet-

FIGURE 12–1: Performance of stocks experiencing unusual insider activity—no lag

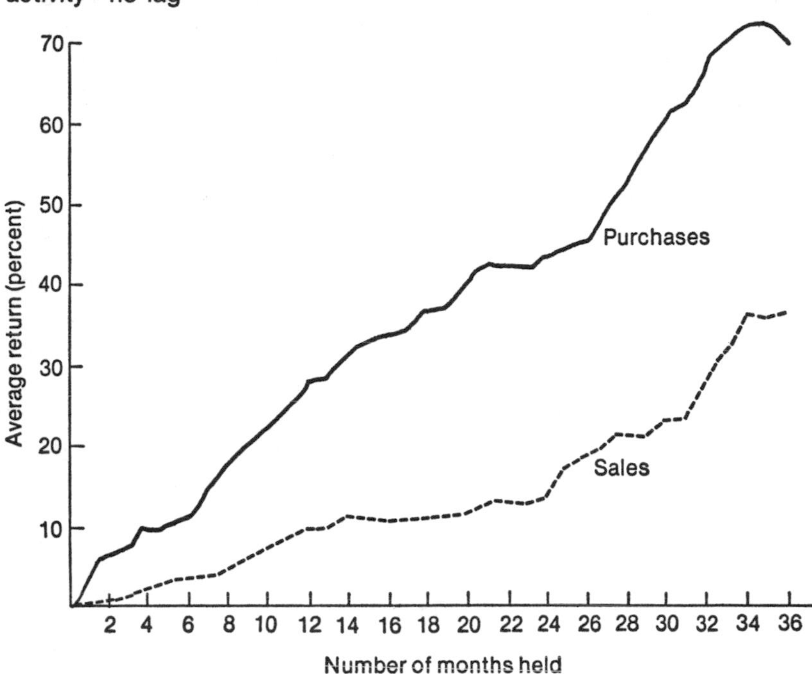

Source: Pratt and DeVere [215].

ter than average investors in their own stocks—a refutation of the strong form of the efficient market hypothesis. What is surprising is that this advantage is available to anyone who reads the *Official Summary of Security Transactions and Holdings*—or listens to someone who does.

EXCHANGE SPECIALISTS

Another group of insiders—the specialists who maintain markets in securities on the floor of a stock exchange—also has confidential information. They know the size and prices of standing buy and sell orders. Under exchange rules, this information is confined to the specialist. So, again, the questions which need to be answered are:

1. Do specialists profit from their privileged information?
2. Do any of their actions provide useful information?

As discussed earlier (Chapter 4), successive intraday price changes on the NYSE do *not* occur in accordance with the random-walk model. The question remains, however, whether the specialists use of the private information on their books is responsible for the nonrandom intraday pattern. This question can be answered by taking a closer look at the behavior of intraday price changes.

There is a pronounced tendency for stock prices to cluster around whole numbers, halves, quarters, and odd one eighths—in that order. M. F. M. Osborne [211] probed this phenomenon by studying what he called "partially reflecting barriers." He hypothesized that if a stock's price is "reflected" back down as it rises to a whole number level, we should find an inordinately large number of daily highs ending in 7/8 fractions. Similarly, if prices are reflected back up as they sink to whole numbers, we should find an abnormally large number of daily lows with 1/8 fractions.

Osborne found such a distribution of prices; that is, whole number and half number price levels acted as partially impenetrable barriers. Thus, many stocks showed daily highs of 7/8 or 3/8 because they were unable to attain the "barrier" price level. Conversely, an inordinate number of lows were observed at price levels just above integers and halves—at 1/8 and 5/8. Thus, as stock prices move either up or down toward whole or half numbers, there is a tendency for prices to reverse. This tendency for prices to reflect off of whole-number "resistance" or "support" points is illustrated in Figure 12–2. Victor Niederhoffer [203, 204] later confirmed Osborne's results for a much larger sample of stocks.

Research conducted by this author (see Hagin [116]) provides further evidence of this phenomenon. Intraday lows and highs for 784 major stocks, classified by price range, are summarized in Table 12–1. The data in the first column of this table were compiled by comparing the number of times over a four-year period each stock's daily high ended with a 1/8 fraction with the number of times its daily low ended with a 1/8 fraction. If the number of lows ending with a 1/8 fraction exceeded the number of highs with a 1/8 fraction, that stock was tallied in the column labeled "more lows at 1/8." The other columns were calculated in a similar fashion.

If prices do not meet resistance at whole numbers, there would be only slight differences between the entries in each column. If, however, prices do tend to be reflected off whole

FIGURE 12–2: Reflection tendency

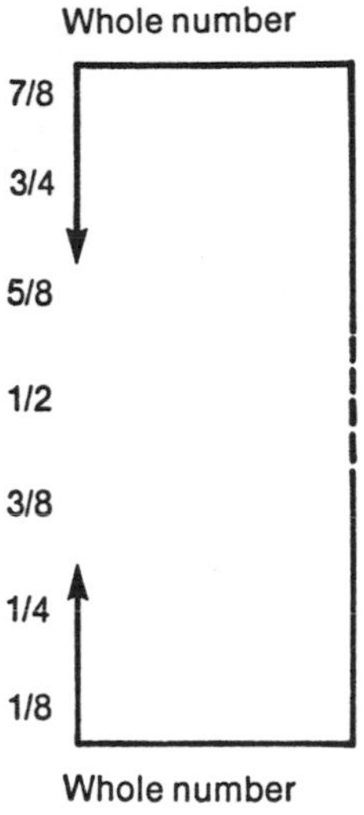

numbers, there would be a predominance of "more lows at 1/8" and "more highs at 7/8" as shown in Figure 12–2.

To best examine the data in Table 12–1, place a sheet of paper across the page so that only the information for the first price range ($0–$9) is visible. For stocks priced in the $0–$9 range, there is no evidence of reflection. In the next price range

TABLE 12–1: Comparison of intraday lows and highs at 1/8 and 7/8 fractional prices for stocks classified by average price range

Average Price Range ($)	*More lows at 1/8*	*More highs at 1/8*	*More lows at 7/8*	*More highs at 7/8*
0–9	60	59	60	57
10–19	90	43	28	108
20–29	102	17	8	112
30–39	132	6	3	135
40–49	108	6	2	113
50–59	70	2	0	73
60–69	40	0	0	40
70–79	23	0	0	23
80–99	12	1	0	13
100–999	9	1	0	9
Total	646	135	101	683

Source: Hagin [116].

($10–$19), however, the excess of more lows at ⅛ and more highs at ⅞ provides overwhelming evidence of reflections. Further, the tendency toward such reflection increases with the price of the stock. Clearly, one would not expect this kind of reflection in a perfectly efficient market.

The specialist system is a curious anomaly. Evolving legal theory holds that *all* parties to a stock transaction must have equal access to information. Yet, the exchanges allow specialists, who trade with the public for their own accounts, to have access to private information. This author has discussed elsewhere (see Hagin [117]) how specialists can use their information on pending buy and sell orders for personal profit. This activity causes the reflection phenomena illustrated in Table 12–1. While it has not been documented, it is reasonable to assume that investors who know that there is an inordinately high probability that a daily high will be at the ⅞ fraction, and an inordinately high probability that a daily low will be at the ⅛ fraction, can use this knowledge to improve their decisions on purchase and sale points.

Chapter 13

Conclusion: Efficient market hypothesis

WEAK FORM

The weak form of the efficient market hypothesis holds that information on the past movements of stock prices and volumes cannot be used to predict future stock prices. In examining the validity of this hypothesis, it is useful to divide the empirical tests into certain categories. First, since any discussion of the weak form of the hypothesis requires an explicit definition of "past," it is useful to discuss three categories of "past"—intraday, between 1 and 40 days, and more than 40 days. Second, since certain results can be statistically significant and still not provide the basis for a profitable investment strategy, it is useful to differentiate between two categories of "significant" research—statistical and practical.

When the evidence in support of the weak form of the efficient market hypothesis is viewed in this context, the conclusions are both clear and consistent. Beginning with the shortest possible time periods (intraday price changes), there is statistical evidence that such changes are not random. While this would imply that someone who could trade without commissions (such as a specialist) might be able to implement inordinately profitable trading strategies, this level of nonrandomness has no practical significance for someone who must pay transaction charges. This research is emphatic in the conclusion that practices such as tape reading are useless!

In the next time interval, the period between 1 and 40 days, there is absolutely no reliable evidence that historical price and volume information is statistically, much less practically,

significant. In the third time interval, in excess of 40 days, there is statistical evidence of the phenomenon of relative strength continuation, where the best performing stocks tend to show above-average performance in subsequent periods. Attempts to translate these statistical phenomena into reliable, practical trading strategies, however, have met with failure.

Thus, two conclusions can be drawn with regard to the weak form of the efficient market hypothesis:

1. The weak form of the efficient market hypothesis is a valid description of the market for anyone who is interested in developing profitable investment strategies from historical price or volume information.
2. There is neither a theoretical foundation nor empirical support for technical analysis based on historical price and volume data.

SEMISTRONG FORM

The most widely used form of fundamental security analysis rests on developing projections of price-earnings multiples and earnings per share. Unfortunately, price-earnings multiplies are subject to wide swings for which there is neither a theoretical nor empirical basis for prediction. Nonetheless, even though the vagaries of price-earnings multiples compromise the basis for this kind of analysis, it can be shown that accurate earnings estimates would provide above-average investment performance.

The semistrong form of the efficient market hypothesis, however, raises serious questions about an analysts' ability to develop useful earnings forecasts. Specifically, this form of the hypothesis holds that the analysis of any publicly available information is pointless because all such information is already reflected in stock prices.

The evidence here is again clear. First, it has been shown that period-to-period earnings changes behave in accordance with a random-walk model. This means that the common practice of basing future earnings projections on historical patterns of earnings changes is of no value.

Second, studies which have examined the behavior of stock prices prior to unexpected earnings changes dramatize that the market is remarkably efficient at accurately anticipating such fluctuations. This evidence indicates that the marketplace is filled with competent analysts who, as a whole, accurately

forecast earnings. In this extremely competitive arena it is doubtful that a few superior earnings forecasters *consistently* "beat the market to the punch."

Dividend information raises a significant challenge to the efficient market hypothesis. There is evidence to support the contention that dividend changes mirror management's largely correct assessment of a firm's future.

A systematic examination of other levels of the information hierarchy reveals only isolated exceptions to a purely efficient market setting. There is evidence, for example, that professional opinions on stocks can cause price movements and that secondary distributions by sellers, whom the market views as "knowledgeable," precede price declines.

STRONG FORM

In its strong form, the efficient market hypothesis holds that even investors with privileged information cannot use that information to develop profitable investing strategies. Not surprisingly, there is little support for this hypothesis. Management insiders do have extra insight into their company's future. Also, there is evidence that stock exchange specialists cause abnormal patterns of fractional price movements.

Significance of the findings

Given the evidence, the stock market can accurately be described as a "nearly efficient" marketplace. Unquestionably, if an opportunity for inordinate profit presents itself in the market, it will not go unnoticed. In such a marketplace one would not expect prices to deviate by much, or for long, from what is perceived to be a "fair" price by the myriad market participants.

The conclusion that the market is "reasonably efficient" is important for two reasons. First, if the market was inefficient (i.e., there were feasible strategies for attaining consistently above-average performances) it would not be necessary to study MPT. But, given the fact that the market is reasonably efficient, it is naïve to assume that the diligent pursuit of traditional forms of analysis will provide above-average returns. Second, a "reasonably efficient" market is a prerequisite for the use of MPT. Without such a high level of efficiency, the theoretical foundation upon which MPT rests would not exist.

PART TWO

MPT: BUILDING BLOCKS

Chapter 14

Forms of risk

Risk is the possibility that the actual return from an investment will differ from the expected return. Embedded in this definition is a subtle, but important, distinction between "risk" and "uncertainty." In situations involving "risk," the probabilities of various outcomes are known. But under "uncertainty," there is no knowledge of the probability distribution of the possible outcomes. In roulette, for example, while there is no way of predicting what the next outcome will be, explicit knowledge is available on the underlying probabilities of all possible outcomes. Hence, in roulette, the exact risk associated with any situation can be calculated. At the other extreme, a prospective investor in a new and unseasoned company has no reliable means of estimating the likelihood of sales, earnings, or stock price distributions. Technically, the latter situation is characterized by uncertainty, not risk.

Recent research has succeeded in eliminating much of the uncertainty previously associated with investment decisions. Much as someone interested in playing roulette might tally the frequency of the various occurrences on a particular wheel in order to derive the probability of certain outcomes, Fisher and Lorie [91, 92, 93] and Ibbotson and Sinquefield [127, 128] have meticulously tallied the results of investing in various markets over varying lengths of time. Through such research, much of the uncertainty and guesswork which would otherwise be associated with investment decision making has now been upgraded to the status of "calculated risk."

While it is useful to bear the distinction between risk and uncertainty in mind, most practitioners do not make this distinction. Thus, from the traditional investment perspective, there are several different kinds of risk: interest-rate, liquidity,

purchasing power, market, and business. Modern portfolio theorists have recast and extended these notions under the rubric of investment risk.

INTEREST-RATE RISK

Most investments provide current income, such as bond interest, common or preferred stock dividends, or rental income from real estate holdings. The relative worth of these returns varies over time as interest rates (the rental charges for money) fluctuate in line with the changing supply of, and demand for, this "commodity."

When interest rates rise, a bond paying a fixed return will become a less desirable investment. Thus, an interest rates rise, bond prices fall. Suppose that the prevailing long-term interest rate is 8 percent. This means that an investor can enter into a long-term contract under which $1,000 can be rented to the issuer of the bond in return for 8 percent, or $80 a year. Once consummated, there is a long-term contractual obligation to accept $80 a year until the end of the "rental period"—when the $1,000 will be returned.

If, however, the investor decides to sell the contract before the end of the rental period, the price that someone else would be willing to pay for it will depend on prevailing interest rates. For example, when prevailing rates are at 10 percent, a contract yielding 8 percent on its face value will be worth less than the 10 percent contracts which are currently available in the market. Similarly, fixed-income contracts increase in value as interest rates decline. Since dividends derived from common stock ownership are similar to the interest derived from bonds, stock prices are influenced by fluctuations in the prevailing interest rates on alternative investments.

LIQUIDITY RISK

Liquidity refers to the ease with which an investment can be converted into cash. Liquidity risk, therefore, represents the possibility of sustaining a loss from current value just by the process of "liquidation," or converting an asset into cash. Generally speaking, shares of an NYSE listed company are highly liquid. Even here, as institutions try to build extremely large positions in a particular stock, the adverse impact on liquidity must be considered.

PURCHASING POWER RISK

We hear a lot about inflation these days, and its threat is indeed a serious one. Since 1967 the average increase in the Consumer Price Index (CPI) has been more than 6 percent per year. To understand and appreciate (or if you prefer, respect) the significance of such an index it is necessary to examine its impact on some "benchmark" item.

There are several ways to measure the historical impact of inflation. One is to contrast current spending requirements with historical requirements. Another is to examine the current worth of "old" money. Both are illustrated in Table 14–1.

TABLE 14–1: Impact of inflation (CPI): 1967–1979

	Year	
	1967	*1979*
Equivalent purchasing power	$1,000	$2,012
Purchasing power of $1,000*	$1,000	$ 476

* Under the assumption of an average annual increase in the Consumer Price Index (CPI) of 6 percent.

These data show that spending $2,012 in 1979 would be the equivalent of spending $1,000, 12 years before. Similarly, it would take a $1,000 bill in 1979 to purchase the same quantity of consumer goods which $476 could have bought in 1967.

Probably the most useful perspective from which to view inflation is to think of it as a *tax on income*. Using $10,000 held in a bank savings account which earns 5 percent annually as an example, consider the scenarios shown in Table 14–2.

Scenario 1 combines annual income consisting of the 5 percent interest payment with 5 percent inflation and zero income tax. Scenario 2 combines an annual interest income of 5 percent with zero inflation and a 100 percent income tax rate. Notice that the year-end purchasing power under each scenario is identical. This means that for an investor who earns 5 percent from a savings account, the effect of 5 percent inflation is equivalent of a 100 percent income tax rate!

Since the inflation rate has averaged more than 6 percent annually since 1967, scenarios 3 and 4 more accurately describe the pretax impact of rising price levels on a 5 percent savings account. Here, for an investor who earns 5 percent, the effect of a 6 percent inflation rate is the same as a 120 percent

TABLE 14–2: Inflation as a tax on income

In each scenario it is assumed that:

Start	$10,000
Plus: Annual income (5%)	500

SCENARIO 1:	Inflation 5% Income tax 0%	SCENARIO 2:	Inflation 0% Income tax 100%
Start	$10,000	Start	$10,000
Plus: Annual income (5%)	500	Plus: Annual income (5%)	500
Less: Inflation (5%)	−500	Less: Inflation (0%)	0
Less: Income tax (0%)	0	Less: Income tax (100%)	−500
Year-end purchasing power	$10,000	Year-end purchasing power	$10,000

SCENARIO 3:	Inflation 6% Income tax 0%	SCENARIO 4:	Inflation 0% Income tax 120%
Start	$10,000	Start	$10,000
Plus: Annual income (5%)	500	Plus: Annual income (5%)	500
Less: Inflation (6%)	−600	Less: Inflation (0%)	0
Less: Income tax (0%)	0	Less: Income tax (120%)	−600
Year-end purchasing power	$ 9,900	Year-end purchasing power	$ 9,900

tax rate. In reality, however, we have both—inflation and taxation. But, of the two, inflation is far more damaging than any tax enacted by legislators.

Unfortunately, tax-exempt investors are also "taxed" by inflation. As a final illustration of the "tax" of inflation, consider a tax-exempt investor who earns 8 percent from a bond portfolio during a year in which the inflation rate is 7 percent. In this case the "tax rate"—the seven-eighths of the return drained away by inflation—is 87.5 percent!

Clearly, the penny postcard, nickel ice cream cone, $800 Ivy League tuition, and $1,000 Chevrolet are long past. Investing in a world with inflation is in some ways an *Alice in Wonderland* situation: "If you want to keep in the same place, you must run. If you want to go someplace else, you must run twice as fast."

MARKET RISK

The market value of sound, well-managed companies can be adversely affected by overall stock market declines. This is not surprising because the fortunes of individual companies, as well as the fortunes of the overall market, are subject to many of the same overall economic forces. (More on this subject later.)

BUSINESS RISK

The degree to which an investment fulfills an investor's expectations depends to some measure on the future prosperity of the business. Unfortunately, not all firms which issue bonds remain solvent long enough to repay their obligations. Similarly, not all firms which issue stock reward their investors with profitable performance.

An investor assumes little business risk in U.S. government bonds or the bonds of broad-based, well-financed, blue-chip corporations such as AT&T. It is very doubtful that these institutions will, in the foreseeable future, become unable to meet their obligations. Yet, all profit-seeking enterprises face some degree of business risk.

Many factors bear on the profitability or ultimate solvency of an enterprise. Some are under the control of the company's management, while others are beyond their control, such as the actions of competitors, changes in demand, and government policies. Some amount, however, of a firm's future is dependent on management's ability to guide the organization successfully in a changing environment. By investing in a company, an investor assumes this risk.

INVESTMENT RISK

When J. P. Morgan was asked what he thought the market would do, he replied that it would "fluctuate." Clearly, as individuals continually reappraise investments, stock prices will move up or down in response to the dynamics of demand and supply. If investors frequently change their minds about a company's outlook, these changes of heart will be reflected in the fluctuations of the stock's price. If investors are consistent in their appraisal of a company, this uniformity of opinion will similarly translate into a stable stock price.

Modern portfolio theorists have sought to quantify these fluctuations under the rubric of investment risk. In keeping with the earlier definition, investment risk is the possibility that the actual return from an investment will differ from the expected return. Since, the magnitude of investment risk can be gauged by the volatility of stock price changes, explicit specifications of investment risk require estimates of the *probability* that variations (from the expected, or mean, return) of a given *magnitude*, will, or will not, occur. Fortunately, information on both the probability and the magnitude of such

volatility is contained in one statistic—the "standard deviation" of expected return.

The standard deviations for a normal distribution are shown in Figure 14–1. The magnitude of variations from the mean is represented by the standard deviations along the bottom of the

FIGURE 14–1: A normal distribution

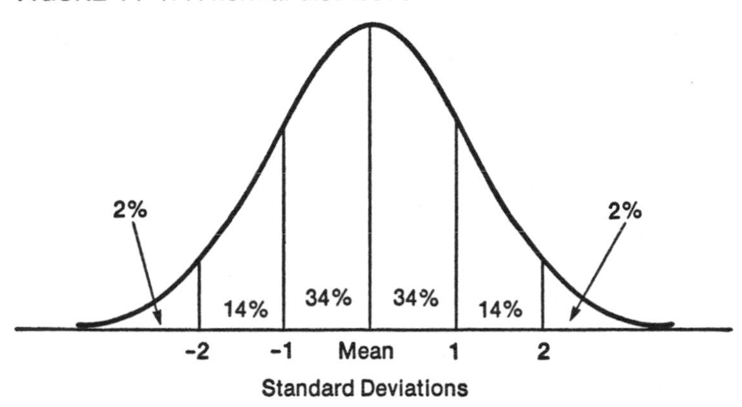

curve. The probability of such variations is represented by the area under the curve. Thus, for normally distributed data, 68 percent of the outcomes (roughly two out of three) will be within the range of plus, or minus, one standard deviation from the mean. Or, again looking at Figure 14–1, 16 percent of the observations (roughly one out of six) will be above plus one standard deviation.

The notion of a standard deviation becomes more meaningful in the following example. Over the 51-year period from the beginning of 1926 through the end of 1976, the mean annual return (dividends plus capital appreciation) for the S&P Composite Index was 9.2 percent. During the same period the standard deviation of annual returns was 22.4 percent. [127] Thus, while the average annual return was 9.2 percent, the return corresponding to plus one standard deviation was 31.6 percent (9.2% + 22.4%), and so on. This situation is shown in Figure 14–2.

An examination of Figure 14–2 reveals that over the 51-year period prior to 1977, while the average annual return was 9.2 percent, the odds were roughly two out of three that the returns in any single year would be between −13.2 percent (one standard deviation below the mean) and +31.6 percent (one standard deviation above the mean). Similarly, since 96 percent of all normally distributed observations fall within plus or

FIGURE 14–2: Historical risk of stock market returns (1926–1976)

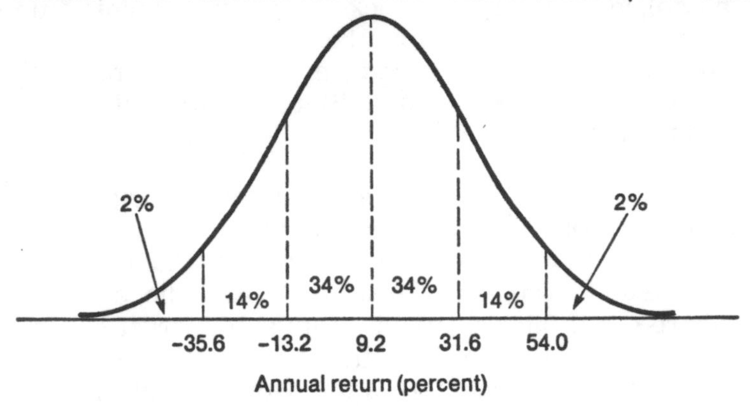

Mean annual return 9.2%
Annual standard deviation 22.4%

Source: Abbotson and Sinquefield [127].

minus two standard deviations, there was better than a 96 percent chance that the returns in any one year were within the range of −35.6 percent (two standard deviations below the mean) and +54.0 percent (two standard deviations above the mean).

Standard deviations can also be used to specify the likelihood that the return in any particular period will be outside of some range. That is, since 16 percent of all normally distributed observations fall below minus one standard deviation, there was a 16 percent chance—roughly one out of every six years—that the return in any single year would be less than −13.2 percent (one standard deviation below the mean).

When dealing with market aggregates, such as the S&P Composite Index, the ex post (historical) measure of risk (the historical standard deviation of return) can reasonably be used as an ex ante (forward-looking) estimate of investment risk. Unfortunately, when dealing with individual stocks, the ex post standard deviation of return is not a reliable guide for predicting future risk.

When working with individual stocks, it is necessary to delve into the three sources of investment risk:

1. *Systematic risk.* Risk that is related to market covariance—the tendency for an individual security's return to fluctuate with the return on the market portfolio.

2. *Extramarket risk.* Risk arising from comovements of homogenous groups of stocks whose movements are independent of those of the market as a whole.
3. *Specific risk.* Risk arising from factors that are specific to the company and, by definition, are unrelated to other companies.

Since the risk arising from extramarket covariance can be eliminated through diversification, many modern portfolio theorists and practitioners concentrate on the prediction of only systematic risk and "residual" risk—the aggregate of specific risk and the risk arising from extramarket covariance.

While these sources of investment risk will be discussed in detail in subsequent chapters, a few words about diversifiable and nondiversifiable risks are in order here. Systematic risk—the risk derived from the tendency for an individual security's return to fluctuate with the return of the market portfolio—is a nondiversifiable risk. Clearly, if an investor held a portfolio with equal proportions of all stocks this risk would still be present. For this reason, systematic risk is said to be a nondiversifiable risk.

Extramarket risk—the risk derived from comovements of homogeneous groups of stocks whose movements are independent of those of the market as a whole—is a diversifiable risk. This means that a portfolio that has an equal representation of all groups can diversify away the risks that are associated with holding only one or more of the homogeneous groups that en toto comprise the market. Specific risk—the risk derived from factors that are specific to a company—is also a diversifiable risk.

This is best understood by thinking of a portfolio composed of all available stocks. Assume that the annual performance of this portfolio was +10 percent. This means that for every security that appreciated more than 10 percent, there had to be another security, or, securities, that had offsetting below-average performance. In such a portfolio the unique characteristics of any company are lost. As a result, the market portfolio did not derive any incremental return (i.e., any return above the 10 percent for holding the market portfolio) from company sources. The performance of the average company, or industry, by definition, is the same as the average performance of the market.

Given that neither individual stocks nor selected homogenous groups of stocks add incremental return to the average

return of the market portfolio, it follows that neither stocks, nor homogenous groups of stocks, add risk to the market portfolio. This means that a portfolio that has an equal representation of all stocks has neither group-related (extramarket) nor security-related (specific) risk—only the market-related (systematic) risk. Thus, two of the three sources of investment risk can be eliminated through proper diversification. Conversely, portfolios that do not match the market possess these risks—as well as these potential sources of excess return.

SUMMARY

The process of investing involves selecting from the available alternatives those investments with the risks and expected returns that best meet the investment objectives. It is a fact of life that in this process one must incur risks in order to attain excess returns. To attain returns in excess of those available from riskfree investments, an investor must incur systematic (market-related) risk. To attain returns in excess of the market's return, an investor must incur risks in excess of the market's purely systematic risk.

Of the wealth of stock market research which has emerged in the last decade, it will become clear in subsequent chapters that the most far-reaching contribution has been the explicit integration of risk into both investment analysis and the measurement of investment performance.

Chapter 15

Professional performance

The first in-depth analysis of the performance of professional investment managers examined mutual funds. At the time only mutual funds, among all institutions, had to disclose their performance figures. Now, bank trust departments, pension funds, and insurance companies have all come under closer scrutiny.

The first comprehensive study of the mutual fund industry, released in 1963, was prepared under the supervision of Professor Irwin Friend and has come to be referred to as the "Wharton School Study of Mutual Funds." The startling conclusion of the analysis was that, on the average, mutual fund performance "did not differ appreciably from what would have been achieved by an unmanaged portfolio consisting of the same proportion of common stocks, preferred stocks, corporate bonds, government securities, and other assets as the composite portfolios of the funds." [100]

In 1965, Friend and Douglas Vickers, also at Wharton, published another study of portfolio performance. They compared the common stock portfolios of 50 mutual funds with 50 randomly selected common stock portfolios over a six-year period. Friend and Vickers reported that "for the six-year period as a whole, from the end of 1957 through 1963, the random portfolios experienced a slightly higher average return than the mutual funds." [102, p. 398] They concluded that "there is still no evidence—either in our new or old tests, or in the tests so far carried out by others—that mutual fund performance is any better than that realizable by random or mechanical selection of stock issues." [102, p. 412] These data prompted Friend and Vickers to remark that their results "raise interesting questions about the apparent inability of professional investment management on the average to outperform the market." [102, p. 413]

Another segment of Friend and Vickers' research raised a crucial issue. During a certain period, the mutual funds performed significantly better than the randomly selected portfolios. Did this mean that mutual fund managers indeed obtained above-average results during that period?

It so happened that the variability of the returns for mutual funds was consistently higher than it was for the randomly generated portfolio returns. The mutual funds were, on the average, riskier than the random portfolios. In such a case, the mutual funds would be expected to do better than average in a year of sharp upward movement for the overall stock market. Could risk differences, asked Friend and Vickers, explain this aspect of their findings? Clearly, there was a need to factor risk into measurements of performance.

TREYNOR AND THE MEASUREMENT OF RISK

Jack Treynor, the editor of the *Financial Analysts Journal*, was the first to incorporate the vital ingredient of risk into a study of investment performance. [271] He devised a way to compare the distinctive risk characteristics of different mutual funds. Prior to Treynor's research, investigators had noted that rates of return for mutual funds typically show wide variations from year to year. The problem was, as it is to a lesser degree even today, to devise a stable risk-related parameter to include in the measurement of "performance." Treynor approached the problem by showing the remarkable stability of a fund's "characteristic line," which can be used to measure risk.

The rate of return history of two hypothetical portfolios over ten years is plotted in Figure 15–1. The horizontal axis records the rate of return for the general market, while the vertical axis measures the return for each fund. Notice that the lines, known as characteristic lines, which are fitted to the points describing the two funds in Figure 15–1 provide two quite different pictures.

Drawn in this way, Treynor's "characteristic lines" illustrate the historical relationships between the rate of return of the portfolio and market over the period studied. The slope of Treynor's characteristic line provides a graphic measure of a fund's volatility in relation to that of the general market. Notice that a steeply sloping characteristic line (such as that of Fund A) means that the historical rate of return for the fund has magnified the general market's return. By contrast, Fund

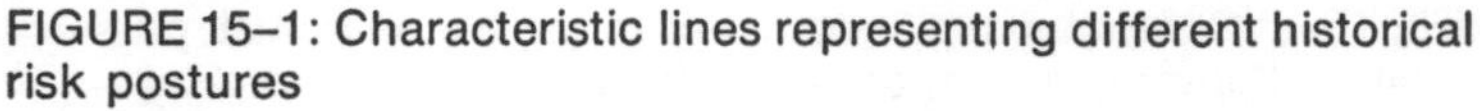

FIGURE 15–1: Characteristic lines representing different historical risk postures

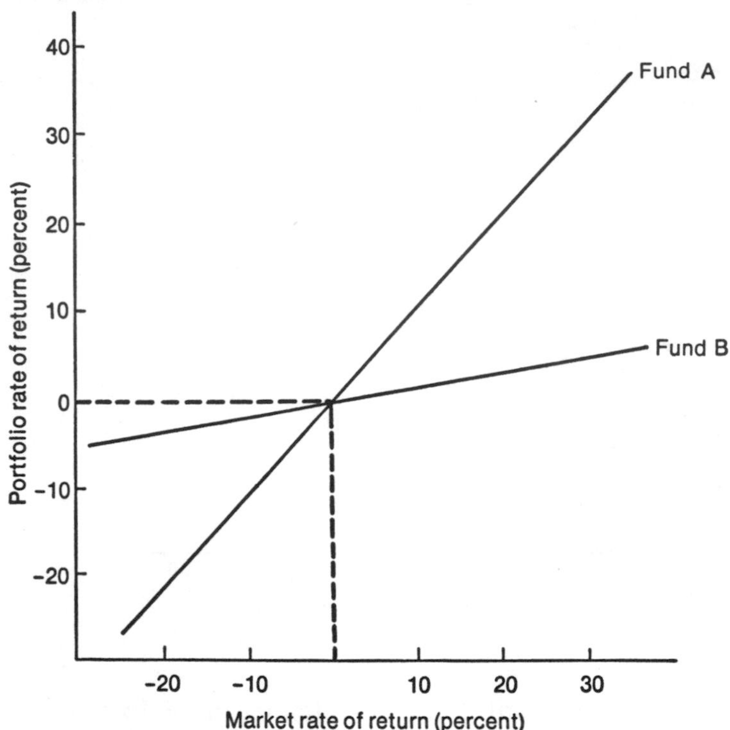

B's characteristic line is less steep than that of Fund A. A characteristic line such as Fund B's indicates less sensitivity to general market fluctuations. Fund B carries a lower component of general market risk.

Treynor observed, "the slope-angle of the characteristic line obviously provides a more refined measure of a fund's volatility than the usual categories of 'balanced fund," 'stock fund,' or 'growth fund.' " [271, p. 66] Treynor reported further that "the range of volatility observed in actual practice is enormous." He found, for example, that a 1 percent change in the rate of return of the Dow Jones Industrial Average was often accompanied by changes in rates of return of certain funds that were more than twice as large.

Besides comparing the historical risk of any two funds, the characteristic line discloses other performance information. Notice that the slopes of the characteristic lines for Fund X and Fund Y in Figure 15–2 are identical. The volatility, or risk, of

FIGURE 15–2: Characteristic lines representing historical risk postures with different average rates of return

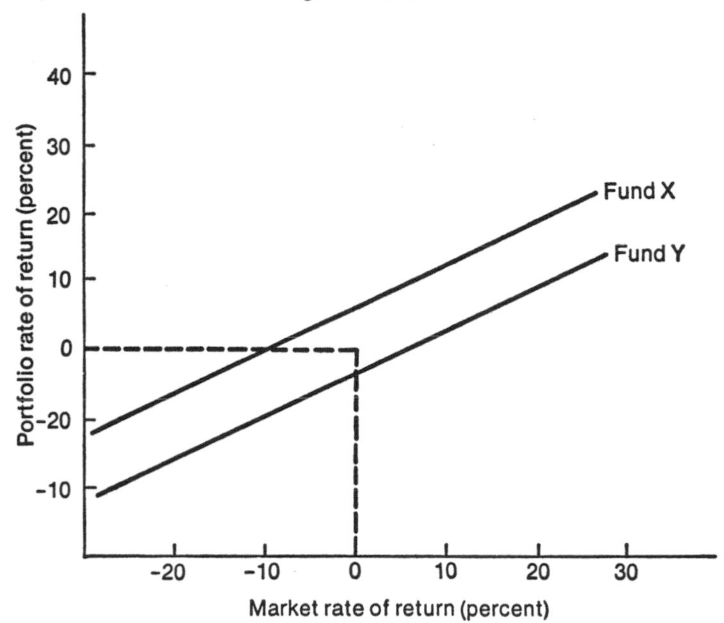

the two funds is equal. Fund X's characteristic line lies above the characteristic line for Fund Y, however. This means that Fund X has historically demonstrated consistently higher returns than Fund Y—in good years and bad. Thus, Treynor's "characteristic line" reflects two distinctive ingredients of a fund's performance history—return and systematic (market-related) risk.

In his now-classic paper, Treynor used this graphic technique to compare the performance of 54 mutual funds. He noted that over a ten-year period (1954–63), roughly 80 percent of the funds studied maintained a constant posture toward systematic risk.

SHARPE'S REWARD TO VARIABILITY MEASURE

William Sharpe also studied the performance of mutual fund portfolios. Sharpe utilized a ratio, similar to that devised by Treynor, which measured the "reward per unit of variability." Like Treynor's measure of performance, Sharpe's statistic

gauged the reward provided to the investor for assuming risk. Sharpe was able to confirm large differences in the way the 34 mutual funds he studied rewarded their investors for assuming risk.

Sharpe also examined the relationship between the efficient market hypothesis and performance. If as the hypothesis holds, elaborate and expensive security analysis is useless, the mutual funds which spend the least on research should show the best net performance records. In Sharpe's words, "the only basis for persistently inferior performance would be the continued expenditure of large amounts of a fund's assets on the relatively fruitless search for incorrectly valued securities." [244, p. 121] Conversely, if security analysis is worthwhile, funds spending the most on such research should have shown better net performance. After much careful investigation, Sharpe reported that "the results tend to support the cynics: good performance is associated with low expense ratios." [244, p. 132]

Sharpe also compared the 34 mutual funds with the Dow Jones Industrial Average, using his reward to variability performance measure. Based on this measure of performance, Sharpe reported that in terms of a reward to risk ratio, the odds were "greater than 100 to 1 against the possibility that the average mutual fund did as well as the Dow Jones portfolio from 1954–1963." [244, p. 137]

Sharpe traced the cause of these remarkably bad mutual fund results to differences between their gross and net performance. He had hypothesized that if the security analysis practiced by Wall Street professionals was indeed useless, the funds' gross performance before fees and expenses would equal that attained from random selection of securities with similar risks. If the hypothesis is correct, it means that, counter to intuition, the investment companies which have spent most heavily on security selection in fact have compiled the worst net performance!

After much careful study, Sharpe reported ". . . all other things being equal, the smaller a fund's expense ratio, the better the results obtained by stockholders." [244, p. 137] On the basis of this evidence, Sharpe was able to conclude, ". . . the burden of proof may reasonably be placed on those who argue the traditional view—that the search for securities whose prices diverge from their intrinsic values is worth the expense required." [244, p. 138]

THE CASE AGAINST "PROFESSIONAL" MANAGEMENT GROWS STRONGER

By 1968, there was a growing body of evidence challenging professional management's ability—as typified by mutual fund results—yet several unanswered questions remained. The 1963 Wharton study, and subsequent research by Friend and Vickers, did not adequately relate performance differences to risk. Treynor and Sharpe examined risk, but their work was not sufficiently comprehensive. A study was needed which analyzed the performance of a large number of mutual funds. Fortunately, investors did not have to wait long.

In 1968, Michael Jensen, building upon the theoretical models derived by Treynor and Sharpe, devised a measure for comparing fund performance across "different risk levels and across differing time periods irrespective of general economic and market conditions." Jensen used this measure to evaluate the "ability of the portfolio manager or security analyst to increase returns on the portfolio through successful prediction of future security prices. . . ." [132, p. 389] In seeking evidence of portfolio managers' predictive ability, Jensen studied the performance of 115 open-end mutual funds in the 1945–64 period. Jensen's measure of performance tested the managers' ability to forecast market behavior as well as price movements of individual issues. His findings are summarized as follows:

> . . . the mutual fund industry (as represented by these 115 funds) shows very little evidence of an ability to forecast security prices. Furthermore, there is surprisingly little evidence that indicates any individual funds in the sample might be able to forecast prices. . . .
>
> The evidence on mutual fund performance . . . indicates not only that these 115 mutual funds were on average not able to predict security prices well enough to outperform a buy-the-market-and-hold policy, but also that there is very little evidence that any individual fund was able to do significantly better than which we expected from mere random chance. It is also important to note that these conclusions hold even when we measure the fund returns gross of management expenses (that is, assume their bookkeeping, research, and other expenses except brokerage commissions were obtained free). Thus on average the funds apparently were not quite successful enough in their trading activities to recoup even their brokerage expenses.
>
> The evidence . . . indicate[s] . . . a pressing need on the part of the funds themselves to evaluate much more closely both the costs and the benefits of their research and trading

> activities in order to provide investors with maximum possible returns for the level of risk undertaken [132, pp. 414–15].

In a subsequent study, Jensen reported

> . . . mutual fund managers on the average are unable to forecast future security prices [133, p. 170]
>
> . . . it appears that on the average the resources spent by the funds in attempting to forecast security prices do not yield higher portfolio returns than those that could have been earned by equivalent risk portfolios selected (*a*) by random selection policies or (*b*) by combined investments in a "market portfolio" and government bonds. [133, p. 170]
>
> [Even though] analysts . . . operate in the securities markets every day and have wide-ranging contacts and associations in both the business and the financial communities . . . the fact [is] that they are apparently unable to forecast returns accurately enough to recover their research and transaction costs. . . . [133, p. 170]

In another study, John O'Brien evaluated the performance of 119 funds during the ten years spanning 1959–68. He concluded that "there are no more managers than predicted by chance occurrence either exceeding or failing to exceed the rate of return predicted for them based upon the level of uncertainty they assume." [208, p. 102]

One of the most extensive research studies of mutual fund performance and that of other institutional investors was published in August 1970 by three faculty members of the Wharton School. In this study Irwin Friend, Marshall Blume, and Jean Crockett reported on the performance of 299 leading funds for the years 1960 through 1968. These researchers reported that:

> The overall annual rates of return on investment in 136 mutual funds [essentially all the larger, publicly owned funds for which data were available] averaged 10.7 percent for the period January 1960, through June 1968 (9.0 percent for the period January 1960, through March 1964, and 12.8 percent for the period April 1964, through June 1968). Unweighted investment in all stocks listed on the Big Board in the same periods would have yielded 12.4 percent (7.0 percent in the first part and 17.8 percent in the second).
>
> * * * * *
>
> When funds were classified by fund size, charges, management expenses, portfolio turnover, and investment objectives, no consistent relationship was found between these factors and investment performance properly adjusted for risk. To the ex-

tent that a relationship exists between performance and sales charges, the funds with the lowest charges, including the "no-load" funds, appear to perform slightly better than the others.

* * * * *

The apparent absence of any consistent relationships between the nonrisk characteristics of mutual funds and their investment performance suggests that, for the industry as a whole, there may be no consistency in the performance of the same fund in successive periods. [103, pp. 19–21]

* * * * *

The performance analysis gave no indication that higher sales charges, management costs, or trading expenses are consistently linked with performance either above or below that of random portfolios. Because no clear payoff results from higher management and trading expenses, a new type of mutual fund and minimal management and trading may be desirable. Such a fund would resemble the fixed or semifixed trusts of former years. These trusts deliberately duplicated the performance of all NYSE stocks or of some other broad range of investments.

This new kind of fund would provide, at a minimal cost, the risk diversification which seems to be the most important continuing service rendered by today's mutual funds. The larger this fund might be, the smaller would be the relative management expenses, and the easier it would be to duplicate the performance of the entire market. Such large funds would become sufficiently well known to the investing public for their shares to be sold at commission rates appreciably lower than the sales loads now charged by mutual funds. [103, p. 23]

CONCLUSION

A long series of research studies dating from 1963 has sought to measure the performance of mutual funds. While the methodology has differed somewhat, the conclusions unanimously cast serious doubt on the "management" ability of mutual funds. Their performance has been no better than could be attained through random stock selection. Despite some debate on research technique, no substantial evidence indicates that mutual funds can outperform the workings of chance.

Chapter 16

Historical performance

In spite of the evidence supporting the existence of an "almost" efficient market, some investment managers do perform better than others. Clearly, when many people "play the game," some must win. Unfortunately, the winner's investment selection process is not necessarily responsible for his or her success. Suppose, for example, that all investment managers were to select their stocks in a completely random fashion—barring a tie, one manager would still outperform the others.

Investors hear much about so-and-so's "expert performance." But how much of the performance is luck, and how much is attributable to astute investment selection? To answer this question, we need to know something about (*a*) what is considered "average," and (*b*) expected variations from "average."

If thousands of investment managers each "randomly" selected one NYSE-traded stock, what results could be expected one year later? One might anticipate the performance of these managers' "selections" to parallel that of the market. It would also be expected, however, that many of these stocks would show widely divergent results, with some better, and others worse, than the average. The distribution of the performance of a large number of one-stock portfolios can be represented by the bell-shaped, or normal, curve shown in Figure 16–1.

An understanding of what can be expected from purely random stock selection provides an important benchmark against which to compare the results obtained by "skilled professionals." As Figure 16–1 shows, purely random selection of stocks produces a cluster of results around some average value. Also, purely by chance, some perform better, and some perform worse, than others.

FIGURE 16–1: Expected distribution of performance for many separate one-stock portfolios

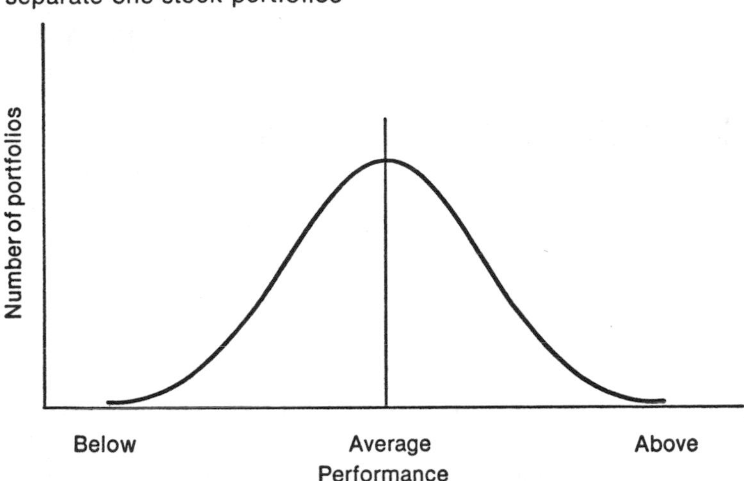

STANDARD DEVIATION

Because the concept of "standard deviation" plays an important role throughout MPT, the salient characteristics of this popular statistical measure should be thoroughly understood. A standard deviation is a measure of variability around a mean (i.e., a mathematical "average"). If it is assumed that the observations of a given characteristic, or value, cluster around the mean in a "normal" fashion, the computed standard deviation has a very convenient property: 68 percent of the values will fall within one standard deviation (plus or minus) from the mean; 95.5 percent of the values will be within two standard deviations from the mean; and 99.7 percent of the values will fall within three standard deviations from the mean.

Because 68 percent is very close to two thirds (66.7 percent), a convenient "rule of thumb" is that the chances are two out of three that an expected value will fall within one standard deviation (plus or minus) of the mean. The key point to remember is that the smaller the standard deviation, the greater is the probability of achieving the expected or "average," result. In turn, a higher likelihood of some average expectation being realized goes hand in hand with a reduction in the standard deviation.

DIVERSIFICATION—AN INTRODUCTION

Suppose that thousands of investment managers were each to buy two-stock portfolios, again using random selection. It would be expected that the average performance of the two-stock investors would again equal that of the overall market, but also that their results should cluster more tightly around that average. Fewer two-stock portfolios would demonstrate the extreme returns exhibited by some one-stock portfolios.

What causes the differing distributions in Figure 16–2? The results for the two-stock investors—the same average performance, but with less variation—do not reflect more accurate forecasts of the market. The investors in this case still could not, on the average, beat the market. They were, however, able to avoid large negative variations through diversification (discussed more fully in Chapter 18). If this example were carried further, it would be shown that holding an increasing number of stocks tends to yield results which increasingly approach the market average. In turn, this market average provides a benchmark against which to measure the *value* of professional investment management.

FIGURE 16–2: Performance outcomes from random selection of one-stock and two-stock portfolios

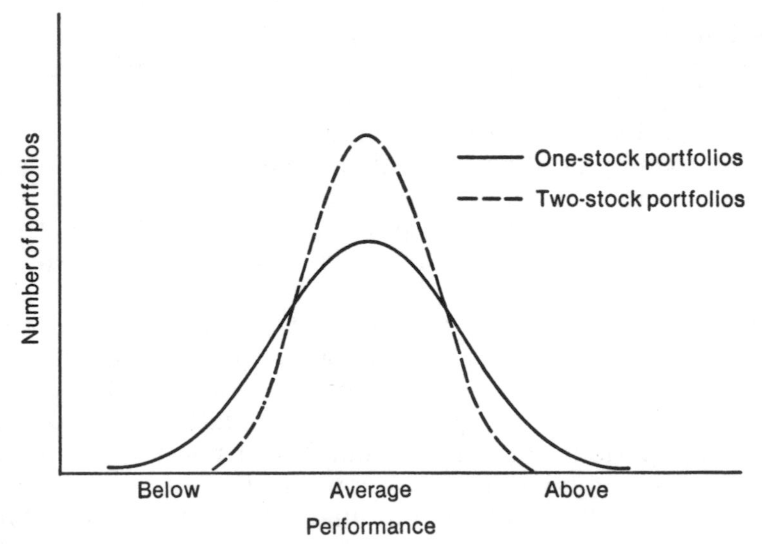

FISHER AND LORIE

The first comprehensive study of the stock market's long-term rate of return was conducted by Lawrence Fisher and James Lorie [91] at the University of Chicago during the mid-1960s. Using an extensive computer-readable file, Fisher and Lorie determined the historical rate of return of all NYSE common stocks between 1926 and 1960. Fisher and Lorie calculated what would have happened if one had held all stocks traded on the NYSE during 22 different, but overlapping, periods between January 1926 and December 1960. Most of the rates of return they reported were greater than 10 percent compounded annually, although the year-to-year returns ranged from a negative 48 percent to a positive 17 percent.

In a subsequent article, Fisher reported the results of an elaborate study of random investments in common stocks. The earlier work, published jointly by Fisher and Lorie, studied all stocks in composite for the specified periods. Fisher's later investigation sought to determine how well an investor would have done by holding individual NYSE stocks. The stocks selected were randomly chosen, as were the buy and sell dates (that is, as though the investor had thrown darts at both stock listings and calendars as the basis for the selections and holding periods).

Fisher generated, by computer, the investment results for multiple combinations of purchases and sales of individual stocks for which data were available. For the 1,715 common stocks in his study, 56,557,538 combinations of stocks and holding periods were tabulated. These results (allowing for brokerage commissions) are shown in Figure 16–3.

Figure 16–3 reveals that annual rates of return exhibited a marked central tendency, or "normal" grouping about the average. Taking brokerage commissions-into account, Fisher reported that "78 percent of the time common stocks yielded a positive net return. Over two thirds of the time, the rate of return exceeded 5 percent . . . [and] the median rate of return was 9.8 percent. . . . Nearly one-fifth of the time, the rate of return exceeded 20 percent per annum, compounded annually." [89, pp. 153–54]

Other conclusions by Fisher are worth noting. The variability of rates of return was much greater for short-term investments than for long-term positions. On the average, the probability of a gain on a long-term investment was greater than 78 percent. Furthermore, "long-term" holdings of more than one

FIGURE 16–3: Frequency distribution of rates of return on investment in each common stock listed on the New York Stock Exchange, 1926–1960, using all possible combinations of month-end purchase and sale dates (based on 56,557,538 cases)

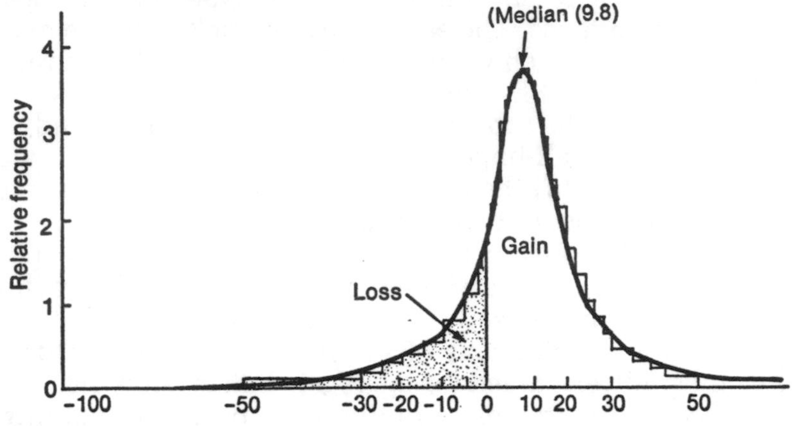

Source: Fisher [89, p. 54].

stock at a time would have yielded, on the average, positive returns far more than 78 percent of the time and, in fact, would have generated returns in excess of 9.8 percent per annum substantially more than half the time. [89, p. 159]

Fisher's work is highly significant. By investing in the most random, haphazard fashion imaginable, an investor would have profited 78 percent of the time during the periods studied. Portfolios of many stocks would be expected to be profitable an even larger percentage of the time. Further, Fisher has shown that risk, or the variation in rates of return, is much greater for short-term investments. Investments held for several years were much less likely to produce absolute losses. Fisher also calculated that the average rate of return, compounded annually, for NYSE common stocks was almost 9.8 percent per annum. In short, using stock price charts, fundamental analysis, or Ouija boards, an investor could have expected to do this well!

Fisher and Lorie's early and now classic studies on average rates of return thus provided important benchmarks for evaluating investment performance. Their finding that the average compounded annual rate of return from NYSE com-

mon stocks was 9.8 percent over the period studied may well be one of the best remembered and most frequently quoted of all investment statistics.

Their more recent studies, however, are of significantly greater importance. The early research dealt with the *average* rates of return which would have been compiled from random investment in NYSE-listed common stocks—*without any indication of risk.* In subsequent research [93] Fisher and Lorie recognized the all-important dimension of risk by providing information on (*a*) the distributions (i.e., riskiness) of returns and (*b*) the effect of diversification on reducing risk.

Specifically, Fisher and Lorie conducted three extensive studies on the variability of returns on investments in common stocks listed on the New York Stock Exchange. One study examined the distributions of returns on *individual* stocks. A second study examined the aggregated distributions of returns on *fixed-size portfolios* of individual stocks over holding periods ranging from 1 to 20 years. A third study examined returns from *different size portfolios* (containing from as few as 6 stocks to as many as 128 stocks).

They found that in general, returns[1] increased with the length of the holding period. These results, while not surprising, verify the precept of MPT that risk increases with the uncertainty of time. They confirm that investors are indeed risk averse and demand (and hence, through their market action, attain) higher rates of return for longer holding periods. (The significance of these findings is discussed in Chapters 19–26.)

Of major importance to other researchers were Fisher and Lorie's observations of positive skewness (relating to the fact that one can occasionally earn more than 100 percent on an investment). Fisher and Lorie also verified this author's (see Hagin [116]) observations of an abnormally high number of very large returns. In their second study, Fisher and Lorie aggregated the distributions. This aggregation, much like tallying the results of a roulette wheel, has provided important information on the historical risk of various investment strategies. With this data, we can ask questions such as, "How frequently would one have realized a gain of more than 20% on an investment in a single randomly selected stock that was held for a randomly selected calendar year between 1946 and 1965?"

---

[1] Fisher and Lorie defined "return" by means of "wealth ratios" (the ratio of the value of an investment at the end of a period to the amount invested).

Another important part of their research has dealt with how increasing the number of stocks in a portfolio can reduce the variability of returns—an important topic which will also be discussed in Chapters 19–26.

Fisher and Lorie's largest tabulation of historical investment results, *A Half Century of Returns on Stocks and Bonds,* was published in 1977. In all, 51 tables provide comparative rates of return on portfolios of NYSE stocks and U.S. Treasury securities, as well as their performance in relation to changes in the Consumer Price Index.

Tables 16–1 and 16–2 have been abstracted from this mass of data in order to contrast the inflation-adjusted returns for

TABLE 16–1: Returns from all NYSE common stocks with equal initial weighting and dividends reinvested (tax-exempt)

	If held until the end of 1976 and purchased at end of				
	1950	*1955*	*1960*	*1965*	*1970*
Current dollars	11.0%	9.4%	9.6%	6.7%	7.1%
Deflated by CPI	7.5	5.5	5.1	1.0	0.5

Source: Fisher and Lorie [94, pp. 24–27].

TABLE 16–2: Returns from holding short-term U.S. Treasury bonds and notes with interest reinvested (tax exempt)

	If held until the end of 1976 and purchased at end of				
	1950	*1955*	*1960*	*1965*	*1970*
Current dollars	3.9%	4.4%	4.7%	5.6%	6.9%
Deflated by CPI	0.6	0.6	0.5	0.0	0.3

Source: Fisher and Lorie [94, pp. 136–37].

common stocks with those on short-term government securities. The period covers the 26-year span from the last trading day of 1950 until the close of 1976. The first line of Table 16–1 shows annualized rates of return that would have been realized by a tax-exempt investor who reinvested all dividends on the assumption that an equal amount had been invested in each of the NYSE common stocks at the beginning of each

designated period. The next line shows annual rates of return *after inflation* (but still before taxes)!

Thus, Table 16–1 shows that over the 26 years from the end of 1950 to the close of 1976, the real (after inflation) annual total return (dividends plus capital appreciation) would have averaged 7.5 percent per year. However, in the more recent 11-year period spanning the end of 1965 to the end of 1976, the real (after inflation) annual rate of return for common stocks averaged only 1.0 percent.

Table 16–2 presents an even more startling picture. *Over the 26-year period from the end of 1950 to the end of 1976, the real (after inflation) return from short-term U.S. Treasury securities has never averaged more than 0.6 percent* (6/10 *of 1 percent*) *per year.*

Clearly, over the "long run," common stocks have provided a superior real rate of return. This is totally consistent with the forthcoming discussion of how one would *expect* assets to be priced. Clearly, common stocks are riskier than short-term government securities. Thus, the only incentive to buy common stocks is that in the "long run," investors should be compensated for the additional risk through higher returns.

Obviously, "the long run" is not a very precise time period. As the famous economist John Maynard Keynes said, "the long run is when we are all dead." Nonetheless, the relationship between risk and long-term average returns is crucial. The only inducement for buying common stocks is that the market's pricing mechanism, over time, will reward investors through higher long-run average returns. Conversely, investors in common stocks should be aware of their riskiness—their likely short-term deviations from the long-run expectation.

Viewed from this perspective, the statistics shown in Tables 16–1 and 16–2 are not at all surprising. They reflect the fact that returns from common stock investments have been both higher and more volatile than those on short-term government securities.

Chapter 17

Expected returns and variance

A market performance study co-written by Roger Ibbotson at the University of Chicago and Rex Sinquefield at the American National Bank and Trust Company of Chicago has attracted considerable attention since its publication in 1977. Basically, Ibbottson and Sinquefield

1. Calculated historical returns and variances during the period 1926–77 for common stocks, long-term U.S. government bonds, long-term corporate bonds, U.S. Treasury bills, and the inflation rate (based on the Consumer Price Index), and
2. Simulated probabilities, future returns, and variances for each of these asset classes for the period 1977–2000.

HISTORICAL RETURNS

Ibbotson and Sinquefield's data on the returns of common stock were derived from a historical analysis of the Standard and Poor's (S&P) Composite Index. This is a market-value weighted index, which means that the weight given each stock corresponds to the market value of that company's outstanding shares. (Although the S&P Composite includes the 500 U.S. stocks with the largest market value, prior to March 1957, the index consisted of 90 of the largest stocks. Nonetheless, the value-weighted data used by Ibbotson and Sinquefield constitute a reasonable proxy for the overall market.)

Figure 17–1 shows comparative growth rates (including capital gains plus dividends or interest income) for three asset classes and inflation (measured by the Consumer Price Index) over a 52-year period. In each case it is assumed that $1 was invested at the end of 1925. Since the vertical scale is

FIGURE 17–1: Comparative growth for inflation and three asset classes, 1926–1977 (assumed initial investment of $1.00 at year-end 1925, includes reinvestment of income without taxes or transaction costs)

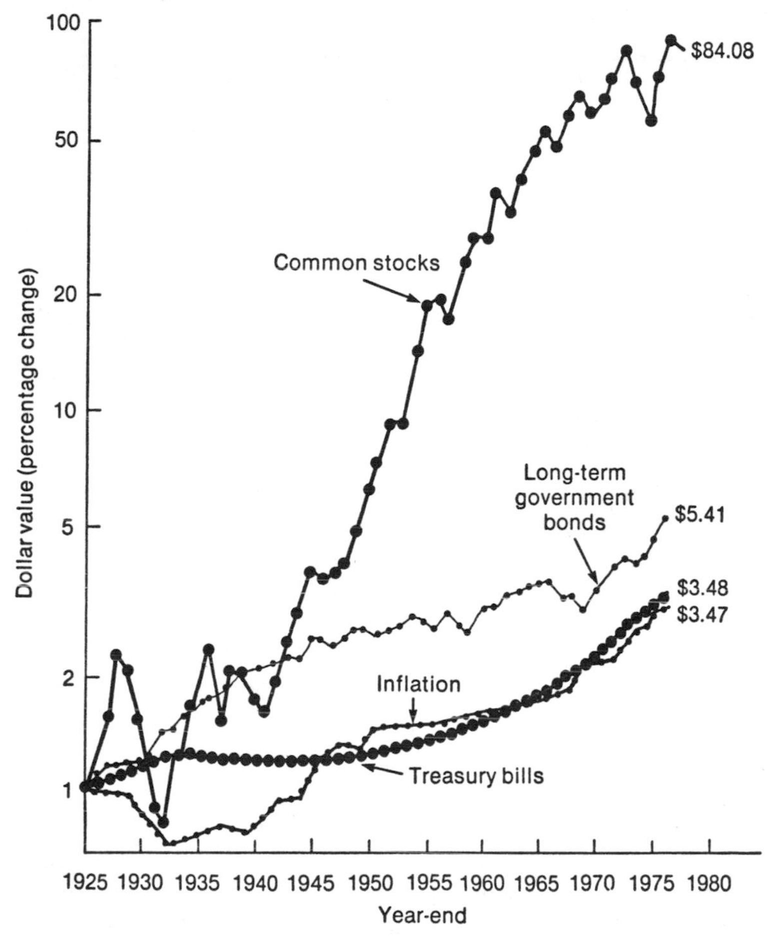

Source: Ibbotson and Sinquefield [127, p. 3].

logarithmic, equal vertical distances represent equal percentage changes.

Figure 17–1 dramatizes the relatively superior long-term performance of common stocks. Specifically, if $1.00 had been invested at year-end 1925 and all subsequent dividends were reinvested (without being taxed and without transaction costs), the $1.00 investment would have been worth $84.08 at year-end 1977. By comparison, at the close of 1977, a dollar put into long-term (20-year) government bonds would be

worth only $5.41—having grown only about one-fifteenth as rapidly as common stocks during the identical period.

Possibly the most discouraging trend portrayed by Figure 17–1 is the difference between the *real* and *nominal* rates of return for U.S. Treasury bills. (A *real* rate of return is an inflation-adjusted return; while a *nominal* return refers only to the pure, unadjusted numerical value). On a nominal (unadjusted) basis, a $1.00 investment in U.S. Treasury bills would have grown to $3.48 over the 52-year period. Inflation took its toll, however. Based on the Consumer Price Index, $3.47 would be necessary at the end of 1977 to equal the purchasing power of $1.00 in 1925. This means that after 52 years, the real (inflation-adjusted) return on an investment in U.S. Treasury bills would have been a paltry $0.01 (still before taxes and costs to reinvest the interest).

Looking only at returns provides just half of the picture. The other key dimension is risk. Before examining the data on the comparative risk of each of the asset classes studied by Ibbotson and Sinquefield, the conceptual difference between an *arithmetic* and a *geometric* mean should be clearly understood.

Consider the following two-year performance record:

Year	*Performance (percentage change)*	*Year-end value of $1*
0	—	$1.00
1	+50%	1.50
2	−50	0.75

What is the average performance? Arithmetically, the average of +50 percent and −50 percent is 0 percent. Yet, a computed average change of zero seems inconsistent with the fact that the initial $1.00 is now worth $0.75. This is the reason for including the geometric mean when reporting average performance. This mean indicates the average annual rate of return which, when compounded annually, would produce the final result. In the above case, the geometric mean is −13.4 percent.[1] Thus, the two-year performance record using the geometric mean would be as follows:

[1] Readers interested in the formula for the calculation of the geometric mean are referred to Ibbotson and Sinquefield [127, p. 8].

Year	Performance (geometric mean)	Year-end value of $1
0	—	$1.00
1	−13.4%	0.87
2	−13.4	0.75

In practice, both measures are useful. When results for a single period are considered, the arithmetic mean is generally used. When the average performance over more than one period is computed, the geometric mean is used.

Returning to the Ibbotson and Sinquefield study, Table 17–1 summarizes the geometric means, the arithmetic means, and

TABLE 17–1: Total annual returns, 1926–1976

Series	Geometric means (percent)	Arithmetic mean (percent)	Standard deviation (percent)
Common stocks	9.2%	11.6%	22.4%
Long-term corporate bonds	4.1	4.2	5.6
Long-term government bonds	3.4	3.5	5.8
U.S. Treasury bonds	2.4	2.4	2.1
Inflation	2.3	2.4	4.8

Source: Ibbotson and Sinquefield [127, p. 10].

the standard deviation (corresponding to the arithmetic mean) for the total returns (with dividends and interest reinvested) for each of five series for the period 1926–76.[2]

The data in Table 17–1 indicate that over the 51-year period spanning 1926 and 1976, stocks returned an average of 9.2 percent per year (compounded annually). During the same period, U.S. Treasury bills returned an average of 2.4 percent, while the Consumer Price Index grew at a nearly offsetting compounded annual rate of 2.3 percent!

These data reveal that while common stocks outperformed other classes of assets, their returns were far more volatile. The standard deviation of common stock annual returns was 22.4 percent. This means that in approximately two out of every

[2] The data illustrated in Figure 17–1 show data through 1977—reflecting the *partial* update (available from the Financial Analysts Research Foundation) of the more complete study that is tabulated in Table 17–1 for the period 1926–76.

three years the return was between −13.2 percent and +31.6 percent (as shown earlier in Figure 14–2).

EQUITY RISK PREMIUM

A concept which will be developed more fully in Chapters 19–26 is that capital markets are dominated by risk-averse investors. Investors could invest solely in risk-free assets such as U.S. Treasury bills. For investors to be persuaded to buy common stocks, they must anticipate higher returns. More specifically, this "excess" return (i.e., the return in excess of the risk-free rate) must be high enough to compensate investors for the assumption of the risk entailed in common stock investments.

The difference between the rate of return available from risk-free assets (such as U.S. Treasury bills) and that on common stocks is called the *equity risk premium*. It is the net return from investing in common stocks rather than U.S. Treasury bills.

This relationship is illustrated by the capital market line shown in Figure 17–2. If an investor assumes no market risk,

FIGURE 17–2: Capital market line

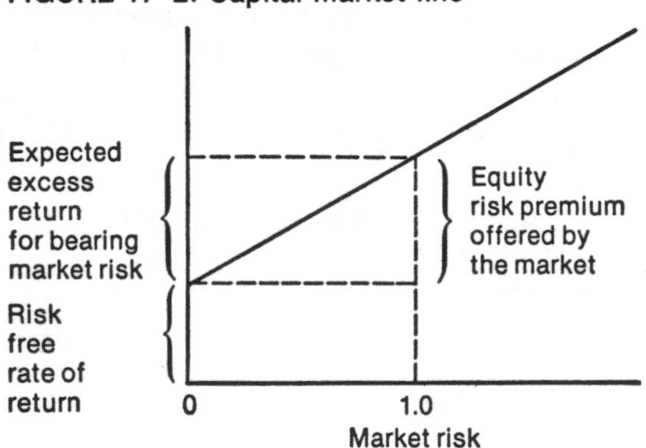

represented by the zero point on the horizontal axis, that investor can obtain the prevailing risk-free rate of return. If an investor invests in the market (i.e., with an investment in all stocks in proportion to their capitalization), represented by 1.0 on the horizontal axis, that investor must *expect* a return that is in excess of the return available without market risk. Otherwise, there would be no reason to invest in the market!

Historical data for the equity risk premium are shown in Table 17–2. (Because of year-to-year compounding effects, the values for the annual equity risk premiums are not precisely equal to the simple differences between the two basic annual returns).

TABLE 17–2: Total annual returns, 1926–1976

Series	*Geometric mean (percent)*	*Arithmetic mean (percent)*	*Standard deviation (percent)*
Equity risk premium	6.7%	9.2%	22.6%

Source: Ibbotson and Sinquefield [127, p. 19].

SIMULATING THE FUTURE

To simulate probabilistic distributions of *future* returns for the period 1977 to 2000, Ibbotson and Sinquefield combined their historical data on the distributions of various rates of return with information on the term structure of interest rates (discussed in Chapter 30). Their simulated inflation figures are shown in Figure 17–3. This study projects the compounded inflation rate to average 5.4 percent over the period 1977–2000 (compared with the historical average annual inflation rate of 2.3 percent over the period 1926–76). Further, according to this study, there is a 5 percent probability (indicated by the

FIGURE 17–3: Inflation—Simulated rate distributions, 1977–2000 (geometric average annual rates)

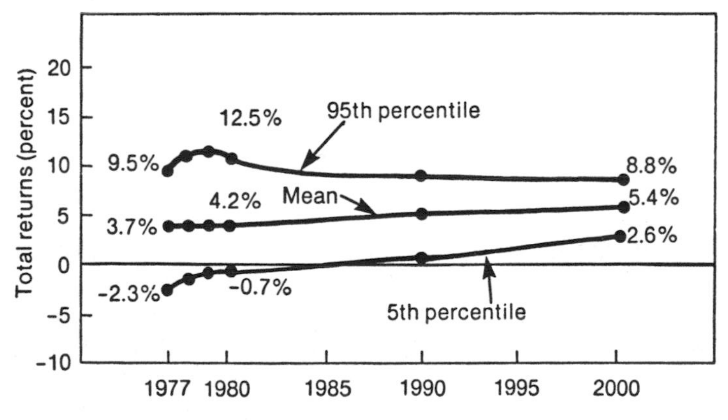

Source: Ibbotson and Sinquefield [127, p. 53].

95th percentile) that, over the length of the forecast period, the inflation rate will average more than 8.8 percent and a 5 percent chance that it will average less than 2.6 percent. On a shorter time horizon, such as the 1977–80 period, the range of probable outcomes is much wider.

Figure 17-4 shows the simulated total return distributions. Specifically, the expected nominal (before inflation) return on

FIGURE 17–4: Common stocks—Simulated total return distributions, 1977–2000 (geometric average annual rates)

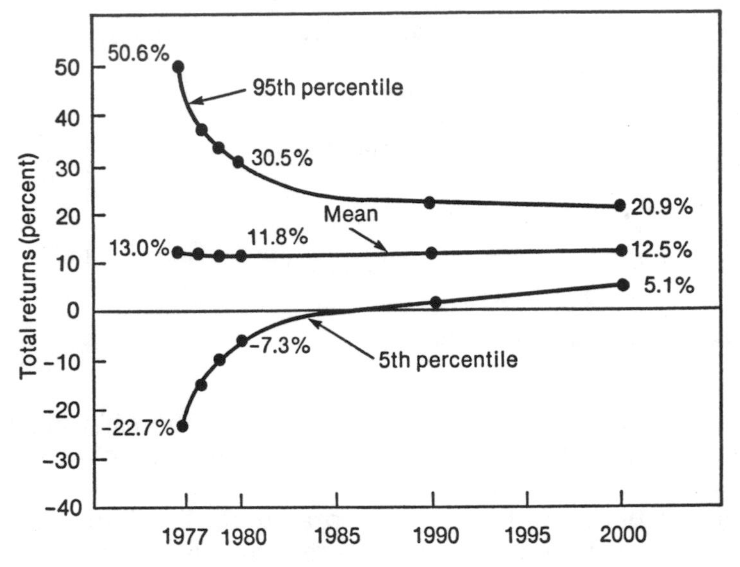

Source: Ibbotson and Sinquefield [127, p. 49].

common stocks for the period is 12.5 percent per year compounded. There is a 5 percent probability that, over the length of the forecast period, the nominal returns will average in excess of 20.9 percent per year. There is also a 5 percent probability that, over the period, the nominal return will average less than 5.1 percent per year. Again, on a shorter time horizon, such as the 1977 to 1980 period, the range of probable outcomes is much wider.

Figure 17–5 portrays the results of an inflation-adjusted simulation of common stock returns by Ibbotson and Sinquefield. Here the expected real (inflation-adjusted) compounded returns on common stocks for the period 1977–2000 work out to 6.8 percent per year. As before, the 95th and 5th

FIGURE 17–5: Common stocks, inflation adjusted—Simulated total return distributions, 1977–2000 (geometric average annual rates)

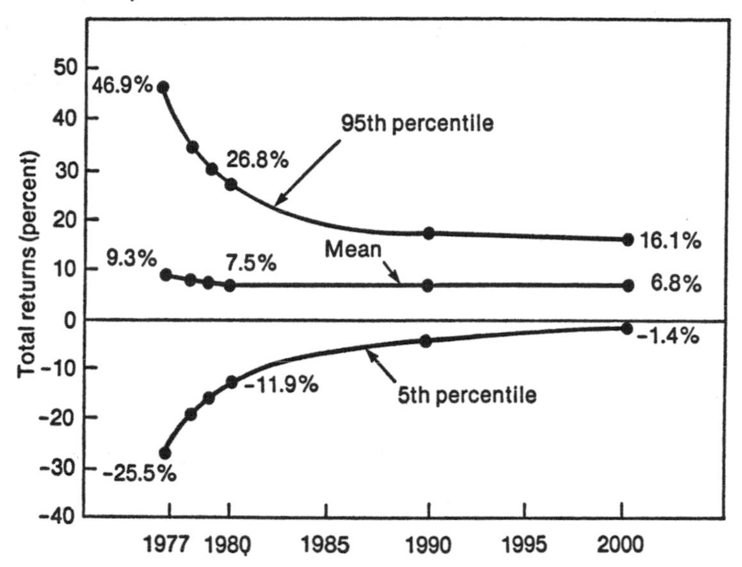

Source: Ibbotson and Sinquefield [127, p. 55].

percentile "funnels" define the range, over increasingly long time periods, within which 90 percent of the inflation-adjusted returns are expected to fall.

One problem with the data presented in Figures 17–3 through 17–5 is that the ever-decreasing width of the probabilistic bands wrongly implies a reduction in uncertainty over time. The graphic representations of the so-called stock and bond wealth indexes in Figures 17–6 and 17–7 illuminate this shortcoming. (A wealth index compares all investments on the assumption that they were worth $1.00 at year-end 1976).

Figure 17–6 shows the simulated distribution of the nominal wealth index for the period 1977–2000. According to this forecast, an investment of $1.00 in common stocks at year-end 1976 will be worth $27.04 at year-end 2000. The dispersion of the simulated results around the mean, or expected value of $27.04, shows that there is a 5 percent probability that in the year 2000 the $1.00 could be worth more than $95.91 and a 5 percent probability that it could be worth $3.27 or less.

Figure 17–7 shows the simulated distribution of the real (inflation-adjusted) wealth index for long-term corporate

FIGURE 17–6: Common stocks—Simulated distributions of nominal wealth index, 1977–2000 (year-end 1976 equals $1.00)

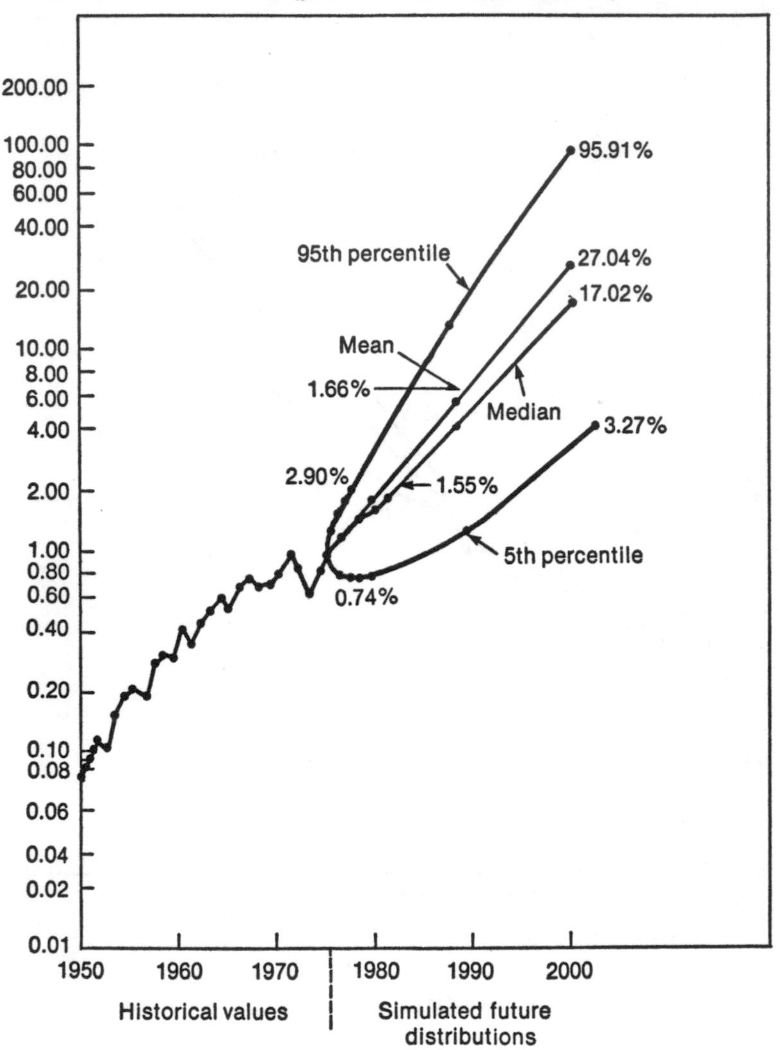

Source: Ibbotson and Sinquefield [127, p. 48].

bonds over the period 1977–2000. Under the forecast, an investment of $1.00 at year-end 1976 has an inflation-adjusted expected value of $6.10 at year-end 2000. Similarly, the simulated results indicate a 5 percent probability that in the year 2000, the $1.00 could be worth more than 9.44 times the initial inflation-adjusted investment. Also, there is a 5 percent proba-

FIGURE 17–7: Long-term corporate bonds—Simulated distributions of wealth index, 1977–2000 (year-end 1976 equals $1.00)

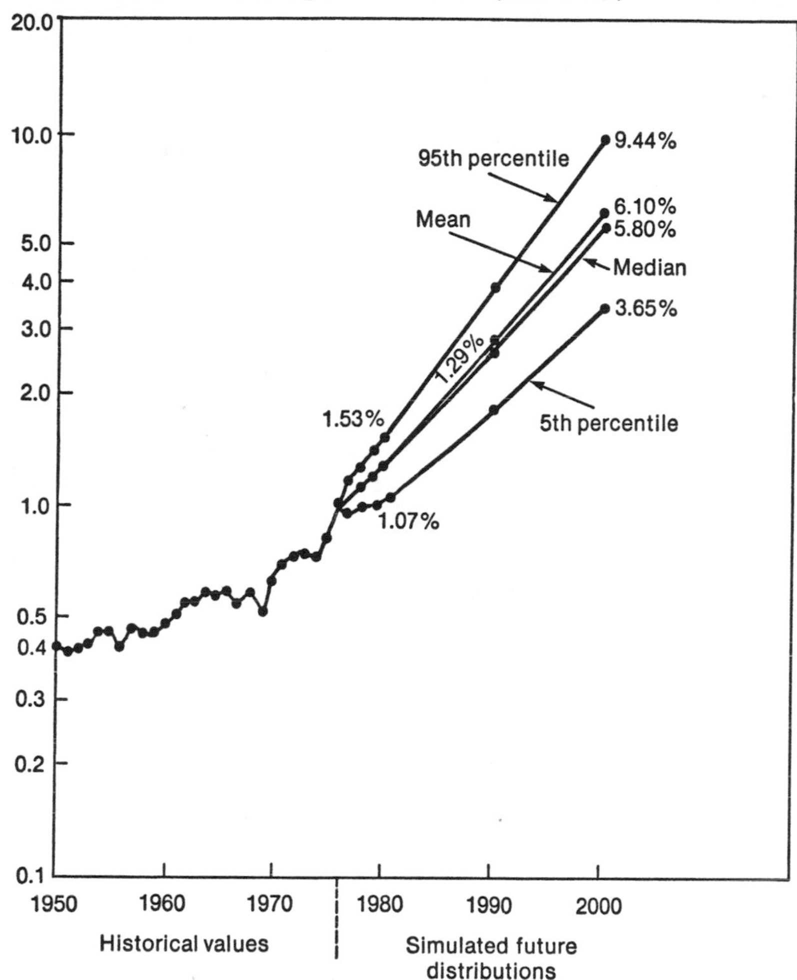

Source: Ibbotson and Sinquefield [127, p. 50].

bility that the inflation-adjusted value of the investment will be worth less than 3.65 times the initial inflation-adjusted amount.

These notions of expected returns will be used in subsequent chapters to provide an important perspective on forward-looking portfolio risk. Before that, however, it is important to understand the relationship between risk and diversification.

Chapter 18

Diversification

Broadly speaking, there are two categories of investors—those who prefer to concentrate their holdings, and those who would rather diversify. Investors who concentrate their assets in a relatively small number of issues typically reason that they can better focus their attention on a limited group of stocks. Conversely, other investors believe that it is difficult to do a consistently better than average job of investment selection. Members of this group typically diversify their holdings among a wide variety of stocks so as to achieve approximately the market's average rate of return.

A BYGONE ERA—PORTFOLIO CONCENTRATION

Most of the "go-go" performers of the 1960s relied on the concentration approach. In this "star" era, those managers with "genius for picking stocks" generated such demand for certain stocks that their recommendations became selffulfilling prophecies and enhanced their reputations even further.

Today's perspective reveals that the go-go investments of the 1960s were concentrated in high-risk glamour stocks. Individually, these stocks would be expected to do well in rising markets and poorly in downturns. Also, portfolios which mainly consisted of a few basically similar companies could be expected to undergo severe declines during a general market downturn—because of the absence of meaningful diversification. This indeed proved to be the case. The supermen of the go-go era ultimately encountered a special kind of kryptonite—a falling market for their glamour stocks.

THE OTHER WAY TO PLAY THE GAME—DIVERSIFY

Many successful investors have adopted the opposite philosophy of diversification. One of the wealthiest and shrewdest investors to espouse a philosophy of diversification was the famous Texan Clint Murchison, Sr. After a roaring start in wildcat oil drilling in the 1920s, Murchison started to diversify his holdings. At one point he was said to control 115 companies stretching from Canada to South America. Murchison undoubtedly had an awareness of industrial and national market "comovements" and protected himself against them through diversification. His philosophy on diversification was a simple one: "Money is like manure—when it stacks up, it stinks; when you spread it around, it makes things grow."

The rationale for stock market diversification is that the overall risk from owning many stocks is lower than the risk of holding a few stocks. The fewer stocks held, the greater the injury if one issue does poorly. The effect of diversification in reducing the overall risk of a portfolio was studied extensively by Jack Gaumnitz [106] in his doctoral dissertation at Stanford University in 1967. Gaumnitz found that until the number of independently chosen securities in a portfolio reached 18, significant reductions in overall risk could be derived by holding more securities.

In 1968, John Evans also studied the effects of diversification in his doctoral dissertation at the University of Washington. Evans randomly constructed 2,400 portfolios which were composed of from 1 to 60 stocks. His findings which are summarized in Figure 18–1, are important.

Evans' calculations show that a portfolio with maximum diversification (that is, equal dollar amounts in all stocks studied) would be expected to have a rate of return fluctuation (hence, risk) of 11.9 percent during a six-month period. Yet, if the investor held only one stock, a six-month variation in the rate of return of approximately 20.5 percent could be expected.

The startling part of Evans' research is what can be expected when an investor places equal dollar amounts in portfolios consisting of two, three, four, five, and ten securities, respectively. Notice in Figure 18–1 that the additional reduction in risk is relatively minor as one moves from a portfolio containing 10 securities to one containing 20 or even 40 securities. In fact, a randomly selected portfolio with equal dollar amounts in just five stocks has only slightly more risk than a portfolio with equal dollar amounts invested in all of Evans's stocks.

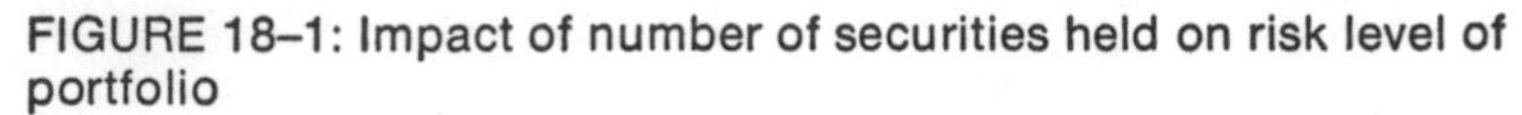
FIGURE 18–1: Impact of number of securities held on risk level of portfolio

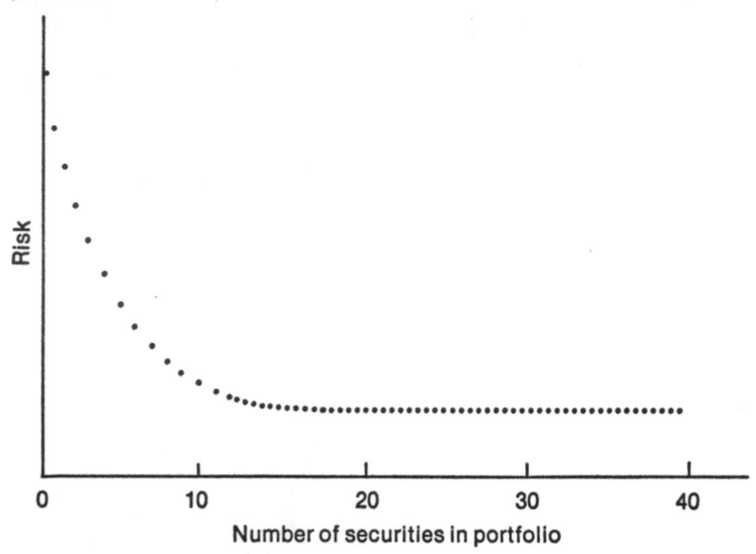

Source: Evans [67, p. 765].

Thus, the importance of portfolio management lies not in the number of holdings, but rather in both the nature and degree of the combined risk of the underlying stocks. Brealey [34] has shown quite dramatically what can happen when one considers both the nature and degree of risk in portfolio composition. He reported that a portfolio containing only 11 securities, which were carefully selected for their risk-diversifying characteristics, would be less risky than a portfolio of 2,000 securities which were selected without regard to risk.

CONCLUSION

A prudent investor must have serious reservations about both the inherent usefulness of traditional forms of security analysis and the ability of investment managers who use these techniques to attain consistent above-average performance. This does *not* mean, however, that prudent investors should disassociate themselves from the stock market. There is strong evidence that there is merit in using diversification to control risk while predicting the collective behavior of groups of securities.

PART THREE

MPT: CONCEPTUAL FOUNDATION

Chapter 19

Capital asset pricing model

In this chapter, two key concepts—efficient capital markets and risk premiums—are brought together in the *capital asset pricing model* (CAPM).

The concept of an efficient capital market leads to the conclusion that prices cannot be expected to diverge "by much" or "for long" from the consensus view of an equitable rate of return for a given level of risk. The rationale of a risk premium is basically that investors must be paid to take any risk above that of a "riskless" investment.

The classical example of a riskless investment is a short-term obligation of the U.S. government. Since the government can always print money, there is no dollar risk with such an instrument. This is not, of course, a truly riskless investment. Any investment which returns a fixed number of dollars is subject to the risks inherent in the fluctuations of the future purchasing power of the dollar. For the time being, however, the notion of purchasing-power risk will be set aside. Unless noted, "risk" will be used in the narrow sense of the dollar risk inherent in market- and company-related investments.

According to the CAPM, investors who select a risk-free investment (such as short-term government securities) can expect to be compensated for the use of their money, but not for market- or company-related risk. This riskless compensation can be thought of as the amount which the government is willing to pay to "rent" money. As such, it is the "pure" (risk-free) interest rate.

Other investors, however, opt for risky investments, including common stocks. Such investors logically expect a higher rate of return as compensation for the risk that they assume. As discussed earlier, the difference between the risk-free rate of return and the total return from a risky investment is called a

risk premium. The capital asset pricing model provides the framework for determining the relationship between risk and return and the amount of the risk premium.

LINEAR RELATIONSHIPS: A KEY PART OF MPT

Since many of the relationships that are examined within the context of MPT are linear in nature, it may be worthwhile to review a little high school math, specifically, the *formula for a straight line.* The basic (zero intercept) equation for a line is

$$Y = \text{Slope}\,X$$

where the *slope* describes the relationship between the two variables. Graphically

$$\text{Slope} = \frac{\text{Units of vertical ``rise''}}{\text{Units of horizontal ``run''}}$$

Using the formula, it is possible to develop explicit definitions of the relationships shown by the lines in Figure 19–1. Inspection of the slope of line *d* shows, for example, that for each

FIGURE 19–1: Linear relationships with a zero intercept

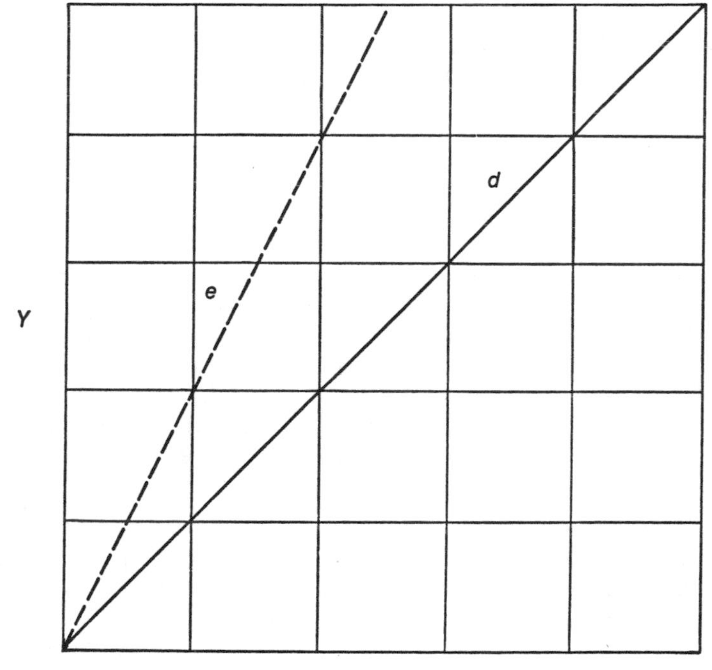

unit of vertical "rise" there is one unit of horizontal "run." Thus, the formula for line d is

$$Y = 1X$$

This means that according to the relationship described by this line, for each unit increase in X there will be a corresponding unit increase in Y. The slope of line e characterizes a relationship between the two variables in which two units of vertical "rise" correspond to one unit of horizontal "run." Thus, the slope of line e (the rise of 2 divided by a run of 1) equals 2. Therefore, the formula for line e is

$$Y = 2X$$

That is, $2X$ is the number of units that Y will increase by for each unit increase in X.

Using the more general form, the equation for a line (with a zero intercept) is

$$Y = bX$$

where b denotes the slope of the line. Note that the greater the value of b, the more rapid the rise of the line.

Figure 19–2 illustrates lines where zero units of X do not

FIGURE 19–2: Linear relationships with a nonzero intercept

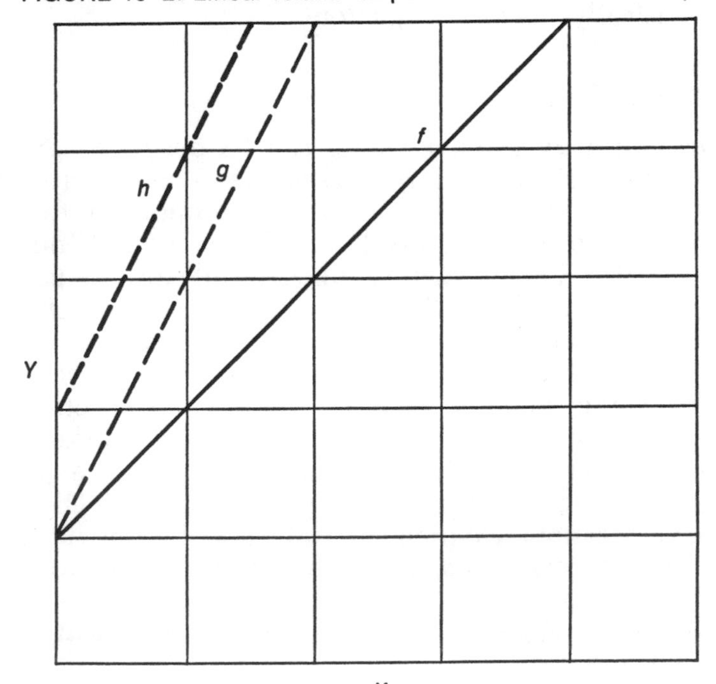

correspond to zero units of Y; i.e., relationships in which the vertical intercept is not zero. To describe these lines, we can use the most general form of the equation for a straight line

$$Y = a + bX$$

where a is the intercept on the vertical axis and b is the slope. Thus, the formula for line f is

$$Y = 1 + 1X$$

The formula for line g is

$$Y = 1 + 2X$$

The formula for line h is

$$Y = 2 + 2X$$

Moving from the general equation to describe a linear relationship between two variables, X and Y

$$Y = a + bX$$

to the equation which represents the linear relationship between a security's expected return and the market's return (discussed in forthcoming sections),

Security's expected return = alpha + beta (market return)

we find basically the same equation!

CAPITAL MARKET LINE

The capital asset pricing model can be portrayed graphically by means of the *capital market line.* Theoretically, the "market" encompasses all securities in proportion to their market value; however, in practice, value-weighted indexes, such as the NYSE or the S&P Composite indexes, are used as proxies for the "market." Given the assumption of an efficient capital market, the pricing of the market portfolio, at any point in time, accurately reflects an equilibrium relationship between the market's consensus of risk and expected return.

Figure 19–3 graphically depicts the capital market line, which represents the relationship between risk and expected return underlying the capital asset pricing model.[1] The horizontal axis measures risk (defined as the standard deviation of return). The vertical axis measures expected return. Note that

[1] For consistency, the notation used here, and in other diagrams, is the same as that of Sharpe [252].

FIGURE 19–3: Capital market line

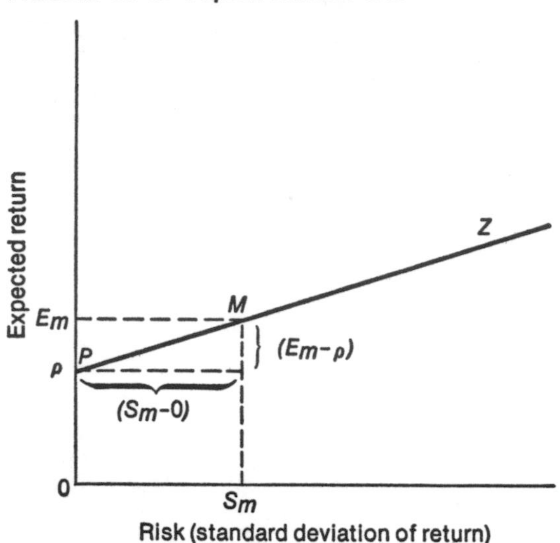

Where

S_m—Standard deviation of market return.
ρ—Riskless rate of interest.
E_m—Expected return of market portfolio.
M—Market portfolio.

and

PMZ—Capital market line.
Slope—Reward per unit of risk borne.

when risk is zero, the expected return is ρ—the riskless rate of interest (return). Note also that the risk of holding the market portfolio (S_m) corresponds to the expected return of the market portfolio (E_m). The difference between the expected return of the market portfolio (E_m) and the expected riskless rate of return (ρ) is the risk premium for the market portfolio.

By assuming that both lending and borrowing are used (explained in detail in Chapter 22), it is possible to select combinations of riskless and risky investments which will plot along line *PMZ*—the capital market line. The slope of the capital market line (the difference between the expected return on the market portfolio and the expected riskless rate of return, divided by the difference in their risks) can be thought of as the expected reward per unit of risk.

Chapter 20

Balancing risk and return

The prudent application of MPT requires significant departures from the "old school" investment selection processes. The most fundamental of these changes is the shift in emphasis from examining the characteristics of individual investments toward the analysis of investments within the context of a complete, appropriately designed portfolio.

MPT has demonstrated that the investment selection process requires far more than just assembling a portfolio of what we believe to be the "best" available securities. Similarly, MPT has shown us that portfolio evaluation should go far beyond simply determining, and then summing, the characteristics of the individual component securities. MPT has demonstrated that investors undertaking either the construction or analysis of portfolios must address the *relationships* between the individual securities which comprise the aggregate portfolio.

RELATIONSHIPS BETWEEN SECURITIES

The relationships between securities which make up a portfolio are easy to understand but difficult to measure. It is obvious to most people, for example, that holding two substantially different securities is less risky than holding a single security. If two quite different securities are held and one suddenly turns "sour," there is a chance that the second security, possibly in a different industry, will turn in an offsetting "good" performance.

But what *is* the chance? The answer to this question depends on the degree to which the two securities can be expected to move together. One would not expect, for example, the same degree of offsetting performance from a two-stock

portfolio drawn from the airline industry, as from a two-stock portfolio representing two widely different sectors of the economy.

Most portfolio managers are intuitively aware of the various kinds of market *comovements*—the tendency for certain stocks, or groups of stocks, to move in the same, or opposite, directions. It is a giant step, however, to move from this intuitive awareness of interrelationships between securities to the development of techniques to measure and forecast these interrelationships. Given the complexity of the problem, it is not surprising that the evolution from modern portfolio *theory*, to practical *applications*, to widespread *acceptance*, and to effective *use* by investment practitioners has spanned more than 25 years.

HARRY MARKOWITZ—THE FATHER OF MPT

The duration of the MPT evolution is best illustrated by the fact that Harry Markowitz (accurately referred to as the father of MPT) published the theoretical foundation for MPT in 1952. [185] In this now classic article, as well as a later book [186], Markowitz set forth the analytical process by which to measure the impact of diversification on risk. While it has taken many years to move from the theory espoused in the 1952 article to widespread acceptance and use by the investment community, Markowitz's work has permanently changed the course of investment-related thought.

Before Markowitz's article, it was more or less taken for granted that the proper way to construct an investment portfolio was just to select the "best securities." It was erroneously assumed that this technique would maximize the expected return for the resultant portfolio. Markowitz correctly pointed out, however, that *the goal of modern portfolio management is not solely to maximize the expected rate of return.* (If this were the only aim, rather than diversifying, investors should concentrate all of their assets in those securities with the highest expected returns—regardless of risk.) Markowitz demonstrated instead that *the objective of modern portfolio management is to maximize what he called "expected utility."*

THE CONCEPT OF UTILITY

The concept of utility is based on the fact that different consumers have different desires, and individuals derive personal

satisfaction in varying ways. Consumers purchase goods which satisfy their needs or desires. To avoid the complex task of attempting to measure the relative importance of these needs and desires, economists have devised the concept of utility. Thus, from the perspective of an economist, purchases are said to provide the consumer with some measure of "utility."

In the context of MPT, the concept of "utility" is used in much the same way. Basically, *utility* embraces "all that an investor wants to get and all that an investor wants to avoid . . . ." [287, p. 291] If we set the complexities aside, "utility" can be viewed as being synonymous with "satisfaction"—as the consumer sees it. If satisfaction is translated into investment terms, each investor's preferred combination of investments depends on his or her preference for positive returns relative to his or her distaste for risk. In turn, then, the goal of all rational investing can be thought of as that of maximizing "satisfaction" (or, in economic jargon, "utility").

The trouble with this definition is that it ends up exactly where it starts. We say that investors seek to maximize utility. But what is utility? It is what investors seek to maximize! Of what use, then, is the economist's assumption that investors seek to maximize utility? The answer is that if all investors are attempting to maximize this thing called utility, all investors must behave in the same way. Consistent behavior by investors means that very specific statements can be made about their aggregate behavior. This, in turn, permits accurate descriptions of their future actions.

A means of somehow measuring utility and determining precisely how much utility someone would attain from a given amount of consumption would be very desirable. Unfortunately, no one has ever been able to devise a satisfactory method for measuring utility. This makes it impossible directly to gauge *marginal utility*—the additional unit of satisfaction the consumer gets for each additional dollar of expenditure.

The inability to measure marginal utility is not a problem, however. Although utility cannot be gauged on an absolute scale, it is possible to evaluate it on a relative scale—much as temperature might be gauged without a thermometer. That is, various states of hot and cold can be distinguished even if the absolute differences cannot be determined. Similarly, a consumer, without an explicit scale of measurement, can still express judgments about relative levels of satisfaction and dissatisfaction. For any individual, these relative judgments can be put in the form of indifference curves.

CLASSIC INDIFFERENCE CURVES

The indifference curve technique is not new. Francis Y. Edgeworth, a British economist, first introduced the concept in the early 1880s. Later, in the 1930s, the approach was popularized by two other British economists, John R. Hicks and R. G. D. Allen. Since then, indifference curve analysis has become a standard and necessary tool of economics.

The significance of the concept lies in the fact that indifference curve analysis eliminates the need to measure utility directly. *Indifference curves* are a graphic representation of consumer tastes and preferences. In Figure 20–1, for example, the consumer is limited to choosing between two commodities—meat and poultry.

Assume that the consumer's household is currently consuming 25 pounds of meat and 20 pounds of poultry per month. This combination is shown as point *E* in Figure 20–1. Notice that any point in quadrant *B* gives the consumer more meat and more poultry—presumably a situation that the con-

FIGURE 20–1: Classic indifference curve

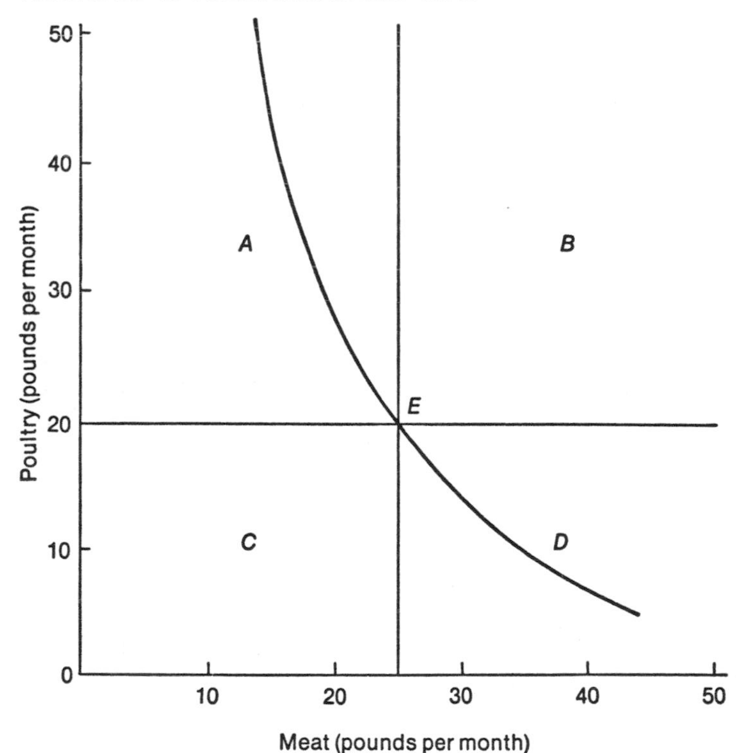

sumer would find preferable. Also notice that any point in quadrant *C* gives the consumer less meat and less poultry—presumably a less desired situation. In quadrants *A* and *D*, it is not as clear what the preferred, or less desirable, situations will be. In quadrant *A* the consumer will receive more poultry and less meat; in quadrant *D*, more meat and less poultry.

The line in Figure 20–1 is the hypothetical consumer's indifference curve. This means that the consumer views all combinations of meat and poultry along this line as *equally satisfactory alternatives.* Specifically, this hypothetical consumer would be indifferent to accepting five pounds less meat in exchange for ten pounds more poultry. Similarly, this con-

FIGURE 20–2: Indifference curves

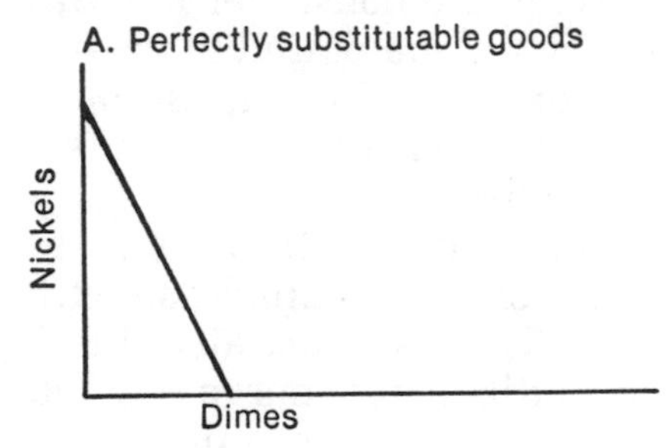

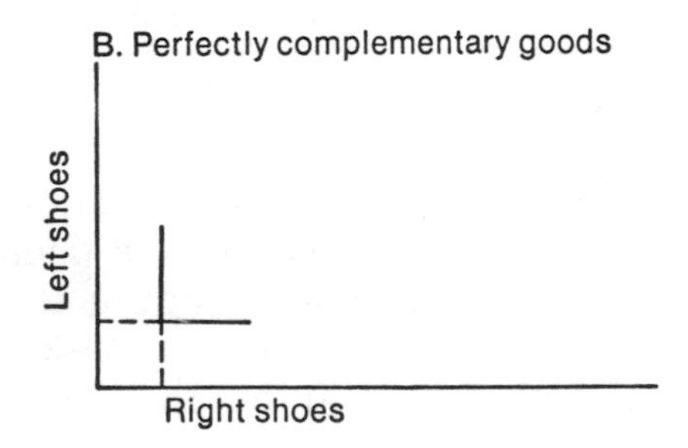

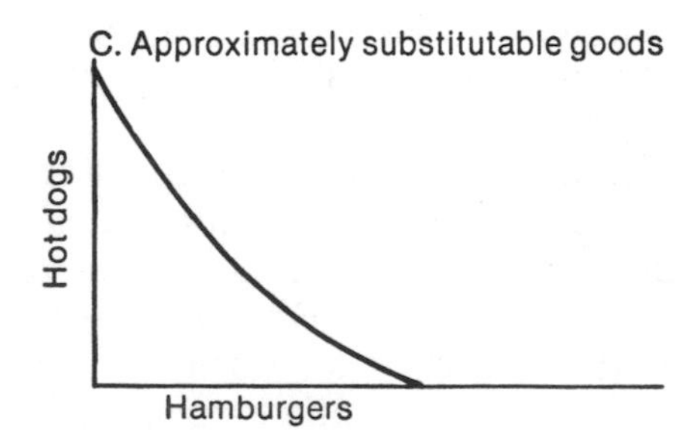

sumer would be willing to substitute ten pounds more meat for ten pounds less poultry. Thus, the consumer is indifferent to any combination of items represented by points *along* the curve.

Technically, the indifference curve represents a single contour line of the investor's utility function. In Figure 20–1 any points above and to the right of the indifference curve give the consumer *more* satisfaction. Similarly, any points to the left and below the curve give the consumer less satisfaction.

The slope of an indifference curve at any point indicates the *marginal rate of substitution*—the rate at which a consumer is willing to substitute one product for another. Between 30 and 40 pounds of poultry, the slope ("rise" divided by the "run") is 2.0. This means that in this range the consumer is willing to substitute two pounds of poultry for one pound of meat. However, between 10 and 20 pounds of poultry, the slope is 1.0. This means that in this range, the consumer views meat and poultry as perfect 1-to-1 substitutes.

The indifference curve for a *perfect substitute* is a straight line; however, as in the case of nickels and dimes, substitution need not be in a 1-to-1 ratio. This is illustrated in Figure 20–2A. By comparison, the indifference curve for *perfect complements*—products which go together as units—is shown in Figure 20–2B. Finally, the shape of an indifference curve for approximately substitutable goods is shown in Figure 20–2C.

INVESTOR'S INDIFFERENCE CURVE

A typical investor's *indifference curve* (or *utility function*) is shown in Figure 20–3. Notice that while economists usually draw indifference curves that are "downward sloping to the right," as they were depicted in Figures 20–1 and 20–2, the curves are "turned" for MPT applications so that the axes can be labeled to match those of the capital market line. Specifically, the horizontal axis shows risk (measured as the standard deviation of return), and the vertical axis plots expected return. This labeling of the axes produces a utility function that is "upward sloping to the right."

To provide a point of reference, the investor's indifference curve in Figure 20–3 has been divided into four quadrants—*A*, *B*, *C*, and *D*. Imagine that an investor's risk is currently *M*—designating the market's level of risk. For this degree of risk, the investor is assumed to receive a "normal" rate of return, *N*. Moving from the intersection of this level of risk and

FIGURE 20–3: Investor's indifference curve

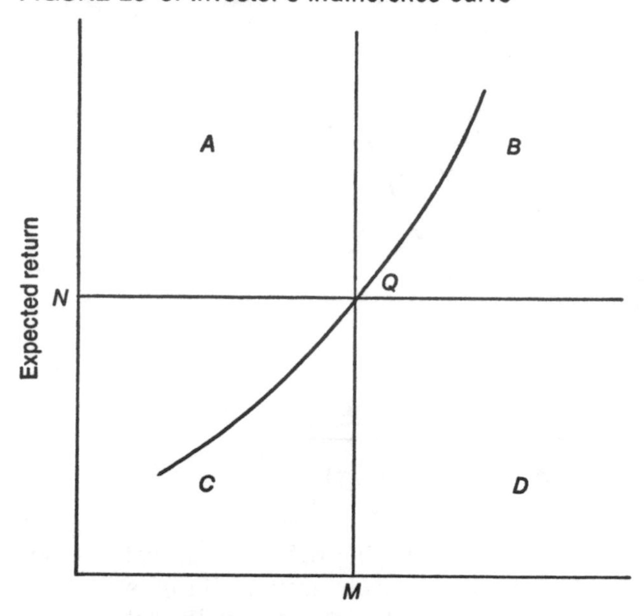

expected return, Q, the investor would prefer any point in quadrant *A*—with a higher expected return and less risk. Conversely, the investor would be less satisfied with any point in quadrant *D*—with a lower expected return and more risk.

As with other indifference curves, the choice of the points in the other quadrants depends on the individual's personal preferences; in this case, the preference for return and the distaste for risk. Thus, moving along the curve in quadrant *B*, this "typical" investor will be willing to accept more risk since the proportionate increases in expected return would progressively exceed the increases in risk. Conversely, moving along the curve in quadrant *C*, the "typical" investor will be willing to accept a lower expected return so long as the proportionate decline in risk progressively exceeds the reduction in expected return.

Importantly, however, by moving to different points along the line, the investor neither increases nor decreases the total level of satisfaction derived from the various combinations of risk and expected return. Hence, the investor is indifferent to being at any point along his or her indifference curve.

Figure 20–4 shows a typical investor's *indifference map*—a

FIGURE 20–4: Investor's indifference map

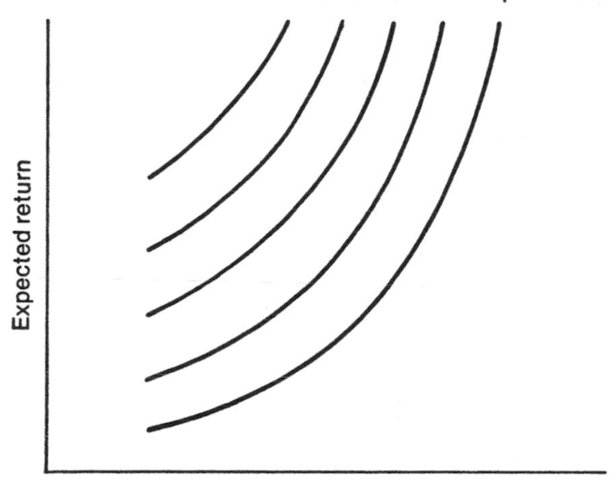

set of indifference curves which profile an investor's willingness to trade off changes in risk against changes in expected return. The important characteristic of an investor's indifference map is that each successive curve moving upward to the left represents a higher level of utility (or, if you prefer, satisfaction).

It should not be presumed that all of the curves on the indifference map are possible. Instead, what the indifference map shows is that depending on the available alternatives, a rational investor would always prefer a higher curve—one with less risk and a greater expected return. Again, given the highest available curve, the investor's personal preferences are such that he or she will be indifferent to any combination of risk or expected return along that particular curve.

Importantly, different investors have varying indifference curves. Figure 20–5 shows two extreme cases in which the indifference curves (in these cases they are actually "lines") labeled 1 through 3 provide different types of investors—"fearless" and "fearful"—with increasing levels of satisfaction. The fearless investor in Figure 20–5A is oblivious to risk since increased satisfaction (moving from indifference curve 1 to 3) is derived solely from increases in expected return—regardless of risk. This investor will select the combination of investments offering the highest expected return. The fearful investor in Figure 20–5B is oblivious to return since increased satisfaction is derived solely from reductions in risk—

FIGURE 20–5: Extreme cases of indifference

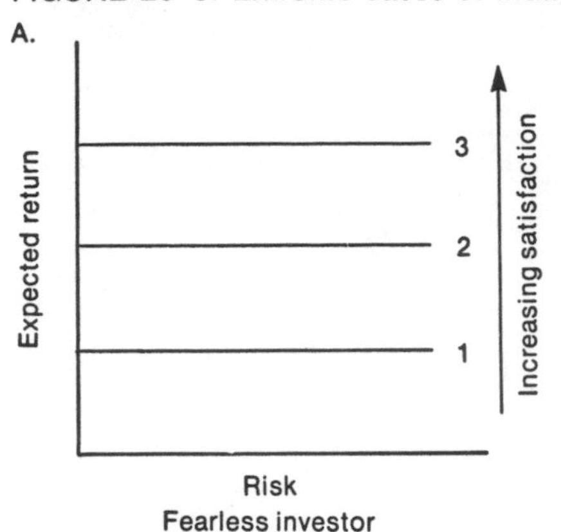

regardless of return. This investor will select the combination of investments offering the lowest risk.

Figure 20–6 illustrates two more typical cases of investor indifference. Both investors are risk averse, but the "adventuresome" investor portrayed in Figure 20–6A is willing to trade relatively smaller increases in incremental expected return for a given increment of risk than the "conservative" investor portrayed in Figure 20–6B.

FIGURE 20–6: Typical cases of indifference

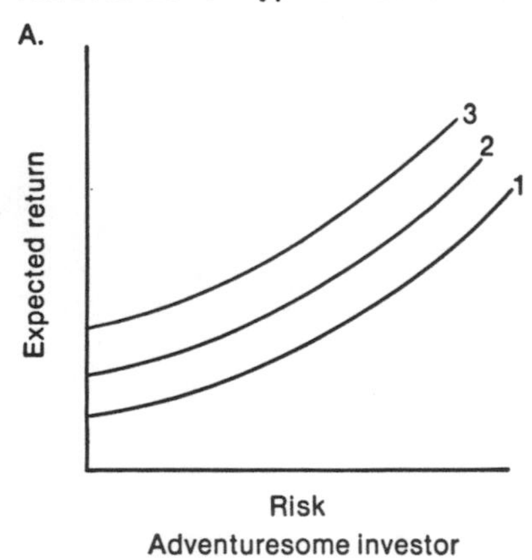

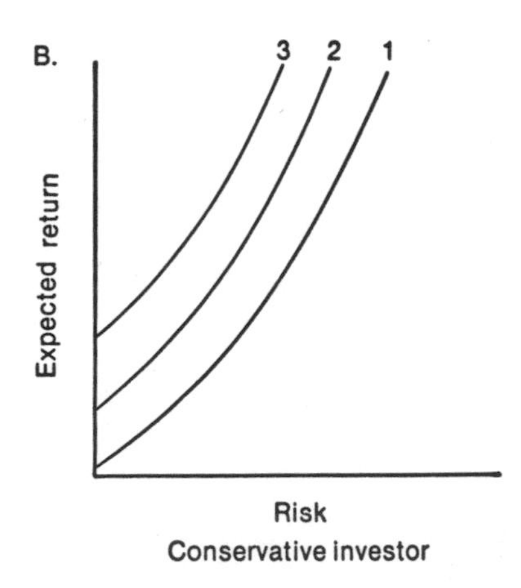

Chapter 21

Markowitz model

To operationalize the concept of "expected utility," Markowitz began with the valid premise that all investors want a combination of high returns *and* low risk. Stated another way, rational investors maximize their "utility" by seeking either (1) the highest available rate of return for a given level of risk. or (2) the lowest level of available risk for a given rate of return.

INEFFICIENT SETS

The relationship between risk and expected return is best illustrated by Figure 21–1. Here "expected return" is plotted on the vertical axis, and "risk" is plotted on the horizontal axis. For now, do not be concerned about how either risk or return is measured. Simply bear in mind that the expected return will increase as one moves up the vertical scale and that risk increases as one moves to the right on the horizontal scale.

Which investment in Figure 21–1 best meets the objective of maximum return with minimum risk? Investment alternatives A and B each have the same expected return, but B carries more risk. Thus, since investment A would be preferred by any rational, risk-averse investor, B can be eliminated from consideration.

Of alternatives A and C, both have the same risk, but A has a higher expected return. Accordingly, alternative C can be eliminated from consideration. A comparison of the two remaining alternatives, A and D, reveals that A has both a higher expected return and a lower risk than D. Thus, investment A—with the highest expected return and the lowest risk—is the preferred alternative.

EFFICIENT SETS

What would happen, however, if these four hypothetical investment alternatives existed in a freely competitive real-

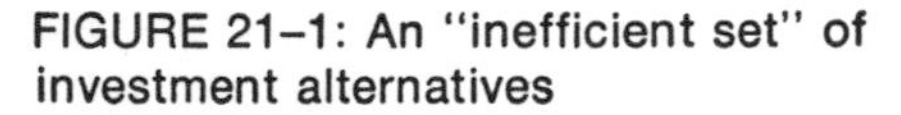

FIGURE 21–1: An "inefficient set" of investment alternatives

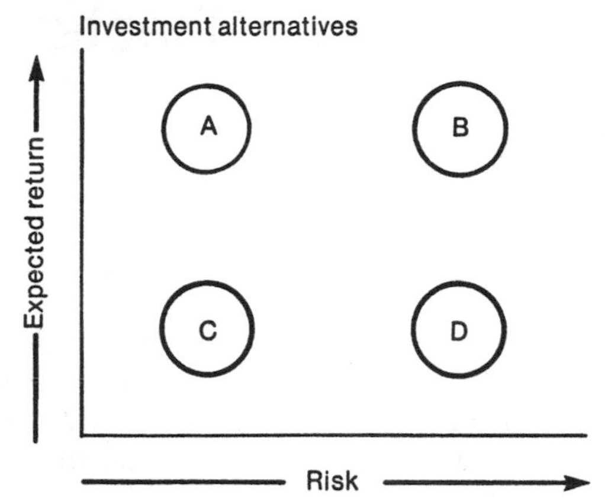

world marketplace (while maintaining the assumption that everyone has the same estimates of expected return and risk)? In a competitive marketplace, since all investors would prefer investment A to the other alternatives, their demand for investment A would drive up its price. But in a real-world marketplace, as the price of investment A increased, the expected return per unit of investment would decrease.

Suppose, for example, that the price of investment A was originally (as shown in Figure 21–1) $1,000 and that its expected return was $80 per year. The return ($80) divided by the cost ($1,000) times 100 gives investment A an expected return of 8 percent. Similarly, suppose that the original price of investment C (as shown in Figure 21–1) was also $1,000, but that its expected return was only $75 per year. The return ($75) divided by the cost ($1,000) times 100 gives investment C an expected return of 7.5 percent. Since A and C have exactly the same level of risk, investment A will be preferred to investment C as long as investment A continues to have a higher expected return. But remember that as the demand for investment A increases, so will its price.

Carrying the example further, suppose that the increased demand for investment A increased its price from $1,000 to $1,066.67. If this occurred, the expected return ($80) divided by the new cost ($1,066.67) times 100 would be 7.5 percent. Since investment C's expected return is also 7.5 percent, the two investments would now be equally attractive on a price basis. (This is an oversimplification because the lack of de-

mand for investment C would drive its price down, in turn increasing its expected return.)

Through what the classical 18th-century economist, Adam Smith [259] referred to as the "invisible hand," prices in competitive markets (such as those for investment securities) quickly adjust to the forces of supply and demand. In keeping with the efficient market hypothesis, these adjustments in price eliminate any market *inefficiencies* whereby one commodity, or investment, is so attractively priced that it is preferred to all others.

Thus, while investors have different risk/return preferences, rational investors will always attempt to find portfolios which provide (*a*) the maximum rate of return for every level of risk, or conversely, (*b*) the minimum level of risk for every possible rate of return. Markets which reflect this goal are said to be *efficient.* Markets containing investments that are "out of line" with this goal, such as alternative D in Figure 21–1, are said to be *inefficient.*

Since inefficiencies are eliminated by competition, the hypothetical investment alternatives depicted in Figure 21–1 would not exist in a competitive marketplace. Instead, as long as everyone used the same estimates for expected return and risk, the "inefficient" marketplace depicted in Figure 21–1 would, through price changes, become "efficient," and the *new* investment alternatives would array themselves as shown in Figure 21–2. The line *XYZ* in Figure 21–2 thus represents the so-called *efficient boundary,* or *efficient set,* of investment alternatives. That is, the investments on this line offer the

FIGURE 21–2: An "efficient set" of investment alternatives

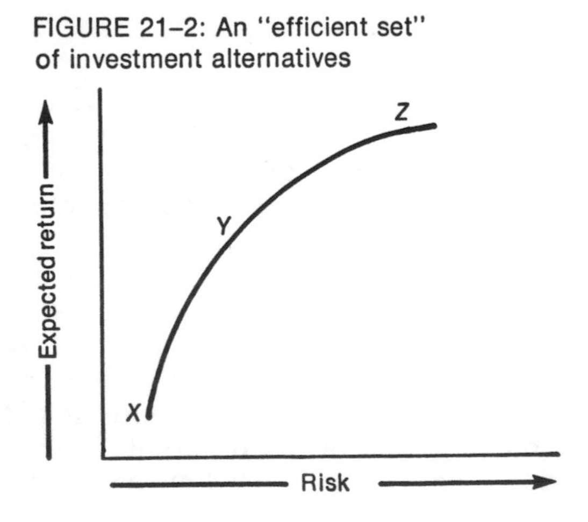

highest level of return for this degree of risk or, alternatively, provide the lowest level of risk for this rate of return.

Readers who are not familiar with the concept of an "efficient set" of investment alternatives are encouraged to note for themselves that in Figure 21–2 (1) any investments to the left of or above line *XYZ* would be *superior* investments, and (2) any investments to the right of, or below, line *XYZ* would be *inferior* investments. Further, readers are reminded that the competitive forces of the marketplace will eliminate—through price changes—any agreed-upon superior or inferior alternatives.

Working from the three investment alternatives depicted in Figure 21–2, suppose it was necessary to select an investment for someone whose investment preferences closely reflect those of a classical "widow" or "orphan." Presumably, this individual would want to attain the *highest available return that is consistent with a minimum level of risk*. Of the three alternatives shown in Figure 21–2, the investment with the lowest risk—the overriding consideration for this person—is investment *X*.

At the other extreme, suppose that an investment must be selected for a classic "speculator." Here, the objective would be to select the alternative with the *lowest available risk that is consistent with the highest expected return*. Of the three hypothetical investments shown in Figure 21–2, the one with the highest expected return—the overriding preference for this person—is investment *Z*. The middle ground between the two extremes—essentially a balance between risk and expected return—is represented by investment *Y*.

RISK AND RETURN—DEFINITIONS

At this point, the terms "expected return" and "risk" require more explicit definitions. One's best estimate of the future return of any investment is the expected value, or mean, of all of the likely returns. It is this mean, or "expected return," that an investor attempts to maximize at each level of acceptable risk. The distributions of the likely returns and the mean, or expected, returns for two hypothetical investments are shown in Figure 21–3.

A comparison of investment A and B reveals that both have the same average, or expected, return. The distributions of the likely, or expected, returns are quite different however. Specifically, investment A has more dispersion, or variance,

FIGURE 21–3: Comparative distributions of likely returns

Investment A

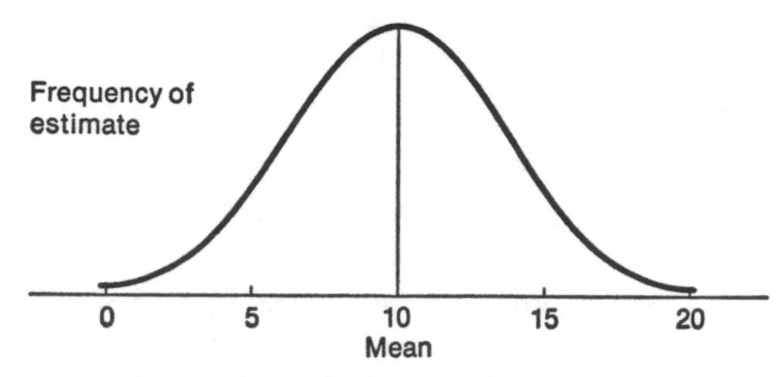

Investment B

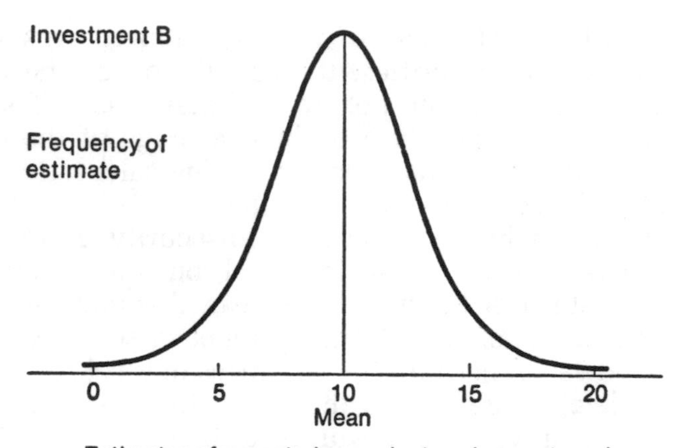

around the mean than the distribution of likely returns for investment B. Thus, based either on a comparison of the graphic representations in Figure 21–3, or on the explicit numerical measures for the variance of the distributions of the expected returns for the two investments, investment B emerges as superior because it offers the same expected return but with less variance of estimated returns.

Figure 21–3 dramatizes the importance of variance. The higher an investment's variance, the more its actual return is likely to deviate from the expected return. From an investor's point of view, the more assurance that the actual results will parallel the expected results, the better the investment. Thus, as we operationalize the maxim that rational, risk-averse investors will always seek investments with a minimum level of risk

for a given level of expected return, it becomes clear that the statistical variance (or its square root, the *standard deviation*) of the distribution of possible expected returns can be used as a measure of risk.

THE MARKOWITZ MODEL

According to Markowitz's formulation, the selection of an efficient portfolio begins with an analysis of three estimates:

1. The *expected return* for each security.
2. The *variance of the expected return* for each security.
3. The possibly offsetting, or possibly complementary, interaction, or *covariance*, of return with every other security consideration.

Beginning with distributions of the expected returns for each of the individual securities, the calculation of the expected return for an aggregate portfolio of these securities is relatively easy. It is merely the weighted average of the expected returns of the individual securities. The calculation of the combined variance is more complicated.

For a situation in which we have a two-security portfolio, assume that each security has an identical, but totally unrelated, expected return of 8 percent per year. Assume further that the variance of the expected returns for *each* security is 2 percent. Also, however, because the variances of the two securities are completely unrelated, a third statistical description can be added—that of zero *covariance* between the two securities.

Thus, investing in either of the two securities separately will produce an expected return of 8 percent with a 2 percent variance of return. It can be shown, however, that if the returns on the two securities are completely unrelated, then the variance in the rate of return if the two securities are combined into a two-security portfolio is only half the variance for each security considered alone. In fact, as long as the expected rates of return of the two stocks are not perfectly correlated, the variance (i.e., risk) of a two-security portfolio will always be lower than the variance of either of the securities considered alone.

To determine the most efficient set from a large number of investments requires what is known as "quadratic programming." (Rather than explain how this is actually done, we will ask the reader to take it on faith that the portfolios resulting from this analysis—which is admittedly taxing for even large-scale computers—do indeed define the efficient set.)

SUMMARY: THE MARKOWITZ MODEL

Markowitz demonstrated that the two relevant characteristics of a portfolio are

1. Its expected return.
2. Some measure of its risk—operationally defined as the dispersion of possible returns around the expected return.

Markowitz also demonstrated that rational investors will choose to hold efficient portfolios; that is, portfolios which maximize each investor's utility by

1. Maximizing expected return for a given degree of risk.
2. Minimizing risk for a given level of expected return.

Markowitz further demonstrated that the identification of efficient portfolios would require information on *each* security's

1. Expected return.
2. Variance of return.
3. Covariance of return with *every other security under consideration.*

Finally, Markowitz demonstrated that once prepared, the foregoing security descriptions could be manipulated by *portfolio optimization* programs (i.e., quadratic programming techniques) to produce an explicit definition of the efficient portfolio in terms of

1. The securities to be held.
2. The proportion of available funds to be allocated to each.

PORTFOLIO OPTIMIZATION PROGRAMS—THE "VALUE ADDED"

It is important to know whether or not portfolio optimization programs generate portfolios which are basically the same as those produced by people who rely on "professional judgment" and "traditional" approaches. In short, are the portfolio optimizers that are derived from MPT really "much ado about nothing"?

While there is a shortage of definitive research data, many organizations which use portfolio optimization techniques to "shadow" professionally constructed portfolios have found a significant number of "inefficient" portfolios (i.e., portfolios that do *not* strike the optimum balance between risk and return). More importantly, given the portfolio selection tech-

niques described here, it is *impossible* to envision a more effective and accurate way to translate a unique set of forecast assumptions and portfolio objectives into an optimal portfolio.

The increasing availability of portfolio optimization programs is causing the traditional role of the portfolio manager to be redefined. *It is an undisputed fact that the translation from security-related forecast assumptions and a set of portfolio objectives and constraints* (*such as no more than 5 percent in any single security, at least four percent yield, and so on*) *to optimal portfolios can be done more effectively, and more accurately, by portfolio optimization programs.*

This does not mean, however, that the job of the portfolio manager will be eliminated by the widespread use of portfolio optimization programs. Quite to the contrary, a portfolio optimization program is merely a tool by which a portfolio manager translates "assumptions" on the risk and return characteristics of a universe of potential investments into a portfolio with certain predefined "characteristics." Both the "assumptions" about the universe of available investments and the "characteristics" of the portfolio must be supplied by the portfolio manager.

Chapter 22

Asset allocation line

William Sharpe extended Markowitz's work in two important dimensions. First, Sharpe broadened the analysis to include riskless assets (such as short-term government securities) and the possibility of borrowing. Second, he developed a simplified model that alleviates the burdensome data collection and computing problems inherent in the Markowitz model. These refinements are discussed, in turn, in the next two chapters.

COMBINING RISKLESS AND RISKY SECURITIES—THE ASSET ALLOCATION LINE

In the earlier discussion of the capital market line, it was stated that various combinations of lending and borrowing will generate a linear continuum of alternative investment possibilities. These return and risk combinations ranged from the risk-free rates of return on a riskless investment through the expected rate of return commensurate with the risk of a fully diversified market portfolio.

As such, the capital market line is a special case of the more general notion of an *asset allocation line.* Although the capital market line employed lending and borrowing to develop a continuum of investment possibilities ranging from risk-free assets to the market portfolio, the same line can be developed to range from risk-free assets to *any* portfolio. The basis for this important notion comes from the work of William Sharpe. Sharpe demonstrated that "when a risky security or portfolio is combined with a riskless one, the risk of the combination is proportional to the amount invested in the risky component." [245, p. 85] Suppose, for example, that an investor divides his or her funds between a common stock portfolio and an insured

(presumably riskless) savings account. Here the only amount "at risk" is the portion in common stock.

This is best illustrated by the hypothetical portfolios shown in Table 22–1. Portfolio A is fully invested in an insured savings account, and the investor is acting as a "lender." For

TABLE 22–1: Investment alternatives: Combinations of risky and riskless holdings

Portfolio designation	*Composition of the portfolio*	*Expected rate of return (percent)*	*Standard deviation of return (percent)*	*Whereby an investor is:*
A..................	100 percent in insured savings account	5.0	0.0	Lender
B	100 percent in common stock portfolio	10.0	20.0	Owner
C	60 percent in portfolio A and 40 percent in portfolio B	7.0	8.0	Lender and owner
D	40 percent in portfolio A and 60 percent in portfolio B	8.0	12.0	Lender and owner
E..................	20 percent in portfolio A and 100 percent in portfolio B	11.0	24.0	Borrower and owner

purposes of illustration, the expected return of portfolio A is assumed to be 5 percent, and the standard deviation of return (the square root of the variance) is assumed to be 0 percent. The "riskless" portfolio appears as point *A* in Figure 22–1.

By comparison, portfolio B in Table 22–1 consists of a portfolio of common stocks, so that an investor purchasing this portfolio of common stocks, is acting as an "owner." In keeping with the valid presumption that a common stock portfolio would carry both a higher expected return and greater risk than an insured savings account, portfolio B is assumed to have an aggregate expected rate of return of 10 percent and a standard deviation of return of 20 percent. (Note these figures are very much in keeping with Ibbotson and Sinquefield's historical data that was discussed in Chapter 17.) Portfolio B is designated as point *B* in Figure 22–1. (The reader is encouraged to "plot" point *B* at the intersection of an expected return

FIGURE 22–1: A hypothetical asset allocation line—Available combinations of risky and riskless investments

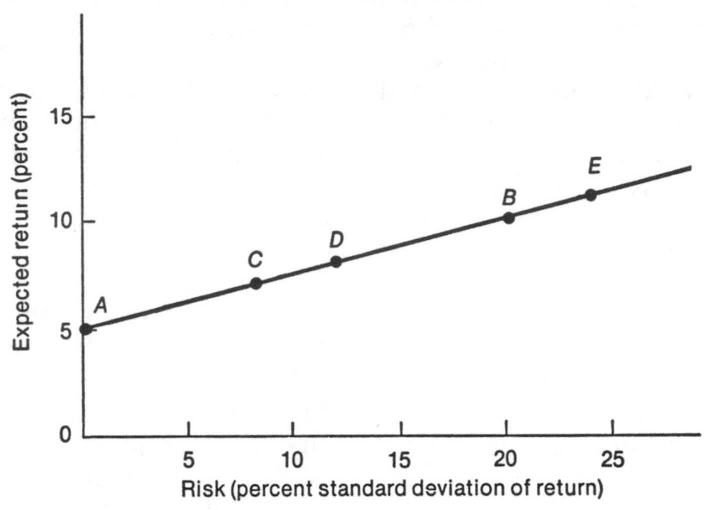

of 10 percent and a standard deviation of return of 20 percent.)

In a situation with two such investment alternatives, an investor could

1. Invest everything in portfolio A.
2. Invest everything in portfolio B.
3. Divide the investment, in any proportion, between the two alternatives A and B.

The latter case, in which funds are divided between the two alternatives, is represented by portfolios C and D in Table 22–1 and Figure 22–1.

Portfolio C, where an investor is acting as both a lender and an owner, was made up by allocating 60 percent of the available funds to portfolio A (an insured savings account) and the remaining 40 percent to portfolio B (a common stock portfolio). Since the expected rate of return for a combined portfolio is merely the weighted average of the component returns, the expected rate of return of portfolio C is 7 percent (i.e., 60 percent of portfolio A's expected return of 5 percent, plus 40 percent of portfolio B's expected return of 10 percent).

Further, since it can be shown that the risk of a portfolio resulting from the combination of a risky security with a riskless one is proportional to the amount invested in the risky security, the standard deviation of return for portfolio C is 8 percent (i.e., 40 percent of the standard deviation of return of

portfolio B). The relationship between risk and expected return for portfolio C is shown as point C in Figure 22–1 (i.e., at the intersection of an expected return of 7 percent and a standard deviation of return of 8 percent).

The relationship between risk and return for portfolio D is calculated in the same way. Table 22–1 shows that portfolio D is similar to portfolio C in that it is constructed from both risky and riskless assets. The proportion of the two types of assets differs from that of portfolio C, however. Specifically, 40 percent of the assets in portfolio D are deployed in portfolio A—the insured savings account. The remaining 60 percent of portfolio D's assets are deployed in portfolio B—a common stock portfolio with an expected rate of return of 10 percent and standard deviation of return of 20 percent.

As with portfolio C, the expected rate of return of portfolio D is merely the weighted average of the component returns, or 8 percent (i.e., 40 percent of portfolio A's expected return of 5 percent, plus 60 percent of portfolio B's expected return of 10 percent). Also, since the risk of portfolio D is proportionate to the amount invested in the risky security, the standard deviation of return for portfolio D is 12 percent (i.e., 60 percent of the standard deviation of return of portfolio B). As with portfolio C, the relationship between risk and expected return for portfolio D is shown as point *D* in Figure 22–1. (Again, the reader is encouraged to "plot" this point).

As now developed, Figure 22–1 illustrates a continuum of investment alternatives—ranging from 100 percent in riskless assets (point *A*) to 100 percent risky assets (point B). That is, an investor could choose to place all his or her assets in a riskless portfolio—point *A*. Alternatively, all of an investor's assets could be placed in the common stock portfolio—point *B*. An investor could, however, select any combination of the first two investment alternatives. All possible combinations of riskless assets (portfolio A) and risky assets (portfolio B) fall on the *asset allocation line ACDB* in Figure 22–1.

Extending this analysis one step further, it is possible to think of the expected return on a *loan* as a riskless investment with a guaranteed loss. Take, for example, the case of a person with $10,000 to invest who, because of a willingness to increase his or her risk through borrowing, takes out a loan of an additional $2,000 with a promise to repay the principal plus interest of 5 percent. This investor could now invest a total of $12,000 in common stock portfolio B. This situation is depicted as portfolio E (where the investor is acting both as a borrower and an owner) in Table 22–1.

The expected rate of return of such a combined portfolio is still the weighted average of the respective component returns. Thus, we have a situation in which the investor is investing 120 percent of his or her available assets in a portfolio that has an expected rate of return of 10 percent, but 20 percent of these available assets are *also* in a portfolio with an expected return of −5 percent. Combining the 12 percent expected return from common stock portfolio B (120 percent of the 10 percent expected return) with the 1 percent expected loss from borrowing (20 percent of the 5 percent negative expected return) indicates an expected return of 11 percent for portfolio E.

Similarly, this investor, through borrowing, will increase the risk (standard deviation of return) to 120 percent of that of the underlying portfolio, or 24 percent. Graphically, portfolio E is shown in Figure 22–1 as point *E* (i.e., the intersection of the 11 percent expected return and the 24 percent standard deviation of return).

Beyond the details of the foregoing example, it is important to note that the *asset allocation line* in Figure 22–1 illustrates the risk and expected return for all possible allocations of assets between a riskless and risky investment. Specifically,

1. Riskless investing through leading—represented by point *A*.
2. Risky investing without lending—represented by point *B*.
3. Any combination of riskless investing *and* risky investing—represented by a continuum of possible points along the line *AB*.
4. Any feasible combination of borrowing and risky investing—represented by the continuum of possible points along the line *BF*.

Figure 22–1 illustrates the important concept that with only three investment alternatives—generally termed risk-free lending, owning, and borrowing—an investor can "mix and match" these alternatives to attain a continuum of possible asset allocations.[1]

[1] An important subject that is beyond the scope of this book deals with the amount of debt that should be used to finance a firm's operations. If investors, through their selection of combinations of investment instruments, can indeed acquire any combinations of debt and equity that they desire, we could presume that this market efficiency would adjust the firm's cost of capital so as to minimize the importance of the firm's internal decisions regarding capital structure. Readers who are interested in this topic are referred to the classic article on the M–M hypothesis by Franco Modigliani and Merton Miller [193].

Chapter 23

Single- and multi-index models

Aside from the omission of the lending and borrowing alternatives, the original Markowitz formulation of the theoretical solution to portfolio selection poses several problems in implementation. Certain simplifications which facilitate implementation are discussed in this chapter.

The "efficient portfolios" resulting from the Markowitz (or any other) model are based on the analysis of estimates of future risk and expected returns which are available at a particular point in time. These estimates, and hence the resultant "efficient portfolios," can be expected to change over time—as price fluctuations raise or lower expected returns and as analysts revise their forecasts of risks and returns.

Thus, the "portfolio selection problem" is not simply that of determining the most efficient portfolios. Instead, investment managers are continually challenged to keep the analysis up to date and to weigh the potential advantages to be derived from changes in a portfolio against transaction costs.

This, in turn, demands both that human resources continually update the required estimates and that the computational resources translate the estimates into efficient portfolios. Logically, the longer one waits to repeat such analysis, the further the once-efficient portfolios can be expected to deviate from the new efficient set. As a result, frequent updates are needed.

Unfortunately, the Markowitz approach requires enormous amounts of both human and computational resources. For example, to evaluate 100 securities, an analyst must prepare 100 timely estimates of both risk and expected return. In addition, *the Markowitz solution requires an explicit estimate of the covariance of returns between each possible pair of securities.* Thus, the evaluation of the covariance between 100 pairs of

securities necessitates the estimation and processing of 4, 550 estimates of covariance.[1]

Aside from the sheer volume of the data, imagine the practical problems facing an expert in the analysis of automobile stocks who is asked to estimate the degree of expected comovement between Ford, American Motors, General Motors, *and* each of 500 other stocks drawn from 60 other industries! Going one step further, even if the automobile analyst prepared such estimates, it would be difficult to place any confidence in their accuracy.

The problem with gathering both this kind and quantity of information was probably best expressed by Markowitz himself when he wrote, "it is reasonable to ask security analysts to summarize their researches in 100 carefully considered expected returns, and 100 carefully considered variances of return. It is not reasonable, however, to ask for [almost] 5,000 carefully and individually considered covariances." [186, pp. 96–97]

To bridge the gap between his theoretical solution and the practical problems of estimating the covariance for each pair of securities under consideration, Markowitz suggested using the relationship between each security's rate of return and the rate of return on a market index as a substitute for explicit data on the covariance of each pair of securities under study. William Sharpe [242] pursued this approach with the so-called single-index model.

There is considerable evidence that securities tend to move with the market. Whether based on such time-honored Wall Street aphorisms as "when they raid the brothel, they take all the girls," or Brealey's less colorful statement, "when the wind of recession blows, there are few companies that do not lean with it" [34, p. 104], it is true that in major market moves, most securities move in the same direction. However, even though securities have many common characteristics and, as a result, tend to move together, their numerous individual and distinguishing properties cause stocks to comove with the market at *different rates.* Accordingly, how *sensitive* a security's price is to changes in the overall market is of crucial importance.

Thus, while the ideal way to select a portfolio would be to develop precise estimates of how every pair of securities under consideration would, or would not, move together, the ap-

[1] The number of pairs which can be drawn from a sample of N securities is $N(N-1)/2$. Thus, the Markowitz analysis of 100 securities requires the estimation and processing of 100(99)/2 covariances—one for each pair of securities.

proach is difficult to implement. To develop an easier to implement alternative, Sharpe focused on the sensitivity of individual stock prices to fluctuations in a single market index—hence, the term "single-index model."

THE INPUTS TO A SINGLE-INDEX MODEL

Aside from reducing the amount of information Sharpe's model requires a significantly different *kind* of information. The Markowitz approach calls for an *unconditional* forecast of the rate of return for each stock. Sharpe's model, on the other hand, employs *conditional forecasts;* that is, forecasts which are conditional on market levels.

It is an important feature of Sharpe's analysis that it does not depend on an absolute forecast of how well a stock will, or will not, perform. Basically, when using the Sharpe approach, security analysts are asked to forecast expected rates of return under several alternative sets of market conditions. Because these analysts are *not* required directly to speculate about future market conditions, the functions of market-level forecasting and company-level forecasting are clearly delineated.

This separation has two major advantages. First, for the investment decision maker, an analyst's forecasts do not represent a composite opinion on both the overall trend of the market and how the security is expected to move within that market context. Imagine the difficulties facing a portfolio manager who receives performance or price estimates from more than 50 security analysts. Each of these estimates may have been derived from the analyst's assumptions about the market, plus his or her outlook for the company. Happily, the Sharpe model separates market- and security-level forecasts.

The second advantage of this separation is that it allows the responsibility for each decision level to be vested with the people who are best qualified to provide each type of forecast. Further, conditional forecasts keep the element of risk in its proper perspective—both as it relates to the security and to the overall market.

Unfortunately, not every organization uses such procedures. In the words of Sharpe, "people continually ask for, and get, single estimates, ignoring the influence of overall market moves and the presence of uncertainty. Such procedures are, however, too simplistic: *most returns are uncertain, and they do depend on market moves.* These two factors are too important to be ignored [italics added in the last sentence]." [252, p. 108]

SUMMARY—SHARPE'S SINGLE-INDEX MODEL

Sharpe's portfolio selection approach does not require estimates of the comovement among individual securities. Instead, the Sharpe approach uses estimates of each security's comovement with *one* general market (single-index) indicator. As a result, the data required to "drive" the Sharpe single-index model is significantly simpler and less burdensome than that required for the Markowitz model. Specifically, the three estimates that are required for each security to be analyzed by the Sharpe approach are:

1. The amount of specific, or nonmarket, return (alpha).
2. A measure of responsiveness to market movements (beta).
3. The variance of the nonmarket return.

MULTI-INDEX MODELS

The Markowitz portfolio selection model can be viewed as the ultimate multi-index model. Since the model is based on the estimation of the covariance between *each* pair of securities, every security is, in fact, an "index," or reference point, for analysis. At the other extreme, Sharpe proposed a single market-related index as the reference point for analysis. Logically, then, there is an entire continuum of possible multi-index models in the "middle ground" between the Sharpe and Markowitz approaches.

Unfortunately, Sharpe's single-index model reflects one disquieting assumption. The model assumes that *the only movements which are common to all securities are related to movements of the overall market.* Other comovements, however, such as those of industries, have been shown to exist [see King, 149, 150]. It is reasonable to expect, therefore, that the use of "middle ground indices," such as those built around significantly different industries, could produce better results than those of a single-index model—without introducing the burdensome data collection and computational problems associated with the Markowitz full covariance approach.

Thus, the limited multi-index approach, while still minimizing data collection requirements offers the advantages of:

1. "Fine tuning" the comovement of homogeneous companies to some subclassification of the general market index.

2. Explicitly estimating the comovements between each pair of subclassifications, in much the same manner as between pairs of individual securities in the Markowitz full covariance approach.

Although it holds out the promise of improved results, the concept of a multi-index model poses a new problem. The market must be segmented into distinctly homogeneous and unrelated groups; that is, securities that are homogeneous in the sense that they move together as a group but are unrelated in that group movements are unrelated. Discouragingly traditional industry classifications—assumed by most people to be the "natural" basis for multi-index classification schemes—have provided disappointing results.

SINGLE- VERSUS MULTI-INDEX MODELS

Kalman Cohen and Jerry Pogue [45] working at the Carnegie Institute of Technology, developed the first multi-index model in the late 1960s. Working with historical data from a fairly large universe of common stocks, they found, surprisingly, that a single-index model usually performed better than their ten-industry, multi-index model.

James L. Farrell, Jr., who now heads the Citibank Investment Management Group, has shown, however, that the reason the Cohen and Pogue multi-index model failed to outperform the single-index model can be traced to deficiencies in their industry indexes. In Farrell's words, "[Cohen and Pogue's] . . . results do not necessarily lead to the conclusion that the single-index model is preferable to the multi-index model. The main implication is that [the] industry indexes [used by Cohen and Pogue] are basically deficient as inputs to the multi-index model." [83, p. 12]

Following Benjamin King's conclusion that stock price movements can be traced to four factors—the market, the basic industry, the industry subgroup, and the company—Farrell reasoned that a broader than industry classification of "growth, cyclical, or stable" characteristics might provide the basis for an improved multi-index model.

Using data on 100 stocks and a technique known as "cluster analysis," Farrell separated stocks into groups or clusters within which price movements were highly correlated, but between which price movements showed little correlation. Four homogeneous groups emerged from this analysis—

growth, cyclical, stable, and, surprisingly, oil stocks. That is, these four groupings of stocks were found to be homogeneous in the sense that intragroup price movements were highly correlated at the same time that there was an insignificant amount of correlation between intergroup price movements. This kind of group homogeneity is the prerequisite for a multi-index portfolio selection model and encouraged Farrell to proceed with the development and testing of a model based on these groups.

A comparison of efficient portfolios generated by a single-index model and Farrell's multi-index model showed that the multi-index model selected "portfolios with lower risk over a broad range of the efficient frontier." Further, the multi-index model diversified more efficiently than the single-index model owing to its facility for distributing the portfolio more evenly across the four homogeneous groups. [83, p. 47]

Having established that his groups remained stable over time, Farrell used historical data from 1961–69 to develop inputs to the two models and then tested their comparative performance against large all-stock mutual funds and the S&P 500 over the period spanning 1970–74. Farrell found that both models outperformed the mutual funds and that his multi-index model outperformed the single-index model.

Chapter 24

Market model

The *market model* provides the conceptual foundation for the single-index model (which is also known as the diagonal model, or the one-factor model). The market model *describes the relationship between returns on individual securities (or portfolios) and the returns on the market portfolio.* Specifically, the market model holds that the returns on an individual security (or portfolio) are linearly related to an index of market returns.

EX POST VERSUS EX ANTE INFORMATION

All investment information is a "before the fact" prediction or an "after the fact" result. Much of the confusion over MPT can be traced to the failure to keep the distinction between "before the fact" estimates and "after the fact" results in mind.

The literature on MPT generally makes the distinction between "before the fact" and "after the fact" by referring to *ex ante* and *ex post* variables. While other terminology might be employed, the academic convention is used here both to familiarize the reader with the quantitative jargon and to parallel the more rigorous discussions of the material.

Much as poker players "ante" before the deal, ex ante is the Latin term used by MPT theorists to indicate "before the fact." Similarly, ex post is taken to mean "after the fact." The need to make this distinction stems from the fact that information such as a stock's beta—its price sensitivity to that of the market—can be an ex ante (i.e., predicted) or an ex post (i.e., historical) value. Moreover, ex post outcomes are occasionally used as estimates for ex ante expectations. This is the case, for example, when historic, or ex post, betas are used as estimates of

future, or ex ante, betas. Thus, when necessary, the distinction between ex ante and ex post information will be made.

CAPM VERSUS MARKET MODEL

The capital asset pricing model (CAPM) discussed in Chapter 19 is a very distinct model. Neither the market model nor the CAPM depends in any way on the other. The CAPM *provides an explicit expression of the expected returns for all assets.* Basically, the CAPM holds that if investors are risk averse, high-risk stocks must have higher expected returns than low-risk stocks. In equilibrium, a security with zero risk will have an expected return equal to that of a riskless asset. Increases in risk beyond that of a riskless asset will be accompanied by proportional increases in expected return.

Thus, the CAPM is indeed a pricing model—it indicates *the price of immediate consumption and the price of risk.* That is, when consumers choose to direct their funds into immediate consumption, they do so in favor of the alternative of investing these funds in riskless securities. The "price" of immediate consumption is consequently the "reward" which could have been earned from waiting. Similarly, when investors choose risky investments, they do so in favor of the alternative of holding riskless investments.

However, in order to attract capital to the risky alternatives, the marketplace must reward investors in proportion to the amount of risk they undertake. Since "price" to the buyer is the "reward" to a seller, these returns can also be thought of as rewards—the reward for waiting and the reward for taking market risk. From the opposite point of view these returns can be thought of as the "price of immediate consumption" and the "price of risk."

While the CAPM is an abstraction and simplification of capital market theory, the market model is not explicitly linked to a particular theory. The market model is merely a description of the relationship which exists between security and market returns. As such, the market model tells us nothing about what *determines* returns. The model merely describes the relationship which has been shown to exist between market and security returns. The construct that is used to describe the market model relationship is the security characteristic line.

SECURITY CHARACTERISTIC LINES

The market model describes the relationship between the return on a security and the overall market (represented by a single market index). The best way to summarize this relationship is through a "*security characteristic line.*" This concept divides a security's "excess return" into two components: (1) market-related (or, systematic), and (2) nonmarket-related (or, residual) return.

"Excess return" as used here is the return that is expected to be derived from the security (during a specified holding period) *less* the estimated return from holding a riskless security (such as a short-term government obligation) during the same period.

Figure 24–1 illustrates the important features of a security characteristic line. The horizontal axis plots excess return on

FIGURE 24–1: Security characteristic line

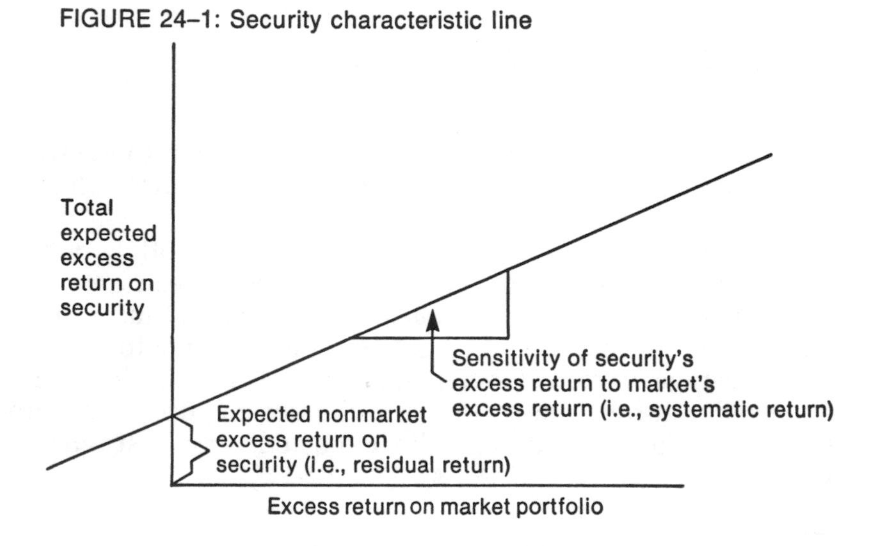

the market portfolio. This is defined as the return on the market portfolio minus the riskless rate of return. The vertical axis measures the excess return on any security. Specifically, the total expected excess return on a security equals the before the fact estimate of the security's return less the riskless rate of return.

The estimation of a security's expected excess return may be best understood from the following verbal representation of the underlying equation:

Since a security's

EXPECTED EXCESS RETURN can be broken down into NONMARKET RELATED (residual) RETURN and MARKET RELATED (systematic) RETURN

it follows that a security's

therefore,

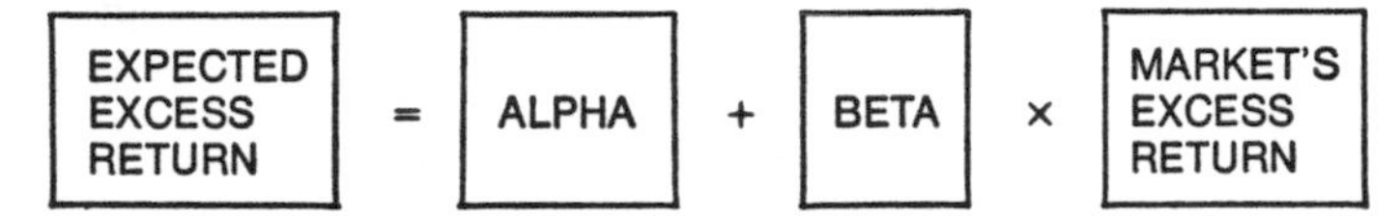

and since the equation for a straight line is:

$$Y = a + bX$$

the values of a security's *alpha* and *beta* represent the vertical intercept and the slope, respectively, of the *security's characteristic line.*[1]

The security characteristic line contains a subtlety which needs to be emphasized. Although *beta* is an estimate of a *relationship* to another variable, *alpha* is an estimate of an *amount*—a specific rate of return. In practice, therefore, alpha is the average, or expected value, of an analyst's *distribution* of expected returns. Accordingly, estimates of alpha are presumed to fluctuate around the expected, or "best guess," value.

---

[1] In specific technical terms:

$$\tilde{R}_i - \rho = [\alpha_i + \tilde{r}_i] + [\beta_{im} (\tilde{R}_m - \rho)]$$

where

$\sim$ = Variable not known in advance.
R_i = Holding period return on security i.
ρ = Riskless rate of return.
α_i = Expected nonmarket excess return on security i.
r_i = Actual deviation from the expected value.
β_{im} = Sensitivity of security i's excess return to the market's excess return.
R_m = Holding period return on the market.
$\tilde{R}_i - \rho$ = Total expected excess return on security i.
$\tilde{R}_m - \rho$ = Excess return on the market portfolio.

Before the fact alpha represents the expected nonmarket excess return. After the fact, however, one should expect the actual results to deviate from this expectation. This is best explained by reference to Figure 24–2. Suppose that the security characteristic line *AB* was drawn at the beginning of a

FIGURE 24–2: Illustration—Nonmarket (residual) variance

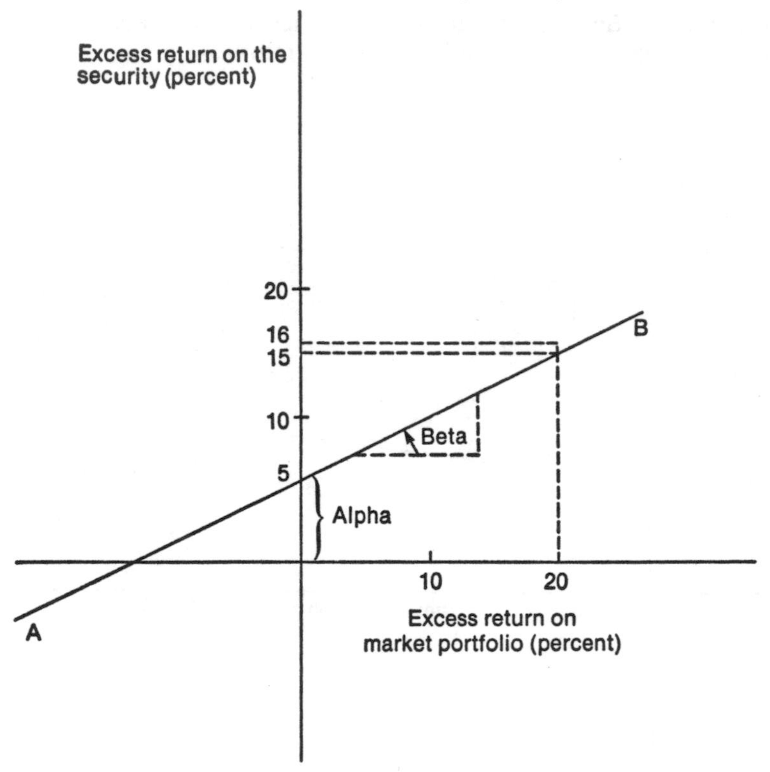

given time period. At the end of that period, it is determined that the estimated beta (the slope of the characteristic line) of 0.5 was correct. Further, it is determined that at the end of the time period, the excess return on the market portfolio was 20 percent and the excess return on the security was 16 percent. The forecast, derived from forward-looking estimates of alpha (5 percent) and beta (0.5), called for an excess return on the security of 15 percent. The discrepancy between the expected and actual results is explained by the difference between the estimated and the actual values for alpha—the nonmarket component of the security's excess return.

The fact that an estimate of alpha is really the mean of a distribution of estimates of nonmarket return is illustrated in Figure 24–3. While both security characteristic lines have the same intercept (alpha) and slope (beta), they present two quite different pictures. The estimate of alpha's dispersion from the expected value is significantly greater in Figure 24–3A than in Figure 24–3B. For this reason, an explicit statement of a secu-

FIGURE 24–3: Security characteristic lines illustrating differences in the variance of estimated nonmarket (residual) returns

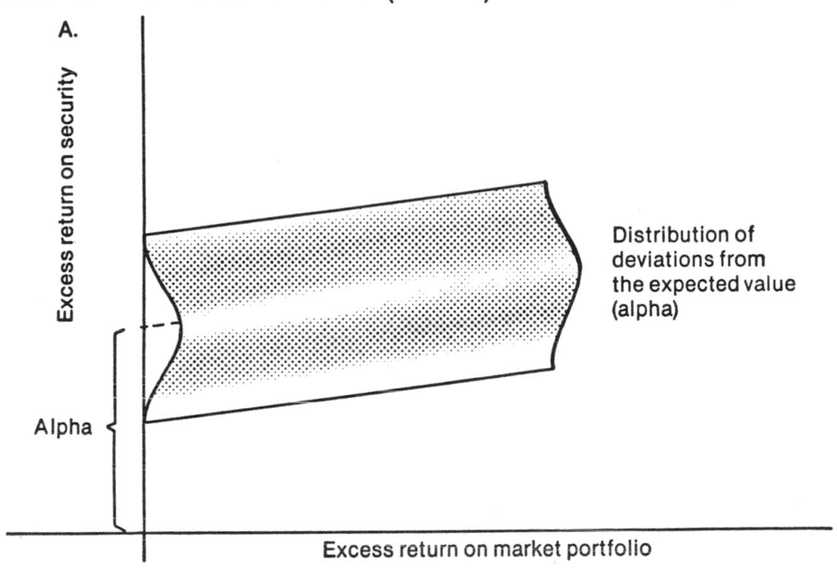

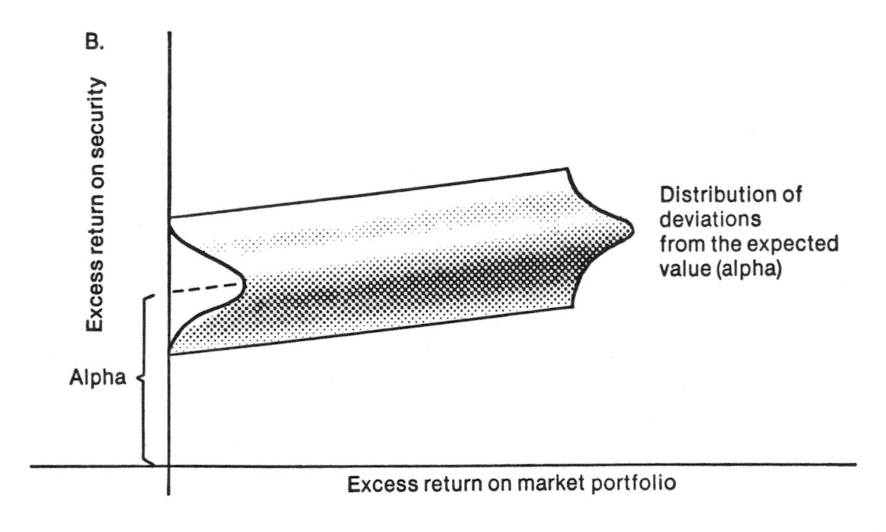

rity's characteristics requires three estimated values: (*a*) alpha, (*b*), beta, and (*c*) an estimate of alpha's dispersion—the variance of the residual component of return (i.e., the amount by which alpha is likely to diverge from its expected value). Looked at another way, since alpha is an estimate of the nonmarket contribution to return, a measure of the dispersion of the residual component of return (typically its standard deviation) is a measure of the security's *nonmarket risk.*

CLASSIFICATION OF RISK

It follows that if a security's excess return can be broken down into two components—alpha (nonmarket related) and beta (market related)—a security's risk can also be divided into the same categories. As discussed earlier, risk, as the term is used within the context of MPT, is the possibility that the actual return from an investment will differ from the expected return. The estimates of risk used by MPT practitioners are attempts to categorize and quantify this lack of assurance that the future will materialize as expected.

Thus, the risk associated with an investment outcome can be broken down into two parts: (1) the *systematic* part related to relationship of the security to the market and (2) the *residual* part related to the deviation between the expected and actual results for the *nonmarket* component of return. Therefore,

TOTAL SECURITY RISK	=	RISK OF THE RESIDUAL (NONMARKET) COMPONENT	+	RISK OF THE SYSTEMATIC (MARKET) COMPONENT

The equation for an expected security characteristic line[2] can be expressed as follows:

EXPECTED VALUE OF A SECURITY'S EXCESS RETURN	=	EXPECTED VALUE OF THE RESIDUAL (NONMARKET) COMPONENT OF EXCESS RETURN	+	EXPECTED VALUE OF THE SYSTEMATIC (MARKET) COMPONENT OF EXCESS RETURN

[2] The formal equation is

$$\text{Exp}(\tilde{R}_i - \rho) = \alpha_i + \beta_{im}\,\text{Exp}(\tilde{R}_m - \rho)$$

(cont.)

Since the standard deviation of the distribution of a security's expected excess returns quantifies the likelihood that deviations of certain magnitudes will occur, it is an appropriate measure of risk.

Conceptually, therefore,

TOTAL SECURITY RISK	=	STANDARD DEVIATION OF THE RESIDUAL (NONMARKET) COMPONENT OF EXCESS RETURN	+	STANDARD DEVIATION OF THE SYSTEMATIC (MARKET) COMPONENT OF EXCESS RETURN

The problem with this conceptually accurate representation is that, mathematically, standard deviations are not additive. However, given the relationship

$$\text{STANDARD DEVIATION}^2 = \text{VARIANCE}$$

and the fact that variances of two independent sources of risk —nonmarket and market—can be combined, it is possible to square the two standard deviations and then combine the two resulting variances. Thus, the equation[3] for a security's risk is

TOTAL SECURITY RISK (VARIANCE)	=	VARIANCE OF THE RESIDUAL (NONMARKET) COMPONENT OF EXCESS RETURN	+	VARIANCE OF THE SYSTEMATIC (MARKET) COMPONENT OF EXCESS RETURN

where:

Exp = Expected value.
$\sim$ = Variable not known in advance.
R_i = Holding period return on security i.
ρ = Riskless rate of return.
R_m = Holding period return on the market.
α_i = Expected nonmarket excess return on security i.
β_{im} = Sensitivity of security i's excess return to the market's excess return.

[3] The formal equation is

$$\text{Var}(\tilde{R}_i - \rho) = \text{Var}(\tilde{r}_i) + \text{Var}[\beta_{im}(\tilde{R}_m - \rho)]$$

---

or

$$\text{Var}(\tilde{R}_i - \rho) = \text{Var}(\tilde{r}_i) + \beta_{im}^2 \text{Var}(\tilde{R}_m - \rho)$$

where:

Var = Variance.
~ = Variable not known in advance.
R_i = Holding period return on security i.
ρ = Riskless rate of return.
R_m = Holding period return on the market.
β_{im} = Sensitivity of security i's excess return to the market's excess return.
r_i = Probability distribution of residual returns for the ith security.

Notice that in the formal equation for the expected value of a security's excess return, alpha is not designated as an "expected value." The reason is that alpha, by definition, is already an expected value. Specifically, alpha is the expected value of a probability distribution of excess security-related returns (designated $\tilde{r}_i$). Thus, the residual (non-market) component of risk in the equation is the variance of $\tilde{r}_i$ (and alpha does not appear in the equation).

Chapter 25

Risk: Classification and measurement

To better understand the classification of risk, it may be useful to imagine a "market portfolio"—one consisting of all outstanding stocks. The total return for accepting the level of risk associated with the market portfolio is the aggregate rate of return society pays to suppliers of risk capital. This return and its associated risk are tied to the overall capital market system. Accordingly, such *returns* are called *systematic* or *market-related* returns. Similarly, the *risk* that is linked to the overall capital market system is referred to as *systematic* or *market-related* risk.

Any risk beyond market-related or systematic risk is known by a variety of names, including residual risk, nonmarket risk, unsystematic risk, and selection risk. Residual merely defines what is "left over." The nonmarket and unsystematic nomenclature parallels the "market" and "systematic" terminology. So-called selection risk pinpoints the source of the risk as coming from selecting investments which are different from the total market. In turn, residual risk can be broken down into *specific risk* (arising from factors that are specific to the company) and *extra-market risk* (arising from components of homogeneous groups whose movements are independent of the market as a whole).

From the perspective of the overall market, each investor's selection risk is always offset by some aggregation of other investors' selection risk. *For the market as a whole, there is no selection risk.* Looked at another way, the capital market system cannot, and does not, reward investment selection. The capital market system only rewards capital market risk. Any gains derived solely from astute investment selection are at the

expense of the investors who have the offsetting selection losses.

PORTFOLIO CHARACTERISTIC LINES

An approach similar to that used to construct a security-related characteristic line can be used to generate a *portfolio characteristic line*[1] where

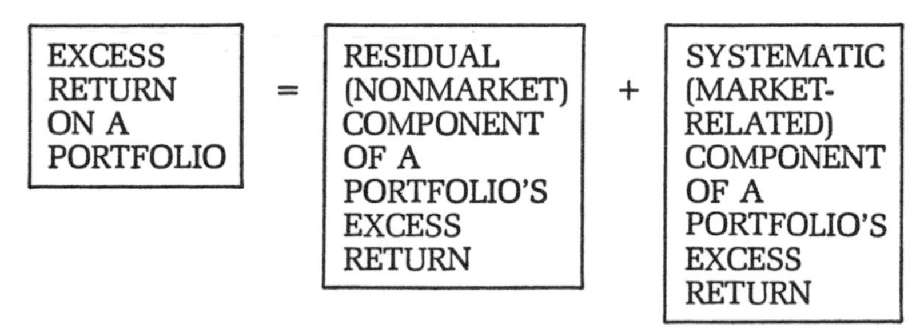

A portfolio's characteristic line is derived from the estimates for the individual securities that comprise the portfolio. In the case of alpha and beta, the relationship is straightforward. A portfolio's alpha is merely the weighted average (using relative market values as weights) of the alpha values of its component securities. Similarly, a portfolio's beta is the weighted average of the beta values of its component securities.

The residual or nonmarket risk of a portfolio (the probability and the amount by which the actual results will deviate from the expectation) is more difficult to estimate. This difficulty arises from the fact that the amount by which the actual nonmarket component of the portfolio's excess return deviates from its expected value, alpha, depends on the degree to which the security-level equivalents of these components are correlated.

---

[1] In technical terms

$$(\tilde{R}_p - \rho) = (\alpha_p + \tilde{r}_p) + (\beta_{pm}(\tilde{R}_m - \rho))$$

where:

$\sim$ = Variable not known in advance.
R_p = Return on portfolio P.
α_p = Expected value of the nonmarket component of portfolio P's excess return.
r_p = Deviation of the actual nonmarket component of portfolio P's excess return from its expected value.
β_{pm} = The sensitivity of portfolio P's excess return to the market portfolio.
R_m = Return on market portfolio.
ρ = Riskless rate of return.

If, for example, a portfolio consists of a few oil stocks, the correlation between the individual securities' nonmarket component of excess return would likely be very high. As a result, nonmarket risk would be very high. If, at the other extreme, the portfolio consists of a well-diversified selection of holdings, it is possible to assume that the deviations of the actual nonmarket component of excess return will be uncorrelated. In this case, the portfolio's nonmarket risk is the weighted average of the variance for the nonmarket component of excess return for its component securities.

R-SQUARED

It has been shown that alpha is the expected value of the nonmarket component of a security's excess return. Alpha is, by definition, uncorrelated with beta—the market-related component of a security's excess return. It has also been shown that a security's total risk consists of two independent components—alpha (nonmarket related) and beta (market related).

The so-called R-squared is a measure of the proportion of the total risk that is market related. Therefore,

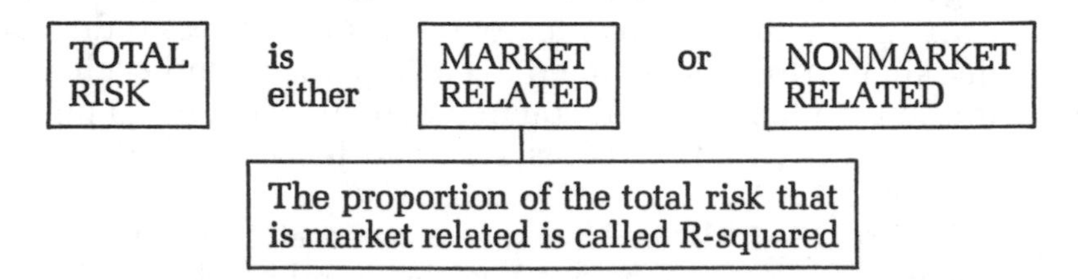

Thus, much as general terms such as alpha and beta have taken on very narrow and explicit meanings within the context of MPT, *R-squared* defines the proportion of either a security's or a portfolio's total risk that is attributable to market risk.

In a portfolio context, R-squared measures the completeness of diversification relative to that of the overall market. The market portfolio, for example, is completely diversified. Thus, in the market portfolio, systematic, or market, risk is the only source of uncertainty. Since R-squared is a measure of the proportion of the total risk that is market risk, the R-squared of the market portfolio is 1.00. Put another way, a portfolio with an R-squared of 1.0 will have zero selection risk. Technically, R-squared is the *coefficient of determination* (R^2).

The formula for computing R-squared, the proportion of total risk (measured by variance) that is attributable to the overall market, is[2]

$$R^2 = \frac{\text{VARIANCE OF THE MARKET COMPONENT OF RETURN}}{\text{VARIANCE OF BOTH COMPONENTS OF RETURN}}$$

The value of R-squared for a typical stock is about 0.30. This means that around 30 percent of a typical stock's behavior (and, hence, risk) is explained by the behavior of the market. On the other hand, the R-squared for a well-diversified portfolio will typically exceed 0.90. *This means that more than 90 percent of a well-diversified portfolio's total price movements can typically be explained by the market's behavior.*

EFFECT OF DIVERSIFICATION

Research examined in Chapter 18 demonstrated that only relatively minor reductions in total risk can be achieved as the size of a portfolio is increased beyond 20 or so unrelated securities. Figure 25–1 goes one step further by showing the relationship between portfolio size and (*a*) total portfolio risk, as well as (*b*) the nonmarket component of total portfolio risk. The assumptions underlying the figure approximate the findings of the empirical studies of market performance. Specifically, the standard deviation of the annual excess return on the market portfolio is assumed to be 20 percent, and each security is assumed to have an R-squared of 0.30. (That is, 30 percent of each security's total risk is assumed to be attributable to the market).

Figure 25–1 shows that the nonmarket component of total portfolio risk "washes out" as the number of securities in a portfolio increases. The significance of this phenomenon is that in well-diversified portfolios, the relevant measure of risk for a security is beta—its relationship to the market, or systematic risk. As illustrated in Figure 25–1 while most nonmarket risk can be diversified away, a significant amount of systematic risk remains. Thus, in a diversified portfolio, the only relevant measure of risk for a security is its volatility. In Sharpe's words, "the unsystematic risk is irrelevant, it will 'wash out' when the security is combined with others." [245, p. 97]

[2] Technically, a security's R-squared value—the proportion of total risk measured by variance attributable to market risk—is

$$R^2 = \frac{\beta_{im}^2 \operatorname{Var}(\tilde{R}_m - \rho)}{\operatorname{Var}(\tilde{R}_i - \rho)}$$

FIGURE 25–1: Effect of diversification on risk

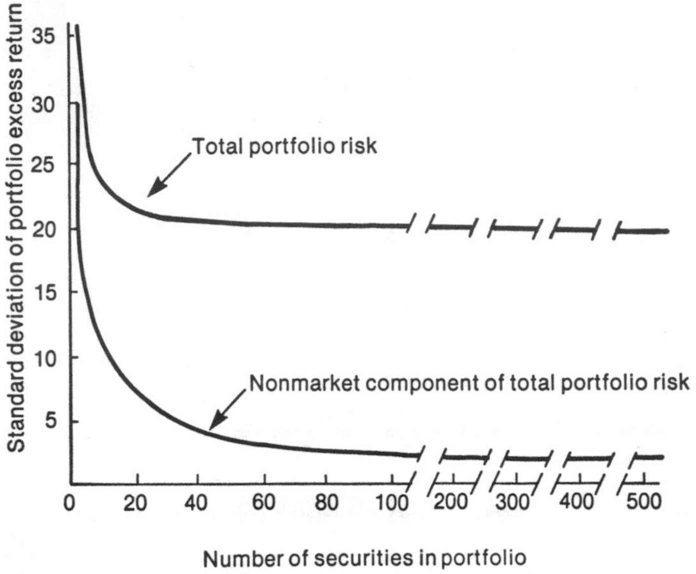

Source: After Sharpe [252, pp. 115–16].

INTERNATIONAL DIVERSIFICATION

It should be clear from the preceding section that diversification reduces risk. While the nonmarket component of risk can be diversified away (by holding the market portfolio), market risk is unavoidable. The only way this systematic market risk can be lowered is to expand the definition of "market" to include other dissimilar markets.

Bruno Solnik [261, 262] has pursued this avenue of research by studying the effect of international diversification on risk. Figure 25–2 contrasts the total risk of portfolios drawn exclusively from securities traded on the New York Stock Exchange with the risk of an international portfolio drawn from exchanges in the United States, the United Kingdom, France, Germany, Italy, Belgium, the Netherlands, and Switzerland. As expected, Solnik's results show that internationally diversified portfolios are much less risky than those limited to NYSE issues.

THE MEANING OF RISK

It is possible to focus too closely on curves that show a progressive reduction of risk. The hazard is that the remaining

FIGURE 25–2: International diversification

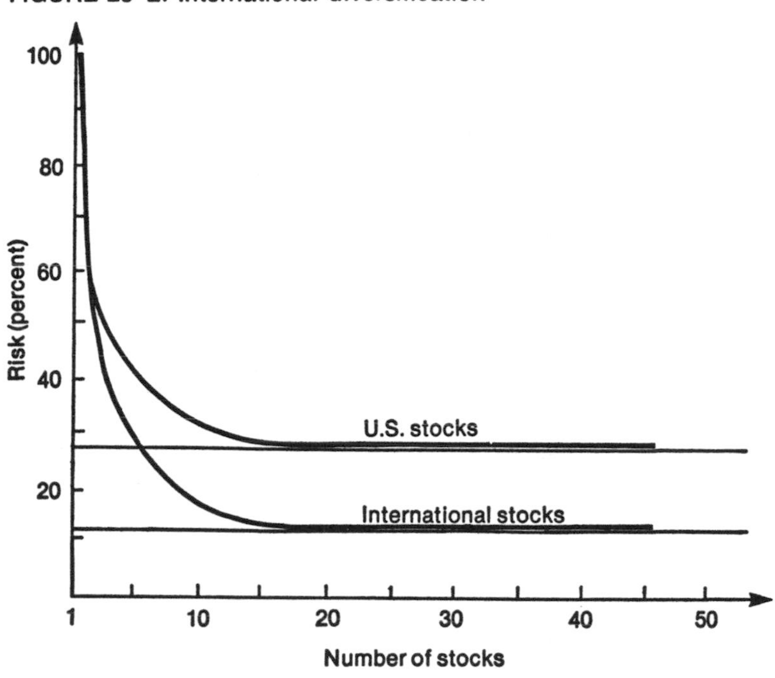

Source: Solnik [261, p. 51].

levels of systematic risk lose their proper perspective. Figure 25–3 shows that the standard deviation of the market (NYSE) portfolio is approximately 20 percent. This means that, on average, in every two out of three years, the market's return will fall within plus or minus 20 percent of the expected return.

Using data from the Ibbotson and Sinquefield study, Figure 25–3 shows a capital market line—the average historical rate of return provided by the marketplace for various levels of risk. On the average, the market portfolio (with a beta of 1.0) has provided an annual return of 9.2 percent. However, given the historical standard deviation of return of 22.4 percent, the market portfolio had a 68 percent probability of providing an annual return of between 31.6 percent (the average of 9.2 percent plus one standard deviation of 22.4 percent) and a negative 13.2 percent (the average of 9.2 percent minus one standard deviation of 22.4 percent). The funnel-shaped pattern in Figure 25–3 illustrates an important concept—the expansion

FIGURE 25–3: Capital market line's "risk funnels"

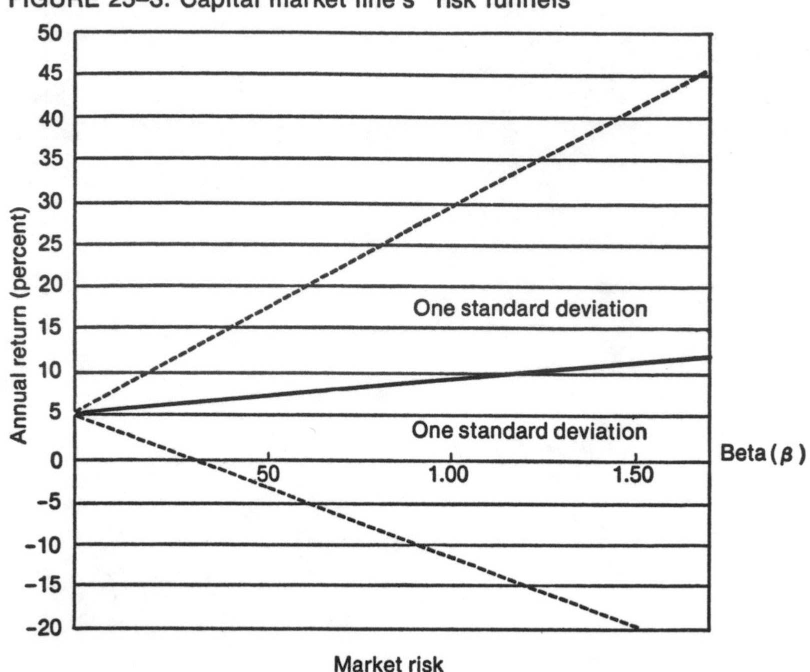

Source: Based on historical data from 1926–1976 taken from Ibbotson and Sinquefield [127].

in total risk (in this case the one standard deviation range) as the level of market risk (beta) increases.

The key point to remember is that the higher the beta, the greater is the standard deviation. While high-beta portfolios can be expected to outperform good markets they can be expected to underperform bad markets. This is, of course, no news to most investors. What is news, however, is that MPT allows these expectations to be quantified in advance!

Chapter 26

Structure of MPT

At this juncture, it may be useful to review the importance of the possibly bewildering array of "hypotheses," "theories," "models," and "lines" that comprise MPT.

THE EFFICIENT MARKET HYPOTHESIS

Early chapters examined the pivotal notion of the efficient market hypothesis in its three forms. The importance of the hypothesis is that if the market is largely inefficient, the study of MPT need not, and in fact, could not proceed. First of all, if the market were inefficient, it would not be necessary to bother with approaches such as MPT. Enormous profits could be realized by detecting and capitalizing on the opportunities posed by the inefficient marketplace. Second, a "relatively" efficient market is a prerequisite for MPT and the existence of "widespread" inefficiencies would invalidate MPT's theoretical foundation.

The research chronicled in earlier chapters established that the market is "reasonably" efficient. Given this research, and the number of astute and knowledgeable competitors, it is logical to assume that the market price for a security will not diverge *by much,* or *for long,* from the market's consensus of an equitable return for a given level of risk.

PORTFOLIO THEORY

Portfolio theory is a *normative* theory. Normative means "normal" or "standard." In economics, a normative theory refers to the "normal" way consumers behave. Accordingly, portfolio theory (or Markowitz theory) delineates the decisions

that will be made by a population of normal investors—each exercising his or her personal preferences.

Specifically, portfolio theory holds that all investors are risk averse. This means that, other things being equal, all rational investors will avoid risk. Thus, faced with the four investment alternatives in Figure 26–1A, all rational investors would choose alternative A—offering the best combination of low-risk and high expected return.

However, as a result of the unanimous preference for alternative A, the inefficiencies depicted in Figure 26–1A will diminish until the available alternatives comprise the efficient set depicted in Figure 26–1B. It should be stressed, however, that portfolio theory says nothing about the way prices of individual assets adjust. The theory describes only the way in which normal investors behave.

Consequently, the importance of portfolio theory is that it provides a normative description of an investor's trade-off between two important dimensions—risk and expected return. This trade-off between what is not wanted (risk) and what is wanted (expected return) can be uniquely represented for any investor by an indifference curve. Figure 26–1C illustrates three indifference curves from a hypothetical investor's indifference map. Moving downward to the right, from curve 1 to 3, each of these curves represents a decreasing level of investor's utility, or satisfaction.

The matching of the available investment alternatives (from the efficient set of alternatives shown in Figure 26–1B) with the investor's most desired alternative (as represented by the highest feasible indifference curve in Figure 26–1C) is the final step in the investment selection process. This selection of the optimal combination of risk and return from the efficient set of many such alternatives is shown in Figure 26–1D.

Importantly, the fact that all investors agree about the optimal combination of risky securities in Figure 26–1B does not mean that all investors will choose the same portfolio. Different sets of indifference curves, representing either more defensive or more aggressive investors, would lead to the selection of different investments from the wide-ranging set of efficient alternatives.

Adding the assumption that every investor can borrow and lend changes the optimal combinations of risk and expected return that are available in the marketplace—the efficient set of investment alternatives on curve *XYZ* in Figure 26–1B. Figure 26–1E shows the asset allocation line—the set of investment

FIGURE 26–1: Portfolio theory—Summary

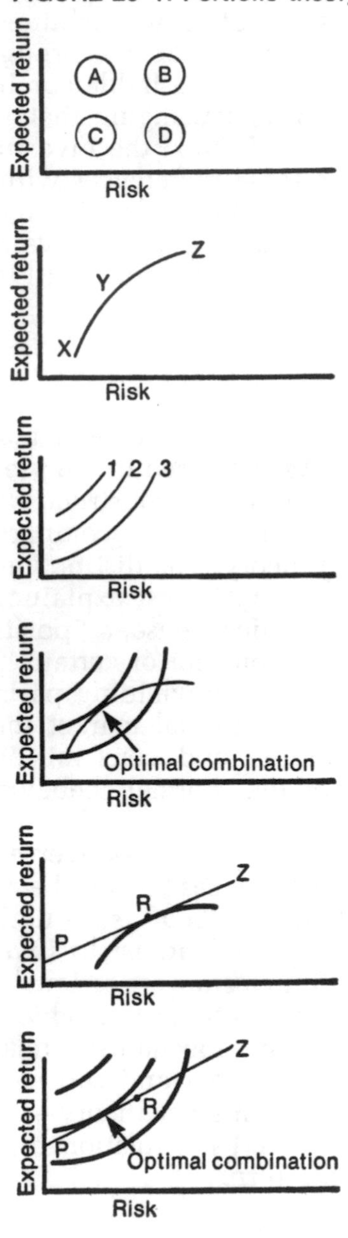

A. Inefficient set of investment alternatives.

B. Efficient set of investment alternatives (without borrowing and lending).

C. Investor's indifference map.

D. Investor's optimal combination of risk and expected return (without borrowing and lending).

E. Asset allocation line (with borrowing and lending) connecting the riskless rate of return and the optimal portfolio.

F. Investor's optimal combination of risk and expected return with borrowing and lending.

alternatives which become available with lending and borrowing. These range from the riskless rate of return, obtained by lending to the Treasury at the riskless rate (point *P*), through to choosing to be fully invested in the most desirable combination of risky investments (point *R*), to leveraging that risky portfolio through borrowing to point Z. Next the investment that best matches the investor's personal preferences with the available alternatives is selected (i.e., the point of tangency between the highest level of investor utility and the available alternatives shown on the asset allocation line *PRZ* in Figure 26–1F.

CAPITAL MARKET THEORY

This theory could appropriately be called "capital market theory based on portfolio theory." As explained in the preceding section, portfolio theory is a normative construct which explains how investors "normally" behave. By comparison, capital market theory is a *positive* theory. The distinction between a normative and a positive theory is best explained by an analogy to a machine. In a mechanical sense, a "positive" mechanism is "definite, unyielding, constant or certain," the outcomes of which are "determined by unyielding parts, or controlled movements." In this sense, capital market theory can be thought of as the unyielding and constant price-setting mechanism that is driven by the "normal" behavior of investors.

Portfolio theory holds that all investors are risk averse and that in satisfying their individual preferences they will act in a consistent, predetermined way. Portfolio theory says nothing about the way prices of individual assets adjust to investor behavior. It follows, however, that if investors are rational, risk averse, and act as portfolio theory suggests (all of which are logical assumptions), the price-setting mechanism relating risk and expected return will be consistent and can be predicted. This is the function of capital market theory—to describe (and, hence, allow us to predict) the relationship between expected risk and expected return.

CAPITAL ASSET PRICING MODEL (CAPM)

William Sharpe has aptly described models as "toy worlds." The advantage of these toy worlds is that key relationships can be defined and analyzed without extraneous information.

Once the key relationships have been dissected and understood, the toy world can then be moved toward the real world by progressively adding more relationships.

One of the most important "toy worlds," or models, of the capital market theory is the capital asset pricing model (a contribution attributable to Sharpe [242], Lintner [168, 167], Treynor [270], and Mossin [197]). Broadly speaking, the simplifying assumptions on which the CAPM is based are:

1. Investors are risk averse and act as portfolio theory suggests.
2. Investors can borrow or lend at the risk-free interest rate.
3. There are no taxes.

Given these assumptions (which are, in fact, not as limiting as they appear), the CAPM provides an explicit statement of the equilibrium expected return on all assets. When the market is in equilibrium, there is no pressure for change. In disequilibrium, investors are dissatisfied with either the securities they hold or the prices of these securities and, as a result, there is pressure for change. At any moment, however, the market is in equilibrium, reflecting the combined influence of all investors' wealth, preferences, and predictions. Whenever disequilibrium occurs because of changes in wealth, preferences, or predictions, these changes are translated to the market and equilibrium is restored.

Thus, the CAPM is the facet of capital market theory that provides an explicit statement of the equilibrium expected return for all securities. Specifically, the CAPM states that the prices of assets in a capital market will be in equilibrium where the expected return on a security is equal to a riskless rate of interest plus a premium that is proportional to the amount of market-related risk—beta. Stated another way, the expected excess return for a security, or portfolio, will come entirely from the market component of return. This is because in equilibrium a security with zero systematic risk (beta) will have the expected return that is available for a riskless asset. Further, in equilibrium, the expected excess return from the nonmarket component is always zero.

According to the CAPM, for efficient portfolios

1. An appropriate measure of risk is the standard deviation of return.
2. In equilibrium, there is a linear relationship between risk and expected return.

FIGURE 26–2: Summary of linear constructs used in MPT

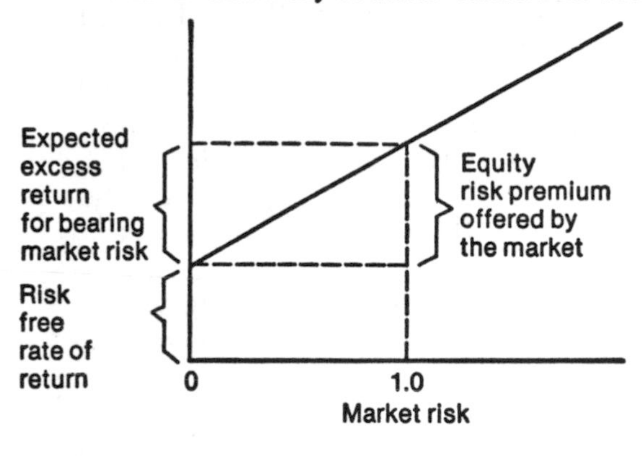

A. *Capital market line*

Concept. The price of immediate consumption and the price of risk (alternatively, the reward for waiting and the reward per unit of risk borne).

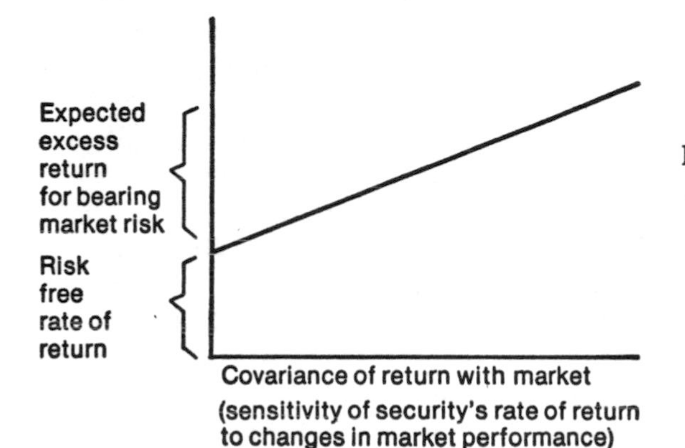

B. *Security market line*

Concept. In equilibrium, *every* security and portfolio will plot along the line.

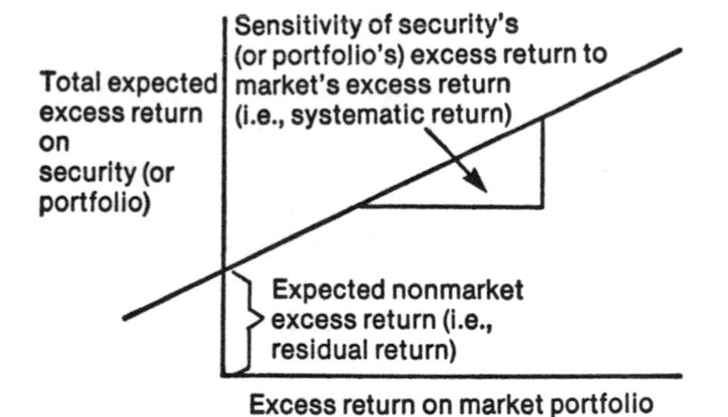

C. *Characteristic line*

Concept. Summarizes the relationship between the excess return on a security (or portfolio) and the excess return on the market.

A construct that is used to portray this relationship between the risk and return of a market portfolio and the riskless rate of return—thereby defining the widely held notions of the price of risk and the price of immediate consumption—is the *capital market line*. Since "price" to the buyer is the same as the "reward" to the seller, these notions can also be thought of as rewards; specifically, the reward per unit of risk borne and the reward for waiting. The format of the capital market line is shown in Figure 26–2A.

The CAPM holds that for individual securities (which may be regarded as highly inefficient portfolios) and portfolios, which are either efficient or inefficient,

1. An appropriate measure of risk is
   a. The covariance between a security's rate of return and that of the market.
   b. The volatility of a security's rate of return relative to changes in market performance.
2. In equilibrium, every portfolio and every security will show a linear relationship between risk and expected return.

The *security market line* is used to portray this relationship between risk and expected return for securities, as well as portfolios. The format of this construct is shown in Figure 26–2B.

In equilibrium, every portfolio and security will plot along the security market line. The market portfolio is no exception. Thus, the capital market line is a special case of the security market line, where the measure of risk used in the security market line (the covariance with the market) turns out to be the market's covariance with itself.

Another construct, the *characteristic line* summarizes the linear relationship between two variables: the market's excess return and a portfolio's or a security's excess return. The values of *alpha and beta* represent the vertical intercept and the slope, respectively, of the line. This relationship is shown in Figure 26–2C.

PART FOUR

MPT: TESTS, EXTENSIONS, AND APPLICATIONS

Chapter 27

Empirical tests

The market model and the capital asset pricing model (CAPM) have been subjected to a considerable amount of testing. The results of these investigations are discussed in this chapter.

TESTS OF THE MARKET MODEL

The market model, sometimes called the diagonal model, hypothesizes that a linear relationship exists between the returns on an individual security or a portfolio, and an index of market returns. To test this hypothesis, Marshall Blume [30] examined the stability of beta coefficients over time. Using successive seven-year periods between July 1926 and June 1968, Blume calculated the correlation between period-to-period betas for portfolios of varying size. He calculated, for example, the correlation between the average beta coefficient which prevailed for the period 1926–33 and that for 1933–40; the correlation between the 1933–40 and 1940–47 betas, and so on. He repeated each calculation for portfolios composed of 1, 2, 4, 7, 10, 20, 35, and 50 securities, respectively. As shown in Table 27–1, the correlations between period-to-period betas are quite high—especially for portfolios containing ten or more securities.

The square of each correlation coefficient in Table 27–1 indicates the percentage variation in the second period's beta that can be explained by the beta of the preceding period. Thus, for individual securities with an average correlation coefficient of approximately 0.60, approximately 36 percent (0.60^2) of the variation in betas can be explained by the historical betas. However, for portfolios with 50 securities, 96 percent of the variation (0.98^2) can be explained by historical betas.

TABLE 27–1: Correlation coefficients of betas for varying size portfolios between successive seven-year time periods

	Correlation of period-to-period betas				
Number of securities per portfolio	*Between 1926–1933 and 1933–1940*	*Between 1933–1940 and 1940–1947*	*Between 1940–1947 and 1947–1954*	*Between 1947–1954 and 1954–1961*	*Between 1954–1961 and 1961–1968*
1	0.63	0.62	0.59	0.65	0.60
2	0.71	0.76	0.72	0.76	0.73
4	0.80	0.85	0.81	0.84	0.84
7	0.86	0.91	0.88	0.87	0.88
10	0.89	0.94	0.90	0.92	0.92
20	0.93	0.97	0.95	0.95	0.97
35	0.96	0.98	0.95	0.97	0.97
50	0.98	0.99	0.98	0.98	0.98

Source: Blume [30].

Thus, for estimating the future betas of large portfolios, simple extrapolations appear to provide extremely accurate forecasts. Furthermore, Gerald Levitz [158] has shown that the forecasting accuracy associated with 30 and 40 security portfolios can be improved by adjusting for the tendency of deviant betas to return to normal.

Basically, the empirical tests support the market model hypothesis. That is, the relationship between security, or portfolio, returns and market returns (the slope of the characteristic line, or beta) remains relatively stable over time. However, *for individual securities or small portfolios, extrapolations of future betas from historical betas do not produce sufficiently accurate forecasts.*

Empirical tests of alpha also support the market model hypothesis. The ex post (after the fact) alpha coefficient is an indication of how a stock has performed with the market-related portions of the total return eliminated. Studies show that *alphas in successive periods are not related.* As a result, historic alphas have no predictive value. This is not surprising. If high alphas tended to be followed by high alphas, investors would choose to hold only stocks with high alphas. This action, however, would bid up the price of high-alpha stocks which, in turn, would lower the return.

TESTS OF THE CAPITAL ASSET PRICING MODEL

The capital asset pricing model states that *in equilibrium,* the expected excess return for a security or portfolio will come

entirely from the market component of return. The verbal representation of this equation is

EXPECTED EXCESS RETURN ON A SECURITY	=	DEGREE TO WHICH THE SECURITY WILL AMPLIFY OR DAMPEN THE MOVEMENT OF THE MARKET (BETA)	×	EXPECTED EXCESS RETURN ON THE MARKET

Thus, the CAPM states that when the market is in equilibrium, there is a linear relationship between the *expected* returns on individual securities and *expected* returns on the market portfolio. The difficulty one encounters in attempting to test this model is that such ex ante (before the fact) expectations are not directly measurable. However, because investors' expectations are what drive the market, an exact test of the CAPM can be based on the study of ex post realizations. Basically, if both the CAPM and the market model are valid, then plots of the ex post returns on assets for any given period should cluster around the *security market line.*[1] The verbal representation of the equation for the security market line is:[2]

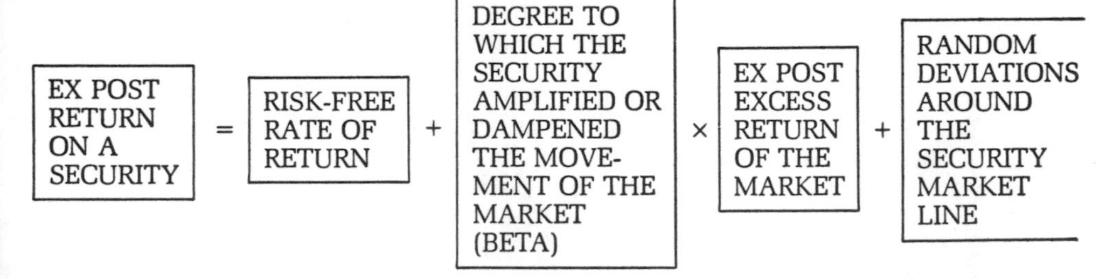

EX POST RETURN ON A SECURITY
=
RISK-FREE RATE OF RETURN
+
DEGREE TO WHICH THE SECURITY AMPLIFIED OR DAMPENED THE MOVEMENT OF THE MARKET (BETA)
×
EX POST EXCESS RETURN OF THE MARKET
+
RANDOM DEVIATIONS AROUND THE SECURITY MARKET LINE

To test the validity of this model, Black, Jensen, and Scholes [26] compared the theoretical and the actual relationships between systematic risk (beta) and average monthly returns for

---

[1] For a technical description of the derivation of the security market line from the market model and the CAPM, the interested reader is referred to Jensen [135, pp. 27–33].

[2] In specific technical terms:

$$R_i = \rho + \beta_{im} (R_m - \rho) + r_i$$

where:

R_i = Holding period return on security *i*.
ρ = Riskless rate of return.
β_{im} = Sensitivity of security *i*'s return to the market's return.
R_m = Holding period return on the market.
r_i = Random deviations.

all 1,952 common stocks listed on the NYSE for the 35-year period spanning 1931–65. In order to handle the massive amount of data, for each year the investigators grouped the securities into ten portfolios of approximately equal size on the basis of that year's beta coefficient. That is, the 195 securities with the highest betas were assigned to one portfolio, the 195 securities with the next highest betas were assigned to another portfolio, and so on.

Figure 27–1 compares the average monthly returns with the systematic risk (beta) for each of the ten different portfolios (denoted by *X*s) over the entire 35-year period. The market portfolio is denoted by the symbol O, and the solid line (the regression line, or line of "best fit," derived from the empirical portfolios) represents the actual relationships. The dashed

FIGURE 27–1: Systematic risk (beta) versus average monthly returns for ten different risk portfolios, and the market portfolio, for the 35-year period 1931–1965

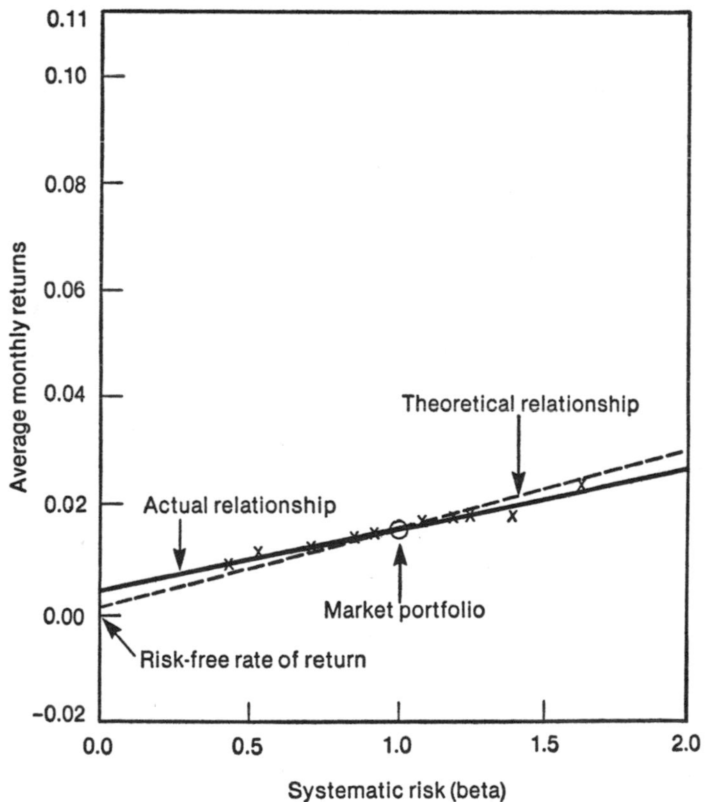

Source: Black, Jensen, and Scholes [26].

line, connecting the average risk-free rate of return and the rate of return on the market portfolio, depicts the theoretical relationship.

If the security market line correctly described reality, the theoretical (dashed) line would match the empirically derived (solid) line. The actual relationship is in fact highly linear (the correlation between return and beta was 0.996), but the actual intercept was higher, and the slope lower, than the theoretical expectation. In practical terms, this means that over the 35-year period, low-risk (low-beta) stocks earned higher returns than implied by the CAPM. Similarly, high-risk (high-beta) stocks showed lower returns than the theory predicts.

Figure 27–2 provides a closer look at the 35-year period studied by Black, Jensen, and Scholes. For four 105-month periods from January 1931 through December 1965, the systematic risk (beta) is plotted against the average monthly returns for the same ten market portfolios and the market portfolio. Here again, the actual relationships do not match the theoretical model. In the post-crash period from January 1931 through September 1939, the low-beta stocks earned less than the model implies and the high-beta stocks earned more. Thus, there is clearly a difference in slope between the theoretical and actual security market lines.

The second difference that can be noted lies in the *direction of the slope* for the actual relationships from April 1957 through December 1965. The security market line is based on the valid assumption that all investors are averse to risk. Nonetheless, the downward sloping security market line during the last 105-month period reveals that, on average, high-risk stocks earned less than low-risk stocks. Clearly, the market did not appropriately compensate investors for the risks they undertook during this period.

Black, Jensen, and Schole's presentation of the security market lines for periods from 1932 to 1965, reproduced in Figures 27–3A through 27–3C, provides further evidence of the discrepancy between the theoretical and actual relationships between risk and return. Although the empirical relationships appear linear, the slope of the line in some periods runs counter to what would be expected. Specifically, the negatively sloped security market lines are inconsistent with the notion that investors are rewarded for risk.

Figures 27–3A through 27–3C also illustrate that the reward that the market provides risk-takers (measured by the slope of the security market line) varies significantly from year to year.

FIGURE 27–2: Average monthly return versus systematic risk for four 105-month subperiods in the interval January 1931–December 1965

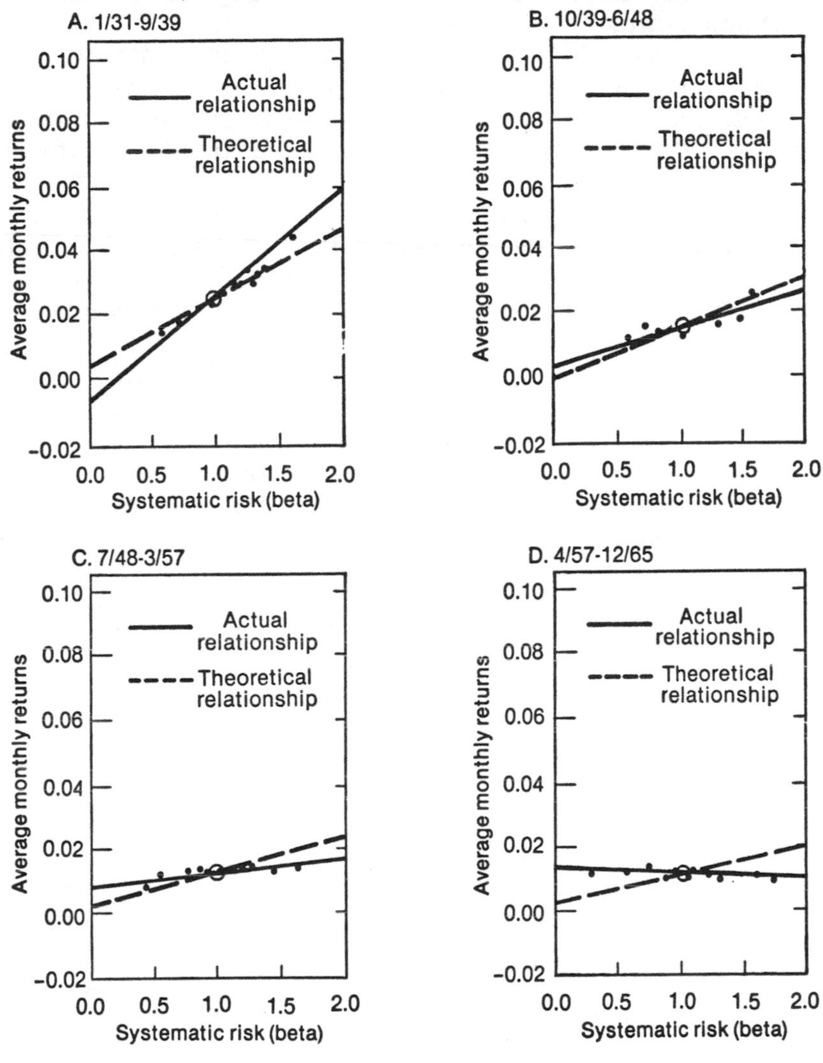

Source: Black, Jensen, and Scholes [26].

Clearly, accurate forecasts of the intercept and slope of this line in future periods could enable an investor to reap substantial profits. Unfortunately, Fama and MacBeth [77] have found that the time sequence of security market lines conforms to a random-walk model. This means that the intercept and slope of future lines cannot be forecast from the pattern of historical changes in these variables.

FIGURE 27–3A: Average monthly returns versus systematic risk for six successive two-year periods from 1932 to 1943.

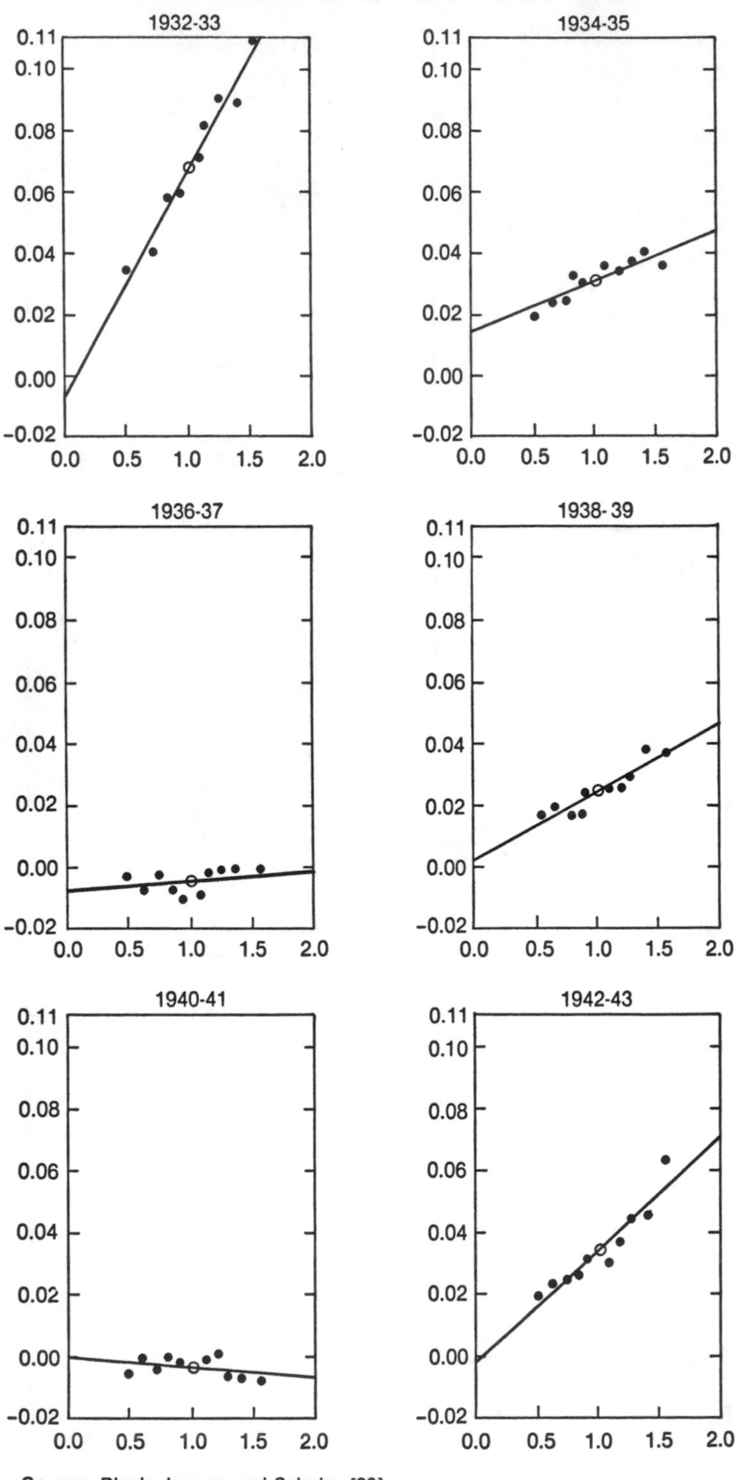

Source: Black, Jensen, and Scholes [26].

FIGURE 27–3B: Average monthly returns versus systematic risk for six successive two-year periods from 1944 to 1955

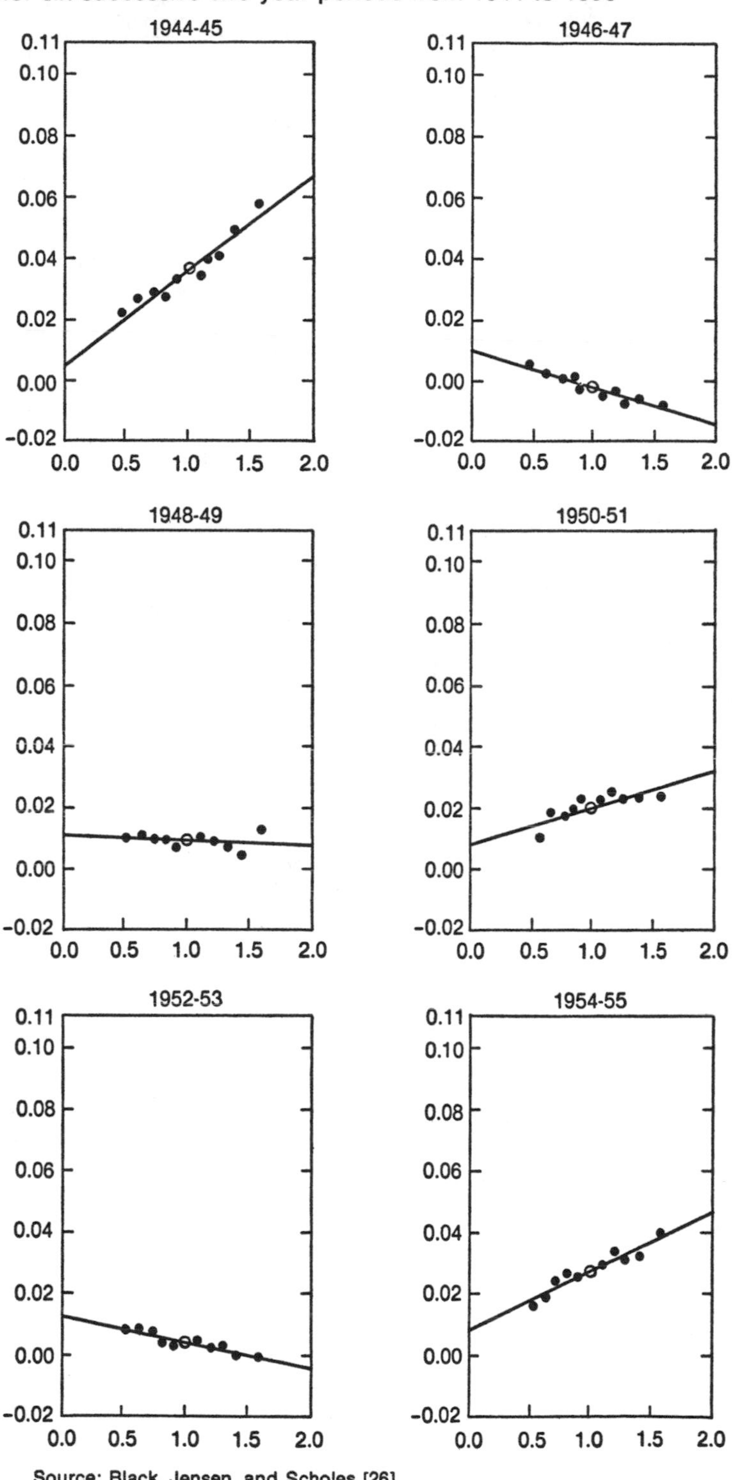

Source: Black, Jensen, and Scholes [26].

FIGURE 27–3C: Average monthly returns versus systematic risk for five successive two-year periods from 1956 to 1965.

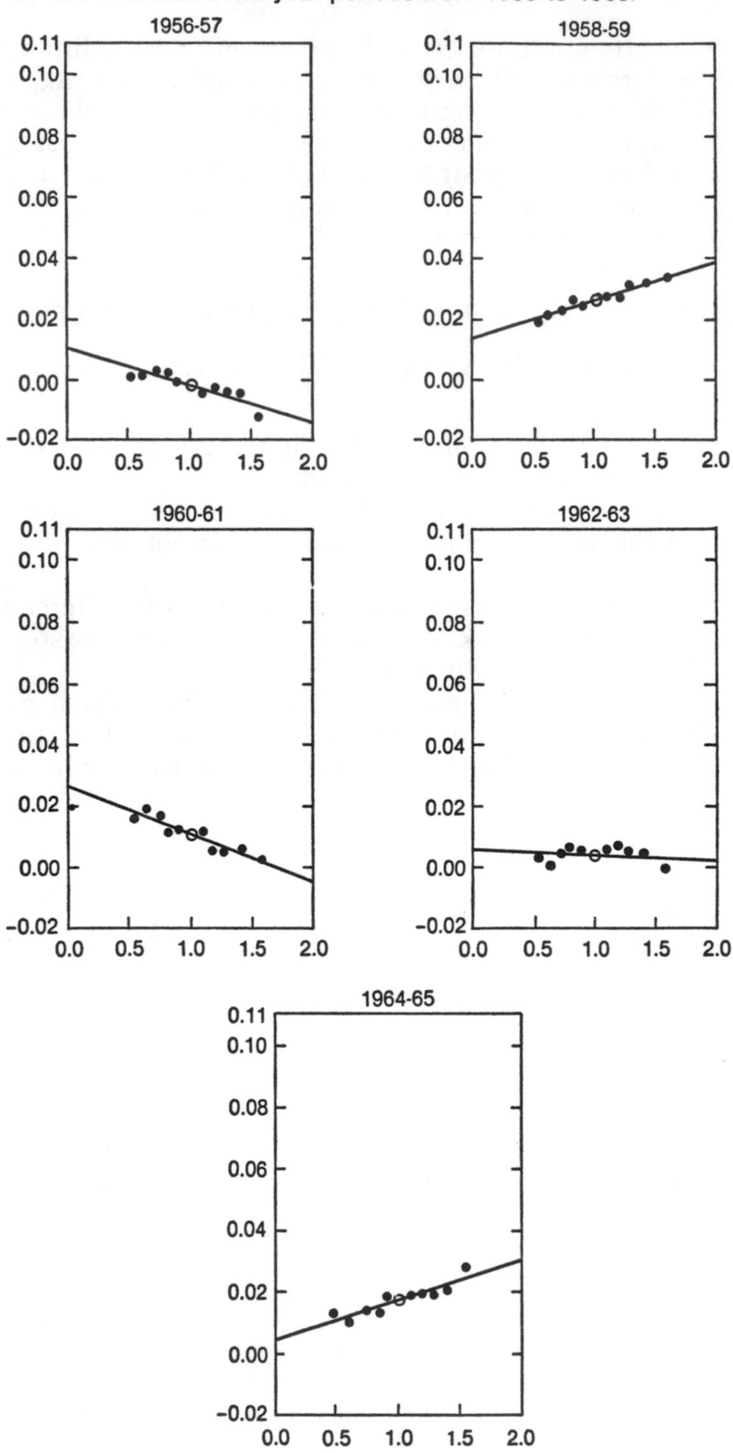

Source: Black, Jensen, and Scholes [26].

In an attempt to describe the observed relationship between risk and return, Black, Jensen, and Scholes [26] suggested a model in which the returns on a zero-beta portfolio are basically, substituted for the riskless rate of interest in the Sharpe-Lintner-Treynor-Mossin CAPM. This model accurately reproduces, but provides no theoretical explanation for empirically observed phenomena.

SUMMARY OF MARKET MODEL AND CAPM TESTS

The conclusions that can be drawn from these empirical tests are as follows:

1. On the average, and in the long run, investors are rewarded for bearing systematic risk.
2. The average relationship between risk and return is linear.
3. On the average, nonsystematic risk is not related to security returns.
4. The CAPM (which states that the zero-risk intercept will be equal to the riskless rate of return) is not consistent with the empirical findings.
5. The joint market model and the CAPM (which predicts that the slope of the security market line will be positive) have not been substantiated by the empirical evidence [see Jensen, 26, pp. 36–7].

Chapter 28

Extensions to the capital asset pricing model

A number of extensions to the basic CAPM have been proposed which seek to explain the empirically observed relationship between risk and return. Michael Brennan [37] and Fischer Black [23] have shown, for example, that the simplifying assumption of riskless borrowing and lending could explain the discrepancies between the theoretical and the observed results.

Other extensions have been formulated by William Fouse at Wells Fargo Investment Advisors. Fouse uses a security valuation model (discussed in Chapter 31) and analysts' estimates of systematic risk to construct ex ante (before the fact) estimates of security market lines. Figure 28–1A represents Wells Fargo's security market lines as plotted on June 30, 1970 and June 30, 1972, respectively. The security market line on June 30, 1970 indicated a market environment in which investors were well rewarded for assuming risks. Two years later, however, on June 30, 1972, the ex ante security market line portrayed an expected relationship under which taking on incremental amounts of risk did not carry the promise of commensurate increases in return.

Figure 28–1B shows the Wells Fargo ex ante security market lines on December 31, 1974 and June 30, 1975. At year-end 1974, market participants were very pessimistic (the Dow Jones Industrials Average closed at 616), and there was widespread aversion to accepting market-related risk. Accordingly, those few people who were willing to assume market risk were rewarded by relatively large expected incremental returns. Within six months, the market, as measured by the Dow Jones Industrial Average, had moved up 263 points to 879. These

FIGURE 28–1: Wells Fargo ex ante security market lines

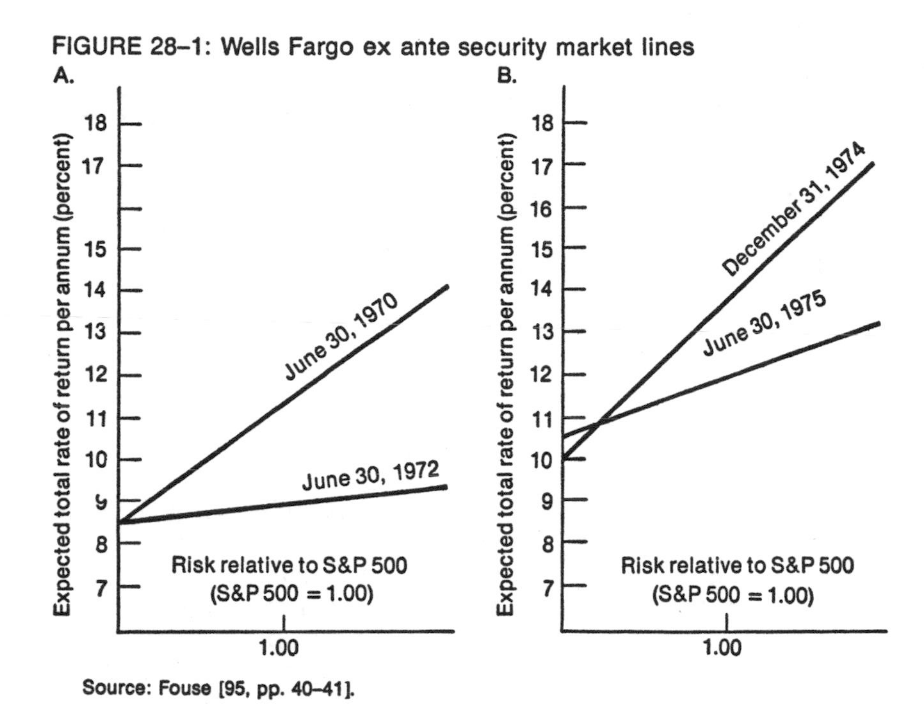

Source: Fouse [95, pp. 40–41].

higher prices are reflected in the lower expected returns for the June 30, 1975 ex ante security market line. Thus, in comparison to the market environment of December 31, 1974, an incremental market risk undertaken on June 30, 1975 carried significantly less promise of incremental returns.

LIQUIDITY MARKET LINE

While market liquidity is not explicitly described by capital market theory, it is conceptually consistent with it. Basically, capital market theory states that investors must be paid to assume risk. It follows, then, that the lower the market liquidity of a stock (i.e., the higher the risk), the higher is the expected return that will be demanded by the marketplace.

Using a liquidity ratio which measures the dollar value of trading required to elicit a 1 percent price variation, Wells Fargo has divided the stocks it analyzes into five liquidity sectors. Figure 28–2 shows the security market lines, called *liquidity* market lines, for each liquidity sector. The family of liquidity lines in Figure 28–2 shows that on December 31,

FIGURE 28–2: Wells Fargo liquidity market lines

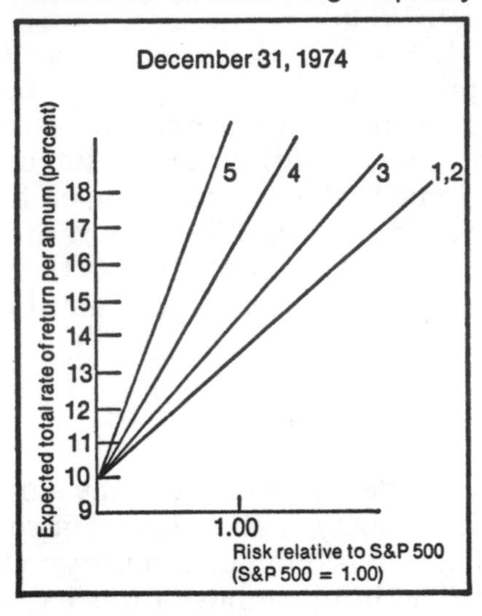

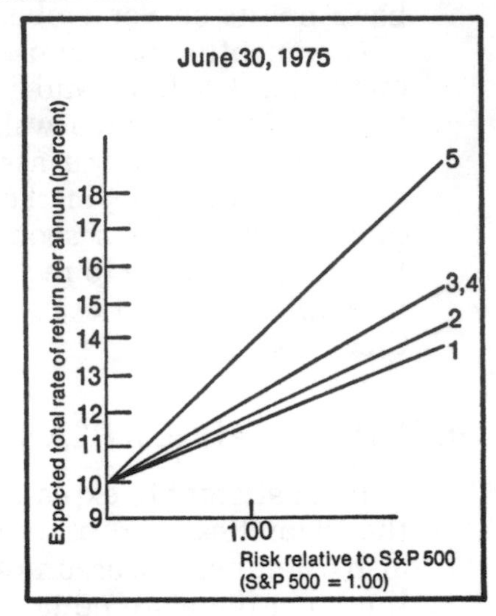

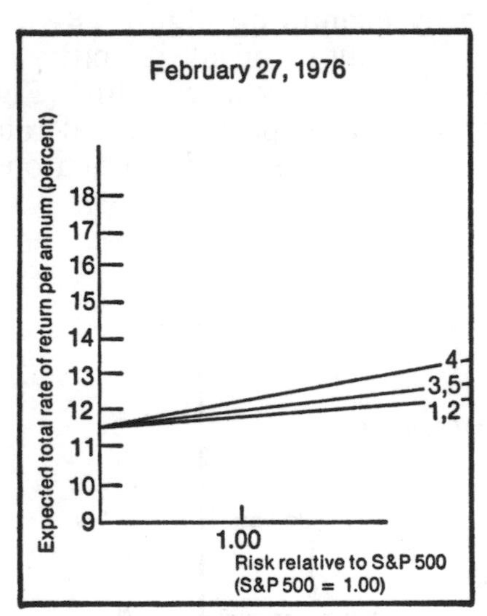

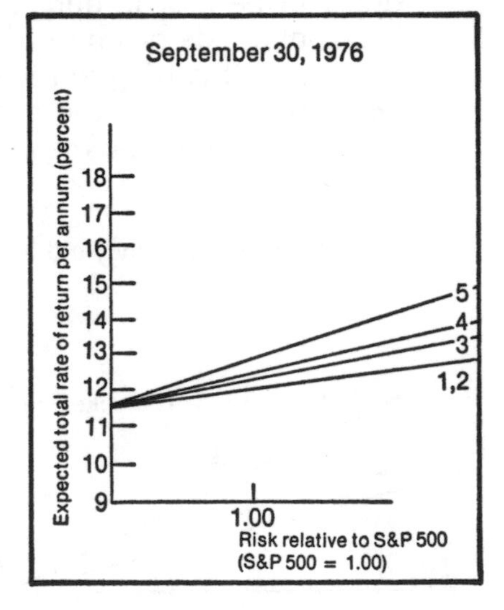

Source: Fouse [96, p. 43].

1974, for a beta of 1.0, there was a 440 basis point[1] spread in expected return between liquidity market lines 1 and 5. This spread had diminished to 230 basis points by June 30, 1975 and narrowed still further to only 50 basis points on February

[1] One hundred basis points is equal to 1 percentage point. Hence, 440 basis points is equal to 4.40 percent.

27, 1976. The liquidity "fan" then reopened to a spread of 190 basis points on September 30, 1976.

Commenting on the usefulness of Wells Fargo's ex ante security market lines and liquidity market lines, Fouse stated: "no particular genius was required to interpret the February 1976 market line and associated liquidity market lines as a signal that the stock market game that had been going on for 15 months was over, or soon would be over. Likewise, it did not require prescience to recognize the winter of 1974 as the time to emphasize equities, and higher risk, less liquid equities at that." [96, p. 45]

SECURITY MARKET PLANE

In an attempt to explain the differences between the slope of the theoretical and observed security market line, Fouse has also examined the assumption, underlying the security market line, that there are no taxes. The implications of this assumption can be best understood by examining Figure 28–3. The horizontal axis has been deliberately reversed to facilitate the merger of this diagram with the security market line. Figure 28–3 assumes that the average total expected annual rate of return from the market portfolio is 15 percent (shown on the

FIGURE 28–3: Security yield line

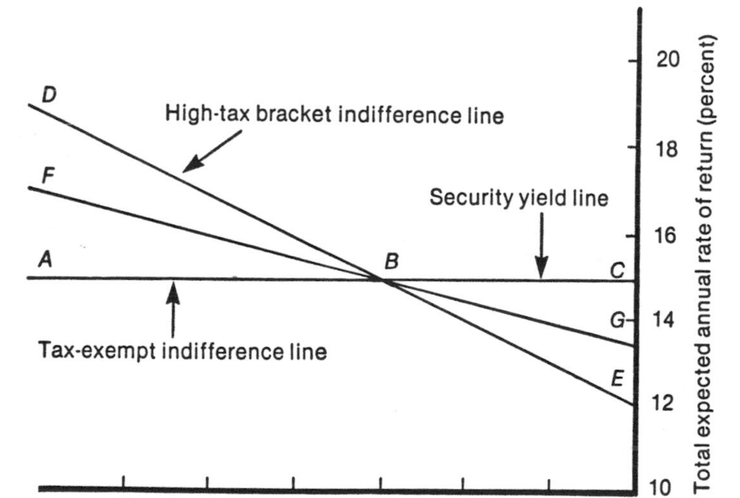

vertical scale), with 6 percent (shown on the horizontal scale), of the total return assumed to be derived from yield and the remaining 9 percent (not shown) derived from capital appreciation. The line *ABC* in Figure 28–3 is the indifference line for a tax-exempt investor. This means that as long as the total expected rate of return is constant at 15 percent, a tax-exempt investor does not care what proportion of the total return is derived from yield.

This is not the case, however, for a tax-paying investor whose yield income is taxed at double the rate levied on capital appreciation. Thus, moving from the assumed average expected yield of the market portfolio (6 percent), most tax-paying investors would be worse off if they received the same total expected return of 15 percent—but with the yield component accounting for a larger proportion of the total return.

Compare, for example, an investment in which all of the expected return is derived from yield with an investment where all of the expected return consists of capital appreciation. If an investor paid twice the taxes on return derived from yield, the aftertax return would be half that obtained from capital appreciation.

The high-tax bracket indifference line *DBE* in Figure 28–3 illustrates that if 50 percent of the yield is taxed away (and, to simplify the illustration, the nonyield portion goes untaxed), an investor will be indifferent to any combination of yield and total expected return along line *DBE*. That is, if all yields are halved by taxes, a 12 percent total return with zero yield leaves 12 percent. Similarly, an 18 percent total return with a 12 percent yield portion that is reduced by half provides an after-tax return of 12 percent.

With an estimate of point *B*—the intersection of the total expected annual rate of return for a universe of stocks and the portion of the total expected return derived from yield—plus a forecast of the slope of the tax indifference line derived from specific tax rates—a specific indifference line can be drawn for any individual.

More importantly, if tax-paying investors demand greater returns from more heavily taxed high-yield stocks, as this implies, high-yield stocks would have to offer investors higher than average total returns. Similarly, under the market's pricing mechanism, a stock with a small portion of its total return consisting of yield could attract sufficient purchasers at a lower than average total return. The relationship between the estimated total return and that portion of total return derived

FIGURE 28–4: Construction of a security market plane

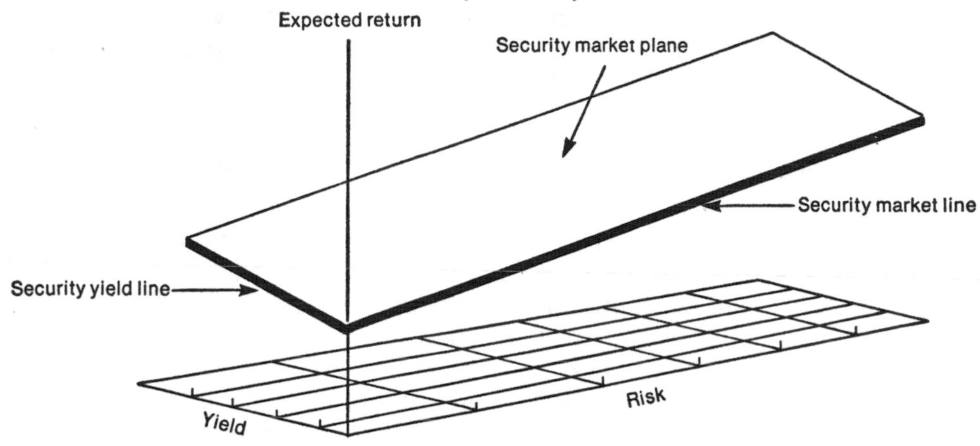

from yield can be portrayed by a *security yield line* such as line *FBG* in Figure 28–3.

The "yield" dimension is not recognized in the risk versus expected return relationship described by the security market line. This shortcoming can be eliminated, however, by expanding the two-dimensional security market line into a three-dimensional *security market plane.*

Figure 28–4 illustrates the features of a security market plane. The two dimensions defining a security market line are risk and total expected return. The addition of a security yield line—the relationship between the yield portion and the total expected return—as the third dimension creates a security market plane.

Chapter 29

Prediction and translation

If current prices in the major investment markets reflect both publicly disseminated and privately held information, these markets can be regarded as efficient. In turn, if major capital markets are efficient, the only predictable portions of the differences between security prices are those which arise from differences in systematic risk. In such a completely efficient market environment, the task of portfolio management would be solely to select an appropriate risk class and then achieve maximum diversification as inexpensively as possible. Further, if the market is truly efficient, actively managed portfolios will perform no better than randomly selected portfolios with the same amount of risk—a conclusion that is supported by empirical studies of performance.

Aside from the lack of evidence that some investors can achieve consistently above-average performance, there is enough evidence of inefficiency that the market must be characterized as "almost" efficient. Even with a limited amount of inefficiency, however, studies of historical performance provide no evidence that these inefficiencies are being translated into profitable investment strategies.

To probe this paradox, it is useful to think of performance in two stages: prediction and translation. Specifically,

1. Can some investors make better than average predictions?
2. If they can, can these better than average predictions be translated into better than average risk-adjusted performance?

The distinction between "prediction" and "translation" is valuable for two reasons. First, it might well be that certain investors have superior predictive ability but that their translation process from thought to action is so ineffective that they

achieve no better than average performance. Second, if the translation process is assumed to be perfect, it is possible, through computer simulations, to determine what amount of *predictive ability* is required to attain a given amount of above-average *performance.*

PREDICTIONS VERSUS RESULTS

Keith Ambachtsheer, who heads Canavest, Inc., has studied both prediction and translation. To study predictive ability, Ambachtsheer asked analysts to rank their predictions in order of *relative* expected price movements. Then, using a ranking scheme from 1 to 5 (where 5 is the largest gain), he compared the ex ante (before the fact) forecasts with the ex post (after the fact) results by the procedure illustrated in Tables 29–1 and 29–2.

TABLE 29–1: Perfectly correlated predictions and results

		↓ Results ↓					
		Relative performance categories					
		1	*2*	*3*	*4*	*5*	*Total predictions in each category*
Predictions →	*Relative performance categories* 1	10					10
	2		20				20
	3			40			40
	4				20		20
	5					10	10
Total results in each category		10	20	40	20	10	

The horizontal rows of Table 29–1 show the ex ante *predictions.* The vertical columns of the table show the ex post *results.* Because predictions and results are perfectly correlated in this case, of the ten before the fact predictions in rating category 1, all ten after the fact results are also in rating category 1. Similarly, each of the other predictions corresponds exactly to the results.

Note that the "average" relative performance category 3 contains the largest number of predictions. The reason for this is that most stocks are assumed to be average performers. Relatively fewer predictions concern stocks which are expected to perform significantly better or worse, than the average. Similarly, the results can be expected to cluster around the average, with relatively fewer especially good or bad performers tallied in the extreme categories.

Table 29–2 portrays quite a different relationship between predictions and results. Here the predictions are the same: 10

TABLE 29–2: Uncorrelated predictions and results

		↓ *Results* ↓					
		Relative performance categories					
		1	*2*	*3*	*4*	*5*	
→ *Predictions* *4* — *Relative performance categories*	*1*	1	2	4	2	1	10
	2	2	4	8	4	2	20
	3	4	8	16	8	4	40
	4	2	4	8	4	2	20
	5	1	2	4	2	1	10
		10	20	40	20	10	

Total results in each category (bottom row); *Total predictions in each category* (right column)

in the first category, 20 in the second, and so on. The results, however, are different. Only one of the ten predictions in relative performance category 1 was accurate. More importantly, since 10 percent of all results were in relative performance category 1, 10 percent of the predictions would be expected to fall there purely by chance. Thus, the pattern portrayed in Table 29–2 is lacking in any correlation between prediction and results.

When data are arrayed in this form, it is relatively easy to calculate the correlations between the predicted relative performance catagories and actual results. Ambachtsheer has labeled the correlation coefficients calculated from such tables as "information coefficients," or ICs.

Table 29–3 illustrates a comparison of *predictions* made on

TABLE 29–3: Comparison of predictions against results

		↓ Results 9–1–78 ↓								
		Relative performance categories								
		1	*2*	*3*	*4*	*5*	*Number of securities*	*After the fact average relative performance category*	*Actual percentage change*	
Predictions (12–1–77) →	*Relative performance categories* *1*	0	4	1	0	0	5	2.2	−1.8	← *Predictions*
	2	3	5	13	1	0	22	2.5	6.5	
	3	2	10	40	18	4	74	3.2	21.5	
	4	0	3	19	12	1	35	3.3	27.9	
	5	0	0	1	4	0	5	3.8	41.0	
Number of securities		5	22	74	35	5				
Before the fact average relative performance category		2.4	2.5	3.1	3.5	3.2				
Actual percentage change		−13.9	−3.8	10.9	48.7	109.1				
		↑ *Results* ↑								

December 1, 1977 (the horizontal rows) with the *results* of those predictions as of September 1, 1978 (the vertical columns). It was estimated as of December 1, 1977 that 5 securities would fall in relative performance category 1, 22 in category 2, 74 in category 3, 35 in category 4, and 5 in category 5. (Category 1 represents the worst relative performers and category 5 the best.) To facilitate comparison of the forecasted ratings, the results are categorized according to the same frequency. That is, the 5 worst performing stocks are placed in result category 1, the 22 next best performers in result category 2, 74 in category 3, and so on.

The first row of Table 29–3 shows that of the five stocks that were predicted to have the worst relative performance (category 1), after the fact four stocks fell in category 2, and one stock was in category 3. Thus, the average after the fact relative performance rating (category) for stocks predicted to be in relative performance category 1 was 2.2. In terms of actual performance, the first row of the extreme right-hand column indicates that the average performance of stocks with before the fact relative performance ratings of 1 turned out to be −1.8 percent over the period.

Moving down the "actual percentage change" column, notice that the changes increase with each of the successively higher rated groups—ranging from −1.8 percent for the predicted worst performers to +41.0 percent for the predicted best performers. Clearly stocks predicted to be in the worst relative performance category 1 turned out to be the worst performers. Also, the stocks predicted to fall in the best relative performance category 5 turned out to be the strongest performers.

Similarly, the column labeled "after the fact average relative performance category" reveals a positive relationship between the predicted and actual ratings. While the relationship is not perfect, stocks predicted to be in the lower relative performance categories were, after the fact, in lower average relative performance categories. The same tendency prevailed for stocks predicted to be in the higher relative performance categories.

The first column of "results" in Table 29–3 shows that the five worst performing stocks (in after the fact performance category 1) had an average before the fact relative performance rating of 2.4. Moving across the row labeled "before the fact average performance category," the numbers tend to increase. This is further evidence of a positive relationship between the predicted and actual results.

Basically, the percentage change column at the far right indicates how the imperfect forecasting would have translated into actual performance. The percentage change column at the bottom of the table indicates what could have been attained from perfect forecasting. Thus, the five worst performing stocks were actually down 13.9 percent. The five stocks that were predicted to be the worst performers were down an average of 1.8 percent. Hence, while not perfect, the predictions illustrated in Table 29–3 have quite good discriminatory ability.

To simplify analysis of the kind of information presented in Table 29–3, the relationship can, as mentioned earlier, be reduced to a single number—the so-called information coefficient (IC). The IC for Table 29–3 is 0.42. While the positive relationship between predictions and results in Table 29–3 is relatively easy to see, it should be emphasized that this is an extremely high IC value. ICs most often range between 0.10 and 0.20 (see Ambachtsheer [4, 5, 6]).

CAN PREDICTIONS OF MODEST QUALITY BE USED PROFITABLY?

Using a computer simulation to make an unerring translation from prediction to action, Stewart Hodges and Richard Brealey [122] found that with an IC of 0.15—the level Ambachtsheer found to be average—an investment manager could, over the long run, outperform an index fund by about 1.5 percent per year. This assumed that forecast revisions and appropriate portfolio revisions took place only once annually. Using a "live" study of 16 forecasting groups (as opposed to a computer simulation) and six-month holding periods, Ambachtsheer also found similar evidence that a modest amount of forecasting ability (i.e., ICs of 0.15) could be used to outperform a market index fund [4].

Basically, the IC argument presented by Ambachtsheer is that a prediction ranked "good" is one that forecasters expect to perform one standard deviation better than the mean. Given Ambachtsheer's assumption that the standard deviation of return for a stock portfolio is around 18 percent, if the IC (i.e., the correlation between the forecaster's expectations and reality) is 0.15, that rate of prediction success multiplied by the prediction will yield the potential success from perfect translation. Thus, if forecasters have a 0.15 success rate (IC) in predicting stocks which will appreciate 18 percent (one standard devia-

tion), their potential success is 0.15 × 18%, or 2.7 percent—before transaction costs.

COMPOSITE FORECASTING

James Farrell and Keith Ambachtsheer [84] have reasoned that two or more separate sources of information can be combined to form a composite IC. By their formulation, if two independent sources of information each have ICs of 0.15, the combined IC would be 0.21.[1]

To illustrate composite forecasting, Farrell and Ambachtsheer developed a composite IC from two well-known valuation services: Value Line and Wells Fargo. Basically, the Value Line valuation approach is based on relative price and earnings estimates, resulting in a one through 5 ranking scheme (where one is best). The Wells Fargo valuation approach is based on a dividend discount model (to be discussed in Chapter 31) which ranks stocks from highest to lowest on the basis of expected risk-adjusted return.

Table 29–4 shows the comparative ICs for the two advisers over six, six-month periods. In addition to the differences portrayed, statistical tests showed that there was close to zero correlation between the two forecasts. Given this statistical independence between the two sets of forecasts, the two were combined, with the Wells Fargo information given twice the weight of the Value Line information. The IC for the combined information (as shown in Table 29–4) averaged 0.152.

TABLE 29–4: Six-month information coefficients

	9/73–3/74	*3/74–9/74*	*9/74–3/75*	*3/75–9/75*	*9/75–3/76*	*3/76–9/76*	*Mean*	*Standard deviation*
Wells Fargo	0.12	0.16	0.01	0.13	0.08	0.31	0.135	0.100
Value Line	0.17	0.04	−0.09	0.16	0.11	0.01	0.067	0.100
Combined	0.17	0.18	0.00	0.16	0.10	0.30	0.152	0.099

Source: Farrell and Ambachtsheer [84].

Next, by setting down careful guidelines, Farrell and Ambachtsheer constructed simulated portfolios from the September 1973 ICs which appear in Table 29–4 and rebalanced each portfolio every six months over the succeeding three-year period. Table 29–5 shows the performance of the three simulated portfolio strategies against both the S&P 500 and the

[1] $IC_{12} = \sqrt{IC_1^2 + IC_2^2}$

TABLE 29–5: Performance results of three simulated portfolio strategies against the S&P 500 and the Becker performance data for pension funds

	9/73 to 9/76 annualized	Performance results					
		3/76 to 9/76	*9/75 to 3/76*	*3/75 to 9/75*	*9/74 to 3/75*	*3/74 to 9/74*	*9/73 to 3/74*
Top Becker Fund	11.9%	—	—	—	—	—	—
Combined: Wells Fargo and Value Line	9.3	7.1	27.4	4.8	43.7	−29.6	− 9.7
Wells Fargo	8.3	8.2	25.2	4.2	42.0	−29.0	−10.8
Value Line	4.8	4.9	27.8	5.4	34.1	−32.1	−10.5
S&P 500 Index	3.3	4.4	25.0	2.7	34.5	−30.8	−11.7
"Universe"	1.8	5.6	19.6	2.3	34.7	−32.2	−10.5
20th percentile Becker Funds	0.8	5.3	26.2	3.1	44.2	−32.2	−14.1
50th percentile Becker Funds	− 2.9	2.5	22.3	−0.3	39.2	−35.2	−17.2
80th percentile Becker Funds	− 5.6	0.8	18.9	−3.4	35.2	−38.4	−20.5
Bottom Becker Fund	−16.1	—	—	—	—	—	—

Source: Farrell and Ambachtsheer [84].

Becker performance data for pension funds. Note that the three simulated portfolios outperformed the S&P 500 and all would have ranked high in the upper 20th percentile of the Becker funds over the period.

It should be noted that the returns on the simulated portfolios were adjusted for transaction costs and management fees. The S&P 500 reflects neither, of course, while the Becker figures exclude management fees. Also, it should be noted that the performance of an index of the universe of stocks from which the simulated portfolios were drawn underperformed the S&P 500. This indicates that the superior performance of the simulated portfolios was based on selection and not an especially favorable universe.

ACTIVE VERSUS PASSIVE MANAGEMENT

Very few people like to be considered average. For most investment managers, being average is just not good enough. But the truth of the matter is that, by any measure, half are below average and half are above average. Over the long haul, common stocks have provided an average compound annual rate of return of nearly 10 percent (excluding commissions and taxes). This is a better record than bonds, savings accounts, and most tangible commodities have shown. Also, common stocks traded on national exchanges are readily transferable. Hence, for some investors, an "average" performance might be a reasonable objective.

For those who consciously decide to seek average performance, MPT has confirmed a very easy way to achieve it: merely spread holdings over many issues and hold them for long periods. For those who opt for this "passive" investment strategy, it is comforting to know that their average results will be *better than half of those "active" investors who try to beat the averages!*

For those who opt for "active" strategies, the concept of ICs can be very useful. *Passive management* is based on a strategy of controlling risk through diversification and providing a fair, risk-adjusted, rate of return. *Active management* is intended to "beat the market." The focal point of the concept of ICs is that *active management can only be justified when an organization*

1. Possesses a measurable degree of predictive ability, and
2. Translates its forecasting ability into investment actions that more than offset the costs associated with the portfolio rebalancing process.

Chapter 30

Valuation theory

A source of popular confusion about MPT should be clarified at this point. MPT holds that estimates of future risk and expected return are the key ingredients in the investment decision process. Accordingly, the task, or even more strongly, the responsibility, of the security analyst is to derive such estimates of future risk and expected return. This does not imply, however, that all users of MPT technology will come out with the same, or even approximately the same, results. Nor does this imply that the role of the security analyst is diminished as a consequence.

While much has been learned about the ways to arrive at estimates of future risk and expected return, it should be emphasized that these are still individually derived forecasts. Different analysts have different preferences for different kinds of information. Further, by analyzing information in different ways, they arrive at independent estimates. As always, analysts are free to exercise their personal prerogatives in making these forecasts.

Accordingly, the application of MPT does not diminish the role of the security analyst. Quite to the contrary, the estimates provided by the security analysts are at the core of the investment decision process. The role of the security analysts has, however, changed dramatically. Before MPT, the job of many security analysts was reduced to (*a*) providing estimates of near-term earnings, (*b*) estimating a future price-earnings ratio, and (*c*) multiplying the estimated earnings by the estimated price-earnings ratio to determine an estimated price. This valuation would be the basis for a purchase or sale recommendation on a stock.

This kind of pre-MPT analysis has two major shortcomings. First, the critically important dimension of risk is omitted.

Second, the variability of price-earnings ratios (illustrated earlier in Figure 7–1) often eclipses the earnings component. Not surprisingly, this kind of analysis prompted the famous economist, John Maynard Keynes, to write

> A conventional valuation which is established as the outcome of the mass psychology . . . is liable to change violently as the result of a sudden fluctuation of opinion due to factors which do not really make much difference to the prospective yield; since there will be no strong roots of conviction to hold it steady. . . .
>
> . . . It might have been supposed that competition between expert professionals, possessing judgment and knowledge beyond that of the average private investor, would correct the vagaries of the ignorant individual left to himself. It happens, however, that . . . [most professional investors] are, in fact, largely concerned, not with making superior long-term forecasts of the probable yield of an investment over its whole life, but with foreseeing changes in the conventional basis of valuation a short time ahead of the general public. They are concerned, not with what an investment is really worth, . . . but what the market will value it at, under the influence of mass psychology, three months or 6 years hence.
>
> . . . The actual, private object of most skilled investment today is "to beat the gun," as the Americans so well expressed it, to outwit the crowd, and pass the bad, or depreciating half-crown to the other fellow.
>
> This battle of wits to anticipate the basis of conventional valuation a few months hence, rather than the prospective yield of an investment over a long term of years, does not even require gulls amongst the public to feed the maws of the professional;—it can be played by professionals amongst themselves. . . . [Professional investing] is, so to speak, a game . . . of Old Maid, of Musical Chairs—a pastime in which he is victor who . . . passes the Old Maid to his neighbour before the game is over, who secures the chair for himself when the music stops. [148, pp. 154–56]

VALUATION APPROACHES

There are two basic approaches to common stock valuation. The *traditional approach* outlined earlier, involves (*a*) estimating a stock's earnings per share (EPS) for the next year or so, (*b*) estimating the price-earnings ratio that is expected to prevail when the estimated earnings are reported, and (*c*) multiplying the estimated future earnings per share by the estimated price-earnings ratio to obtain the estimated future

price.[1] While most people who use this approach stop here, the estimated dividend flow can be incorporated into the analysis to obtain an estimate of the rate of return for the forecast period.

There are serious questions over the usefulness of any of the myriad forms of this analytical approach. First, it omits any explicit estimate of risk. Second, the considerable evidence in support of the semistrong form of the efficient market hypothesis (discussed in Part One) leads to the resounding conclusion that no information of real value can be derived from such analysis!

Approaching the problem of security valuation from a different perspective, *classical value theory*—the basis for security valuation within the context of MPT—focuses on the *true*, or *intrinsic*, value of an asset. Specifically, classical value theory holds that the value of a financial asset is the discounted sum of all future income flows that will be received by the owner of the asset.

The seminal notion that the *intrinsic value* of an asset is derived from the discounted present value of the asset's future stream of "cash" flows was first advanced by Irving Fisher [87] at Yale around the turn of the century. Later, John Burr Williams described what might be called the pure theory in his classic 1938 book *The Theory of Investment Value*. [286] More recently, Nicholas Molodovsky [195], the late editor of the *Financial Analysts Journal*, crusaded for more widespread use of the technique.

The application of intrinsic value theory to the valuation of common stocks is relatively easy. It merely involves calculating and then summing the present values of the future payments anticipated by the holder of the stock.

PRESENT VALUE

The concept of *present value* is best understood by referring to some examples. Suppose you were considering the purchase of a contract under which you would receive a guaranteed payment of $1,000 one year from today. How much would you currently pay for a guaranteed $1,000 one year from today? The answer to this question depends on the "price of money"—that is, the interest rate that you expect to prevail during the period.

[1] Mathematical purists should note that the product of two expected values will not equal the expected value of the product if there is a correlation between the two original estimates.

TABLE 30–1: Present value of $1

Years into the future	Discount rate 5.0%	6.0%	7.0%	8.0%	9.0%
1	0.952 381	0.943 396	0.934 579	0.925 926	0.917 431
2	0.907 030	0.889 996	0.873 439	0.857 339	0.841 680
3	0.863 838	0.839 619	0.816 298	0.793 832	0.772 183
4	0.822 703	0.792 094	0.762 895	0.735 030	0.708 425
5	0.783 526	0.747 258	0.712 986	0.680 583	0.649 931
6	0.746 215	0.704 961	0.666 342	0.630 170	0.596 267
7	0.710 681	0.665 057	0.622 750	0.583 490	0.547 034
8	0.676 839	0.627 412	0.582 009	0.540 269	0.501 866
9	0.644 609	0.591 899	0.543 934	0.500 249	0.460 428
10	0.613 913	0.558 395	0.508 349	0.463 194	0.422 411
11	0.584 679	0.526 788	0.475 093	0.428 883	0.387 533
12	0.556 837	0.496 969	0.444 012	0.397 114	0.355 535
13	0.530 321	0.468 839	0.414 964	0.367 698	0.326 179
14	0.505 068	0.442 301	0.387 817	0.340 461	0.299 246
15	0.481 017	0.417 265	0.362 446	0.315 242	0.274 538
16	0.458 112	0.393 646	0.338 735	0.291 891	0.251 870
17	0.436 297	0.371 364	0.316 574	0.270 269	0.231 073
18	0.415 521	0.350 344	0.295 864	0.250 249	0.211 994
19	0.395 734	0.330 513	0.276 508	0.231 712	0.194 490
20	0.376 890	0.311 805	0.258 419	0.214 548	0.178 431
21	0.358 942	0.294 155	0.241 513	0.198 656	0.163 698
22	0.341 850	0.277 505	0.225 713	0.183 941	0.150 182
23	0.325 571	0.261 797	0.210 947	0.170 315	0.137 781
24	0.310 068	0.246 979	0.197 147	0.157 699	0.126 405
25	0.295 303	0.232 999	0.184 249	0.146 018	0.115 968
26	0.281 241	0.219 810	0.172 196	0.135 202	0.106 393
27	0.267 848	0.207 368	0.160 930	0.125 187	0.097 608
28	0.255 094	0.195 630	0.150 402	0.115 914	0.089 548
29	0.242 946	0.184 557	0.140 563	0.107 328	0.082 155
30	0.231 377	0.174 110	0.131 367	0.099 377	0.075 371
31	0.220 360	0.164 255	0.122 773	0.092 016	0.069 148
32	0.209 866	0.154 957	0.114 741	0.085 200	0.063 438
33	0.199 873	0.146 186	0.107 235	0.078 889	0.058 200
34	0.190 355	0.137 912	0.100 219	0.073 045	0.053 395
35	0.181 290	0.130 105	0.093 663	0.067 635	0.048 986
36	0.172 657	0.122 740	0.087 536	0.062 625	0.044 941
37	0.164 436	0.115 793	0.081 809	0.057 986	0.041 231
38	0.156 605	0.109 239	0.076 457	0.053 691	0.037 826
39	0.149 148	0.103 056	0.071 455	0.049 713	0.034 703
40	0.142 046	0.097 222	0.066 780	0.046 031	0.031 838
41	0.135 282	0.091 719	0.062 412	00.42 621	0.029 209
42	0.128 840	0.086 527	0.058 329	0.039 464	0.026 797
43	0.122 704	0.081 630	0.054 513	0.036 541	0.024 584
44	0.116 861	0.077 009	0.050 946	0.033 834	0.022 555
45	0.111 297	0.072 650	0.047 614	0.031 328	0.020 692
46	0.105 997	0.068 538	0.044 499	0.029 007	0.018 984
47	0.100 949	0.064 658	0.041 588	0.026 859	0.017 416
48	0.096 142	0.060 998	0.038 867	0.024 869	0.015 978
49	0.091 564	0.057 546	0.036 324	0.023 027	0.014 659
50	0.087 204	0.054 288	0.033 948	0.021 321	0.013 449
60	0.053 536	0.030 314	0.017 257	0.009 876	0.005 681
70	0.032 866	0.016 927	0.008 773	0.004 574	0.002 400
80	0.020 177	0.009 452	0.004 460	0.002 119	0.001 014
90	0.012 387	0.005 278	0.002 267	0.000 981	0.000 428
100	0.007 605	0.002 947	0.001 152	0.000 455	0.000 181

The arithmetic of converting a known future value—in this illustration $1,000—into an equivalent present value is called *discounting*. The first line of Table 30–1 shows the present value of $1, one year from today, discounted at selected interest rates. Assume, for example, that the going interest rate for a riskless investment which will be held exactly one year is 8 percent. Given this assumption, we can use Table 30–1 to derive the equivalent present value of a contract under which we would be guaranteed $1,000 one year from today. Specifically, the Table 30–1 value at the intersection of line one (corresponding to one year into the future) and column four (corresponding to an 8 percent discount rate) is 0.925926—the space between the two numbers in the table having been added only for reading simplicity. This means that if you invested $0.925926 today and received an 8 percent annual rate of return, your investment would appreciate to $1.00 one year from now (i.e., the original investment of $0.925926 plus the 8 percent return, or 0.074074, equals $1.00). Conversely, and more in keeping with financial jargon, you could say that "the present value of $1.00, discounted at 8 percent for one year, is $0.925926."

The present value of any amount can be readily obtained from multiplying the *discount factor* in Table 30–1 by the amount in question. Thus, to determine the answer to the initial question—the present value of $1,000 discounted at 8 percent for one year—we merely need to multiply $1,000 by the *discount factor* in Table 30–1 to obtain the answer of $925.93. That is, given an interest rate of 8 percent, the discount factor of 0.925926 from Table 30–1 times $1,000 indicates that $925.93 today is equivalent to $1,000 one year from today.

We can extend this kind of analysis, using the discount factors from Table 30–1, to determine the present value of any future stream of payments. How much, for example, is a bond worth which one year from today will pay $50, two years from today will pay another $50, and three years from today will pay a final $50 plus $1,000?

The calculation of the present value of such a bond is shown in Table 30–2. Using the discount factors from Table 30–2 and an assumed annual discount (interest) rate of 8 percent, we can determine that the present value of $50 one year from today is $46.30. Similarly, using the discount factor for two years, we can determine that the present value of $50 two years from today is $42.87. Finally, based on the discount factor for three years, we can determine that the present value of the final

TABLE 30–2: Present value of a bond (based on an 8.0 percent annual discount rate)

Payment date	*Amount*	×	*Discount factor*	=	*Present value*
One year from today	$50		0.925926		$ 46.30
Two years from today	$50		0.857339		42.87
Three years from today	$1,050		0.793832		833.52
Total present value					$922.69

payment of $1,050 is $833.52. Summing each of these present values, we arrive at an aggregate present value of $922.69.

An important advantage of this type of valuation is that the analyst can use any combination of assumptions about different spot and forward interest rates. (*Spot prices* and *spot rates* refer to prices or rates for the *current time period. Forward rates,* or *forward prices,* on the other hand, refer to rates, or prices, that apply to *future contract periods*.) The relationship between the prevailing spot rate and various forward rates is shown by both the shape and the level of the current *yield curve.*

YIELD CURVES

Yield curves provide a visual representation of the current *term structure of interest rates.* Quite simply, the term structure of interest rates refers to the relationship (i.e., the "structure") of the different rates of return that are currently available on interest-bearing investments that are made for different periods of time (or, if you prefer, different "terms"). Generally, moving further into the future, higher rates of return will be required to compensate investors for the increased risk that is associated with longer term investments. Fortunately, however, life in the real world of investing is much more exciting than one might posit for the "general" case. Thus, at any moment in time both the shape and the level of the yield curve (reflecting the current term structure of interest rates) are important elements in security valuation.

Figures 30–1, 30–2, and 30–3 show the characteristic shape of the yield curve under three "classic" interest rate scenarios. The use of specific numbers in these figures has been avoided in order to concentrate on the alternative "shapes." The vertical scale of the yield curve denotes increasing interest rates (in

FIGURE 30–1: Rising yield curve

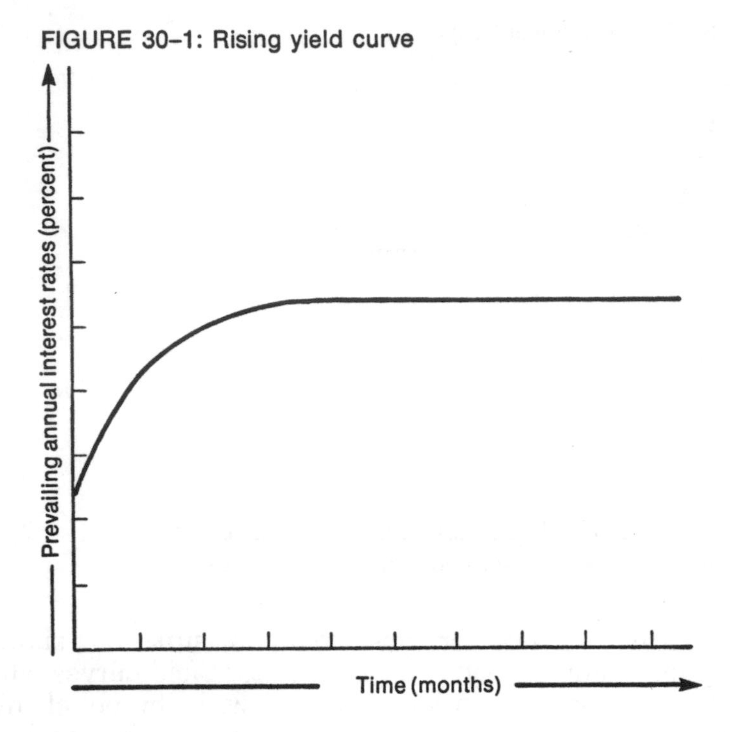

percentages) and the horizontal scale denotes increasing time (in months).

Basically, the shape of the yield curve depends on the marketplace's assessment of the future course of short-term rates. Figure 30–1 shows the so-called *rising yield curve*. This curve,

FIGURE 30–2: Flat yield curve

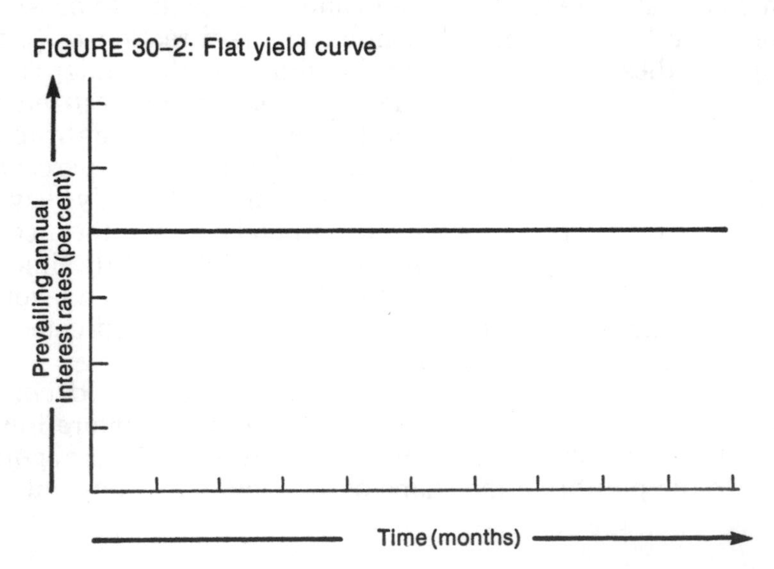

FIGURE 30–3: Inverted yield curve

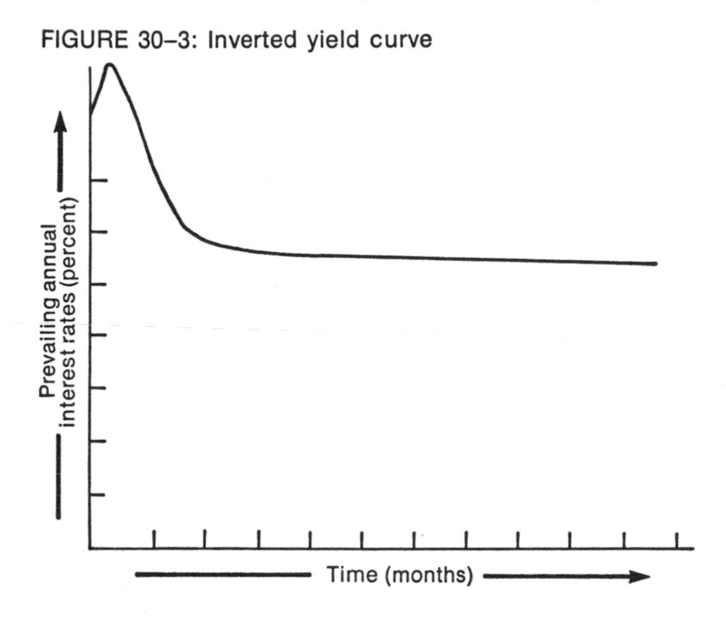

depicting the "normal," or most common, situation, shows that long-term rates exceed short-term rates. Yield curves with this general shape tend to be associated with the belief that short-term interest rates will remain low. In this climate, borrowers are willing to pay higher rates for long-term funds and lenders will demand higher rates for long-term obligations than for short-term obligations.

Figure 30–2 shows a relatively *flat yield curve.* The interest rate scenario accompanying a flat yield curve would be one in which all rates are relatively high and, as a result, the prospective lender's uncertainty is slanted in the direction of "how long will these levels hold?" In this situation, the lender is not faced with the question of where to "get" the highest return. Instead, in a climate where short-term rates are thought to be "temporarily" high, the lender faces what he or she perceives to be the risk of lower rates. In this climate, the only way to "hold on to" the prevailing rates is to make a long-term commitment. Since the traditional risk associated with time is offset by the possibility of a decline in the current high level of rates, the same rate prevails for all maturities, as indicated by the yield curve in Figure 30–2.

Figure 30–3 shows an *inverted,* or humped, *yield curve.* Here the yields offered for long-term commitments are lower than those available on short-term commitments. Again, going back to the point that the shape of the yield curve depends on

the market's assessment of the future for short-term rates, a downward sloping curve means that the high short-term rates are being viewed as transitory. As an example, suppose that the return on one-month government securities is 10 percent and the yield on two-year government securities is 9 percent. The downward sloping yield curve which would depict this situation really indicates that, at this moment, the "market" believes the 10 percent short-term rate will not prevail in this climate. In fact, an equitable two-year return—in the face of the "temporary" 10 percent on one-month loans—is only 9 percent.

Yield curves are important because they offer a perspective on the rates that are available for various holding periods. In addition, they underline the importance of building estimates of forward interest rates into investment analysis.

The dramatic changes that can occur in yield curves in a period as short as one year are illustrated in Figure 30–4. In December 1977, the yield curve was a classic "rising" shape.

FIGURE 30–4: Government securities yield curves (yield to maturity—Treasury bills, notes and bonds)

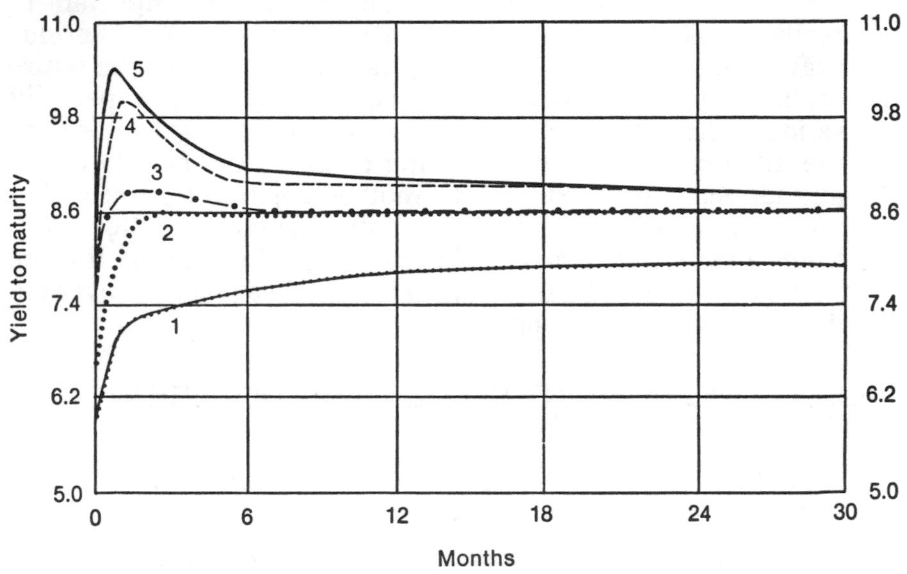

1 December 16, 1977
2 June 16, 1978
3 September 20, 1978
4 November 20, 1978
5 December 21, 1978

Source: Merrill Lynch, *Capital Market Monitor,* December 26, 1978, p. 5.

Six months later, the curve was the same basic shape, but three-month obligations had risen more than 100 basis points (100 basis points equal 1 percentage point). By December 1978, the curve was a classic "inverted," or "humped," shape.

YIELD TO MATURITY

It is important to clarify the difference between forward interest rates and yield to maturity figures. *Forward interest rates*, on the one hand, refer to the current prevailing rates for contracts in specific future, or "forward," time periods. The notion of a forward interest rate is important because it allows us to enter into a contract today that is based on the interest rate that one assumes will prevail during any future (forward) separately segmented time period. *Yield to maturity*, on the other hand, represents the average annualized rate of return that will prevail over the entire multi-period duration of an investment.

Because the yield to maturity figure reduces the returns on different kinds of investments of different durations to a single average interest rate, it is the most commonly used measure of return for bonds. It is a useful number, but it is important to realize that the yield to maturity figure has a serious drawback—it assumes a constant rate of return over the entire duration of the investment. This shortcoming can be especially serious when there are wide differences in forward rates (i.e., the different rates currently being charged for specific future periods, such as "next year"). Another important point is that yield curves do not portray the term structure of "forward" interest rates. Yield curves plot yield to maturity, which is the average annualized rate of return that will be received over the duration of the investment.

CALCULATING PRESENT VALUE USING DIFFERENT FORWARD INTEREST RATES

We have seen that the present value of a known future payment can be determined from the equation:

Present value = Discount factor × Future payment

The equation for the above discount factor is

$$\underset{\text{(year 1)}}{\left(\frac{1}{1+r}\right)} \quad \underset{\text{(year 2)}}{\left(\frac{1}{1+r}\right)} \quad \underset{\text{(year 3)}}{\left(\frac{1}{1+r}\right)} \cdots \underset{\text{(year n)}}{\left(\frac{1}{1+r}\right)}$$

where r is the interest rate in each year for any number of years. If we make the assumption that r is constant from year to year, we can easily compute the discount factors that appear in Table 30–1. Take, for example, the problem of determining the discount factor for five years at 9 percent. It is simply

$$\left(\frac{1}{1.09}\right)\left(\frac{1}{1.09}\right)\left(\frac{1}{1.09}\right)\left(\frac{1}{1.09}\right)\left(\frac{1}{1.09}\right) = 0.649931$$

the value that appears in Table 30–1.

While the above analysis is appealing because of its simplicity, it is unreasonable to assume that interest rates will remain the same for the next five years. Thus, while we might believe that the "average" rate for the next three years will be 9 percent, we might estimate that the year-to-year rates will be 11 percent, 10 percent, 9 percent, 8 percent, and 7 percent. These assumptions can be used to determine the appropriate discount rate by merely changing r, the year-by-year interest rate, in the above equation. Specifically,

$$\left(\frac{1}{1.11}\right)\left(\frac{1}{1.10}\right)\left(\frac{1}{1.09}\right)\left(\frac{1}{1.08}\right)\left(\frac{1}{1.07}\right) = 0.65205$$

Assuming that we were calculating the present value of $100,000 five years hence, under these two procedures (i.e., using an average discount rate and using specific year-by-year rates) the comparative values would be:

$65,020.50 based on year-by-year forecasts
versus
$64,993.10 based on the average value

Obviously, the two procedures yield strikingly similar results and, as a result, little advantage is gained from explicit estimates of year-to-year changes. This has important implications for the construction of valuation models.

Chapter 31

Valuation models

For a riskless asset (i.e., a noncallable default-free bond such as a short-term government security), information on the structure of forward interest rates can be used to discount the cash flows produced. The aggregate present value of these discounted cash flows will equal the present value of the bond. The valuation of risky assets, such as common stocks, requires two changes in this approach:

1. Since there is some possibility that scheduled payments will not be made, *the analysis must be based on "expected" cash flow.*
2. Since the risk is, by definition, greater than that for holding a riskless asset, *the "expected" cash flow must be discounted on the basis of a higher forward structure of interest rates (i.e., one that reflects the additional risk).*

Once the above changes are incorporated into the analysis, the technique of appropriately discounting, and then summing, the expected cash flows can be used to value common stocks. However, before proceeding with an example of this valuation procedure, two points need to be emphasized:

1. In this analysis, only *cash* that is received by the investor is used in the valuation process.
2. Since many streams of future dividends can reasonably be expected to continue "forever," the analysis must deal with the discounted present value of an *infinite series of dividend payments.*

Each of these points deserves some elaboration.

DIVIDENDS NOT EARNINGS

The consideration only of dividends, makes a clear decision not to analyze company earnings. While this is perplexing to

some people, the relevance of dividends versus earnings as a source of value, and in turn, a basis for analysis, is, in the words of William Sharpe, "a repeated but somewhat pointless controversy." [252, p. 302] The rationale for calculating the intrinsic value of a share of common stock from its dividends, instead of earnings per share, is that the only value that is ever *received* by the stockholder, is the dividend. From this perspective, earnings are important only in so much as they provide dividends.

The validity of dividend-based stock valuation can be better appreciated on considering what can be done with a firm's *earnings*. Basically, aftertax earnings can be used for financing

1. Net new investments in plant and equipment.
2. Purchases of outstanding shares of the company's common stock.
3. Dividend distributions to shareholders.

It is important to realize that management's decision to invest (or not to invest) in new plant and equipment does not depend on company earnings. Corporate managers make new investment decisions, just like everyone else, on the merits of the proposed project. That is, net new investments are made because the expected returns on these investments are forecast to be in excess of those on available alternatives with similar risks. Also, once management concludes that an investment should be made (again, based on its expected risk and reward), the project can be financed in a variety of ways—only one of which is through retained earnings.

Setting aside the second possible use of earnings—to purchase outstanding shares of the company's common stock—the rationale for basing valuation models on future dividend streams can be better understood by reference to Figure 31–1.

Figure 31–1 illustrates that earnings can be used to increase a firm's assets. Net new investments create assets which can be combined with other resources, such as labor, to produce future earnings. Typically, in a company's early years—while it has internal investment opportunities, such as expansion to meet the demands of a growing market—earnings are channeled into net new investment.

What is confusing about the notion of a dividend discount model is that while a company might not pay dividends, it clearly has "value." The validity of the dividend discount model can best be illustrated by an example. Imagine a company which expects annual earnings of $1 per share far into

FIGURE 31–1: Disposition of earnings—two of the choices

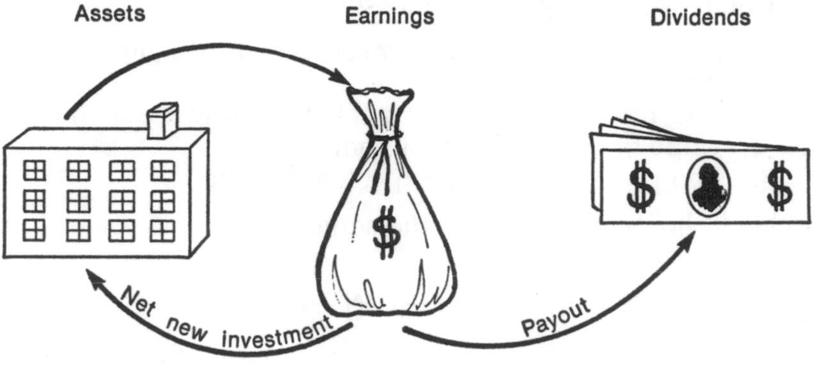

the future. Suppose, further, that in order to sustain this constant flow of expected earnings, the net new investment in plant and equipment will have to be increased at the rate of $1 per share per year. In this rather farfetched example, since an amount equal to each year's earnings must be continually channeled into net new investments, there is never any hope of a sustainable payout and, hence, no value.

Nor can a firm increase the value of its shares simply by increasing the payout ratio (the portion of earnings that is paid out as dividends). Astute analysts would "flag" such dividend increases as detracting from the amount which would otherwise be channeled into net new investments and which, in turn, would increase the expected growth in earnings per share.

This overly simplified example brings out two important points:

1. For any nondividend-paying stock, the market presumption is that "eventually" earnings are going to outpace the company's need for additional plant and equipment. When this happens, earnings will exceed the funds that are channeled into net new investments creating the capacity to pay *dividends.*
2. Focusing one's attention on the present value of a forecasted stream of earnings can be misleading. The variable of interest is the present value of expected earnings *net of any investment that is required to produce the earnings.* And, as can be noted from Figure 31–1, earnings less net new investments equal *dividends.*

According to valuation theory, the value of an equity can be calculated through three measures:

1. The present value of expected earnings net of required investment.
2. The present value of expected earnings less the present value of required investment.
3. The present value of expected dividends.

Each, however, produces the same result!

SUSTAINABLE DIVIDEND GROWTH RATE

The concept of sustainable dividend growth provides a useful understanding of the relationship between a company's return on equity, reinvestment rate, dividend payout ratio, and dividend growth rate. The *reinvestment rate* is the percentage of return that is retained by the company for reinvestment. Typically, the amount that is not reinvested is paid out in dividends. This amount is referred to as the *dividend payout ratio.*

Theoretically, a company's *sustainable dividend growth rate* is its return on equity times its reinvestment rate. This is best understood by referring to Table 31–1. The first line of

TABLE 31–1: Concept of sustainable dividend growth

Equity pool	*Return on equity*	*Return*	*Reinvestment rate*	*Reinvestment amount*	*Dividend amount*	*Dividend growth rate*
$10,000.00	12%	$1,200.00	60%	$720.00	$480.00	—
10,720.00	12	1,286.40	60	771.89	514.56	7.2%
11,491.84	12	1,379.02	60	827.41	551.61	7.2

this table shows a 12 percent return on an initial equity pool of $10,000 and a 60 percent reinvestment rate. In this situation, 60 percent of the first period's return ($720) is carried forward to the second period, and 40 percent of the return ($480) is paid out as dividends. Notice, however, that if the return on equity and reinvestment ratio remain constant in the subsequent periods, dividends will grow by the return on equity (12 percent) times the reinvestment rate (60 percent), or 7.2 percent per period.

DISCOUNTING INFINITE INCOME STREAMS

The second point that requires elaboration concerns the problem of determining the present value of an *infinite stream of expected dividends.* While this might appear to present an insurmountable difficulty, the fact is that the present value of increasingly more distant dividends becomes progressively less important. This is best illustrated by reference to Table 31–2.

Table 31–2 shows the present value of $1 for annual discount rates ranging from 10 percent to 14 percent for future periods up to 100 years. (Table 30–1 showed the same information for annual discount rates ranging from 5 percent to 9 percent.) The table value for $1 can also be thought of as the decimal equivalents for the discounted present value of any amount. Using the 12 percent discount rate as an example, notice how rapidly the present value of a future stream of dividends declines further out into the future.

Specifically, using a 12 percent discount factor, Table 31–2 shows that a payment to be received in five years has a present value that is worth only $0.57 (or 57 percent), of that future payment. Similarly (with a 12 percent discount rate), a payment that will be received in ten years has a present value worth only 32 percent of the future payment. Going even further into the future to, say 25 years (using the 12 percent discount rate), the present value of such a payment is only about 6 percent of the future payment.

From a slightly different perspective, consider the present value of an annual annuity of $1. Using the 12 percent discount rate in Table 31–2, note that the present value of $1 in one year is 89 cents and the present value of $1 in 20 years is $0.10. This means that even if the discount factor did not fall further beyond the 20th year, the annuity's contribution to present value from the 20th to the 29th year would be roughly the same as the contribution derived from the 1st year. In reality, however, by the 30th year, the present value of the dollar has decreased to $0.03. Even if this discount factor did not fall (which of course it does), the annuity over the next 30 years would make roughly the same contribution to the present value as next year's dollar.

Thus, while the valuation of common stocks based on an infinite stream of future dividends might at first appear to pose an unmanageable problem, the fact that the present values become progressively smaller further into the future (unless

TABLE 31–2: Present value of $1

Years in the future	*Discount rate*				
	10.0%	*11.0%*	*12.0%*	*13.0%*	*14.0%*
1	0.909 091	0.900 901	0.892 857	0.884 956	0.877 193
2	0.826 446	0.811 622	0.797 194	0.783 147	0.769 468
3	0.751 315	0.731 191	0.711 780	0.693 050	0.674 972
4	0.683 013	0.658 731	0.635 518	0.613 319	0.592 080
5	0.620 921	0.593 451	0.567 427	0.542 760	0.519 369
6	0.564 474	0.534 641	0.506 631	0.480 319	0.455 587
7	0.513 158	0.481 658	0.452 349	0.425 061	0.399 637
8	0.466 507	0.433 926	0.403 883	0.376 160	0.350 559
9	0.424 098	0.390 925	0.360 610	0.332 885	0.307 508
10	0.385 543	0.352 184	0.321 973	0.294 588	0.269 744
11	0.350 494	0.317 283	0.287 476	0.260 698	0.236 617
12	0.318 631	0.285 841	0.256 675	0.230 706	0.207 559
13	0.289 664	0.257 514	0.229 174	0.204 165	0.182 069
14	0.263 331	0.231 995	0.204 620	0.180 677	0.159 710
15	0.239 392	0.209 004	0.182 696	0.159 891	0.140 096
16	0.217 629	0.188 292	0.163 122	0.141 496	0.122 892
17	0.197 845	0.169 633	0.145 644	0.125 218	0.107 800
18	0.179 859	0.152 822	0.130 040	0.110 812	0.094 561
19	0.163 508	0.137 678	0.116 107	0.098 064	0.082 948
20	0.148 644	0.124 034	0.103 667	0.086 782	0.072 762
21	0.135 131	0.111 742	0.092 560	0.076 798	0.063 826
22	0.122 846	0.100 669	0.082 643	0.067 963	0.055 988
23	0.111 678	0.090 693	0.073 788	0.060 144	0.049 112
24	0.101 626	0.081 705	0.065 882	0.053 225	0.043 081
25	0.092 296	0.073 608	0.058 823	0.047 102	0.037 790
26	0.083 905	0.066 314	0.052 521	0.041 683	0.033 149
27	0.076 278	0.059 742	0.046 894	0.036 888	0.029 078
28	0.069 343	0.053 822	0.041 869	0.032 644	0.025 507
29	0.063 039	0.048 488	0.037 383	0.028 889	0.022 375
30	0.057 309	0.043 683	0.033 378	0.025 565	0.019 627
31	0.052 099	0.039 354	0.029 802	0.022 624	0.017 217
32	0.047 362	0.035 454	0.026 609	0.020 021	0.015 102
33	0.043 057	0.031 940	0.023 758	0.017 718	0.013 248
34	0.039 143	0.028 775	0.021 212	0.015 680	0.011 621
35	0.035 584	0.025 924	0.018 940	0.013 876	0.010 194
36	0.032 349	0.023 355	0.016 910	0.012 279	0.008 942
37	0.029 408	0.021 040	0.015 098	0.010 867	0.007 844
38	0.026 735	0.018 955	0.013 481	0.009 617	0.006 880
39	0.024 304	0.017 077	0.012 036	0.008 510	0.006 035
40	0.022 095	0.015 384	0.010 747	0.007 531	0.005 294
41	0.020 086	0.013 860	0.009 595	0.006 665	0.004 644
42	0.018 260	0.012 486	0.008 567	0.005 898	0.004 074
43	0.016 600	0.011 249	0.007 649	0.005 219	0.003 573
44	0.015 091	0.010 134	0.006 830	0.004 619	0.003 135
45	0.013 719	0.009 130	0.006 098	0.004 088	0.002 750
46	0.012 472	0.008 225	0.005 445	0.003 617	0.002 412
47	0.011 338	0.007 410	0.004 861	0.003 201	0.002 116
48	0.010 307	0.006 676	0.004 340	0.002 833	0.001 856
49	0.009 370	0.006 014	0.003 875	0.002 507	0.001 628
50	0.008 519	0.005 418	0.003 460	0.002 219	0.001 428
60	0.003 284	0.001 908	0.001 114	0.000 654	0.000 385
70	0.001 266	0.000 672	0.000 359	0.000 193	0.000 104
80	0.000 488	0.000 237	0.000 115	0.000 057	0.000 028
90	0.000 188	0.000 083	0.000 037	0.000 017	0.000 008
100	0.000 073	0.000 029	0.000 012	0.000 005	0.000 002

the growth in dividend payments matches or exceeds the discount rate) resolves the potential difficulty.

Using this approach the value of a share of common stock is the sum of the *discounted* present value of the estimated future stream of *dividends*. Specifically, "estimated future dividend" replaces "1" in the numerator of the discounting formula discussed in Chapter 30. Thus, the present value of next year's dividend is

$$\frac{\text{Next year's dividend}}{1 + r}$$

where r is the discount, or interest, rate. Similarly, the present value of the dividend expected the year after next is

$$\frac{\text{Second-year dividend}}{(1 + r)(1 + r)}$$

Based on general algebraic notation, where d_1 is next year's expected dividend, d_2 is the expected dividend two years hence, and so on, the present value of a common stock becomes

$$\text{Present value} = \frac{d_1}{1 + r} + \frac{d_2}{(1 + r)^2} + \frac{d_3}{(1 + r)^3} + \ldots \text{ and so on indefinitely}$$

In summary, classical valuation theory states that

PRESENT VALUE can be derived from the DISCOUNT RATE and DIVIDEND STREAM

Notice that in the foregoing "equation," a discount rate and a dividend stream is used to arrive at a present value. Using some algebraic manipulation, however, the "equation" can be rewritten so that the

IMPLICIT DISCOUNT RATE can be derived from the PRESENT VALUE and DIVIDEND STREAM

Using this transformed equation, with estimates of (*a*) present value and (*b*) the future dividend stream, it is possible to calculate the stock's *implicit discount rate*—the expected rate of total return that equates the current price with the forecasted dividend stream.

Basically, the implicit discount rate for a stock is the same as the yield to maturity for a bond. Given a security's price and

its dividend stream, implicit discount rate, or *implied return*, is calculated as if it was a bond with an infinite stream of coupon payments. The resultant figure, the *implicit discount rate*, is considered by MPT proponents such as William Fouse, of Wells Fargo Investment Advisors, to be "*the single most important piece of information to have about a common stock*" (italics added). [96, p. 40]

Two things are required to calculate a security's implied return—the present value of the security and a long-term estimate of the security's dividend stream. Obviously, the present value (the current market price) is readily available. A forecast of the long-term dividend stream is usually developed from analyst's inputs to a dividend growth model.

DIVIDEND GROWTH MODELS

Dividend growth models provide an analytical framework for determining the value of a share of stock from estimated growth rates in the components of value—earnings and payout ratios. Most dividend growth models divide the future into three stages: (*a*) a time period that is within the analyst's forecast horizon, (*b*) a variable-length normalizing period, and (*c*) an infinitely long period of normal growth.

Basically, the period within the analyst's forecast horizon is defined as an "explicit" growth stage. For the explicit forecast period, analysts provide year-by-year estimates of expected dividends and earnings. For the variable length normalizing period, analysts estimate (*a*) the length of the "normalizing" period, (*b*) the transitional earnings growth rate, (*c*) the transitional dividend payout ratio, and (*d*) the "pattern" of change in the earnings growth rate during the normalizing period. The most distant stage, beyond the analyst's forecast horizon and the "normalizing" period, is assumed to be an infinitely long period during which the growth of the company is equal to that of the economy. These stages are illustrated in Figure 31–2.

Several observations about growth models are relevant here. First, as illustrated in Table 31–2, the present value of progressively more distant dividends rapidly decreases to the point of insignificance. Thus, forecast errors in more distant time periods have a minimal impact on expected rates of return. Second, dividend growth models are used for the relative valuation of a universe of securities. In this valuation process, near-

FIGURE 31–2: Growth model forecast periods

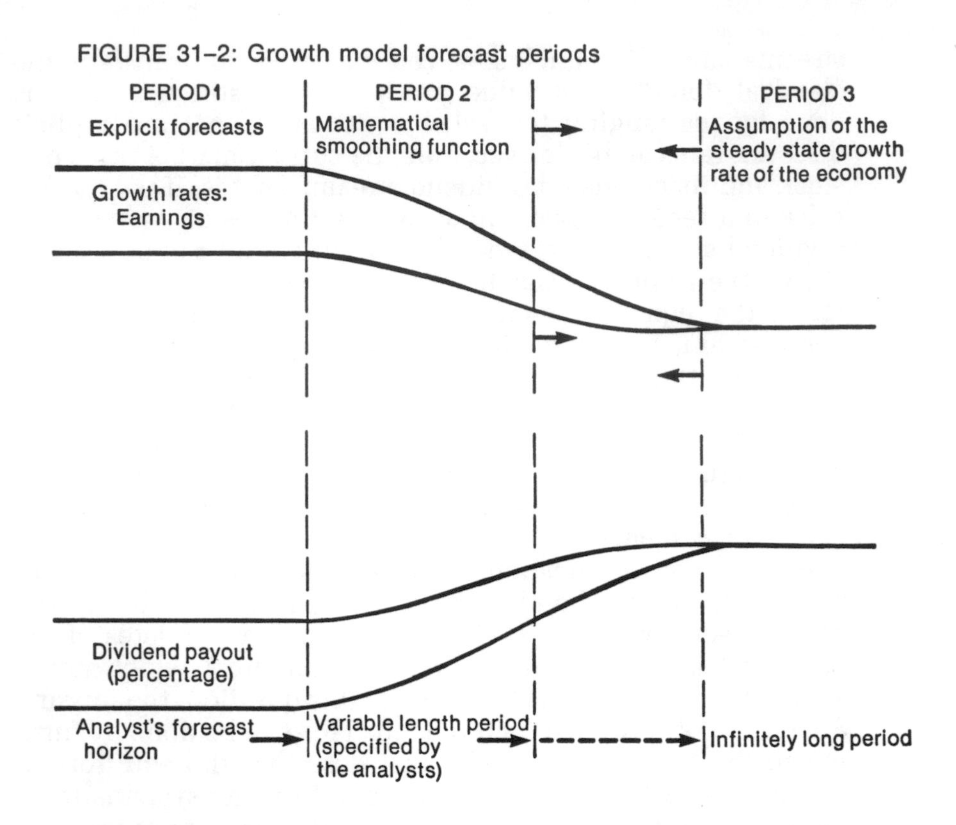

term estimates, at which superior security analysts should be able to demonstrate their forecasting abilities, are the most important. Similarly, since all dividends are assumed to grow at the same rate in the most distant forecast period, the assumptions in this period do not alter the relative valuations.

Finally, it should not be construed that this kind of forecasting requires an infinite forecasting horizon. Today's market price reflects today's consensus expectation. Tomorrow's market prices will reflect tomorrow's consensus expectations. Thus, today's forecasts need to predict tomorrow's consensus—not a perpetual forecast!

THE LINK BETWEEN MPT AND VALUATION THEORY

Classical investment value theory defines the value of an investment as the discounted present value of the future stream of payments derived from ownership. The *dividend discount model* shows how estimates of future dividend

streams and discount rates can be used to translate the classical definition of value into practical estimates. This is done by rearranging the value equation so that an implicit discount rate can be derived from the current market price of a stock and its estimated dividend stream. That is, if the market price of a security is combined with estimates of its expected dividend stream, the dividend discount model can be used to derive the *implicit discount rate*—the expected rate of total return that equates the current price with the forecasted dividend stream. This implicit discount rate provides an *expected rate of return for a security.*

In MPT, estimating a security's expected rate of return solves only half the problem. Consider, for example, two bonds with identical maturities and the expected rates of return of 10 percent and 12 percent, respectively. Which bond is the better investment?

Answering this question requires a comparative measure of the risk of the two bonds. The situation is no different in the case of security analysis. Given comparative estimates of expected rates of return (or implicit discount rates), which stocks are the best investments? To answer this question, the missing dimension of risk must be provided. This can be done by turning to the CAPM—the model that describes the equilibrium relationship between expected rate of return and systematic, or market-related, risk. This model holds that an appropriate discount rate for any asset can be derived from two factors: (*a*) the risk-free rate of return and (*b*) an additional, or premium, return that is commensurate with the asset's risk.

Determining the first factor—the risk-free rate of return—is relatively easy. It is merely the return that can be earned without incurring risk. Conceptually, the risk-free rate of return is the rate for the pure rental of money plus an inflation hedge. The risk-free rate of return is only part of the equation, however. For an estimate of the other component—the risk premium—we can turn to capital market theory. This theory holds that the risk premium of each stock is a linear function of systematic risk, or beta.

The link between MPT and valuation theory is shown in Figure 31–3. That is, valuation theory says that the value of an asset depends on the expected future stream of dividends and an appropriate discount rate. In turn, the CAPM says that the discount rate depends on the risk-free rate of return and the risk premium. Since the risk-free rate is easily determined, the missing element is quantification of the appropriate risk pre-

FIGURE 31–3: The link between MPT and valuation theory

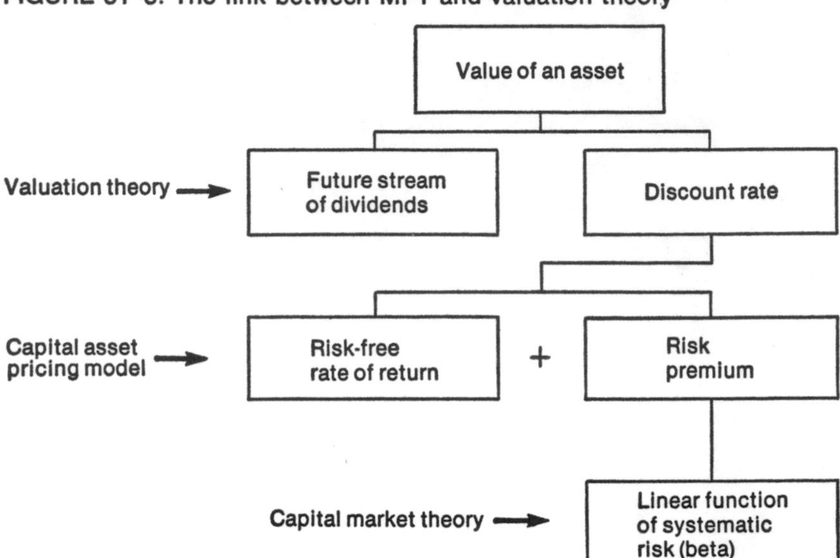

mium. Capital market theory holds, however, that the risk premium is a linear function (i.e., it can be represented by a straight line) of systematic risk.

A forward-looking estimate of systematic risk is an ex ante estimate of beta. Thus, with estimates of the future stream of dividends, the risk-free rate of return, and beta, the equilibrium expected rate of return of any asset can be determined. Herein lies the enormous significance of beta in security valuation.

Much progress has been made in improving the forecast reliability of beta coefficients by introducing company fundamentals into the analysis. Accordingly, before turning to the subject of betas, and their prediction, it will be useful to focus on the comparative analysis of company fundamentals.

Chapter 32

Company fundamentals

It would be difficult to find two identical companies. Clearly, Ford is different from General Motors; IBM is different from Control Data, and so on. But *how* do these companies differ? And how do these differences translate into differing risk and return expectations?

To answer the first question—how companies differ—a comparative analysis of company fundamentals is required. Generally speaking, *fundamentals* encompass all of the accounting-related data which appear on a company's financial statements. Techniques which facilitate this kind of comparative analysis are presented in this chapter.

Specifically, the goal here is to (*a*) clarify some often confusing accounting terms, (*b*) suggest a convenient technique that can be used for balance sheet and income statement comparisons, and (*c*) illustrate a system of ratios which link data on the balance sheet and the income statement. The graphic techniques presented here were largely developed by my long-time colleague, Chris Mader—holder of the Anvil Award for Teaching Excellence at the Wharton School of Finance.

BALANCE SHEET

Within the accounting profession, different terms are used to describe the same thing. Each of the following terms, for example, refers to the same document:

Balance sheet
Statement of financial condition
Position statement
Statement of net worth
Statement of assets, liabilities, and owners' equity

The balance sheet (as it is most commonly known) is the basic financial statement for a firm. It shows, on the left-hand side of the page, what the company owns (valued at acquisition cost plus installation minus accumulated depreciation) and, on the other side of the page, the sources of the funds that were used to acquire those assets.

By definition, the total amounts represented on each side of a balance sheet are numerically equal—they balance. Specifically, the equation for a balance sheet is

(Left side) (Right side)
Assets = Liabilities + owners' equity
(What is owned) (How it was funded)

An asset is something of sustained value that is owned by the company. The value of an asset (as it appears on the balance sheet) is cost plus installation minus accumulated depreciation. It is important to note that this definition and valuation convention can result in a very misleading picture of a company. Consider, for example, all of the things that are of value to a company but are not "owned" (and, hence, cannot be called "assets"). Obviously, management and employees are not "owned." In an accounting sense, people are resources which are leased or rented. And since leased resources are not "owned," they do not appear on the balance sheet. Thus, for example, the value of IBM's highly trained technical and sales personnel is not reflected on the company's balance sheet.

Another way in which balance sheets can be misleading stems from the convention of valuing assets at cost plus installation. Consider, for example, the current market value of real estate purchased 15 years ago. (Only since March 23, 1976, has the Securities and Exchange Commission's Rule 3–17, Regulation SX required firms with over $100 million in sales to provide unaudited estimates of the value of their assets at *replacement cost.*)

The final thing to remember about a balance sheet is that it is a static picture of an enterprise "as of the close of business on a particular day." Clearly, if you know that you are going to have your picture taken on December 31, you will do whatever you can to look your best on that day.

In spite of the definitional problems, the balance sheet can be useful in the comparative analysis of companies. A technique which will facilitate this comparison is to represent the two sides of the balance sheet as two equally tall columns of money. Graphically, these can be thought of as two tall build-

ings, such as New York's World Trade Towers. This columnar representation is shown in Figure 32–1.

Next, it is useful to think of the data to be analyzed in terms of percentages—not the typically incomprehensible absolute

FIGURE 32–1: World Trade Towers representation of a "typical" balance sheet

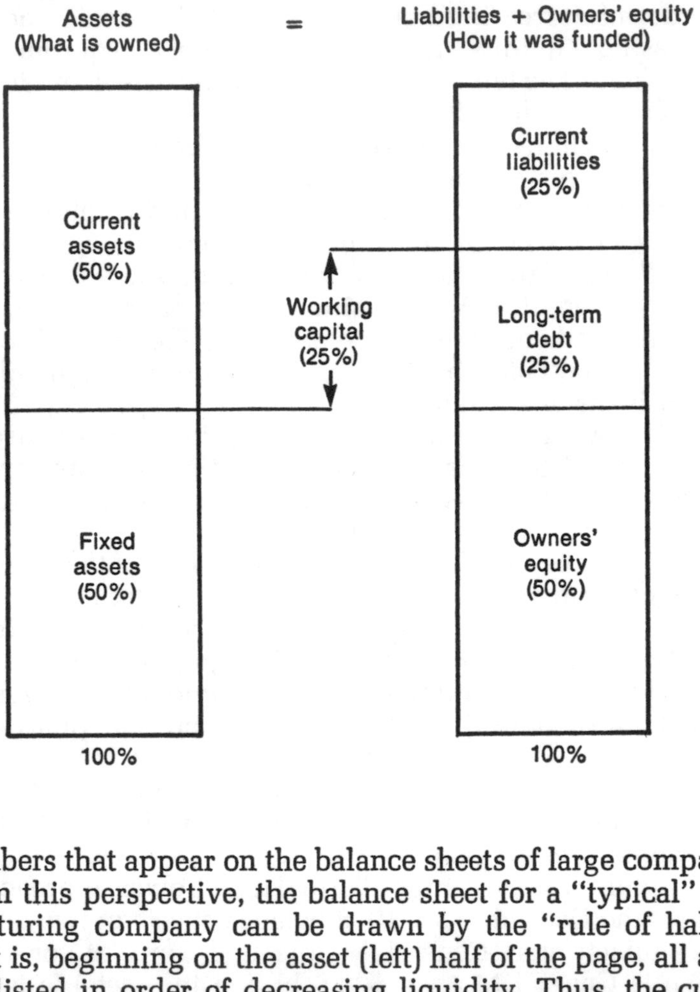

Assets (What is owned) = Liabilities + Owners' equity (How it was funded)

Current assets (50%)

Fixed assets (50%)

100%

Working capital (25%)

Current liabilities (25%)

Long-term debt (25%)

Owners' equity (50%)

100%

numbers that appear on the balance sheets of large companies. From this perspective, the balance sheet for a "typical" manufacturing company can be drawn by the "rule of halves." That is, beginning on the asset (left) half of the page, all assets are listed in order of decreasing liquidity. Thus, the *current assets* (those most likely to be converted into cash during an operating cycle) are shown first, followed by the fixed assets. Fixed assets are those things of long-term usefulness to the firm which are not likely to be converted to cash, or consumed, within the next operating cycle. Based on the rule of halves, a

typical manufacturing company would have half current and half fixed assets.

Within each of the broad categories of current and fixed, assets are listed in order of decreasing liquidity. Current assets, in order of decreasing liquidity, include accounts such as cash, marketable securities, accounts receivable, and inventories. The inventory category is, in turn, broken down into finished goods, work-in-process, and raw materials, also in order of decreasing liquidity. The fixed assets, in order of decreasing liquidity, include items such as equipment, plant, and land. The typical division between current and fixed assets is shown in the left side of Figure 32–1.

The right half of the balance sheet shows how the purchases of the assets appearing on the left side of the balance sheet were funded. Basically, there are two funding alternatives. Assets can be purchased with borrowed money (representing *liabilities* of the company) or capital invested by stockholders (*owners' equity*). Again, using the rule of halves, a typical mix of debt and equity will be one-to-one. That is, half of the right side of the balance sheet amounts consists of liabilities and half is owners' equity.

Following much the same convention that was used on the left side of the balance sheet, liabilities are listed in order of "term" or nearness of the obligation. Thus, short-term debt obligations appear first, with owners' equity coming last. Based on the rule of halves once more, half of the liabilities of a typical firm are current and half are long-term.

A representation of a balance sheet derived from the rule of halves appears in Figure 32–1. This graphic format can also be used to depict working capital—the amount by which the current (most liquid) assets exceed the current (most pressing) liabilities. Other data, such as the percentage of owners' equity—what is owned (assets) minus what is owed (liabilities)—can also readily be derived from this kind of graphic presentation.

Figure 32–2 uses the World Trade Tower approach to contrast the December 31, 1978 balance sheets of two automobile manufacturers—General Motors and Ford Motor Company. While General Motors ($30.6 billion in assets) is larger than Ford ($22 billion in assets), the step-by-step comparison of each balance sheet category is now very easy. The tower comparison reveals, for example, that General Motors's assets were more liquid. General Motors had 59 percent of its assets in the

FIGURE 32–2: Comparative balance sheets

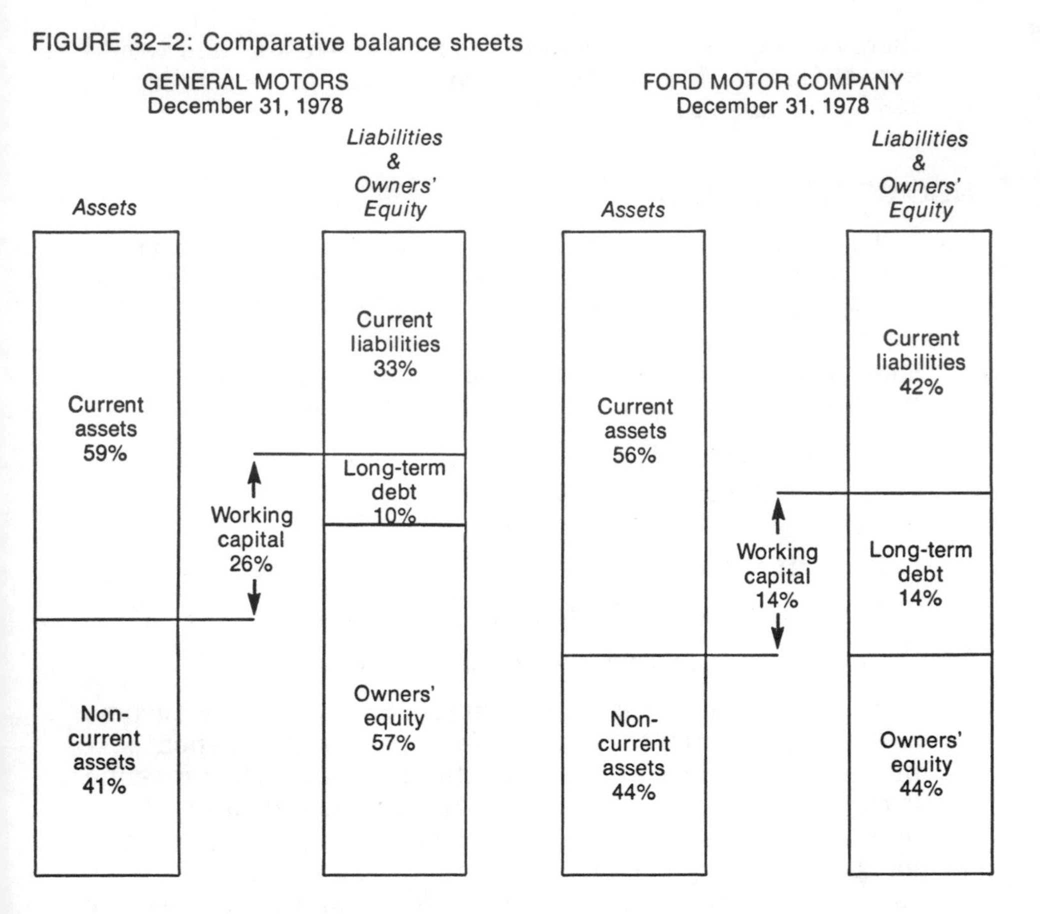

current category compared to 56 percent for Ford. The fact that General Motor's working capital accounts for 26 percent of its assets, versus Ford's 14 percent, shows that money is tighter at Ford.

Debt represents 43 percent of General Motors' liabilities and equity, against 56 percent for Ford. Thus, in terms of three comparisons—(*a*) asset liquidity, (*b*) working capital, and (*c*) the debt to equity ratio—General Motors has the stronger balance sheet. Clearly, on the basis of these fundamentals, General Motors is more attractive. Knowing nothing else, but assuming a reasonably efficient market, one would be surprised to find both General Motors and Ford priced equally. In fact, if they were, it might reasonably be concluded that General Motors was undervalued (or Ford was overvalued, or both). But, alas,

there are few such surprises in the market—just as one would expect General Motors' price-earnings ratio on December 31, 1978 was almost twice Ford's.

INCOME STATEMENT

The income statement (as it is most commonly known) is used to report managerial performance over time. It is a *dynamic* statement reflecting the progress (or lack of progress) of the firm. By comparison, the balance sheet is a *static*, or snapshot, picture of the firm's financial condition at a single point in time. Terms used interchangeably here are

Income statement
Profit and loss statement
P&L
Operating statement

The basic equation for the income statement is

$$\text{Income} = \text{Revenue} - \text{Expenses}$$

No one can disagree with so simple a definition for income as everything brought in (revenue) less everything spent (expenses). Yet, there are many subtleties regarding *when* revenue is recognized as such and *which* expenses should, at that time, be matched against it. To compound matters, income statements are also replete with many different terms that mean the same thing. There is no difference, for example, between the following:

Revenues
Sales
Turnover (in Europe)
Gross income
"The top line"

Similarly, there is no difference between

Income
Profit
Earnings
Net income
"The bottom line"

The income statements of different companies can also be

compared using the World Trade Tower approach. It merely requires the algebraic rearrangement of the basic equation from

$$\text{Income} = \text{Revenue} - \text{Expenses}$$

to

$$\text{Revenue} = \text{Expenses} + \text{Income}$$

In this format, we can convert any company's numerical percentages and represent each side of the equation as easily comparable "towers," as shown in Figure 32–3.

FIGURE 32–3: World Trade Tower representation of a "typical" income statement

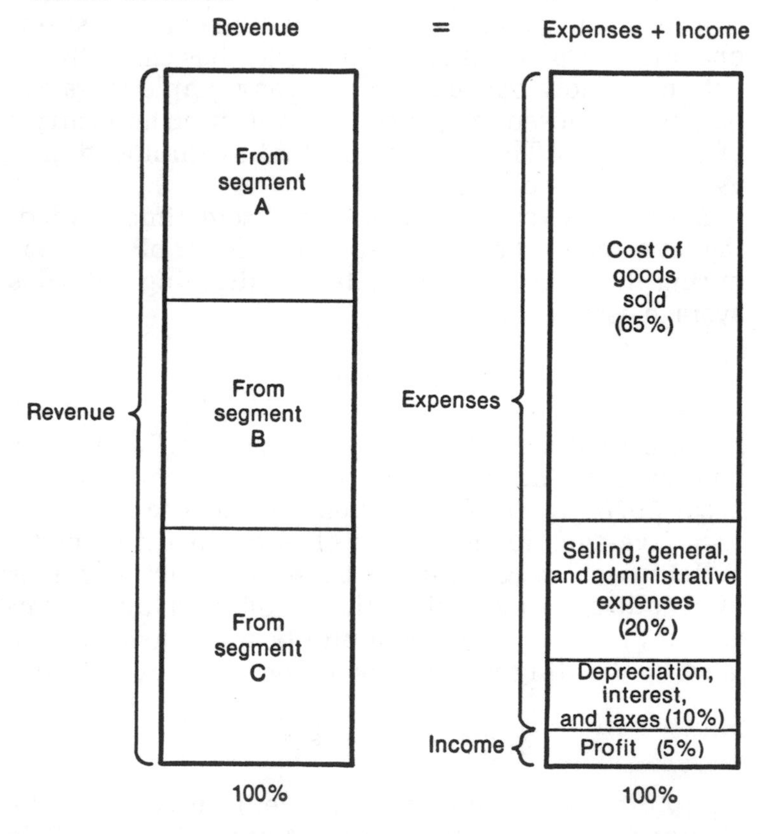

Under the segment accounting rules now in effect (for audited companies), whenever 10 percent or more of a company's revenues are from a given line of business (such as a sales division or a rental segment), the revenues from that seg-

ment must be reported separately. Thus, the revenue (left-hand) column is merely a graphic representation of the percentages of the company's revenue that are derived from each major segment of its business. Similarly, the expenses and income (right) column, breaks out the percentages of the company's expenses by various categories. And, last but not least, the bottom of the right-hand column shows the amount that is left after expenses are subtracted from revenues—net aftertax profit, or income.

FINANCIAL ANALYSIS

Financial analysis is the study of the interrelationship between an enterprise's financial structure (balance sheet) and its operating results (income statement). Basically, the task is to determine how efficiently a company employs its assets and how it has chosen to finance the acquisition and carrying costs of those assets. The key system of ratios employed in this analysis is explained below.

Asset turnover. Asset turnover (sometimes called operating leverage) is the ratio of sales per dollar of assets employed during the year. It is calculated by dividing net sales by the average assets. Thus,

$$\text{Asset turnover} = \frac{\text{Sales}}{\text{Assets}}$$

In fiscal 1978 (ended June 30), for example, Tandy Corporation had an asset turnover ratio of 2.06. This means that during fiscal 1978, Tandy Corporation generated $2.06 in sales for each (average) dollar's worth of assets that it owned.

Return on sales. Return on sales (sometimes abbreviated ROS and sometimes called the operating margin, or net profit margin) is the percentage of profit earned on sales. It is calculated by dividing net income, or earnings, by net sales. Thus,

$$\text{Return on sales} = \frac{\text{Earnings}}{\text{Sales}}$$

Continuing with the same example, in fiscal 1978 the Tandy Corporation had a return on sales of 6.2 percent. This means that the Tandy Corporation earned 6.2 cents in net (aftertax) profit for each dollar of sales.

Return on assets. Return on assets (sometimes abbreviated ROA) is the percentage of net profit earned on total assets. It is the product of asset turnover and return on sales:

Asset turnover × Return on sales = Return on assets

$$\frac{\text{Sales}}{\text{Assets}} \times \frac{\text{Earnings}}{\text{Sales}} = \frac{\text{Earnings}}{\text{Assets}}$$

Note that when the fraction representing "asset turnover" is multiplied by the fraction representing "return on sales," the "sales" terms in the two fractions cancel each other. Thus, return on assets can be calculated either by multiplying asset turnover by return on sales or by merely dividing earnings by assets. The Tandy Corporation had a return on assets of 12.8 percent in fiscal 1978–12.8 cents for each dollar of assets.

Financial leverage. Financial leverage is the measure of how many dollars of assets are held in relation to each dollar of stockholders' equity—in other words, how much of a company's asset base is financed with stockholders' equity and how much with borrowed funds. It is calculated by dividing average assets by average stockholders' equity. Thus,

$$\text{Financial leverage} = \frac{\text{Assets}}{\text{Equity}}$$

During fiscal 1978, the leverage ratio for Tandy Corporation was 3.39, indicating that the company employed $3.39 of assets for each dollar of stockholders' equity.

Return on equity. Return on equity (sometimes abbreviated ROE)—a key measure of the profitability of an equity investment—is the net income earned by a company expressed as a percentage return on the stockholders' investment. Its relationship to return on assets and financial leverage is as follows:

Return on assets × Financial leverage = Return on equity

$$\frac{\text{Earnings}}{\text{Assets}} \times \frac{\text{Assets}}{\text{Equity}} = \frac{\text{Earnings}}{\text{Equity}}$$

Note that when the fraction representing "return on assets" is multiplied by the fraction representing "financial leverage," the "asset" terms in each fraction are canceled out. Thus, return on equity can be calculated either by multiplying return on assets by the financial leverage ratio or merely by dividing earnings by equity. For fiscal 1978, the Tandy Corporation had a whopping aftertax return on equity of 43.6 percent—the highest in the firm's history and unequaled by any other major retailer or electronics and computer company.[1]

[1] For further analysis of these data, the interested reader is referred to the Tandy Corporation annual report. It may be obtained without charge by writing Tandy Corporation, Shareholder Relations, 1800 One Tandy Center, P.O. Box 17180, Fort Worth, Texas 76102; or by telephone (817) 390–3091.

We can gain much insight into the Tandy Corporation by arraying the *system* of financial ratios which produces return on equity in the format shown in Table 32–1.

The sources, data, and relationships expressed by this system of ratios can be summarized as shown below:

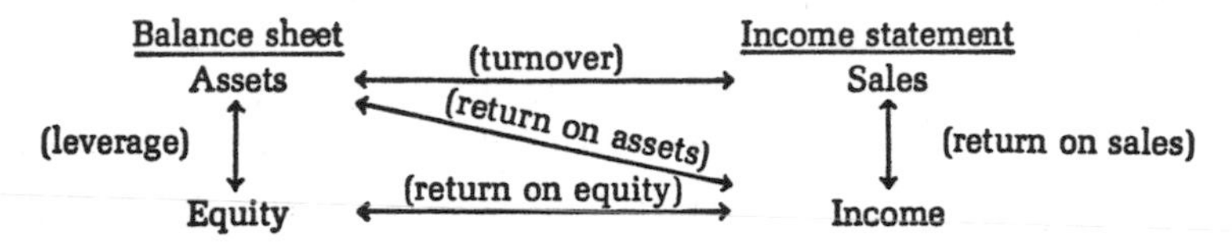

Thus, leverage provides a measure of the balance sheet relationship between the assets and equity. Turnover, return on assets, and return on equity define relationships between key items on the balance sheet and income statement. Finally, return on sales provides a measure of the relationship between sales and income on the income statement.

Given these relationships and the data presented in Table 32–1, the interrelationships which produced Tandy's final return on equity figure can be probed. Moving from left to right across the 1978 line, it is apparent that asset turnover (sales/assets) is down slightly from fiscal 1977. Reference to the balance sheet shows that total assets increased over the year from $475 million to $553 million—for an average of $514 million for fiscal 1978. Reference to the income statement shows that sales rose from $953 million in fiscal 1977 to $1,065 million in fiscal 1978. Thus, both assets and sales showed year-to-year increases, but sales per average dollar of assets employed (measured by the *asset turnover* ratio) declined.

Moving to the next column, it is evident that *return on sales* (income/sales) has also decreased. Since income is the difference between sales and expenses, the expense items on the income statement can be scrutinized for an explanation of the drop in the return on sales figure. The expense figures show that part of the decline in return on sales stems from a year-to-year doubling of interest expense—from roughly $15 million to $30 million. Further probing reveals that the bulk of this incremental interest expense reflects an increase in debt issued to repurchase the company's common stock. The rationale behind this financing decision was that the profit margins of the company were running in excess of the interest costs on the new debt. Thus, the repurchase of shares with borrowed funds was expected to enhance the return on equity.

The fourth column of Table 32–1 shows a significant increase in *financial leverage* during fiscal 1978, following the

TABLE 32–1: Illustrative system of key financial ratios for the Tandy Corporation

	Asset turnover (operating leverage)	×	*Return on sales (net margin)*	=	*Return on assets*	×	*Financial leverage*	=	*Return on equity*
	Sales / Average assets	×	*Net income / Sales*	=	*Net income / Average assets*	×	*Average assets / Average equity*	=	*Net income / Average equity*
1972	1.39	×	3.9%	=	5.4%	×	1.61	=	8.7%
1973	1.34	×	4.4	=	5.9	×	2.06	=	12.2
1974	1.47	×	3.6	=	5.3	×	2.41	=	12.8
1975	1.71	×	5.1	=	8.7	×	2.53	=	22.0
1976	2.04	×	8.7	=	17.7	×	2.18	=	38.6
1977	2.16	×	7.3	=	15.8	×	2.37	=	37.2
1978	2.06	×	6.2	=	12.8	×	3.39	=	43.4

Source: Tandy Corporation's June 30, 1978 *Annual Report.*

stock repurchase program. The result, in the final column, is a return on equity of 43.4 percent.

With the financial data on Tandy Corporation arrayed in the format of Table 32–1, it is possible to "go beyond" *return on equity* by disecting the system of financial ratios that produce it. The asset turnover column reveals, for example, that the amount of sales generated per dollar of assets has remained fairly constant since fiscal 1976. By comparison, the company's return on sales has fallen since 1976. The product of the first two ratios, return on assets, has similarly fallen since 1976. The information in the next column, shows that Tandy increased its financial leverage. Finally, the product of return on assets and financial leverage produces return on equity.

Clearly, the objective here is not to comment on the investment merits of Tandy Corporation, but rather to provide some insight into how the fundamental risk and return characteristics of a company can change over time. Importantly, MPT has addressed the subject of how changes in an investment's fundamentals can alter its potential risks and returns. Barr Rosenberg's pioneering work in this area is discussed in the next chapter.

Chapter 33

Prediction of beta

Systematic risk, measured by beta coefficients, is the risk which cannot be eliminated by diversification. Thus, beta prediction—the only estimate of risk in a well-diversified portfolio—has a pivotal role in MPT.

EX POST BETAS

Ex post or backward-looking, betas are best understood by imagining an experiment in which pairs of market and security returns are plotted, with the market return on the horizontal axis and the security's return on the vertical axis. The slope of a regression line fitted through these points measures the degree to which market returns, on average, have been associated with the security's returns.

Caution needs to be exercised in interpreting an historical beta. First, it cannot be assumed that the true beta is fixed over time. Quite the contrary, there is reason to expect that beta does change. Second, historical beta is merely an estimate of the "true" underlying beta. During any historical period, the observed combinations of market and security returns that are used to calculate a historical beta represent the "true" beta, plus or minus random factors which are unique to a security. Third, historical betas should not obscure the fact that while historical betas are useful when interpreting historical performance, prediction requires betas that are ex ante, forward-looking, estimates.

BETA DOES NOT DESCRIBE A CAUSAL RELATIONSHIP

Much of the confusion surrounding beta can be avoided by remembering that beta does not describe a causal relationship. A certain level of market return does not result in a certain

level of security return. Instead, both market and security returns depend on a third variable—the economy. Economic events cause systematic changes in both security and market prices.

Properly viewed, beta reflects the fact that both market and security returns depend on common events. Thus, the most logical way to forecast beta is to quantify the relationship between market and security returns and these factors. What, for example, is the relationship between changes in the expected rate of inflation and the returns of both individual securities and the market? Compared to the market, which securities are sensitive to inflation and which are not?

BETA FORECASTING AND SECURITY ANALYSIS

Approached from this perspective, beta forecasting is strikingly similar to security analysis. Conventional security analysis recognizes two components of return: (*a*) that arising from events which bear particularly on the company in question and (*b*) the component resulting from events which affect the economy, or the market, as a whole. The sum of these two components is the total expected return.

The lack of certainty surrounding the events which solely impact a company is the specific risk. However, since the events specific to individual firms tend to cancel out through diversification, on the average, specific returns do not add to market return. Consequently, the uncertainty which is not specific to individual companies—the nonspecific risk—accounts for almost all of a portfolio's risk. This nonspecific risk—that inherent in the economy and shared by other companies—cannot be diversified away. Nonetheless, the nonspecific risk can be estimated from a prediction of the amount of economy-related uncertainty surrounding the security return—in other words, beta.

Traditionally, of the two components of risk and return, security analysis has emphasized the specific, company-related, factor. The age-old quest for misvalued securities has tended to focus on events which are specific to individual firms. Yet, most of the risk and return in a portfolio are linked to the market. In turn, the market component of risk and return for a security is derived from the economic events which impact on many stocks. It follows that one of the most fruitful areas of research has dealt with the extension of fundamental security analysis that is concerned with the relationship between a se-

curity's return and nonspecific, economywide events—so-called *fundamental betas.*

ROSENBERG'S FUNDAMENTAL BETAS

Barr Rosenberg has pioneered in the prediction of fundamental betas through *relative response coefficients.* Basically, a relative response coefficient is the ratio of the expected response of a security to the expected response of the market if both the security and the market are impacted by the same event. For example, if the event is inflation, those stocks which react to inflation in the same way as the market will have a high relative response coefficient for this event. Similarly, stocks that are not as sensitive to inflation as the market will have a low relative response coefficient for inflation.

Suppose, that an investor is interested in studying the impact of future energy and inflation developments on the market and on two stocks. Assume that there is an equal likelihood that future events in each of these areas will turn out to have favorable, unchanged, or unfavorable implications. This situation, plus the "relative response" which each event-outcome combination is expected to elicit, are depicted in Table 33–1.

TABLE 33–1: Contributions to return for hypothetical event-outcome sequences

		Percentage contribution to return		
Event	*Outcome*	*Market*	*Stock A*	*Stock B*
Energy.........	Favorable	+6	+4	+8
	Unchanged	0	0	0
	Unfavorable	−6	−4	−8
Inflation	Favorable	+3	+6	0
	Unchanged	0	0	0
	Unfavorable	−3	−6	0

Source: Rosenberg and Guy [227].

Stock A is expected to respond two thirds as much as the market to an energy-related event, while stock B is anticipated to react one third more strongly than the market. To an inflation event, stock A is expected to respond twice as much as the market, while stock B is not expected to show any reaction to inflation events.

The relationships portrayed in Table 33–1 can be used to contrast the expected values and variances of returns on securities with those of the market when both are impacted by the same macroeconomic events. In this illustration, the expected (average) impact of these two events on market return is zero, and the variance is 30 percent.[1] The variance of future market returns can be separated into the variances generated by each of the two events. In this illustration, energy uncertainties cause 24 percentage points of the variance in market returns. Similarly, the variance caused by inflation uncertainty amounts to 6 percent.

DETERMINATION OF BETA

In general terms, a security's beta is determined by

1. The proportional contributions of various categories of economic events to market variance.
2. The relative response of security returns to these same events—the relative response coefficients.

More specifically, the beta for any security is the weighted average of its relative response coefficients, each weighted by the proportion of total variance in market returns due to that event.[2]

In the example in Table 33–1, energy is the greatest source of uncertainty (variance). Thus, in the calculation of beta, energy uncertainty receives proportionately more emphasis. In terms of response to the two economic events, stock B is expected to be volatile in a changing energy situation. It is not

[1] To assist the reader who wishes to pursue this subject in more detail, the numerical example used here is identical to that used by Rosenberg and Guy. The interested reader can find the procedure used to calculate this variance (as well as other information) in [227, pp. 63–4].

[2] In technical terms

$$B_{im} = \sum_{j=1}^{J} \left(\frac{V_j}{\sum_{j=1}^{J} V_j} \right) \gamma_{ji}$$

where

B_{im} = Beta for security i.
V_j = Contribution of the economywide event j to the market variance in any period.
γ_{ji} = Ratio of the response of security i and the market to event j—the relative response coefficient.

surprising, therefore, that the betas for stocks A and B are 0.9 and 1.1, respectively.[3]

BETAS VARY OVER TIME

The importance of the foregoing discussion of the composition of beta is that a security's beta will change when

1. The variance contributed by the various categories of economic events changes.
2. The response coefficients change.

Also, to the degree that these changes can be predicted or explained, beta can be predicted or explained.

The preceding chapter on company fundamentals discussed the capital structures of firms. Clearly, as a firm becomes more or less leveraged (i.e., the proportion of debt in its capitalization structure increases or decreases, respectively), its relative response coefficient to virtually all economic events will increase or decrease. As a result, its beta will also rise or fall (after Rosenberg and Guy [227]).

HISTORICAL VERSUS FUTURE BETA VALUES

It is important to remember that the "true" beta is never observed. Before the fact, ex ante, predictions of the true value can be derived from properly weighted relative response coefficients. With after the fact data on the historical relationship between risk and return, it is possible to develop a regression line which serves as an estimate of the underlying true beta value that produced these results. In practice, both ex ante and ex post betas have specific uses.

The choice of historical or future beta values depends on the proposed application. When the beta is to be used for ex post performance evaluation, the coefficient is used to estimate the portion of total return which was derived from market and nonmarket components. In this case, since there is no need to be concerned with forward-looking, ex ante, estimates for individual securities, backward-looking, ex post, betas are appropriate.

The process of calculating backward-looking betas is conceptualized in Figure 33–1. After the relationship between his-

[3] Again, the interested reader will find an explanation of the calculation of these numbers in [227].

FIGURE 33–1: Calculation of backward-looking betas

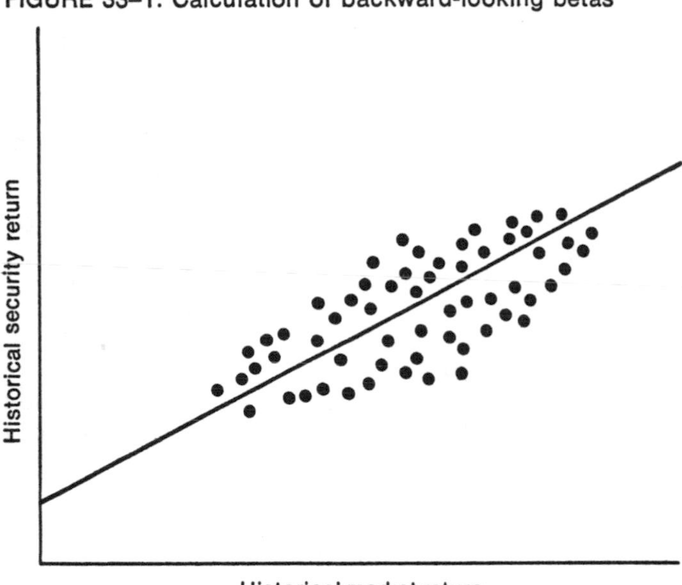

torical pairs of market and security returns has been plotted, a regression line, or "least squares" line of best fit, is calculated. In mathematical terms, such lines are plotted so as to minimize the sum of the squared distances between them and the points of observation, hence, the term "least squares" regression estimate. The slope of the least squares regression line is the ex post beta coefficient.

Sample ex post betas and other historical information are shown in the sample page drawn from a *Merrill Lynch Market Sensitivity Report,* reproduced as Table 33–2. During the historical period covered by the report (60 months), Allis Chalmers had a *beta* of 0.94—indicating that it was not as sensitive to the market as the average stock in the S&P 500 Index. Allis Chalmer's *alpha* was 2.13 during the same period—indicating a positive nonmarket-related return of 213 basis points. The R-squared of 0.27 indicates that during the period studied, 27 percent of the variance in Allis Chalmer's price was attributable to the market.

The *residual standard deviation* is a summary measure of the distances from the plotted points to the regression line. The residual standard deviation is an ex post measure of the security's specific, or nonmarket, risk that was present during the

TABLE 33–2: *Merrill Lynch Market Sensitivity Report:* 2/27/79 (for the first 30 stocks—alphabetical by ticker symbol—in the *S&P 500 Index*)

Ticker symbol	*Security name*	*Price (1–31–79)*	*Beta*	*Alpha*	*R-squared*	*Residual standard deviation*	*Standard error: Beta*	*Standard error: Alpha*
ACF	ACF INDUSTRIES, INC.	30.38	1.06	−0.27	0.47	5.83	0.15	0.75
AMF	AMF, INC.	17.50	1.22	−0.04	0.41	8.13	0.21	1.05
ARA	ARA SERVICES, INC.	41.00	1.15	−0.44	0.46	6.70	0.17	0.87
ASA	ASA LTD.	25.38	0.74	−0.19	0.05	11.54	0.29	1.49
ABT	ABBOTT LABORATORIES	33.50	1.17	1.72	0.55	5.79	0.15	0.75
AMT	ACME CLEVELAND CORP.	20.25	0.85	0.90	0.16	8.58	0.22	1.11
AET	AETNA LIFE & CASUALTY	42.25	1.16	0.63	0.39	7.92	0.20	1.02
AHN	AHMANSON, H.F. & CO.	22.50	1.35	1.43	0.31	11.35	0.29	1.47
ANK	AKZONA INC.	13.13	0.91	−0.46	0.19	8.83	0.22	1.14
ACV	ALBERTO CULVER CO.	8.00	1.00	0.04	0.20	9.89	0.25	1.28
AL	ALCAN ALUMINUM LTD.	36.38	0.79	0.31	0.16	7.51	0.19	0.97
ACD	ALLIED CHEMICAL CORP.	30.00	1.13	−0.52	0.48	6.35	0.16	0.82
ALS	ALLIED STORES CORP.	22.63	1.11	1.42	0.35	7.97	0.20	1.03
AH	ALLIS-CHALMERS CORP.	30.75	0.94	2.13	0.27	7.50	0.19	0.97
APC	ALPHA PORTLAND INDS.	16.63	0.88	0.44	0.15	9.73	0.25	1.26
AA	ALUMINUM CO. OF AMERICA	51.13	0.80	0.30	0.18	7.44	0.19	0.96
AGM	AMALGAMATED SUGAR CO.	17.00	0.54	−0.24	0.01	8.72	0.22	1.13
AMX	AMAX, INC.	51.13	0.96	0.23	0.31	7.14	0.18	0.92
AMR	AMERICAN AIRLINES	11.88	1.39	0.95	0.33	11.42	0.29	1.48
AT	AMERICAN BRANDS	50.25	0.83	0.51	0.55	3.43	0.09	0.44
ABC	AMERICAN BROADCASTING	35.38	1.21	1.69	0.33	9.34	0.24	1.21
AC	AMERICAN CAN CO.	36.63	0.68	0.49	0.27	4.24	0.11	0.55
ACY	AMERICAN CYANAMID CO.	25.38	1.04	0.37	0.55	4.94	0.13	0.64
AEP	AMERICAN ELEC POWER	22.75	0.81	−0.13	0.29	5.58	0.14	0.72
AXP	AMERICAN EXPRESS CO.	29.50	1.49	−0.41	0.64	6.68	0.17	0.86
AGI	AMERICAN GENERAL INS.	27.38	1.21	1.21	0.49	6.87	0.17	0.89
AHP	AMERICAN HOME PRODUCTS	27.50	1.09	−0.48	0.44	6.51	0.17	0.84
AHS	AMER HOSPITAL SUPPLY	25.88	1.54	−0.26	0.58	7.77	0.20	1.00
AMI	AMERICAN MEDICAL INT'L.	28.50	1.59	3.45	0.45	10.47	0.27	1.35
AMO	AMERICAN MOTORS CORP.	6.13	0.84	−0.56	0.07	12.81	0.33	1.65

period. The greater a particular stock's residual standard deviation, the greater is the effect of company-related events on the price of the stock. Given that the data are monthly and that roughly two thirds of the deviations fall within plus or minus one standard deviation, Allis Chalmer's residual standard deviation of 7.50 indicates that in roughly two out of every three months, Allis Chalmer's price was within plus or minus 7.50 percent (750 basis points) of the price estimated by the beta of the regression line and the level of the market at the time. In analyzing this number, remember that for a single stock the market accounts for only about 30 percent of total uncertainty. That is, for the average stock, the monthly R-squared—the portion of the total variance attributed to the market—is around 30 percent. With the remaining 70 percent of the monthly risk, on the average, coming from nonmarket sources, it is not surprising to find ex post monthly residual standard deviations of the magnitude of those in Table 33–2.

The regression procedure used to calculate alpha and beta (shown conceptually in Figure 33–1) relies on sampling to estimate the "true" underlying values. It follows that the greater the number of cases included in the sample, the smaller any errors between the "sample estimated" and the "true" value will be. The *standard error of estimate* provides an estimate of the probable extent of this kind of error. Thus, Allis Chalmer's standard error of beta of 0.19 indicates that there is a 68 percent chance (i.e., plus or minus one standard deviation) that the "true" beta is within ±0.19 of the estimated value. Similarly, the standard error of alpha of 0.97 indicates that there is a 68 percent chance that the "true" alpha is within 97 basis points of the estimated alpha.

ADJUSTED BETAS

There is much evidence (see Blume [31]) that over time, deviant betas regress to normal. Accordingly, many services which provide historical betas (such as the report in Table 33–2), "adjust" for this regression tendency, so that the historical figures will more closely approximate the "true" forward-looking beta.

USE OF BETA FOR PORTFOLIO SELECTION

To quote Rosenberg and Guy, ". . . an accurate prediction of beta is the most important single element in predicting the

future behavior of a portfolio." [227, p. 65] That is, in the portfolio context, the relevant risk of a security lies in its impact on the risk of a portfolio. Further, the risk of a well-diversified portfolio is almost exclusively linked to the sensitivity of its component securities to future market moves. For this purpose, backward-looking betas are inappropriate.

Instead, it is necessary to (*a*) consider the *sources* of such future moves, (*b*) project the security's *reaction* to such sources, and (*c*) assign *probabilities* to the likelihood of each possible occurrence. This process, in turn, requires a thorough understanding of (*a*) the economics of the relevant industry, (*b*) both operating leverage and financial leverage of the company (see the discussion in Chapter 32), and of (*c*) other fundamental factors with meaningful relative response coefficients.

As mentioned earlier, Barr Rosenberg has pioneered in developing fundamentally derived betas that have been shown to be more accurate than historically derived estimates. To calculate fundamentally based predictions of beta and residual risk, Rosenberg uses the following categories of information:

1. *Market variability.* This index measures the impact of certain factors on the relationship between the market variability of returns and security returns. Such factors include:
   a. Historical beta.
   b. Historical standard deviation of residual return.
   c. Share turnover rate.
   d. Trading volume divided by the standard deviation of return.
   e. Average monthly price range.
2. *Earnings variability.* This index measures the variability of earnings. (Needless to say, earnings variability contributes to risk.) Among the descriptors used here are:
   a. Variability (coefficient of variation) of annual earnings per share.
   b. Typical proportion of earnings that are extraordinary items.
   c. Variability (coefficient of variation) of cash flow.
   d. Earnings covariability with total corporate earnings.
   e. The "Beaver" beta: regression coefficient between normalized earnings-price ratio of the firm and normalized earnings-price ratio of the economy.
   f. A measure of the absence of earnings diversification across industries.

   g. Reported foreign operating income as a percentage of total operating income.
3. *Low valuation and "unsuccess."* This index is designed to measure the variability of returns (risk) inherent in consistently low-market-valuation stocks with dismal operating records. These factors include:
   a. Growth in earnings per share.
   b. Delta earnings: a measure of proportional changes in adjusted earnings per share.
   c. "Relative strength" rate of return.
   d. Indicator of very low current earnings.
   e. Ratio of book value of equity per share to stock price.
   f. Applicable federal tax rate.
   g. Average proportional cut in dividends.
   h. Return on equity.
4. *Immaturity and smallness.* This index differentiates between the older and larger firms—which have accumulated substantial fixed assets and have a more secure economic position and a lower degree of risk—and the small, younger, and riskier firms. Among the descriptors in this index are:
   a. Logarithm of total assets.
   b. Capitalization: market value of common equity.
   c. Market share.
   d. Ratio of net plant to gross plant.
   e. Ratio of gross plant to common equity.
   f. Ratio of estimated net plant in current dollars to common equity.
   g. Number of prior years of available monthly prices.
   h. Earnings history.
5. *Growth orientation.* This index measures the risk associated with the so-called high-multiple stocks. Among the descriptors used are:
   a. A measure of normal payout.
   b. Dividend yield.
   c. Asset growth rate.
   d. Variability of capital structure.
   e. Earnings-price ratio.
6. *Financial structure.* This index measures financial risk by incorporating leverage (long-term debt and equity as a percentage of book value), coverage of fixed charges, the ratio of debt to total assets, liquidity, and net monetary debt. In general, the more highly leveraged a financial structure, the greater is the risk to the common stockholders. These factors include:

   a. Book leverage: book value (long-term debt plus preferred equity) divided by market book value (common equity).
   b. Market leverage: book value (long-term debt plus preferred equity) plus market value (common equity) divided by market value (common equity).
   c. Ratio of total debt to assets.
   d. Estimated probability of noncoverage of fixed charges, using a trend value for current operating income.
   e. Ratio of typical cash flow to current liabilities.
   f. Liquidity of current financial position.
   g. Potential dilution.
   h. Proportional adjustment to earnings for inflation.
   i. Tax liability adjustment to net monetary debt.

7. *Other characteristics.* In addition to these six risk indexes, Rosenberg uses special variables for each industry group to account for risk that is typical of the industry itself and cannot be explained by the preceding six indexes. These include factors such as:
   a. NYSE listing.
   b. Commodities exchange listing.
   c. Raw material ownership.
   d. Producers goods manufacturers.
   e. Retailers.
   f. Wholesalers.
   g. Coefficient of variation of quarterly earnings about trend.
   h. Ratio of plant to total sales.
   i. Estimated probability that operating income may fall below fixed charges.
   j. Ratio of intangibles to market value (or equity).
   k. S&P quality rating and indicator for its existence.
   l. Operating leverage.
   m. Variability of operating income.
   n. Growth rate of operating income.
   o. Operating profit margin.
   p. Mean retained earnings per dollar of assets.
   q. Rate of growth of total sales.
   r. Estimate of nonsustainable growth.
   s. Marketability (annual trading volume).
   t. Negative returns in the past.
   u. Variability of proportional earnings growth rate.
   v. Variability of earnings-price ratio.
   w. Rate of return on investment.
   x. Growth valuation adjustments.

EXTRAMARKET COVARIANCE

Basically, Rosenberg's research provides a more refined decomposition of risk and return. The simple decomposition of return (and risk) is

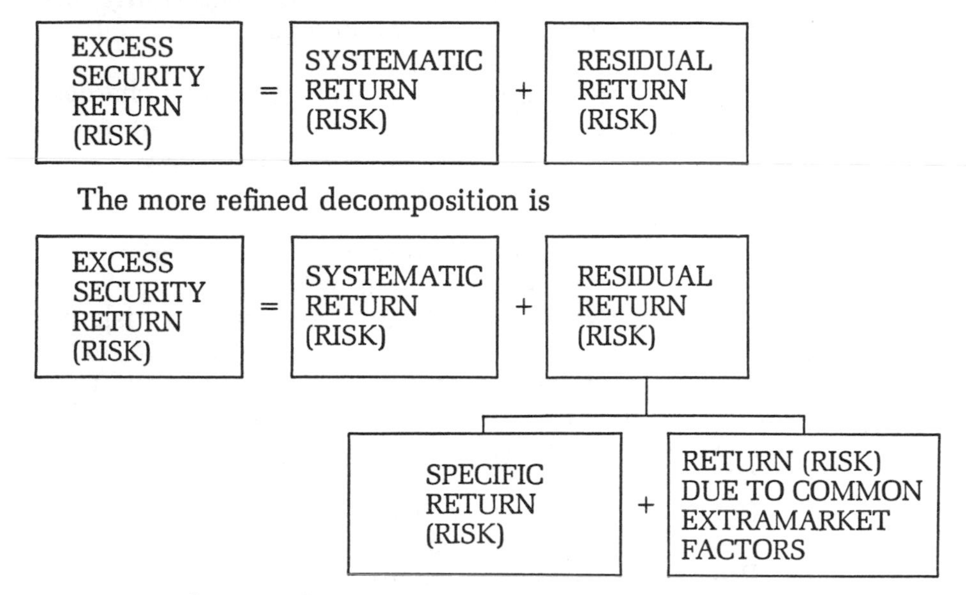

As discussed earlier, systematic risk is the degree to which security returns are related to market moves. The measure of systematic risk is beta. Systematic return, equal to the security beta times the market excess return (the excess of market return over the risk-free rate) is the component of return arising from systematic risk. The residual return is merely any remaining return that cannot be explained by the systematic return. The residual risk can, however, be further broken down into specific risk and extramarket covariance.

Specific risk is the uncertainty in the return that arises from events that are specific to the firm. Specific risk is unrelated to events that impact on other firms and is sometimes referred to as the "unique" risk or "independent" risk of the company (see Rosenberg et al. [233, p. 88]).

Extramarket covariance is the remaining component of residual risk. It is manifested as a tendency of related assets to move together in a way that is independent of the market as a whole. The term "covariance" refers to the tendency of stock prices to move together, or "covary." The term "extramarket" means that these comovements are *not* related to the movements of the market as a whole. Extramarket covariance can be

thought of as the middle ground between systematic and specific risk. Systematic risk impacts all firms. Specific risk impacts only one firm. Extramarket covariance impacts a homogeneous group of firms, such as those belonging to a certain industry or those with large capitalizations.

For individual stocks specific risk is most important, accounting for about 50 percent of the total risk, with the remainder about equally divided between systematic risk and extramarket covariance. For a well-diversified portfolio, systematic risk is likely to be 80 or 90 percent of the total risk.

For portfolios with concentrations of stocks in certain industry groups, or classes of stocks such as interest-sensitive stocks, extramarket covariance is very important. Thus, the construction of prudent, well-reasoned portfolios requires the prediction of all three aspects of risk—systematic, specific, and extramarket. It is noteworthy in this regard that the Rosenberg prediction scheme derives estimates of both market returns and extramarket covariances from a single underlying model. (The interested reader will find a general explanation of this procedure in Rosenberg and Guy [227] and a detailed explanation in Rosenberg [233]).

EMPIRICAL TESTS OF FUNDAMENTAL BETAS

Rosenberg and Marathe [229] have compared the forecasting accuracy of the so-called fundamental betas with the predictive power of historically derived and regression-adjusted betas (vis-à-vis the Merrill Lynch procedure) over 230 months with an average of 1,200 firms studied in each month. Using historically derived and regression-adjusted values as a benchmark, Rosenberg and Marathe compared the predictive power of each of their various prediction rules. These comparisons are summarized in Table 33–3.

Based only on their market variability descriptors, there were significant increases in predictive power (when compared with the historically derived and regression-adjusted values). Specifically, the use of their market variability descriptors added 57 percent to the predictive power for beta and 22 percent to the predictive power for the residual standard deviation. What is most striking, however, is that by using only fundamental information—with no market variability descriptors whatsoever—Rosenberg and Marathe obtained 45 percent and 10 percent improvements in the predictive power of beta and the residual standard deviation, respectively.

TABLE 33–3: A comparison of the forecasting accuracy of historically derived betas and Rosenberg and Marathe's fundamentally derived betas

	Predictive power	
Values derived from	*Beta (percent)*	*Residual standard deviation (percent)*
Historically derived and regression adjusted	100%	100%
Using only market variability descriptors	157	122
Using only fundamental descriptors	145	110
Using the complete prediction rule	186	132

Source: Rosenberg and Marathe [229, p. 134].

When both market variability information and fundamental information were combined into their complete decision rule, the results were little short of remarkable. There was an 86 percent improvement in the predictive power for beta and a 32 percent increase in the predictive power for the residual standard deviation. Thus, the so-called fundamental betas provide the linch pin between theory and application.

Chapter 34

Inflation and valuation

The most provocative financial article to appear in the last decade was published in 1979 by Franco Modigliani and Richard Cohn. In this article, Modigliani, a world-famous financial theorist, alleges that ". . . because of inflation-induced errors, investors have systematically undervalued the stock market by 50 percent." [192, p. 24] Since the Modigliani-Cohn position is destined to stir much debate, the basic points of their arguments are summarized in this chapter.

MODIGLIANI AND COHN'S THESIS

Theoretically, equity investments represent claims against physical assets whose real (inflation-adjusted) returns should be unaffected by inflation. Moreover, many equity investments represent claims against levered assets (those partially funded by debt). In inflationary times, these debts have the advantage that they are repaid with devalued currencies.

In reality, however, equities have not provided the much-sought hedge against inflation. In nominal (noninflation-adjusted) terms, the market indices have not progressed since the upward inflationary spiral started in the late 1960s. In real (inflation-adjusted) terms, the major market indices have declined by almost half over the same period.

The explanation for the dismal performance of the equity investments over the last 15 years must, by definition, rest with the investor perception that real (inflation-adjusted) earnings have decreased and/or the fact that investors demand a higher earnings capitalization rate.

As discussed in Chapter 7, a common valuation procedure concentrates on the "multiple" that the market places on a company's earnings. The reciprocal of the earnings multiple is

the *earnings capitalization rate.* Thus, a company that is priced at an earnings multiple of five has an earnings capitalization rate of 20 percent (1/5). Similarly, a company that is priced at an earnings multiple of 20 has an earnings capitalization rate of 5 percent (1/20).

The earnings capitalization rate is the rate of return demanded by the marketplace for capital. As illustrated in the preceding examples, earnings multiples are inversely related to earnings capitalization rates. Thus, earnings multiples are depressed if investors demand higher rates of return for the use of their capital.

By this formulation, the market price of a stock is equal to its earnings divided by its earnings capitalization rate. It follows, therefore, that the price of a stock will fall when either earnings decrease or capitalization rates increase.

Using this formulation, most analysts place the responsibility for the market's dismal performance since the late 1960s on the inflation-adjusted earnings component. Citing such evidence as the fact that adjusted earnings of industrial corporations *declined* from $38.2 billion in 1967 to $30.2 in 1977, this conclusion seems warranted.

Modigliani and Cohn disagree. While they contend that it is proper to adjust earnings downward, they contend that analysts should factor in the *beneficial* effect that inflation has on the company's debts.

An outstanding explanation of how inflation reduces reported earnings—even though true earnings are unaffected—is provided by Stanford Rose's interpretation of Modigliani and Cohn's work.

> . . . Suppose the rate of inflation is zero, and a company with earnings before taxes and interest charges of $100 borrows $1,000 from a bank for a one-year period. Since there is no inflation, the company pays the real rate of interest—say, 3 percent. So pretax profits equal $100 minus $30 in interest, or $70.
>
> Now assume that the inflation rate suddenly jumps to 8 percent. If the company's loan is a variable-rate obligation, the bank immediately raises its interest charge to 11 percent—3 percent plus the 8 percent inflation premium. Interest charges thereupon rise from $30 to $110.
>
> In an accounting sense, the company's $70 profit has temporarily turned into a $10 loss. In a real sense, however, nothing whatever has happened to profits. At the end of the year, the company pays the bank back the $1,000. But since inflation has eroded the value of this repayment by 8 percent, its "real"

> worth is $80 less, or only $920. If that $80 were added back into company profits, these would remain at the original $70. Unfortunately, according to generally accepted accounting principles, corporations must sock earnings for interest expenses, but they cannot adjust them upward for repayments made in depreciated dollars (or for the higher nominal values of assets bought with the loan proceeds). So the profits of industrial corporations seem to be much lower than they actually are.
>
> Consider some data for 1977, which is the most recent year for which true corporate profits can be estimated. The debt owed by the average industrial corporation in that year amounted to about five times its annual profits. But the real burden of that debt obviously fell by the 1977 rate of inflation, or by about 7 percent. In order to measure corporate profits accurately, it is therefore necessary to raise reported earnings by approximately 35 percent—the rate of inflation times the amount of outstanding net debt. Since the Department of Commerce estimates that understated depreciation and phony inventory gains reduced 1977 reported profits by about a third, the required adjustments just about cancel out.
>
> The widely publicized notion that true corporate profits decline sharply during a period of high inflation turns out to be a myth. [222, p. 139]

In all, Modigliani and Cohn explored three possible explanations for the apparent contradiction between the theoretical ability of equities to hedge against inflation, and the reality that they have not. First, they examined the possibility that inflation-adjusted profits may actually have deteriorated. Second, they examined the possibility that inflation has boosted required capitalization rates (the rates of return demanded by equity investors in exchange for the use of their capital). Third, they examined the possibility that "in the presence of unaccustomed and fluctuating inflation . . . [investors] price equities in ways that fail to reflect their true economic value." [192, p. 25]

CORPORATE PROFITABILITY AND THE LEVEL OF THE MARKET

To analyze the real (inflation-adjusted) profitability of corporate capital Modigliani and Cohn studied two measures of return on capital: corporate value added and return on replacement cost. To measure corporate value added they calculated total return as "the sum of interest plus after-tax profits adjusted to eliminate the effect of paper gains on inventories

and to reflect depreciation on a replacement, rather than an historical cost basis." [192, p. 25] Except for the mid-60s bulge, Modigliani and Cohn found this series to be basically "trendless . . . [and] from 1975 on, . . . [to be] not significantly different from, and certainly not lower than, that prevailing from the beginning of the 1950s through the first half of the 1960s." [192, p. 25] Similarly, they found historical returns on replacement costs (the ratio of the total return used in the first series to the estimated replacement cost) to be "roughly flat with a bulge in the mid-60s." [192, p. 25]

On the basis of this evidence, Modigliani and Cohn conclude that, despite inflation, corporate profits have *not* declined over the last decade. In reconciling this conclusion with the popular view that inflation has eroded profits, Modigliani and Cohn emphasized two important points. First, the mid-1960s represented a period of unprecedented returns on capital and should not be used as a reference point. Second, earnings per share—a readily available and popular measure of return—underestimate true corporate profits.

Modigliani and Cohn also addressed the popular claim that inflated profits precipitate inflated taxes on the real (inflation adjusted) profits. They correctly point out, however, that this claim "fails to recognize . . . that stockholders are not taxed on that part of their return that consists of depreciation of debt. In other words, they are allowed to deduct their entire interest expense even though the portion of it corresponding to the inflation premium is really a return on capital. Because of this the share of pretax operating income paid in taxes declines with the rate of inflation." [192, p. 27]

Thus, our tax system erroneously taxes inflated profits while, at the same time, erroneously reducing the inflated profits by classifying a portion of return of capital as an interest expense. For the market as whole (although not necessarily for individual firms) these effects tend to cancel out, leading Modigliani and Cohn to conclude that the failure of equities to provide a hedge against inflation cannot be traced to taxation or a deterioration in corporate profitability.

As a second possible explanation for the failure of equity investments to provide the theoretical hedge against inflation, Modigliani and Cohn evaluated the possibility that the earnings capitalization rate demanded by the marketplace should be systematically raised as inflation increases (i.e., the price-earnings ratios should be systematically lowered).

Theoretically, an equity's nominal (noninflation-adjusted)

growth fully reflects the rate of inflation. If the price earnings ratio remains constant, say at 5, a 10 percent earnings increase will translate into a 10 percent price increase. Conversely, if earnings growth parallels the rate of inflation, the only way market values will not pace the rate of inflation is if the market applies a lower earnings multiple to the inflated earnings.

Basically, in an inflationary environment, interest rates rise by the rate of inflation (to compensate lenders for the erosion of the real purchasing power of their claims). This means that there are two equivalent ways to determine the value of a firm in the world of inflation: (1) to capitalize real (inflation-adjusted) profits at the real capitalization rate, or (2) discount the stream of nominal (not inflation-adjusted) earnings at an appropriate nominal discount rate. In Modigliani and Cohn's words "if either valuation is done correctly, the real value of the firm will be found to be unaffected by inflation." [192, p. 29]

Again, quoting from Rose

> Instead of discounting future earnings by the real rate of interest—2 or 3 percent, plus an appropriate risk premium—investment advisers have been discounting them by 7 or 8 percent, plus the risk premium. Thus, a mistake in evaluating the numerator of the stock-valuation ratio gives rise to another, and even more serious, mistake in evaluating the denominator, the capitalization rate . . . [and, as a result] . . . stock values have been scissored by rapid changes in both numerators and denominators. [222, p. 140]

The magnitude of this "scissoring" effect is enourmous. According to Modigliani and Cohn, "each percentage point of inflation typically reduces market value by a staggering 13 percent relative to what it would be if valued rationally . . . [and as a result of the failure of the investment community to recognize the errors in traditional valuation] as of year-end 1977 . . . the actual market value [of the S&P index] was only 46 percent of its correct value." [192, p. 33]

Chapter 35

Conclusion

Modern portfolio theory-based applications include:

1. Security valuation.
2. Portfolio optimization.
3. Asset allocation.
4. Performance measurement.

Basically, MPT holds that there is a forecastable relationship between risk and return. Moving from this premise, MPT first asserts that by discarding the traditional approaches to security analysis, it is possible accurately to forecast expected return, as well as the key risk relationships that are inherent in expected returns. After first using MPT techniques to derive estimates both of expected returns and risk relationships for individual investments, MPT can then be used to construct portfolios which uniquely balance an investor's willingness to assume risks with the investor's desire for larger and larger returns. The third area to which MPT has been applied is asset allocation—basically analyzing investment alternatives to determine the combination of available assets that best matches investor preferences.

The first three applications include varying elements of classification, estimation, and control of risk. The fourth, and final, application uses MPT compatible techniques for the continuous assessment of investment performance against the MPT-derived estimates.

While many people perceive "their" favorite security (or, securities) as somehow "unique," there is no evidence to support the hypothesis that in toto, organized securities markets operate in this fashion. [237, p. 198] The reality is that organized securities markets operate in a very organized way.

The gap between theory and practice which long charac-

terized the investment profession is rapidly disappearing. As a result, people are becoming less naïve. Today, there is a growing awareness that if one investment manager consistently outperforms the risk-adjusted averages, others must consistently underperform the same average. Logically, as the "losers" in what Keynes called the "game of investing" become aware of their underperformance, they will change managers. In their selection of a new manager, they will choose either a firm that can provide the fair rate of return inherent in a "passive" strategy, or one of the consistent "winners." In either case, however, the population of naïve investors that any consistent "winners" must depend upon for their above-average returns will shrink.

Beyond the new words like quants (those who apply quantitative investment techniques), super-quants, pseudo-quants, and even turncoat-quants (those who purportedly understand MPT but make a living out of lobbying against it), prudence is no longer defined as performance. *Prudence is a methodology that allows investors to classify, estimate, and control risk and return.*

Bibliography

1. Alexander, Sidney S. "Price Movements in Speculative Markets: Trends or Random Walks," *Industrial Management Review*, vol. 2, no. 2 (May 1961), pp. 7–26. Reprinted (and expanded) in Paul H. Cootner, ed., *The Random Character of Stock Market Prices*. Cambridge, Mass.: M.I.T. Press, 1964, pp. 199–218 and 338–372.
2. Altman, E., B. Jacquillat, and M. Levasseur. "La Stabilité tu Coefficient Beta," *Analyse Financière*, no. 16, 1st Trimestre (1974), pp. 43–54.
3. Andersen, Theodore A. "Trends in Profit Sensitivity," *Journal of Finance*, vol. 28, no. 4 (December 1963), pp. 637–46. Reprinted in James Lorie and Richard Brealey, ed., *Modern Developments in Investment Management: A Book of Readings*. 2d ed. Hinsdale, Ill.: Dryden Press, 1978, pp. 659–68.
4. Ambachtsheer, Keith P. "Profit Potential in an 'Almost Efficient' Market," *Journal of Portfolio Management*, vol. 1, no. 1 (Fall 1974), pp. 84–87.
5. ——. "Can Selectivity Pay in an Efficient Market?" *Journal of Portfolio Management*, vol. 2, no. 4 (Summer 1976), pp. 19–22.
6. ——. "Where Are the Customers' Alphas?" *Journal of Portfolio Management*, vol. 4, no. 1 (Fall 1977), pp. 52–56.
7. Arditti, Fred D. "Risk and the Required Return on Equity," *Journal of Finance*, vol. 22, no. 1 (March 1967), pp. 19–36.
8. Babcock, Guildord C. "The Concept of Sustainable Growth," *Financial Analysts Journal*, vol. 26, no. 3 (May–June 1970), pp. 108–44.
9. ——. "The Trend and Stability of Earnings per Share." *Proceedings of the Seminar on the Analysis of Security Prices*, University of Chicago, November 1970.
10. Bachelier, Louis. *Théorie de la Speculation*. Paris: Gauthier–Villars, 1900. Translation by A. James Boness, reprinted in Paul H. Cootner, ed., *The Random Character of Stock Market Prices*. Cambridge, Mass.: M.I.T. Press, 1964, pp. 17–78.
11. Ball, Philip, and John W. Kennelly. "The Informational Content of Quarterly Earnings. An Extension and Some Further Evidence," *Journal of Business*, vol. 45, no. 3 (July 1972), pp. 403–15.

12. Ball, Ray, and Philip Brown. "An Empirical Evaluation of Accounting Income Numbers," *Journal of Accounting Research*, vol. 6, no. 2 (Autumn 1968), pp. 159–78. Reprinted in James Lorie and Richard Brealey, ed., *Modern Developments in Investment Management: A Book of Readings*. 2d ed. Hinsdale, Ill.: Dryden Press, 1978, pp. 559–78.

13. Ball, Ray, and Ross Watts. "Some Time Properties of Accounting Incomes," *Journal of Finance*, vol. 27, no. 3 (June 1972), pp. 663–82.

14. Barker, C. Austin. "Effective Stock Splits," *Harvard Business Review*, vol. 34, no. 1 (January–February 1956), pp. 101–06.

15. ———. "Stock Splits in a Bull Market," *Harvard Business Review*, vol. 35, no. 3 (May–June 1957), pp. 72–79. Reprinted in E. Bruce Fredrikson, ed., *Frontiers of Investment Analysis*. Scranton, Pa.: International Textbook Co., 1965, pp. 540–51.

16. Bauman, W. Scott. "Performance Objectives of Investors." Occasional Paper No. 2. Financial Analysts Research Foundation, 1975.

17. ———. "Evaluation of the Portfolio Management System." Occasional Paper No. 3. Financial Analysts Research Foundation, 1975.

18. Beaver, William H. "Financial Ratios as Predictors of Failure," *Journal of Accounting Research*, Autumn supplement 1966, pp. 71–111.

19. ———. "Market Prices, Financial Ratios and the Prediction of Failure," *Journal of Accounting Research*, vol. 6, no. 2 (Autumn 1968), pp. 179–92.

20. Beaver, William, and James Manegold. "The Association between Market-Determined and Accounting-Determined Measures of Systematic Risk: Some Further Evidence," *Journal of Financial and Quantitative Analysis*, vol. 10, no. 2 (June 1975), pp. 231–84.

21. Beaver, William, Paul Kettler, and Myron Scholes. "The Association between Market Determined and Accounting Determined Risk Measures," *Accounting Review*, vol. 45, no. 11 (October 1970), pp. 654–82.

22. Bergstrom, Gary L. "A New Route to Higher Returns and Lower Risks," *Journal of Portfolio Management*, vol. 2, no. 1 (Fall 1975), pp. 30–38.

23. Black, Fischer. "Capital Market Equilibrium with Restricted Borrowing," *Journal of Business*, vol. 45, no. 3 (July 1972), pp. 444–55.

24. ———. "Yes, Virginia, There Is Hope: Tests of the Value Line Ranking System," *Financial Analysts Journal*, vol. 29, no. 5 (September–October 1973), pp. 10–14.

25. ———. "The Investment Policy Spectrum: Individuals, Endowment Funds and Pension Funds," *Financial Analysts Journal*, vol. 32, no. 1 (January–February 1976), pp. 23–31. Reprinted in James Lorie and Richard Brealey, ed., *Modern Developments in Investment Management: A Book of Readings*. 2d ed. Hinsdale, Ill.: Dryden Press, 1978, pp. 397–405.

26. Black, Fischer, Michael C. Jensen, and Myron Scholes. "The Capital Asset Pricing Model: Some Empirical Tests," in Michael C. Jensen,

ed., *Studies in the Theory of Capital Markets.* New York: Praeger Publishers, Inc., 1972.

27. Black, Fischer, and Myron Scholes. "The Effects of Dividend Yield and Dividend Policy on Common Stock Prices and Returns," *Journal of Financial Economics,* vol. 1, no. 1 (May 1974), pp. 1–22.

28. Blume, Marshall E. "The Assessment of Portfolio Performance—An Application to Portfolio Theory." Unpublished Ph.D. dissertation, University of Chicago, 1968.

29. ______. "Portfolio Theory: A Step towards Its Practical Application," *Journal of Business,* vol. 43, no. 2 (April 1970), pp. 152–73.

30. ______. "On the Assessment of Risk," *Journal of Finance,* vol. 26, no. 1 (March 1972), pp. 1–10. Reprinted in James Lorie and Richard Brealey, ed., *Modern Developments in Investment Management: A Book of Readings.* 2d ed. Hinsdale, Ill.: Dryden Press, 1978, pp. 432–41.

31. ______. "Betas and Their Regression Tendencies," *Journal of Finance,* vol. 30, no. 3 (June 1975), pp. 785–96.

32. Blume, Marshall E., and Irwin Friend. "Risk, Investment Strategy, and Long-run Rates of Return," *Review of Economics and Statistics,* vol. 61, no. 3 (August 1974), pp. 259–69.

33. Bower, Dorothy H., and Richard S. Bower. "Test of a Stock Valuation Model, *Journal of Finance,* vol. 25, no. 5 (May 1970), pp. 483–92.

34. Brealey, Richard A. *An Introduction to Risk and Return from Common Stock Prices.* Cambridge, Mass.: M.I.T. Press, 1969.

35. ______. *Security Prices in a Competitive Market.* Cambridge, Mass.: M.I.T. Press, 1971.

36. Breen, William. "Low Price-Earnings Ratios and Industry Relatives," *Financial Analysts Journal,* vol. 25, no. 4 (July–August 1969), pp. 125–27.

37. Brennan, Michael J. "Capital Market Equilibrium with Divergent Borrowing and Lending Rates," *Journal of Financial and Quantitative Analysis,* vol. 6, no. 4 (December 1971), pp. 1197–1205.

38. Brown, Philip, and Ray Ball. "An Empirical Evaluation of Accounting Income Numbers," *Journal of Accounting Research,* vol. 6, no. 3 (Autumn 1968), pp. 159–78.

39. Brown, Philip, and Victor Niederhoffer. "The Predictive Content of Quarterly Earnings," *Journal of Business,* vol. 41, no. 4 (October 1968), pp. 488–97.

40. Buffett, Warren E. "How Inflation Swindles and Equity Investor," *Fortune,* vol. 95, no. 5 (May 1977), pp. 250–67.

41. Cagan, Phillip. "Common Stock Values and Inflation—The Historical Record of Many Countries," National Bureau of Economic Research, Report No. 13, March 1974.

42. Cohen, A. W. *The Chartcraft Method of Point and Figure Trading.* Larchmont, N.Y.: Chartcraft, Inc., 1963.

43. ______. *Technical Indicator Analysis by Point and Figure Technique.* Larchmont, N.Y.: Chartcraft, Inc., 1963.

44. Cohen, Jerome B., Edward D. Zinbarg, and Arthur Zeikel. *Investment Analysis and Portfolio Management.* Homewood, Ill.: Richard D. Irwin, Inc., 1973.

45. Cohen, Kalman J., and Jerry A. Pogue. "An Empirical Evaluation of Alternative Portfolio Selection Models," *Journal of Business,* vol. 40, no. 2 (April 1967), pp. 166–93.

46. ______. "Some Comments concerning Mutual Fund versus Random Portfolio Performance," *Journal of Business,* vol. 41, no. 2 (April 1968), pp. 180–90.

47. Colker, S. S. "An Analysis of Security Recommendations by Brokerage Houses," *Quarterly Review of Economics and Business,* vol. 3, no. 2 (Summer 1963), pp. 19–28.

48. Cootner, Paul H. "Stock Prices: Random vs. Systematic Changes." *Industrial Management Review,* vol. 3, no. 2 (Spring 1962), pp. 24–45. Reprinted in Paul H. Cootner, ed., *The Random Character of Stock Market Prices.* Cambridge, Mass.: M.I.T. Press, 1964. Reprinted in E. Bruce Fredrikson, ed., *Frontiers of Investment Analysis.* Scranton, Pa.: International Textbook Co., 1965, pp. 489–510.

49. ______. "Stock Market Indexes: Fallacies and Illusions," *Commercial and Financial Chronicle,* vol. 204, no. 6616 (September 29, 1966), pp. 18–19. Reprinted in James Lorie and Richard Brealey, ed., *Modern Developments in Investment Management: A Book of Readings.* 2d ed. Hinsdale, Ill.: Dryden Press, 1978, pp. 94–100.

50. Cootner, Paul H., ed. *The Random Character of Stock Market Prices.* Cambridge, Mass.: M.I.T. Press, 1964.

51. Copeland, R. M., and R. J. Marioni. "Executives' Forecasts of Earnings per Share vs. Forecasts of Naïve Models," *Journal of Business,* vol. 45, no. 4 (October 1972), pp. 497–512.

52. Cowles, Alfred. "Can Stock Market Forecasters Forecast?" *Econometrica,* vol. 1, no. 3 (July 1933), pp. 309–24.

53. ______. "A Revision of Previous Conclusions Regarding Stock Price Behavior," *Econometrica,* vol. 28, no. 4 (October 1960), pp. 909–15. Reprinted in Paul H. Cootner, ed., *The Random Character of Stock Market Prices.* Cambridge, Mass.: M.I.T. Press, 1964, pp. 132–38.

54. Cowles, Alfred, and Herbert F. Jones. "Some À Posteriori Probabilities in Stock Market Action," *Econometrica,* vol. 5, no. 3 (July 1937), pp. 280–94.

55. Cragg, J. G., and Burton G. Malkiel. "The Consensus and Accuracy of Some Predictions of the Growth of Corporate Earnings," *Journal of Finance,* vol. 23, no. 1 (March 1968), pp. 67–84.

56. Crowell, Richard. "Earnings Expectations, Security Valuation and the Cost of Equity Capital." Unpublished Ph.D. dissertation, Massachusetts Institute of Technology, 1967.

57. Cushing, Barry. "The Effects of Accounting Policy Decision on Trends in Reported Corporate Earnings per Share." Ph.D. dissertation, Michigan State University, 1969.

58. Darling, P. G. "The Influence of Expectations and Liquidity on Dividend Policy," *Journal of Political Economy*, vol. 65, no. 3 (June 1957), pp. 209–24.

59. Darvas, Nicholas. *How I Made $2,000,000 in the Stock Market.* Larchmont, N.Y.: American Research Council, 1960.

60. Douglas, George W. "Risk in the Equity Market: An Empirical Appraisal of Market Efficiency." Unpublished Ph.D. dissertation, Yale University, 1967.

61. Durand, David. "Growth Stocks and the Petersburg Paradox," *Journal of Finance*, vol. 12, no. 3 (September 1957), pp. 348–63. Reprinted in James Lorie and Richard Brealey, ed., *Modern Developments in Investment Management: A Book of Readings.* 2d ed. Hinsdale, Ill.: Dryden Press, 1978, pp. 492–507.

62. Edwards, Robert D., and John Magee. *Technical Analysis of Stock Trends.* 4th ed. Springfield, Mass.: John Magee, 1962.

63. Elton, Edwin J., and Martin J. Gruber. "Marginal Stockbroker Tax Rates and the Clientele Effect," *Review of Economics and Statistics*, vol. 52, no. 1 (February 1970), pp. 68–74.

64. ———. "Improving Forecasting through the Design of Homogeneous Groups," *Journal of Business*, vol. 44, no. 4 (October, 1971), pp. 432–50.

65. Elton, Edwin J., Martin J. Gruber, and Manfred W. Padberg. "Optimal Portfolios from Simple Ranking Devices," *Journal of Portfolio Management*, vol. 4, no. 3 (Spring 1978), pp. 15–18.

66. Evans, John L. "Diversification and the Reduction of Dispersion: An Empirical Analysis." Unpublished Ph.D. dissertation, University of Washington, 1968.

67. Evans, John L., and Stephen H. Archer. "Diversification and the Reduction of Dispersion: An Empirical Analysis." *Journal of Finance*, vol. 23, no. 12 (December 1968), pp. 761–67.

68. Fama, Eugene F. "The Behavior of Stock Market Prices," *Journal of Business*, vol. 38, no. 1 (January 1965), pp. 34–105.

69. ———. "Risk, Return and Equilibrium: Some Clarifying Comments," *Journal of Finance*, vol. 23, no. 3 (March 1968), pp. 29–40.

70. ———. "Efficient Capital Markets: A Review of Theory and Empirical Work," *Journal of Finance*, vol. 25, no. 2 (May 1970), pp. 383–417. Reprinted in James Lorie and Richard Brealey, ed., *Modern Developments in Investment Management: A Book of Readings.* 2d ed. Hinsdale, Ill.: Dryden Press, 1978, pp. 109–53.

71. ———. "Risk, Return and Equilibrium," *Journal of Political Economy*, vol. 79, no. 1 (January–February 1971), pp. 30–55.

72. ———. "Components of Investment Performance," *Journal of Finance*, vol. 27, no. 5 (June 1972), pp. 551–67. Reprinted in James Lorie and Richard Brealey, ed., *Modern Developments in Investment Management: A Book of Readings.* 2d ed. Hinsdale, Ill.: Dryden Press, 1978, pp. 448–65.

73. ———. "A Note on the Market Model and the Two Parameter

Model," *Journal of Finance*, vol. 28, no. 5 (December 1973), pp. 1181–86.

74. ———. "The Empirical Relationship between the Dividend and Investment Decisions of Firms," *American Economic Review*, vol. 44, no. 3 (June 1974), pp. 304–18.

75. Fama, Eugene F., and H. Babiak. "Dividend Policy: An Empirical Analysis," *Journal of the American Statistical Association*, vol. 63, no. 12 (December 1968), pp. 1132–61.

76. Fama, Eugene F., and Marshall E. Blume. "Filter Rules and Stock Market Trading," *Journal of Business*, vol. 39, no. 1, pt. 2 (January 1966), pp. 226–41.

77. Fama, Eugene F., and James D. MacBeth. "Risk, Return, and Equilibrium: Empirical Tests," *Journal of Political Economy*, vol. 81, no. 3 (May–June 1973), pp. 607–36.

78. Fama, Eugene F., Lawrence Fisher, and Michael C. Jensen. "The Adjustment of Stock Prices to New Information," *International Economic Review*, vol. 10, no. 1 (February 1969), pp. 1–21. Reprinted in James Lorie and Richard Brealey, ed., *Modern Developments in Investment Management: A Book of Readings*. 2d ed. Hinsdale, Ill.: Dryden Press, 1978, pp. 177–97.

79. Fama, Eugene F., Lawrence Fisher, Michael C. Jensen, and Richard Roll. "The Adjustment of Stock Prices to New Information," *International Economic Review*, vol. 10, no. 2 (February 1969), pp. 1–21.

80. Farrar, Donald Eugene. *The Investment Decision under Uncertainty*. Englewood Cliffs, N.J.: Prentice-Hall, Inc., 1962.

81. Farrell, James L., Jr. "Analyzing Covariation of Return to Develop Homogeneous Stock Groupings," *Journal of Business*, vol. 47, no. 2 (April 1974), pp. 186–207.

82. ———. "Homogeneous Stock Groupings: Implications for Portfolio Management," *Financial Analysts Journal*, vol. 31, no. 3 (May–June 1975), pp. 50–62.

83. ———. "The Multi-Index Model and Practical Portfolio Analysis." Occasional Paper No. 4. Financial Analysts Research Foundation, 1976.

84. Farrell, James, and Keith Ambachtsheer. "Can Active Management Add Value?" Unpublished paper, 1979.

85. Ferber, Robert. "Short-run Effects on Stock Market Services on Stock Prices," *Journal of Finance*, vol. 13, no. 1 (March 1958), pp. 80–95.

86. Ferguson, Robert. "Active Portfolio Management," *Financial Analysts Journal*, vol. 31, no. 3 (May–June 1975), pp. 63–72.

87. Fisher, Irving. *The Rate of Interest*. American Economic Association, 1907.

88. Fisher, Lawrence. "Determinants of Risk Premiums on Corporate Bonds," *Journal of Political Economy*, vol. 67, no. 3 (June 1959), pp. 217–37. Reprinted in James Lorie and Richard Brealey, ed., *Modern Developments in Investment Management: A Book of Readings*. 2d ed. Hinsdale, Ill.: Dryden Press, 1978, pp. 727–47.

89. ———. "Outcomes for 'Random' Investments in Common Stocks Listed on the New York Stock Exchange," *Journal of Business*, vol. 3, no. 4 (April 1965), pp. 149–61.

90. ———. "Using Modern Portfolio Theory to Maintain an Efficiently Diversified Portfolio," *Financial Analysts Journal*, vol. 31, no. 3 (May–June 1975), pp. 73–85.

91. Fisher, Lawrence, and James H. Lorie. "Rates of Return on Investments in Common Stocks," *Journal of Business*, vol. 37, no. 1 (January 1964), pp. 1–21. Reprinted (in part) in E. Bruce Fredrikson, ed., *Frontiers of Investment Analysis*. Scranton. Pa.: International Textbook Co., 1965, pp. 159–76.

92. ———. "Rates of Return on Investments in Common Stocks: The Year-by-Year Record, 1926–1965," *Journal of Business*, vol. 41, no. 3 (July 1968), pp. 291–316. Reprinted in James Lorie, and Richard Brealey, ed., *Modern Developments in Investment Management: A Book of Readings*. 2d ed. Hinsdale, Ill.: Dryden Press, 1978, pp. 16–41.

93. ———. "Some Studies of Variability of Returns on Investment in Common Stocks," *Journal of Business*, vol. 43, no. 2 (April 1970), pp. 99–134. Reprinted in James Lorie and Richard Brealey, ed., *Modern Developments in Investment Management: A Book of Readings*. 2d ed. Hinsdale, Ill.: Dryden Press, 1978, pp. 42–77.

94. ———. *A Half Century of Returns on Stocks and Bonds*. Chicago: University of Chicago, Graduate School of Business, 1977. Reprinted (in part) in James Lorie and Richard Brealey, ed., *Modern Developments in Investment Management: A Book of Readings*. 2d ed. Hinsdale, Ill.: Dryden Press, 1978, pp. 78–93.

95. Fouse, William L. "Risk and Liquidity: The Keys to Stock Price Behavior," *Financial Analysts Journal*, vol. 32, no. 3 (May–June 1976), pp. 35–45.

96. ———. "Risk and Liquidity Revisited," *Financial Analysts Journal*, vol. 33, no. 1 (January–February 1977), pp. 40–5.

97. Fouse, William F., William W. Jahnke, and Barr Rosenberg. "Is Beta Phlogiston?" *Financial Analysts Journal*, vol. 30, no. 1 (January–February 1974), pp. 70–80.

98. Francis, Jack Clark. "Do Some Stocks Consistently Lead or Lag the Market?" Working Paper No. 5-12. Rodney L. White Center for Financial Research, University of Pennsylvania, n.d.

99. Friedman, Milton, and Anna J. Schwartz. *Monetary History of the United States, 1867–1960*. Princeton, N.J.: Princeton University Press, 1963.

100. Friend, Irwin, et al. *A Study of Mutual Funds*. Prepared for the Securities and Exchange Commission by the Securities Research Unit, Wharton School of Finance and Commerce, University of Pennsylvania. Washington, D.C.: U.S. Government Printing Office, 1962.

101. Friend, Irwin, and Marshall Blume. "Risk and the Long-Run Rate of Return on NYSE Common Stocks." Working Paper No. 18-72, The Wharton School of Finance and Commerce, Rodney L. White Center for Financial Research, 1972.

102. Friend, Irwin, and Douglas Vickers. "Portfolio Selection and Investment Performance," *Journal of Finance*, vol. 20, no. 2 (September 1965), pp. 391–415.

103. Friend, Irwin, Marshall Blume, and Jean Crockett. *Mutual Funds and Other Institutional Investors: A New Perspective*. New York: McGraw-Hill Book Company, 1970.

104. Friend, Irwin, James Longstreet, Ervin Miller, and Arleigh Hess. *Investment Banking and the New Issues Market*. New York: New York World Publishing Company, 1967.

105. Furst, R. W. "Does Listing Increase the Market Price of Common Stock?" *Journal of Business*, vol. 43, no. 4 (April 1970), pp. 174–80.

106. Gaumnitz, Jack E. "Investment Diversification under Uncertainty: An Examination of the Number of Securities in a Diversified Portfolio." Unpublished Ph.D. dissertation, Stanford University, 1967.

107. Gaviria, Nestor G. "Inflation and Capital Asset Market Prices: Theory and Tests." Unpublished Ph.D. dissertation, Graduate School of Business, Stanford University, 1973.

108. Godfrey, Michael D., Clive W. J. Granger, and Oskar Morgenstern. "The Random-Walk Hypothesis of Stock Market Behavior." *Kyklos*, vol. 17, fasc. 1 (1964), pp. 1–30.

109. Graham, Benjamin, David L. Dodd, and Sidney Cottle. *Security Analysis*. 4th ed. New York: McGraw-Hill Book Company, 1951.

110. Granger, Clive W. J. "What the Random-Walk Model Does Not Say," *Financial Analysts Journal*, vol. 26, no. 3 (May–June 1970), pp. 91–93.

111. Granger, Clive W. J., and Oskar Morgenstern. "Spectral Analysis of New York Stock Market Prices," *Kyklos*, vol. 16 (1963), pp. 1–27. Reprinted in Paul H. Cootner, ed., *The Random Character of Stock Market Prices*, Cambridge, Mass.: M.I.T. Press, 1964.

112. Grayson, C. Jackson. "Decisions under Uncertainty: Drilling Decisions by Oil and Gas Operators," Division of Research, Harvard Business School, 1960. Chapter 10, "Utility," reprinted in James Lorie and Richard Brealey, ed., *Modern Developments in Investment Management: A Book of Readings*. 2d ed. Hinsdale, Ill.: Dryden Press, 1978. pp. 275–309.

113. Green, David, Jr., and Joel Segall. "Brickbats and Straw Men: A Reply to Brown and Niederhoffer," *Journal of Business*, vol. 41, no. 4 (October 1968), pp. 498–502.

114. ______. "The Predictive Power of First Quarter Earnings Reports," *Journal of Business*, vol. 40, no. 1 (January 1967), pp. 44–55.

115. ______. "Return of Straw Man," *Journal of Business*, vol. 43, no. 1 (January 1970), pp. 63–65.

116. Hagin, Robert L. "An Empirical Evaluation of Selected Hypotheses Related to Price Changes in the Stock Market." Unpublished Ph.D. dissertation, University of California (Los Angeles), 1966.

117. Hagin, Robert L. (with Chris Mader). *The New Science of Investing*. Homewood, Ill.: Dow Jones-Irwin, Inc., 1973.

118. Hakansson, Nils H. "Capital Growth and the Mean-Variance Approach to Portfolio Selection," *Journal of Financial and Quantitative Analysis*, vol. 6, no. 1 (January 1971), pp. 517–58.

119. Hanna, M. "Short Interest: Bullish or Bearish?—Comment," *Journal of Finance*, vol. 23, no. 6 (June 1968), pp. 520–23.

120. Hausman, Warren H. "A Note on the Value Line Contest: A Test of the Predictability of Stock-Price Changes," *Journal of Business*, vol. 42, no. 3 (July 1969), pp. 317–20.

121. Hausman, Warren H., R. R. West, and J. A. Largay. "Stock Splits, Price Changes, and Trading Profits: A Synthesis," *Journal of Business*, vol. 44, no. 1 (January 1971), pp. 69–77.

122. Hodges, Stewert D., and Richard A. Brealey. "Portfolio Selection in a Dynamic and Uncertain World," *Financial Analysts Journal*, vol. 29, no. 2 (March–April 1973), pp. 50–65. Reprinted in James Lorie and Richard Brealey, ed., *Modern Developments in Investment Management: A Book of Readings*. 2d ed. Hinsdale, Ill.: Dryden Press, 1978, pp. 348–63.

123. Homa, Kenneth E., and Dwight M. Jaffee. "The Supply of Money and Common Stock Prices," *Journal of Finance*, vol. 26, no. 5 (December 1971), pp. 1045–66.

124. Horrigan, James. "The Determination of Long-Term Credit Standing with Financial Ratios," *Journal of Accounting Research*, Autumn supplement 1966, pp. 44–62.

125. Houthakker, Hendrik S. "Systematic and Random Elements in Short-Term Price Movements," *American Economic Review*, vol. 51, no. 2 (May 1961), pp. 164–72.

126. Ibbotson, Roger G. "Price Performance of Common Stock New Issues," *Journal of Financial Economics*, vol. 2, no. 3 (September 1975), pp. 235–72.

127. Ibbotson, Roger G., and Rex A. Sinquefield. *Stocks, Bonds, Bills and Inflation: The Past (1926–1976) and the Future (1977–2000)*. Charlottesville, Va.: Financial Analysts Research Foundation, 1977.

128. ______. "Stocks, Bonds, Bills and Inflation: Year-by-Year Historical Returns (1926–74)," *Journal of Business*, vol. 49, no. 1 (January 1976), pp. 11–47.

129. Jaffe, Jeffrey F. "Special Information and Insider Trading," *Journal of Business*, vol. 47, no. 3 (July 1974), p. 410–29.

130. James, F. E., Jr. "Monthly Moving Averages—An Effective Investment Tool?" *Journal of Financial and Quantitative Analysis*, vol. 3, no. 3 (September 1968), pp. 315–26.

131. Jensen, Michael C. "Random Walks: Reality or Myth—Comment," *Financial Analysts Journal*, vol. 23, no. 6 (November–December 1967), pp. 77–85.

132. ______. "The Performance of Mutual Funds in the Period 1945–64," *Journal of Finance*, vol. 23, no. 2 (May 1968), pp. 389–416. Reprinted in James Lorie and Richard Brealey, ed., *Modern Developments in Investment Management: A Book of Readings*. 2d ed. Hinsdale, Ill.: Dryden Press, 1978, pp. 231–58.

133. ——. "Risk, the Pricing of Capital Assets, and the Evaluation of Investment Portfolios," *Journal of Business*, vol. 42, no. 4 (April 1969), pp. 167–247.

134. ——. "Capital Markets: Theory and Evidence," *Bell Journal of Economics and Management Science*, vol. 3, no. 2 (Autumn 1972), pp. 357–98.

135. ——. "Tests of Capital Market Theory and Implications of the Evidence." Research Paper No. 1. Financial Analysts Research Foundation, 1975.

136. Jensen, Michael C., ed. *Studies in the Theory of Capital Markets*. New York: Praeger Publishers, 1972.

137. Jensen, Michael C., and George A. Benington. "Random Walks and Technical Theories: Some Additional Evidence," *Journal of Finance*, vol. 25, no. 2 (May 1970), pp. 469–81.

138. ——. "Random Walks and Technical Theories: Some Additional Evidence," *Journal of Finance*, vol. 25, no. 2 (May 1970), pp. 469–81. Reprinted in James Lorie and Richard Brealey, ed., *Modern Developments in Investment Management: A Book of Readings*. 2d ed. Hinsdale, Ill.: Dryden Press, 1978, pp. 164–76.

139. Jiler, William L. *How Charts Can Help You in the Stock Market*. New York: Commodity Research Publication Corp., 1962. Reprinted (in part) in Bill Alder, ed., *The Wall Street Reader*. New York: The World Publishing Co., 1970, pp. 15–23.

140. Joy, O. Maurice, Robert H. Litzenberger, and Richard W. McEnally. "The Adjustment of Stock Prices to Announcements of Unanticipated Changes in Quarterly Earnings," *Journal of Accounting Research*, vol. 15, no. 2 (Autumn 1977), pp. 207–25.

141. Kaish, S. "Odd-Lot Profit and Loss Performance," *Financial Analysts Journal*, vol. 25, no. 9 (September–October 1969), pp. 83–92.

142. Kaplan, Robert S., and Richard Roll. "Investor Evaluation of Accounting Information: Some Empirical Evidence," *Journal of Business*, vol. 45, no. 2 (April 1972), pp. 225–57.

143. Kaplan, Robert S., and Roman L. Weil. "Risk and the Value Line Contest," *Financial Analysts Journal*, vol. 29, no. 4 (July–August 1973), pp. 56–62.

144. Kendall, Maurice George. *The Advanced Theory of Statistics*. London: Griffin, 1943.

145. ——. "The Analysis of Economic Time Series—Part I: Prices," *Journal of the Royal Statistical Society*, Series A (General), vol. 116, pt. 1 (1953), pp. 11–25. Reprinted in Paul H. Cootner, ed., *The Random Character of Stock Market Prices*, Cambridge, Mass.: M.I.T. Press, 1964, pp. 85–99.

146. Kewley, T. J., and R. A. Stevenson. "The Odd-Lot Theory as Revealed by Purchase and Sales Statistics for Individual Stocks," *Financial Analysts Journal*, vol. 23, no. 5 (September–October 1967), pp. 103–06.

147. ——. "The Odd-Lot Theory for Individual Stocks: A Reply," *Fi-*

nancial Analysts Journal, vol. 25, no. 1 (January–February 1969), pp. 99–104.

148. Keynes, John Maynard. *The General Theory of Employment Interest and Money.* London: Macmillan and Company, 1936.

149. King, Benjamin F. "The Latent Statistical Structure of Security Price Changes." Unpublished Ph.D. dissertation, University of Chicago, 1964.

150. ———. "Market and Industry Factors in Stock Price Behavior," *Journal of Business*, vol. 39, no. 1, pt. 2 (January 1966), pp. 139–90.

151. Kisor, Manown, Jr., and Van A. Messner. "The Filter Approach and Earnings Forecasts," *Financial Analysts Journal*, vol. 25, no. 1 (January 1969), pp. 109–15.

152. Kisor, Manown, Jr., and Victor Niederhoffer. "Odd-Lot Short Sales Ratio: It Signals a Market Rise." *Barron's* September 1, 1969, p. 8.

153. Klein, D. J. "The Odd-Lot Stock Trading Theory." Ph.D. dissertation Michigan State University, 1964.

154. Klemkosky, Robert C., and John D. Martin. "The Effect of Market Risk on Portfolio Diversification," *Journal of Finance*, vol. 30, no. 1 (March 1975), pp. 147–54.

155. Kraus, Alan, and Hans Stoll. "Price Impacts of Block Trading on the New York Stock Exchange," *Journal of Finance*, vol. 27, no. 3 (June 1972), pp. 569–88.

156. Latané, Henry Allen, and Donald L. Tuttle. "An Analysis of Common Stock Price Ratios," *Southern Economic Journal*, vol. 33, no. 1 (January 1967), pp. 343–54.

157. Lessard, Donald F. "World, Country and Industry Relationships in Equity Returns: Implications for Risk, Reduction through International Diversification," *Financial Analysts Journal*, vol. 32, no. 1 (January–February 1976), pp. 31–38.

158. Levitz, Gerald D. "Market Risk and the Management of Institutional Equity Portfolios," *Financial Analysts Journal*, vol. 30, no. 1 (January–February 1974), pp. 53ff.

159. Levy, Haim. "Equilibrium in an Imperfect Market: A Constraint on the Number of Securities in the Portfolio," *American Economic Review*, vol. 68, no. 4 (September 1978), pp. 643–58.

160. Levy, Robert A. "An Evaluation of Selected Applications of Stock Market Timing Techniques, Trading Tactics and Trend Analysis." Unpublished Ph.D. dissertation, The American University, Washington, D.C., 1966.

161. ———. "Random Walks: Reality or Myth," *Financial Analysts Journal*, vol. 23, no. 6 (November–December 1967), pp. 129–32.

162. ———. "Random Walks: Reality or Myth—Reply," *Financial Analysts Journal*, vol. 23, no. 1 (January–February 1968), pp. 129–32.

163. ———. "On the Short-Term Stationarity of Beta Coefficients," *Financial Analysts Journal*, vol. 27, no. 6 (November–December 1971), pp. 55–62.

164. ______. "A Note on the Safety of Low P/E Stocks," *Financial Analysts Journal*, vol. 29, no. 1 (January–February 1973), p. 57.

165. Lintner, John. "Distribution of Incomes of Corporation among Dividends, Retained Earnings and Taxes," *American Economic Review*, vol. 46, no. 5 (May 1956), pp. 97–113.

166. ______. "Dividends, Earnings, Leverage, Stock Prices and the Supply of Capital to Corporations," *Review of Economics and Statistics*, vol. 44, no. 8 (August 1962), pp. 243–69.

167. ______. "The Valuation of Risk Assets and the Selection of Risky Investments in Stock Portfolios and Capital Budgets," *Review of Economics and Statistics*, vol. 47, no. 2 (February 1965), pp. 13–37.

168. ______. "Security Prices, Risk, and Maximal Gains from Diversification," *Journal of Finance*, vol. 20, no. 12 (December 1965), pp. 587–615.

169. ______. "Inflation and Security Returns," *Journal of Finance*, vol. 30, no. 2 (May 1975), pp. 259–80.

170. ______. "Inflation and Common Stock Prices in a Cyclical Context," National Bureau of Economic Research, 53rd Annual Report, September 1973. Reprinted in James Lorie and Richard Brealey, ed., *Modern Developments in Investment Management: A Book of Readings*. 2d ed. Hinsdale, Ill.: Dryden Press, 1978, pp. 669–82.

171. Lintner, John, and Robert Glauber. "Higgledy Piggledy Growth in America." Unpublished paper prepared for the Seminar on the Analysis of Security Prices, University of Chicago, May 1967. Reprinted in James Lorie and Richard Brealey, ed., *Modern Developments in Investment Management: A Book of Readings*. 2d ed., Hinsdale, Ill.: Dryden Press, 1978, pp. 594–611.

172. Logue, Dennis Emhardt. "An Empirical Appraisal of the Market for First Public Offerings of Common Stock." Unpublished Ph.D. dissertation, Cornell University, 1971.

173. Lorie, James, and Richard Brealey, ed. *Modern Developments in Investment Management: A Book of Readings*. 2d ed. Hinsdale, Ill.: Dryden Press, 1978.

174. Lorie, James H., and Mary T. Hamilton. *The Stock Market: Theories and Evidence*. Homewood, Ill.: Richard D. Irwin, Inc., 1974.

175. Lorie, James H., and Victor Niederhoffer. "Predictive and Statistical Properties of Insider Trading," *Journal of Law and Economics*, vol. 11, no. 4 (April 1968), pp. 35–53.

176. McDonald, John G. "Objectives and Performance of Mutual Funds, 1960–1969," *Journal of Financial and Quantitative Analysis*, vol. 9, no. 3 (June 1974), pp. 311–44.

177. McDonald, John G., and A. K. Fisher. "New Issue Stock Price Behavior," *Journal of Finance*, vol. 27, no. 1 (March 1972), pp. 97–102.

178. McKibben, Walt. "Econometric Forecasting of Common Stock Investment Returns: A New Methodology Using Fundamental Operating Date," *Journal of Finance*, vol. 27, no. 5 (May 1972), pp. 371–80.

179. Malkiel, Burton G. "Equity Yields, Growth, and the Structure of

Share Prices," *American Economic Review*, vol. 53, no. 12 (December 1963), pp. 1004–30.

180. Malkiel, Burton G., and John G. Cragg. "Expectations and the Structure of Share Prices," *American Economic Review*, vol. 40, no. 4 (September 1970), pp. 601–17.

181. Malkiel, Burton G., and Richard E. Quandt. *Strategies and Rational Decisions in the Securities Options Market*. Cambridge, Mass.: M.I.T. Press, 1969.

182. Mandelbrot, Benoit. "The Variation of Certain Speculative Prices," *Journal of Business*, vol. 36, no. 4 (October 1962), pp. 394–419. Reprinted in Paul H. Cootner, ed., *The Random Character of Stock Market Prices*, Cambridge, Mass.: M.I.T. Press, 1964, pp. 307–37.

183. ______. "Forecasts of Future Prices, Unbiased Markets, and 'Martingale' Models," *Journal of Business*, vol. 39, no. 1, pt. 2 (January, 1966), pp. 242–55.

184. ______. "The Variation of Some Other Speculative Prices," *Journal of Business*, vol. 40, no. 4 (October 1967), pp. 393–413.

185. Markowitz, Harry M. "Portfolio Selection." *Journal of Finance*, vol. 7, no. 1 (March 1952), pp. 77–91. Reprinted in E. Bruce Fredrikson, ed., *Frontiers of Investment Analysis*. Scranton, Pa.: International Textbook Co., 1965, pp. 353–66, and Reprinted in James Lorie and Richard Brealey, ed., *Modern Developments in Investment Management: A Book of Readings*. 2d ed., Hinsdale, Ill.: Dryden Press, 1978, pp. 310–24.

186. ______. *Portfolio Selection: Efficient Diversification of Investments*. New York: John Wiley & Sons, Inc., 1959.

187. May, A. Wilfred. "Current Popular Delusions about the Stock Split and Stock Dividend," *The Commercial and Financial Chronicle*, vol. 184, no. 5586 (November 15, 1956), p. 5.

188. ______. "On Stock Market Forecasting and Timing," *The Commercial and Financial Chronicle*, vol. 186, no. 5690 (Thursday, November 14, 1957), p. 5. Reprinted in Richard E. Ball, ed., *Readings in Investments*, Boston: Allyn and Bacon, Inc., pp. 380–92.

189. Mayor, T. H. "Short Trading Activities and the Price of Equities: Some Simulation and Regression Results," *Journal of Financial and Quantitative Analysis*, vol. 3, no. 9 (September 1968), pp. 283–98.

190. Merjos, A. "New Listings and Their Price Behavior," *Journal of Finance*, vol. 25, no. 9 (September 1970), pp. 783–94.

191. Miller, Merton H., and Franco Modigliani. "Dividend Policy, Growth, and the Valuation of Shares," *Journal of Business*, vol. 34, no. 4 (October 1961), pp. 411–33. Reprinted in James Lorie and Richard Brealey, ed., *Modern Developments in Investment Management: A Book of Readings*. 2d ed. Hinsdale, Il.: Dryden Press, 1978, pp. 508–30.

192. Modigliani, Franco, and Richard A. Cohn. Inflation, Rational Valuation and the Market," *Financial Analysts Journal*, vol. 35, no. 2 (March–April 1979), pp. 24–44.

193. Modigliani, Franco, and Merton Miller. "The Cost of Capital, Corporate Finance, and the Theory of Investment," *American Economic Review*, vol. 48, no. 3 (June 1958), pp. 261–97.

194. Modigliani, Franco, and Gerald Pogue. "An Introduction to Risk and Return," *Financial Analysts Journal*, vol. 30, no. 2 (March–April 1974), p. 68.

195. Molodovsky, Nicholas. *Investment Values in a Dynamic World: Collected Papers of Nicholas Molodovsky*. Homewood, Ill.: Richard D. Irwin, Inc., 1974.

196. Moore, Arnold B. "A Statistical Analysis of Common Stock Prices." Unpublished Ph.D. dissertation, University of Chicago, 1962.

197. Mossin, Jan. "Equilibrium in a Capital Asset Market," *Econometrica*, vol. 34, no. 10 (October 1966), pp. 768–83.

198. ———. *Theory of Financial Markets*. Englewood Cliffs, N.J.: Prentice-Hall, Inc., 1973.

199. Murphy, Joseph E., Jr. "Relative Growth of Earnings per Share—Past and Future," *Financial Analysts Journal*, vol. 22, no. 6 (November–December 1966), pp. 73–76.

200. ———. "Return, Payout and Growth," *Financial Analysts Journal*, vol. 23, no. 3 (May–June 1967), pp. 91–96.

201. Nerlove, Marc. "Factors Affecting Differences among Rates of Return on Individual Common Stocks," *Review of Economics and Statistics*, vol. 50, no. 8 (August 1968), pp. 312–31.

202. Newell, Gale E. "Revisions of Reported Quarterly Earnings," *Journal of Business*, vol. 44, no. 3 (July 1971), pp. 282–85.

203. Niederhoffer, Victor. "Clustering of Stock Prices," *Operations Research*, vol. 13, no. 2 (March–April 1965), pp. 258–65.

204. ———. "A New Look at Clustering of Stock Prices," *Journal of Business*, vol. 39, no. 2 (April 1966), pp. 309–13.

205. ———. "The Predictive Content of First Quarter Earnings Reports," *Journal of Business*, vol. 43, no. 1 (January 1970), pp. 60–62.

206. Niederhoffer, Victor, and M. F. M. Osborne. "Market Making and Reversal on the Stock Exchange," *Journal of the American Statistical Association*, vol. 61, no. 316 (December 1966), pp. 887–916.

207. Niederhoffer, Victor, and Patrick Regan. "Earnings Changes, Analysts' Forecasts, and Stock Prices," *Financial Analysts Journal*, vol. 28, no. 3 (May–June 1972), pp. 65–71. Reprinted in James Lorie and Richard Brealey, ed., *Modern Developments in Investment Management: A Book of Readings*. 2d ed. Hinsdale, Ill.: Dryden Press, 1978, pp. 548–58.

208. O'Brien, John W. "How Market Theory Can Help Investors Set Goals, Select Investment Managers and Appraise Investment Performance," *Financial Analysts Journal*, vol. 26, no. 4 (July–August 1970), pp. 91–103.

209. Osborne, M. F. M. "Brownian Motion in the Stock Market," *Operations Research*, vol. 7, no. 2 (March–April 1959), pp. 145–73. Re-

printed in Paul H. Cootner, ed., *The Random Character of Stock Market Prices*. Cambridge, Mass.: M.I.T. Press, 1964, pp. 100–28.

210. ______. "Periodic Structure of Brownian Motion of Stock Prices," *Operations Research*, vol. 10, no. 3 (May–June 1962), pp. 345–79. Reprinted in Paul H. Cootner, ed., *The Random Character of Stock Market Prices*, Cambridge, Mass.: M.I.T. Press, 1964, pp. 262–96.

211. ______. "Reply to 'Comments on Brownian Motion in the Stock Market,'" *Operations Research*, vol. 7, no. 2 (March–April 1959); pp. 807–11.

212. Pettit, Richardson R. "Dividend Announcements and Security Performance," Preliminary Working Paper, Rodney L. White Center for Financial Research, Wharton School of Finance and Commerce, University of Pennsylvania, February 19, 1971.

213. Praetz, Peter D. "The Distribution of Share Price Changes," *Journal of Business*, vol. 45, no. 1 (January 1972), pp. 49–55.

214. Pratt, Shannon P. "Relationship between Risk and Rate of Return for Common Stocks." Unpublished D.B.A. dissertation, Indiana University, 1966.

215. Pratt, Shannon P., and C. W. DeVere. "Relationship between Insider Trading and Rates of Return for NYSE Common Stocks, 1960–1966." Unpublished paper prepared for the Seminar on the Analysis of Security Prices, University of Chicago, (May 1968).

216. ______. "Relationship between Insider Trading and Rate of Return for NYSE Common Stocks, 1960–66." Unpublished paper prepared for the Seminar on the Analysis of Security Prices, University of Chicago (May 1968). Reprinted in James Lorie and Richard Brealey, ed., *Modern Developments in Investment Management: A Book of Readings*. 2d ed. Hinsdale, Ill.: Dryden Press, 1978, pp. 259–70.

217. Press, S. James. "A Compound Events Model for Security Prices," *Journal of Business*, vol. 40, no. 7 (July 1967), pp. 317–35.

218. Reilly, F. K. "Price Changes in NYSE, AMEX, and OTC Stocks Compared," *Financial Analysts Journal*, vol. 27, no. 2 (March–April 1971), p. 54.

219. Reilly, F. K., and K. Hatfield. "Experience with New Stock Issues," *Financial Analysis Journal*, vol. 25, no. 5 (September–October 1969), pp. 73–82.

220. Roberts, Harry V. "Stock Market 'Patterns' and Financial Analysis," *Journal of Finance*, vol. 14, no. 1 (March 1959), pp. 1–10. Reprinted in Paul H. Cootner, ed., *The Random Character of Stock Market Prices*. Cambridge, Mass.: M.I.T. Press, 1964, pp. 7–16. Reprinted in Richard E. Ball, ed., *Readings in Investments*, Boston: Allyn and Bacon, Inc., 1965, pp. 369–79. Also reprinted in James Lorie and Richard Brealey, ed., *Modern Developments in Investment Management: A Book of Readings*. 2d ed. Hinsdale, Ill.: Dryden Press, 1978, pp. 154–63.

221. Rogoff, Donald L. "The Forecasting Properties of Insiders' Transactions." Unpublished Ph.D. dissertation, Michigan State University, 1964.

222. Rose, Stanford. "The Stock Market Should Be Twice as High as It Is." *Fortune*, vol. 99, no. 5 (March 12, 1979), pp. 138–44.

223. Rosenberg, Barr. "The Behavior of Random Variables with Nonstationary Variance and the Distribution of Security Prices." Research Program in Finance, Working Paper No. 11. Berkeley: Institute of Business and Economic Research, University of California, 1972.

224. _____. "Extra Market Components of Covariance among Security Prices," *Journal of Financial and Quantitative Analysis*, vol. 9, no. 2 (March 1974), pp. 263–94.

225. _____. "Security Appraisal and Unsystematic Risk in Institutional Investment." *Proceedings of the Seminar on the Analysis of Security Prices*, University of Chicago, vol. 21, no. 2 (November 1976), pp. 171–237.

226. _____. "Institutional Investment with Multiple Portfolio Managers." *Proceedings of the Seminar on the Analysis of Security Prices*, University of Chicago, vol. 22, no. 2 (November 1977), pp. 55–160.

227. _____. "Performance Measurement and Performance Attribution." *Proceedings of the Seminar on the Analysis of Security Prices*, University of Chicago, vol. 23, no. 1 (May 1978), pp. 69–119.

228. Rosenberg, Barr, and James Guy. "Prediction of Systematic Risk from Investment Fundamentals," *Financial Analysts Journal*, vol. 32, no. 3 (May–June 1976), pp. 60–72, and vol. 32, no. 4 (July–August 1976), pp. 62–70.

229. Rosenberg, Barr, and Michel Houglet. "Error Rates in CRISP and COMPUSTAT Data Bases and Their Implications." *Journal of Finance*, vol. 29, no. 9 (September 1974), pp. 1303–10.

230. Rosenberg, Barr, and Vinay Marathe. "Prediction of Investment Risk: Systematic and Residual Risk." *Proceedings of the Seminar on the Analysis of Security Prices*, University of Chicago, vol. 20, no. 1 (November 1975), pp. 85–225.

231. _____. "Common Factors in Security Returns: Microeconomic Determinants and Macroeconomic Correlates." *Proceedings of the Seminar on the Analysis of Security Prices*, University of Chicago, vol. 21, no. 2 (May 1976), pp. 61–115.

232. Rosenberg, Barr, and Walt McKibben. "The Prediction of Systematic Risk in Common Stocks," *Journal of Financial and Quantitative Analysis*, vol. 8, no. 3 (March 1973), pp. 317–33.

233. Rosenberg, Barr, and Andrew Rudd. "The Yield/Beta/Residual Risk Tradeoff." Research Program in Finance Working Paper No. 66. Berkeley: Institute of Business and Economic Research, University of California, November 1977.

234. Rosenberg, Barr, Michel Houglet, Vinay Marathe, and Walt McKibben. "Components of Covariance in Security Returns." Research Program in Finance Working Paper No. 13. Berkeley: Institute of Business and Economic Research, University of California, 1973 (rev. 1975).

235. Ruff, R. T. "The Effect of Selection and Recommendation of a Stock of the Month," *Financial Analysts Journal*, vol. 19, no. 2 (March–April 1965), pp. 41–43.

236. Samuelson, Paul A. "Proof That Properly Anticipated Prices Fluctuate Randomly," *Industrial Management Review*, vol. 6, no. 2 (Spring, 1965), pp. 41–49.

237. Scholes, Myron S. "A Test of the Competitive Hypothesis: The Market for New Issues and Secondary Offerings." Unpublished Ph.D. dissertation, Graduate School of Business, University of Chicago, 1969.

238. ———. "The Market for Securities: Substitution versus Price Pressure and the Effects of Information on Share Prices," *Journal of Business*, vol. 45, no. 2 (April 1972), pp. 172–211. Reprinted in James Lorie and Richard Brealey, ed., *Modern Developments in Investment Management: A Book of Readings*. 2d ed. Hinsdale, Ill.: Dryden Press, 1978, pp. 198–230.

239. Seneca, Joseph J. "Short Interest: Bearish or Bullish?" *Journal of Finance*, vol. 22, no. 3 (March 1967), pp. 67–70.

240. ———. "Short Interest: Bullish or Bearish?—Reply," *Journal of Finance*, vol. 23, no. 3 (March 1967), pp. 524–27.

241. Sharpe, William F. "A Simplified Model for Portfolio Analysis," *Management Science*, vol. 9, no. 2 (January 1963), pp. 277–93. Reprinted in James Lorie and Richard Brealey, ed., *Modern Developments in Investment Management: A Book of Readings*. 2d ed. Hinsdale, Ill.: Dryden Press, 1978, pp. 325–41.

242. ———. "Capital Asset Prices: A Theory of Market Equilibrium under Conditions of Risk," *Journal of Finance*, vol. 19, no. 3 (September 1964), pp. 425–42. Reprinted in James Lorie and Richard Brealey, ed., *Modern Developments in Investment Management: A Book of Readings*. 2d ed. Hinsdale, Ill.: Dryden Press, 1978, pp. 366–83.

243. ———. "Risk Aversion in the Stock Market," *Journal of Finance*, vol. 20, no. 9 (September 1965), pp. 416–22.

244. ———. "Mutual Fund Performance," *Journal of Business*, vol. 39, no. 1, pt. 2 (January 1966), pp. 119–38.

245. ———. "Linear Programming Algorithms for Mutual Fund Portfolio Selection," *Management Science*, vol. 13, no 7 (March 1967), pp. 449–510.

246. ———. *Portfolio Theory and Capital Markets*. New York: McGraw-Hill Book Company, 1970.

247. ———. "Risk, Market Sensitivity and Diversification," *Financial Analysts Journal*, vol. 28, no. 1 (January–February, 1972), pp. 74–79. Reprinted in James Lorie and Richard Brealey, ed., *Modern Developments in Investment Management: A Book of Readings*. 2d ed. Hinsdale, Ill.: Dryden Press, 1978, pp. 342–47.

248. ———. "Bonds versus Stocks: Some Lessons from Capital Market Theory," *Financial Analysts Journal*, vol. 29, no. 6 (November–December 1973), pp. 74–80.

249. ———. "Imputing Expected Security Returns from Portfolio Composition," *Journal of Financial and Quantitative Analysis*, vol. 9, no. 3 (June 1974), pp. 463–72.

250. ———. "Likely Gains from Market Timing," *Financial Analysts Journal*, vol. 31, no. 2 (March–April 1975), pp. 60–69.

251. ———. "Adjusting for Risk in Portfolio Performance Measurement," *Journal of Portfolio Management*, vol. 1, no. 2, (Winter 1975), pp. 29–34. Reprinted in James Lorie and Richard Brealey, ed., *Modern Developments in Investment Management: A Book of Readings*. 2d ed. Hinsdale, Ill.: Dryden Press, 1978, pp. 442–47.

252. ———. *Investments*. Englewood Cliffs, N.J.: Prentice-Hall, Inc., 1978.

253. Sharpe, William F., and Guy M. Cooper. "Risk-Return Classes of New York Stock Exchange Common Stocks," *Financial Analysts Journal*, vol. 28, no. 2 (March–April 1972), pp. 46–56. Reprinted in James Lorie and Richard Brealey, ed., *Modern Developments in Investment Management: A Book of Readings*. 2d ed. Hinsdale, Ill.: Dryden Press, 1978, pp. 384–94.

254. Sharpe, William F., and Howard B. Sosin. "Risk, Return and Yield: New York Stock Exchange Common Stocks, 1928–1969," *Financial Analysts Journal*, vol. 30, no. 2 (March–April 1976), pp. 33–42.

255. Shelton, John P. "The Value Line Contest: A Test of the Predictability of Stock Price Changes," *Journal of Business*, vol. 40, no. 3 (July 1967), pp. 251–69.

256. Shenker, Israel. "Professors Top Wall Street's Stock Advice," *The New York Times*, Saturday, March 11, 1972, p. 37.

257. Shiskin, Julius. "Systematic Aspects of Stock Price Fluctuation." Unpublished paper prepared for the Seminar on the Analysis of Security Prices, University of Chicago (May 1967). Reprinted in James Lorie and Richard Brealey, ed., *Modern Developments in Investment Management: A Book of Readings*. 2d ed. Hinsdale, Ill.: Dryden Press, 1978, pp. 640–58.

258. Slutsky, Eugene. "The Summation of Random Causes as the Source of Cyclic Processes," *Econometrica*, vol. 5, no. 2 (April 1937), pp. 105–46.

259. Smith, Adam. *An Inquiry into the Nature and Causes of the Wealth of Nations*. 2d ed. vol. 1, bk 2. London: Methuen and Company, Ltd., 1904.

260. Smith, Randall D. "Short Interest and Stock Market Prices," *Financial Analysts Journal*, vol. 24, no. 6 (November–December 1968), pp. 151–54.

261. Solnik, Bruno H. "The International Pricing of Risk: An Empirical Investigation of the World Capital Market Structure," *Journal of Finance*, vol. 29, no. 2 (May 1974), pp. 364–78.

262. ———. "Why Not Diversify Internationally Rather Than Domestically?" *Financial Analysts Journal*, vol. 30, no. 4 (July–August 1974), pp. 48–54.

263. Stigler, George J. "Public Regulation of the Securities Markets," *Journal of Business*, vol. 37, no. 2 (April 1964), pp. 117–42.

264. Stoffels, J. D. "Stock Recommendations by Investment Advisory Services: Immediate Effects on Market Pricing," *Financial Analysts Journal*, vol. 22, no. 3 (March 1966), pp. 77–86.

265. Taussig, F. W. "Is Market Price Determinate," *Quarterly Journal of Economics*, vol. 35, no. 5 (May 1921), pp. 394–411.

266. Telser, L. G. "A Critique of Some Recent Empirical Research on the Explanation of the Term Structure of Interest Rates," *Journal of Political Economy*, vol. 75, no. 4 (August 1967), pp. 546–61. Reprinted in James Lorie and Richard Brealey, ed., *Modern Developments in Investment Management: A Book of Readings*. 2d ed. Hinsdale, Ill.: Dryden Press, 1978, pp. 711–726.

267. Tobias, Andrew. *The Only Investment Guide You'll Ever Need*. New York: Harcourt Brace Jovanovich, 1978.

268. Tobin, James. "Liquidity Preference as Behavior Towards Risk," *Review of Economic Studies*, vol. 25, no. 2 (February 1958), pp. 65–85.

269. ———. "The Theory of Portfolio Selection," in F. H. Hahn and F. P. R. Brechling, eds., *The Theory of Interest Rates*. London: Macmillan Company, 1965, pp. 3–51.

270. Treynor, Jack L. "Toward a Theory of Market Value of Risky Assets." Unpublished manuscript, 1961.

271. ———. "How to Rate Management of Investment Funds," *Harvard Business Review*, vol. 43, no. 1 (January–February 1965), pp. 63–76. Reprinted in David A. West, ed., *Readings in Investment Analysis*, Scranton, Pa.: International Textbook Co., pp. 137–58.

272. ———. "The Trouble with Earnings," *Financial Analysts Journal*, vol. 28, no. 5 (September–October 1972), pp. 41–43. Reprinted in James Lorie and Richard Brealey, ed., *Modern Developments in Investment Management: A Book of Readings*. 2d ed. Hinsdale, Ill.: Dryden Press, 1978, pp. 612–16.

273. ———. "The Coming Revolution in Investment Management," in James L. Becksler, *Methodology in Finance–Investments*. Lexington, Mass.: Lexington Book's, P. C. Heath and Company, 1972. Reprinted in James Lorie and Richard Brealey, ed., *Modern Developments in Investment Management: A Book of Readings*. 2d ed. Hinsdale, Ill.: Dryden Press, 1978, pp. 424–41.

274. Treynor, Jack L., and Fischer Black. "How to Use Security Analysis to Improve Portfolio Selection," *Journal of Business*, vol. 46, no. 1 (January 1974), pp. 66–86.

275. Valentine, Jerome L. "Investment Analysis and Capital Market Theory." Occasional Paper No. 1. Financial Analysts Research Foundation, 1975.

276. Van Horne, James C. "New Listings and Their Price Behavior." *Journal of Finance*, vol. 25, no. 9 (September 1970), pp. 783–94.

277. Van Horne, James C., and George G. C. Parker. "Technical Trading

Rules: A Comment," *Financial Analysts Journal*, vol. 24, no. 4 (July–August 1968), pp. 128–32.

278. Vasicek, Oldrick A. "A Note on Using Cross-Sectioned Information in Bayesian Estimation of Security Betas," *Journal of Finance*, vol. 28, no. 5 (December 1973), pp. 1233–39.

279. von Neumann, John, and Oskar Morgenstern. *The Theory of Games and Economic Behavior*. New York: John Wiley & Sons, Inc., 1940.

280. Wagner, W. H., and S. C. Lau. "The Effect of Diversification on Risk," *Financial Analysts Journal*, vol. 27, no. 6 (November–December 1971), pp. 48–57.

281. Wallich, Henry C. "What Does the Random-Walk Hypothesis Mean to Security Analysis?" *Financial Analysts Journal*, vol. 24, no. 2 (March–April 1968), pp. 159–62.

282. Walter, James. "Dividend Policies and Common Stock Prices," *Journal of Finance*, vol. 11, no. 1 (March 1956), pp. 29–41.

283. Watts, Ross. "The Information Content of Dividends," *Journal of Business*, vol. 46, no. 2 (April 1973), pp. 191–211.

284. West, Richard R. "Mutual Fund Performance and the Theory of Capital Asset Pricing: Some Comments," *Journal of Business*, vol. 41, no. 4 (April 1968), pp. 230–34.

285. Whitbeck, Volkert S., and Manown Kisor, Jr. "A New Tool in Investment Decision Making," *Financial Analysts Journal*, vol. 19, no. 3 (May–June 1963), pp. 55–62. Reprinted in E. Bruce Fredrikson, ed., *Frontiers of Investment Analysis*, Scranton, Pa.: International Textbook Co., 1965, pp. 335–50. Reprinted in James Lorie and Richard Brealey, ed., *Modern Developments in Investment Management: A Book of Readings*. 2d ed. Hinsdale, Ill.: Dryden Press, 1978, pp. 531–47.

286. Williams, John Burr. *The Theory of Investment Value*. Cambridge, Mass.: Harvard University Press, 1938. Reprinted (in part) in James Lorie and Richard Brealey, ed., *Modern Developments in Investment Management: A Book of Readings*. 2d ed., Hinsdale, Ill.: Dryden Press, 1978, pp. 471–91.

287. Williamson, J. Peter. *Investments: New Analytic Techniques*. New York: Praeger Publishers, 1970.

288. Working, Holbrook. "A Random-Difference Series for Use in the Analysis of Time Series," *Journal of the American Statistical Association*, vol. 29, no. 185 (March 1934), pp. 11–24.

289. ______. "New Ideas and Methods for Price Research," *Journal of Farm Economics*, vol. 38, no. 5 (December 1956), pp. 1427–36.

290. ______. "Note on the Correlation of First Differences of Averages in a Random Chain," *Econometrica*, vol. 28, no. 4 (October 1960), pp. 916–18. Reprinted in Paul H. Cootner, ed., *The Random Character of Stock Market Prices*, Cambridge, Mass.: M.I.T. Press, 1964, pp. 129–31.

291. Wu, Hsiu-Kwang. "Corporate Insider Trading, Profitability and Stock Price Movement." Unpublished Ph.D. dissertation, University of Pennsylvania, 1963.

Periodical references

292. *Financial Analysts Journal*, vol. 32, no. 5 (September–October 1976).

293. *Fortune*, vol. 74, no. 1 (July 1, 1966).

Glossary

Accruals. Expenses charged against current operations but not requiring cash payment until some future date. Thus bond interest may be accrued on the corporation's books each month, although it usually is paid only at six-month intervals.

Accrued interest. Interest accrued on a bond since the last interest payment was made. The buyer of the bond pays the market price plus accrued interest.*

Acid test ratio. A measure of financial liquidity (also known as the quick assets ratio): quick assets (current assets less inventories) divided by current liabilities.

Across-the-market samples. Stock market data can be collected in two ways: "sequentially" or "across-the-market." A sequential sample is data on a particular stock collected over time. An across-the-market sample records data on a group of stocks during a single time period. Thus, an across-the-market sample can be drawn from *one* financial page of a newspaper.

Active management. A style of investment management which seeks to attain above-average risk-adjusted performance.

Alpha. The nonmarket-related component of a security's return in the equation relating the risk premium on an asset to the risk premium on the market. Its expected value is zero, but its actual value may differ from zero. It is this possibility that explains investors' efforts to identify under-valued or over-valued securities, i.e., those with nonzero alphas.

AMEX. An abbreviation for the American Stock Exchange.

Amortization. Accounting for expenses or charges as applicable rather than as paid. Includes such practices as depreciation, depletion, write-off of intangibles, prepaid expenses, and deferred charges.*

Entries marked with an asterisk (*) are included with the permission of the New York Stock Exchange from the *Glossary: The Language of Investing*, New York: New York Stock Exchange, Inc., 1978.

Annual report. The formal financial statement issued yearly by a corporation. The annual report shows assets, liabilities, earnings—how the company stood at the close of the business year, how it fared profit-wise during the year, and other information of interest to sharehowners.*

Arbitrage. A technique employed to take advantage of differences in price. If, for example, ABC stock can be bought in New York for $10 a share and sold in London at $10.50, an arbitrageur may simultaneously purchase ABC stock in New York and sell the same amount in London, making a profit of $0.50 a share, less expenses. Arbitrage may also involve the purchase of rights to subscribe to a security, or the purchase of a convertible security—and the sale at or about the same time of the security obtainable through exercise of the rights or of the security obtainable through conversion.*

Asset allocation models. The MPT application area that addresses the problem of the amount of assets to be allocated among various investment alternatives.

Asset turnover (sometimes called operating leverage). The ratio of sales per dollar of assets employed during the year. It is calculated by dividing net sales by the average assets. As such, it provides a comparative link between a key balance sheet item (assets) and a key item on the income statement (sales).

Assets. Everything a corporation owns or due to it: cash, investments, money due it, materials and inventories, which are called current assets; buildings and machinery, which are known as fixed assets; and patents and goodwill, called intangible assets.*

Auction market. The system of trading securities through brokers or agents on an exchange such as the New York Stock Exchange. Buyers compete with other buyers while sellers compete with other sellers for the most advantageous price.*

Averages (market). Market averages measure changes in the aggregate value of a group of securities which serve as a "proxy" for the price changes of the market. (See Dow Jones Industrial Average, NYSE Common Stock Index, and S&P 500.)

Balance sheet. A condensed financial statement showing the nature and amount of a company's assets, liabilities, and capital on a given date. In dollar amounts the balance sheet shows what the company owned, what it owed, and the ownership interest in the company of its stockholders.

Basis point. One hundred basis points equal 1 percent. Thus, a basis point is 1/100 of 1 percent. Accordingly, 50 basis points is the same as 1/2 of 1 percent, 10 basis points is the same as 1/10 of 1 percent, 200 basis points is the same as 2 percent, etc.

Bea.. Someone who believes the market will decline.

Bear market. A declining market.

Bearer bond. A bond which does not have the owner's name registered on the books of the insurer and which is payable to the holder.

Beta coefficient. The beta coefficient measures sensitivity of rates of return on a portfolio, or on a particular security, to general market movements. If the beta is 1.0, a 1 percent increase in the return on the market will result, on average, in a 1 percent increase in the return on the particular portfolio or asset. If beta is less than 1.0, the portfolio or asset is considered to be less risky than the market. Beta is the regression coefficient of the rate of return on the market in the market model.

Bid and asked. Often referred to as a quotation, or quote, the "bid" is the highest price anyone is willing to pay for a security at a given time, the "asked" is the lowest price anyone will take at the same time.*

Block. A large holding or transaction of stock—popularly considered to be 10,000 shares or more.*

Blue chip. A company known for the quality and wide acceptance of its products or services, and for its ability to make money and pay dividends.*

Blue sky laws. A popular name for laws enacted to protect the public against securities frauds. The term is believed to have originated when a judge ruled that a particular stock had about the same value as a patch of blue sky.*

Board room. A room in a broker's office where prices of leading stocks used to be posted on a board throughout the market day. Today such price displays are normally electronically controlled, although most board rooms have replaced the board with the ticker and/or individual quotation machines.*

Bond. Basically an IOU or promissory note of a corporation usually issued in multiples of $1,000. A bond is evidence of a debt on which the issuing company usually promises to pay the bondholders a specified amount of interest for a specified length of time, and to repay the loan on the expiration date. In every case a bond represents debt—its holder is a creditor of the corporation and not a part owner as is a shareholder.*

Bond interest coverage. A measure of bond safety: total income divided by annual interest on bonds (or earnings before interest and taxes divided by annual interest on bonds).

Bond ratio. A measure of long-term financial risk and leverage: long-term debt divided by total capitalization.

Book value. An accounting term determined from adding all of a company's assets then deducting all debts and other liabilities, plus the liquidation price of any preferred issues. The sum arrived at is

divided by the number of common shares outstanding and the result is book value per common share. Book value of the assets of a company or a security may have little or no significant relationship to market value.*

Broker. An agent who handles orders to buy and sell securities. commodities, or other property for a commission.*

Brokers' loans. Money borrowed by brokers from banks or other brokers for a variety of uses. The money may be used by specialists and to help finance inventories of stock they deal in; by brokerage firms to finance the underwriting of new issues of corporate and municipal securities; to help finance a firm's own investments; and to help finance the purchase of securities for customers who prefer to use the broker's credit when they buy securities.*

Bull. One who believes the market will rise.*

Bull market. An advancing market.*

Call. See Option.

Callable. A bond issue, all or part of which may be redeemed by the issuing corporation under definite conditions before maturity. The term also applies to preferred shares which may be redeemed by the issuing corporation.*

The capital asset pricing model. (CAPM). Describes the way prices of individual assets are determined in markets where information is freely available and reflected instantaneously in asset prices—that is, efficient markets. According to this model prices are determined in such a way that risk premiums are proportional to systematic risk, which is measured by the beta coefficient. As such, the CAPM provides an explicit expression of the expected returns for all assets. Basically, the CAPM holds that if investors are risk averse, high-risk stocks must have higher expected returns than low-risk stocks.

Capital gain or capital loss. Profit or loss from the sale of a capital asset. A capital gain, under current federal income tax laws, may be either short-term (12 months or less) or long-term (more than 12 months). A short-term capital gain is taxed at the reporting individual's full income tax rate. A long-term capital gain is subject to a lower tax.*

Capital market line. A graphic portrayal of the average rate of return provided by the marketplace for various levels of risk. The capital market line in the Sharpe model is the line from the risk-free rate of return that is tangent to the efficient frontier of risky assets. It describes the relationship between expected rates of return on efficient portfolios and risk. All efficient portfolios lie on this line if lending and borrowing are permissible at the (same) risk-free rate.

Capital stock. All shares representing ownership of a business, including preferred and common.

Capital structure. The division of the capitalization between bonds, preferred stocks, and common stock. Where common stock represents all, or nearly all the capitalization, the structure may be called "conservative." Where common stock represents a small percentage of the total, the structure is called "leveraged".

Capitalization. Total amount of the various securities issued by a corporation. Capitalization may include bonds, debentures, preferred and common stock, and surplus. Bonds and debentures are usually carried on the books of the issuing company in terms of their par or face value. Preferred and common shares may be carried in terms of par or stated value. Stated value may be an arbitrary figure decided upon by the directors or may represent the amount received by the company from the sale of the securities at the time of issuance.*

Cash flow. Reported net income of a corporation plus amounts charged off for depreciation, depletion, amortization, and extraordinary charges to reserves, which are bookkeeping deductions and not paid out in actual dollars and cents.*

Characteristic lines. The market model describes the relationship between the return on a security and the overall market (represented by a single market index). This relationship can be summarized, for either a security or a portfolio, with a characteristic line. The slope of the line indicates the security's (or the portfolio's) sensitivity to the market's return. The intercept indicates the nonmarket (residual) component of return. In specific technical terms the equation for a security characteristic line is:

$$\tilde{R}_i - \rho = \alpha_i + \beta_{im} (\tilde{R}_m - \rho) + \tilde{r}_i$$

where

$\sim$ = Variable not known in advance.
R_i = Holding period return on security i.
ρ = Riskless rate of return.
α_i = Expected nonmarket excess return on security i.
r_i = Actual deviation from the expected value.
β_{im} = Sensitivity of security i's excess return to the market's excess return.
R_m = Holding period return on the market.
$\bar{R}_i - \rho$ = Total expected excess return on security i.
$\tilde{R}_m - \rho$ = Excess return on the market portfolio.

Classical security analysis. Security analysis based on the valuation techniques popularized by the late Benjamin Graham. The major shortcoming of this approach is that it does not quantify risk.

Closed-end investment company. (See investment company.)

Cluster analysis. A statistical procedure that is used to discern groups (or "clusters") of stocks within which price movements are

highly correlated but between which price movements show little correlation.

Coefficient of determination. See correlation coefficient and r-squared.

Coefficient of variation. The coefficient of variation is the standard deviation divided by the mean, or

$$\sqrt{\frac{\Sigma(x_i - \bar{x})^2}{N}} \Big/ \bar{x}.$$

It is a measure of the *relative* spread of a distribution about its mean. Coefficients of variation can be compared, since they are relative measures. For example, if the standard deviation of a distribution of rates of return were 2 percent, and the mean were 5 percent, the coefficient of variation would be 0.02/0.05 or 0.4 percent.

Collateral. Securities or other property pledged by a borrower to secure repayment of a loan.*

Commission. The broker's fee for purchasing or selling securities or property as an agent.*

Common stock. Securities which represent an ownership interest in a corporation. If the company has also issued preferred stock, both common and preferred have ownership rights. The preferred normally is limited to a fixed dividend but has prior claim on dividends and, in the event of liquidation, assets. Claims of both common and preferred stockholders are junior to claims of bondholders or other creditors of the company. Common stockholders assume the greater risk, but generally exercise the greater control and may gain the greater reward in the form of dividends and capital appreciation. The terms common stock and capital stock are often used interchangeably when the company has no preferred stock.*

Compounding. The arithmetic process of finding the final value of an investment or series of investments when compound interest is applied. That is, interest is earned on the interest as well as on the initial principal.

Conglomerate. A corporation that has diversified its operations, usually by acquiring enterprises in widely varied industries.*

Consolidated balance sheet. A balance sheet showing the financial condition of a corporation and its subsidiaries.*

Consumer price index (CPI). Measures the average change in the prices of a fixed market basket of goods and services over time. At the end of 1978 the expenditure categories that comprised the CPI were: food and beverages 19.2 percent, housing 44.3 percent, apparel and upkeep 5.5 percent, transportation 17.8 percent, medical care 5.0 percent, entertainment 4.0 percent, and other goods and services 4.2 percent.

Continuous compounding. The annual rate of return compounded continuously is the natural logarithm ($\log_e$) of the ratio of the value of the investment at the end of the year to the value at the beginning. For example, if the wealth ratio were 1.1, its natural logarithm would be 0.09531. The annual rate of return compounded continuously would be 9.531 percent. This is easily converted to an annual rate of return compounded annually using the formula $e^x - 1$, where x is the annual rate compounded continuously. If the period is other than one year, the annual rate compounded continuously can be found by dividing the logarithm of the wealth ratio by the number of years in the period.

Convertible. A bond, debenture, or preferred share which may be exchanged by the owner for common stock or another security, usually of the same company, in accordance with the terms of the issue.*

Correlation coefficient. A measure of the relationship between two variables where the "relationship" is the degree to which the two variables move together. If the relationship can be thought to hold in the future, the correlation coefficient can be interpreted as a measure of the degree to which knowing the value of one variable can be used to predict the value of the other. The correlation coefficient is the square of 1 minus the unexplained variance of one variable (i.e., given its relationships to the other) divided by its total variance. Symbolically, for the variables, x_i and x_j

$$\rho_{ij} = \sqrt{1 - \frac{S_{i \cdot j}^2}{S_i^2}}.$$

The square of the correlation coefficient is the coefficient of determination. It measures the percentage of the total variance of *i* explained by its relationship to *j*.

Coupon bond. Bond with interest coupons attached. The coupons are clipped as they come due and are presented by the holder for payment of interest.*

Covariance. A measure of the degree to which two variables move together. A positive value means that on average, they move in the same direction. The covariance is related to, but not the same as, the correlation coefficient. It is difficult to attach any significance to the absolute magnitude of the covariance. Symbolically, the covariance between two variables, x_i and x_j, is

$$\frac{\Sigma(x_i - \bar{x}_i)(x_j - \bar{x}_j)}{N}.$$

The covariance is also equal to $p_{ij}\sigma_i\sigma_j$, so its magnitude depends not only on the correlation, but also the standard deviations of the two variables. Stated alternatively, the correlation coefficient is the covariance standardized by dividing it by the product of σ_i and σ_j.

Covering. Buying a security previously sold short.*

Cumulative preferred stock. Stock having a provision that if one or more dividends are omitted, the omitted dividends must be paid before dividends may be paid on the company's common stock.*

Curb exchange. Former name of the American Stock Exchange. The term comes from the market's origin on a street in downtown New York.*

Current assets. Those assets of a company which are reasonably expected to be realized in cash, or sold, or consumed during the normal operating cycle of the business. These include cash, U.S. Government bonds, receivables and money due usually within one year, and inventories.*

Current liabilities. Money owed and payable by a company, usually within one year.*

Current ratio (also known as the working capital ratio). Measure of financial liquidity: current assets divided by current liabilities.

Current yield. Annual bond interest divided by market price per bond.

Day order. An order to buy or sell securities which, if not executed, expires at the end of the trading day on which it was entered.*

Dealer. An individual or firm in the securities business acting as a principal rather than as an agent. Typically, dealers buy for their own account and sell to a customer from this inventory. The dealer's profit or loss is the difference between the price paid and the price they received for the same security. The dealers' confirmation must disclose to the customer that they acted as principal. The same individual or firm may function, at different times, either as broker or dealer.*

Debenture. A promissory note backed by the general credit of the issuing company.*

Depletion accounting. Natural resources, such as metals, oil, gas and timber, which conceivably can be reduced to zero over the years, present a special accounting problem. Depletion is an accounting practice consisting of charges against earnings based upon the amount of the asset taken out of the total reserves in the period for which accounting is made. A bookkeeping entry, it does not represent any cash outlay nor are any funds earmarked for the purpose.*

Depreciation. Normally, charges against earnings to write off the cost, less salvage value, of an asset over its estimated useful life. It is a bookkeeping entry and does not represent any cash outlay nor are any funds earmarked for the purpose.*

Diagonal model. See Single-index model.

Differencing interval. An important factor in tests of the weak form of the efficient market hypothesis. This form of the hypothesis holds

that the direction of future price changes cannot be predicted from the pattern of "historical" price changes. The differencing interval defines "historical" (such as "day-to-day", or "after a volume surge") in the empirical tests of this form of the hypothesis.

Dilution. An increase in the number of common shares without a corresponding increase in the company's assets. Most convertible issues are protected against this contingency by an "antidilution clause," which reduces the conversion price in the event of dilution.

Diminishing marginal utility of wealth. Marginal utility is the amount of additional satisfaction associated with an additional amount of something such as money or wealth. If successive increments in satisfaction decline as the level of wealth increases, there is diminishing marginal utility. This implies risk aversion, because, at a given level of wealth, the gain in utility associated with some increment in wealth is less than the loss in utility associated with a decrement of the same amount of wealth.

Director. Person elected by shareholders to establish company policies. The directors appoint the president, vice presidents, and all other operating officers. Directors decide, among other matters, if and when dividends shall be paid.*

Discount. The amount by which a preferred stock or bond may sell below its par value. Also used as a verb to mean "takes into account" as the price of the stock has discounted the expected dividend cut.*

Disequilibrium. See Equilibrium.

Dispersion. The spread of a distribution about its average, or mean value. The greater the spread, the greater the variability. It can be measured either absolutely or relatively. Common absolute measures are the standard deviation and the variance. The most common measure of relative dispersion is the coefficient of variation (the standard deviation divided by the mean).

Diversification. The spreading of investments over more than one company or industry to reduce the uncertainty of future returns caused by unsystematic risk.

Dividend. Broadly defined, any distribution of cash or property to corporate shareholders.

Dividend growth models. An analytical framework for determining the value of a share of stock from estimated growth rates in the components of value—earnings and dividend payout ratios.

Dividend payout ratio. The earnings reinvestment rate is the percentage of return that is retained by a company for reinvestment. Typically, the amount that is not reinvested (or used to purchase outstanding shares of the company's common stock) is paid out in dividends. This amount (dividends per share divided by earnings per share) is referred to as the dividend payout ratio.

Dividend yield. Annual dividends per share divided by market price per share.

Double taxation. Short for "double taxation of dividends." The federal government taxes corporate profits once as corporate income; any part of the remaining profits distributed as dividends to stockholders may be taxed again as income to the recipient stockholders.*

Dow Jones Industrial Average (DJIA). A popular price-weighted market index of 30 large industrial companies. Price-weighted means that an increase of 10 percent in the price of a $10 stock has twice the effect of a 10 percent increase of a $5 stock.

Dow theory. A theory of market analysis based upon the performance of the Dow-Jones industrial and transportation stock price averages. The theory says that the market is in a basic upward trend if one of these averages advances above a previous important high, accompanied or followed by a similar advance in the other. When the averages both dip below previous important lows, this is regarded as confirmation of a basic downward trend. The theory does not attempt to predict how long either trend will continue.*

Down tick. See Up tick.

Drunkard's walk. See Random-walk model.

Earnings capitalization rate. The return (earnings) demanded by the marketplace for equity capital. It is easily calculated by inverting the company's price-earnings ratio. For example, a company with an earnings multiple of 5 has an earnings capitalization rate of $^1/_5$, or 20 percent.

Earnings per share. Net income less preferred dividends divided by shares of common outstanding.

Earnings report. A statement—also called an income statement—issued by a company showing its earnings or losses over a given period. The earnings report lists the income earned, expenses and the net result.*

Efficient. The term used to describe both the speed and accuracy of the process whereby the market, through its participants, translates new information on the economy an industry, or an enterprise, into security prices. An "efficient" market is one in which new information is quickly and accurately reflected in the price of the stock. Conversely, an "inefficient" market is one in which information is not quickly and accurately translated into security prices.

Efficient frontier. The efficient frontier is the locus of all efficient portfolios. If neither lending nor borrowing is allowed, it is that part of the boundary of the feasible set that includes only efficient portfolios of risky assets. If lending and borrowing are permissible, the efficient frontier is the line drawn from the risk-free rate to the point

of tangency on the efficient frontier of risky assets. This line is called the capital market line.

Efficient market. See Efficient.

Efficient market hypothesis. The assertion that in a market with numerous investors who prefer high returns over low returns, and low risk over high risk, "information" is of no value. In such a market, an investor can attain no more, nor less, than a fair return for the risks undertaken. The three forms of the efficient market hypothesis are: (1) weak form: a market in which historical price data cannot be used to predict future price changes (see Technical analysis); (2) semistrong form: a market in which all publicly available information is efficiently (i.e., quickly and accurately) impounded on the price of a stock and, hence, a market in which no amount or item of publicly available information can be used to predict future price changes (see Fundamental analysis); and (3) strong form: a market in which even those with privileged (non-public) information cannot obtain superior investment results.

Efficient portfolio. An efficient portfolio is one that is fully diversified. For any given rate of return, no other portfolio has less risk, and for a given level of risk, no other portfolio provides superior returns. All efficient portfolios are perfectly correlated with a general market index, except portfolios with beta coefficients above 1.0 and which do not achieve that relatively high risk by levering an efficient portfolio. Such portfolios lie on the curved frontier of portfolios consisting exclusively of risky assets.

Empirical tests. Tests based on studies of actual data.

Equilibrium. A market condition in which there is no pressure for change. In disequilibrium, investors are dissatisfied with either the securities they hold or the prices of these securities and, as a result, there is pressure for change. At any moment, however, the market is in equilibrium, reflecting the combined influence of all investors' wealth, preferences, and predictions.

Equity. The ownership interest of common and preferred stockholders in a company.

Equity risk premium. The difference between the rate of return available from risk-free assets (such as U.S. Treasury bills) and that available from assuming the risk inherent in common stocks.

ERISA (Employee Retirement Income Security Act of 1974). This law requires that persons engaged in the administration, supervision, and management of pension monies have a *fiduciary responsibility* to ensure that all investment-related decisions are made: (1) with the care, skill, prudence and diligence . . . that a prudent man . . . *familiar with such matters* (italics added) would use. . . . , (2) *by diversifying the investments . . . so as to minimize risk.* (italics added) . . . This wording mandates two significant changes in tradi-

tional investment practice: (1) the age-old "prudent man" rule has been replaced by the notion of a prudent "expert," (2) the notion of a prudent investment has been replaced by the concept of a prudent *portfolio*.

Ex ante. The term is used to distinguish forward-looking, or predicted, variables.

Ex post. The term is used to distinguish backward-looking, or historical, variables.

Excess return. The return derived from a security (during a specified holding period) less the return from holding a riskless security (such as a short-term government obligation) during the same period.

Exchange acquisition. A method of filling an order to buy a large block of stock on the floor of the Exchange. Under certain circumstances, a member-broker can facilitate the purchase of a block by soliciting orders to sell. All orders to sell the security are lumped together and crossed with the buy order in the regular auction market. The price to the buyer may be on a net basis or on a commission basis.*

Exchange distribution. A method of selling large blocks of stock on the floor of the Exchange. Under certain circumstances, a member-broker can facilitate the sale of a block of stock by soliciting and getting other member-brokers to solicit orders to buy. Individual buy orders are lumped together and crossed with the sell order in the regular auction market. A special commission is usually paid by the seller; ordinarily the buyer pays no commission.*

Ex-dividend. A synonym for "without dividend." The buyer of a stock selling ex-dividend does not receive the recently declared dividend. Every dividend is payable on a fixed date to all shareholders recorded on the books of the company as of a previous date of record. For example, a dividend may be declared as payable to holders of record on the books of the company on a given Friday. Since five business days are allowed for delivery of stock in a "regular way" transaction on the New York Stock Exchange, the Exchange would declare the stock "ex-dividend" as of the opening of the market on the preceding Monday. That means anyone who bought it on and after Monday would not be entitled to that dividend.*

Expected rate of return. The expected rate of return on an asset or portfolio is the weighted arithmetic average of all possible outcomes, where the weights are the probabilities that each outcome will occur. It is the expected value or mean of a probability distribution.

Ex-rights. Without the rights. Corporations raising additional money may do so by offering their stockholders the right to subscribe to new or additional stock, usually at a discount from the prevailing market price. The buyer of a stock selling ex-rights is not entitled to the rights.*

Extra. The short form of "extra dividend." A dividend in the form of stock or cash in addition to the regular or usual dividend the company has been paying.*

Extramarket covariance. The tendency for homogeneous groups of stocks to move together but in a way that is independent of the market as a whole.

Extramarket risk. Risk arising from comovements of homogeneous groups of stocks whose movements are independent of those of the market as a whole.

Face value. The value of a bond that appears on the face of the bond, unless the value is otherwise specified by the issuing company. Face value is ordinarily the amount the issuing company promises to pay at maturity. Face value is not an indication of market value. Sometimes referred to as par value.*

Feasible set. The feasible or attainable set includes all individual securities and all combinations (portfolios) of two or more of these securities available to the investor within the limits of the available capital.

Filter rules. Rules based on the assumption that trends exist in stock prices but that these patterns are obscured by insignificant fluctuations, or market "noise". The filter precept is utilized to justify a procedure whereby all price changes smaller than a specified size are ignored. The remaining data are then examined. A typical filter rule might be: if the stock price advances 5 percent (signaling a breakout), buy and hold the stock until it declines by 5 percent (signaling the start of a reversal). At that time, sell the stock held and sell short an equal amount until the stock again moves up 5 percent. Under such a rule, all moves of less than 5 percent are ignored. Filter techniques seek to discover "significant moves" by studying price changes of a given magnitude, irrespective of the length of time between them.

Financial leverage. The measure of how many dollars of assets are held in relation to each dollar of stockholders' equity—in other words, how much of a company's asset base is financed with stockholders' equity and how much with borrowed funds. It is calculated by dividing average assets by average stockholders' equity. As such, it provides a comparative link between two key balance sheet items, assets and equity.

Fiscal year. A corporation's accounting year. Due to the nature of their particular business, some companies do not use the calendar year for their bookkeeping. A typical example is the department store which finds December 31 too early a date to close its books after the Christmas rush. For that reason many stores wind up their accounting year January 31. Their fiscal year, therefore, runs from February 1 of one year through January 31 of the next. The fiscal year of other

companies may run from July 1 through the following June 30. Most companies, though, operate on a calendar year basis.*

Fixed assets. See Assets.

Fixed charges. A company's fixed expenses, such as bond interest, which it has agreed to pay whether or not earned, and which are deducted from income before earnings on equity capital are computed.*

Flat income bond. This term means that the price at which a bond is traded includes consideration for all unpaid accruals of interest. Bonds which are in default of interest or principal are traded flat. Income bonds, which pay interest only to the extent earned are usually traded flat. All other bonds are usually dealt in "and interest," which means that the buyer pays to the seller the market price plus interest accrued since the last payment date.*

Floor. The trading area where stocks and bonds are bought and sold on an exchange.

Forward interest rate. The prevailing interest rate for a contract in a specific future, or "forward," time period.

Full covariance model. See Markowitz model.

Fundamental analysis. Analysis based on factors such as sales, earnings, and assets that are "fundamental" to enterprise. The usefulness of fundamental analysis is challenged by the semistrong form of the efficient market hypothesis which holds that the analysis of publicly available fundamental information cannot improve an investor's rate of return.

Funded debt. Usually interest-bearing bonds or debentures of a company. Could include long-term bank loans. Does *not* include short-term loans, preferred or common stock.*

General mortgage bond. A bond which is secured by a blanket mortgage on the company's property, but which may be outranked by one or more other mortgages.*

Geometric mean. The geometric mean is the nth root of the product of n observations. It is the correct measure to use when averaging annual rates of return, compounded annually, over time. In calculating the average of rates of return, it is necessary to take the geometric mean of wealth ratios in order to allow for negative rates. The average rate of return is then the geometric mean minus one. For example, if the annual rates of return for two years were 10 percent and 8 percent, the average annual rate of return would be

$$\sqrt[2]{1.1 \times 1.08} - 1$$

or .0899. If the annual rates for two years were 100 percent and −50 percent, the average annual rate of return would be

$$\sqrt[2]{2.0 \times 0.5} - 1 = 0.0.$$

Growth stock. Stock of a company with a record of growth in earnings at a relatively rapid rate.

Holding company. A corporation which owns the securities of another, in most cases with voting control.

Implied return. See Implicit discount rate.

Implicit discount rate. Basically, the implicit discount rate (or implied return) for a stock is the same as the yield to maturity for a bond. It is the expected average annualized rate of return that equates the current price with the forecasted dividend stream.

Inactive stock. An issue traded on an exchange or in the over-the-counter market in which there is a relatively low volume of transactions. Volume may be no more than a few hundred shares a week or even less.*

Indenture. A written agreement under which bonds and debentures are issued, setting forth maturity date, interest rate, and other terms.*

Independence (statistical). If two variables are statistically independent, changes in the two variables are unrelated. Knowledge of the changes in one is of no value in predicting the other. (The weak form of the efficient market hypothesis asserts the statistical independence of successive price changes.)

Index. A statistical yardstick expressed in terms of percentages of a base year or years. For instance, the Federal Reserve Board's index of industrial production is based on 1967 as 100. An index is not an average.*

Indifference curve. An indifference curve represents combinations of, say, risk and return, that are equally valued. For risk averters, indifference curves are convex from below when return is measured on the vertical axis and risk on the horizontal axis. The shape varies with the risk-return preferences of the individual.

Information coefficients (IC's). The term used to describe the correlation coefficients derived from tabulations of ex ante predictions of performance and ex post results.

Institutional investor. An organization whose primary purpose is to invest its own assets or those held in trust by it for others. Includes pension funds, investment companies, insurance companies, universities, and banks.*

Intangible assets. See Assets.

Interest. Payments a borrower pays a lender for the use of the lender's money. A corporation pays interest on its bonds to its bondholders.*

Interest coverage. The number of times that interest charges are earned, found by dividing the (total) fixed charges into the earnings available for such charges (either before or after deducting income taxes).

Interest-rate risk. When interest rates rise the market value of fixed-income contracts (such as bonds) declines. Similarly, when interest rates decline the market value of fixed-income contracts increases. Interest-rate risk is the risk associated with these fluctuations.

Internal rate of return. Term analogous to the familiar yield to maturity on a bond. The internal rate of return is the rate of discount which makes the net present value of an investment equal to zero. In the case of a bond,

$$P_o - \sum_{t=1}^{N} \frac{I_t}{(1 + i)^t} + \frac{P_N}{(1 + i)^N} = 0,$$

where P_o is the initial price, P_N is the terminal price, I_t is the interest in year t, i is the internal rate of return.

Intrinsic value. The value that asset "ought" to have as judged by an investor. Discrepancies between current market value and intrinsic value are often the basis of decisions to buy or sell the asset.

Inventories. Current assets representing the present stock of finished merchandise, goods in process of manufacture, raw materials used in manufacture, and sometimes miscellaneous supplies such as packing and shipping material. These are usually stated at cost or market value, whichever is lower.

Investing. To forego present spending in exchange for expected future benefits. Since today's price is known, investing entails a certain sacrifice in hopes of attaining an uncertain future benefit.

Investment bankers. Also known as underwriters they stand between the corporation issuing new securities and the public. The usual practice is for one or more investment bankers to buy outright from a corporation a new issue of stocks or bonds. The group forms a syndicate to sell the securities to individuals and institutions.*

Investment company. A company or trust which uses its capital to invest in other companies. There are two principal types: the closed-end and the open-end, or mutual fund. Shares in closed-end investment companies are readily transferable in the open market and are bought and sold like other shares. Capitalization of these companies remains the same unless action is taken to change, which is seldom. Open-end funds sell their own new shares to investors, stand ready to buy back their old shares, and are not listed. Open-end funds are so called because their capitalization is not fixed; they issue more shares as people want them.*

Issue. Any of a company's securities, or the act of distributing such securities.*

Least-square regression line. Minimizes the sum of the squares of the vertical deviations of observations from a line drawn through

them. For example, if a regression line is fitted to points representing pairs of values of x_i and x_j, the equation is

$$x_i = a + bx_j.$$

The squared vertical distances of the actual values of x_i from the theoretical values, given its relationship to x_j are minimized. The mean values of x_i and x_j will always be a point on the regression line.

Leverage. The effect on the per-share earnings of the common stock of a company when large sums must be paid for bond interest or preferred stock dividends, or both, before the common stock is entitled to share in earnings. Leverage may be advantageous for the common stock when earnings are good but may work against the common when earnings decline. Example: Company A has 1,000,000 shares of common stock outstanding, no other securities. Earnings drop from $1,000,000 to $800,000 or from $1 to 80 cents a share, a decline of 20 per cent. Company B also has 1,000,000 shares of common but must pay $500,000 annually in bond interest. If earnings amount to $1,000,000, there is $500,000 available for the common or 50 cents a share. But earnings drop to $800,000 so there is only $300,000 available for the common, or 30 cents a share—a drop of 40 per cent. Or suppose earnings of the company with only common stock increased from $1,000,000 to $1,500,000—earnings per share would go from $1 to $1.50, or an increase of 50 per cent. But if earnings of the company which had to pay $500,000 in bond interest increased that much—earnings per common share would jump from 50 cents to $1 a share, or 100 per cent. When a company has common stock only, no leverage exists because all earnings are available for the common, although relatively large fixed charges payable for lease of substantial plant assets may have an effect similar to that of a bond issue.*

Liabilities. All the claims against a corporation. Liabilities include accounts and wages and salaries payable, dividends declared payable, accrued taxes payable, fixed or long-term liabilities such as mortgage bonds, debentures, and bank loans.*

Lien. A claim against property. A bond is usually secured by a lien against specified property of a company.*

Limit order. An order to buy or sell a stated amount of a security at a specified price, or at a better price.

Liquidation. The process of converting securities or other property into cash. The dissolution of a company, with cash remaining after sale of its assets and payment of all indebtedness being distributed to the shareholders.*

Liquidity. The ability of the market in a particular security to absorb a reasonable amount of buying or selling at reasonable price changes.

Liquidity is one of the most important characteristics of a good market.*

Liquidity market line. A security market line for a group of stocks with approximately the same market liquidity.

Liquidity ratio. A measure of financial liquidity: cash plus marketable securities divided by current liabilities.

Liquidity risk. The possibility of sustaining a loss from current market value by the process of liquidation, or converting the investment into cash.

Logarithmic change. The use of absolute and percentage price changes can be confusing. Clearly, a $1 price change for a $10 stock is 10 percent while a $1 price change for a $100 stock is only 1 percent. Also, if a stock rises from $50 to $100 it appreciates 100 percent. However, if the stock then falls from $100 back to the original $50 the decline is only 50 percent. Since the difference between two logarithms measures the rate of change (instead of the magnitude of change) logarithms eliminate the confusion that arises when dealing with absolute price changes. By definition, a logarithm of a number is the power to which the base (say 10) must be raised to yield that number. Thus, the base 10 logarithms for 10, 100 and 1000 are 1, 2 and 3 respectively. If the price of one stock appreciated from $10 to $100 its absolute appreciation would be $90. If another holding appreciated from $100 to $1000 its absolute appreciate would be $900. In each case, however, the difference between the logarithms is 1—indicating that the rate for change from $10 to $100 is the same as from $100 to $1000.

Long. Signifies ownership of securities: "I am long 100 U.S. Steel" means the speaker owns 100 shares.*

Margin. The amount paid by the customer when using credit to buy a security. Under Federal Reserve regulations, the initial margin required in the past years has ranged from 50 percent of the purchase price all the way to 100 percent.*

Market model. Describes the relationship between the returns on individual securities (or portfolios) and the returns on the market portfolios. Specifically, the market model holds that returns on an individual security (or portfolio) are linearly related to an index of market returns. As such, the market model provides the conceptual foundation for the single-index portfolio selection model. (See Characteristic lines.)

Market order. An order to buy or sell a stated amount of a security at the most advantageous price.*

Market portfolio. Includes all risky assets in proportion to their market value. In the capital asset pricing model, it is the optimum portfolio of risky assets for all investors. Graphically, it is located at

the point of tangency of a line drawn from the risk-free rate of return to the efficient frontier of risky assets.

Market price. In the case of a security, market price is usually considered the last reported price at which the stock or bond sold.*

Markowitz model. Delineates the decisions that will be made by a population of normal investors—each exercising his or her personal preferences.

Maturity. The date on which a loan or a bond or debenture comes due and is to be paid off.*

Mean absolute deviation. The mean absolute deviation is the average of the absolute values (the signs are disregarded) of the deviations of a group of observations from their expected value. Symbolically it is

$$\frac{\Sigma|x_i - \bar{x}|}{N}.$$

Median. The median of a distribution is the value that divides the number of observations in half. If the distribution is normal, the mean and the median will coincide. If the distribution is not normal and has positive skewness, the mean will exceed the median. If the skewness is negative, the mean will be below the median.

Member corporation. A securities brokerage firm, organized as a corporation with at least one member of the New York Stock Exchange, Inc. who is an officer and a holder of voting stock in the corporation.*

Member firm. A securities brokerage firm organized as a partnership and having at least one general partner who is a member of the New York Stock Exchange, Inc.*

Member organization. This term includes New York Stock Exchange Member Firm *and* Member Corporation.*

Modern investment theory (MIT). See Modern portfolio theory.

Modern portfolio theory (MPT). The theoretical constructs that enable investment managers to classify, estimate, and control the sources of risk and return. In popular usage, the term is not limited to "portfolio" theory. Instead, the term encompases all notions of modern investment, as well as portfolio, theory. Accordingly, MPT is synonymous with such terms as new investment technology (NIT) and modern investment theory (MIT).

Modigliani-Cohn thesis. The hypothesis that inflation has an advantageous impact on a corporate debt that (with other inflation-related factors) has been systematically overlooked by investment analysts.

Modigliani-Miller (M-M hypothesis). The hypothesis that the market pricing mechanism will adjust a firm's cost of capital so as to

minimize the importance of the firm's internal decisions regarding capital structure.

Multi-index model. A portfolio selection model that is based on the relationship between each security's rate of return and the rate of return of homogeneous groups of securities that move together as groups but whose group movements are unrelated.

Multiple correlation. A measure of the relationship between one variable (the dependent variable) and two or more other variables (the independent variables) simultaneously. It is an extension of simple correlation to include more than one independent variable.

Municipal bond. A bond issued by a state or a political subdivision, such as county, city, town, or village. The term also designates bonds issued by state agencies and authorities. In general, interest paid on municipal bonds is exempt from federal income taxes and state and local income taxes within the state of issue.

Mutual fund. See Investment company.

NASD. The National Association of Securities Dealers, Inc. An association of brokers and dealers in the over-the-counter securities business organized to "adopt, administer and enforce rules of fair practice and rules to prevent fradulent and manipulative acts and practices, and in general to promote just and equitable principles of trade for the protection of investors."*

NASDAQ. An automated information network which provides brokers and dealers with price quotations on securities traded over-the-counter. NASDAQ is an acronym for National Association of Securities Dealers Automated Quotations.*

Negotiable. Refers to a security, title to which is transferable by delivery.*

Net asset value. A term usually used in connection with investment companies, meaning net asset value per share. It is common practice for an investment company to compute its assets daily, or even twice daily, by totaling the market value of all securities owned. All liabilities are deducted, and the balance divided by the number of shares outstanding. The resulting figure is the net asset value per share.*

Net change. The change in the price of a security from the closing price on one day and the closing price on the following day on which the stock is traded. The net change is ordinarily the last figure on the stock price list. The mark +1⅛ means up $1.125 a share from the last sale on the previous day the stock traded.*

Net quick assets. A measure of financial liquidity: quick assets (current assets minus inventories) minus current liabilities.

New investment technology (NIT). See Modern portfolio theory.

New issue. A stock or bond sold by a corporation for the first time. Proceeds may be used to retire outstanding securities of the company, for new plant or equipment, or for additional working capital.*

New York Stock Exchange composite index. See New York Stock Exchange common stock index.

Nominal return. The nominal return on an asset is the rate of return in monetary terms, i.e., unadjusted for any change in the price level. The nominal return is contrasted with the real return which is adjusted for changes in the price level.

Noncumulative. A preferred stock on which unpaid dividends do not accrue. Omitted dividends are, as a rule, gone forever.*

Nonmarket risk. See Residual risk.

"Normalized" earnings. The earnings one would expect in a "normal" or mid-cyclical year. There is no general agreement about the best way to normalize earnings, but it is not uncommon to use a moving average for three, four, or five or more years. Normalized earnings are sometimes called "steady-state" earnings.

Normative theories. Normative means "normal" or "standard". In economics, a normative theory refers to the way investors "normally" behave. In this context, portfolio theory is a normative theory—it specifies how normal risk-averse investors will behave.

NYSE. An abbreviation for the New York Stock Exchange.

NYSE Common Stock Index. A value-weighted index (one where the weight given each stock corresponds to the market value of the company's outstanding shares) of all common stocks listed on the New York Stock Exchange.

Odd lot. An amount of stock less than the established 100-share unit or 10-share unit of trading: from 1 to 99 shares for the great majority of issues, 1 to 9 for so-called inactive stocks.*

Off-board. This term may refer to transactions over-the-counter in unlisted securities, or to a transaction involving listed shares which was not executed on a national securities exchange.*

Offer. The price at which a person is ready to sell. Opposed to bid, the price at which one is ready to buy.

One-factor model. See Single-index model.

Open-end investment company. See Investment company.

Operating leverage. See Asset turnover.

Optimizers. See Portfolio optimization.

Option. A right to buy (call) or sell (put) a fixed amount of a given stock at a specified price within a limited period of time. The purchasers of options hope that the stock's price will go up (if they

bought a call) or down (if they bought a put) by an amount sufficient to provide a profit greater than the cost of the contract and the commission and other fees required to exercise the contract. If the stock price moves in the opposite direction, the price paid for the option is lost entirely. Individuals who write (sell) options are obliged to deliver or buy the stock at the specified price.*

Over-the-counter. A market for securities made up of securities dealers who may or may not be members of a securities exchange. Over-the-counter is mainly a market made over the telephone. Thousands of companies have insufficient shares outstanding, stockholders, or earnings to warrant application for listing on the New York Stock Exchange, Inc. Securities of these companies are traded in the over-the-counter market between dealers who act either as principals or as brokers for customers. The over-the-counter market is the principal market for U.S. Government and municipal bonds.*

Owners' equity. Capital invested by stockholders.

Paper profit. An unrealized profit on a security still held. Paper profits become realized profits only when the security is sold.*

Par. In the case of a common share, par means a dollar amount assigned to the share by the company's charter. Par value may also be used to compute the dollar amount of the common shares on the balance sheet. Par value has little significance so far as market value of common stock is concerned. Many companies today issue no-par stock but give a stated per share value on the balance sheet. In the case of preferred shares and bonds, however, par is important. It often signifies the dollar value upon which dividends on preferred stocks, and interest on bonds, are figured. The issuer of a 6 percent bond promises to pay that percentage of the bond's par value annually.*

Participating preferred. A preferred stock which is entitled to its stated dividend and, also, to additional dividends on a specified basis upon payment of dividends on the common stock.*

Passive management. A style of investment management that seeks to attain average risk-adjusted performance.

Performance index. A "total return" index of investment performance. A performance index differs from the popular market indexes, or so-called averages (such as the Dow Jones Industrial Average) in that the popular measures do *not* include the return derived from dividends and other distributions to shareholders.

Performance measurement. The MPT application area involved with the measurement of risk-adjusted performance.

Point. In the case of shares of stock, a point means $1. If ABC shares rises 3 points, each share has risen $3. In the case of bonds a point means $10, since a bond is quoted as a percentage of $1,000. A bond

which rises 3 points gains 3 percent of $1,000, or $30 in value. An advance from 87 to 90 would mean an advance in dollar value from $870 to $900 for each $1,000 bond. In the case of market averages, the word point means merely that and no more. If, for example, the Dow-Jones Industrial average rises from 870.25 to 871.25, it has risen a point. A point in this average, however, is not equivalent to $1.*

Portfolio. Holdings of securities by an individual or institution. A portfolio may contain bonds, preferred stocks and common stocks of various types of enterprises.*

Portfolio characteristic line. See Characteristic line.

Portfolio optimization. Starting with a universe of securities that has been valued in terms of (a) expected return, (b) variances of expected return, and (c) covariance of return with every other security under consideration, the process of portfolio optimization involves selecting the portfolio that minimizes risk for a given level of risk. In practice, the computerized optimization programs can impose manifold constraints on the characteristics of the resultant portfolio. Typical constraints would be that the resultant portfolio have no more than 5 percent of the portfolio's value in a single stock, that the average current yield be at least 4 percent per annum, etc.

Positive theories. A positive theory is best described by an analogy to a machine. In a "positive" machine, the outcomes are determined by the mechanism. In a similar sense, a positive theory describes a mechanism that can be used for prediction. Portfolio theory is a positive theory. Basically, portfolio theory holds that if investors are risk averse and act as portfolio theory suggests, the price-setting mechanism relating risk and expected return will be consistent and can be predicted.

Preferred stock. A class of stock with a claim on the company's earnings before payment may be made on the common stock and usually entitled to priority over common stock if the company liquidates. Usually entitled to dividends at a specified rate—when declared by the Board of Directors and before payment of a dividend on the common stock—depending upon the terms of the issue.*

Premium. The amount by which a preferred stock, bond or option may sell above its par value. In the case of a new issue of bonds or stocks, premium is the amount the market price rises over the original selling price. Also refers to a charge sometimes made when a stock is borrowed to make delivery on a short sale. May refer, also, to redemption price of a bond or preferred stock if it is higher than face value.*

Present value. The actual value discounted at an appropriate rate of interest. The discounting reflects the productivity of capital and the risk premium. For example, the present value of a share of stock, V_0, is the stream of future payments discounted to perpetuity, or,

$$\sum_{t=1}^{\infty} \frac{P_t}{(1 + i)^t}$$

where P_t are the payments in period t and i is the rate of discount.

Price-earnings ratio. The price or a share of stock divided by earnings per share for a 12-month period. For example, a stock selling at $50 a share and earning $5 a share has a price earnings ratio, or P/E, of 10.

Primary distribution. Also called primary offering. The original sale of a company's securities.*

Principal. The person for whom a broker executes an order, or a dealer buying or selling for his own account. The term "principal" may also refer to a person's capital or to the face amount of a bond.

Probability distribution. A distribution of possible outcomes with an indication of the subjective or objective probability of each occurrence.

Prospectus. The official selling circular that must be given to purchasers of new securities registered with the Securities and Exchange Commission so investors can evaluate those securities before or at the time of purchase. It highlights the much longer Registration Statement filed with the Commission. It warns the issue has not been approved (or disapproved) by the Commission and discloses such material information as the issuer's property and business, the nature of the security offered, use of proceeds, issuer's competition and prospects, management's experience, history, and remuneration and certified financial statements. A preliminary version of the prospectus, used by brokers to obtain buying indications from investors, is called a red herring. This is because of a front-page notice containing a large red legend warning that the document is preliminary and "subject to completion or amendment".*

Proxy. Written authorization given by a shareholder to someone else to vote at a shareholders meeting.*

Proxy statement. Information required by SEC to be given stockholders as a prerequisite to solicitation of proxies for a security subject to the requirements of Securities Exchange Act.*

Quick assets. Measure of financial liquidity: current assets minus inventories.

Quotation. Often shortened to "quote." The highest bid to buy and the lowest offer to sell a security in a given market at a given time.*

Rally. A brisk rise following a decline in the general price level of the market or in an individual stock.*

Random selection. Random selection is similar to picking stocks by throwing darts at a stock listing. Technically, random selection means that each element in the relevant population has a known and positive probability of selection.

Random-walk model. The name historically given to the weak form of the efficient market hypothesis. A random walk implies that there is no discernible pattern of travel. The size and direction of the next step cannot be predicted from the size and direction of the last or even from all the previous steps. Random walk is a term used in mathematics and statistics to describe a process in which successive changes are statistically independent. The serial correlation is zero.

Real return. An inflation-adjusted return. (See Nominal return.)

Record date. The date on which one must be registered as a shareholder on a stock book of a company in order to receive a declared dividend or, among other things, to vote on company affairs.*

Red herring. See Prospectus.

Redemption price. The price at which a bond may be redeemed before maturity, at the option of the issuing company. Redemption value also applies to the price the company must pay to call in certain types of preferred stock.

Refinancing. Same as refunding. New securities are sold by a company and the money is used to retire existing securities. Object may be to save interest costs, extend the maturity of the loan, or both.*

Reflection. A situation in which stock prices are believed to reverse as if they are "reflected" away from certain "resistance" or "support" levels.

Registered bond. A bond which is registered on the books of the issuing company in the name of the owner. It can be transferred only when endorsed by the registered owner.

Registered representative. In a New York Stock Exchange Member Organization, an employee who has met the requirements of the Exchange as to background and knowledge of the securities business. Also known as an account executive*.

Registration. Before a public offering may be made of new securities by a company, or of outstanding securities by controlling stockholders—through the mails or in interstate commerce—the securities must be registered under the Securities Act of 1933. Registration statement is filed with the SEC by the issuer. It must disclose pertinent information relating to the company's operations, securities, management and purpose of the public offering. Securities of railroads under jurisdiction of the Interstate Commerce Commission, and certain other types of securities, are exempted. On security offerings involving less than $300,000, less information is required. Before a security may be admitted to dealings on a national securities exchange, it must be registered under the Securities Exchange Act of 1934. The application for registration must be filed with the exchange and the SEC by the company issuing the securities. It must disclose pertinent information relating to the company's operations, securities and management.*

Regression analysis. Regression or correlation analysis is a statistical technique for estimating the relationship between one variable (dependent variable) and one or more other variables (independent variables). The relationship estimated, usually a least-squares regression equation, is often used to predict the value of the dependent variable, given the values of the independent variable, or variables.

Regression coefficient. A regression coefficient indicates the responsiveness of one variable to changes in another. If the relationship between two variables is described by a straight line, the regression coefficient is the slope of the line. The regression coefficient between rates of return on an asset and rates of return on the market is called the beta coefficient.

Regular way delivery. Unless otherwise specified, securities sold on the New York Stock Exchange are to be delivered to the buying broker by the selling broker and payment made to the selling broker by the buying broker on the fifth business day after the transaction. Regular way delivery for bonds is the following business day.*

Regulation T. The federal regulation governing the amount of credit which may be advanced by brokers and dealers to customers for the purchase of securities.*

Regulation U. The federal regulation governing the amount of credit which may be advanced by a bank to its customers for the purchase of listed stocks.*

Reinvestment rate. The percentage of a company's earnings that are retained for investment.

REIT. Real Estate Investment Trust, an organization similar to an investment company but concentrating its holdings in real estate investments. Generally REIT's are required to distribute as much as 90 percent of their income.*

Relative response coefficients. Used in the calculation of the so-called "fundamental" betas, a relative response coefficient is the ratio of the expected response of a security to the expected response of the market if both the security and the market are impacted by the same event.

Relative strength continuation. Generally referred to as merely "relative strength," this is the occasionally observed tendency for stocks that have either above-average or below-average performance in one period to *continue* that performance in the "next" period.

Replacement cost accounting. Balance sheets tend to be misleading because they typically value assets at cost plus installation. To overcome this problem assets can be valued at replacement cost. For fiscal years ending on or after December 25, 1979 the Financial Accounting Standards Board requires approximately 1,350 of the largest U.S. corporations to report supplementary information based

on constant (inflation-adjusted) dollars and current (replacement) costs.

Residual risk. The aggregate of specific risk and the risk arising from extramarket covariance.

Residual standard deviation. A summary measure of the distances from the plotted points to a "least squares" regression line. The residual standard deviation is an ex post measure of a security's specific, or non-market, risk.

Resistance level. A price level that is believed to pose a barrier to upward price movements.

Return. See Yield.

Return on assets (sometimes abbreviated ROA). The percentage of new profit earned on total assets. As such it provides a comparative link between a key item on the balance sheet (assets) and a key item on the income statement (income).

Return on equity (sometimes abbreviated ROE). A key measure of the profitability of an equity investment—is the net income earned by a company expressed as a percentage return on the stockholders' investment. Its relationship to return on assets and financial leverage is as follows:

$$\text{Return on assets} \times \text{Financial leverage} = \text{Return on equity}$$

$$\frac{\text{Earnings}}{\text{Assets}} \times \frac{\text{Assets}}{\text{Equity}} = \frac{\text{Earnings}}{\text{Equity}}$$

As such it provides a comparative link between a key balance sheet item (equity) and a key income statement item (income).

Return on sales. Return on sales (sometimes abbreviated ROS and sometimes called the operating margin, or net profit margin) is the percentage of profit earned on sales. It is calculated by dividing net income, or earnings, by net sales. As such it provides a comparative link between two key items on the income statement—earnings and sales.

Reward to variability ratio. The reward-to-variability ratio is the risk premium on an asset per unit of risk as measured by the variability or standard deviation.

Rights. When a company wants to raise more funds by issuing additional securities, it may give its stockholders the opportunity, ahead of others, to buy the new securities in proportion to the number of shares each owns. The piece of paper evidencing this privilege is called a right. Because the additional stock is usually offered to stockholders below the current market price, rights ordinarily have a market value of their own and are actively traded. In most cases they

must be exercised within a relatively short period. Failure to exercise or sell rights may result in actual loss to the holder.*

Risk aversion. All rational investors can be characterized as being "risk averse." This means that for any level of return a rational investor will prefer the lowest level of available risk. Similarly, for any given level of risk a rational investor will prefer the highest level of available return. Basically risk aversion means riskiness matters and is disliked. A risk averter will hold a portfolio of more than one stock in order to reduce risk for a given expected return. Technically, the utility function of a risk averter will depend on rate of return and risk and will not be linear. This implies diminishing marginal utility of wealth. This implies that a risk-averse investor will incur additional risk only in exchange for an expected higher rate of return.

Risk-free asset. Typically a noncallable, default-free bond such as a short-term government security. While such an asset is not risk-free in an inflation sense, it is (under the rationale that the government can always print money) risk-free in a dollar sense.

Risk-free rate of return. The risk-free rate of return is the return on an asset that is virtually riskless. For example, Treasury bills maturing in one year have a precisely predictable nominal rate of return for one year. The risk premium on an asset is the rate of return in excess of the risk-free rate. The risk-free rate is normally used in portfolio theory to represent the rate for lending or borrowing.

Risk neutrality. Risk neutrality means risk does not matter. A risk-neutral investor cares only about rate of return and would hold a portfolio of one asset—the one with the highest expected rate of return. Risk neutrality implies constant marginal utility of wealth. The utility function for such an investor is linear.

Risk premium. On an asset, the actual return minus the risk-free rate of return. In the capital asset pricing model, the risk premium for any asset is proportional to its beta—the measure of sensitivity to general market movements. If R_i is the rate of return on an asset, and ρ is the riskless rate, $R_i - \rho$ is the risk premium.

Risk-reward spectrum. A construct used to illustrate that (in a rational market place) higher and higher anticipated rewards are always accompanied by incremental increases in risk (measured as the deviations between expected and actual results). The left end of the spectrum represents the lowest risk investment—typically short-term government obligations. Moving to the right on the spectrum—through a continuum of common stock investments—each incremental increase in expected return is accompanied by an incremental increase in risk.

R-squared (R^2). The proportion of a security's (or a portfolio's) total risk that is market related. Technically, R-squared is the coefficient of determination.

Round lot. A unit of trading or a multiple thereof. On the NYSE the unit the trading is generally 100 shares in stocks and $1,000 par value in the case of bonds. In some inactive stocks, the unit of trading is 10 shares.*

Rule of "72". A convenient technique for either mental or pencil-and-paper *estimation* of compound interest rates—derived from the fact that a 7.2 percent return per year is the interest rate that will double the value of an investment in ten years. Hence, "years to double" an investment with a given annual rate of return can be estimated by dividing the "rate of return" into 72. For example, if an investment's annual return is 6 percent, its value will double in *approximately* 12 years (72 ÷ 6). If an investment's annual return is 9 percent, its value will double in *approximately* eight (72 ÷ 9) years. Similarly, the "rate of return" that will double the value of an investment in a given number of years can be estimated by dividing the number of "years to double" into 72. For example, the value of an investment will double in six years if the annual rate of return is *approximately* 12 percent (72 ÷ 6).

Rule of halves. The benchmark for a "typical" balance sheet. That is, on the left side half the assets are current and half are fixed. On the right side, half is in the liability category and half is in the owner's equity category. Further, the rule of halves can be applied to the liability category where "typically" half are current and half are long-term.

Runs. A sequence of price changes in the same direction. The number of runs in a sequence of price changes is the number of reversals in sign plus one. Thus, if a series of price changes is described as zero, positive and negative, the sequence + + + − + + + + − − 0 − − would have six runs.

Sampling. Sampling is the process of selecting a subset of a population. It may or may not be random. The usefulness of a sample depends upon its representativeness, or the degree to which one can make inferences about the excluded population on the basis of the sample.

S&P 425. An index of the 425 industrial stocks that comprise the S&P 500.

S&P 500. A composite index of 500 stocks—425 industrials with the remainder railroads and utilities. In contrast to the Dow Jones Industrial Average (DJIA) the weighting of the relative importance of the component stocks in the S&P 500 corresponds to the market value of the company's outstanding shares.

Seat. A traditional figure-of-speech for a membership on an exchange.*

SEC. The Securities and Exchange Commission, established by Congress to help protect investors. The SEC administers the Securities

Act of 1933, the Securities Exchange Act of 1934, the Securities Act Amendments of 1975, the Trust Indenture Act, the Investment Company Act, the Investment Advisers Act, and the Public Utility Holding Company Act.*

Secondary distribution. Also known as a secondary offering. The redistribution of a block of stock some time after it has been sold by the issuing company. The sale is handled by a securities firm or group of firms and the shares are usually offered at a fixed price which is related to the current market price of the stock.*

Security characteristic line. See Characteristic lines.

Security market line. A construct used to portray the relationship between risk and return. In equilibrium, every security will plot on this line.

Security market plane. A three dimensional diagram that incorporates the security market line and the security yield line.

Security valuation models. Typically based on the precept that the value of a share of common stock is the sum of the discounted present value of the estimated future stream of dividends.

Selection risk. See Residual risk.

Semistandard deviation. The semistandard deviation is analogous to the standard deviation, but only the observations below the mean are taken into account. The deviations, $(x_i - \bar{x})$, are all negative. The measure is relevant if one is interested only in downside or adverse risk.

Separation theorem. States that the choice of an optimum portfolio is independent of, or separate from, the optimal combination of *risky* assets. The latter is the same for all investors if lending and borrowing are allowed. Individual needs determine only the amount of borrowing or lending.

Serial correlation. Measures the degree to which what happens "next" in a series of events (such as price changes) is related to what happened previously. Since the weak form of the efficient market hypothesis (also known as the random-walk model) holds that a stock's "next" price change cannot be predicted from its previous price changes, the serial correlation of period-to-period price changes (such as day-to-day or week-to-week) is frequently used to test this hypothesis.

Settlement. Conclusion of a securities transactions in which a customer pays a debit balance owed to a broker or receives from the broker the proceeds from a sale.*

Short covering. Buying stock to return stock previously borrowed to make delivery on a short sale.*

Short position. Stocks sold short and not covered as of a particular date. On the NYSE, a tabulation is issued once a month listing all

issues on the Exchange in which there was a short position of 5,000 or more shares and issues in which the short position had changed by 2,000 or more shares in the preceding month.*

Short sale. Short sales are made by people who expect the market to go down. In a regular securities transaction, shares are bought first and sold later. In a short transaction, the sale comes first, the purchase later. A short sale is effected by borrowing stock through a broker and selling it at the current market price. The proceeds of the sale are then held as collateral for the loan of the stock. To close out the short position the borrowed stock must be replaced. This is done by buying an equivalent number of shares at the then current market price. If a short sale is made at $100 and the short can later be closed by buying the stock at $90, there will be a $10 per share profit (before any intervening interest on the loan and repayment of any individual income).

Single-index model. A portfolio selection model which uses the relationship between each security's rate of return and the rate of return on a market index as a substitute for explicit data on the covariance of each pair of securities under study.

Sinking fund. Money regularly set aside by a company to redeem its bonds, debentures, or preferred stock from time to time as specified in the indenture or charter.*

SIPC. Securities Investor Protection Corporation which provides funds for use, if necessary, to protect customers' cash and securities which may be on deposit with a SIPC member firm in the event the firm fails and is liquidated under the provisions of the SIPC Act. SIPC is not a Government Agency. It is a non-profit membership corporation created, however, by an Act of Congress.*

Skewness. Skewness is a measure of the asymmetry of a distribution. A normal distribution is symmetrical and has no skewness. If there are more observations to the left of the mean, the skewness is positive; if more to the right, negative.

Specialist. A member of the New York Stock Exchange, Inc. who has two functions. First, to maintain an orderly market insofar as reasonably practicable, in the stocks in which he or she is registered as a specialist. In order to maintain an orderly market, the Exchange expects the specialist to buy or sell for his or her own account, to a reasonable degree, when there is a temporary disparity between supply and demand. Second, the specialist acts as a broker's broker. When a commission broker on the Exchange floor receives a limit order, say, to buy at $50 a stock then selling at $60—it is not practical to wait at the post where the stock is traded to see if the price reaches the specified level. In such cases the order can be left with the specialist, who will try to execute it in the market if and when the stock declines to the specified price. There are about 400 specialists on the NYSE.*

Speculator. One who is willing to assume a relatively large risk in the hope of gain.*

Split. The division of the outstanding shares of a corporation into a larger number of shares. A 3-for-1 split by a company with 1 million shares outstanding results in 3 million shares outstanding. Each holder of 100 shares before the 3-for-1 stock split would have 300 shares, although the proportionate equity in the company would remain the same: 100 parts of 1 million are the equivalent of 300 parts of 3 million.*

Stable Paretian distribution. There is considerable evidence that stock price changes are not "normally" distributed but rather approximate what is known as a "stable Paretian" distribution. Basically, this distribution is used to accommodate the abnormally large number of "large" price changes.

Standard deviation. The standard deviation is a commonly used measure of dispersion. It is the square root of the variance. It is based on deviations of observations from the mean and is therefore in the same units as the observations. A measure of relative dispersion is the standard deviation divided by the mean (the coefficient of variation). This is often useful in comparing distributions that differ substantially in the magnitude of the numbers. The formula for the standard deviation, σ, is

$$\sqrt{\frac{\Sigma(x_i - \bar{x})^2}{N}}.$$

Standard error (of estimate). Provides a probabilistic measure of the differences between "true" and "sample estimated" values (of alpha and beta).

Standard and Poor's Index. See S&P 425 and S&P 500.

Stock ahead. Sometimes an investor who has entered an order to buy or sell a stock at a certain price will see transactions at that price reported on the ticker tape while his or her own order has not been executed. The reason is that other buy and sell orders at the same price came in to the specialist ahead of this order and had priority.*

Stock dividend. A dividend paid in securities rather than cash. The dividend may be additional shares of the issuing company, or in shares of another company (usually a subsidiary) held by the company.*

Stockholder of record. A stockholder whose name is registered on the books of the issuing corporation.*

Stop limit order. A stop order which becomes a limit order after the specified stop price has been reached.*

Stop order. An order to buy at a price above or sell at a price below the current market. Stop buy orders are generally used to limit loss or

protect unrealized profits on a short sale. Stop sell orders are generally used to protect unrealized profits or limit loss on a holding. A stop order becomes a market order when the stock sells at or beyond the specified price and, thus, may not necessarily be executed at that price.*

Street. The New York financial community in the Wall Street area.*

Street name. Securities held in the name of a broker instead of the customer's name are said to be carried in a "street name." This occurs when the securities have been bought on margin or when the customer wishes the security to be held by the broker.*

Support level. A price level that is believed to pose a barrier to downward price movements.

Sustainable dividend growth rate. The theoretical rate at which dividends can grow (derived from the product of the company's return on equity and earnings reinvestment rate).

Syndicate. A group of investment bankers who together underwrite and distribute a new issue of securities or a large block of an outstanding issue.

Systematic risk. Risk that is related to market covariance—the tendency for an individual security's or a portfolio's return to fluctuate with the return on the market portfolio. It can be estimated statistically from the market model. The percentage of total variability that is systematic is given by the coefficient of determination and the degree of responsiveness to market movements is measured by beta.

Take-over. The acquiring of one corporation by another—usually in a friendly merger but sometimes marked by a "proxy fight". In "unfriendly" take-over attempts, the potential buying company may offer a price well above current market values, new securities, and other inducements to stockholders. The management of the subject company might ask for a better price or fight the take-over or merger with another company.*

Technical analysis. Analysis based on the study of historical price and volume data. The usefulness of technical analysis is challenged by the weak form of the efficient market hypothesis which holds that the analysis of historical price and volume information is a useless endeavor.

Tender offer. A public offer to buy shares from existing stockholders of one public corporation by another company or other organization under specified terms good for a certain time period. Stockholders are asked to "tender" (surrender) their holdings for stated value, usually at a premium above current market price, subject to the tendering of a minimum and maximum number of shares.*

Thin market. A market in which there are comparatively few bids to buy or offers to sell or both. The phrase may apply to a single security

or to the entire stock market. In a thin market, price fluctuations between transactions are usually larger than when the market is liquid. A thin market in a particular stock may reflect lack of interest in that issue or a limited supply of or demand for stock in the market.*

Third market. Trading of stock exchange listed securities in the over-the-counter market by non-exchange member brokers and all types of investors.*

Tick. The term used to describe price changes between successive securities transactions. An "up" tick (also called a plus tick) designates a transaction at a higher price than the preceding trade. A "zero-plus" tick is a term used for a transaction at the same price as the preceding trade but higher than the preceding different price. A stock may be sold short only on an up tick, or on a "zero-plus" tick. A down tick, or "minus" tick, is a term used to designate a transaction made at a price lower than the preceding trade. A "zero-minus" tick is a transaction made at the same price as the preceding sale but lower than the preceding different price.

Tick (cumulative). The most sensitive indicator of intraday market activity. Tick measures the net difference of the total number of stocks that have traded up in price from their previous trade and the total number of stocks that have traded down in price from their previous trade.

Ticker. The instruments which display prices and volume of securities transactions within minutes after each trade.

Time-weighted return. Pursuant to the recommendations set forth in the 1968 report by the Bank Administration Institute entitled "Measuring the Investment Performance of Pension Funds" most performance figures are "time weighted." "Time weighting" eliminates the effect of periodic additions and withdrawals that are beyond the control of the investment manager. The time-weighted rate of return is a weighted average of the internal rates of return for subperiods dated by the contribution or withdrawal of funds from a portfolio at the time of each cash inflow or outflow and the dates on which these occur. Rates of return on mutual fund shares are time-weighted rates of return.

Tipees. Persons who come into possession of confidential information. The law holds that a tipee receiving "material inside information" becomes a de facto insider and must either disclose the information publicly or refrain from trading on it. Since it is illegal to enter into securities transactions on the basis of information that is not publicly available, all parties to securities transactions are guaranteed equal access to the same material facts.

Tips. Supposedly "inside" information on corporation affairs.*

Total return. Total return means that all dividends and income are

added, and fees, such as brokerage commissions, are subtracted from the aggregate value of a portfolio to arrive at the true measure of "total" performance.

Trader. One who buys and sells for short-term profit.*

Transfer. This term may refer to two different operations. For one, the delivery of a stock certificate from the seller's broker to the buyer's broker and legal change of ownership, normally accomplished within a few days. For another, to record the change of ownership on the books of the corporation by the transfer agent. When the purchaser's name is recorded on the books of the company, dividends, notices of meetings, proxies, financial reports and all pertinent literature sent by the issuer to its securities holders are mailed direct to the new owner.*

Transfer agent. A transfer agent keeps a record of the name of each registered shareowner, his or her address, the number of shares owned, and sees that certificates presented for transfer are properly cancelled and new certificates issued in the name of the transferee.*

Treasury stock. Stock issued by a company but later reacquired. It may be held in the company's treasury indefinitely, reissued to the public, or retired. Treasury stock receives no dividends and has no vote while held by the company.*

Treynor index. The Treynor index of performance is the reward per unit of risk as measured by volatility or beta. It indicates the rate of return on the market index required to make the expected rate of return on a portfolio equal to the risk-free rate.

Turnover rate. The volume of shares traded in a year as a percentage of total shares listed on an Exchange, outstanding for an individual issue or held in an institutional portfolio. In 1975, the turnover rate on the New York Stock Exchange was 21%.*

Underwriter. See Investment banker.

Unlisted. A security not listed on a stock exchange. (See Over-the-counter).

Unsystematic risk. The variability not explained by general market movements. It is avoidable through diversification. Only inefficient portfolios have unsystematic risk. (See Residual risk).

Utility function. It describes the relationship for an individual between various amounts of something such as wealth and the satisfaction it provides. If one's preferences are known, the utility functions can often be approximated by precise mathematical equations. The signs and values of its derivatives indicate the direction and magnitude of changes in utility associated with changes in the amount of the good possessed.

Valuation models. See Security valuation models.

Variance. The variance of a distribution is a measure of variability based on squared deviations of individual observations from the mean value of the distribution. Its square root, the standard deviation, is a commonly used measure of dispersion. The formula for the variance is,

$$\sigma^2 = \frac{\Sigma(x_i - \bar{x})^2}{N}.$$

If the distribution is of future outcomes that are now known with certainty, the variance is a weighted average of the squared deviations and the weights are the probabilities of occurrence. That is,

$$\sigma^2 = \Sigma P_i [x_i - E(x)]^2.$$

Volatility. That part of total variability due to sensitivity to changes in the market. It is systematic and unavoidable risk. It is measured by the beta coefficient. Efficient portfolios have no additional risk, and volatility is the only source of variability in rates of return.

Volume. The number of shares traded in a security or an entire market during a given period. Volume is usually considered on a daily basis and a daily average is computed for longer periods. Record daily volume on the New York Stock Exchange is 81,620,000 shares on October 10, 1979. Average daily volume during 1977 was 20,928,000 shares.*

Voting right. The stockholder's right to vote his or her stock in the affairs of the company. Most common shares have one vote each. Preferred stock usually has the right to vote when preferred dividends are in default for a specified period. The right to vote may be delegated by the stockholder to another person.*

Warrant. A certificate giving the holder the right to purchase securities at a stipulated price within a specified time limit or perpetually. Sometimes a warrant is offered with securities as an inducement to buy.*

Wealth ratio. A wealth ratio is the terminal value of an investment divided by its initial value. It is used in calculating rates of return. The wealth ratio is expressed as W_t/W_o where W_t refers to the terminal value and W_o to the initial value. The annual rate of return compounded continuously is

$$\frac{\log_e \left(\frac{W_t}{W_o}\right)}{n},$$

where n is the number of years in the period. The annual rate of return compounded annually is $e^x - 1$, where x is the annual rate compounded continuously.

Weighting. The specification of the relative importance of each of a group of items that are combined. For example, stocks included in indexes may be equally weighted or weighted according to value.

When issued. A short form of "when, as and if issued." The term indicates a conditional transaction in a security authorized for issuance but not as yet actually issued. All "when issued" transactions are on an "if" basis, to be settled if and when the actual security is issued and the Exchange or National Association of Securities Dealers rules the transactions are to be settled.*

Wire house. A member firm of an exchange maintaining a communications network linking either its own branch offices, offices of correspondent firms, or a combination of such offices.*

Working capital. Measure of financial liquidity: current assets minus current liabilities.

Yield. Also known as return. The dividends or interest paid by a company expressed as a percentage of the current price. A stock with a current market value of $40 a share paying dividends at the rate of $2.00 is said to return 5 percent ($2.00 ÷ $40.00). The current return on a bond is figured the same way. A 6 percent $1,000 bond selling at $600 offers a current yield return of 10 percent ($60 ÷ $600).*

Yield curve. A visual representation of the term structure of interest rates.

Yield tilt fund. An alternative to a pure index fund, a yield tilt fund diversifies its holdings among a universe of stocks that is "tilted" in the direction of higher yield—such as the high-yield stocks that comprise the S&P 500. Yield tilt funds are based on the assertion that, since dividend income is taxed at higher rates, the market must compensate for this taxation by providing higher returns for the high-yield segment of the market. If this assertion is true, tax-exempt investors could benefit from this market inefficiency by investing in high-yield stocks.

Yield-to-maturity. The average annualized rate of return that will prevail over the entire multi-period duration of an investment.

Index

R

S